A Companion to Tudor B

This book is dedicated to
Anne K. Tittler *and* Lynn Langer Meeks

A Companion to
Tudor Britain

Edited by

Robert Tittler and Norman Jones

THE
HISTORICAL
ASSOCIATION
THE VOICE FOR HISTORY

⊛WILEY-BLACKWELL
A John Wiley & Sons, Ltd., Publication

Library of Congress Cataloging-in-Publication Data

A companion to Tudor Britain / edited by Robert Tittler and Norman
Jones.
  p. cm. – (Blackwell companions to British history)
Includes bibliographical references and index.
ISBN 978-1-4051-8974-3 (alk. paper)
1. Great Britain – History – Tudors, 1485–1603 – Handbooks, manuals, etc.
2. Tudor, House of – Handbooks, manuals, etc. I. Tittler, Robert. II.
Jones, Norman L. (Norman Leslie), 1951– III. Title. IV. Series.

DA315.C66 2004
941.05–dc22
                                                            2003021512

A catalogue record for this book is available from the British Library.

Set in 10/12pt Galliard by SNP Best-set Typesetter Ltd., Hong Kong

1 2009

BLACKWELL COMPANIONS TO HISTORY

This series provides sophisticated and authoritative overviews of the scholarship that has shaped our current understanding of the past. Defined by theme, period and/or region, each volume comprises between twenty-five and forty concise essays written by individual scholars within their area of specialization. The aim of each contribution is to synthesize the current state of scholarship from a variety of historical perspectives and to provide a statement on where the field is heading. The essays are written in a clear, provocative, and lively manner, designed for an international audience of scholars, students, and general readers.

A Companion to International History
1900–2001
Edited by Gordon Martel

A Companion to Western Historical Thought
Edited by Lloyd Kramer and Sarah Maza

A Companion to Gender History
Edited by Teresa A. Meade and Merry E. Wiesner-Hanks

BLACKWELL COMPANIONS TO BRITISH HISTORY

A Companion to Roman Britain
Edited by Malcolm Todd

A Companion to Britain in the Later Middle Ages
Edited by S. H. Rigby

A Companion to Tudor Britain
Edited by Robert Tittler and Norman Jones

A Companion to Stuart Britain
Edited by Barry Coward

A Companion to Eighteenth-Century Britain
Edited by H. T. Dickinson

A Companion to Nineteenth-Century Britain
Edited by Chris Williams

A Companion to Early Twentieth-Century Britain
Edited by Chris Wrigley

A Companion to Contemporary Britain
Edited by Paul Addison and Harriet Jones

A Companion to the Early Middle Ages: Britain and Ireland
Edited by Pauline Stafford

BLACKWELL COMPANIONS TO EUROPEAN HISTORY

A Companion to Europe 1900–1945
Edited by Gordon Martel

A Companion to Eighteenth-Century Europe
Edited by Peter H. Wilson

A Companion to Nineteenth-Century Europe
Edited by Stefan Berger

A Companion to the Worlds of the Renaissance
Edited by Guido Ruggiero

A Companion to the Reformation World
Edited by R. Po-chia Hsia

A Companion to Europe Since 1945
Edited by Klaus Larres

In preparation

A Companion to the Medieval World
Edited by Carol Lansing and Edward D. English

BLACKWELL COMPANIONS TO AMERICAN HISTORY

A Companion to the American Revolution
Edited by Jack P. Greene and J. R. Pole

A Companion to 19th-Century America
Edited by William L. Barney

A Companion to the American South
Edited by John B. Boles

A Companion to American Indian History
Edited by Philip J. Deloria and Neal Salisbury

A Companion to American Women's History
Edited by Nancy A. Hewitt

A Companion to Post-1945 America
Edited by Jean-Christophe Agnew and Roy Rosenzweig

A Companion to the Vietnam War
Edited by Marilyn B. Young and Robert Buzzanco

A Companion to Colonial America
Edited by Daniel Vickers

A Companion to 20th-Century America
Edited by Stephen J. Whitfield

A Companion to the American West
Edited by William Deverell

A Companion to American Foreign Relations
Edited by Robert D. Schulzinger

A Companion to the Civil War and Reconstruction
Edited by Lacy K. Ford

A Companion to American Technology
Edited by Carroll Pursell

A Companion to American Immigration
Edited by Reed Ueda

A Companion to African-American History
Edited by Alton Hornsby, Jr

BLACKWELL COMPANIONS TO WORLD HISTORY

A Companion to the History of the Middle East
Edited by Youssef M. Choueiri

A Companion to Latin American History
Edited by Thomas Holloway

A Companion to Japanese History
Edited by William M. Tsutsui

A Companion to Russian History
Edited by Abbott Gleason

Contents

PART IV CULTURE

Plates

Maps

Contributors

Malcolm Airs is Professor of Conservation and the Historic Environment at the University of Oxford and a Fellow of Kellogg College. He was the founding president of the Institute of Historic Building Conservation and has published extensively on both architectural history and historic conservation. He is the author of *The Tudor & Jacobean Coutry House* (1995) and *Tudor and Jacobean* in the 'Buildings of Britain' series (1982).

Joseph S. Block is a professor in the Liberal Studies Department at California State Polytechnic University in Pomona, California. Currently he is serving as president of the Pacific Coast Conference on British Studies. He is the author of *Factional Politics and the English Reformation, 1520–1540* (1993) and is one of the contributing-editors of *State, Sovereigns and Society in Early Modern England* (1998).

Lesley B. Cormack is a professor in the Department of History and Classics at the University of Alberta. Her research interests include history of geography in early modern England, images of empire, and the social context of the scientific revolution. She is the author of *Charting an Empire: Geography at the English Universities, 1580–1620* (1997) and has recently co-edited *Making Contact: Maps, Identity, and Travel* (2003).

Peter Cunich lectures in European history at the University of Hong Kong. He is currently working on a financial history of the Court of Augmentations and is Director of the Monastic Database Project. He has written extensively on the dissolution of the monasteries and its aftermath.

Jane E. A. Dawson is John Laing Lecturer in the History and Theology of the Reformation in the Department of Ecclesiastical History at the University of Edinburgh. She is the author of *The Politics of Religion in the Age of Mary, Queen of Scots: The Earl of Argyll and the Struggle for Britain and Ireland*, and editor of *Campbell Letters 1559–83*, as well as numerous articles on Reformation Scotland. She is presently working on a book on the creation of Protestant Scotland.

David Dean, who taught at Goldsmiths College, University of London from 1983–1994, is currently Professor of History and Director of the Centre for Public History at Carleton University, Ottawa. The author of *Law-Making and Society in Late Elizabethan England* (1996), he has published numerous articles on Elizabethan parliaments and governance and co-edited *Interest Groups and Legislation in Elizabethan Parliaments* (1989), *The Parliaments of Elizabethan England* (1990) and *Parliament and Locality,*

1660–1939 (1998). He is presently writing a history of England in the 1590s for Blackwell.

Alan Dyer was born and brought up near Stratford-upon-Avon and studied up to doctoral level at the University of Birmingham. His PhD thesis on the city of Worcester in the sixteenth century was published in 1974. Since 1965 he has lectured at the University of Wales, Bangor. He has published on various aspects of the early modern English town, and on the phenomenon of urban decline in the later middle ages. He has also researched and written about disease in the sixteenth century (plague, and the sweating sickness) and its population history.

Steven G. Ellis is Professor of History and Head of Department at the National University of Ireland, Galway. His publications include *Tudor Ireland: Crown Community and the Conflict of Cultures 1470–1603*; *Tudor Frontiers and Noble Power: the Making of the British State*; and *Ireland in the Age of the Tudors: English Expansion and the End of Gaelic Rule, 1447–1603*. He is currently completing *The Making of the British Isles, 1450–1660*.

Michael Graham is an associate professor of History at the University of Akron. His publications include *The Uses of Reform: "Godly Discipline" and Popular Behavior in Scotland and Beyond* (1996), which was awarded the Roland Bainton Prize for History and Theology by the Sixteenth Century Studies Conference. He has also been a James Cameron Faculty Fellow at the Reformation Studies Institute, University of St Andrews, where the bulk of his contribution to this volume was written. He earned his PhD from the University of Virginia in 1993.

David Grummitt completed his PhD on Calais under the early Tudors in 1997. He has published on Henry VII, Anglo-French relations, Calais and warfare and military service in England in the fifteenth and early sixteenth centuries and is editor of *The English Experience in France, c. 1450–1558*. He has co-authored, with Steven Gunn and Hans Cool, a major comparative study

of the impact of war on the polities of England and the Habsburg Netherlands between 1477 and 1559, due to be published in 2004. He is currently a Research Fellow on the 1422–1504 section of the History of Parliament.

DeLloyd J. Guth has researched, taught and published diversely since completing his doctoral thesis. He is currently Professor of Law and Canadian Legal History, Faculty of Law, University of Manitoba, Winnipeg, and Recurrent Visiting Professor of Medieval Law, Central European University, Budapest. An activist for legal archives, and quondam curator to the Supreme Court of Canada, he also continues primary research in English legal history from the Wars of the Roses to the Restoration. His most recent book is *Family Law in the Medieval World: An International Survey* (2000).

Steve Hindle is Professor in the Department of History at the University of Warwick. He is the author of *The State and Social Change in Early Modern England, 1550–1640* (2000); and of several articles on the governance of rural parishes in the sixteenth and seventeenth centuries; and co-editor with Paul Griffiths and Adam Fox of *The Experience of Authority in Early Modern England* (1996). He has just completed a monograph entitled *On the Parish?: The Micro-Politics of Poor Relief in Rural England, c.1550–1730* (forthcoming).

R. W. Hoyle is Professor of Rural History at the University of Reading. He has written widely on aspects of sixteenth-century history such as public finance (including taxation and the management of the crown's estate), rural society and the politics of the North of England. His most recent book is *The Pilgrimage of Grace and the Politics of the 1530s* (2001).

Peter Iver Kaufman is Professor of Religious Studies and faculty co-ordinator of the Johnston and Carolina Scholars Program at the University of North Carolina, Chapel Hill. His publications on early modern religious reform include *Redeeming*

Politics (1990), *Prayer, Despair, and Drama: Elizabethan Introspection* (1996), and *Thinking of the Laity in Late Tudor England* (forthcoming).

Alexandra F. Johnston is Professor of English at the University of Toronto and director of Records of Early English Drama (which she was instrumental in founding) since 1975. She was co-editor with Margaret Rogerson of the first of the REED series, the *Records of York* (1979), is one of the four co-editors of the Oxford University and City records to be published in 2004 and is preparing the records of Berkshire, Buckinghamshire and Oxfordshire for a future REED volume. She has written extensively on many aspects of early English drama.

Norman Jones is Professor and Chair of History at Utah State University. He has held visiting fellowships at Harvard University, the Huntington Library, and Christ Church and Lincoln College, Oxford. His publications include *Faith by Statute: Parliament and the Settlement of Religion, 1559* (1982), *God and the Moneylenders: Usury and Law in Early Modern England* (1989), *The Birth of the Elizabethan Age: England in the 1560s* (1992), and *The English Reformation: Religion and Cultural Adaptation* (2002). He co-edited *Interest Groups and Legislation in Elizabethan Parliaments* (1989) and *The Parliaments of Elizabethan England* (1990).

Anne Laurence is Professor of History at the Open University and author of *Women in England 1500–1760: A Social History* (1995). She is currently working on a comparative study of women in the different nations of the British Isles in the seventeenth century.

Ben R. McRee earned his doctorate at Indiana University and teaches medieval and early modern British history at Franklin & Marshall College in Lancaster, Pennsylvania. His research interests lie in the religious and urban history of the late medieval and early Tudor periods, particularly as they have intersected in the activities of urban religious gilds. Results of that work have appeared in the *Journal of British Studies*, *Speculum*, the *English Historical Review*, and other periodicals. He is currently working on an examination of the office of mayor in late-medieval Norwich.

John Milsom, editor of the journal *Early Music*, has written widely on the relationship of music and society in the Tudor period, and has been particularly interested in the role of popular song and singing.

Catherine F. Patterson is Associate Professor of History at the University of Houston in Houston, Texas, where she teaches British and European history. She received her PhD degree from the University of Chicago. Her publications include *Urban Patronage in Early Modern England: Corporate Boroughs, the Landed Elite, and the Crown, 1580–1640* as well as articles in the *Journal of British Studies*, *History* and *Midland History*.

David Potter obtained his PhD from he University of Cambridge with a thesis on Anglo–French diplomacy in the Renaissance. He then concentrated his research interests on French History in the 15th and 16th centuries and has continued to publish on Anglo–French diplomacy in the 16th century, military history (including studies in French on mercenaries in French service). He is author of *War and Government in the French Provinces: Picardy 1470–1560* (1993), *A History of France, 1460–1560: the Emergence of a Nation State* (1995), *The French Wars of Religion: Selected Documents* (1998) *Un homme de guerre au temps de la Renaissance: la vie et les lettres d'Oudart du Biez, maréchal de France et gouverneur de Picardie et de Boulogne (vers 1475–1553)* (2001) and many articles on the nobility, politics and military organization of late medieval and early modern France and England. He has edited *France in the Later Middle Ages* (2003) and *Foreign Intelligence and Information Gathering in Elizabethan England: Two English Treatises on the State of France, 1579–84* (forthcoming, 2004).

William Sheils teaches History at the University of York, specializing in the Reformation and British Social History in the early modern period. He has published widely on the English Reformation, on both Puritans and Catholics, and has written a textbook, *The English Reformation 1530–1570* (1989). He has been editor of *Studies in Church History*, and has also edited with Sheridan Gilley a *History of Religion in Britain* (1994). He is currently completing an edition of an estate book of the archbishopric of York covering the period 1620 to 1760.

Robert Tittler teaches at Concordia University, Montreal, and has been Visiting Professor of History at Yale. He chairs the Executive Board of Records of Early English Drama. His most recent books explore the politics and political culture of post-Reformation urban communities: *Architecture and Power: The Town Hall and the English Urban Community, 1500–1640* (1991), *The Reformation and the Towns in England: Politics and Political Culture, 1540–1640* (1998) and *Townspeople and Nation: English Urban Experiences, 1540–1640* (2001). He is currently completing a book on English civic portraiture in the same era.

Joseph P. Ward is an associate professor of History at the University of Mississippi. He is the author of *Metropolitan Communities: Trade Guilds, Identity, and Change in Early Modern London* (1997); the editor of *Britain and the American South: From Colonialism to Rock and Roll* (2003); and co-editor of *The Country and The City Revisited: England and the Politics of Culture, 1550–1850* (1999) and *Protestant Identities: Religion, Society, and Self-Fashioning in Post-Reformation England* (1999).

Retha Warnicke is Professor of History at Arizona State University. Her previous publications include *Women of the English Renaissance and Reformation* (1983); *The Rise and Fall of Anne Boleyn: Family Politics at the Court of Henry VIII* (1989); and *The Marrying of Anne of Cleves: Royal Protocol in Tudor England* (2000). She is currently writing a biography of Mary, Queen of Scots.

Daniel Woolf is Professor of History and Dean of the Faculty of Arts at the University of Alberta, Edmonton. He has previously taught at McMaster University and Dalhousie University. Among his books are *The Idea of History in Early Stuart England* (1990), *Reading History in Early Modern England (2000)*, and *The Social Circulation of the Past* (2003). In addition he has co-edited several volumes of essays and is the author of articles in journals such as the *American Historical Review* and *Past and Present*.

Jenny Wormald is a Fellow in Modern History at St Hilda's College, Oxford. She formerly taught in the Department of Scottish History, University of Glasgow. She has published *Court, Kirk and Community: Scotland, 1470–1625* (1981, reprinted 1991); *Lords and Men in Scotland: Bonds of Manrent, 1442–1603* (1985); *Mary Queen of Scots: a Study in Failure* (1988, republished as *Mary Queen of Scots: Politics, Passion and a Kingdom Lost*, 2001); and articles on late medieval and early modern Scotland and Britain.

Preface and Acknowledgements

The opportunity to compile and edit a volume of this sort has been both a privilege and a challenge. The privilege has been the opportunity to put forth, in something of a cubist form, a series of perspectives about Britain in the Tudor era which have emerged over the course of our research careers. Though one of us has been somewhat more taken up with questions of politics and religion, and the other with questions regarding social groupings and cultural expressions, this volume has allowed us to establish a comfortable meeting place on the broad issues, and to define the contents of the volume accordingly.

The challenge has been to find the right people to share with us compatible perspectives on specific issues: those who were not only expert in what we considered the important subjects, but also willing and able to devote substantial efforts to the work and meet firm deadlines. Though we had also hoped to have an opening essay treating the British landscape, which seemed an obvious backdrop for the scenes to follow, the ultimate shape of the volume otherwise conforms pretty closely to our initial vision.

Our first debt must be to Tessa Harvey, who initially invited us to take on this task for Blackwell, and to Andrew MacLennan, Blackwell's Consultant Editor, who applied his usual but quite extraordinary skills to helping us define the shape of the whole at the outset. Blackwell's supporting editorial cast of Angela Cohen, Helen Lawton, and Tamsin Smith took us in hand from there and helped us see the whole to its completion. We are grateful to them as well as to Julia Pope, who pitched in with some of the indexing, and to Janey Fisher, our meticulous copy-editor. Our greatest debt must be to our contributors and colleagues in print. Virtually all of them put their shoulders to the wheel; many did so in the face of competing commitments, serious illness, changes in employment, or other personal distractions. It is one thing to envision how a thing should work, but quite another to build it and make it run: we are pleased to have done the former, but it is they who have done most of the rest. Our final debt must be to our wives. Even having had to share each of us with the other, they are still speaking to us.

Robert Tittler and Norman Jones

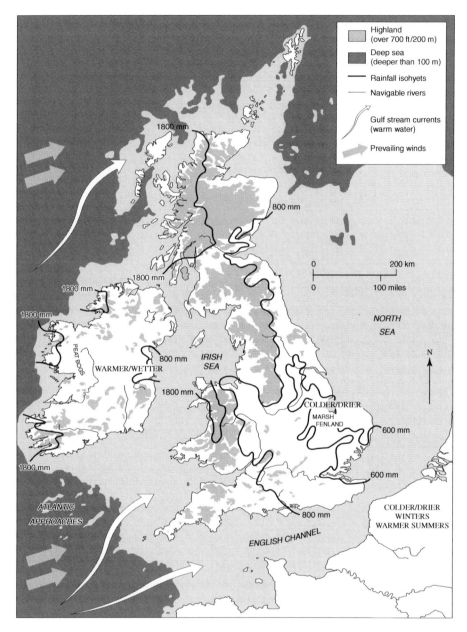

Map 1 Physical Geography of the British Isles
Source: Nicholls, *A History of the Modern British Isles, 1529–1603* (Oxford, 1999), p. xxi

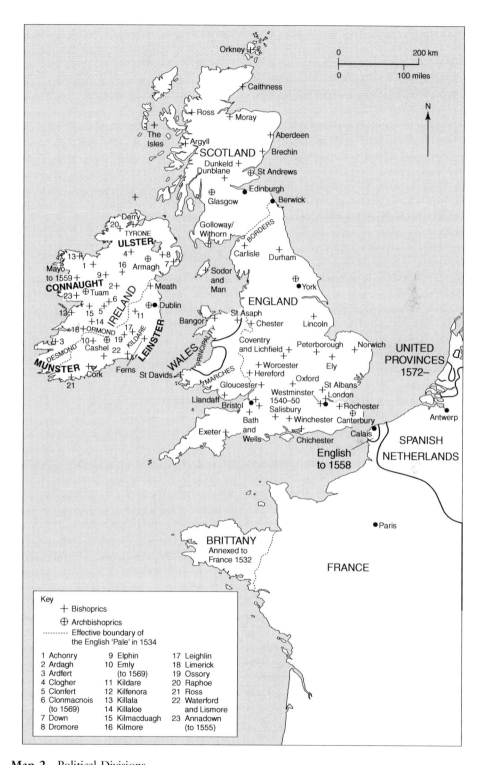

Orkney

+ Caithness

0 ___ 200 km
0 ___ 100 miles

N

+ Ross + Moray

The
Isles + Argyll + Aberdeen

SCOTLAND + Brechin
Dunkeld +
Dunblane ⊕ St Andrews
+

⊕ Edinburgh
Glasgow ● Berwick

Derry
20 + Golloway/
TYRONE Withorn BORDERS
ULSTER
4 + ⊕ +8 + Carlisle + Durham
13 + 1 + 16 Armagh 7 +
Mayo 9 + + Sodor
to 1559 + 2 + + Meath and ⊕ York
CONNAUGHT Man
23 + ⊕ Tuam + 6
12 + 15 5 ⊕ ● Dublin ENGLAND
+ 3 + 10 + 11 Bangor + St Asaph Lincoln
+ 14 IRELAND + + Chester
+ 18 ORMOND 17 LEINSTER WALES Coventry Peterborough + Norwich
DESMOND 19 KILDARE and Lichfield +
Cashel 22 PRINCIPALITY + Worcester + Ely
MUNSTER + Hereford + Oxford UNITED
Cork Ferns St Davids + Gloucester + St Albans PROVINCES
21 MARCHES Westminster + London 1572–
Llandaff 1540–50 ⊕ Rochester
Bristol + Salisbury
Bath + + Winchester Canterbury Antwerp
Exeter + and + Chichester Calais
Wells English SPANISH
to 1558 NETHERLANDS

BRITTANY
Annexed to
France 1532 FRANCE

● Paris

Key
  + Bishoprics
  ⊕ Archbishoprics
------ Effective boundary of
       the English 'Pale' in 1534
1 Achonry   9 Elphin   17 Leighlin
2 Ardagh   10 Emly   18 Limerick
3 Ardfert   (to 1569)   19 Ossory
4 Clogher   11 Kildare   20 Raphoe
5 Clonfert   12 Kilfenora   21 Ross
6 Clonmacnois   13 Killala   22 Waterford
  (to 1569)   14 Killaloe   and Lismore
7 Down   15 Kilmacduagh   23 Annadown
8 Dromore   16 Kilmore   (to 1555)

Map 2 Political Divisions
Source: Nicholls, *A History of the Modern British Isles, 1529–1603* (Oxford, 1999), p. xxii

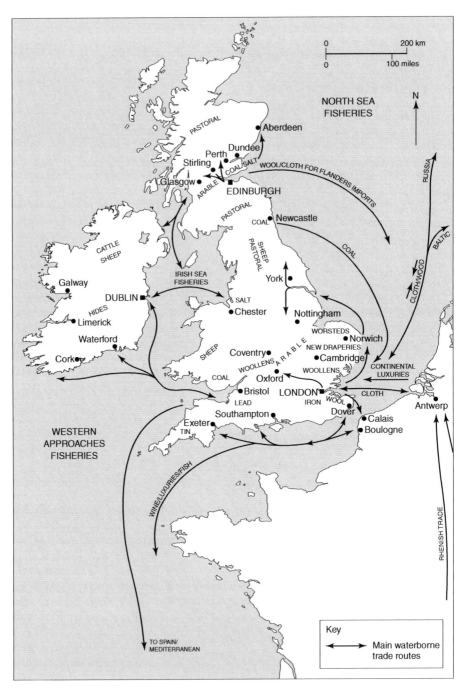

Map 3 Towns and Trades
Source: Nicholls, *A History of the Modern British Isles, 1529–1603* (Oxford, 1999), p. xxiii

Introduction

ROBERT TITTLER AND NORMAN JONES

In bringing forth this volume of essays we are well aware that the title 'Tudor Britain' will strike some readers as a misnomer. Both in its chronological and geographic implications, its choice requires an explanation. We take the dynastic designation 'the Tudors' as a precise form of shorthand to designate the period embraced by this volume. We intend it to announce that our coverage begins in the 1480s, and not to imply that it deals only with the kingdom of England and its Celtic satellites. To understand the sixteenth century we thought it essential to start with the reigns of Henry VII of England (1485–1509), and James IV (1488–1513) of Scotland. It was logical to conclude the book in 1603 when James VI of Scotland succeeded Elizabeth Tudor to become James I of England, thereby bringing the Tudor dynasty to a close.

In addition, we take 'Britain' to define our geographic limits. Of course we recognize that sixteenth-century Scotland and England were autonomous and independent nations, whose political histories had been and continued to be shaped by mutual antagonisms. The era under consideration begins in Scotland with the death of James III in 1488 during a rebellion repudiating his pro-English policies. His son, James IV, died at the Battle of Flodden in 1513, struck down by English billmen. His successor, James V, died in 1542, a week after being defeated by the English at Solway Moss. The 1540s saw the 'Rough Wooing' as English troops, attempting to convince the Scots to marry their infant Queen Mary Stewart to Edward Tudor, sacked Edinburgh, devastated Dundee, and ended with the massacre of Scots after the battle of Pinkie in 1547. This maladroit policy drove the Scots into close alliance with the French, and made them players against the English and Spanish in the Habsburg–Valois struggle that ended in 1559. In 1560 English forces, making common cause with rebellious Scots, besieged Leith and forced the French to withdraw from Scotland, securing the dominance of the Protestant Lords of the Congregation. By 1568 Mary Stewart had been driven out of Scotland to a refuge in England, where her awkward presence as a Catholic Queen of Scotland and next-in-line to the English crown served as a potential threat to the Elizabethan state. Elizabeth kept her under house arrest, and eventually made the difficult decision to have her executed for treason in 1587. Ironically, this century of Anglo-Scottish conflict ended with the peaceful accession of James VI of Scotland to the throne of England in 1603.

Yet when Blackwell and the Historical Association agreed to produce a series of 'Companions to British History', they wished to represent recent historiographical thinking,[1] which treats the parts of the British archipelago as interrelated units, and they accordingly chose to call this volume 'Tudor Britain'. In accepting the invitation to edit this work, we accepted the challenge of producing an inclusive and integrated volume while acknowledging the reality that there was no pan-Britannic state in the sixteenth century. We have thus taken 'Britain' in the title to recognize the scholarly concern, which we ardently share, to ensure that the histories of the various parts of the isles are linked together as much as possible as distinctive but nevertheless highly interactive parts. We have chosen the subjects of the essays which follow so as to reflect these possibilities. Our colleagues have been encouraged to take an integrated approach where that has seemed warranted by their subjects, and to remain traditionally insular where it has not.

We have also encouraged discussion, where the subject has warranted it and where secondary scholarship has made it possible, of the principality of Wales and the kingdom of Ireland, as well as of those areas which were nominally and formally a part of the kingdoms of Scotland and England, such as the border country and the Isles, but which were not effectively governed by either. Wales had been annexed by the English crown under Edward I in 1284, but not until the Act of Union passed by the English parliament in 1536, reinforced by another broad Act of 1543, did Wales begin to become integrated with the English administrative system and to gain representatives in parliament. Ireland had a similarly long period of subjugation to the kingdom of England, not being able, at the opening of our period, to hold its parliament without the assent of the English crown, nor being master of its own destiny in most other respects. After the earl of Kildaire's unsuccessful rebellion of 1533–4, Henry VIII imposed direct rule, setting out to bring the Irish under as strict control as he could manage, and adopting the anomalous title of King of Ireland in 1541 to symbolize his intent.

Both the Scottish and English monarchies shared a troubled relationship with Gaelic-speaking regions they claimed to control. In Scotland, the Borders, the Highlands and the Isles were dominated by powerful clans such as the Douglases and the Campbells who resisted royal control. The Tudors shared the problem of the Borders and the Isles with the Stewarts, since their common national border passed through the area dominated by the Border families such as the Dacres. In the Irish Sea the Clan Donald, the Lords of the Isles, controlled ground claimed by both kingdoms, from Antrim in Ireland to the Hebrides and the Earldom of Ross. The last powerful Lord of the Isles, Donald Dubh, who could command thousands of men and scores of ships, died in 1545, while negotiating an alliance with Henry VIII against the Scottish kingdom.

Although historians recognize the interrelated nature of the political history of the British Isles, the historiographical traditions of the region have developed in different ways. This, too, has had to be taken into account in organizing the volume at hand. With their nation's political, constitutional and diplomatic history having been fleshed out in close detail for a very long time, English historians have, in recent decades, invested much more effort in research outside these areas than have historians of Scotland, Ireland and Wales. As David Cannadine and others have pointed out, the energy expended by English historians from the 1970s to the 1990s on some of the newer methodologies was not mirrored by most historians of Scotland, Wales or Ireland. They were more interested in exploring their own national traditions, and they did so largely through more traditional approaches. The result has been an impressive expansion of the political history of Scotland, Wales and Ireland, but (with the notable exception of women's history) less progress on social, economic, environmental or cultural histories.

Notwithstanding this somewhat uneven disposition of current secondary scholarship, we have striven to encourage reflections on the whole of the British Isles, and on the broad, virtually holistic range of subjects which are increasingly intrinsic to the study of the past. We mean to acknowledge that over the past few decades 'history' as we were taught it has been greatly influenced and fundamentally changed by its close contact with other disciplines: especially with the social sciences (chiefly sociology and anthropology) in the 1970s and 1980s, with philosophy and literature since then, and perhaps with the Fine Arts poised in the wings to take their turn in years to come. Lines of demarcation in academic institutions, long quite rigid, have yielded substantially and often quite fruitfully to interdisciplinary thinking on all fronts. Perhaps these tendencies have unfolded sooner and more naturally in universities outside the British Isles. There, undergraduate education itself has long been more inter- or multi-disciplinary, the student clientele has had a less specialized but also broader preparation, and narrow sub-specialties within such fields as 'English history' have not found as fertile soil. As one of us has expressed at greater length elsewhere,[2] and in the teaching and research in which we both engage, we share a firm commitment to these developments. We have structured this volume accordingly.

Our Table of Contents will thus look a lot different and more inclusive than it would have done even a decade ago. The general public may be surprised to find some of our chosen topics on the list, as they certainly do not reflect what would have been taught, probably under the rubric of 'Tudor England', until quite recently. Having in both cases begun our professional careers with very traditional, nationally oriented, English rather than British, and rather narrowly political training, we understand this well.

In partial consequence of this perspective, it is only somewhat coincidental that Canadians, Americans, Australians, New Zealanders and a resident of Hong Kong join English, Irish and Scots contributors to this volume, all having been encouraged to bring their diverse sensibilities to the task. The questions we have asked together, and the ways in which we have tried to answer them, reflect the influences of our own experiences as members of different political and cultural traditions within the English-speaking scholarly community. None of us have mastered all its corners, but this volume strives at least to offer what we have learned about different subjects within different traditions.

In the belief that all human activities are played out and shaped by the context of the land we inhabit, we had earnestly hoped to begin this volume with an essay on the topography of the British Isles and its implications for the history of the era under discussions. However, in the challenging course of bringing together the work of more than two dozen colleagues in a finite period of time, some disappointments are bound to accrue. It is a cause of considerable regret that the chapter which we had commissioned on this subject has not been produced.

We have divided the discussions into four parts which seemed to us to reflect best the breadth and scope of the subject. Part I takes up the more traditional issues of government and its institutions, though not all the essays handle their subjects in traditional ways. The opening three chapters in Part I establish the basic narrative of political development at the national level and in England. We recognize that these chapters look suspiciously like the traditional approach to 'Tudor England' which we wish to move beyond, but we expect them to serve most readers as familiar points of reference for what follows. The rest of the chapters in Part I work outwards from this beginning to consider two important subjects relative to national government: the royal courts (chapter 4) and legal systems (chapter 5).

We wish then to broaden our overview of political issues by moving downwards and outwards from the English centre with which we began: to the government of the counties of England and Wales (chapter 6) and of towns and cities (chapter 7), thence to the nature of governance in the more disparate regions of the area, the Borders, Marches and Irish Pale (chapter 8). Then we turn to the politics and government of Scotland itself (chapter 9), to political relations between England and Scotland (chapter 10) and finally to British relations with the wider world (chapter 11).

These chapters concern the structures and strategies by which people were governed, but only by implication do they refer to English, Irish, Scottish and Welsh people themselves. We designed Part II to respond to that need. Reflecting our shared convictions about the centrality of the Reformation experience, in all its parts, we decided to begin with questions of belief. Against the description of traditional religious beliefs and practices (chapter 12), we consider the nature and implications of the Reformation for questions of land ownership and the authority which comes with it (chapter 13), the Elizabethan period of accommodation and definition (Chapter 14), and then the emerging traditions of Catholic resistance and Protestant Dissent (chapters 15 and 16) before offering an overview of the Scottish experience by itself (chapter 17).

Part III of the volume has been devoted to particular types of people, their characteristic activities, and the circles in which they moved: we hope we have labelled it appropriately as concerning 'people and groups'. Here we deal with economic activity in both agrarian and urban contexts (chapters 18 and 19), with urban society itself at both the metropolitan and provincial levels (chapters 20 and 21), and with the role of women in all of these social settings (chapter 22).

Finally, we have considered it essential to address the remarkable cultural outpouring of this era in all its major forms. We do this not in the hope of making definitive statements about the nature of particular media in and of themselves, a task for which there are other 'Blackwell Companion' volumes, but rather to describe each medium in its broader social context. We begin with an innovative chapter (chapter 23) on how contemporaries remembered their past, and how such collective memories shaped perceptions of ethnic, regional and national identities within the British Isles. We move from there to discussions of individual media of expression in their appropriate social and political contexts. Chapters on drama and theatre, on portraiture, on architecture and on music (chapters 24–7) all of them firmly rooted in the social context of the era, reflect some of the most fertile and intriguingly inter-disciplinary developments of recent scholarship. In our view it has now become imperative to include them in any broad treatment of the age. And though it is also sometimes neglected, we feel that a discussion of science and technology (chapter 28) is an equally appropriate, indeed, vital part of the whole.

In sum, we have tried to represent the state of current scholarship on that wide range of issues which now constitute the history of the British Isles in the period bounded by the Tudor dynasty of England. At the request of our publishers, who hope to make this volume accessible to the general reading public as well to academics and their students, we have avoided a plethora of footnotes. Essential references to specific points have been provided in note form, along with bibliographies listing specific sources of each essay. In addition, we hope that the non-specialist will find the selected additional bibliographies of each essay to be useful guides to further reading.[3]

NOTES

1. See especially Edwin Jones's *The English Nation: The Great Myth* (Stroud, 1998) and Norman Davies's *The Isles: A History* (Oxford, 1999).
2. Robert Tittler, 'Early Modern British History: Here and There, Now and Again', *Albion*, 31, 2 (Summer 1999) pp. 190-206.
3. The rendering of spellings in either original or modernized form has been left to the individual contributors.

PART I

Government and Politics

INTRODUCTION

The study of government and politics in sixteenth-century Britain has been stood on its head since the days of G. R. Elton and J. D. Mackie. In the mid-twentieth century historians were emphasizing the processes of centralization from the top down. Classically spelled out in Elton's *The Tudor Revolution in Government* of 1953 and adumbrated in terms of 'rising' monarchies, these arguments held that the intentions of monarchs and ministers were key. Currently, as the scholars writing here suggest, the emphasis has shifted from the top and the centre to the peripheries. We are now asking how government and politics worked in practice, day to day, in the hands of the thousands of men who made the state work. This mystery is caught in the phrase 'self-government by royal command,' a seeming contradiction that made sense on the ground more than in theory.

The historiography of English royal government has been evolving, changing our understand of how Henry VII actually ruled and undermining the assumption that Henry VIII and his ministers were the great innovators. David Grummitt, writing on Henry VII, and Joe Block, writing on Henry VIII, show us an early Tudor system of governance that was less 'modern' than once thought, and yet still innovative.

Forms of government and political processes varied widely across the Isles and across time. Of course, the national governments of Scotland and England had separate political systems, varying within themselves as well as between one another. Consequently, there are times when it is appropriate to make the unit of government the level of analysis, so that corporate towns are treated as distinct from counties, the royal courts as distinct from the law courts. Catherine Patterson demonstrates that towns throughout the two realms had similar governmental issues and that town governors were depended upon and empowered by their crowns to maintain control. The work on English county government has been so intense over the last few decades that the English counties were deemed worthy of a chapter of their own. However, we asked Steven Ellis to delineate rule and politics in the home counties from rule and politics in the Marches and Borders. Foreign relations are, of course, very important to understanding national politics. Because the main site of international conflict in sixteenth-century Britain was the border running from Carlisle to

Newcastle on Tyne, we deemed it important to have Jane Dawson's distinct chapter on Anglo-Scottish relations. British relations with the rest of the world were as much economic as military and political, and, as the Reformation progressed, those relations were increasingly influenced by ideological values. David Potter's exploration of these topics demonstrates the rapid and important changes occurring across the century, including the Plantation of Ireland and the first stirring of North American settlement.

One way to think about government and politics is to explore structures. This still useful approach was exemplified by the work of G. R. Elton, whose 'points of contact' argument, stressing the roles of court, parliament, and privy council, has been a starting-point for many scholars. There is, however, another way to look at government and politics. Using the lens of political culture we can explore the values, intellectual assumptions and social forces that underlie political behaviour. In the sixteenth century two important value systems operated in conjunction with politics and governmental systems, religion and the law. Religion is taken up in the 'Belief' section of this collection, but the law and the men of the law are DeLloyd Guth's brief because their way of construing the possible set bounds around the politically feasible. Just as importantly, the places of political interaction operated according to values that shaped the politically possible. Retha Warnicke's article on royal Courts exemplifies this: methods of access to the royal person, the power of ministers and favourites, gender, where and when one ate, whom one knew, concepts of honour and myriad other things shaped the political life of courtiers and of countries. David Dean's exploration of Elizabethan politics shows us how political decisions were deeply connected to small things like the jewellery worn by ladies-in-waiting.

When seen through the lens of political culture, the English, Scottish, Welsh and Irish experiences come into bolder relief. Scotland and England had different royal Courts, putting the monarch in a different relation to the courtiers and demonstrating differing cultural influences. Ireland, of course, had no Court at all, which, one suspects, made monarchical government even more dependent on the willing co-operation of local magnates. As Steve Ellis suggests, Henry VIII's failure to grasp this contributed to many of the Tudor regime's problems in Ireland and the North. If monarchical rule required points of contact, the more isolated parts of both realms had poor connections.

Differing legal systems created different political and governmental cultures, too. The imposition of English law on Wales through the Act of Union (1536–43) integrated it into the realm in ways that Ireland, which had its own parliament, never experienced. And, once again, the legal reach of the central courts in both nations became weaker the further people were from Westminster and Edinburgh. As Steven Ellis notes, London was a logical capital for the Angevin kingdom with all of its French possessions, but it was an inefficient place from which to rule the North, Wales and Ireland. By the same token, ruling the Western Isles from Edinburgh was not easy, either.

The picture of government and politics that emerges here is like meeting a long-lost family member. There is something familiar about it, but it is a stranger nonetheless. It is our hope that these chapters will encourage readers to continue comparing and contrasting political communities in the British Isles, moving political history away from *res gestae* toward things done in the web of values and social systems. It was, after all, their political value systems that held nations together despite religious revolutions, despite child monarchs and childless queens, despite economic crises, and all the rest.

CHAPTER ONE

The Establishment of the Tudor Dynasty

DAVID GRUMMITT

On 1 August 1485 Henry Tudor, earl of Richmond, led a small group of followers from exile in France to lay claim to the English throne. He landed at Milford Haven in South Wales on 7 August and three weeks later defeated Richard III at the battle of Bosworth and was proclaimed Henry VII, the first Tudor king of England.

Henry Tudor was an unlikely king.[1] He had been an exile in Brittany and later France since June 1471 when he and his uncle, Jasper, had fled England on the collapse of the restored monarchy of Henry VI. Henry Tudor's Lancastrian credentials, through his mother's Beaufort blood and the fact of his grandfather Owen's marriage to Katherine of Valois, widow of Henry V, made him a potential rallying-point for opposition to the Yorkist Edward IV. In exile Henry had been the plaything of princely diplomacy. In 1471 he and Jasper had probably planned to go to the court of the French king, Louis XI, where Jasper was a pensioner, but storms had forced them to the coast of Brittany. In Brittany Henry proved a useful bargaining counter for Duke Francis II, who sought English help against his feudal overlord the king of France. In 1475 Edward IV had requested the return of the exiled Tudors, ostensibly to marry Henry to one of his own daughters, and Henry had even been put aboard a ship at St Malo bound for England. At the last minute he feigned illness and escaped capture and an uncertain fate in England.

The death of Edward IV on 9 April 1483 transformed Henry's position. Soon after the king's death the throne, which had passed to his nine-year-old son Edward V, was usurped by Edward IV's brother Richard, duke of Gloucester. Richard, whose own grasp on the throne was less than secure, was keen to gain control of Henry Tudor as a potential rival but was unable or unwilling to offer the military assistance that would induce Francis to hand him over. When, in October 1483, Richard's ally in the usurpation, the duke of Buckingham, led a rebellion, mainly comprised of former servants of Edward IV, against the king, Duke Francis gave Henry assistance in assembling a fleet to return to England to make his claim. The expedition was a disaster and Buckingham's rebellion a fiasco: Henry failed to make landfall and Richard redoubled his efforts to secure the most dangerous threat to his throne. The Buckingham debacle did, however, have one important and positive outcome. Henry

was joined by a new group of Yorkist exiles, men like Sir Giles Daubeney, and this
gave his opposition to Richard a new and powerful dimension. In September 1484,
however, he was again forced to flee Brittany. The Breton government had brokered
a deal with Richard and so Henry was forced to flee to France, disguised as a servant,
to escape being returned to England.

There Henry was able to forge an unlikely coalition between die-hard Lancastrians and disaffected Yorkists that made his claim a real threat to Richard III. At Rennes
cathedral on Christmas Day 1483 Henry solemnly promised to take Elizabeth,
daughter of Edward IV, as his queen and was acclaimed king of England by the exiles.
Nevertheless, Henry's position was far from assured and his accession to the English
throne as distant as ever. The new French king, Charles VIII, played an ambiguous
game: while he encouraged Henry to use the English royal title it is now clear that
he did little in practice to assist his claim to the throne. When Henry and the exiles
set sail to claim the English throne they did so at the head of a motley army paid for
not by the French king but by money borrowed from a French nobleman.[2] Equally,
when Henry faced Richard III across the fields of the Leicestershire/Warwickshire
border on the morning of 22 August he did so not at the head of a large group of
individuals who had flocked to his banner to oust a usurping tyrant but as a fugitive
whose time for flight had ended. Henry Tudor won the battle of Bosworth more by
luck than by judgement: Richard III's ill-advised adherence to chivalric practice and
the skill of Tudor's French pikemen won the day against all the odds.[3]

Few English kings can have been as ill-prepared for kingship as Henry Tudor. He
had, he told the French chronicler Commynes, been on the run since the age of five;
he had had none of the training in English government, justice and war that had, for
instance, been Henry V's kingly apprenticeship. What he did have, however, was a
hard upbringing in the realities of fifteenth-century diplomacy and politics. He had
studied the kingship of the French kings at first hand. His models were, therefore,
continental: one commentator would later observe that he 'would like to govern in
the French fashion'. But this is to confuse Henry VII's character and style of kingship. The personal nature of Henry's rule, his suspicion of others and the absolute
trust he placed in those who had stood by him in exile were distinctly his, products
of his unique upbringing. Moreover, Henry had to innovate to survive; to establish
the Tudor dynasty he had to redefine the English medieval system of monarchy and
governance.

The sense that Henry VII's accession heralded the beginnings of a new age of
peace, reconciliation and stable and effective government has been reflected in the
historiography. Equally, however, there is confusion: was Henry the last medieval or
the first early modern king of England? This is compounded by the fact that the
sources for the reign are more scattered and 'medieval' in character than for the later
Tudors. Early perceptions of the reign were dominated by Francis Bacon's *History
of the Reign of King Henry VII*, published in 1622 for the future Charles I. However,
Bacon's picture of an apolitical and bureaucrat king was written to reflect his own
disappointment at a failed career at court. Bacon's account, devoid of high politics,
reinforced the impression that Henry's reign was distinct from those of his Lancastrian and Yorkist predecessors, whose reigns were dominated by dynastic confrontation and noble rebellion. This was reinforced by the largely institutional nature of
the first serious studies of Henry's reign: writing in the early twentieth century,
A. F. Pollard argued that Henry VII distanced himself from the petty squabbles of

the nobility that had characterized the disastrous rule of the Henry VI and, by asserting princely power, laid the foundations for the 'despotism' of Henry VIII. The 'new
monarchy', therefore, was based upon bureaucratic innovation and a desire to make
the nobility subservient to the royal will.

From the mid-1950s, however, this orthodoxy was gradually eroded away and the
first Tudor was relocated within a late-medieval context. First, Geoffrey Elton suggested that the real transition to a modern state took place during the 1530s and
that Henry VII still governed an essentially medieval realm in an essentially medieval
way. Later, Bertram Wolffe argued that many of Henry's fiscal innovations actually
had their origins in the estate management of the Yorkist kings. Henry, then, was
transformed from the dynamic founder of the 'new monarchy' into a lacklustre
medieval king. The standard biography of the reign, S. B. Chrimes's *Henry VII*, first
written in 1972 but reissued as recently as 1999, struggles to identify exactly what
it was that Henry achieved: 'His was not an original mind; he was no great innova-
tor. He was rather a highly skilful builder on existing foundations . . . In the ultimate
analysis, the quality of Henry VII was not that of a creator, but rather of a stabiliser,
for lack of whom ships of state are apt to founder'.[4] Anyone reading this account will
be struck by how little Chrimes appeared to know of what actually happened during
the reign. The interaction between the king and the political nation – that is, the
landowning classes, nobility and gentry – has become accepted by historians of the
fifteenth century as the acid test of the success of any reign. Studying Henry VII by
this criterion one can judge the novelty of his reign and his success in establishing
the Tudor dynasty. Historians who study Henry's reign in these terms can be placed
in two very distinct categories. First, there are those who see Henry's reign as part
of a process of state-building, started under Edward IV and largely completed by the
end of Elizabeth's reign.[5] Although local stresses did occur, Henry brought strong
kingship and through that exorcised many of the ghosts of the fifteenth century. On
the other hand, Christine Carpenter has argued that Henry fundamentally misun-
derstood the nature of late medieval political society and the need to govern with
and through the land-owning elite. Judged by these standards, she asserts, Henry
was an incompetent monarch who was lucky to pass on the throne intact to his son.[6]

Thus recent historiography has tended to play down the novel aspects of Henry
Tudor's accession. Nevertheless, it did mark the beginning of a new dynasty that
would rule England for over a century. This chapter, therefore, will consider five areas
and determine to what extent Henry's policies were new and laid the foundations of
the Tudor monarchy. These are:

1) the ideas and influences behind Henry's kingship;
2) his relationship with the nobility;
3) the impact of Tudor rule on local political society;
4) administration and change in the machinery of government; and
5) his last years and the legacy of his reign.

Ideas and Influences

Henry's victory at Bosworth was undoubtedly against the odds. It was therefore
important for him to assert quickly the foundations of his claim to the throne and
define the nature of his kingship to the political nation.[7] After the battle, Henry

marched to London and in a service at St Paul's Cathedral gave thanks for his victory. However, the banners presented here asserted a hereditary right to the throne rather than the more obvious divine judgement in battle: first, the arms of St George, a traditional English symbol; second, the red dragon, not a narrowly Welsh symbol but a banner employed by previous English kings from Richard the Lionheart to Edward III; and, finally, the dun cow, a banner which highlighted Henry's Beaufort, Lancastrian blood but which also had Neville associations. This was a dubious claim but one which became the foundation of the Tudor title. The hereditary claim to the throne was also apparent in Henry's first parliament, summoned to meet at Westminster on 7 November 1485. In parliament the new king addressed the Commons and proclaimed his right to the throne, not only by divine right as revealed by his victory at Bosworth but also by hereditary title. An act of attainder was passed against King Richard and his closest followers which, crucially, dated Henry's accession to 21 August, the day before Bosworth. This, in theory, could have important ramifications for landowners who supported their king in battle, risking forfeiture if their then lord was defeated in battle; and was thus a controversial and potentially unpopular move. Nevertheless, it demonstrated Henry's desire to assert his authority over the political nation. Henry's first parliament lasted until the beginning of March. Before it closed the new king had made good his promise and married, on 18 January 1486, Elizabeth of York. Henry had therefore established a claim to the throne based on right inheritance, united the houses of York and Lancaster through marriage, and symbolically lifted the crown above the warring factions of the Wars of the Roses.

These priorities were reflected in several demonstrations of Henry's concept of kingship. In the first five years of the reign he ordered a new coinage and built a new warship, the *Sovereign*, making much use of the arched imperial crown which signified more than mere kingly power. He also emphasized the sacral nature of kingship: his proposed effigy at the heart of Westminster Abbey on top of the shrine of Edward the Confessor would have shown him receiving the crown from God. Henry was able to juxtapose various images of kingship in an attempt to broaden the appeal of the new Tudor monarchy. For example, the symbol of the crown in a hawthorn bush, evidence of God's judgement on the field at Bosworth, was not forgotten and became one of the standard Tudor icons, adorning the architecture commissioned by the king and his followers, books and other visible media. Similarly, a chorus of Welsh poets heralded Tudor's accession as the fulfilment of the ancient prophesies concerning the vanquishing of the Anglo-Saxons by the British, drawing attention to Henry's Welsh ancestry.

Nevertheless, it would be wrong to make too much of a new symbolic rhetoric to define Tudor kingship. The English use of the arched imperial crown had its origins in the Lancastrian dual-monarchy of Henry V. Similarly, the house of York had frequently employed 'British' propaganda for its own ends and Edward IV's 'British' credentials, established via genealogies linking him, through the Mortimers, with Llewellyn, Prince of Wales, and eventually to the mythical founder of Britain, Brutus, were equal to Henry's. Other Tudor icons therefore drew attention to more tangible and immediate justifications of the dynasty. The Beaufort portcullis, the Richmond greyhound and Tudor Rose, for example, stressed Henry's dynastic legitimacy and the conciliation with the Yorkist polity achieved through his marriage to Elizabeth. When on 19 September 1486 an heir, Arthur, was born his birth was celebrated as the guarantee of dynastic security and confirmation that the realm would never again fall into civil war. Despite this strong emphasis on continuity and legitimacy, however, it is clear that Henry brought a new sense of direction to the English crown. This was most apparent in his dealings with the landowning classes. The remainder of this chapter will, therefore, deal with how Henry's policies towards the political elites established the Tudor dynasty firmly on the throne of England.

Crown and Nobility

To the historians writing in the nineteenth and early twentieth centuries one of Henry Tudor's greatest achievements was to rescue England from the damage caused by noble factions and the 'over-mighty subject' during the Wars of the Roses. S. T. Bindoff considered that the principal problem facing Henry in 1485 was 'how to suppress the magnates' and J. R. Lander stated that the first Tudor was so successful in achieving this end that, by 1509, the parliamentary peerage had been cowed into the impotency that would characterize them throughout the sixteenth and early seventeenth centuries.[8] Although the nobility continued to enjoy a role both in the government of the localities and at court there nevertheless remains the feeling amongst historians that Henry was somehow less inclined to see the nobility as his natural partners in government than were his Lancastrian and Yorkist predecessors. In reality the situation was less clear-cut. What Henry was concerned with primarily was the augmentation of the crown's authority and the security of the Tudor dynasty on the English throne. At times this clashed with the interests of not only the nobility but the landed classes as a whole. However, other factors, not only royal policy, were also at work in explaining the apparent decline of noble fortunes between 1485 and 1509.

First, it is far from clear that the majority of the nobility saw themselves as having a national political role. The nobility as a whole had largely remained aloof from the events of 1470–1, when Edward IV had been deposed by his erstwhile ally, the Earl of Warwick, and the Lancastrian Henry VI briefly restored to the throne, and had also acquiesced in Richard III's usurpation in 1483. At Bosworth only five of the fifty-five nobles summoned to parliament in 1484 turned out for Richard III, while Henry was accompanied on the battlefield by only one peer, that die-hard Lancastrian loyalist the earl of Oxford. Similarly at Stoke two years later, apart from the attainted earl of Lincoln and Viscount Lovel, only two peers supported the pretender Lambert Simnel (posing as Edward, earl of Warwick, the son of Edward IV's brother, George, duke of Clarence), while only seven members of the nobility took the field for Henry. It seems as if Lord Mountjoy's deathbed advice to his son in 1485 not to seek to be 'great about princes' was a sentiment with which the nobility generally had some sympathy. Indeed, when noblemen did exercise power at a local level it was only with the king's approbation or even at the king's command. For example, on Henry's accession Lord Stanley, instrumental in the victory at Bosworth and related to the new king by marriage, was made earl of Derby and he and his family rewarded with new influence in the North-West and North Wales; Jasper Tudor became duke of Bedford and enjoyed the 'rule' of the South Wales and the Marches; equally, Giles Daubeney, a supporter of Henry in exile, was made Lord Daubeney and given the command of Calais and, later, regional power in the South-

West through the grant of royal offices there. In many ways this can be seen as a continuation of the policies of Edward IV but the scale of the influence enjoyed by Derby, Daubeney or Bedford cannot really be compared to the independence that Edward IV allowed the duke of Gloucester in the North or even Lord Hastings in the Midlands.

Equally, circumstances also militated against independent noble power-bases in the localities. The 4th earl of Northumberland, for instance, had been imprisoned in the Tower for his support of Richard III at Bosworth and was only slowly allowed to recover his family's traditional lands and offices in the North. However, when he was murdered in 1489, attempting to collect a royal tax, he was replaced by the earl of Surrey as the king's lieutenant of the North. Surrey, who had also supported Richard in 1485, needed the king's favour to recover his family's position in their traditional region of influence, East Anglia, and thus proved a subservient, yet effective, royal representative in the North. Although Henry employed the nobility in their tradi-tional role as the links between the localities and the centre, their power was increas-ingly made dependent upon royal favour or replaced altogether by royal servants. Perhaps the clearest example of the way in which Henry attacked entrenched noble power was in Lancashire and Cheshire where, from the 1490s, the Stanley family and their servants were systematically excluded from duchy and palatinate offices.

Moreover, Henry did not significantly add to the ranks of the nobility; at the same time the existing nobility was allowed to dwindle through attainder and natural wastage. In the first years of the reign there was a small rush of peerage creations – six new barons, for example, between September 1485 and November 1488 – but these were mainly rewards for service at Bosworth and, with the exception of Daubeney, were revivals of titles in abeyance. Similarly, amongst the higher peerage only Jasper Tudor was raised to the rank of duke while Philibert de Chandee's cre-ation as earl of Bath was merely a recognition of the Frenchman's service at Bosworth and was not accompanied by grants of lands in England. This was in contrast to Edward IV who had created a new nobility to serve him as leaders of local society. Also under Henry VII those peers, like the earls of Lincoln, Warwick and Suffolk, who were attainted were not replaced. Other peers, like the 5th earl of Northum-berland, the earls of Kent and Thomas, Lord Burgh, were either minors, lunatics or not equipped with the skills which enabled them to command influence in political society, making them neither a threat nor a tool of royal government.

As well as an apparent reluctance to create new nobles, Henry also demonstrated that he was inherently wary of the aristocracy as potential rivals for local power and influence. This was apparent in his use of financial bonds to regulate his relations with the nobility and the greater gentry. This device, a form of suspended fine for the performance of some agreed task or as an insurance against bad behaviour, was a commonplace in late-medieval society but their use under Henry VII multiplied greatly. It was apparent from the beginning of the reign but was restricted to those who were obvious potential threats to the new regime: in the North, for instance, old Yorkists like Sir John Conyers were almost immediately placed under heavy bonds for good behaviour, while Thomas Grey, marquis of Dorset, whose loyalty had always been in question despite him being a companion in exile, was required in 1492 to provide sureties for his good behaviour to the tune of £10,000. From about 1500, however, Henry extended the system to those who did not pose any ostensible threat.

In 1507 George Neville, Lord Abergavenny, one of Henry's key lieutenants in Kent, was fined the enormous sum of £100,000 for illegal retaining, although the king agreed to commute this to a £5,000 fine. By 1509 some 75 per cent of the nobility had entered into a bond of some sort. Some historians, notably J. R. Lander, have taken this as part of a deliberate policy by the king to have his greatest subjects in his financial power. While these bonds fulfilled a primarily political purpose, Henry also showed a ruthless determination to exact all the crown's rights as feudal overlord and to acquire more land under the crown's direct control. Henry's reign, therefore, witnessed a change in the political role and importance of the ancient nobility *vis-à-vis* the rest of the political nation and that, in part, was due to deliberate royal policy. This is apparent by the fact that Henry's first parliament was attended by thirty-four of the fifty-five lords eligible to be summoned (although six were minors); by the time of the first parliament of his son's reign there were only forty-one lords eligible to be summoned. The bare figures point to the decline of the nobility under Henry VII and corresponding rise in the importance of the crown and royal affinity that would be a defining feature of the early Tudor polity.

Centre and Locality

Some of the changes apparent in the government of the localities and the dynamic between locality and centre have already been touched upon. It is in his management of local political society that Henry VII might be seen as most distinct from his predecessors and this has come in for most of the recent criticism of him. Traditionally the crown relied primarily on the nobility to enforce its will in the localities but in counties where there were no resident magnates, for example in Kent or Nottinghamshire, the gentry had taken the lead and the crown had established direct links with them by recruitment into the royal household or by using the offices available on the crown lands, such as on the duchy of Lancaster estates. As the fifteenth-century political commentator Sir John Fortescue noted: 'the myght off the lande, aftir the myght off the grete lordes theroff stondith most in the kynges officers. Ffor thai mowe best rule the contreis wher as ther offices ben . . .'[9] It was the spread of rule through the 'kynges offices' to areas usually under the sway of 'grete lordes' which was, crudely speaking, one of the defining features of Henry's reign and an important stage in the establishment of the Tudor dynasty.

Office on the crown lands, therefore, was of prime importance in establishing a greater royal authority in the localities. Stewardships of land conferred the right to command the service of the tenants (the *manraed*). Crucially, it was this system that allowed the crown, through its office-holders, to raise armies both for defence against rebels, as in 1497, or for wars against France and Scotland, as in 1492 and 1496. As the crown's landed estate was increased by feudal accident, forfeiture or purchase so the potential for the crown, through its estate officers, to intervene more directly in local affairs also increased. Moreover, new laws against retaining – that is, the handing out of livery and badges and payment of fees to any who were not immediate household servants – in 1487 and 1504 made it illegal for anybody to retain either the king's officers or his tenants. The number of special licences the crown granted to its officials to hand out the king's livery and by these means extend the crown's authority became instantly more visible and apparent in the shires. The epitome of the licensed retinue is the 1,300 or so men in the retinue of Thomas Lovell, Henry's first treasurer of the chamber and a leading councillor throughout the reign. Lovell's retinue was built around crown office. About a third of the retinue came directly from crown tenants, while a fifth were from monastic and episcopal stewardships, which had been granted to Lovell by those eager to exploit his position as somebody influential with the king and whose favour in local affairs was sought after. A further portion was from the followings of individual gentlemen already members of the retinue, some of whom also enjoyed crown office, while a sixth of the retinue was comprised of the tenants of the Roos estates in Lincolnshire. Lovell's marriage to Isabel Roos, a royal ward, was doubtless facilitated by the king in his desire to bring the Roos lands and their tenants under royal influence.

There was, of course, a tendency for crown officials to use their local influence to their own ends, just as the retinues of magnates in the fifteenth century had taken advantage of the protection of their lords for their own good, and this explains partly the unrest in some areas that has triggered recent scholarly criticism of Henry's policies. William Sandes in Hampshire, Sir Edward Darell in Berkshire and Edward Belknapp in Warwickshire have all recently been highlighted as crown officials who abused their positions and thus destabilized local society. Perhaps the most damning example of this tendency, however, is Henry's grant to Lord Daubeney of a near monopoly of crown office in the South-West. This excluded the local gentry from influence and the backlash was apparent in their failure to turn out for the king and fight against the Cornish rebels in 1497. Henry's natural tendency, unlike Edward IV, was to support the royal official rather than the local interest in these cases. This may have damaged local harmony in the short term but, crucially, in the long term reinforced the view that the crown was the ultimate authority. Moreover, it is by no means apparent that the growth of the royal affinity in the localities was a bad thing for local order and government everywhere. In Kent, for example, it was the weakness of the crown's agent there, Sir Richard Guildford, that caused unrest rather than the crown's policies *per se*.

Rather than seeing Henry's policy towards the localities as a ham-fisted attempt to go against the established norms through which local political society operated, we should perhaps see the growth of the royal affinity as part of a deliberate policy to strengthen the crown and establish the Tudor dynasty. In the same way as Henry attempted to maximize the financial yield of the crown lands, so he sought to exploit fully their human potential. If this at times trampled on existing local structures of power it was a price the king, and it seems most of local society, was willing to pay. Tudor policy was successful in as much as it ensured that more force was mobilized for the king than for his enemies in the two significant tests of Henry's kingship: at Stoke in 1487 when he defeated the pretender, Lambert Simnel; and at Blackheath ten years later when the king faced the Cornish rebels.

Finance and Administration

While the present state of our knowledge about the effect of Henry's governance on local political society is limited, the same cannot be said of the institutions through which he ruled. Traditionally, the study of the council and financial machinery has been the main focus of Tudor historians. Paradoxically it has now become accepted as a commonplace that it was in his bureaucracy that Henry was most like his Yorkist predecessors. However, the most recent work on the king's counsel and royal finances suggests that there was something distinctive and new in Tudor rule.

The process of counselling the monarch – that it was done effectively and, more importantly, seen to be done effectively – was one of the necessary lubricants for the proper functioning of political society. The importance to Henry of the king's council has never been beyond doubt. Chrimes saw Henry's council as conventionally medieval. There were no council committees, no court of Star Chamber nor Council Learned in the Law in an institutionalized sense. Councillors met in the Star Chamber at Westminster or 'learned counsel' (the contemporary term for lawyers) deliberated over legal matters but they were not committees as we, or indeed later sixteenth-century governments, would understand them. Henry VII's council was large and amorphous: 227 men were styled king's councillors during the reign, including two-thirds of the nobility, although the council usually met as a working party of about two dozen.

We can identify four levels on which counsel operated during Henry's reign. First, in the seven parliaments (in 1485, 1487, 1489, 1491, 1495, 1497 and 1504) and the five Great Councils (in 1485, 1487, 1488, 1491 and 1496) he summoned, Henry took counsel from and sought the approbation of the community of the whole realm. Henry's Great Councils, assemblies of the nobility not constrained by the formality of summoning and convening a parliament comprised of king, lords and commons, in particular became a forum in which the king appealed to the realm for assistance. Grants of taxation made in Great Councils were later confirmed and legalized in parliament. All but the parliament of 1504 were summoned in times of domestic or international crisis and were linked to the accepted necessity of asking approval for the granting of taxation.[10] Second, there were meetings of the council proper where the principal office-holders and sometimes the king met to discuss the everyday business of government. It was in these circumstances that the key royal officials, the treasurer, chancellor, keeper of the privy seal, and advisers, Sir Reginald Bray (d. 1502), Sir Thomas Lovell and, later in the reign, Richard Empson and Edmund Dudley, saw to the execution of the royal will. Thirdly, there was the informal counsel which characterized effective government in a personal monarchy. This could happen at a number of levels: for example, in 1492 Henry took informal counsel on a very grand scale by calling an impromptu meeting of the commanders of his army outside Bologna to discuss terms for the settlement of the war with France, or in a very private context by taking counsel from courtiers and attendants in the King's Chamber or on a hunting trip. The individuals closest to the king offered counsel by means of all these methods; the process of counselling the monarch was not yet fully institutionalized as it would be later in the sixteenth century. The men denounced by Perkin Warbeck (who claimed he was Richard, duke of York, Edward IV's younger son) in 1497 as evil counsellors and 'caitliffs and villains of low birth' – Bishop Fox, the keeper of the privy seal, Sir Reginald Bray, Sir Thomas Lovell, Sir John Risley, Oliver King, Henry's secretary, Sir Richard Empson, Sir Richard Guildford and Sir John Turberville – represented a mix of high officers of state, household servants and companions in exile, demonstrating that the principal determinant of who counselled Henry lay with the king himself.

The final way in which counsel was given in Henry's reign, however, is the most interesting and reveals a significant innovation in the way in which government operated. John Watts has argued that Henry's reign saw a removal of much of the personal character of late-medieval government. Using the blueprint for government given by Sir John Fortescue in the 1470s, the lawyers in Henry's counsels – individuals like Dudley, Empson, Bray and Risley – exploited the king's unfamiliarity with the norms of government and took over much of the day-to-day business, allowing government to function with a minimum of interference from the king. The Council Learned in the Law and, in financial matters, the general surveyors epitomized this development. They met regularly without the king's supervision – the general surveyors met at Blackfriars or in the Prince's chamber at Westminster – to interpret and implement the king's will. Unlike the barons of the exchequer the general surveyors were not constrained in their dealings by the cumbersome process of common law. Although Watts is correct to identify the growth of largely independent conciliar courts later in Henry's reign, his explanation for its cause is probably mistaken. Henry did not relinquish any aspect of the royal prerogative nor did the king's will cease to be the principal motor of central government. Any examination of the documents which Henry's government created leaves no doubt that it was the king who was behind the formulation and execution of policy: his sign manual, annotations and notes in his own hands are a commonplace throughout the administrative records of the reign. Royal government expanded its ambitions and responsibilities massively during the reign to intervene at every level of national and provincial life, and thus the conciliar committees represented the fact that in the burgeoning Tudor state the king was forced to delegate certain aspects of the princely role in government. Nevertheless, despite these bodies, government remained primarily an instrument of the king's will throughout the reign.[11]

Changes in the priorities of government, driven by Henry's own will, are perhaps most apparent in matters of national finance. The regime's policy was summarized by Geoffrey Elton and his appraisal remains valid today. He observed how Henry exploited every possible source of income open to the crown, including feudal rights, fines on penal statutes and the chasing up of royal debts. 'Henry', it seems, 'was not only calling for his dues but pressing hard upon all landowners'.[12] The extent to which he pursued the crown's prerogative rights and sought to increase its wealth was unquestionably novel. However, historians have, in the main, accepted the view that there was nothing new about the means and methods of administration that the king employed. Henry's 'chamber system' – in which the crown's income was augmented and based primarily upon the revenues of the crown lands paid directly to the king's chamber rather than the exchequer, the ancient body which handled national finance – was nothing more than a utilization of the system of estate management used by most magnates and introduced on a national level by Edward IV during the 1460s.

Nevertheless, it seems that the way in which Henry Tudor perceived national finance was fundamentally different to his late-medieval predecessors. The survival of Henry's chamber accounts and a mass of other related accounts allows us to reconstruct in detail the machinery by which the royal revenues were expanded and strengthened. Between 1461 and 1485 the Yorkists had essentially continued, albeit in an extended form, the normal practice of late-medieval state finance. Edward IV used his private wealth, in the form of the crown lands and especially the lands of March and York, alongside the public revenue as an additional source of royal authority much as the Lancastrians kings had in times of crisis. This, however, did not represent a financial re-foundation of royal government. Many royal estates were alienated in the 1460s; wardships, such as that of the future Talbot earl of Shrewsbury, were not exploited financially but used to foster royal authority in the localities; acts of resumption, which aimed to return royal land granted by the profligate Henry VI, were tempered by the need to maintain the support of the aristocracy. Furthermore, the Yorkist kings conspicuously failed to employ these private resources effectively for national expenditure, for example the war with Scotland in the early 1480s, or transfer those funds effectively from king to king.

When compared with these precedents it is clear that the role of the chamber in national finance under Henry VII was very different. The commonplace distinctions between ordinary and extraordinary revenue and expenditure, and the public resources of the crown and the king's private revenues, were gradually undermined during Henry's reign. Similarly, the functions of the Exchequer, which handled the public revenues derived principally from taxation and the customs, and the king's chamber, which collected and spent his private wealth (mainly in the form of the crown lands), were merged. This change may have been caused partly by the king's lack of experience of the usual patterns of English medieval government, and may have been linked to his exposure to continental forms of royal authority. It was also recognition, however, of more deep-rooted inadequacies in the fiscal resources of late-medieval monarchy. Henry effectively combined his private sources of income with those that pertained to the crown, such as feudal prerogatives, the crown's ancient demesne lands, the profits of justice and national taxation to provide a consolidated royal revenue. Once under the control of the king's chamber, all these sources were applied equally to whatever expenditure Henry felt increased the authority and security of the Tudor dynasty.[13]

Henry VII's Last Years

Perhaps the most frequent charge levelled against Henry VII is that his policies became, as the reign wore on and especially after 1504, increasingly avaricious, unjust and resented. Polydore Vergil and the London *Great Chronicle* considered the king's greed as a vice which threatened to nullify all his greatest achievements. This theme was taken up with great vigour in a debate between Geoffrey Elton and J. P. Cooper. Elton refuted the chroniclers' claim while Cooper maintained that Henry's policies were rapacious and prejudicial to the liberty of the subject. Central to these arguments was the role of the king's ministers, especially the Council Learned and its most infamous members, Edmund Dudley and Richard Empson. Dudley and Empson have been largely exonerated by modern historians and indeed, Dudley's so-called 'petition' makes it clear that it was Henry himself who formulated and drove policy, especially from about 1500 when his own failing health and the reality of possible dynastic failure hit home. As Dudley himself noted, the king's purpose was to 'have as many persons in his danger at his pleasure' through his use of bonds and exploitation of feudal rights and penal statutes.[14]

Of course, in a personal monarchy government policy was primarily determined by the king's character. Henry VII was, it seems, an unusually cautious man even for an age where political events were often determined by treachery and sudden volte-faces. In exile he had been a pawn of European power politics and his primary loyalty was to those who had stood by him in exile. Almost to the end of the reign those who had been his companions in France and Brittany – Guildford, Daubeney, Bray and Lovell – were his most trusted companions. Those whom he had any reason to distrust – for example, the marquis of Dorset, who had tried to contact Richard III in 1485 – remained under a cloud for the rest of reign (as it turned out an eventually fatal cloud for Dorset). Traditional loyalties and chivalric values, it seemed, were also dangerous under Henry: in 1495 Sir William Stanley, the chamberlain of Henry's own household, whose intervention had been decisive at Bosworth, was executed for his complicity in the Perkin Warbeck conspiracy. His was said to have in his possession a Yorkist livery collar, granted to him as steward of Edward, prince of Wales's household, and to be foolish enough to state that if a son of Edward IV was really still alive his loyalty to Henry would be compromised. There is no evidence, however, that Stanley had ever acted treasonably. Henry's natural suspicion also acted in the opposite way: in 1504 the treasurer of Calais, Hugh Conwey – another of Henry's companions in exile – reported that the king was prone to believe that reports of treasonable activities were made 'but of envy, yll wille and malis'. That belief saved Conwey's skin the following year when Henry dismissed a report, probably correctly, by one John Flamank of treasonable words by members of the Calais garrison.

There is undeniable evidence, however, that Henry became increasingly suspicious and that his policies to augment the financial security of the crown did, at times, compromise good government and the liberty of the subject. This is shown clearly by the list of those who 'had a hard end' in Dudley's petition and by the king's policies in Calais, where the wool merchants, who paid for the defence of the town, were chased for the payment of their debts to the crown to the detriment of their ability to pay the town garrison's wages. Several historians have attributed this change of policy to the king's sense of dynastic insecurity, apparent from 1502 with the death of his eldest son, Prince Arthur, and, in the following year, of his queen. However, these policies were also apparent earlier in the reign: for example, the defection of Edmund de la Pole, earl of Suffolk to the continent and his emergence as a Yorkist claimant to the throne in 1501 had its roots in Henry's financial exploitation of the de la Pole family.[15]

More important than Henry's domestic disaster in the apparent change of direction in royal policy around the turn of the century may be the king's failing health. It is clear, from the so-called 'Flamank Information' (a report of an alleged conversation in September 1504 between the officers of the Calais garrison concerning the succession), that the king had been close to death in 1499 and during the next few years he suffered from bouts of recurrent incapacity. The chamber accounts show that for weeks at a time the Court stopped its regular perambulations around Henry's southern hunting lodges and other sources confirm that Henry was close to death in the springs of 1507 and 1508 before his demise in April 1509. Changes in royal policy, therefore, may represent the gradual shift from the king personally directing government to ministers interpreting what they perceived to be the royal will. Vergil notes as well that the king's physical illness was accompanied by a mental decline in the last three years of his life so it may be that the royal will was more ambiguous in these last years.

There are indeed signs that there were tensions at Court and around the king's person during the last years of his reign. In 1505 Sir Richard Guildford was dismissed from his role as comptroller of the household, thus losing his role at Court and proximity about the king, for unknown reasons. He left for pilgrimage to Jerusalem where he died the following year. In the same year Lord Daubeney was disgraced, ostensibly because he had embezzled funds while lieutenant of Calais; in his will he complained of the king's decision to force him into hefty financial penalties for his supposed misdemeanour. In 1507 Sir James Hobart, the attorney-general and one of the king's closest counsellors, was also dismissed for an unknown cause. At the same time, the chamber accounts reveal the growing influence of Empson and Dudley, Sir John Hussey, master of the wards, and Edward Belknap, surveyor of the prerogative, about the king: in March 1508, for example, all the payments made by the treasurer of the chamber were annotated with Empson, Dudley or Hussey's name suggesting their influence at the heart of power.

The tensions of Henry's last years were soon revealed in the wake of his death. The king's death was kept secret for thirty-six hours to enable a court coup in which the king's older and aristocratic counsellors, led by the treasurer, the earl of Surrey and Bishop Fox, keeper of the privy seal, engineered the arrest and subsequent execution of Empson and Dudley. This led to the establishment of a broad, noble-led council to advise the young Henry VIII.[16] In the first year of the new reign a general pardon was issued and many of those who had been subject to bonds under Henry VII successfully petitioned to have them cancelled – in all, 175 were cancelled up to 1515. Nevertheless, many of Henry VII's policies survived, albeit in modified form. His financial policy continued almost intact: the series of acts of parliament between 1510 and 1512 which named John Heron, Henry's treasurer of the chamber, as the general receiver of the crown's revenues and established the auditing activities of the general surveyors in law were a peculiarly English attempt to recognize the significance of the change that had occurred in the nature of royal government. The expansion of the royal household's role in government and greater intervention in local affairs remained a constant feature of Tudor government. This must have been so because those who had a stake in royal government, including, significantly, men like Thomas Howard, earl of Surrey (whose father the duke of Norfolk had been killed fighting for Richard III at Bosworth) recognized their benefit for the good government of the realm: 'Henry succeeded because his leading subjects wanted him to succeed; he did not govern in despite of them'.[17]

K. B. McFarlane once pronounced that 'The only New Monarchy that England ever had came in with William the Conqueror' but, as Steven Gunn has reminded us, 'neither a man nor a monarchy need be completely or uniquely new to be significantly new'.[18] There were enough aspects of Henry VII's rule to make the advent of the Tudor dynasty in 1485 a significant new start in English history. That is not to say that things changed overnight: we know that there were significant continuities of personnel and institutions, men like John, Lord Dynham, Henry's first treasurer of England between 1486 and 1501, were inveterate survivors who moulded themselves successfully to the very different politics of Edward IV's, Richard III's and Henry VII's reign. Nevertheless, the fact that Henry was an outsider without first-hand experience of the nature of the late-medieval English polity made some change inevitable. Moreover, the nature of that change was permanent and provided the foundations for a distinctly Tudor political culture. Politics, especially in the last years of the reign, became more court-centred; the crown succeeded in intervening and imposing its will on local political society more effectively; and the efficiency of government was increased by the new developments in the financial administration and the way in which the council interpreted and implemented the king's will. These were all features that characterized Tudor government throughout the sixteenth century. If we accept that strong central government is a good thing, then we might concur with S. T. Bindoff who concluded that Henry was 'the most uniformly successful of English kings';[19] however, if we perceive no inherent problems in the way in which medieval England was governed then we might consider Henry's rule disastrous for landowning society and his survival, and that of his dynasty, more due to good luck than good judgement. Good king or bad king, Henry VII's reign had, in many ways, prepared the British Isles for the more momentous changes of the remainder of the sixteenth century.

NOTES

1. For Henry Tudor's early life see Griffiths and Thomas, *Making of the Tudor Dynasty*, pp. 39–86.
2. Jones, 'The myth of 1485'.
3. Jones, *Bosworth 1485*, esp. ch. 6.
4. Chrimes, *Henry VII*, pp. 319, 322.
5. See especially Gunn, *Early Tudor Government* for this approach.
6. Carpenter, *Wars of the Roses*, ch. 11.
7. The symbolism of Henry's reign is discussed in Anglo, *Images of Tudor Kingship*, ch. 2 and Gunn, *Early Tudor Government*, ch. 4.
8. Bindoff, *Tudor England*, p. 66; Lander, 'Bonds, coercion and fear'. For discussions of the role of the nobility see Pugh, 'Henry VII and the English nobility' and the case studies by Luckett ('Crown patronage and political morality') and Cunningham ('Henry VII, Sir Thomas Butler and the Stanley family').
9. Quoted in Luckett, 'Crown office and licensed retinues', p. 237.
10. For Henry's Great Councils and their link with parliament see Holmes, 'The Great Council in the reign of Henry VII'.
11. Watts, '"A New Ffundacion of is Crowne": monarchy in the reign of Henry VII'.
12. Elton, 'Rapacity and remorse', pp. 23–4, 32.
13. Grummitt, 'Henry VII, Chamber finance and the "New Monarchy"'.
14. Harrison, 'Petition of Edmund Dudley', pp. 88–94. For the debate in the *Historical Journal* over Henry's character see Elton, 'Rapacity and remorse', countered in J. P. Cooper, 'Henry VII's last years reconsidered', with Elton's reply in 'Henry VII: a restatement'.
15. Grummitt, "For the surety of the Towne and Marches'; Jones, 'Sir William Stanley'.
16. Gunn, 'Accession of Henry VIII'.
17. Horrox, 'Yorkist and early Tudor England', p. 489. McFarlane, *Nobility of Later Medieval England*, p. 283.
18. Gunn, 'Sir Thomas Lovell', p. 153.
19. Bindoff, *Tudor England*, p. 66.

BIBLIOGRAPHY

Anglo, Sydney, *Images of Tudor Kingship* (London, 1992).
Bindoff, S. T., *Tudor England* (London, 1960).

Carpenter, Christine, *Locality and Polity: A Study of Warwickshire Landed Society, 1401–1499* (Cambridge, 1992).

Carpenter, Christine, *The Wars of the Roses: Politics and the Constitution c. 1437–1509* (Cambridge, 1997).

Chrimes, S. B., *Henry VII* (London, 1972; 2nd edn. New Haven, 1999).

Condon, Margaret, 'Ruling elites in the reign of Henry VII', in C. D. Ross, ed., *Patronage, Pedigree and Power in Late Medieval England* (Gloucester, 1979), pp. 109–42.

Cooper, J. P., 'Henry VII's last years reconsidered', *Historical Journal*, 2 (1959), 103–29.

Cunningham, Sean, 'Henry VII and rebellion in North-Eastern England, 1485–1492: bonds of allegiance and the establishment of Tudor authority', *Northern History*, 32 (1996), 45–60.

Cunningham, Sean, 'Henry VII, Sir Thomas Butler and the Stanley family: politics and the assertion of royal influence in north-western England, 1471–1521', in Tim Thornton, ed., *Social Attitudes and Political Structures in the Fifteenth Century* (Stroud, 2000), pp. 220–41.

Elton, G. R., 'Henry VII: rapacity and remorse', *Historical Journal*, 1 (1958), 21–39.

Elton, G. R., 'Henry VII: a restatement', *Historical Journal*, 4 (1961), 1–29.

Griffiths, R. A. and Thomas, Roger S., *The Making of the Tudor Dynasty* (Gloucester, 1985).

Grummitt, David, 'Henry VII, 'Chamber finance and the "New Monarchy": some new evidence', *Historical Research*, 72 (1999), 229–43.

Grummitt, David, ' "For the Surety of the Towne and Marches": early Tudor policy towards Calais 1485–1509', *Nottingham Medieval Studies*, 44 (2000), 184–203.

Gunn, S. J., 'The accession of Henry VIII', *Bulletin of the Institute of Historical Research*, 64 (1991), 278–88.

Gunn, S. J., 'The courtiers of Henry VII', *English Historical Review*, 108 (1993), 23–49.

Gunn, S. J., *Early Tudor Government, 1485–1558* (Basingstoke, 1995).

Gunn, S. J., 'Sir Thomas Lovell (c. 1449–1524): a new man in a new monarchy?', in John L. Watts, ed., *The End of the Middle Ages* (Stroud, 1998), pp. 117–53.

Harrison, C. J., 'The petition of Edmund Dudley', *English Historical Review*, 87 (1972), 82–94.

Harriss, G. L., 'Medieval government and statecraft', *Past and Present*, 24 (1963), 1–39.

Holmes, P., 'The Great Council in the reign of Henry VII', *English Historical Review*, 101 (1986), 840–62.

Horrox, Rosemary, 'Yorkist and early Tudor England', in Christopher Allmand, ed., *The New Cambridge Medieval History.* Vol. 7, *c. 1415–c. 1500* (Cambridge, 1998).

Jones, Michael K., *Bosworth 1485: Psychology of a Battle* (Stroud, 2002).

Jones, Michael K., 'Henry Tudor and the myth of 1485' in David Grummitt, ed., *The English Experience in France: War, Diplomacy and Cultural Exchange, c. 1450–1558* (Aldershot, 2002), pp. 85–105.

Jones, Michael K., 'Sir William Stanley of Holt: politics and family allegiance in the late fifteenth century', *Welsh History Review*, 14 (1988), 1–22.

Jones, Michael K. and M. G. Underwood, *The King's Mother: Lady Margaret Beaufort, Countess of Richmond and Derby* (Cambridge, 1992).

Lander, J. R., 'Bonds, coercion and fear: Henry VII and the peerage', in J. G. Rowe and W. H. Stockdale, eds, *Florilegium Historiale: Essays Presented to Wallace K. Ferguson* (Toronto, 1971), pp. 328–67.

Luckett, D. A., 'Crown office and licensed retinues in the reign of Henry VII', in Rowena Archer and Simon Walker, eds, *Rulers and Ruled in Late Medieval England* (London, 1995), pp. 223–38.

Luckett, D. A., 'Crown patronage and political morality in early Tudor England: the case of Giles, Lord Daubeney', *English Historical Review*, 110 (1995), 578–95.

McFarlane, K. B., *The Nobility of Later Medieval England* (Oxford, 1973).

Morgan, D. A. L., 'The king's affinity in the polity of Yorkist England', *Transactions of the Royal Historical Society*, 5th Series, 23 (1973), 1–25.

Pollard, A. J., *Late Medieval England, 1399–1509* (London, 1999).

Pugh, T. B., 'Henry VII and the English nobility' in G. Bernard, ed., *The Tudor Nobility* (Manchester, 1992), pp. 49–110.

Storey, R. L., *The Reign of Henry VII* (New York, 1968).

Watts, John, "A New Ffundacion of is Crowne': monarchy in the reign of Henry VII', in B. Thompson, ed., *The Reign of Henry VII* (Stamford, 1995), pp. 31–53.

Wolffe, B. P., *The Royal Demesne in English History: The Crown Estate in the Governance of the Realm* (London, 1971).

FURTHER READING

The standard biography of Henry VII's reign remains S. B. Chrimes, *Henry VII* (1999), but R. L. Storey's *The Reign of Henry VII* (1968) is also useful. Two recent textbooks on late-medieval England offer interesting but opposing views of Henry from a medievalist's point of view: Tony Pollard's *Late Medieval England, 1399–1509* (1999) is reasonably positive about the reign while a hostile account of Henry can be found in Christine Carpenter's *The Wars of the Roses* (1997). A proper assessment of Henry's achievements can only be achieved by an understanding of the late-medieval polity. Essential to this are the essays by G. L. Harriss 'Medieval government' (1963) and D. A. L. Morgan, 'The king's affinity in the polity of Yorkist England' (1973). Most recent accounts have stressed the continuities through the period 1450–1509; important in this regard is the work of B. P. Wolffe, especially his *The Royal Demesne in English History* (1971), but see also S. J. Gunn, *Early Tudor Government* (1995). However, for recent suggestions that the reign had important, distinctive features see Grummitt, 'Henry VII, chamber finance and the "New Monarchy"' (1999). For Henry's relationships with the elites see Margaret Condon, 'Ruling elites' (1979) and Pugh, 'Henry VII and the English nobility' (1992). More local studies are needed but see Cunningham, 'Bonds of allegiance' (1996), 'Henry VII and the Stanley family' (2000), Luckett, 'Crown patronage' (1995) and the final chapter of Carpenter's *Locality and Polity* (1992). For the politics of Henry's reign and especially the rebellions of the 1480s and 1490s see Ian Arthurson's *The Perkin Warbeck Conspiracy* (1994) and Michael Bennet's *Lambert Simnel and the Battle of Stoke* (1987). The nature of Henry's court and its role in politics is explored in Gunn, 'The courtiers of Henry VII' (1993).

Chapter Two

The Rise of the Tudor State

Joseph S. Block

The focal point of this chapter, located as it is between one chapter titled 'The Establishment of the Tudor Dynasty' and another titled 'Elizabethan Government and Politics', will be to track the major changes in the functioning of central government over the first half of the sixteenth century, with an emphasis on the reign of Henry VIII. While this might seem to be a most conventional assignment, new questions about the structure and purpose of government in general, as well as in sixteenth-century England, have redefined and reinvigorated our interest in institutions of central government such as the monarchy, the household, and the Council.

Any study of government must at some point take up the question, 'Why should anybody obey anyone?'. What was the nexus of power within society, and how was power made manifest from the top downward and the centre outwards? Government relies on the consent of the governed in order to function. Moreover, 'the rise of the Tudor state', itself, implies that something new had been created, either from nothing, or from the ruins of something that had earlier fallen, or on top of something already built and now being extended. This examination recognizes that central government had changed significantly by the middle of the sixteenth century, and whatever one chooses to call these changes, they were fundamental and could not be reversed. England eventually emerged from over a century of reformation and revolution a Protestant rather than a Catholic realm in which central governmental power had shifted from the full sovereignty of the crown in partnership with the nobility and the church to the sovereignty and initiative of the king-in-parliament, an elemental reorganization of the body politic. The story of this transformation during the reign of Henry VIII will be the subject of my contribution to this volume.

Questions about the structure of central government have created significant debates among historians, particularly since 1953 when Sir Geoffrey Elton surveyed the constitutional scene and pronounced a *Tudor Revolution in Government*. His argument, founded on a preference for state activism, a dislike of Henry VIII, and a passion for controversy, held that changes attendant on the break from Roman religious jurisdiction came so fast and cut so deeply into the political fabric of the nation that 'revolution' was the only term able to describe it. According to Elton, England before the 1530s was medieval. By the end of the decade, the revolution was deeply embedded, and by 1550 England had assumed a modern identity.[1]

Challenges to Elton's vision have played down the impact of administrative changes in the 1530s. Many of the specific elements supporting the idea of a revolution in government have been modified or discarded. The state as a positive force in people's lives is much debated. As we examine the period, it will not be necessary to delve too deeply into this longstanding historiographical clash, but the discussion may serve as a guide in our attempt to discover a vision of the rise of the Tudor state which is satisfying to the historical imagination of contemporary scholars and students alike.

Our story begins with the ascent to the English throne of Henry VIII who on 22 April 1509, not yet eighteen years old, succeeded his father. By 1520 Henry had reached his twenty-ninth year, had married, fathered a legitimate daughter and an illegitimate son, fought a war, and had governed his realm for more than a decade. That year is a good time from which to take our first look at Henry's kingdom, free from the distractions caused by the Wars of the Roses on one side and the Reformation yet to come on the other. English government could still be described as medieval, but this is not to say primitive. Patronage, good lordship and pageantry tied together noble households and the king, a great landowner in his own right. Patronage, especially, acted as a binding force between king and nobility. Both parties preferred the carrot to the stick. Real power came from combining territorial influence with offices held from the crown.

Peasants for their part were expected to obey the law as well as their lords who owned the land they worked. In addition, the church exercised a powerful authority over individuals. Alongside aristocratic power stood the secular authority of the church and its princes. One-third of the land in England lay under the hands of the church. Monasteries alone controlled one-fifth of all land with a net annual income of £136,000. The church as a whole enjoyed about £270,000 yearly, considerably more than the revenue of the crown. Most importantly, the church commanded the minds of women and men through the confessional, the pulpit, images, relics and ceremonies. Not surprisingly, the church pervaded every aspect of national life.[2]

By the beginning of Henry's reign, government was highly developed and sophisticated. Edward IV had begun the process of restoring effective government, and Henry VII made it the centrepiece of his reign. The aristocracy was persuaded to renounce adventures in civil war in favour of their traditional place in society as the party of law and order. Monarchy, convinced of the political utility of living of its own, attended to the state of royal finances and made available the resources necessary to govern. Regionalism slowly began to respond if not to yield to central authority. The nobility, so often involved in factional opposition to one king or another, were encouraged, while playing their traditional roles, to stay out of dangerous plots and schemes. The crown developed new jobs for them, and patronage offered opportunities for advancement with minimal risk. Thus the central authority increased its influence over the nobility by creating a partnership that benefited all and reduced the perceived need for conflict. Official, centralized authority combined with tight local control over peasants by men who possessed land, and social status provided governance for regions as well as the realm itself.[3]

These restorative achievements fitted well with the duties of monarchy, often said to consist of the defence of the realm, maintenance of the law, and provision of justice.

This homily on kingship applied particularly to Henry VII, who had attained the throne through victory in civil war and in the early years wore his crown precariously. Henry VII successfully passed the crown to his son because he satisfied the political nation by governing effectively. A medieval or early modern English king occupied a complex position. He was lord of his domain, which was the entire kingdom. At the same time, the commonwealth over which he presided obliged him to consider his subjects. He should listen to his natural advisers, pay attention to local concerns, and respect the traditional commitment of kings to rule in the interest of the entire realm.

The ability to handle both local and central political affairs made for effective kingship. The well-remembered and long-lamented reign of Henry VI reminded his successors of the price of failure. And why were kings obeyed? Peasants, of course, had little choice. They lived lives of obedience bounded by poverty and lack of potency. Their lords by comparison lived lives of plenty but were often haunted by the spectre of rebellion. Sixteenth-century England experienced endemic violence and disorder. All men of wealth, fearing unrest and upheaval from below, saw a clear mutual interest with the king in controlling the peasantry. A strong king brought to this partnership effective government and the power wrought by the symbolic imagery of a divinely appointed monarchy.[4]

Participation in central government also offered lucrative rewards. Crown servants of Henry VII, such as Sir Reynold Bray and Edmund Dudley, counted their annual revenues in thousands of pounds and enjoyed influence over several counties by virtue of grants of land from a grateful monarch.[5] These fortunes may not have been characteristic, but clearly in the minds of the aristocracy crown service wedded to landed wealth represented the pathway to preferment in the early Tudor world. In addition, Tudor monarchs found power to rule in their considerable non-material authority. They paraded their semi-divine qualities and advertised their place in the world as representatives as well as protectors of their subjects. Various Court ceremonials gave the appearance of a universe apart, while the public nature of celebrations themselves made it appear that anyone might have access to the royal presence.[6] When everything went as planned, it was good indeed to be the king.

Almost any book that deals with the rise of the Tudor state opens the reign of Henry VIII with a version of the same mantra. Henry VII left his son 'a safe throne, a full treasury, a functioning machinery of government, and a reasonably ordered and prosperous country.'[7] The ability to govern well allowed Henry VII to enjoy the throne; it produced a sense of satisfaction in the political nation. The king paid his own way, showed good political judgment, and coped well with the everyday matters of government.[8]

The king personally functioned as the mainspring of government. Henry VIII, despite his lack of experience, knew well from his first day on the throne that he stood at the centre of all things. Throughout the Tudor century, political theorists shared the belief that the prince exemplified England. Thomas Starkey, in his *Dialogue between Pole and Lupset*, placed the king at the centre of the body politic. He stated that the king was the heart of the state. 'From the princes and rulers of the state cometh all laws, order and policy, all justice, virtue and honesty.'[9] Throughout the reign, other writers echoed Starkey, and the metaphor would remain a commonplace for many years.

Henry VIII certainly concurred with those who placed him at the heart of English government, but he had little stomach, himself, for the hard and tedious grind of day-to-day governance. Two central institutions under the king's rule took part in governing the realm. The King's council was the driving force of central government. It exercised formal administrative authority. The royal household or Court, on the other hand, developed, ad hoc, a host of its own offices, rivalling and at times surpassing the old, established administrative centres.

In the early years of his reign, Henry relied on the council provided by his father to handle the crown's administrative business. The council served *de facto* in a regency capacity while Henry learned to stand on his own. Then in 1512 Thomas Wolsey, the first of Henry VIII's two great ministers, emerged to dominate the Tudor political scene. Wolsey's career trajectory was nothing short of meteoric. A royal chaplain during the latter years of Henry VII's reign, Wolsey became royal almoner on Henry VIII's accession. From there his promotions dramatically accelerated. He became bishop of Lincoln in 1514, archbishop of York later in the same year, and, pushed by the king, cardinal in September 1515. When Archbishop Warham resigned as lord chancellor in December of 1515, Wolsey was given the Great Seal. Finally, in 1518 the cardinal capped his list of major promotions with appointment as *Legate a Latere*.[10]

Wolsey served as the king's chief minister for fifteen years, and it often seemed that the cardinal overshadowed the monarch, but neither ever doubted who was in charge. Wolsey satisfied Henry, and the king allowed him to replace the council as his chief source of political advice. If Henry chose to intervene, as he did from time to time, Wolsey never forgot his place. But as long as he enjoyed the king's favour, nothing on earth could diminish Wolsey's agency. In the normal run of business, finance, justice, the church or the activities of the council, Henry left responsibility on his minister's shoulders.

Wolsey focused on integrating the kingdom and making it responsive to the king's will. A major tool in this enterprise was the creation of the Tudor subsidy, a system of direct taxation. Traditionally, taxation reflected an agreed-upon theory of reciprocal rights and responsibilities. The king was expected to provide the realm with protection and justice. When an extraordinary event, usually military, became too expensive to be borne from the king's ordinary revenues, parliament was expected to meet its obligation to grant the king, through taxation, sufficient money to meet the emergency.

Taxes took two different forms. A system of levying fifteenths and tenths on moveable property had been in effect from early in the fourteenth century. This was an indirect tax that charged a fifteenth of the value of rural property and a tenth of the value of urban property. All land was exempt. Values had been fixed in 1334 and remained about at the same level nearly two centuries later. The advantage of the system lay in the fact that it provided a simple tax with a fixed yield on communities rather than individuals. The community decided how to assess and collect this tax, which by the early Tudor period amounted to about £30,000. No one welcomed taxation, but tradition supported fifteenths and tenths, and parliament represented the political nation when called upon to impose this tax.[11] Inflation and changes in the geographical balance of wealth rendered necessary a new form of taxation, and Wolsey brought forward a plan between 1512 and 1515 for direct taxation based on assessments of the current wealth of individuals. The subsidy of 1514 alone raised about £100,000. The fact that this financial plan could be envisioned much less imposed is indicative of the successful centralization of royal power under Wolsey.[12]

The council also underwent revision under the cardinal's controlling hand. It continued to function and remained under the personal control of the king, but Henry VIII, unlike his father, did not preside in person. Wolsey made few institutional changes at first, but unsurprisingly the importance of the council's business declined to the level of the routine and was handled by politicians below the first rank in status and importance. When Henry declined not to make political decisions himself, Wolsey, rather than the council, took the initiative in the name of the king. Wolsey not only took policy-making functions from the council, he diverted the councillors' energies into judicial work. Legal institutions had become strained past their limits as landowners went to law rather than to war to solve disputes with their neighbours. By 1520 the courts, particularly the equity courts, had difficulty handling the quantity of suits reaching them. The number of cases in the court of Star Chamber and their visibility convinced some later writers that the court had its origins in 1520. In fact, the court, which was the council sitting in its judiciary capacity in the suite called Star Chamber, had been in business at least from the reign of Henry VII. Wolsey, without specific legal training, nevertheless valued the court as a way of increasing the authority of central government. In addition, it gave the cardinal a stage of his own upon which to perform.[13] Wolsey, as chancellor, already presided over his own court of Chancery where he used his position to soften the common law in the name of equity. During this same period of the cardinal's judicial initiatives, the court of Requests began meeting in the palace of Westminster, offering a rough-and-ready justice in suits brought by poor men, and Wolsey gave to the council licence to oversee these actions as well. Wolsey thus continued the centralizing labours begun by Edward IV and Henry VII. By his actions, the territorial feuds of magnate politicians fought on fifteenth-century battlefields became focused instead on the king's courts and the king's Court.

The household or Court comprised the other centre of power in the kingdom. Definition is somewhat confusing. Suffice to understand that the 'court' and the royal 'household' are two different words for a single collective, and that in whatever vocabulary we prefer, it had a history of at least 200 years by the time of the foundation of the Tudor dynasty. The centralization of government from the mid-fifteenth century meant that access to royal power became the key to political influence as well as to admission to the royal largesse.[14] For those who were courtiers, the Court represented the 'chief preoccupation of their official lives'. All of their attention focused on the person of the monarch. Catching his eye or ear, wisdom suggested, could make a career. Losing access could mean the end of whatever one held dear, including life itself. The Court became the clearing house for royal service and patronage opportunities and remained a most important arena for politics. Those who would participate came to Court to join in the battle.[15]

Much has been made about the differences between Court, council and privy chamber. Various historians have argued that decisive political power resided in the Court, where everybody who was anybody gathered to compete for influence and the attendant rewards, or the council, the body of formal advisers to the king, or the privy chamber, where the groom of the stool and other servants presided over the king's most personal activities. The current consensus, I believe, is to focus less on which set of rooms held sway and more on the individuals who for whatever reason dominated royal government. In any case, the king's government remained highly personal, and the competence of the king who directed government mattered most. Kings, particularly Henry VIII, rarely exercised direct control over administrative institutions. He surrounded himself with courtiers, many of whom held offices in the household or on the council. His function was to preside over 'the great game of politics'. Whether courtier politicians found themselves in the household, one of the great offices, the council, or the privy council mattered far less than the fact that they were courtier politicians, players in the game, and as such, could gain or lose all on a single throw of the dice.

During the reign of Henry VIII, his two chief ministers, Thomas Wolsey, 1512 to 1529, and Thomas Cromwell, 1532 to 1540, in turn monopolized political power. They shaped institutions to fit their style of leadership and determined which governmental institutions were to be used to express the will of central government. Wolsey enjoyed significantly more freedom than did Cromwell, because Henry intervened less in affairs before the divorce crisis than he did afterwards. Until the pursuit of the divorce, known as 'the King's Great Matter', began in earnest in the summer of 1527, Wolsey kept his monarch quite satisfied. The cardinal's competence allowed the king to enjoy his pastimes with little concern for royal business. Henry's trust gave Wolsey the opportunity to develop policy that contributed to the centralizing of English government. Always the consummate politician, Wolsey continued the firm rule of Henry VII, and focused political attention on the king's Court, rather than on the ambitions of territorial magnates.[16]

Personal rather than institutional authority, however, carries its own burdens and risks. The game of politics, unlike the government of the realm, required access to the monarch's person, and exclusion mattered so much because the battle for advantage might come down to 'catching the king's ear or the queen's eye.'[17] Certainly Wolsey kept an eye on courtiers close to the king. After 1518 he worked assiduously to control who might see the king. The privy chamber and the council attendant on Henry represented likely sources of stiff competition to the cardinal's monopoly of power and influence. In January 1526, Wolsey moved against the gentlemen of the privy chamber to keep these noblemen from generating significant political opposition. He proposed a scheme for the reform of the royal household. The Eltham Ordinance of 1526 envisioned a reform of the council that would have created a small, workable body, attendant upon the king wherever he went. This was Wolsey's effort to reduce the political influence of the privy chamber, staffed with many of Henry's friends and resistant to his leadership. But this plan did not leave the drawing board during the cardinal's lifetime. This attendant council would have exercised immense power had it ever been established, and a decade later Thomas Cromwell, Wolsey's successor, revisited the cardinal's scheme for conciliar reform.[18]

Wolsey's dominance foundered in 1527 when Henry VIII demanded that his minister obtain for him a divorce from Catherine of Aragon so that he could marry Anne Boleyn with whom he had fallen in love. This was problematical for Wolsey, since only an annulment secured from the pope could meet Henry's requirements – an extremely unlikely outcome. The first moves in the divorce action revealed the impasse. Henry loved Anne, but also required a legitimate male heir to perpetuate the Tudor dynasty. The pope, Clement VII, could not move from under the thumb of Charles V, Holy Roman Emperor and king of Spain; and Charles, Catherine of Aragon's nephew, would not countenance her removal. The pope, who had recently witnessed the sack of Rome by the emperor's Lutheran troops, could in no way sanction Henry VIII's demand to have his first marriage declared invalid. For two years the English king challenged and cajoled Clement VII. The pope on his part offered a series of compromises and even toyed with the idea of allowing Henry to enter a bigamous marriage with Anne Boleyn. But Henry was adamant; his heir must be legitimate beyond dispute; only a legal annulment would suffice. Finally, the pope authorized a legatine court to be held at Blackfriars in London to decide the matter, but at the moment when a verdict seemed about to be pronounced, on 31 July 1529, the papal legate, Cardinal Campeggio, adjourned the proceedings and removed the case to Rome. The next stage of the divorce began – without Cardinal Wolsey.

Wolsey's inability to deliver the divorce left him vulnerable to his enemies, and Henry's anger made inevitable the minister's fall from power. The king could only hate those whom he had ceased to love, and only death from illness on his journey to the Tower of London spared Wolsey a more public and ignominious fate. With the cardinal gone, other important consequences became discernable. Reaching for divorce, Henry shattered England's unity with Catholicism. The beginnings of the Reformation brought a revolution in ecclesiastical polity that would end Roman jurisdiction in England. Anticlericalism, endemic among the populace, was embraced by the king, who needed allies in his struggle against the pope. And his need insured that the constitutional revolution would go forward. Those men who wanted a profound change in the country's religious life would also find opportunity in the king's Great Matter. Ministers of the crown would shape the enthusiasm for reform and slowly begin the process of re-weaving a Protestant commonwealth from the shredded fabric of a formerly united Christendom.[19]

The king had intended few if any of these outcomes. At almost any point along the way he would have been happy to have had papal co-operation in his marital plans, but with or without Rome's blessing, Henry would have his Anne; they would wed, and the sons she would bear would be legitimate in the eyes of all. Although it seemed clear that independence from Rome loomed as the only course to Henry's goal, the king had not developed an effective tactical approach. Nor could he be sure of convincing his subjects to join him in this endeavour. Obedience to the royal power of a godly king was one thing; risking eternity in hell might cause people to pause in their enthusiasm for their king's passion.

For those who had abandoned the church in England, the divorce represented an unprecedented opportunity for change. England had a long history of anticlericalism connected to the failures of the post-plague church to meet the spiritual needs of many in its flock. Some had experimented with Lollardy and remained faithful to this alternative to orthodoxy. Others, particularly the most educated, identified themselves with Erasmus and Thomas More, neither of whom broke with the church, and yet numbered themselves among its harshest critics. And then there was Luther, who beginning in 1517 presented a persuasive theological challenge to the Catholic church. Justification by faith alone convinced many that centuries old ritual and practice could be abandoned in favour of a scripture-based reliance on the grace of God alone as the road to salvation. A religious life that had evolved over a period of centuries now could be changed by the conscious acts of men and women. New institutions could promote a new religious life. 'In their actions lay the thrust of their hope – the renewal of a fondly imagined golden age of Christian life'.[20]

In 1530, most of these changes lay in the future. The king's attention remained tightly focused in the moment. In November 1529, Henry turned to parliament and encouraged its members to express their anticlerical feelings through a legislative attack on papal authority in England. This 'Reformation parliament' began enacting statutes striking at lucrative sources of papal income. They also attacked abuses in the church such as pluralism and non-residence, longstanding practices that had denied the laity access to the sacraments essential for their spiritual welfare. In addition, a petition complaining about Roman ecclesiastical jurisdiction in England came into the hands of a rising star on the Tudor political horizon: Henry was about to turn to a new favourite, one who had the ability to secure the divorce by bringing to the commonwealth the vision of an independent Church of England.

Thomas Cromwell had been Wolsey's chief lieutenant for several years. He came from the same social milieu that had produced his mentor; his father worked as a cloth worker in Putney, where Cromwell was born about 1485. He spent much of his adolescent and early adult life in Italy and the Netherlands where he learned soldiering and business. When he returned to England in about 1512, he took up the study of common law and entered Wolsey's service where he became closely identified in all the cardinal's business affairs and matters of policy. Surviving his master's fall, Cromwell entered the king's service and by 1531 had entered the inner circle of the king's advisers.[21] Henry appointed him to the office of principal secretary early in 1534. The office of principal secretary had grown in importance during the late medieval period, but Cromwell took it into new territory as he used the position to solidify his administrative and political power. He became the first king's secretary to organize the work of the council. With an expanded staff that seemed to be everywhere, collecting information and facilitating public business, Cromwell gained an unchallenged supremacy in all of the central government's institutions.[22]

As Cromwell quickly rose to a pre-eminent position in Henrician politics and government, he authored a series of statutes passed by parliament between 1532 and 1536, redefining the relationship between church and state. This series of statutes were intended by Cromwell to free Henry from Catherine and make him available to Anne. The Act in Conditional Restraint of Annates threatened to deprive the pope of revenues he received from English bishops. And, if the pope retaliated by refusing to consecrate new bishops, the statute specified that English authority alone would be sufficient to induct them. Then Cromwell returned to the Reformation parliament's petition known as the Commons' Supplication against the Ordinaries. He used it as the foundation from which to demand the formal surrender of the English church to Henry VIII. Convocation, the church's legislative body, could not meet without express permission from the king. New canons required royal assent. A royal commission would review old canons and remove those in conflict with the king's prerogative.

Henry, however, was still married to Catherine, and time suddenly became of the essence. Anne had finally allowed the king to share her bed, and by the end of 1532 she was pregnant. Thomas Cranmer, soon to be archbishop of Canterbury, secretly married the couple on 24 January 1533. Cromwell used statute as the engine to break the constitutional connection between England and Rome. The Act in Restraint of Appeals became law in April 1533. No appeal could be made from the king's jurisdiction to Rome. All spiritual cases were to be judged in England. The preamble of this momentous Act vigorously asserted that England was an empire governed by one supreme head and king. Cranmer, a key political ally, was consecrated as archbishop of Canterbury in March 1533, by the end of May he had pronounced null and void the marriage of Henry and Catherine and declared that of Henry and Anne to be legal and binding. Catherine was removed from the Court to live the remaining three years of her life in internal exile. Anne Boleyn's coronation took place on Whit Sunday 1533, and on 7 September of the same year the new queen gave birth to a healthy girl, Elizabeth, much to the displeasure of the king.

Cromwell had little time to reflect upon the birth of another Tudor daughter. Additional legislation had to be enacted by parliament to complete the break with Rome. Between 1534 and 1536 several statutes received parliamentary sanction. The Succession Act, passed in the spring of 1534, put Cranmer's declaration of Henry and Anne's lawful marriage into statutory form. It became treasonous to deny the king's right to reign or to slander his marriage. This Act together with the later Act Against Papal Authority required most crown officials to take an oath affirming their support of the break with Rome. The Act for the Submission of the Clergy made law the 1532 surrender, giving parliamentary authorization to the king's actions limiting the ability of the church to act as an independent force. The Dispensations Act put the issuance of special privileges into the hands of English church authorities and limited the travel of monks. The heresy law was revised so that critics could speak out against papal authority. In the second session of 1534 the Act of Supremacy was passed. Henry now became supreme head of the Church of England. A Treasons Act established penalties for those who might challenge Henry's supremacy.[23]

Cromwell's statutory campaign articulated a new role for central government. By moving the headship of the church from the pope to the king, Cromwell had vested responsibility for the spiritual and social well-being of the English people with purely national institutions. Their collective will was to be expressed in statute, the sovereign voice of the king in parliament. Not only did the royal supremacy satisfy the passion of a king for a new wife, it expressed and encouraged the collective will of the commonwealth to explore and determine different spiritual possibilities.

Cromwell had little opportunity to reflect on his successful undertaking. Henry appointed him vicegerent in spirituals, and Cromwell set about to give substance and identity to the royal supremacy. He faced a daunting task. The English people had to be persuaded to follow the king away from Rome and toward an uncertain spiritual future. Cromwell sponsored an intense propaganda campaign. He used his considerable patronage resources to encourage uniformity and obedience. The printing press and the pulpit became major tools in the operation. The royal supremacy did not proceed without opposition from those who preferred the old-time religion with or without the pope. Defiance carried risk, and death awaited those who persisted in their resistance to the Supremacy. Thomas More swiftly followed John Fisher, the obdurate bishop of Rochester, to martyrdom, both of them prosecuted as traitors. The law of treason set out in 1534 and 1536 covered not only actions directed against the king, but also words written or spoken against anything of or emanating from the royal estate. All who spoke out against the king's policies might find themselves in serious trouble.

To return to the question, then, Why should anybody obey anyone? Perhaps because the alternative for the disobedient was certain detection and prosecution, or so it seemed; and the only potential remedy was rebellion. The failure of the Pilgrimage of Grace seemed to prove the futility of this approach. Thousands of people died in a struggle that is noted as the most serious threat to Henrician rule but which in the end led to little more than the tightening of central control over remoter parts of the realm. At a constitutional level, the royal supremacy made necessary changes in central government. Everything that had its origin in Roman jurisdiction required replacement. Old institutions strained by the burden of the Supremacy had to be refashioned or replaced. Moreover, since monasticism was both incompatible with the new religion and an easy target to be stripped of its great wealth, mechanisms for collecting and disposing of the spoils had to be developed. In addition, parliamentary participation in the process of establishing the royal supremacy meant that political relationships had to be reorganized or created. New men came to the fore with a different sense of the connections between church and state, and their vision required accommodation.

The 1530s witnessed the reorganization of central governmental administration under Cromwell's innovative hand. The chancellorship, a keystone of Wolsey's career, held no great appeal for Cromwell. After Thomas More's resignation, Sir Thomas Audley, a competent administrator with little political weight, succeeded to the post. Instead of the highly visible office, Cromwell chose to vest his power in the office of principal secretary to which he had been appointed by the king in 1534. He also received the offices of vicegerent for spirituals in 1535 and became lord privy seal in 1536. From these relatively modest positions, Cromwell seized the opportunity to achieve undefined yet unlimited authority in financial administration along with most other areas of central governance.

Historians are still very much occupied in trying to understand the origins, substance and implications of Cromwell's work in reshaping Henrician administrative institutions. Some things are clear. The period of Cromwellian influence, lasting from 1532 to 1540, accompanied a wide-ranging set of changes in the way business was conducted. Government administration became more bureaucratic, and whether Cromwell invented these procedures or borrowed them from the past, once in place they persisted. Financial expedients were of great importance. Money that had been collected in England only to be redirected to Rome now went to London and had to be accounted for. Cromwell created the court of First Fruits and Tenths to collect the clerical taxes on new appointments and the yearly tax on clerical benefices. The 1534 Act for the Payment of First Fruits led to the collection of £46,052 in 1535 and £51,770 in 1536, a significant increase in revenue from this source.[24] By 1540 the crown had realized £406,415 in first fruits and tenths.[25]

In 1536, the court of Augmentations was established to deal with the enormous amount of wealth in land and moveable property that came to the king as a result of the dissolution of the monasteries. After passage of the Act for the Dissolution of the Lesser Monasteries, commissioners for the court began immediately to take charge of the wealth of the affected houses. They surveyed the land, collected the moveable assets, moved the monks and nuns to other religious houses or returned them to secular lives. A second phase of visitations began in 1538 when parliament dissolved the greater monasteries. Cromwell's commissioners moved quickly. The execution of several abbots for treason ended resistance, and by 1540 the process had been completed. Enormous amounts of money came to the crown from the dissolution. In the first eight years of its history, the court of Augmentations collected almost £900,000. Some of this wealth came from the sale of the lands, some of it came from rents. In any event, Cromwell had produced incredible cash reserves for the crown, and a host of real-estate opportunities for members of the political nation. It is not surprising, therefore, that English monasticism *in extremis* could call upon few defenders.

A host of other governmental and administrative reforms contributed to Cromwell's historical reputation for managerial achievement. The king's council, so important to Cromwell's predecessors, also received the minister's reforming attention. Until Cromwell became principal secretary in 1534, the council looked and acted as much the same institution it had been under Edward IV and Henry VII. The number of councillors and their functions fluctuated. Some members rarely attended; others formed the heart of the council, handling all important business as well as advising the king. Wolsey had attempted to reduce competition for the king's attention by focusing responsibility for policy formation on himself and diverting the work of the council into the legal business associated with the courts of Star Chamber and Requests. The cardinal had envisioned in the Eltham Ordinance of 1526 a much more efficient body with twenty regular members who would meet regularly with the king in his dining chamber. Private suits would be shifted away from the council to leave its officers, the most important in the realm, free to give attention to the most important issues of government and administration. This important reform never took place during Wolsey's lifetime, and the council had enjoyed a brief non-ministerial rejuvenation between Wolsey's fall and Cromwell's successful rise to power. When Cromwell looked to reorganizing the structure of the king's council, however, he followed the same line of thinking as that espoused by his mentor a decade earlier.

Cromwell began his reorganizing efforts during a series of intense political crises. We cannot know what his plans might have been if they could have been put into play in quieter times. But, by the spring of 1537, we can say that the king's council had taken on a new shape. Still the formal heart of English central government, Cromwell's plan for the council, however, did not embrace a desire to have it speak with a single voice. Rather, he seemed more interested in continuity of personnel and the regular attendance of men who would take responsibility for the business of the crown. Cromwell, make no mistake, spoke in the dominant voice until his fall in 1540. But by that time, the reformed council, with a formal written record of its own, had become an institution along lines that he had created.[26]

Whether or not the emergence of a privy council and the host of other administrative changes in government during Cromwell's ministry constitute a revolution in government has never seemed to me to be a particularly engaging question. The broader issue of the impact of the break from Roman jurisdiction, however, argues 'revolution' without qualification. Some may still play down the impact of the royal supremacy, but its political significance is certain. The most important contribution of the Supremacy to the future was the way in which it had been produced. England had been connected to Rome by a series of agreements between kings and popes. The connection was broken by statute passed by parliament with the participation of the king. The Act of Appeals had argued that England possessed a national sovereignty that owed allegiance to none outside the realm. On the strength of this statutory preamble, parliament claimed the right to legislate on behalf of the nation. The political nation had taken a giant step away from any restraining authority and established itself as the exclusive sovereign of England.

By the time Cromwell fell in 1540, the Tudor state had been largely refashioned. When Henry VIII died in 1547, his legacy to his son resembled in many respects his own inheritance. England remained an agricultural country farmed by men and women as their ancestors had for generations. Common people obeyed their lords in much the same fashion as they always had. And despite a quarter of a century of religious ferment, most also obeyed their God in much the same manner as they always had. Elements of the future, however, can easily be discerned. For example, more people now occupied traditional villages and fields than in 1509. The population continued to recover its numbers, and prices rose in response to increased numbers of mouths to feed. The landscape had changed. Monasteries now lay in ruins. The monks and nuns who had given colour and depth to Catholicism were gone. Reformation began to be seen in other areas as well. Images so important in reinforcing faith had begun to disappear, seen as idolatrous at best and fraudulent at worst. People's politics probably reflected universal themes. Henry alive probably attracted jokes and comments about his six wives. The king dead, however, must have chilled the more aware, whatever their station in life. Edward VI was but a young boy and must have reminded people of the stories they had heard about the minority of Henry VI. Waiting in the wings were Mary, Elizabeth, and the unknown.

By 1550, many of people's worst fears had been experienced. Rivalries among magnate politicians accompanied Edward's accession. Even to his unconditional supporters, his poor health must have been a concern. Cromwell had tried to enrich the crown and strengthen central government, but he had been dead for ten years, and those that followed had neither the talent nor the political will to build solid political institutions on the foundations he had designed. Money intended to endow the crown had been spent in war. The monastic land upon which the endowment depended had been sold. Population growth, economic inflation, political conflict, religious tumult, all added to a sense of uncertainty that could only be overturned from the top. Another eight years would pass before the daughter so repugnant to Henry VIII would come to the throne to restore the fortunes of the Tudor dynasty.

As I noted in the first paragraph of this essay, the idea of the 'Rise of the Tudor State' at first seems based on an old-fashioned approach to historical studies. This is due, primarily, to the nature of the historiography that underlies the topic. Few if any historians working today would discuss the Tudor state by looking first at its institutions. We would all begin, middle, and end with discussions of the individuals who held power and their relationships with each other. We might choose to view these scenes from a theoretical perspective in order to make connections with current concerns and approaches to texts. This is not to say that these are better methodologies, only that they are ours at the beginning of this century.

In the middle of the last century, the reign of Henry VIII belonged, almost exclusively, to G. R. Elton who researched and wrote in the field of administrative history. This is not the place to rehearse Elton's work in depth. Suffice to say that his impact over a career that spanned over forty years, a large shelf filled with his books, and more than seventy graduate students has been significant. Anyone working in the Tudor field has had to deal with Elton's ideas about central administration. Since he argued that the 1530s represent a watershed between medieval and modern, and that Thomas Cromwell was singularly responsible for a 'revolution in government', many, as we might expect, have found cause to disagree.

First David Starkey discovered the privy chamber. He has shown us the links between the personal and the political. His book, *The Reign of Henry VIII*, is subtitled 'personality and politics', and in the introduction Starkey insists that this isn't a book about Henry VIII: 'It is about the great game of politics over which he presided.' His chapters begin with a structural overview and immediately turn to 'a blow by blow account of the game'. As anyone who has seen his recent television biography of Henry VIII knows, Starkey has taken the 'game' over the top. Nevertheless, his original contributions made in the 1970s have opened up valuable areas for further investigation. He has done much to repopulate the Henrician Court.[27]

John Guy, another of Elton's students, also has helped to move the study of Henrician administrative history away from the revolution in government. He has argued persuasively in *Tudor England* that until we are able to look at Tudor politics and administration through fresh eyes, we will never be able to understand the significance of the Henrician Age in particular or of the Tudor era in general.[28] I might add that it may be time to let Sir Geoffrey rest in peace for a while and allow future generations to discover his work on their own. Starkey's book was published in 1985, Guy's in 1988. Their research has added much to our understanding of the details of early Tudor government and politics, but reactive theses that proclaim 'no revolution in government' won't serve to take us much beyond Elton's 'revolution in government'. It is worth noting our audiences. Our undergraduate freshmen, the class of 2006, were born in 1984 and 1985. It is time to be thinking about a new synthesis.

Another Elton student, Susan Brigden, may have taken significant steps in the direction of a new narrative. Her Penguin history of the Tudors, *New Worlds, Lost Worlds*, reads almost like a play. Instead of being set in Elton's universe, Professor Brigden has widened the context of her text to that of an examination of the English Renaissance and Reformation. She discusses an England that shares its history with Ireland and Scotland, an England on the edge of Europe, an English people who lived as much in their imagination as do the people reading her book. It is a work that gives as much credit to 'awe and excitement' as it does to a quality of research that is evident but clearly the tool rather than the product. She places cabbages in the same sentence as kings and invites readers to a more active participation in the creation of meaning. These are her new worlds of the sixteenth century, the lost worlds that preceded the Tudor dynasty's involvement with religion and other intellectual innovations, that opened up for the explorers of souls as well as the seas.[29] If indeed we can move in these lost worlds or those of our own creative enterprise, there is much of interest to be encountered, and we may even be able to encourage our students to accompany us on the journey.

NOTES

1. Elton, *Tudor Revolution in Government*.
2. Williams, *The Tudor Regime*, Introduction.
3. Gunn, *Early Tudor Government*, p. 13.
4. Elton, *Studies in Tudor and Stuart Politics and Government*, vol. III, p. 56.
5. Gunn, *Early Tudor Government*, p. 32.
6. Elton, *The Tudor Constitution*, pp. 12–13.
7. Elton, *England under the Tudors*, p. 69.
8. Brown, *The Governance of Late Medieval England*, p. 2.
9. Mayer, *Thomas Starkey and the Commonweal*, p. 128.
10. Loades, *Politics and Nation*, p. 113.
11. Schofield, 'Taxation and the Political Limits of the Tudor State', p. 230.
12. Slavin, *The Precarious Balance* pp. 102–3.
13. Loades, *Politics and Nation*, p, 115.
14. Gunn, *Early Tudor Government*, p. 34.
15. Elton, *Studies in Tudor and Stuart Politics and Government*, vol. III, pp. 44–56.
16. Guy, *Tudor England*, p. 85.
17. Elton, *Studies in Tudor and Stuart Politics and Government*, vol. III, p. 46.
18. Guy, *Tudor England*, pp. 103–4.
19. Slavin, *The Precarious Balance*, p. 140.
20. Slavin, *The Precarious Balance*, p. 117.
21. Lockyer, *Tudor and Stuart Britain*, pp. 38–9.
22. Gunn, *Early Tudor Government*, p. 53.
23. Guy, *Tudor England*, pp. 127–36.
24. Loades, *Politics and Nation*, p. 144.
25. Slavin, *The Precarious Balance*, p. 145.
26. Guy, *Tudor England*, pp. 159–61; Loades, *Politics and Nation*, pp. 149–50.
27. Starkey, *The Reign of Henry VIII*, p. 8.
28. Guy, *Tudor England*, p. vii.
29. Brigden, *New Worlds, Lost Worlds*, pp. x–xi.

BIBLIOGRAPHY

Brigden, Susan, *New Worlds, Lost Worlds: The Rule of the Tudors, 1485–1603* (New York, 2000).
Brown, A. L., *The Governance of Late Medieval England 1272–1461* (Stanford, 1989).
Elton, G. R., *England under the Tudors* (3rd edition, London, 1991).
Elton, G. R., *Studies in Tudor and Stuart Politics and Government*, vol. III (Cambridge, 1983).
Elton, G. R., *The Tudor Constitution* (Cambridge, 1965).
Elton, G. R., *The Tudor Revolution in Government* (Cambridge, 1953).
Gunn, S. J., *Early Tudor Government, 1485–1558* (New York, 1995).
Guy, John, *Tudor England* (Oxford, 1988).
Loades, David M., *Politics and Nation, England 1450–1660* (5th edition, Oxford, 1999).
Lockyer, Roger, *Tudor and Stuart Britain 1471–1714* (2nd edition, New York, 1985).
Mayer, Thomas, *Thomas Starkey and the Commonweal: Humanist Politics and Religion in the Reign of Henry VIII* (Cambridge, 1989).
Schofield, Roger, 'Taxation and the political limits of the Tudor state', in Claire Cross, David Loades and J. J. Scarisbrick, eds, *Law and Government under the Tudors* (Cambridge, 1988).

Slavin, Arthur Joseph, *The Precarious Balance: English Government and Society* (New York, 1973).
Starkey, David, *The Reign of Henry VIII: Personalities and Politics* (London, 1985).
Williams, Penry, *The Tudor Regime* (Oxford, 1979).

FURTHER READING

The most useful of the general surveys that cover the rise of the Tudor state are Susan Brigden, *New Worlds, Lost Worlds: The Rule of the Tudors, 1485–1603* (2000) and John Guy, *Tudor England* (1988), See also D. M. Loades, *Politics and Nation: England 1450–1660*, 5th edn (1999), and G. R. Elton, *England under the Tudors*, 3rd edn (1991).

In recent years a number of books have been published that offer essays which comment effectively on the rise of the Tudor State. These include: *Law and Government under the Tudors*, ed. C. Cross, D. M. Loades and J. J. Scarisbrick (1988); *Revolution Reassessed*, ed. C. Coleman and D. R. Starkey (1986); *Tudor Political Culture*, ed. Dale Hoak (1995); *The Reign of Henry VIII*, ed. Diarmaid MacCulloch (1995); and *Reassessing the Henrician Age*, ed. Alastair Fox and John Guy (1986).

The structure of medieval and early modern government are concisely and usefully covered by A. L. Brown, *The Governance of Late Medieval England 1272–1461* (1989), and S. J. Gunn, *Early Tudor Government 1485–1558* (1995). See also G. R. Elton, *The Tudor Constitution* (1965) and Penry Williams, *The Tudor Regime* (1979).

The best biography of Henry VIII remains J. J. Scarisbrick, *Henry VIII* (1968). For Thomas Wolsey, see P. Gwynn, *The King's Cardinal: The Rise and Fall of Thomas Wolsey* (1990), and S. J. Gunn and P. G. Lindley eds, *Cardinal Wolsey: Church, State and Art* (1991). Thomas Cromwell has been treated most fully in several books and articles written by G. R. Elton. A good starting point would be *Reform and Renewal: Thomas Cromwell and the Common Weal* (1973).

CHAPTER THREE

Elizabethan Government and Politics

DAVID DEAN

At 9pm on 21 November 1596 Bartholomew Steer, a carpenter living in the village of Hampton Gay, Oxfordshire, went up to Enslow Hill overlooking the River Cherwell where, according to popular memory, there had been a rebellious gathering in 1549. Only a few men joined him and after two hours they gave up and returned home. Arrested, charged and found guilty under the treason laws, two of the conspirators were executed on 11 June 1597, symbolically on Enslow Hill. The others died in prison, possibly as the result of torture. The severity of the government's response to this aborted rising, occasionally described by historians (adopting a nomenclature which reflects the worst fears of the authorities) as the 'rebellion of 1596', indicates the fragility of Elizabethan government at a time of distress. Yet it also demonstrates the stability of the Elizabethan regime. Despite severe economic hardship, few among the poorer and middling sort were willing to join the conspiracy. This 'rebellion', like every other during Elizabeth's long reign, was a failure.[1]

The history of the rising reveals much about Elizabethan attitudes towards government and authority. In the autumn of 1596 England was in the grip of the worst subsistence crisis of the century. The privy council itself noted that the poorer sort had suffered 'great misery and extremity'. Yet when local authorities wanted to prevent grain leaving Oxfordshire the government refused, worried that depriving London markets of grain would provoke food riots like those led by apprentices in 1595. Meanwhile, between forty and sixty men visited Henry, Lord Norris at Rycote, who as lord lieutenant was responsible for law and order in the county. They asked him to help the poor, but warned if he did nothing 'they would seek remedy themselves, and cast down hedges and ditches, and knock down gentlemen'.

Steer, then employed by Lord Norris, took it upon himself to make the threat a reality with a plot to seize weapons, attack landowners and march to London where the apprentices would undoubtedly join them. The conspirators sought support from friends and relatives, neighbours and those they encountered in the mills, markets and fairs of the Cherwell valley. The rising was timed for the Sunday after Accession Day, 17 November, one of the key festivals of Elizabethan England, a time of bell-ringing and rejoicing, which would not only give them further recruitment opportunities but would ensure Norris's absence at Court. However, when a servant informed his land-lord of the plot, the alarm was raised and the deputy-lieutenant, himself one of their targets, made the arrests with the assistance of justices and village constables. What began as a plea for assistance and then an assault on enclosures had turned into a violent assault on property and persons – a conspiracy against all authority.

Although Norris tried to play down the uprising, the privy council took a much more serious view of the matter. Aware of the apprentice-led riots a year earlier, receiving reports of unrest in Essex, Kent and the west country and concerned at the possibility of gentry leadership, the council ordered Norris 'to take order with the justices and other gentlemen of ability, honest farmers and other officers' to sup-press any disturbances. Those arrested were brought to London for interrogation by a committee led by attorney-general Sir Edward Coke who was instructed to dis-cover whether the plotters had support from any gentlemen 'that do favour the com-monalty'; or demobilized soldiers. Coke reported to Sir Robert Cecil, recently appointed principal secretary, that the rising was serious enough to merit charges of treason under the act of 1571 and although all the legal requirements of that statute were not met, the defendants were indicted at the assizes by a jury which included two of their intended targets and tried before a special commission of Oxfordshire men at Westminster which included a man whose son would marry Steer's landlord's daughter a year later. Found guilty, the men were transferred to the care of the high sheriff of Oxfordshire, another prospective victim, who supervised their execution.[2]

The history of the Enslow Hill rising demonstrates that in Elizabethan England property was the key to power. As the privy council's instructions made clear, all property-owners were responsible for maintaining the peace, even though those holding key offices in the local government, such as deputy-lieutenant, sheriff or justice of the peace, were particularly bound to do so through oaths of office. These men also provided an essential network of authority with links all the way to the privy council. That the treason law could be interpreted to include attacks on property as well as waging rebellion against the queen is perhaps the ultimate proof that land-owning and political power went hand in hand.[3]

Elizabeth knew this well. At the age of twenty-five she inherited the throne from her Catholic half-sister Mary. No one was in any doubt that a new regime would be put in place. A few days before Mary died, her husband (King Philip II of Spain)'s ambassador paid a visit to the heir apparent hoping to discover who would be in and who would be out. He reported with some dismay that 'I am very much afraid that she will not be well-disposed in matters of religion, for I see her inclined to govern through men who are believed to be heretics and I am told that all the women around her definitely are.'[4] He was correct, for Elizabeth quickly appointed men to her privy council who were not only Protestants, but included some who been strong oppo-nents of Mary's government. Moreover, Elizabeth was ruthless in trimming Mary's large council of thirty down to nineteen, a level similar to what it had been in the faction-ridden years of Thomas Cromwell's ascendancy.

Several nobles retained their places on the privy council because they would provide stability through their extensive landholdings. They included four of ancient lineage: Henry FitzAlan, earl of Arundel and lord steward; Edward Stanley, earl of Derby; Francis Talbot, earl of Shrewsbury and Lord President of the North; and Edward Clinton, Lord Clinton and lord admiral. These men dominated the political landscapes of Lancashire and Cheshire, Nottinghamshire, Derbyshire, Yorkshire and the North. Also retained was William Herbert, earl of Pembroke, a recent Tudor creation whose rise to power through marriage (to the Parrs, the family of Henry VIII's last wife) and property speculation (purchasing former monastic lands) led to his emergence as a major landowner in South Wales and Wiltshire. Thomas Howard, duke of Norfolk, dominated East Anglia, but his deeply held Catholic beliefs kept him off the council until 1562. By contrast, the fervent Protestant Francis Russell, earl of Bedford, who preferred exile to living in England under Mary, brought his extensive west-country properties into government.

Elizabeth knew her privy council needed noblemen whose prominence depended on their lineage, status and property holdings, men who considered it their born right to rule. In this she differed little from her grandfather, the first Tudor, when he had seized the crown in 1485. However, the early Tudors also promoted men who owed their position to royal favour and patronage secured through ability, knowledge, service and experience rather than landholding. Such men were essential for good government and would become her most trusted advisers. They included her surveyor of lands Sir William Cecil (principal secretary, a post he had held under her Protestant half-brother Edward VI) and her steward Sir Thomas Parry (comptroller, and later treasurer, of the household, and master of the court of wards, an office which allowed him to manage the property of any under-age heir of a royal tenant). Others were Sir Edward Rogers (who had supported Sir Thomas Wyatt's revolt against Mary and spent time in the Tower as had Elizabeth herself) and her relatives Sir Richard Sackville and the Marian exile Sir Francis Knollys. Her great-uncle, William, Lord Howard of Effingham, retained the office of lord chamberlain; he, like Lord Admiral Clinton, was a Marian councillor who had befriended Elizabeth. Two exclusions from the privy council are revealing. Robert, Lord Dudley (later earl of Leicester) had to wait until 1562 to be promoted to the council, having failed to obtain his desired goal of royal consort. The new archbishop of Canterbury, Matthew Parker, was perhaps expected to be too busy with the religious settlement to have time for ordinary conciliar business. On the other hand, perhaps this was another signal that Elizabeth's regime would differ from her half-sisters, for neither Parker nor his immediate successor Edmund Grindal became privy councillors. Indeed, of the fifty-eight men who so served only one was a cleric, Archbishop John Whitgift, who was appointed in 1586.

Elizabeth's privy council was thus small, secular, Protestant and packed with men whom she felt she could trust to provide her with good counsel. At its heart was Cecil, the principal secretary who provided the vital link with the queen, who rarely attended meetings. It was to be one of the most remarkable political relationships in the history of England, lasting nearly forty years. Cecil rarely lost the confidence of his queen and was rewarded with a peerage, becoming Lord Burghley in 1571. Promoted to the more prestigious and lucrative office of lord treasurer in 1572, he never relinquished his role as Elizabeth's chief minister and adviser that he undertook as secretary in 1558. His relative, Sir Nicholas Bacon, was made lord keeper of the great seal, also in 1558. Cecil's later influence is reflected in the appointments of his friends, Sir Walter Mildmay (chancellor of the exchequer, in 1566) and Sir Thomas Smith (secretary, 1572) and especially in the careful grooming of his second son Robert first as a privy councillor (1591) and then as principal secretary (from 1596).

Cecil, Bacon, Knollys, Rogers, Clinton, Howard, Dudley, Mildmay – these men were the core of the early Elizabethan privy council, regular in their attendance, diligent in their efforts. Most were commoners, holding key offices in the central administration. Bacon, as lord keeper (and any successor holding the higher office of lord chancellor) was the head of the Chancery, an institution responsible for the Great Seal of England which authenticated diplomatic dispatches, official orders, writs and grants. The Chancery was responsible for issuing writs summoning members of the House of Lords to attend parliament and writs to the sheriffs of each county to hold elections for members of the House of Commons. The lord chancellor managed the Lords for the government. Cecil, as principal secretary, held the other essential authorizing instruments, the signet and the sign manual (a stamp of the royal signature). He controlled an office that was the nerve centre of government both for foreign and domestic affairs. Mildmay, as chancellor of the exchequer and under-treasurer was responsible for the nation's finances, both receiving revenues and auditing expenditures. He also played a vital role, as did Cecil, in managing the House of Commons.

Elizabeth was opposed to novelty and as her reign proceeded the privy council shrank in size; at one time in the 1590s it numbered only ten. As men failed to outlive their queen, others with similar outlooks and backgrounds took their place: relatives, sons and heirs, loyal men of proven service. Elizabeth's cousin, Henry Carey, Lord Hunsdon, had been entrusted in the late 1560s with the important tasks of securing the border with Scotland and suppressing the rebellion of the northern earls of 1569 before joining the council in 1577. His son George joined in the 1590s, as had Sackville's son Richard, Lord Buckhurst and Howard's son Charles, Lord Howard of Effingham in the 1580s. Sir James Croft, who had shared jail with Elizabeth during Mary's reign, served as governor of Berwick and warden in the Scottish marches before becoming comptroller of the household and a privy councillor in 1570. Leicester's brother Ambrose, made earl of Warwick in 1561 and a councillor in 1573, had served well as master of the ordnance since 1560, led English troops to relieve the Huguenots at Le Havre in 1562, was a commissioner inquiring into Mary Stewart, Queen of Scots, in 1568 and a judge in the trial of the duke of Norfolk in 1572. Sir Francis Walsingham, who became principal secretary in 1573, was a Marian exile, learned in the law and a skilled diplomat, and enjoyed Burghley's patronage. Sir John Fortescue, a relative of the queen who had become master of the wardrobe on her accession, spent years in loyal household service before becoming chancellor of the exchequer and a privy councillor in 1589 while Sir Thomas Egerton served as attorney-general and Master of the Rolls before joining the council in 1596 as lord keeper.

As the numbers shrank so too did the role of the nobility, particularly those with regional power bases. Only two such men were appointed in the middle years of the reign, George Talbot, earl of Shrewsbury and Henry Stanley, earl of Derby. None were appointed in the 1590s and Elizabeth's perceived failure to reward her nobility contributed to Robert Devereux, earl of Essex's revolt against her in 1601. Only after it was suppressed were Shrewsbury's son and heir Gilbert, and Edward Somerset, earl of Worcester, appointed to the council. The old nobility thus lost political influence during the queen's reign. As the archbishop of York, pondering the leadership of the Council of the North towards the end of the reign remarked, 'the race of nobles the Queen found at her accession has passed away.'[5]

Indeed, the pattern of new creation reflected the pattern of appointments to the privy council in that they were rewards for royal service. Dudley became earl of Leicester (1564), Cecil, Lord Burghley (1571), Sackville, Lord Buckhurst (1567), Clinton, earl of Lincoln (1572), Charles Howard (who succeeded his father as Lord

Howard of Effingham and Lord Admiral) earl of Nottingham (1597). Besides Whitgift, only Sir Christopher Hatton looks different, for rather than long service he made it to the council table through good looks and courtly behaviour ('by the galliard' as a fellow courtier put it).[6] Thus the core of the privy council in the 1570s, 1580s and 1590s looked not all that very different from that of the 1560s. Moreover, although Elizabeth's privy council saw a steady decline in the nobility, most privy councillors had substantial country houses. The magnificent homes built by Burghley (Burghley House and Theobalds) and Hatton (Holdenby) were testaments to their political power both at Westminster and in the country.

The privy council was the most important policy-making and administrative institution of Elizabethan government. It was, in the words of Thomas Norton, a man used by the council to help influence the city of London and parliament, 'the wheels that hold the chariot of England upright'. By the end of the reign it was meeting almost daily and the range of business it conducted was enormous. In the week following their first dispatch concerning the Oxfordshire rising, the council also dealt with matters such as recusancy in Ely and Suffolk, wardship, dispatching troops and supplies to Normandy and Ireland, training soldiers in Suffolk, grain shortages in Shrewsbury, relief for maimed soldiers, inmates of a London prison, the appointment of a high sheriff in Dorset and a private case involving debt.[7]

As well as letters and written instructions, Elizabeth and her privy council had a legislative power, the proclamation. Proclamations were the most regular form of legislation at the crown's disposal simply because the council was always in session whereas parliament, whose statutes were the highest form of law in the country, met only occasionally. Although proclamations had limited powers, for example they could not deprive people of property or declare people traitors, they covered an impressive range of social, economic and administrative matters. Elizabeth's reign saw a much larger number dealing with economic and social matters than had been the case under Mary (62 per cent compared to 22 per cent) and many less concerning religion (7 per cent compared to 13 per cent).[8] Proclamations could be used to handle emergencies, for example to stop people coming to London to attend trials when plague broke out in 1593. In 1596 proclamations were issued in the hope of enforcing parliamentary statutes on rogues and vagabonds and on wool-winding; regulating wages in Chester; enforcing orders for marketing grain and prohibiting unlicensed manufacture or sale of starch; ordering justices to punish people carrying forged papers; licensing collections for poor prisoners; and ordering the better keeping of the peace on the Scottish border, of hospitality, and of castles, forts and ports.[9]

Unlike the privy council, parliament was not a regular part of Elizabethan government for it met only occasionally. It was, however, as Secretary Sir Thomas Smith argued, the 'most high and absolute power of England'. Here the monarch, the 'barony for the nobility and lords', 'the knights, esquires, gentlemen and commons for the lower part of the common wealth' and the bishops for the clergy 'be present to advertise, consult and show what is good and necessary for the common wealth. Perhaps Bishop John Aylmer put it better: England was a mixed monarchy best 'seen in the parliament house'.[10] The two houses of parliament, the upper chamber or House of Lords and the lower chamber or House of Commons, met in the palace of Westminster and Elizabeth summoned it on average once every three and a half years, with each meeting lasting around ten or eleven weeks. By Elizabeth's reign significant changes had taken place in the composition of both houses. In the Lords, the Reformation had seen the disappearance of the heads of the monasteries, leaving only the bishops sitting with the secular nobles, of whom by 1558 over one-third were recent (post-1529) creations. While the Lords shrank over the Tudor period, the Commons grew, settling down to 462 MPs by the end of Elizabeth's reign. More and more gentry were securing seats ostensibly representing towns; a process described by historians as 'the gentry invasion of the boroughs.'[11]

Political and religious developments, particularly in the reign of Henry VIII, had made regular consultation of Lords and Commons by the monarch a necessary part of government. By Elizabeth's reign the crown was expected to obtain parliamentary approval for raising revenues beyond those supplied by ordinary means (for example customs dues and rents). These extraordinary revenues voted by both houses of parliament were known as fifteenths and tenths (a fixed tax on moveables voted in the first parliament of the reign for life) and subsidies (occasional taxes based on incomes, which were however rapidly diminishing because of outdated assessments). Just as important as regularizing parliamentary taxation for the history of state formation was the reformation of religion under Henry VIII and his children. Between 1529 and 1536 Henry VIII and his advisers engineered the transfer of authority over the church from the papacy to the crown through parliamentary statute rather than proclamation and in order to carry the changes any further, as Edward VI wished, or to reverse matters, as Mary Tudor desired, would have to be done through parliament.

Therefore, by Elizabeth's reign parliament had well-established advisory, tax-granting and law-making functions. All statutes had to have royal approval; the queen could veto any proposed law however much the Commons and Lords were in agreement that it was necessary. Parliament was in many ways an event, called into existence as the monarch saw fit and whose advice (in the form of petitions) or recommendations (in the form of proposed laws) were to be accepted as she saw fit. Yet parliament shared characteristics with the other institutions of government. In Elizabeth's reign it always met in the same place, there were well-established rules for proceedings and debates, and it had a body of permanent officials who kept its records safe in between parliaments.

The need to call it for the approval of extraordinary taxes and for changes in laws established by earlier statutes meant that no monarch could rule successfully without it. Moreover, parliament had an extremely important role as what G. R. Elton called a 'point-of-contact' between crown and subject. It provided a rare opportunity for the queen to address, and privy councillors to discuss matters of importance with, men selected to attend on behalf of their boroughs and shires. Members of parliament attended from counties which would, for reasons of distance and expense, never see a royal progress or had few local men placed at Court or holding office in the central administration. These men would not only return able to explain why certain new laws were necessary and should be put into effect, they also carried letters, raised problems, listened to gossip in and around the council, the Court and even the central law courts. Parliament also provided occasion for political display. The opening procession was as magnificent as a royal entry, the queen's opening and closing of parliament was heavily laden with rituals of power, and the speeches offered by herself and her lord chancellors were opportunities for nation-building.

Historians in recent years have not only emphasised parliament's role as political theatre, as a public forum of considerable importance, but also as a law-making body that had a profound effect on Elizabethan society and economy. Elizabeth called thirteen parliaments during her reign. They considered over 950 legislative proposals and over 400 new laws were enacted. Many regulated industry, trade, agriculture, fishing and manufacturing. Others governed life, as in laws concerning religion, witchcraft, slander or providing poor relief. The criminal law was reformed, revised, expanded. Many of these had important and long-lasting consequences. The Poor Laws passed in the parliaments of 1597–8 and 1601 established workhouses and thus governed the regulation of the poor in England for over two hundred years. The plethora of new laws placed considerable strain on those local officials expected to enforce them.

The emphasis on parliament's legislative functions was in itself a reaction to an earlier view of parliament, which located its importance as a forum for opposition to the government's moderate and tentative steps towards establishing Protestantism. J. E. Neale argued that radical Protestants (known as puritans) fought in parliament against the Anglican compromise preferred by Elizabeth and most of her councillors: a church which retained elements of Catholicism such as bishops and clerical vestments while insisting upon a Protestant theology. Their parliamentary campaigns against bishops, ecclesiastical courts, vestments and the Anglican prayer book led to their seeking to dominate parliament and develop strategies that lay the foundation for effective parliamentary opposition to royal absolutist tendencies in later years. Neale's insistence upon an organized puritan party has now been discredited for a number of reasons. Puritans, or as historians now prefer, 'godly Protestants', never formed a coherent party although they certainly were at times a vocal if small group. It is hard to describe them as an organized opposition when several members of the privy council itself shared their views. Archbishop Whitgift's attacks on the radical Protestants known as presbyterians provoked much anger among some of his fellow privy councillors as it did among godly Protestants in the country.

Although Neale's critics have rightly emphasized parliamentary taxation and legislation as its main business, some may have gone too far in asserting that parliament had no political role. Not only were laws politically charged, as evidenced by those seeking to control the poor or regulate behaviour, but lobbying for the success of a particular bill, even ones concerning matters such as agriculture and fishing, trade and manufacturing, might be contentious and provoke political controversy. Increased taxation, especially during the years of war with Spain after 1585, proved very contentious, leading to criticism of the government in the parliaments of 1593, 1597–8 and 1601. In these last two parliaments anger was voiced at the queen's granting of monopolies of trade and manufactures to her courtiers.

Parliament could also play an important role in pressuring the queen to act, even against her own inclinations. In the 1560s the council was especially preoccupied with the issue of the queen's marriage. Cecil and other councillors encouraged an association between the need for the queen to marry and the granting of a subsidy in 1563 and 1566. Norton, who had penned a pamphlet urging the debarring of Mary Stewart and the settling of the succession on Catherine Grey, co-authored (with Thomas Sackville) the play *Gorboduc* which promoted the Dudley marriage by showing the horrible consequences of an unsettled succession.[12] Elizabeth managed to ignore conciliar and parliamentary pressure to marry (indeed, her courtships were a key part of her diplomacy). She ended Dudley's aspirations (even suggesting he marry Mary

Stewart – who married Henry, Lord Darnley instead) and promoting him to the privy council instead of her marriage bed. Elizabeth 'settled' the succession by doing nothing, thus tacitly acknowledging the right of Mary's son James (b. 1566).

Mary Stewart's escape to England in 1568 (fleeing Scotland after being implicated in the murder of Darnley) proved to be the issue around which her council mounted the most vigorous campaign in parliament to pressure the queen into doing something that the normal channels of advice and counsel had failed to achieve. As a Catholic claimant to Elizabeth's throne, soon given a boost by the pope's Bull declaring Elizabeth a heretic and requiring all good Catholics to support her overthrow, the privy council desired Mary gone for good. Norfolk, one of their own, foolishly plotted to marry Mary himself. In the parliament of 1572 the council used all its power to encourage both Lords and Commons to demand Norfolk's and Mary's deaths. As one MP put it, Mary had to be dealt with either by 'an axe or an act'. Elizabeth gave them Norfolk, but she refused to budge on Mary. Only after many years of hard work, notably by Secretary Walsingham, was enough evidence assembled to secure Mary's trial and execution for high treason in 1587. The parliament of 1586–7 was used to pressure Elizabeth and even then it was a close-run thing. Elizabeth signed Mary's death warrant, Secretary William Davison rushed it to Burghley and before Elizabeth changed her mind Mary was dead. Davison was sent to the Tower before being pensioned off while Burghley was temporarily banished from Court.

The national nightmare was the assassination of their sovereign queen. In 1584 hundreds of Protestants across the realm signed a Bond of Association, swearing to pursue to the death anyone seeking the queen's harm and to resist anyone benefiting from her death by way of succession. The Bond was supported in a parliamentary act of 1584–5 entitled 'for the Queen's safety' and when Burghley contemplated the horrible – how to govern England without Elizabeth – he put parliament at the centre of an interim government alongside the privy council and the main administrative and judicial officers. And it was in parliament that the political nation would sort through rival claimants and decide who should be the new ruler.[13]

If the privy council was the most important administrative institution of government and parliament the most important legislative body, the Court was the most visible. Not only was the Court in constant session, it was mobile, for Elizabeth renewed the summer progress when the Court left its normal residence in and around London and visited towns, villages and estates in the countryside. It was the turn of Essex and Hertfordshire in 1571. Hatfield was visited on 7 August, then Audley End and Saffron Walden where she was met by the town's officials, who knelt before her and offered her 'a cup of silver, double gilt, with a cover weighing 46 ounces . . . and a case to put it in' as well as payments to her footmen, porters, trumpeters and other servants. The earl of Leicester, Burghley and Smith (who was born in the town) each received a sugar loaf. By mid-September she was at Marks Hall, belonging to Walter Devereux, Viscount Hereford (soon to become the 1st earl of Essex), then with Lord Rich at Lees and finally to Hunsdon House, her cousin's home. Before Elizabeth returned to Richmond Palace Burghley had a chance to show off his new house at Theobalds where she was presented with a book of verses and a picture of the house itself.[14]

Several key players in the Elizabethan political world first enjoyed power and influence through their position at court. Lord Robert Dudley may not have secured a position as privy councillor at the beginning of the reign, but he did become Master of the Horse responsible for protecting the queen every time she left a royal palace and so a very public statement of trust. Hatton used the Court as a springboard to becoming privy councillor and ultimately lord chancellor. Essex dazzled at Court before seeking prominence through military success. As the royal household provided the most personal service to the queen, men who held its most important offices, such as the lord chamberlain, vice-chamberlain and comptroller, often became key advisers on the privy council: Knollys and Croft in the early part of the reign, Sir Thomas Heneage and Sir John Stanhope towards the end. Only a few influential courtiers failed to get such office, among them Sir Walter Raleigh.

The political aspirations of the nobility and gentry of England were channelled into the Elizabethan Court; at least two-thirds of the nobility attended at one time or another and perhaps as many as sixty leading gentlemen were residents. Here access to and influence on the monarch was the key to political success and sometimes even the privy council could find its carefully laid-out plans undermined by such influence. When William Cecil accused Heneage of unwarranted meddling in politics, the latter protested that he never spoke against a decision of the privy council and only offered the queen advice when 'it pleased her to ask mine opinion.'[15] Jockeying for position at Court was essential for those seeking power and absence proved a major stumbling block to political aspirations. This was the fate of Sir Francis Bacon, whose impolitic complaint about the level of taxation in the parliament of 1593 led to his being excluded from Court. In choosing military glory as a path to influence, his friend and patron Essex absented himself from Court, helping others to engineer his downfall when he became lord lieutenant of Ireland.

Prominence at Court could also prove crucial in settling local disputes and securing prestigious posts, property and patronage in the shires. In the early 1590s a power struggle developed in Nottinghamshire between the long-established Talbots, earls of Shrewsbury, and the Stanhopes. The queen's cousin Buckhurst warned Shrewsbury to beware the courtier brothers John and Michael Stanhope for 'the near place they hold to her Majesty and that which is above all the rest, the especial favour which her Majesty doth bear unto them will always prevail with so great advantage against you.' Factions in Wiltshire could all draw upon connections at Court, which was one reason why the county experienced very divisive politics over many years.[16]

Noble and gentry women had one important advantage over the male courtier, for they had greater access to the more intimate and private rooms of the Court. The privy chamber, although formally managed by the lord chamberlain, was Elizabeth's refuge from the male-dominated public rooms of the Court such as the presence chamber. The gentlewomen of the privy chamber and ladies of the bedchamber were a very select group of women who would assist the queen in routine daily activities. At the beginning of the reign Elizabeth chose them with no less care than she did privy councillors, and close intimates included Catherine (née Carey), Lady Knollys and Blanche Parry. Many of those attending the queen were wives of leading noblemen and gentry such as Elizabeth, Lady Clinton and Anne, Lady Carey (who soon became Lady Hunsdon).

Leicester petulantly complained in 1569 that Elizabeth had heard the news of Norfolk's plan to marry Mary Stewart from 'some babbling women'. Years earlier his rival, Thomas Radcliffe, earl of Sussex, who as lord chamberlain was responsible for room allocations at Court, sought to delay the arrival of Leicester's sister Mary, Lady

Sidney, by offering her unsuitable rooms. Evidently he was concerned that she would use her position as lady-in-waiting to influence the queen in her brother's favour. However, the women of Elizabeth's Court ran into trouble if they directly intervened in politics. When Catherine Ashley and Dorothy Broadbelt wrote to the Swedish Court encouraging a match with King Eric XIV in opposition to Dudley's aspirations, they found themselves placed under close confinement, a warning to all women in the privy chamber not to meddle with affairs of state, at least without the knowledge and approval of their sovereign. More subtle means could be used to better effect. Mildred, Lady Cecil, wife of secretary Sir William Cecil, provocatively wore a jewel in the shape of a two-headed eagle, the device of the Habsburgs, intending to promote the case for the queen's marriage to the Archduke Charles, youngest son of the Habsburg emperor Ferdinand I.[17]

However much Elizabeth desired her privy chamber to be a refuge from politics, a political system so dependent on access to the monarchy meant that there was always a role, if not for direct political action, for political involvement. Individual courtiers, and even those outside the Court, approached the women of the privy chamber for help in putting a word in the queen's ear, to offer her a petition or deliver a letter at a quiet moment. When Burghley was in disgrace over what the queen saw as her councillor's betrayal in hastening the execution of Mary Stewart, he received a comforting letter from Frances, Lady Cobham, chief gentlewoman of the privy chamber: 'if you will write I will deliver it. I do desire to be commanded by you. Others here in presence do speak for themselves.' For men such as Dudley, Burghley, Robert Cecil and his rival Essex, it was essential to have friends and supporters in the privy chamber. If it could not be a centre for political activity as it had under Henry VIII, it was still an arena in which to seek influence and secure reward. In this way the correspondence of the Talbot family, earls of Shrewsbury in the 1590s, bears comparison with the Lisle letters of the 1530s with their reports of agents at Court attempting to solicit the queen.[18]

Robert Beale, the clerk of the privy council who wrote a treatise on the office of principal secretary, advised that connections with the privy chamber were essential: 'learn before your access, her Majesty's disposition by some in the Privy Chamber with whom you must keep credit'. He also advised that the secretary should avoid overburdening himself with suits by referring them to others in the chamber or household. The Court was a lively place with hundreds of people dining at the queen's expense, many more providing services to them and others seeking their support in obtaining a royal favour. Social connections were important here, and more so the system of patronage. In order to keep a patron happy service had to be offered and gifts sent. Disaster could strike when a client lost the favour of his or her patron or lost a patron through death. Burghley's death in 1598 caused a major rupture in the system of clientage and patronage of Elizabethan England. It was a tragedy which one client, the dean of Gloucester, described as casting him 'in the dirt and dust of indignity and disgrace'. In his desperate letter to Robert Cecil asking him to replace his father as patron, he offered Archbishop Whitgift, the lord admiral and the lord chamberlain as references – itself a reflection on just how important Cecil had become as the dispenser of patronage. In the meantime he sent Cecil two Worcestershire cheeses 'as a present, small in quantity but in quality excellent.' This was not a bribe, for Cecil was free to choose whether to act or not; gifts were simply good political practice as attested by the carefully detailed lists of the New Year's gifts the queen received from her courtiers and officials.[19]

If the Court failed to fulfil the ambitions of the political nation, and if those ambitions found no other arena in which to flourish, the result could be political crisis. The Catholic Thomas Percy, earl of Northumberland, came from a family of ancient lineage but at the beginning of Elizabeth's reign was stripped of posts that had long been held by the Percies, the wardenships of the East and Middle Marches. To add insult to injury the first went (eventually) to the anti-Marian exile Bedford and the latter to Sir John Forster, a long-standing local rival. Similarly, the descendant of a Yorkshire family of long standing, Richard Norton, was dropped from the Council of the North (the only person to lose his position). They, along with another leading Catholic nobleman, Leonard Dacre, brother to Thomas, Lord Dacre, conspired to raise a rebellion with the aim of destroying Elizabeth and replacing her with Mary Stewart. Drawing the head of another ancient northern family, Charles Neville, earl of Westmorland, into the revolt, the rebellion of the northern earls of 1569 was to be the most serious of the reign. Religion was clearly a major cause, with the rebels rallying around banners displaying the five wounds of Christ, the emblem of an earlier rebellion in the North, the Pilgrimage of Grace. Prominent too were the standards of the Percies and Nevilles, for most of those joining the revolt came from their estates. Besides being a Catholic uprising, this was a revolt led by the traditional ruling families of the North opposed to the new political order centred at the Court and council in Westminster.

If the revolt of the earls can be seen as one of the last gasps of the declining feudal aristocracy, who sought political power by raising an army based on their own tenants and wrestling control of the crown from another's hands, the last rebellion of the reign demonstrates just how Court- and council-centred politics had become. Elizabeth's favourite, Essex, fought hard to gain power through his personal relationship with the queen and by demonstrating his worth through military success and an expertise in foreign intelligence. Yet he found his political ambitions blocked by the Cecils and their supporters in the Court and on the council. His failure to obtain the attorney-generalship for his friend Francis Bacon (it went to Coke, the Cecil candidate) in 1594; Cecil's appointment as principal secretary in 1596; and the queen's insistence that he share the glory of his victory at Cadiz with Lord Howard of Effingham were all blows to the earl's prestige, reputation and political power. When the Queen elevated Howard to the earldom of Nottingham, which gave him precedence over Essex, the latter flew into a rage and left Court, returning only when he was created earl marshal, thus restoring him to superiority over Nottingham. Burghley's death might have opened possibilities for Essex, but Robert Cecil simply moved into his father's position of authority at both Court and council. Essex even failed to get Burghley's lucrative post of master of the court of Wards. From at least 1595 the Court was beset with intrigue as the Essex and Cecil factions struggled for supremacy. Rumours and libels became the common currency of political discourse. Soon after his appointment to Ireland, Essex wrote to Lord Willoughby apologising for being a patron 'that can procure nothing for himself or for any of his friends'. He then summed up the transition from aristocratic-centred to Court-centred politics that had occurred over the course of the reign: 'the court is the centre; but methinks it is the fairer choice to command armies than honour'.[20]

Essex sought a return to political power through military success, but it was not to be. Elizabeth saw his negotiations with the Gaelic leader of the Irish revolt against English rule known as the Nine Years War (1594–1602), Hugh O'Neill, 2nd earl of Tyrone as an admission of failure at best, treasonous at worst. With his enemies able to influence the queen daily, the earl rushed back to England only to find himself put under house arrest and once released, banned from Court. When the queen refused the renewal on his lease on the duties on sweet wines, Essex could no longer endure his inability to enjoy what he considered to be his right by birth and service, influence over the queen. Other young noblemen and gentlemen soldiers shared his resentment over Cecil's monopoly of power, including Henry Wriothesley, earl of Southampton, in disgrace for getting one of the queen's maids of honour pregnant and marrying her without royal permission. Essex and his followers hatched a plot to seize control of the queen, the Court and the council. He wrote to the heir apparent, James VI of Scotland, for support and a signal for the rising was to be a performance of Shakespeare's *Richard II*, with its story of the deposition of a ruling monarch by an injured martial aristocrat. Ordered to Court, Essex chose rebellion instead, but strong support in the City failed to materialize and he was tried for high treason and executed. Southampton's death sentence was reprieved and he achieved political prominence in the next reign through astute politicking at Court, council and parliament.

Although the competition between Essex and Cecil ended so disastrously for the former, it is true to say that the two men differed only occasionally as far as domestic or foreign policy was concerned. Although there was certainly serious jockeying for power and influence in the 1560s between Sussex and Dudley, and between the latter and William Cecil, often the differences were small compared to the factional disputes of the 1530s or 1550s. Leicester and Burghley were both actively supportive of the Protestant cause abroad. They agreed that a French marriage alliance in the 1570s was worth pursuing and both felt it was necessary to intervene in support of the Dutch rebels in the 1580s, although they disagreed on the strength, and extent, of the commitment. If the longevity of Elizabeth's councillors, courtiers and gentlewomen is striking, so too is their ideological hegemony. More often as not councillors were in agreement among themselves, but found their sovereign reluctant to act upon their advice and counsel. Burghley wrote himself a memorandum in 1575 in which he listed all the things 'her Majesty's forbearing and delays hath produced not only inconveniences and increases of expenses, but also dangers.' Over many of the key issues of the reign the councillors formed a united front against a queen who was hesitant and conservative: marriage and the succession, intervention on behalf of protestants in France and the Netherlands, the threat of Mary Stewart, war and succession politics in the last decade of the reign. This perspective, argued by historians such as Simon Adams, corrects an earlier emphasis on a faction-ridden council and Court, factions encouraged by Elizabeth whose policy was to 'divide-and-rule'.[21]

However clear the main structures of central government seem, it is important to remember that Elizabethan government was also informal, personal and fluid. Institutional boundaries were often blurred; one individual might hold several offices at once; and changes in personnel could lead to new arrangements as individuals struggled for fees, rewards and influence. Men like Burghley and Walsingham saw their archives as personal papers, not as official state documents, and their spy networks competed with each other rather than becoming a single department of state. Nor were the structures of government static. Over such a long reign, and especially in the context of the tremendous upheavals in sixteenth-century Europe, government was always responsive to events. Competing ideas and vocabularies provided a rich dynamic for both politics and the theories and practice of government, as in the tension between Elizabeth's belief in herself as imperial ruler and the desire of councillors and parliament men to influence matters of state.

It is also important to recognize limitations of central authority. As Patrick Collinson has argued, in many ways the political landscape of Elizabethan England might be best described as a confederation of gentry republics.[22] For most of England's inhabitants their experience of authority lay in their encounters with local officials such as justices of the peace, constables and churchwardens. Lacking a standing army or a regular police force, the government depended almost entirely on the co-operation of local magistrates and rulers to get anything done. On one estimate, this 'political society' comprised some 2,500 men, from justices of the peace through to the most influential magnate.[23] To this we must add those men further down the social scale who helped secure order, particularly high constables and petty constables, and those who did so in their parishes, such as churchwardens. Authority was negotiated with these elites, who were relatively free to choose whether to enforce, modify or simply ignore statutes passed in parliament or orders from the privy council. The frequency with which central authorities pleaded for the proper enforcement of its instructions and proclamations and even, in the 1590s, for the ruling elite to assess themselves properly for taxes, reveal the limitations of Elizabethan government.

Institutional innovations were rare, but there were some. The lord lieutenancy was a military office introduced under Mary but used extensively and creatively by Elizabeth not only to organize the nation for war, but for law and order. London's provost marshals had similar duties in the City. These changes seemed necessary in part because England was at war with Spain and war brought financial hardship and resentment. Some issues were longstanding, such as irritation over purveyance, the means whereby the Court supplied itself by requiring sales of supplies at cheap prices or even seizure. The mustering, training and billeting of soldiers, money demanded for ships, compulsory loans to the government, and more frequent subsidies all added tensions in localities across England. The government worked hard to keep itself informed. Beale noted that the secretary had to keep good records of the nation and its inhabitants: lists of nobles, gentry and officials, of Catholic recusants and merchants; notes on tax assessments, the whereabouts and amounts of ordnance and ships; detailed maps of each county and town. Throughout the 1590s Burghley and Cecil amassed a vast archive of information that was another important contribution to the process of state formation in early modern England.

Yet the successful exercise of power and authority demanded a recipriocity from those called upon to behave in certain ways and to obey particular laws. Stability did not only depend on authority being successful in binding men, women and children to its will, it also required their co-operation and participation. In this way forms of resistance are especially revealing. At the lower levels of the social order it seems clear that those for whom punitive laws were designed – vagabonds, beggars, prostitutes, demobilized yet armed soldiers, Catholic recusants – had some ability to negotiate their treatment by strategies which involved kinship and neighbourhood, household and community. Justices might as easily turn a blind eye to a regular offender they knew well in the interest of community peace or in response to a notion of fairness held by the community, no matter how often they might receive a letter from the privy council admonishing them to enforce the laws more strictly. Local solutions were found without reference to central authority and on occasion, as in the village of Swallowfield, those of the lower sort devised solutions in a parliamentary way. Even rioters might use the language of obedience, loyalty, responsibility – the same vocabulary drawn upon by those seeking to enforce order. Although he won the argument, several judges dissented from Coke's use of the treason laws against the Oxfordshire rebels.

Elizabeth was both a woman and a monarch. In a society which often described political authority through the image of the body, with the monarch as its head and the lowest orders, peasants and artificers, as the feet, this fact was not unproblematic. At the heart of government was the royal household and the bedrock of Elizabethan society was the household. However, while authority in the household was male, in the royal household between 1558 and 1603 it was female and Elizabeth's councillors certainly struggled intellectually and practically with the queen's often-exercised right to refuse their counsel. Convincing France, and more generally Europe, that the English monarch had the same authority whether the occupant of the throne was man or woman was one of the chief motivations behind Smith's discussion of the English state, *De Republic Anglorum*; her authority at home was promoted in a variety of ways, drawing on a wide range of verbal and visual vocabulary. In parliament she invoked her femininity, identifying herself as the mother of her people. At Tilbury, addressing the forces waiting for the arrival of the Spanish Armada, she deliberately played on her gender, noting that while she might have the body of a woman, she had the heart and stomach of a King. Scriptural and classical references were made in the performances that attended her at Court and on progress. Elizabeth was celebrated in image, prose and verse as the English Deborah, as Astraea, Minerva and Diana. Her minted profile jingled in the purses of her subjects. Some might have a cheap print of the queen in her regal majesty; one of 1563 was listed as 'Loe here the pearl, whom God and man doth love.' Paintings carried powerful visual metaphors, symbols and representations, such as the pelican, a bird who pierced its own breast to feed its starving fledglings with her own blood, or the phoenix, the bird which rose from the fire unharmed. Nicholas Hilliard, known best for his miniatures of the queen and her courtiers, made some remarkable medals, given to courtiers, favourites and as rewards to officials. One struck in the late 1580s shows Elizabeth in profile, on the reverse an ark jostled by storms but remaining ever steady. In another, made after the Armada's defeat, a crowned Elizabeth is shown in a frontal pose, holding sceptre and the orb surmounted by a cross. On the reverse is a bay tree, a symbol of fortitude and perseverance, on an island surrounded by turbulent waves that pitch ships back and forth. In the heavens winds and thunder, even lightning, attempt to shatter the tree but it remains steadfast.[24]

The ship of state might endure perilous seas but God's faith in his Elizabeth, the leader of the English nation, was a message repeated time and time again in music, word and image. None perhaps is more striking though than the famous Ditchley portrait, painted for Sir Henry Lee, Elizabeth's champion courtier. It depicts the queen in a magnificent dress holding a fan and a glove. Pearls fall from her neck, two huge rubies adorn her necklace and she wears a gold earring in the shape of a celestial sphere. Elizabeth, ruler of the cosmos, attracts brilliant sunshine on her right while dark clouds flee her presence. She stands firmly on a map of England, as accurate as those produced by Christopher Saxton in his *Atlas of the Counties of England* commissioned by

Burghley as a tool of statescraft. Her feet are squarely situated on Oxfordshire, Lee's county, and the painting was probably commissioned around 1592 when we know the queen visited his house at Ditchley while on progress.[25] One wonders how much Lee pondered that painting after the 'rebellion' of Steer and his followers, men who had planned to destroy his little part of the queen's England. Yet they too protested that they meant no harm to the queen, that they sought only to rectify a grievous ill, a matter which their social betters in parliament sought to remedy by legislation in 1597–8 but in a way that ensured that authority and power remained firmly in the hands of the propertied. The last word on the relative success and stability of Elizabethan government might be that it was another forty-four years before some Englishmen suggested that all men born in England should participate in the government of the realm and not just those with a propertied 'fixed interest' in it, a view shaped by their experience of royal absolutist tendencies and civil war.

NOTES

1. Walter, 'Rising of the people', 90–143; Manning, *Village Revolts*, pp. 221–9.
2. Walter, 'Rising of the people', 95–8, 126–8; Manning, *Village Revolts*, pp. 200–10; Archer, *Pursuit of Stability*, pp. 1–9.
3. Bellamy, *Treason*, pp. 78–81; Walter, 'Rising of the people', 126–30.
4. Rodríguez-Salgado and Adams, 'Feria's dispatch', p. 331. On Council membership see MacCaffrey, *Shaping of the Elizabethan Regime*, pp. 27–40; *Making of Policy*, pp. 436–9; and *War and Politics*, pp. 25–6; Pulman, *Privy Council*, pp. 18–51; Williams, *Tudor Regime*, pp. 454–5.
5. MacCaffrey, *War and Politics*, p. 458.
6. Naunton, *Fragmenta Regalia*, p. 67, attributing the saying to Sir John Perrot.
7. Graves, *Elizabethan Parliaments*, p. 56; *Acts of the Privy Council* (1596–7), pp. 361ff.
8. Youngs, *Proclamations of the Tudor Queens*, p. 13.
9. Hughes and Larkin, *Tudor Royal Proclamations*, pp. 118–22, 125–7, 158–72.
10. Smith, *De Republica Anglorum*, p. 78; Collinson, *Elizabethan Essays*, p. 19.
11. Graves, *Tudor Parliaments*, pp. 7–8, 45–9, 69–73, 100–1, 117–18, 132–4; and *Elizabethan Parliaments*, pp. 28–32.
12. Doran, *Monarchy and Matrimony*, pp. 55–65; Elton, *Parliament of England*, pp. 355–74; Graves, *Thomas Norton*, pp. 78–146.
13. Collinson, *Elizabethan Essays*, pp. 48–56.
14. Nichols, *Progresses*, Vol. 1, pp. 280–91.
15. Haigh, *Elizabeth I*, pp. 91, 92.
16. MacCaffrey, 'Talbot and Stanhope', p. 79; Wall, 'Patterns of politics', 947–63.
17. Wright, 'A change in direction', pp. 154, 167; Adams, *Leicester and the Court*, p. 38; Doran, *Monarchy and Matrimony*, p. 34; Croft, *Patronage Culture and Power*, pp. 286–8.
18. Wright, 'A change in direction', pp. 165, 166–7; Byrne, *Lisle Letters*.
19. Read, *Mr Secretary Walsingham*, vol. 1, pp. 423–43; HMC, *Salisbury Manuscripts*, XII, p. 456; Nichols, *Progresses*, vol. 2, pp. 249–76; vol. 3, pp. 1–25.
20. MacCaffrey, *War and Politics*, p. 523.
21. Haigh, *Elizabeth I*, p. 77; Adams, *Leicester and the Court*, pp. 13–67; Hammer, *Polarisation of Elizabethan Politics*, pp. 356–61.
22. Collinson, *Elizabethan Essays*, pp. 31–57.
23. MacCaffrey, 'Place and patronage', pp. 98–9.

24.   Howarth, *Images of Rule*, pp. 104–5, 111–12; Strong, *Cult of Elizabeth*, Watt, *Cheap Print*, p. 352.
25.   Strong, *Gloriana*, pp. 135–41.

BIBLIOGRAPHY

Adams, Simon, *Leicester and the Court: Essays on Elizabethan Politics* (Manchester, 2002).

Archer, Ian, *The Pursuit of Stability: Social Relations in Elizabethan London* (Cambridge, 1991).

Bellamy, John, *The Tudor Law of Treason: An Introduction* (London, 1979).

Byrne, Muriel St Clare, ed., *The Lisle Letters* (London, 1983).

Collinson, Patrick, *Elizabethan Essays* (London, 1994).

Croft, Pauline, ed., *Patronage, Culture and Power: The Early Cecils* (New Haven and London, 2002).

Doran, Susan, *Monarchy and Matrimony: The Courtships of Elizabeth I* (Routledge, London, 1996).

Elton, G. R., *The Parliament of England, 1559–1581* (Cambridge, 1986).

Graves, Michael A. R., *Elizabethan Parliaments 1559–1601* (2nd edition, London, 1996).

Graves, Michael A. R., *Thomas Norton: The Parliament Man* (Oxford, 1994).

Graves, Michael A. R., *The Tudor Parliaments: Crown, Lords and Commons, 1485–1603* (London, 1985).

Haigh, Christopher, *Elizabeth I* (2nd edition, London, 1998).

Hammer, Paul E. J., *The Polarisation of Elizabethan Politics: The Political Career of Robert Devereux, 2nd Earl of Essex, 1585–1597* (Cambridge, 1999).

Historical Manuscripts Commission, *Calendar of Salisbury Manuscripts at Hatfield House* (London, 1910).

Howarth, David, *Images of Rule: Art and Politics in the English Renaissance, 1485–1649* (Berkeley, 1997).

Hughes, Paul L. and Larkin, James F., *Tudor Royal Proclamations*, vol. III, *The Later Tudors (1588–1603)* (New Haven and London, 1969).

MacCaffrey, Wallace, *Elizabeth I: War and Politics 1588–1603* (Princeton, NJ, 1992).

MacCaffrey, Wallace, 'Place and patronage in Elizabethan politics', in S. T. Bindoff, J. Hurstfield and C. H. Williams, eds, *Elizabethan Government and Society: Essays Presented to Sir John Neale* (London, 1961), pp. 95–126.

MacCaffrey, Wallace, *Queen Elizabeth and the Making of Policy, 1572–1588*, (Princeton, NJ, 1981).

MacCaffrey, Wallace, *The Shaping of the Elizabethan Regime: Elizabethan Politics 1558–1572*, (London, 1969).

MacCaffrey, Wallace, 'Talbot and Stanhope: an episode in Elizabethan politics', *Bulletin of the Institute of Historical Research*, 33 (1960), 73–85.

Manning, Roger B., *Village Revolts: Social Protest and Popular Disturbances in England, 1509–1640* (Oxford, 1988).

Naunton, Sir Robert, *Fragmenta Regalia, or Observations on Queen Elizabeth, Her Times & Favorites*, ed. John S. Cerovski (Washington, DC, 1985).

Nichols, John, *The Progresses and Public Processions of Queen Elizabeth* (3 vols, London, 1823).

Pulman, Michael Barraclough, *The Elizabethan Privy Council in the Fifteen-Seventies* (Berkeley, 1971).

Read, Conyers, *Mr Secretary Walsingham and the Policy of Queen Elizabeth* (3 vols, Oxford, 1925).

Rodríguez-Salgado, M. J. and Adams, Simon, eds and trans., 'The Count of Feria's dispatch to Philip II of 14 November 1558', *Camden Miscellany*, XXVIII, Camden Fourth Series, 29 (1984), 303–44.

Smith, Sir Thomas, *De Republica Anglorum*, ed. Mary Dewar (Cambridge, 1982).

Strong, Roy, *The Cult of Elizabeth: Elizabethan Portraiture and Pageantry* (Berkeley, 1977).

Strong, Roy, *Gloriana: The Portraits of Queen Elizabeth I* (London, 1987).

Wall, Alison, 'Patterns of politics in England, 1558–1625', *Historical Journal*, 31 (1988), 947–96.

Walter, John, 'A "rising of the people"? The Oxfordshire Rising of 1596', *Past and Present*, 107 (1985), 90–143.

Watt, Tessa, *Cheap Print and Popular Piety, 1550–1640* (Cambridge, 1991).

Williams, Penry, *The Tudor Regime* (Oxford, 1979).

Wright, Pam, 'A change in direction: the ramifications of a female household, 1558–1603', in David Starkey, ed., *The English Court from the Wars of the Roses to the Civil War* (London, 1987), pp. 147–72.

Youngs, Frederick A., *The Proclamations of the Tudor Queens* (Cambridge, 1976).

FURTHER READING

Stephen Alford, *The Early Elizabethan Polity: William Cecil and the British Succession Crisis, 1558–1569* (1998).

David Dean, *Law-Making and Society in Late Elizabethan England: The Parliament of England, 1584–1601* (1996).

Ian Dunlop, *Palaces and Progresses of Elizabeth I* (1962).

G. R. Elton, *Studies in Tudor and Stuart Politics and Government* (4 vols, 1974–92).

A. Fletcher and D. MacCulloch, *Tudor Rebellions* (4th edn, 1997).

Michael A. R. Graves, *Burghley* (1999).

Paul Griffiths, Adam Fox and Steve Hindle (eds), *The Experience of Authority in Early Modern England* (1996).

John Guy, *Politics, Law and Counsel in Tudor and Early Stuart England* (2000); and (ed.), *The Reign of Elizabeth I: Court and Culture in the Last Decade* (1995).

T. E. Hartley, *Elizabeth's Parliaments: Queen, Lords, and Commons, 1559–1601* (1992).

Richard Helgerson, *Forms of Nationhood: The Elizabethan Writing of England* (1992).

Dale Hoak (ed.), *Tudor Political Culture* (1995).

Mervyn James, *Society, Politics and Culture: Studies in Early Modern England* (1986).

Carol Levin, *Heart and Stomach of a King: Elizabeth and the Politics of Sex and Power* (1994).

David Loades, *Power in Tudor England* (1997); *The Tudor Court* (1986); and *Tudor Government: Structures of Authority in the Sixteenth Century* (1997).

Marjorie Keniston McIntosh, *Controlling Misbehaviour: England 1370–1600* (1998).

A. N. McLaren, *Political Culture in the Reign of Elizabeth I: Queen and Commonwealth 1558–1585* (1999).

J. E. Neale, *Elizabeth I and Her Parliaments* (2 vols, 1953, 1955); and *The Elizabethan House of Commons* (1949).

Conyers Read, *Lord Burghley and Queen Elizabeth* (1960); and *Mr Secretary Cecil and Queen Elizabeth* (Jonathan Cape, London, 1955).

Judith M. Richards, 'Love and a female monarch: the case of Elizabeth Tudor', *Journal of British Studies*, 38 (April 1999), 133–60.

A. G. R. Smith, *The Government of Elizabethan England* (1967).

R. Malcolm Smuts, *Culture and Power in England, 1585–1685* (1999).

Alison Wall, *Power and Protest in England 1525–1640* (2000).

Frances A. Yates, *Astraea: The Imperial Theme in the Sixteenth Century* (1975).

CHAPTER FOUR

The Court

RETHA WARNICKE

Because personal monarchs governed the British Isles in the early modern period, a knowledge of their Courts is essential to an understanding of contemporary politics and culture. These rulers, who stood atop their realms' social and political hierarchies, used the routine and protocol of Court life to demonstrate and validate their superior status and to confirm their membership among the royal dynasties of Christendom. At their most basic level, Courts were where rulers happened to be, whether at a palace or hunting lodge or on progress, except for an occasional, short journey, sometimes incognito, like that of Henry VIII's greeting of Anne of Cleves at Rochester in 1540. Functioning within structures that were similar to those of noble households, only larger and more complex, Court officials not only housed, fed, transported and entertained their monarchs, but also extended hospitality to visitors. In early Tudor England, some noblemen, such as Edward Stafford, third duke of Buckingham, still attempted to imitate this largess, but with an annual income of only 5,000 pounds sterling, or less, they could not match royal expenditure. Before turning to the Courts' physical location and departments, this essay will briefly recount the ruling families of the British Isles. It will end with an examination of Court theatrical display, the patronage that forged a link between central and local government, and factional politics.

All the British Isles monarchs in the sixteenth century were relatives of Henry VII, the first Tudor, who died in 1509. Except for his son-in-law, James IV of Scotland, who married his daughter Margaret Tudor, the other rulers were Henry's descendants. A knowledge of who they were is important to Court history, for their personal qualities, especially their ages and sex, shaped cultural and political developments. Since Edward VI and the Scottish monarchs who succeeded James IV until 1625 were minors at their accession, their regents' ambitions also influenced Court developments. Moreover, activities at the Court of Henry VII, who was a spectator at entertainments, varied from those at that of his youthful son, who regularly participated in masques and athletic competitions. The Courts of the married queens regnant, Mary Stuart and Mary Tudor, who had to be concerned with not only their husbands' politics but also with the possibility of childbirth, differed from that of the unwed Elizabeth, who utilized marriage proposals in her diplomacy. One key difference in these monarchs' reputed powers was that only English rulers, who touched for scrofula, claimed a special quasi-sacerdotal status. On Good Friday, the early Tudors also blessed cramp rings that allegedly healed epilepsy and other disorders.

By Henry VII's and James IV's accessions, both England and Scotland had identifiable capitals. In England, the central judicial courts, parliament, and the treasury were located at Westminister with the Tower of London, of course, situated nearby. After the residential part of Westminster Palace burned down in 1512, the Tudors lacked a major palace at the capital until 1529 when Henry VIII seized York Place, later called Whitehall, from Thomas, Cardinal Wolsey. In Scotland, parliament and other great assemblies met at Edinburgh, and the court of session was located there from the reign of James V. The capital was also the home of Holyrood Palace and Edinburgh Castle.

Despite possessing these capitals, rulers remained peripatetic. Several factors account for their journeys, which were tedious undertakings, for attendants had to pack belongings in carts and transport them from palace to palace every few weeks except during the height of winter. Concern about sanitation was a prime consideration, for dwellings that housed hundreds had to be aired and cleaned out. So serious was this problem that an ordinance of 1526 banned all dogs, except a few small spaniels, from the English Court.[1] As the royal entourage consumed vast amounts of food and supplies, it needed to relocate to other areas to replenish its larder. Some monarchs also went on progresses to assert royal prestige and to make themselves known to their subjects. James VI even recommended that rulers visit their entire realms once every three years. Progresses offered subjects opportunities to seek redress of grievances, and in Scotland monarchs were expected personally to support the activities of local justiciars and sheriffs. An epidemic such as the plague could force rulers to change their locations, and personal inclinations sometimes motivated their travels. Henry VIII hunted during the summer months; Elizabeth went on progresses, despite their additional expense, partly for entertainment and partly to elude officials, who sought to press their demands upon her.[2] Increasingly, her travels evoked criticism, for her purveyors had the right to purchase supplies at fixed rates, which inflation had made quite favorable to the crown. By the 1590s most counties had compounded with her government for fixed fees to replace purveyance. Finally, monarchs visited their children who resided in satellite courts.

The Tudor Court, excluding the stables, was divided into the household, the hall and service areas, under the control of the lord steward, the great chamber under the supervision of the lord chamberlain, and the privy chamber under the charge of the groom of the stool.[3] The Eltham Ordinances of 1526 and the Cromwellian Ordinances of 1539–40 directed two major reorganizations of the Court. A primary aim of the former was to limit expenses by reducing the number who received allotments of food and supplies. The Cromwellian regulations, among other goals, reorganized the council and raised salaries to offset the effects of inflation.

Although only a few courtiers amassed fortunes, Henry VIII was a better-paying employer than his noblemen. His early modern successors, however, failed to increase salaries, with the result that Queen Anne was still paying the same level of wages to her officials in 1702 as he had in 1540. This frozen scale did not deter office-seekers because rulers adopted strategies to counter inflation, for example, increasing food allotments and granting several posts to some officeholders. In 1553, William, earl of Pembroke, held thirty-eight separate positions, besides his membership in the privy chamber, all of which earned him about 200 pounds sterling yearly.[4]

The lord steward, supported by the treasurer, comptroller, and master of the household, supervised a staff of some 300 in twenty service departments: the buttery and cellar, pantry, kitchen and larder, and others, each of which was run by a sergeant who was supported by yeomen, grooms, and various servants. Except for the laundresses, the household was a male establishment. Twice a day, at 10:00 a.m. and 4:00 p.m., the lord steward oversaw the distribution of food on communal tables in the great chamber for those who had diet rights and ate at crown expense. By Elizabeth's reign, many officers were illegally avoiding these tables and enjoying separately prepared meals in their lodgings, a practice that kitchen servants and chamber staff encouraged because they could sell the surplus food from communal tables, which was their perquisite, for profit. Besides diet, the lord steward supplied some individuals with 'bouge of Court': prescribed portions of bread, ale and wine, as well as of fuel and torches; the size of these varied according to the individual's rank. In addition, some employees earned cash payments, the amounts of which also differed greatly with some menial workers receiving little or no payments at all. The household's duties and obligations help to explain why its budget formed the largest single peacetime expenditure, rising from about 16,000 pounds sterling at the beginning of Henry VIII's reign to 55,000 pounds sterling in Elizabeth's.

Among other tasks, the lord steward supervised the work of the cofferer, who headed the financial office, known as the board of greencloth, so named because of the colour of the baize on the counting table. The lord steward also administered common-law jurisdiction ex officio in Court sessions as needed, and, along with the comptroller, became an ex officio member of the privy council.

The great chamber, which was headed by the lord chamberlain and his assistant, the vice-chamberlain, was also a male establishment. In 1526, seventy-three gentlemen officers of the chamber claimed bouge of Court and 273 obtained wages without bouge. Assisted by his vice-chamberlain, gentlemen ushers and a treasurer, the lord chamberlain oversaw the public rooms, the guard chamber, and the presence chamber, where the ruler sat under a canopied throne on days of state, conducted visitors to the monarch, arranged the progresses, and supervised the work of the masters of the revels, of the tents, and of ceremonies, and the surveyor of works. Related to his department but not under his control were the jewel house and the Chapel Royal. The lord chamberlain, who could also appoint court lodgings, and the vice-chamberlain became ex officio members of the privy council.

Many in the chamber worked three-month shifts, thus quadrupling the number who could claim office without greatly increasing costs. In addition, some 150 unpaid esquires and knights of the body extraordinary, members of prominent families, ran errands in the chamber and escorted visitors around. Other personnel, whose positions were anomalous since they may not have been accountable to the lord chamberlain, included players, artists and artificers.

Because the aristocracy had free access to the public rooms, the crown established a security force. The 200 or so yeomen of the guard, in shifts of about fifty and headed by a captain, policed the guard room and the precincts of the Court under the supervision of the vice-chamberlain. Fifty gentlemen pensioners, working in quarterly shifts, and led by a captain and a lieutenant, stood at attention in the presence chamber.

About 1495, to afford the monarch more privacy, the privy chamber separated from the chamber and eventually developed into a complex department.[5] Beyond the privy chamber were located the bedchamber and privy galleries and lodgings, including libraries and closets. In Elizabeth's reign a withdrawing room was inserted between the privy chamber and the privy apartments, offering her even greater privacy. Although technically, the privy chamber fell under the lord chamberlain's jurisdiction, the groom of the stool, as the department's first gentleman, was in charge de facto and controlled access there; he also served as keeper of the privy purse. In 1526, one nobleman, the groom of the stool, and five other gentlemen, two gentlemen ushers, four grooms, the king's barber, and a page completed the personnel. By 1547, the membership had increased to twenty-eight, and two of its number had assumed the title of chief gentlemen, one of whom was always groom of the stool. Both chief gentlemen served as ex officio members of the privy council. Only these individuals, who worked on a six weeks' tour of duty, had the right to enter this department. Others, except for some designated officials, had to await royal summons for admission. At night two gentlemen slept in the privy chamber.

The establishment of this department permitted Tudor monarchs the opportunity to eat alone and avoid meal ceremonial, except on occasions when they hosted banquets. By Elizabeth's reign, this division had led to the fiction of her dining daily in state in the presence chamber. A lavishly set table had an empty chair for the monarch, whose place was served dinner as though she were present, her staff closely following the protocol for attending to her needs from food-tasting to ceremonial bowing. Subsequently, they delivered the meal to her private quarters.

It was in 1518 that gentlemen were first appointed to the privy chamber, possibly in response to the appointment of gentlemen to the French chamber in 1515. Like Francis I, Henry utilized them for public duties, and the Ordinances of Eltham specified that they should be skilled in rhetoric and capable of delivering messages to foreign princes as necessary. Their close proximity to the king's body endowed them with a special status, as they were seen as representing his authority and charisma. However, their primary responsibility remained seeing to his private needs: only they were to dress him or to touch his royal person.

With Mary's and Elizabeth's accessions, members of the privy chamber were no longer employed on governmental assignments, for these rulers necessarily appointed mostly females to their privy chambers. During her reign, Elizabeth assigned to it only two gentlemen but eight gentlewomen. These women, along with six maids of honour, joined the outer court under the lord chamberlain's supervision while four ladies of the bedchamber assumed charge of her private needs.

Besides female visitors and the laundresses, the other women at court were the monarch's relatives and their servants. For example, Henry VII's and Henry VIII's consorts had female attendants whose presence added a small number of women at Court. Their daughters, upon reaching an appropriate age, also resided with their parents and siblings.

When Tudor monarchs worshipped at the Chapel Royal, they marched to it in formal procession.[6] The members of this entourage belonged to the elite: key noblemen, the lord keeper with the great seal, and other senior officers carrying the sword of state and sceptre. Behind them followed the monarch with various personal attendants. They marched from the privy chamber into the presence chamber, past the great chamber and then through the gallery into the Chapel Royal. Although daily services were held in their chapels, since rulers also employed privy chaplains, they usually processed to chapel only on Sundays and special feast days. In some of her palaces, Elizabeth walked between a line of visitors who knelt on both knees as she passed.

The Scottish court also had officers who provided their monarchs with basic domestic needs and entertainment. The major differences between the English and Scottish courts were their size and structure, for in 1590, for example, the court of James VI was about one-third the size of Elizabeth's, and its departments more nearly resembled the French structure, which lacked a privy chamber, than its English counterpart. This was not surprising because from the late thirteenth century Scotland and France had often been military allies. When he visited France in 1536, moreover, James V was favourably impressed by French culture; his marriages to two Frenchwomen and his widow Mary of Guise's decision to send their heir, Mary Stuart, to France must also have influenced this acculturation process.

In the absence of a privy chamber, one man served both as lord chamberlain and as first gentleman of the chamber, in charge of the king's personal needs; thus, the chamber's entire staff served directly in his bedchamber. Without a barrier between the bedchamber and the chamber, the Scottish Court developed a more casual style than the English one and provided freer and easier access to its monarchs. James VI, who advised his heir, Henry, that only tyrants ate in private, also had a cabinet beyond the bedchamber where he worked. Obviously, during the years of Mary's personal rule in Scotland, the female in charge of her personal needs could not also function as her lord chamberlain.

A hierarchical ritual developed around the Scottish monarchs' meals, for their food was never intended for their nourishment only. Leftovers were distributed downward through the Court hierarchy in a prescribed chain, elite status being defined by who received food directly from the royal table.[7] In England, in contrast, leftovers from the monarch's private table were distributed to the poor as alms.

Some members of the crown's council also resided at Court. Some 227 councillors of Henry VII have been identified, but many, especially the forty-four who did not attend a recorded meeting, probably held only honorific titles. After Henry VIII's accession, the council underwent a pragmatic restructuring into what was ultimately called the privy council. The Eltham Ordinances provided for twenty councillors to attend the king, but in practice so many exceptions were made that only two actually resided at Court. As the principal secretary and keeper of the privy seal, Thomas Cromwell reduced the council to about nineteen members, but it did not gain bureaucratic routine until after his execution in 1540 when a clerk began to keep minutes of its meetings.[8] These took place almost daily where and when the king determined, usually in a room assigned for them, which was removed from the Court's outer chamber to the privy lodgings. Despite this proximity, Henry never attended the meetings and, like his father, continued to seek advice from individuals or small groups of councillors, as he pleased. After his death, substantial changes were made in the council membership that grew to some forty by Mary's death. Her sister, Elizabeth, returned it to the pattern of their father's reign but later further reduced its size.

In 1545 in Scotland, a clerk began to keep a register of the privy or secret council meetings, which also took place at Court. Mary of Guise, the mother of, and from 1554 the regent for, Mary Stuart, attended its meetings regularly. When Mary returned to her realm in 1561, after the death of her husband, Francis II, she met with the council infrequently. Perhaps, she was following French practice, for in the mornings, for example, her father-in-law, Henry II, consulted with a few advisers and avoided the formal meetings of the council in the afternoon. Only eighteen years old, Mary may also have been learning about the business of governing, for her son, James VI, likewise met with his council infrequently during the first years after 1585, when he was about her age. Only in the 1590s did his attendance become regular.[9]

Many studies have emphasized the Court's importance as a theatre, for its outer magnificence rather than its inner domesticity has appealed to a wide range of interdisciplinary scholars. The splendour of Renaissance Courts, which also awed contemporaries, was an irresistible attraction: monarchs drew around them scholars, musicians, artists, actors and craftsmen to produce entertainment. Essential instruments of power, the festivities and drama confirmed the abstract permanence of the monarchy and the legitimacy of the dynasty; they formed authentic aspects of Court life, and rulers who ignored them jeopardized their honour and reputation at home and abroad. The sumptuous entertainments had two major settings: dynastic and state occasions and traditional religious and secular feasts.

Some spectacles achieved special brilliance because the crown co-ordinated religious rites with secular ceremonies, especially civic entries. Two noteworthy examples were the marriage of Catherine of Aragon and Arthur, prince of Wales, and the coronation of Elizabeth.[10] On 12 November 1501, Catherine entered London on a richly caparisoned horse. Amidst trumpet fanfare and cannon shots, she rode from Southwark over London Bridge, along Fenchurch Street to Cornhill and then to Cheapside, where the lord mayor welcomed her, and then to St Paul's for a thanksgiving service. Having decorated the streets with draperies, the Londoners entertained her with six Christian and allegorical pageants on the way to St Paul's. The first, a tabernacle of the saints, housed St Catherine and St Ursula, who foretold the princess's arrival at a celestial court. Obviously, the first saint represented the bride, and as St Ursula brought to mind the constellation Ursa Minor, which is adjacent to Arcturus, a medieval name for Ursa Major, she represented the bridegroom. The practice of citizens welcoming personages in entries, which were modelled after ancient Roman triumphs, can be traced back to the thirteenth century in England, although the earliest were simple affairs without pageants. By the Tudor period, they had become increasingly elaborate, and it is interesting that scholars have rated those of 1501 as the century's most distinguished productions.

Two days later Arthur and Catherine exchanged vows outside St Paul's and then entered the cathedral for the nuptial mass. A bridge was erected, about five feet off the ground, from the west door of St Paul's over the nave to the choir. Decorated in red worsted, it ended at steps leading to a platform on which sat the king and queen at one end, the lord mayor and aldermen on the other end, and at its centre Catherine and Arthur.

Between 19 and 25 November, the wedding party attended several banquets and tournaments to celebrate the occasion. The initial banquet merits attention because it introduced into England entertainments, called disguisings, which adopted the

Burgundian practice of employing pageant-cars to transport masquers and scenery into court. As these also included allegorical costuming, drama, music and dancing, they displayed all the ingredients of the later masque. In the third pageant on the 19th, disguised knights of the Mount of Love, who emerged from a great hill or mountain, playfully attacked a fortress, the castle of beauty, which housed ladies who ended the battle and the pageant by surrendering and dancing with their conquerors.[11]

Tournaments also played an important role in these festivities, although neither Arthur nor his father participated in the ones honouring his marriage. After women began to witness tournaments in the thirteenth century, the competitions gained renown for their pageantry in which combatants often wore disguises, some based on romance characters. In 1501, Buckingham, the prince's champion, issued the customary challenge for the tournament to be held at Westminster. At the tilt-yard was displayed England's first tree of chivalry on which the combatants hung their shields in the Burgundian manner. They erected richly decorated pavilions, Henry Bourchier, earl of Essex's, for example, was in the form of a green mountain with a lady sitting on its top. During the games, warriors jousted with rebated lances on the tilt-yard, competed in tourneys in the open fields with sharp spears, and fought on foot at barriers with swords and spears.

English coronations were likewise associated with entries and elaborate entertainments. On 14 January 1559, the eve of Elizabeth's coronation, her household staff, lesser officers of state, the bishops, peers and foreign ambassadors marched into London ahead of the king of arms, the lord high steward, bearing the sword of state, the earl marshal, and the high constable. The queen, having spent the previous two nights at the Tower, came next in a chariot with a canopy borne over her head by four knights. Following her were the master of the horse, her ladies, and peers' wives and daughters. Processions like these validated the social and political hierarchy, emphasized the monarch's position at the head of the nobility, and served to inculcate social discipline. The pageants began at Fenchurch Street with a child's welcoming speech, but Elizabeth had to silence the roaring crowd to hear him. Her close attention to his words and to the succeeding pageants served as evidence to her people of her love for them. At the upper end of Gracechurch Street, actors, who stood amidst red and white roses on several stages to form her family tree, were dressed as Henry VII, Elizabeth of York, Henry VIII, Anne Boleyn and Elizabeth. At the Little Conduit in Cheap, she kissed the Bible presented to her and placed it on her breast to proclaim her Protestantism. Later, at Ludgate, a pageant, recognizing her as a female monarch, referred to her as Deborah, the judge and restorer of the house of Israel.

The next day, she was crowned at Westminster Abbey. At the end of the medieval period, some monarchs began to emphasize this sacred rite to offset the emperor's prestige and to affirm their own independent status. Signs of this assertive attitude were their adoptions of the closed or imperial crown and the title of Majesty. In some sense, their authority was tied to the existence and display of this insignia. After her coronation, Elizabeth hosted a banquet that lasted from 3:00 p.m. to 1:00 a.m. As was customary, the monarch's champion, in this case, Sir Edward Dymoke, rode into the building and flung down his gauntlet, signalling that he was prepared to fight any challenger to her accession. At the banquet's end, a play or masque was probably held since the master of the revels received funds for his expenses. Jousting had been planned at the Whitehall tilt-yard the next day, but the exhausted queen post-poned the games until the 17th.

For entertainment, Elizabeth's master of the revels developed a regular schedule, which derived from a popular tradition of celebrations that predated the Tudor period. Dramas and some masques in which Elizabeth, unlike her father, did not par-ticipate, were commonly produced during the liturgical festivals of the church year: the twelve days of Christmas, St Stephen's, St John's, Innocents', New Year's, Twelfth Night or Epiphany, Candlemas, and Shrovetide (Sunday, Monday and Tuesday before Ash Wednesday).

Jousting also remained popular at her court, and, from the 1570s, her champion, Sir Henry Lee, associated games at the Whitehall tilt-yard with her accession anniver-sary. Annually, on 17 November, splendidly dressed knights jousted in front of her to honour her as their monarch and unattainable mistress, thereby affirming her female rule with a male competition.

The century's grandest spectacle occurred in the pale of Calais at what was cele-brated as the Field of Cloth of Gold. There for three weeks in June 1520, the Courts of Henry VIII and Francis entertained each other while exploring the possibility of an alliance. The English at Guisnes and the French at Ardres visited each other and competed in glorious display. To supplement housing at Guisnes Castle for Henry and his entourage, a vast, highly ornate tent or palace with a banqueting hall and chapel and some 400 pavilions were constructed. Allegories and symbolism decorated the chambers of these temporary buildings, which possessed drapery and furniture of cloth of gold and other precious materials. The two Courts indulged in masques, ban-quets, concerts, ecclesiastical ceremonies, athletic competition and other festivities.

In sixteenth-century Scotland, the coronations of its rulers were not elaborate affairs associated with entries, primarily because the new monarchs were children whose governments faced the threats of foreign and civil wars. Behind the scenes, while preparations for their coronations were pushed forward, factions competed for control of them and their realms. The coronations of queens consort offered better opportunities for display, and that of Margaret Tudor is particularly well documented.

On 7 August 1503, James IV met Margaret, dressed in cloth of gold and heavily jewelled, outside Edinburgh. James dismounted from his horse, kissed his bride who rode in a litter, and remounted without putting his feet in the stirrups. As they approached the city, two knights entertained them with a mock joust over a lady, first on horseback with spears and then on foot with swords. When they reached the city gates, singing angels presented them with the keys to Edinburgh, recalling the Advent liturgy with Edinburgh representing the New Jerusalem. In the centre of the town, the streets of which were decorated with tapestries, they drank wine from the foun-tain and, further on, were greeted by four virtues, Justice, Force, Temperance and Prudence. Musicians played as they passed on to the Canongate, to the Church of the Holy Cross, and finally, to Holyrood Palace. The next day, after their wedding at Holyrood chapel, Margaret was crowned and anointed. With trumpets blaring, the royal party walked to the banqueting hall while people danced and sang in the streets lit with bonfires. For four days the festivities continued with the production of morality plays, tournaments, dances and concerts.

Another celebration that utilized elaborate entertainments was the baptism of Henry, heir to the Scottish throne, on 30 August 1594, six months after his birth.

The affair drew on the standard chivalric festival style of the 1580s that developed in England. On the first day, a tilting tournament took place and on the third day, after the baptism, a banquet was held, which featured pageants that employed elaborate machinery, including a ship, eighteen feet in length, on which stood three gods and six goddesses.[12]

Producing these entertainments required increased royal patronage of the arts. Henry VIII employed Hans Holbein the younger, who decorated the long gallery at Whitehall, in the process creating the first art gallery in England. Elizabeth gathered at her Court a large musical establishment, apart from the Chapel Royal where Thomas Tallis and William Byrd created their compositions. In Scotland, Sir David Lindsay of the Mount served James V as Lyon King of Arms, the chief heraldic officer, and staged many spectacles, including Mary of Guise's receptions at St Andrews and Edinburgh in 1538. His plays and poetry entertained the court and remained popular long after his death.

Besides patronizing the arts, monarchs rewarded and advanced their subjects to secure their service and obedience. At royal disposal were material advantages, offices, lands, pensions and monopolies, which were distributed to the aristocracy, the politically active class that numbered about 2,500 by Elizabeth's reign. This patronage was one aspect of the reality that Court politics were based on personal relationships and that those who won the monarch's favour reaped the greatest rewards.[13] At stake for the clientage was not only the possibility of amassing fortunes, but also of gaining community pride, a sense of worth and personal honour, the hallmark of nobility.

Through those with access to Court, suitors pressed their petitions; sometimes this practice resulted in a frantic competition and even to the seeking of positions before the present holder had died. In their quest for patronage, suitors employed agents or they themselves acted to obtain intelligence for use in winning largesse from royal favourites within a surveillance system that dominated all levels of Court culture. Roger Ascham recalled that Sir Anthony Denny, a privy councillor, warned him of the dangers lurking there:

> The corte, Mr. Ascam, is a place so slipperie, that dewtie never so well done, is not a staffe stiffe enough to stand by alwaise very surelie; where ye many tymes repe most unkyndness where ye have sown greatest pleasurs, and those also readye to do you moch hurt to whom yow never intended to think any harme. . . .[14]

Petitioners usually sought the support of more than one favourite for advancement: they realized that success was more likely if they persuaded two or three patrons to further their suits, and they recognized that some individuals had better opportunities than others to obtain particular preferments, such as, for example, financial gifts, which might require the lord treasurer's approval. Access to rulers was the asset that counted, and suitors were even known to petition humble crown servants. Although female attendants of the queens regnant and consort did not hold public positions, they engaged in this patronage network. Since successful suitors paid patrons handsomely, royal favourites sought to build up an extensive clientage in order to win benefits for themselves. In practice, monarchs were concerned enough about outbreaks of violence to spread rewards widely in order to avoid the discontent that could erupt into rebellions. Although Wolsey and Sir William Cecil held important positions at Henry's and Elizabeth's Courts, for example, royal favour extended beyond them to win the good will of the political class.

The Court was a crucial point of contact with the aristocracy in the countryside. Important offices at Court and in the country were reserved for the peerage: lords lieutenancies, military commands, and some household, chamber and council positions. Tudor monarchs expanded their Courts at the expense of the peerage, whose household splendour could no longer rival theirs. Since the patronage that revolved around royal Courts was absorbing their patronage networks, the peers needed to win the monarch's favour in order to retain influence in local appointments. By Elizabeth's reign, their occasional Court attendance was expected, and if a peer failed to come at her summons, she considered it as a treasonable act.

Like the peers, the greater gentry served in county positions, and, as deputy lieutenants and justices of the peace, they answered to the privy council for their administrative and judicial duties. Although Court attendance also contributed to their success, as local landlords they had to limit their employment to part-time positions; they also visited Court occasionally, and some hired agents to act for them there. Their sons and younger brothers, who before the Tudor century might have been employed in noble households, sought careers at Court, mostly in the chamber. The early Tudors greatly broadened the basis of their rule by utilizing these service gentry, and although the county remained the focal point of the aristocracy, something like a national political elite developed around the Court.

Through the numerous individuals who visited or who were resided at their Courts, monarchs extended their influence into the country, for the aristocracy carried information about royal views on education and religion and about Court fashions and events back home with them. It became obvious, too, that Court office, even esquire extraordinary of the body, translated into higher social status in the localities. Whether true or not, many believed that a courtier could rely upon royal support in any dispute or controversy.

A hotly debated topic in modern scholarship concerns the nature of political factions at Henry VIII's Court. One theory explains that factional politics coincided with Anne Boleyn's ascendancy, that they were based on religious ideology, and that their focus was the privy chamber.[15] Another, more subtle theory, argues that factions were rooted in their adherents' political interests, but that they could be tinged with ideology, and that it was only after the king favoured a faction leader that his or her policies were adopted. At first, it was the individual that attracted him, not the ideology.[16]

These theories have elicited many critical responses, for they not only rely heavily on the writings of resident ambassadors, who mostly reported unconfirmed rumours in their dispatches, but they also offer a rather cynical view of the character of the king, who appears politically manipulated, possessing no deep policies and lacking command of his Court. That depiction does not take into consideration his reputation in the Tudor century. For example, in 1592, Robert Beale, clerk of the Privy Council, wrote a treatise with instructions for a principal secretary in which he utilized the following story:

> It is reported of K[ing] Hen[ry] 8 that when S[ir] William Peter, at the first time that
> he was Secretarie, seemed to be dismaied for that the K[ing] crossed and blotted out

manye thinges in a wrightinge w[hi]ch he had made, the K[ing] willed him not to take it in evill parte, for it is I, sayd he, that made both Crumwell, Wriotheslie and Pagett good Secretaries and so must I doe to thee.

Beale explained: 'The Princes themselves knowe best their owne meaninge and ther must be time and experience to acquainte them w[i]th their humours before a man can doe anie acceptable service.'[17]

Another problem is that these theories misrepresent Tudor practice by assuming that individuals could be assigned to factions by some kind of ideological test. Everyone was expected to follow Henry's lead on religious matters, a topic that greatly interested him and that intersected with diplomatic matters. The various official acts concerning his church seem to have responded more directly to events abroad than to domestic issues. If courtiers did not support the royal supremacy in 1534, the doctrinal conservatism in 1539, and some Erasmian reform, for example, they were rusticated or imprisoned. How much Erasmian reform various individuals advocated was a personal not a factional policy.

The modern assignment of some individuals to factions can on closer investigation be disproved. Thomas Howard, third duke of Norfolk, for example, allegedly protested against the royal marriage of his niece, Anne Boleyn, because he headed a conservative faction that challenged her evangelical one, but he actually reaped great rewards from her liaison. His daughter Mary wed the king's illegitimate son, Henry Fitzroy, duke of Richmond; his son Henry, earl of Surrey, travelled as Richmond's companion to France; Norfolk was admitted to the Order of St Michael, the French equivalent of the Order of the Garter. Another alleged leader of the duke's faction was Stephen Gardiner, bishop of Winchester, but no evidence confirms that they were political allies. Norfolk's faction was also supposedly hostile to Cromwell's evangelical following, but, in 1538, Cromwell acted in legal and personal matters as the agent of Norfolk, who planned to appoint him a godfather to his grandson, except that the child was born prematurely and had to be immediately christened.

In assuming, moreover, that the usual pattern of the patronage network was manifested by an inflexible grouping of individuals around a person who was in competition with another patron and his following, these theories not only underestimate the fluidity of politics at courts, which contained so many part-time employees and visitors, but also over-emphasize the significance of the limited access to the king in his privy lodgings. While the right of entry to the privy chamber was important, surely admissions were at his discretion, for he was not isolated there as though he were in prison. When he visited his consorts, for example, they and their attendants could seek favours from him. Moreover, one of his favourite gambling companions was actually the sergeant of the kitchen.

The close, personal association of the members of the privy chamber with Henry, although their appointments were initially based on royal favour, could breed his contempt for them, for even indiscreet speech constituted an offence. In 1538, when Sir Francis Bryan, a long-time member of the privy chamber, offended Henry, the king called him a drunkard and rusticated him.

It is also true that some vital information shared with the privy councillors was usually withheld from members of the privy chamber who were not on the council. When in 1540, at Rochester, Henry wondered whether Anne of Cleves had the features of an unmarried woman, he disclosed some of his concerns to his privy-chamber escort, but he waited until he could assemble select privy councillors at Greenwich to discuss how to resolve this crisis. All with access to royal secrets took oaths not to reveal them to others, and to do so endangered their lives.

Finally, in response to the theory that factions manipulated the king, it must be noted that officials were expected to wait for their monarchs to seek their advice before they offered it. According to authors of contemporary treatises, rather than impress upon a ruler some new unsought-after policy, courtiers were more likely to flatter royal opinions in the hope of winning greater rewards for their clients and of extending their patronage networks.

When rigid factions emerged, it was not over the usual patronage competition but over control of crown policies. They were composed of individuals who were personally bound to one leader and who viewed themselves as opposed to all other leaders and their personal followings. Not only could this kind of competition disrupt Court life, but it could also result in uprisings against the government. Virtually all contemporary treatises warned monarchs of this danger. These factional struggles erupted at three specific times in the sixteenth century: a minor's accession, a queen regnant's marriage, and late in an aged monarch's reign. After Edward VI's accession in 1547, his younger uncle, Thomas, Lord Seymour of Sudeley and lord admiral, competed with his older uncle, Edward Seymour, duke of Somerset and lord protector, for control of his government.[18] Sudeley married Henry's widow, Catherine Parr, gained control of Elizabeth who resided with her, and subsequently obtained custody of Jane Grey, another royal claimant. He then attempted to entice Edward away from Somerset's influence with bribes of money. These machinations led to his execution in 1549, but the fratricide which John Dudley, future duke of Northumberland, had encouraged made Somerset vulnerable to his faction. After capturing control of the privy chamber and with it the king, Northumberland ordered the arrest of Somerset and his brother-in-law, Sir Michael Stanhope, the chief gentleman of the privy chamber. They were executed in 1552.

For much of the sixteenth century, factional struggles, similar to that of Edward VI's reign, flourished in Scotland. The minorities of James V, Mary, and James VI, and the absence abroad of Mary left the realm to the governance of regents, some of whom were assassinated. Abductors seized all three monarchs to gain control of their governments, although at the time of Mary's seizure, she, unlike the others, was an adult. Only in the 1590s did James VI extend royal power over the earls and end this violence. He informed his son that royal honour demanded that kings employ their nobility in all their important business.

The question of a queen regnant's marriage was deeply contentious, for in this patriarchal society her male subjects doubted the ability of women, identified as the weaker sex, to govern, and expected royal husbands to become the realm's actual rulers. In the sixteenth century, only four marriages of British Isles queens regnant occurred, and all generated revolts. In 1554, Mary Tudor's decision to wed Philip of Spain led to Thomas Wyatt the Younger's uprising. Similarly, the three marriages of Mary Stuart ended in rebellions. Some observers blamed the one in 1558 to Francis II for the successful Protestant challenge to her mother's French-dominated regency. When, in 1565, the widowed Mary wed Henry Lord Darnley, her former adviser and illegitimate half-brother, James Stewart, earl of Moray, revolted against her. Her final marriage to James Hepburn, earl of Bothwell, in 1567 led to the warfare that cost her the throne.

In the 1560s, when negotiations were under way for Elizabeth to wed Charles, archduke of Austria, factional politics threatened her court.[19] Her strength of character combined with the willingness of two of her favourites, Sir William Cecil and Robert Dudley, earl of Leicester, to co-operate together for the common good despite their disagreements over the viability of this Catholic suitor, ended the threat. Given this and subsequent disputes concerning the candidates she considered, and given the violence directed against other royal bridegrooms, it is not surprising that Elizabeth seemed to equate her political survival with the unmarried state.

Finally, aged monarchs sometimes began to lose control of their Courts. Most scholars describe the competition between Sir Robert Cecil and Robert Devereux, earl of Essex, in the last years of Elizabeth's reign as a vicious factional struggle. Essex's failure to win her support for his policies and his loss of patronage led to his abortive rebellion to remove Cecil from power. Executed in 1601, Essex seemed to have lacked the flexibility needed to accept the rejection of his goals and the aged Elizabeth seemed incapable of persuading him of the risks involved in challenging her decisions. By 1601, others appeared impatient with her longevity: Henry Clinton, earl of Lincoln, for example, refused to receive her when she arrived at his home on a progress.

At the end of her father's reign, it is possible to find competition that approaches the extreme of the 1590s, but scholars are still debating its meaning, for an understanding of it has been obscured by the providential narrative of John Foxe, who identified, among others, Norfolk and Winchester as leaders of a conservative faction in opposition to the reforming party led by Edward, the future Somerset, and Thomas Cranmer, archbishop of Canterbury. But if it were factional politics that led to Norfolk's and Surrey's arrest in 1546, these were not essentially ideological, for some of Surrey's connections were Protestants, and the Howards were not Winchester's allies. The Seymours, as blood relatives of the young Edward, and the Howards – or at least Surrey – both hoped to dominate his regency. Surrey claimed that privilege for his family because his father, whose life was saved by Henry's death, was the realm's senior nobleman.

The crime for which Surrey died, that he had illegally quartered the royal arms on his coat of arms, was fictitious, but Henry validated it, even editing the paper that outlined the case in his own hand.[20] Surrey actually had two valid claims to the royal arms: the Howards were descendants of Thomas of Brotherton, a son of Edward I, and they possessed the right to display Edward the Confessor's arms, which had been granted by Richard II to their Mowbray ancestors, the first dukes of Norfolk.

The crown's real concern may have been that Surrey's maternal grandfather was Buckingham, a descendant of Edward III, who had been executed in 1521 for treasonable ambitions. With reference to the duke's lineage, it is interesting that late in Henry VII's reign when he was ill, depositions were taken of conversations at Calais in which Buckingham was named as a possible successor to the king, but in which the royal heir, the future Henry VIII, was ignored. Was it religious politics then that manipulated Henry into supporting Surrey's condemnation, or was it primarily his concern for young Edward's security? The deaths of Edward IV's sons had, after all, enabled the Tudor accession, and the recent publication of Sir Thomas More's study of Richard III reminded its readers of those events.

The details of an earlier incident in Henry's reign offer some insights. In 1538, he approved of Cromwell's arranging a marriage between Mary Howard, widow of Richmond, and Thomas Seymour, but after Surrey protested, the plan was dropped. In light of this controversy, Henry's reasonable conclusion would have been that the earl, who blocked his sister's marriage, would resist co-operating with the Seymours under any circumstance. When Norfolk attempted to ease tensions in 1546 by resurrecting this match, Surrey again opposed it.

By then, the ailing king seems to have suspected that Surrey possessed his maternal grandfather's ambitions, and he must have been troubled about the earl's disdain for young Edward's blood relatives at a time when the selection of his regency council was underway. An obvious appointment to it was the prince's eldest maternal uncle, who had no independent royal claim and whose authority would, it might seem, depend on protecting his nephew's sovereignty. Henry may well have anticipated that Surrey's ambitions would lead him into conflict with the regency council. The continuation of his dynasty was Henry's prime goal, but whether the king, whose death was imminent, fully understood the heraldic charges is not clear, for his editorial comments outlining them have errors that indicate he suffered from a somewhat confused state of mind. Nevertheless, it can be argued that the intricacies of the case may have eluded him but that the dangers of factional politics at a minor's accession had not.

The early modern Court has attracted much recent scholarship. Since the debate over Court factions will continue to generate more research on this topic, it would be useful to have further demographic studies of the privy council and of the privy chamber. Identification of their members, of the other offices they held, of their access to patronage at Court and in the county, and of their connections to each other make possible a greater clarification of court politics. Many scholars will continue to examine the social and cultural impact of royal patronage and to study the splendour of Court culture but more should be done on the ritual of daily royal life. Particularly fascinating is the work of scholars across several fields, who have developed an interest in the political and cultural significance of the presence of queens regnant and consort and their female attendants at the Courts, which were essentially male establishments presiding at the top of a patriarchal hierarchy.

NOTES

1. Nichols, ed. *Ordinances and Regulations*, 150.
2. Cole, *The Portable Queen*, pp. 1–22.
3. Loades, *Tudor Court*, pp. 40–2.
4. Braddock, 'The rewards of office-holding'.
5. Starkey, 'Intimacy and innovation'.
6. Kisby, ' "When the king goeth a procession" '.
7. Gibson and Smout, 'Food and hierarchy in Scotland'.
8. Guy, 'The privy council: revolution or evolution'.
9. Goodare and Lynch, 'James VI: universal king?', p. 4.
10. Kipling, *Enter the King*, for all the entries discussed in this section.
11. Howard, ' "Ascending the Riche Mount": performing hierarchy and gender in the Henrician masque', *has identified this as a 'mock rape'*.

12. Lynch, 'Court ceremony and ritual'.
13. MacCaffrey, 'Place and patronage in Elizabethan politics'.
14. Ellis, ed. *Original Letters*, pp. 13–14.
15. Starkey, *The Reign of Henry VIII*, p. 29.
16. Ives, 'Henry VIII: the political perspective', p. 30.
17. Read, *Mr Secretary Walsingham*, vol. 1, p. 439.
18. Hoak, 'The king's privy chamber'.
19. Adams, 'Favourites and factions at the Elizabethan Court'.
20. Moore, 'The heraldic charge against the earl of Surrey'.

BIBLIOGRAPHY

Adams, Simon, 'Favourites and factions at the Elizabethan Court', in John Guy, *The Tudor Monarchy* (London, 1997), pp. 253–74.
Braddock, Robert C., 'The rewards of office-holding in Tudor England', *Journal of British Studies*, 14 (1975), 29–47.
Cole, Mary, *The Portable Queen: Elizabeth I and the Politics of Ceremony* (Amherst, 1999).
Ellis, Henry, ed., *Original Letters of Eminent Literary Men of the Sixteenth, Seventeenth, and Eighteenth Centuries* (London, 1843).
Gibson, A. and T. C. Smout, 'Food and hierarchy in Scotland, 1550–1650', in Leah Leneman, ed., *Perspectives in Scottish Social History: Essays in Honour of Rosalind Mitchison* (Aberdeen, 1988), pp. 32–52.
Goodare, Julian and Lynch, Michael, 'James VI: universal king?', in J. Goodare and M. Lynch, eds, *The Reign of James VI* (East Linton, 2000).
Guy, John, 'The privy council: revolution or evolution', in Christopher Coleman and David Starkey, eds, *Revolution Reassessed: Revisions in the History of Tudor Government and Administration* (Oxford, 1986), pp. 59–86.
Hoak, Dale, 'The king's privy chamber, 1547–1553', in Deloyd Guth and John McKenna, eds, *Tudor Rule and Revolution: Essays for G. R. Elton from his American Friends* (Cambridge, 1982), pp. 87–108.
Howard, Skiles, '"Ascending the Riche Mount": performing hierarchy and gender in the Henrician masque', in Peter Herman, ed., *Rethinking the Henrician Era: Essays on Early Tudor Texts and Contexts'* (Urbana, 1994), pp. 16–39.
Ives, Eric, 'Henry VIII: the political perspective', in Diarmaid MacCulloch, ed., *The Reign of Henry VIII: Politics, Policy and Piety* (Basingstoke, 1995).
Kipling, Gordon, *Enter the King: Theatre, Liturgy and Ritual in the Medieval Civic Triumph* (Oxford, 1998).
Kisby, Fiona, '"When the king goeth a procession:" chapel ceremonies and services, the ritual year, and religious reforms at the early Tudor Court, 1485–1547', *Journal of British Studies*, 40 (2001), 44–75.
Loades, David, *The Tudor Court* (London, 1986).
Lynch, Michael, 'Court ceremony and ritual during the personal reign of James VI', J. Goodare and M. Lynch, eds, *Reign of James VI* (East Linton, 2000), pp. 71–92.
MacCaffrey, Wallace, 'Place and patronage in Elizabethan politics', in S. Bindoff, J. Hurstfield, and C. Williams, eds, *Elizabethan Government and Society* (London, 1961), pp. 95–126.
Moore, Peter, 'The heraldic charge against the earl of Surrey, 1546–47', *English Historical Review*, 116 (2001), 557–83.
Nichols, John, *A Collection of Ordinances and Regulations for the Government of the Royal Household, Made in Divers Reigns* (London, 1790).
Read, Conyers, *Mr Secretary Walsingham* (3 vols, Oxford, 1925).

Starkey, David, 'Intimacy and innovation: the rise of the privy chamber, 1485–1547', in D. Starkey et al., *The English Court from the Wars of the Roses to the Civil War* (London and New York, 1987), pp. 71–118.
Starkey, David, *The Reign of Henry VIII: Personalities and Politics* (London, 1985).

FURTHER READING

Stephen Alford, *The Early Elizabethan Polity: William Cecil and the British Succession Crisis, 1558–69* (1988).
Ronald Asch and Adolf Burke (eds), *Princes, Patronage and Royalty, 1450–1800* (1977).
John Archer, *Sovereignty and Intelligence: Spying and Court Culture in the English Renaissance* (1993).
Susan Doran, *Monarchy and Matrimony: The Courtships of Elizabeth I* (1996).
Carol Edington, *Court and Culture in Renaissance Scotland: Sir David Lindsay* (1994).
G. R. Elton, (ed.), *Studies in Tudor and Stuart Politics and Government* (4 vols, 1974–92).
Antonio Guevara, *The Diall of Princes*, trans. Sir Thomas North (1968).
S. J. Gunn, *Early Tudor Government, 1485–1558* (1995).
John Guy (ed.), *The Reign of Elizabeth I: Court and Culture in the Last Decade* (1995).
R. Christopher Hassel, *Renaissance Drama and the English Church Year* (1979).
Dale Hoak, *The King's Council in the Reign of Edward VI* (1976).
R. A. Houlbrooke, 'Debate: Henry VIII's wills: a comment', *Historical Journal*, 37 (1994), 891–9.
Gordon Kipling, *The Triumph of Honour: Burgundian Origins of the English Renaissance* (1977).
R. J. Knecht, *Renaissance Warrior and Patron: The Reign of Francis I* (1994).
Michael Lynch (ed.), *Mary Stewart, Queen in Three Kingdoms* (1988).
A. A. MacDonald, Michael Lynch and Ian Cowens (eds), *The Renaissance in Scotland: Studies in Literature, Religion, History, and Culture* (1994).
Joycelyne Russell, *The Field of Cloth of Gold: Men and Manners in 1520* (1969).
Narasingha Prosad Sil, *Tudor Placement and Statesmen: Select Case Histories* (2001).
Beatrice White (ed.), *The Eclogues of Alexander Barclay from the Original Edition by John Cawood* (1928).
Janet Williams (ed.), *Stewart Style, 1513–1542: Essays on the Court of James V* (1996).

CHAPTER FIVE

Law

DeLloyd J. Guth

Rule of law, and its legal-judicial system, offered remarkable contrasts in Tudor England and Stuart Scotland. The late medieval, pre-Reformation way of living was under a plurality of laws: royal common law, church canon law, and local customary laws – whether the rural landlord's manorial law or the municipal laws of cities and boroughs. In theory the various jurisdictions did not coincide; but in reality, for example in debtor–creditor actions, any plaintiff could sue the same defendant for the same claim at the same time in any of these law courts. Competitive and complicated as the legal systems could be, nevertheless both kingdoms had had settled systems of governance based on law since at least the twelfth century. By the late fifteenth century, both had survived violent dynastic struggles for family control of the monarchy: the Wars of the Roses, York against Lancaster in England since 1455; and, since 1466, the embattled James III in Scotland against the Boyds of Kilmarnock and then against his own brothers, Albany and Mar. By the 1490s an uneasy dynastic peace returned to each nation. Then in 1503, James IV wed Henry VII's daughter, Margaret Tudor, and that marriage would justify the merger of English and Scottish monarchies, when James VI rode south (1603) to replenish the exhausted Tudor bloodline, as James I of England. But neither then nor now has a merger of English and Scottish laws occurred.

In England, the separate royal, central common law had become much more associated with what each royal parliament routinely produced. The English common law offered a network of courts of first resort, some recently created by parliament, such as the Star Chamber or the Court of Wards, for English men and women. The several English church reformations (1529, 1553 and 1559) were all legislated by royal parliaments. These also attempted to reduce the intrusiveness of canon law courts in ordinary lives. Similarly pre-empted were the customary courts of law, more often rural manorial and hundred jurisdictions, where one sued debtors, bullies or local profiteers. As the Tudor century's demographic shift became a one-way ride into cities, towns and boroughs, more people became more secularized and more subject to royal (i.e., common law) regulation. The legal pluralism continued but in England the competitive balance already favoured the common law.

North of that ever-shifting Anglo-Scottish border, a weaker monarchy and less centralized government left the king first-among-equal clan chieftains and left the law more localized among landlords. A Scot lived under a mix of romanized Anglo-Norman principles, feudal property rules and mainly local customs. These enforced a quasi-military and clan-based, lord–tenant, patron–client legal culture. Added to this mix was a church law, universal to both pre-Reformation England and Scotland, that claimed control over entry into eternal heaven or hell, by enforcing its moral and liturgical rules. The Scottish kirk had its one-and-only Reformation (1560) as a result of a decisive series of parliamentary acts. Canon law and its church courts had previously played an aggressive, pervasive role in Scotland. After 1560 much of this jurisdiction transferred to the secular Court of Session, but with the old church's law enforced with the new Calvinist fervour. Law in sixteenth-century Scotland would remain a mix of local and royal rules, but more rural-landlord than urban-commercial, and more private than public.

The same could be said for law in Wales, but with one huge exception. Its forced union into England's common law regime, by parliamentary statutes of 1536 and 1543, changed both process and personnel for Welsh ways of governance. Ever since Edward I (1272–1320) had conquered the Cambrian dales, law and order had come to depend more directly on how closely local Welsh elites positioned themselves with English royal power and patronage. The Celts in Ireland would learn in the 1640s the same lesson that the Welsh learned in the 1540s: that England's common law was the vehicle for validating the invading, transplanted English landlords. From Anglesey in the north down to Gower Anglicana, rustic poverty, reformed religion and English-style local governance had fixed Wales alongside Ireland as first jewels in England's 'imperial' crown.

In the course of the sixteenth century, then, both England and Scotland evolved discrete monarchies that relied on cabinet-like ministerial ways for creating policies and enforcing laws; on an entrenched parliamentary procedure for law-making; on a self-confident – albeit crown-dependent – judiciary to resolve disputes peacefully according to royal rules; on a nationalized church with a laity of landlords and merchants, increasingly defining public morals and enforcing parish discipline; on an expanding criminal law power in the royal magistracy, sitting routinely at quarter-sessions and assizes; as well as on a popular migration into towns and cities that made borough customs matter more and rural manorial customs less. As for the expertise needed to service these trends, the numbers of English and Scottish lawyers multiplied, and the printing press made their specialized case reports and treatises more available and authoritative. By 1600 the rule of law, as a pacifying alternative to group force and individual violence, had entrenched itself in the British Isles, increasingly on royal terms. In resolving their conflicts, therefore, most sixteenth-century people had learned to choose law courts over battlefields and back alleys, to rely on rule-based procedures more often than on vigilantes and handknives.

Definitions and Sources of Law

The historian's first duty is to ask if 'law' meant the same thing at the end of the six-teenth century as it did at the beginning, when Elizabeth I's grandfather, Henry VII, invaded and seized the throne in 1485. That duty is relatively easy for us to discharge in the twenty-first century. We have the best access yet to Tudor-Stuart-era evidence in archives and printed texts that convey the processes, results and mentalities behind their legal systems. Our difficulty as researchers, therefore, is the one within ourselves, as the distant observers: how can we ensure that what we find and describe in their sixteenth-century words about 'law' remains true to their meaning, especially if our present meaning of 'law' is different?

Our views of law exist in realities unimaginable to sixteenth-century men and women: first of all, most nations – although neither England nor Scotland – now have written constitutions, even declarations of 'rights'; there is no legal pluralism, only single and uniform sets of laws (whether for criminal or civil pleadings); we have only one chain of inferior-to-superior-to-supreme courts (with appeals from lower judgments); institutionalized legislatures meet regularly; popular voting for legislators is open to all citizens, albeit more recently to women; social equality, non-discrimination and disestablished religions are legally protected; lawyers are available to (almost) everyone; permanent administrative tribunals exist for everything from child welfare to investment fraud; and quasi-military police forces, as well as parking-meter attendants and crown prosecutors, enforce the law. None of this would make sense to anyone living in Tudor-Stuart Britain, even when we think that we see pre-modern seeds for our twenty-first century in their sixteenth-century legal realities.

Most councillors to the first two Tudor kings were five centuries closer than us to ancient meanings and nuances of 'law'. They studied that revived classical learning about law, and much else, that we label Renaissance humanism, modelled on texts from Athens and Rome. Thomas More's Book II of *Utopia* (1516), and even Edmund Dudley's *Tree of Commonwealth* (1510), echoed the defining ideas of Cicero's classical Roman law: 'the highest reason, implanted in Nature, . . . when firmly fixed and fully developed in the human mind, is Law . . . whose natural function it is to command right conduct and forbid wrongdoing.' The other part of law was justice, which Cicero said was also rooted in that same Nature; however, it could transcend those commands and prohibitions that were enacted in written law or recognized as custom. Justice therefore stood for 'right reason' which made all good men love fairness and seek equity for its own sake, particularly in a case where literal application of the law led to an unjust result. Even so, Cicero reminded Quintus, 'it is rather ignorance of the law than knowledge of it that leads to litigation' in the first place.[1]

These were precisely the definitional points that Christopher St German made in his first eleven chapters of *Doctor and Student* (1523). There were at least four originating 'laws' :

(1) the law eternal, emanating from the divine will, known by human reason, divine revelation and the order of a prince;
(2) the law of reason, alias 'the lawe of nature of resonable creature . . . wryten in the herte' of each individual;
(3) the law of God, in both the Hebrew Bible and New Testament, but not necessarily in the church's canon law; and
(4) the law of man, meaning that 'in every lawe posytyve well made is somwhat of the lawe of reason and of the lawe of god,' articulated in positive commands and negative penalties.[2]

All this added to Cicero the medieval Christian terms of reference, which St German borrowed heavily from the French Renaissance theologian Jean Gerson, and before him, from Thomas Aquinas. Both Thomas More and Christopher St German offered the late-medieval, pre-Reformation last gasps for 'law', defined as a fusion of the spiritual and temporal, sacred and secular, sources of authority.

St German's dialogue next addressed 'the lawe of Englande' as it existed in the 1520s. Thomas Cardinal Wolsey was then at the pinnacle of legal and ecclesiastical powers, Thomas More was hunting Lutherans when not sitting as an equity judge in the Duchy of Lancaster, and Henry VIII was recently named papal Defender of the Faith, loyal to Rome but flirting with Anne Boleyn. This 'law of Englande is groundyd upon syxe pryncypall groundes.' Again we get the law of reason, the law of God, but also four vague categories of 'dyvers generall customes of the realme', and then 'dyvers pryncyples that be called maximes', followed by 'dyvers partyculer customes', and lastly 'divers statutis made in Parlyamentes by the kynge & by the common Councell of the realme.' St German made clear that the first two types of law held pre-eminence over the final four. Parliamentary statutes came significantly last, as enacted when the other five 'semyd not to be suffycent' (i.e., merely supplementary), at least prior to the Reformation parliament (1529–36).[3] He made no explicit reference to case law and to precedent, certainly not in modern 'common law' terms.

But the references to customs, first in general and secondly in particular, plus the legal maxims, were St German's ways of recognizing a pre-eminent role for judge-made law in late medieval England. The legal reasoning was still deductive, with royal judges applying to individual cases the more universal customs and maxims that they knew in advance, unlike our inductive 'common law' reasoning based on selective precedential case law. St German's royal judges did not grow the law by linkage, one case judgment after another, to form an inductive chain of variously applied prior case judgments and statutes, which would harden into one discernible line for an authoritative rule, in the modern fashion. According to St German, in the 1520s judges still began each case with the appropriate rule, known 'by common learning'.[4] Like their medieval predecessors, early Tudor judges knew the customs and maxims in advance of any case, which was what the law-learning culture in their four Inns of Court was all about: students attended readings, learned cases from the year books, memorized writ formularies and studied statutes.

However, at least one other pre-Reformation dialogue writer, Thomas Starkey (d. 1538), found too many confusions in the varieties of law which St German and others praised. Starkey urged consolidation of the laws of nature, reason, custom and 'other lawys wryten & devysyd by the polytyke wytte of man' into a civil law that was not 'dyverse & varyabull'.[5] And that was what the English parliamentary Reformation era, 1529–59, did try to produce.

By stark contrast to St German's pre-Reformation law, the post-Reformation English law described by Thomas Smith in *De Republica Anglorum* (1565), had a far different sense of authority and legal reasoning. His treatise focused on a civil law originating in parliament and crown courts, not on abstract jurisprudence and the roles of reason, nature and God as sources of law. Smith (1513–77) asked how the common law was administered and altered, who the actual officials were who did such things, and about particular subordinates created by English law, such as wives, children and servants. How much of this was new, how much still ancient, by the early years of Elizabeth I's reign? New law or old law did not matter to Smith because parliament had become his centre of gravity for English sovereignty, effectively omnicompetent, though not quite omnipotent.

Still, Smith was not far off the modern view of parliamentary supremacy. St German, Starkey and Smith were experienced, credible insiders to the English legal system, separated in time by the several Reformation parliaments, 1529 to 1559. What a difference this made. Listen to Sir Thomas Smith's view of law: 'The Parliament abrogateth olde lawes, maketh newe, giveth orders for thinges past, and for thinges hereafter to be followed, changeth rights, and possessions of private men, legittimateth bastards, establisheth formes of religion, altereth weightes and measures, giveth formes of succession to the crowne. . . .' Statute law 'is the Princes and whole realmes deede. . . . And the consent of the Parliament is taken to be everie mans consent.'[6]

The law's sovereignty now rested on a secular source, the monarch-in-parliament. Smith's early Elizabethans recognized parliament as capable of doing what it pleased, albeit well within policy perimeters drafted and managed – sometimes tightly, sometimes generously – by the queen and her council. The focal period for the law's definitional change, then, was that thirty years between St German and Smith. Another generation later, by the 1590s, Smith's view was commonplace, whether personified by Sir Edward Coke (1552–1634) or Sir Francis Bacon (1561–1626). These robust competitors tended to locate the source of law according to whatever officer's hat each wore at the time.

When Coke wore the attorney-general's hat, he argued monarchy as a source of law; later as chief justice of common pleas it was judge-made case law, including the earth-shaking notion of judicial review of statute; and lastly as opposition leader in the House of Commons, the source was parliament. When he allowed law to be based on reason, it was because it agreed with his own reason; and the same could be said for the roles of nature and god. Still, his 'Proeme' to the *Third Part* of his *Institutes* made clear that 'pleas of the crown . . . for the most part [are] grounded upon, or declared by statute Lawes.' And for all of his absolute faith in judge-made common law, Sir Edward Coke could end his *Institutes* invoking his favorite aphorism: 'Blessed be the amending hand.'[7] Law was neither immutable nor incorruptible, and best not vested in a single person or institution. Coke was never a royal sycophant, which was probably why Queen Elizabeth I preferred him to Bacon and definitely why her 'divine right'-believing successor, James I, did the opposite.

When Bacon served as lord chancellor, and earlier as solicitor-general, he promoted equity and royal prerogative, even at the expense of Coke's kind of case law. But Bacon fancied himself more thinker than lawyer, one who could cross-examine nature and apply scientific method to law, in search of first principles and applied maxims. He built on St German's categories of law, rather than on Coke's practitioner's approach. In his *Brief Discourse Upon the Commission of Bridewell* (before 1587), Bacon emphasized that 'Maxims are the foundations of the Law, and the full and perfect conclusions of reason,' alongside and informing statutes and customs. In the *Case of the Post-Nati* (1608), directly related to Scots born after their Stuart king, James VI, had become the English king, James I, Bacon argued: 'for as the common law is more worthy than the statute law; so the law of nature is more worthy than them both.' He even supplied twenty-five maxims, each based on cited year-book and reported cases, as well as statutes; and he loved to spout aphorisms, paradoxes, formularies and repartees, as deductive rules to live by.[8]

Changes in English law across the Tudor century came as a matter both of thinking and of doing. Late medieval legal-judicial culture had emphasized transcendental sources such as nature, reason and God, while late-Elizabethans thought in terms of more earthly origins, of a legal positivism rooted in man-legislated statutes and man-adjudicated reported cases. This early-to-late Tudor contrast in law can be seen in other definers of law, many of them lawyers and judges, some chroniclers such as Polydore Vergil and Edward Hall, as well as scholars such as Thomas Elyot, William Lambarde and Richard Hooker. No parallel shift occurred in sixteenth-century Scottish views of law and would not until a hundred years later, beginning with James Dalrymple, Viscount Stair (1619–95).

This did not signify Scottish backwardness or English superiority but only the continuing difference between an increasingly case-based, judge-made, statute-bound English common law and that Scottish equivalent, which was a mix of Roman and feudal laws, by way of France and the Netherlands, combined with local customs and royal statutes. Stuart Scotland had legal authors as learned as the Tudor commentators; but, of course they had a different law, with different sources, to describe.

At the start of the sixteenth century, Scottish law was far more mixed and pragmatic than the English, sharing only their universal church's pre-Reformation canon law. Even their basic medieval legal treatise, *Regiam Majestatem*, which borrowed heavily from England's *Glanvill* (*c.* 1190), conceded that writing down all of the realm's laws was then (*c.* 1318) 'a wholly impossible task' because 'of the recorders' ignorance as well as the profusion and confusion of cases.'[9] Reading this seven centuries later, what is most intriguing is that late medieval Scots thought it desirable to collect all of their laws and statutes, a desire that would repeat itself well into the modern era. No Tudor Englishman, except perhaps Thomas Starkey, suggested such a similar need for a single collection of England's laws, although Coke's *Institutes* was an attempt of sorts, but not begun until years after Elizabeth I's death (1603).

Scotland's jumble of laws needed collectors rather than commentators. By the end of the sixteenth century its definition of law had remained consistent with that of Robert the Bruce (1274–1329): 'lawis, statutis, and ordinances, to be perpetuallie and inviolablie keipit and observit within his haill realme.' By the 1580s Sir James Balfour could declare that 'the law is devydit in thre partis.' Natural law, 'written be the finger of God . . . in the heart of man', and 'the law of God is that quhilk [which] is reveillit'; but, after this pious introductory paragraph, what mattered for the rest of the text was 'the law positive . . . made be man allanerlie [alone].'[10] The Scots spent far less time conceptualizing the law and much more in collecting, but not codifying, it. Sixteenth-century Scots, from start to finish, saw law in hard-nosed positive terms of what was legislated, adjudicated and manipulated.

This meant that they defined law more in monarchic terms, in keeping with the continental European, Roman law traditions. And unlike the English, Scottish jurisprudents actually debated openly whether or not monarchs held authority from on high, descending as inherent to the victor or heir of the office, or ascending from the community below, as an agent of sovereign subjects who could lawfully buttress, banish or behead them. John Mair, a contemporary of St German, More and Starkey, emphatically argued the latter view. George Buchanan's *De Jure Regni apud Scotos* (1578) justified deposing Mary Queen of Scots (1567). Adam Blackwood's *Apologia pro Regibus* (1581) countered by bringing Jean Bodin's French view of absolute royal sovereignty to Scotland. Of course the greatest proponent of this was Mary's son, James VI, who wrote a sermonette on the *Trew Law of Free Monarchy* (1598) and for whom the source of secular law was ultimately himself, as the divinely conceived choice.

Abundant original evidences for the many sources and definitions of law, as well as for its actual workings and failings in sixteenth-century legal systems, survive in the separate National Archives of England and Wales (London), of Scotland (Edinburgh), and in the National Library of Wales (Aberystwyth). Mountains of parchment and paper await the reader of plea rolls and courtbooks, offering a court's total context for lawyer's printed reports of highly select individual case judgments. Tracking down cathedral and parish records, as well as those in modern cities and towns, allows one to reconstruct how canon and customary law courts operated and to identify the poor souls who fell foul of religious rules and local by-laws. Study the books and essays by contemporaries like St German or Balfour as treatises on how the law was supposed to work. Then, only then, can one confidently begin to understand law in Tudor Britain, in its own words and institutions, starting with its law-makers.

Royal Parliaments and Statute Law

Royal and ecclesiastical legislative assemblies appeared throughout twelfth-century Western Europe, with parliaments not occurring in England until the second half of the thirteenth century. Edward I (1272–1307) regularized them there but also carried off Scotland's public records, which probably included evidence of its contemporary parliamentary acts. By 1485 both countries had routine institutions meeting only when the crown called them. In England's bi-cameral parliament, only its upper chamber of lay and spiritual nobles continued what had been one original parliamentary function: to act as a court of law, receiving petitions and adjudicating disputes by peers. Scotland's uni-cameral parliament, however, continued to make that juridical function its primary purpose.

In England, members summoned by name sat in the upper House of Lords, whether of secular or spiritual seniority. Writs of summons sent to the sheriffs for unnamed representatives gave no directions as to how such members of the House of Commons should be selected, only that they be landed knights of the counties or burgesses of the boroughs. Allegations of pre-election thuggery, false ballot counts and partisan mayhem came before the Tudor Court of Star Chamber; but with an electorate limited to landholding males, regardless of how 'rotten' a borough was, any challenge to a Tudor sheriff's election return sought damages rather than an overturn of the result, as John Baker has recently shown. The crown managed parliaments, not elections. When a Thomas Cromwell or William Cecil promoted a crown candidate in a particular constituency, the motive was partisan patronage, not ideological strategy. The English parliament's purpose was law-making, mainly by private bills but with a crown-controlled agenda for public bills that made tax grants assessed on personal property, not on land, the priority.

Over the century the English Commons increased in membership from 296 to 462. Beginning with the addition of Wales after 1536, there were thirty-four new members under Edward VI, twenty-five during Mary I's reign and sixty-two more with Elizabeth I.[11] The first Reformation parliament opened in 1529 with 310 members of the Commons, seventy-four knights from thirty-seven counties and 236 burgesses from 117 boroughs. Each constituency sent two members, except for London's four, with contested elections almost as rare as whale sightings in the Thames. Local landlords sorted out most nominees in advance of any poll, which was limited by statute of 1430 to the more substantial freeholders of land worth at least forty shillings. In Henry VIII's Reformation parliament the knight was usually a 'courtier-cum-local magnate' and most burgesses were actually resident in their towns, prominent as merchants or civic officers.[12] This changed dramatically by the end of Elizabeth I's reign, when almost 88 per cent of burgesses were actually rural country gentlemen. Contrast all of this with a pre-Reformation House of Lords that, in the 1529 parliament, totalled 107 members, fifty being bishops and abbots, and fifty-seven lords temporal (dukes, marquises, earls, viscounts and thirty-eight barons). That parliament permanently removed thirty-one abbots, by abolishing the monasteries, thus ensuring an Elizabethan House of Lords that was 'effectively secularised' and 'amenable to control by the Crown,' according to Sir Geoffrey Elton.[13]

The products, parliamentary statutes, became in Tudor England the ultimate laws because, when their tripartite makers, the monarch-lords-commons, agreed, a bill became a statute, the highest instrument of sovereign authority. There was no single parliament throughout a reign, only intermittent, separate parliaments called when the royal council needed them. Henry VII called seven during his twenty-four-year reign, meeting for a total of less than one year. His son held the most: nine sat for an overall 183 weeks between 1509 and 1547. Edward VI's minority council called two in six years but 'Bloody' Mary I reluctantly faced five in four years. Elizabeth I called ten, meeting almost 140 weeks in thirteen sessions during her forty-five-year reign, also with a decreasing sense of royal enthusiasm. None could match Henry VIII's reign for law reform and basic productivity: from 1509 to 1531, 148 out of 203 statutes were public bill enactments (i.e., not private-interest bills); but in the next eight years of Thomas Cromwell's management, over 200 public acts passed, out of 333, including those that purged the pope's authority, nationalized Christianity and put massive monastic revenues into royal coffers. Elizabethan parliaments looked lazy by comparison. Her forty-five-year rule brought enactment of only seventy-nine more statutes than Cromwell's eight years in power had generated.[14] There were high turnover rates of members, hence few professional parliamentarians; but at least increasingly uniform procedural rules existed over the century to ensure stable consistency in creating, amending and abolishing laws.

The same was true for Scotland, on a smaller scale, where the first recorded parliament which included burgesses sat in 1326. Unlike England, the late medieval parliaments in Scotland had delegated most powers to quasi-permanent committees, including a Committee for Causes, from which the judicial Court of Session emerged.

Whereas the English parliament of 1529 met first at Blackfriars monastery, within the City of London, then adjourned to Westminster Hall, the Scottish parliament by 1500 always sat at Edinburgh in a three-storeyed courthouse called the Old Tolbooth. It had shops, booths and tapestried walls on all sides, until converted into a gaol when the New Tolbooth replaced it in 1564. By 1500 England's parliament existed for legislative purposes but Scotland's was still primarily the occasion for public presentation of complaints and causes to the king and three estates (clergy, barons and burghs). Auditors would be appointed to hear the parties and to examine evidence and witnesses, before parliament made the judgment. While England's parliament mirrored rigid social hierarchy, Scotland's three estates sat as distinct groups but within a uni-cameral assembly that recognized the one-man, one-vote, simple majority rule on all bills and lawsuits. All members of the Scottish parliament had to wear uniform dress patterned by royal prescription, something utterly alien to English lords and commons. Even more unlike England, the Scottish sessions were open to the public, at least from the 1570s onwards. No women sat in either country's parliament, and Roman Catholics were disqualified from both after the 1560s.

Scottish monarchs called parliament much more routinely than did the Tudors, suggesting greater royal dependency and decentralized power. In the case of Mary Queen of Scots (1542–87) in the nineteen years of her minority and absence there were seventeen parliaments; she then called five during her six-year independent reign; and her son, James VI, placed on the throne aged one year, needed almost annual sittings. Between 1488 and 1587, the total membership averaged sixty-eight per parliament: twenty clergy and thirty barons, while the burgh commissioners grew from twelve in 1489 to thirty a century later. The big exception was the Reformation parliament of 1560, which John Knox and Calvinist supporters packed with 106 'petty barons'. After this, the role of the laird (a royal tenant-in-chief), as having an inherent right to a parliamentary seat, all but disappeared. As late as 1567 the thirteen bishops remained split almost evenly between Protestant and Catholic, but none of the latter existed after that. Of the twenty-seven abbots and seventeen priors of monasteries in pre-Reformation Scotland, most still held their parliamentary seats in 1597, as leaders from the legally established Presbyterian kirk of Scotland (1592). The number of burgh seats remained stable, with fifty in 1488 and seventy by 1600. Legislation from 1469 forbade the popular election of burgh representatives, which left selection in the hands of town councillors. Post-Reformation Scottish parliaments showed a marked attempt at royal management, with all major crown officers (such as the chancellor, treasurer, keeper of the privy seal, comptroller, justice clerk) prominently sitting.

Scotland retained a legislative institution, the royal convention, between the smaller privy council and the full parliament, which usually meant exclusion of burgh commissioners. Called less and less during the sixteenth century, the convention existed mainly to recognize changes of monarchs and to authorize taxation. Regarding the latter, the crown was expected to live from its own resources; but when an exceptional grant had to be made, the three estates assessed themselves as a bloc and then each decided how to distribute the burden. Unlike England, where parliamentary taxes were levied only on moveables, in Scotland the grant was based on land valuations. But taxation remained third on the list of Scottish parliamentary priorities, while in England's House of Commons it had a growing primacy of purpose, as a bargaining device for *quid pro quo* politics.

Because the Scottish parliaments made adjudication of disputes their primary business, their litigants could sue at first instance in both civil and criminal matters, particularly if their land-holdings were subject to crown and parliamentary grants. Its centrality in the judicial system meant that all trial judgments could also be appealed to it from all lower courts, even from seemingly administrative-type tribunals as high as the Lords-in-Council. That appellate process and status existed in only a severely limited way in England, to the House of Lords. More often the English judges, not the losing litigants, took tough cases into the exchequer chamber, seeking consensus. When the Scottish parliament exercised its secondary function, as legislator, it mainly renewed or revised previous acts or reformed procedural law.

The first Tudor king, Henry VII, allowed Richard Pynson to print texts of statutes in 1497; similarly, but not until 1541, James V ordered Thomas Davidson to print extracts (only) of acts passed in 1540. England continued to publish each parliament's full text enactments but would not attempt to create any official collection of statutes in force. Mary Queen of Scots, however, commissioned Scotland's first comprehensive collection of legislated law in 1566. Her six commissioners held authority

> ... to visie, sight and correct the laws of this realm made by the queen and her predecessors, by the advice of the three estates in parliaments held by them, beginning at the books of law called *Regiam Majestatem* and *Quoniam Attachiamenta*. ... So that no others but the said laws seen, mended and corrected by her said counsellors and commissioners ... shall ... have place, faith or authority to be alleged and rehearsed before any of her judges or justices whatsoever in judgment and outwith.[15]

This official version of royal parliamentary law began with enactments from 1424 but did not include customary or judge-made case law. This comprehensive approach continued with commissions in 1587, 1592 and 1598, all without parallel in England.

Crown Courts and Case Law

Throughout the sixteenth century all European countries, except the Swiss cantons, remained monarchist. Each had at least one royal dynastic family claiming control by inheritance over medieval crown executive powers. Chief among these were undivided, sometimes undifferentiated, powers to make, to enforce and to offer for dispute-resolution the accumulation of royal parliamentary statutes and recognized customs of the realm. England and Scotland separately developed a law common to each realm that royal officials administered in all localities, as agents of royal judges, wherever the royal writ – purchased by the plaintiff – issued and 'doth run'. The biggest difference between the two was that the royal common law's hegemony in England was a first in Europe, originating even before *Magna Carta* (1215), while in Scotland the royal consolidation did not occur until after 1532.

The powers to impose and to apply royal laws required that all subjects have access to royal law courts. Both countries had these in abundant varieties and venues, but again the differences could be dramatic. England's common-law system by 1485 offered four royal courts at Westminster Hall, plus itinerant royal justices travelling throughout the realm, and robust professional, self-regulating corps of lawyers and judges. All this expanded exponentially by 1603, partly at the expense of competing church, municipal, manorial and baronial jurisdictions. Scotland's pre-sixteenth century royal system of courts was based on committees of the king's council and in parliament. After Henry VIII's forces killed James IV and most of his nobles at

Flodden (1513), the regent Albany fled to France, leaving Scotland divided into four royal judicial districts under the control of numerous lords of council and session. Compared with England this was juridical chaos, making a mockery of the Edinburgh parliament's declaration in 1503 that only 'common law' should govern Scotland. This was the context explaining why Scottish royal justice barely competed with local and church courts, both in civil and criminal pleadings, and why 1532 became such a vital turning-point in Scottish judicial history.

All courts of law exist to service plaintiffs, civil and criminal, by offering to resolve disputes by peaceful, rule-based procedural alternatives to self-help acts of seizure, detention, defamation or mutilation in the name of restitution, revenge or right-eousness. Before the Criminal Justice Act (1587) regularized justice-ayres, to be held regionally in the spring and the autumn before royally appointed justiciars, they too often produced only war-lord local justice among the nobility and other landlords, with most thugs finding patron protectors. Even the best contemporary reports indicated that feuds and self-help operated commonly outside the law's reach. Inside the criminal law system, the indicted and convicted offender faced judicialized death by beheading, hanging, drowning, burning or torture. More minor offences also brought judicialized violence: mutilation, flogging, banishment, fines, forfeitures, the stocks and imprisonment. Whether this meant that Scottish criminal justice offered overkill or tit-for-tat, the message was clear: don't get caught, get good local lordship!

Scottish 'common law' for civil pleadings did not suffer such decentralized distortion. Cases brought by complainants before the Council or parliament, 1478 to 1532, were registered in the *Acta Dominorum Concilii*; but this record in no way yielded the sorts of quantifiable detail that English common-law plea rolls did. In 1532 the College of Justice Act instituted 'ane college of cunning and wise men, both of spirituale and temporal estate, for the doing and administration of justice.'[16] This fifteen-member court received papal recognition in 1535, as an independent, professional jurisdiction that effectively replaced parliament's first-instance trial activities. Twenty-six procedural rules of court, drafted by the judges, had been signed by James V at Edinburgh on 27 May 1532. This Court of Session, modelled in part on the Parlement of Paris and possibly the *Collegio dei Giudici* of Pavia, by the 1590s had full jurisdiction over all civil matters, including all actions involving the crown, as well as feudal property disputes and grants. It could order payment of debts, performances, damages, removals and restitutions, even reductions in parliamentary grants and in its own decrees. Unfortunately, systematic records of case files and pleadings do not survive, as they largely do for England, so we cannot measure patterns and effectiveness of central, royal court business.

By marked contrast, England had central, royal courts of common law in orderly, operational place since at least the 1190s. The *curia regis* soon divided into courts of the exchequer, then the King's Bench and Common Pleas, followed by growth of an equity jurisdiction in Chancery after the mid-fourteenth century. By 1485 the two parties in any lawsuit either travelled to Westminster Hall, in Middlesex, west of London, to appear before royal judges in person or by attorney, or (*nisi prius*) the judges rode to them, itinerantly at fixed semi-annual assize locations. English common law was applied locally in law-and-order prosecutions at county quarter-sessions before the justices of the peace. The court of King's/Queen's Bench took cognisance of all criminal cases, initiated mainly by indictment and tried by juries; and it welcomed a diversity of civil cases, including those by writs of trespass alleging violence (*vi et armis*) against the royal peace (*contra pacem domini regis*), as well as all personal actions initiated by bill. The Tudor court of Common Pleas invited every variety of civil disputes between subjects, where the crown had no stake in your case or you could not fictively allege this. Wherever the crown had a revenue interest, one could sue before the barons of the Exchequer, where most prosecuting informants alleged import-export smuggling or penal statute violations, such as retainder or usury. An action in these three common law courts began by purchasing the correct royal writ, each uniquely identifying the form of action that ordered the sheriff to summon the defendant. The Chancery, however, initiated civil actions by bills of petition, and its masters then sub-pœnaed the defendants and resolved disputes, not by applying the common law but by invoking 'equity and conscience'. By Henry VIII's reign, however, Chancery process and its 'decrees and orders' were growing into more predictable formulae.[17]

From our twenty-first-century observation deck, the case-counts alone confirm the rule of law: overwhelming quantities and varieties of lawsuits and broad public participation in the Tudor legal systems. Virtually all defendants at common law had the right to trial by jury, which meant that a huge number of male citizens had to be on call for every court day. Between 1490 and 1560, the population replacement rate remained stable but the numbers of cases initiated in the courts of King's Bench and Common Pleas grew two and one-half times, from 2,000 to 5,300 annually. Then, under Elizabeth I, the adult population doubled but yearly numbers of initiated cases quadrupled, and would hit 30,000 by 1640. The Exchequer under Henry VII had 1,782 cases over twenty-four years, with a slower but more steady growth for the rest of the Tudor century. The Chancery simply exploded in numbers and varieties of petitory bills filed between the 1480s and 1603.[18] Not every lawsuit pre-empted resorts to violence, but these numbers alone posited an extraordinary social commitment to rule of law, certainly contrasted with continental Europeans; and the common law courts offered only one system among several, to user-fee-paying plaintiffs at all levels.

This boom within English common law courts occurred alongside other royal courts, four that operated regionally and at least nine other new ones. There were busy palatine courts, exercising jurisdictions reserved to the crown over lands and tenants of the earldom of Chester (since 1237); of the duchy of Lancaster (since 1265) and of the palatinate of Lancaster (since 1351); of the feudal bishops of Durham (after 1536); and of the duchy of Cornwall (since 1337). The first two Tudors added five conciliar and four statutory courts. Henry VII's council, exercising prerogative powers, expanded the court of Star Chamber, initially to prosecute public riot and corruption, and created the court of Requests, initially for 'poor men's civil causes'. The two courts grew in popularity and clientele, because these petitory, in-person alternatives to common-law writ courts were reputedly faster and cheaper, perhaps more arbitrary, but usually saved you the cost of hiring a lawyer. The other three conciliar courts were regional, short-term experiments for the border areas: Henry VII's Council for the Marches of Wales and Henry VIII's Council of the North, against the Scots, and his short-lived Council of the West.

The Reformation parliament created four statutory courts, mainly to administer its nationalized church's properties: the court of Augmentations (1536), the court of First Fruits and Tenths (1540), the court of Wards and Liveries (1540), and the court of General Surveyors (1542). Again, procedurally and substantively these jurisdictions targeted new areas of royal revenues and grants, with all but the third being merged into the Exchequer after 1554.[19] All four stood as reminders of how economically and land-powerful the pre-Reformation church had been and the post-Reformation crown had become.

This plethora of courts and cases suggested law and order as a Tudor growth industry, at least for civil cases. Most attempts at law reform, by parliamentarians and judges, however, ended in frustration. In an agrarian economy with land as primal wealth, legislators held the law of real property to a virtual standstill but judges promoted a near revolution, recognizing the new roles in common law of the use, the trust and the will for family land settlements. The Statute of Uses (1535) and Statute of Wills (1540) had failed, as would dozens of Elizabethan bills for reforms that landlords in both Houses blocked. Elizabethan merchant interests supported what became the modern basis for bankruptcy law but also promoted the savagery of imprisonment for debt or for mercantile insurance disputes, in a century that knew no banks. In contracts and torts, two medieval centuries of debt and trespass actions would culminate in the gradual recognition, between the 1490s and Slade's Case (1602), of enforceable obligations: a mutual *assumpsit* to act required performance. The purpose in all such civil pleadings was restitution or compensation, so the adversarial winners and losers focused on things, mainly material but also spiritual, such as reputation and promises.

The purpose pursued in criminal pleadings was punishment; and the justification was based on the common-law obligations to keep the peace, to reject violence and to protect *meum et tuum* (what's mine is mine and yours is yours). To do the opposite, breaking the peace by using violence to take away anything not rightfully yours, was deemed evil in itself; but such types of acts were few in number: treason, homicide, robbery, larceny and burglary, rape, arson and embezzlement. All were felonies, for which the penalty was death; but, unlike Scotland, in England many endangered felons found escape by way of benefit of clergy, sanctuary, abjuration, purchased pardons, outlawry, and 'there but for the grace of god go I' juries! The impact of this necessarily miserable cul-de-sac in law, with its routine bloodshed, can never be measured accurately or humanely, beyond counting only those criminal acts reported and prosecuted, as tips of society's icebergs, regarding incidences of violence.

Canon and Customary Laws

If the central, royal, common-law courts of criminal and civil pleadings did not ensnare you, then the church, municipal, manorial and baronial courts might still seriously complicate your life. Alternatively the latter continued to offer local venues – more neighbourly, but not necessarily more friendly – for settling old scores, creating official records of transactions, claiming rights, prosecuting wrongs, contriving remedies and enforcing peace-promising settlements. The twelfth century had brought consolidation and regularizing of canon and customary legal systems in both countries, and the entrenching of England's common law. By 1485 in Scotland the local landlord-based jurisdictions had remained more vigorously intrusive, thanks to the weaker central institutions of kingship.

The pre- and post-Reformation churches simply expelled external Roman control, for England from the 1530s and Scotland in the 1560s. By 1600, however, there was still little structural change (for example, both retained bishops but allowed a married priesthood) and even fewer canon-law reforms either in substance or in enforcement. Traditionally the canon-law courts operated upwardly, with local archdeacons visiting parishes and deans overseeing cathedral chapters, and all were answerable upon appeal to the bishop's 'court of audience'. These lowest-level courts called upon the local laity to name fellow sinners, mainly to root out and publicly punish fornicators and adulterers. Religious reformers never challenged the validity or necessity for such church powers to continue. The issue was simply about control and, indeed, Elizabethan Puritans and Scottish Presbyterians were all the more keen to use these local courts to do God's work on earth, even if Calvin's God alone knew which sinners were predestined for salvation. Unlike England, by 1600 the kirk, not the king, was the primary prosecutor of most Scottish criminal, penal and moral offenders; and the judicial session's registers read like modern tabloid newspapers!

Above such local church courts, one episcopal consistory court operated in each diocese, where canon law and litigation focused largely on marriage and succession (probate or intestate) issues. Defamation, as when someone called a woman a priest's whore, was often real; but the even more prolific accusations of perjury were usually nothing more than covers for actions of debt, wherein the alleged defaulter had broken his word. The church's two biggest jurisdictions, over all matrimonial and testamentary matters, would continue until secularized in the nineteenth century, into what are now the family (common law) and probate (Chancery) divisions in each country. One could appeal from the bishop's consistory to the archbishop's provincial court and then to the papal rota court in Rome, before the Reformation. After, a court of High Commission adjudicated English church appeals, with final appeal to the High Court of Delegates. The Thirty-Nine Articles articulated the new faith but the law remained largely what Rome had developed. In Scotland, the General Assembly Act (1592) fulfilled the presbyterianizing that parliament's earlier Papal Jurisdiction Act (1560) necessitated: it abolished the papal hierarchy of courts and created a new, decentralized system of parish presbyteries and synods, with a general assembly, all devoted to rigorous enforcement of the First Book of Discipline. Thomas Cromwell's and Thomas Cranmer's 'anglican' church retained Rome's downward authoritarian structure, while John Knox's 'kirk' emerged by 1600 as a much more upwardly participatory institution, at least for the 'godly' sorts.

Municipal law, in English boroughs and Scottish burghs, dealt with local contractual, market, labour and product-quality regulation. It also made a routine of social and moral disciplines on urban residents and visitors, often duplicating the church court invigilations. Everything from debtor–creditor actions and forestalling in market price manipulation (buy low, hold to create scarcity, sell high) to gossiping, fornication, the size of a loaf of bread and the quality of a pint of beer appeared routinely in the municipal court records. There were over 500 royally chartered English boroughs by 1600. In Scotland as of 1488 there were fifty-two royal and seventy-eight non-royal burghs which grew by 1600 to sixty-nine and 185, respectively. English boroughs usually held two annual courts leet, to enforce regulations, and then monthly sessions for civil suits; Scottish burghs had a head court meeting three times each year: Michaelmas, Yule and Whitsun. The aldermen and the dozens

of presentment jurors passed their own legislation, exercised summary market jurisdiction, prosecuted property owners who failed to keep their parts of the borough
clean and in repair, annually elected bailiffs and constables, supervised the night-
watchers who enforced the curfews, and adjudicated actions of debt, trespass and
deceit. The City of London held three weekly courts, with losers routinely filing bills
of appeal into the royal Chancery: the court of Hustings heard real (land) actions
and both the sheriff's court and the mayor's court adjudicated personal actions. While
craft aristocracies exerted control in larger towns, sometimes through their own law
courts, the merchant gilds dominated most boroughs/burghs and even in the 1580s
the twelfth-century *Leges Burgorum* was still cited for authority across Scotland. These
urban elites were always disputatious, often fractious, but they still resorted to the
legal systems for debtor–creditor recoveries.

Politically, however, by 1603 control over most of their burgess seats in the central
government's parliament had slipped into gentry hands, of surrounding rural landlords. Finally, municipal law in the form of collected customs offered a classic example
of what Alan Watson has called 'legal transplants',[20] whereby Edinburgh, Aberdeen
and London were often models for other towns in Scotland and England, while copy-
cat Welsh boroughs looked to Hereford's royal charter and by-laws as their model.

The more ancient, rural counterpart to the chartered English borough had been
the hundred, as a subdivision within the shire, administered by the sheriff. Both
offered public jurisdictions, alongside private landlord courts of the manor and the
barony; but hundred and sheriff courts barely existed after 1485, used mainly for
small debts. By then, the crown commissioned county justices of the peace, sitting
in quarter-sessions four times annually and more frequently in petty sessions, often
presided in parallel to, and even in competition with, borough courts. The sheriff
remained the royal financial and administrative agent, especially for executing all
common-law court writs; but in Scotland he also retained judicial powers in his own
court and even began to act as a quasi-crown prosecutor in post-Reformation Courts
of Session.

In England the sessions were the spokes radiating from the royal hub at
Westminster Hall, bringing the wheel of common law throughout the countryside.
There, twice each year, judges from the three central courts rode to the several assize
towns to preside with local justices of the peace (JPs) over 'pleas of the crown' and
lawsuits (*nisi prius*) deferred from Westminster Hall back to the parties' locality. Such
regular courts were supplemented, when crises required, by irregular sittings of JPs
and Westminster judges on commissions of gaol delivery, *oyer et terminer* (to hear
and determine), and even for environmental matters regarding sewers and marshes.
All this signified how the central pre-empted the local law: the royal common law
saying to all subjects, if you cannot get justice from your landlord or borough, we
bring ours to you!

Most English and Scottish peoples still encountered law immediately in manorial
and baronial courts, owned and operated by their landlords. In Scotland, nobles and
barons secured parliamentary protection in 1567 for their medieval privileges, which
included holding court to adjudicate disputes between themselves and their tenants
(in other words, conflict of interest!), and between tenants, in matters of debt, pos-
sessory claim and minor bloodshed. Court books survive to show that losers could
appeal to the sheriff's court and that all proceedings had broad participation of the

parties, witnesses, presenting jurors and local functionaries. In England the manorial courts in the sixteenth century still played a special role in recording 'immemorial' copyhold estates, which had become the most pervasive way for medieval
subsistence folks to hold land, as tenants-at-will, sometimes heritable; by the early
sixteenth century common law recognized copyhold, and then protected it by
century's end. Manor courts thrived throughout Tudor England, often enforcing
borough-leet sorts of social regulations and always offering contract and tort relief,
rather like modern small-claims courts, for resident and non-resident tenants.

Lawyers, Literature and Education

If the rule of law was so popularly rooted and robustly growing in sixteenth-century
Britain, how much can be explained by the existence and activities of a legal profession? Viewed from the common law, the answer has to be 'a great deal'; but viewed
from countryside manors and boroughs, the answer remains obscured. Legal historians have consistently skewed the answer by focusing on pleaders and attorneys in
England's Westminster Hall, if only because common-law plea rolls offer easy access
to quantifiable data about them. The ratios told the story, as case-counts outpaced
population growth and lawyer-counts outpaced both: between 1485 and 1603 the
numbers of attorneys enrolled in Common Pleas and King's Bench grew, from about
200 to 1,000 at any given time, with the greatest growth after the 1570s; and the
number of pleaders went from 100-plus in the 1530s to nearly 450 a century later.
A lot of someones obviously needed and paid for such specialist skills, in hopes of
peaceful, enforceable winnings; but none of this explains why so many ordinary
people resorted to litigation, inside and outside the common law, why they willingly,
actively served time and 'truth' in courtrooms at all levels, and why they needed
lawyers in the first place.

To answer this one needs to know what sixteenth-century lawyers offered, by way
of services, that any do-it-yourself litigant could not do: learned professional expertise *versus* observed lay knowledge. Did going to any law court require knowing its
substantive law, for pleading purposes? or only its procedural rules and formularies,
either from the litigant's experience, as participant and observer in previous courtrooms, or from an outside advising attorney or document draftsman? The truth was
that most litigation, in both England and Scotland, then as now, ended on determination of fact and only unusually on the authority of law. England dramatically
expanded public access to courts that focused on summary fact-finding, and less on
law-defining: equity, prerogative and sessional jurisdictions. Such realities must have
encouraged litigants to appear in person, without lawyers, to 'prove the facts' in every
variety of law court. One suspects that, alongside lawyer-counts, we should be counting the un-lawyered litigants who appeared and pleaded in person.

For those who needed lawyers there were several ranks of expertise available in
England. The top pleaders were serjeants-at-law, half of whom could expect calls to
the bench after twenty years in ordinary practice. Next, the utter-barristers were
senior members of one of the four Inns of Court (Gray's, Lincoln's, Inner Temple,
Middle Temple).[21] They took turns as benchers and readers in the Inns, knew the
law in principle and how minutely to apply it, pleaded it in common-law jurisdictions using Law French, not English vernacular, and mastered its medieval Latin

vocabulary. Nevertheless, the vast majority of England's litigants did not need or use counsel. Still, it is lawyer's literature that survives, extending their eyes, ears and emphases to us: the late-medieval year books and, after 1536, the law reports, selected and published case-law records, mainly excerpting arguments, occasionally noting judgments, for these two types of pleaders. Over 300 collections of unprinted law reports, gathered by individual barristers and judges, survive from the Tudor common-law cases, two-thirds after 1575.

The rest of England's legal profession, at least 95 per cent, remained in the shadows, as solicitors, attorneys, scriveners and clerks. Most were local men, coming up to London to train for several years in one of eight Inns of Chancery, associated earlier in medieval times with the royal Chancery as *scriptorium*. Their apprentice-ships in these drafting and formulary schools emphasized the practical services clients needed, advising basic strategies for possessions and relationships, and then making that advice literal, and legally enforceable.[22] By 1585 there were, at any given time, 750 students in the Inns of Chancery, some training to be attorneys and clerks, others as young gentlemen and soon-to-be-heirs, with a small number hoping for entry to an Inn of Court. Any Elizabethan town had a half-dozen such attorneys, plying their profession from their homes, the parish church or the pub and market. While most students at the Inns of Court by 1603 had attended university (where no English law was taught!), and spent some time at an Inn of Chancery, most Inns of Chancery lads entered directly from local grammar schools.

Legal services were further supplied by the civil lawyers, albeit never more than a tenth of the numbers of common lawyers. In 1539 a royal order stopped the study of canon law in Oxford and Cambridge but a year later Henry VIII created a pro-fessorship in civil law. Remembering that family and inheritance laws survived the Reformation within the church and mainly outside the common law, ordinary folk still had to rely on canon law for routine matters regarding birth, marriage, bastardy, death, tithes, defamation and probate. The civilian profession divided into advocates, equivalent to common-law barristers, and proctors, or attorneys. Their schooling took place in Doctors Commons, founded in 1490, and their courtroom practice included dozens of church courts, the university courts, and royal courts of Admi-ralty and of Chivalry. The busiest civilian court was the Court of Arches, the highest trial court for the archdiocese of Canterbury. By 1590, the two civilian courts in Cambridge, for example, heard 150 cases annually, mainly for debt, trespass and assault; both sat at Trinity Hall, the vice-chancellor's court as a criminal jurisdiction and the commissary's court for civil suits.[23]

Unlike common-law education in England, controlled centrally in London inns by the professional bar and bench since the fourteenth century, Scotland located its civil- and canon-law studies in its universities (St Andrews, Glasgow, Aberdeen, and after 1555 Edinburgh). After 1560 canon law became an atrophied source, the legal profession became secularized and legal-judicial families began what would become dynasties. Advocates, or pleaders, came mainly from families of lairds, such as Henryson, Balfour, Skene and Sharp. Most studied law in French universities (Poitiers, Paris, Toulouse) after learning 'perfect' Latin at grammar school and having three years of Scottish university legal studies. Procurators, or attorneys, limited themselves to representing litigants and usually were knowledgeable about substan-tive law, also from university studies. For the third level, notaries, law was a 'practick', mainly a craft apprenticed by endless copying of forms from protocol books and chancery drafts. Parliament repeatedly tried to regulate the quality of notarial personnel and practices, evidently with mixed success before 1603. As with English solicitors, the Scottish notary was the universal draught-horse of the legal system, doing its land-conveyancing, certifying the literal records for minutes of proceedings, drafting contracts, betrothals, marriage bargains and inheritances, as well as countless varieties of charters, writs and all other legal instruments, royal and local.[24]

Conclusion

Earlier historians used the terms 'Tudor despotism' and 'Stuart absolutism' in debates about sixteenth-century Britain's political structure, often when they disliked the ways in which the religious Reformations developed; but none can contest the vigorous existence in each country of the 'rule of law'. The criteria used throughout this chapter for 'rule of law' have been:

(1) a conceptual, theoretical framework for sources of authority, be they divine, natural, positive, customary, or any combinations of these, that provided the rationale for public confidence in law as a best alternative in dispute resolution;
(2) a law-making institution, be it monarchy, aristocratic council, elected legislature or pure democracy, by which rules were declared and reformed, based on past experience and present necessity;
(3) a system of adjudicatory and administrative courts, both horizontal (trial) and vertical (appeal), with fixed, universally applicable procedures and doctrinal, substantive rules; and
(4) a balance of professional and lay people to operate these three elements, be they jurisprudents, pleaders, attorneys or notaries on the one hand or, on the other, ordinary folk committed to orderly lives as witnesses, plaintiffs, defendants, jurors, contractors, heirs, or tenant servants.

Both Tudor England and Stewart Scotland fulfilled these criteria, albeit often differently and with varying degrees of effectiveness. Given the awesome cornucopia of legal-judicial archives awaiting any student of sixteenth-century Anglo-Scottish cultures, one cannot avoid concluding that law was at the heart of their human condition.

ACKNOWLEDGEMENT

The author gratefully acknowledges careful readings of the penultimate draft by Alan Watson, Sir John Baker and Norman Jones, but remains accountable for this final product.

NOTES

1. Cicero, *De Legibus*, p. 317.
2. St German, *St German's Doctor and Student*, pp. 9, 13, 21, 27.

3. Ibid., pp. 31, 73.
4. Baker, *Introduction to English Legal History*, p. 226.
5. Starkey, *Dialogue between Pole and Lupset*, p. 11; in 1575, Sir Nicholas Bacon made a strong argument for consolidating and abridging statute law, which both the royal council and common lawyers also ignored (see Tittler, *Nicholas Bacon*, pp. 79–80).
6. Smith, *De Republica Anglorum*, pp. 78–9.
7. Coke, *Third Part of the Institutes*, p. 82; and *The Fourth Part*, p. [366], quoting Edmund Plowden (1518–85).
8. Spedding et al., *Works of Francis Bacon*, pp. 509, 647.
9. Cooper, ed., *Regiam Majestatem*, pp. 57–8.
10. Balfour, *Practicks of Sir James Balfour*, p. 1. By the eighteenth century the jurisprudential tendencies reversed. Scottish law would be a leader in the European Enlightenment, while English law paid little heed to theory and was more of a mass and mess of unabridged statutory, customary and case laws.
11. Elton, *Tudor Constitution*, p. 243.
12. Lehmberg, *Reformation Parliament 1529–1536*, pp. 9–13, 19, 37.
13. Elton, *Tudor Constitution*, p. 242.
14. Ibid., p. 228.
15. Walker, *Legal History of Scotland*, vol. III, p. 365.
16. Ibid., p. 509.
17. *Guide to the Contents of the Public Record Office*, pp. 7, 45, 114, 133.
18. Brooks, *Pettyfoggers and Vipers*, pp. 48–74.
19. *Guide to the Contents of the Public Record Office*, pp. 80, 86, 150, 172–86.
20. Watson, *Legal Transplants*, pp. 29–30 and, regarding Scotland, pp. 36–56.
21. Prest, *The Inns of Court*, p. 7, noting that '. . . the rate of annual admissions to the inns quadrupled between 1500 and 1600.'
22. Their basic copybooks identified their tasks and services, for example: [John Waylye], *Tenour and Forme of Indentures* (1550), and John Rastell's legal vocabulary (1523).
23. O'Day, *The Professions in Early Modern England*, pp. 159–60.
24. Walker, *Legal History of Scotland*, vol. III, pp. 373–94.

BIBLIOGRAPHY

Bacon, Francis, *The Works of Francis Bacon*, ed. James Spedding, Robert L. Ellis and Douglas D. Heath (London, 1859), vol. VII.

Baker, John H., *An Introduction to English Legal History* (4th edition, London, 2002).

Balfour, James, *The Practicks of Sir James Balfour of Pittendreich*, ed. Peter G. B. McNeill (Edinburgh, 1962).

Brooks, Christopher W., *Pettyfoggers and Vipers of the Commonwealth: The 'Lower Branch' of the Legal Profession in Early Modern England* (Cambridge, 1986).

Cicero, Marcus Tullius, *De Legibus*, trans. Clinton W. Keyes (London, 1928).

Coke, Edward, *The Third Part of the Institutes of the Laws of England* [and] *The Fourth Part* . . . (London, 1644).

Cooper, Thomas Mackay, ed., *Regiam Majestatem and Quoniam Attachiamenta* (Edinburgh, 1947).

Elton, G. R., *The Tudor Constitution* (Cambridge, 1960).

Guide to the Contents of the Public Record Office, Vol. I, *Legal Records, etc.* (London, 1963).

Lehmberg, Stanford E., *The Reformation Parliament 1529–1536* (Cambridge, 1970).

O'Day, Rosemary, *The Professions in Early Modern England, 1450–1800: Servants of the Commonweal* (Harlow, 2000).

Prest, Wilfrid R., *The Inns of Court under Elizabeth I and the Early Stuarts, 1590–1640* (London, 1972).

Rastell, John, *The Exposicions of Termys of Law of England and the Nature of the Writts* (London, 1523).

St German, Christopher, *St German's Doctor and Student*, ed. T. F. T. Plucknett and J. L. Barton (London, 1974).

Smith, Thomas, *De Republica Anglorum*, ed. Mary Dewar (Cambridge, 1982).

Spedding, James, Ellis, Robert L. and Heath, Douglas D., *The Works of Francis Bacon* (London, 1859), vol. VII.

Starkey, Thomas, *A Dialogue between Pole and Lupset*, ed. T. F. Mayer (London, 1989).

Walker, David M., *A Legal History of Scotland*, vol. III, *The Sixteenth Century* (Edinburgh, 1995).

Watson, Alan, *Legal Transplants: An Approach to Comparative Law* (2nd edition, Athens, GA, 1993).

Waylye, John, *An Introduction to the Knowlege and Understandyng aswel to make as also to perceyve the Tenour and Forme of Indentures: Obligations, Quyttances, Bylles of Payment, Letters of Lycence, Letters of Sale, Letters of Exchange, Protections, Supplycatyons, Complayntes, a Certificat, and the copy of save condyte* (London, 1550).

FURTHER READING

L. W. Abbott, *Law Reporting in England 1485–1585* (1973).

John H. Baker, *The Legal Profession and the Common Law: Historical Essays* (1986); and *The Oxford History of the Laws of England, VI: 1483–1558* (2003).

John H. Baker and S. F. C. Milsom (eds), *Sources of English Legal History: Private Law to 1750* (1986).

John G. Bellamy, *Criminal Law and Society in Late Medieval and Tudor England* (1984).

James S. Cockburn, *History of English Assizes, 1558–1714* (1972).

David M. Dean, *Law-Making and Society in Late Elizabethan England: The Parliament of England, 1584–1601* (1996).

David M. Dean and Norman L. Jones (eds), *The Parliaments of Elizabethan England* (1990).

G. R. Elton, *The Parliament of England 1559–1581* (1986); *Policy and Police: The Enforcement of the Reformation in the Age of Thomas Cromwell* (1972); and *Reform by Statute: Thomas Starkey's Dialogue and Thomas Cromwell's Policy* (1970).

C. H. S. Fifoot, *History and Sources of the Common Law: Tort and Contract* (1949).

Michael A. R. Graves, *Early Tudor Parliaments* (1990).

Charles M. Gray, *Copyhold, Equity, and the Common Law* (1963).

Alan Harding, *A Social History of English Law* (1966).

Richard H. Helmholz, *Roman Canon Law in Reformation England* (1990); and *Select Cases on Defamation to 1600* (1985), vol. 101.

Ralph A. Houlbrooke, *Church Courts and People During the English Reformation, 1520–1570* (1979).

Martin Ingram, *Church Courts, Sex and Marriage in England, 1570–1640* (1987).

Eric W. Ives, *The Common Lawyers in Pre-Reformation England: Thomas Kebell, a Case Study* (1983).

W. J. Jones, *The Elizabethan Court of Chancery* (1967).

Henry A. Kelly, *The Matrimonial Trials of Henry VIII* (1976).

Brian P. Levack, *The Civil Lawyers in England 1603–1641* (1973).

Hector McKechnie (ed.), *An Introductory Survey of the Sources and Literature of Scots Law* (1936).

Hector L. MacQueen (ed.), *The College of Justice: Essays by R. K. Hannay* (1990); and (ed.), *Miscellany Four* (2002).

G. C. H. Paton (ed.), *An Introduction to Scottish Legal History* (1958).

O. F. Robinson, T. D. Fergus and W. M. Gordon, *European Legal History: Sources and Institutions* (1994).

Jenny Wormald, *Court, Kirk and Community: Scotland 1470–1625* (1981).

CHAPTER SIX

County Government in England

STEVE HINDLE

The polity over which the Tudors assumed control at the end of the fifteenth century, although notoriously destabilized by the political violence characteristic of an aristocracy who recognized ineffective kingship when they saw it, had long been considered one of most centralized and bureaucratized states in medieval Europe. During the thirteenth and fourteenth centuries, the central courts rained hailstorms of writs every year upon county sheriffs who were required to enrol, copy and forward them to subordinate officers within their jurisdictions and to endorse, reply and return the originals to the central authority which had issued them.[1] The early Tudors therefore inherited a financial and judicial infrastructure that provided the basis for the incremental, episodic process of incorporating the peripheries into a unified stable sovereign state.[2] In this respect, the Tudor achievement was two-fold: first to pacify their over-mighty subjects, especially in the far north where provincial magnates enjoyed a very ambiguous relationship with the crown; and second to transform them and their clients into servants of the regime in the localities. Both the Tudor peace and the creation of a series of loyal and obedient local elites were achieved, even more remarkably, on the cheap. The Elizabethan regime was staffed by a salaried bureaucracy of only 1,200 officials, a tiny cadre of officeholders dwarfed by that of France where the central and local government of Henri IV was carried out by between forty and fifty thousand paid officials, many of whom inherited their offices. Much of Tudor governance was, perforce, carried out by amateurs who volunteered their service out of a combination of desire for national or local recognition of their honour and prestige and of an ethos of public duty which was derived partly from the tradition of classical republicanism mediated through the humanist curricula of grammar schools and universities and partly from indigenous habits of political participation in the institutions of manor, parish and county.

The texture of Tudor local government varied not only between regions but also between counties within regions (perhaps also even between areas within counties such as Gloucestershire or Warwickshire), and was shaped both by the depth and breadth of political participation and by the quality of social relations between those who participated. The presence or absence of a dominant magnate family such as the

Howards in East Anglia, the Stanleys in the north-west or the Percies in the far north; the fate of the estates of wealthy ecclesiastical foundations broken up as a result of the disendowment of the church; the geographical distribution of gentry seats; the existence of factional strife, whether driven by conflicts of ideology or of personality, among the resident gentry; the willingness, perhaps even the enthusiasm, of more humble householders to shoulder office-holding responsibility when their social superiors proved unwilling, or unable, to do so: all these factors (and more) might influence the exercise and experience of authority in the localities. These factors were, moreover, not only structural but also dynamic, and the nature of county governance undoubtedly changed over the course of the century, sometimes very rapidly, and occasionally even unexpectedly. Norfolk provides perhaps the best single example of a revolution in local government, with the destruction of the duke of Norfolk in 1572 transforming the political environment from one of unchallenged aristocratic supremacy to one of endemic petty conflict between gentry factions untrammelled by considerations of patronage.[3] The impact of the duke's fall in neighbouring Suffolk could not, however, have been more different, with the protestant gentry easing themselves into a position of collective leadership virtually unopposed by what was left of the Howard affinity.[4] In some respects Elizabethan Suffolk, dominated at it was by an oligarchy of godly gentlemen, had more in common with the consensus that prevailed in distant Northamptonshire than it had with neighbouring Norfolk. As these examples show, even adjacent county elites might respond in radically different ways to the contingencies of national politics. Nor should it be assumed that internecine strife between gentry families was invariably fuelled by religious difference. To be sure, the political complexion of a county like Kent might gradually be disfigured by the rise of ideological politics in the Elizabethan and early Stuart periods.[5] On the other hand, however, the antagonism between the Grey and Hastings families in Leicestershire long predated the Reformation and extended into the crisis of the mid-seventeenth century.[6] The resulting picture of county governance in Tudor England (and Wales) is, by definition, a mosaic, but nevertheless one in which certain patterns are clearly discernible.

This chapter describes and analyses three of these patterns in turn: first, the social profile of participation in county government; second, the obligations and responsibilities of those who participated; and third, the character of relations between the crown and the peripheries. It will conclude by suggesting that although participation was one of the defining structural characteristics of Tudor local government, Englishmen were developing habits of association and obedience which had taken on a momentum of their own by the end of the sixteenth century. The paradox of state formation in this period was that the strengthening of the hands of local elites only served to reinforce, and was in turn reinforced by, the growing authority of central government. The county, and even the parish, elites of England were to a very large extent self-governing, but theirs was 'self-government at the king's command'.[7]

Bearing Rule: The Social Profile of Participation in Local Government

Who, then, should the king command to bear rule on his behalf? The answer to this question fluctuated over the course of the sixteenth century. The problem was first posed against the background of the Wars of the Roses, a cycle of instability and law-lessness created by a nobility which paradoxically, in Henry VII, provided the first Tudor monarch, and yet at the same time ensured that he and his successors would always be suspicious of them. Magnates had, of course, been the natural choice as county governors throughout the medieval period. On the one hand, their presence in the counsels of monarchs, in the House of Lords, and at the royal court ensured that they might easily communicate the grievances of their affinities to the crown. On the other, their local knowledge; their ties of kinship and patronage with the provincial gentry; and the natural deference that they might command from their tenants ideally suited them to broker royal authority in the shires. The danger was that their substantial local standing might serve as a power base independent of royal patronage, which (if combined with financial strength) might allow them – as Richard, duke of York, Edward, earl of March and Henry, earl of Richmond had done – to outface, and perhaps even militarily outmatch, the monarch. Accordingly Henry VII placed little trust in his nobility, preferring instead a dual strategy of highly selective patronage to reliable 'known men' such as the earls of Oxford or Derby or the duke of Bedford, who were trusted with extraordinary powers in their own local-ities, with a more general campaign of political terror against those aristocrats whose loyalty might be suspect.

Over time, however, both crown and nobility came to recognize that fear and intimidation were not the most stable of platforms for a successful working relation-ship. Henry VIII persuaded his aristocracy that their interests were best served by dancing attendance on him at Court at Whitehall, and in return he allowed them to exercise authority on his behalf in the provinces. Successful politicians, like the Talbot earls of Shrewsbury, the Brandon dukes of Suffolk and the Howard dukes of Norfolk, recognized the advantages of playing this political game and accordingly cultivated an ethos of service that eventually found reward in grants of office even in regions far removed from their own estates. By the mid-sixteenth century, it was possible for noblemen like Edward Seymour, duke of Somerset or John Dudley, duke of Northumberland to achieve political supremacy precisely *because* of their service to the crown. By the end of the Elizabethan period, moreover, influence on the council and at Court was an indispensable supplement to landed wealth if an aristocrat wished to dominate the politics of his county. The earlier Tudors had therefore created an office-holding aristocratic elite, whose administrative expertise and military prowess was exercised in the provinces on behalf of the crown; an elite that was, moreover, ideally at least, synonymous with the ancient nobility. Even in the late sixteenth century, however, Elizabeth showed a marked reluctance to create new peers, reflect-ing a residual suspicion of the ambiguous loyalties of aristocrats that her grandfather would easily have recognized.

Royal mistrust of aristocrats as potential governors of the localities had always been latent: noble houses were, after all, just as vulnerable to the accidents of minority and lunacy as was the crown itself. This suspicion was, however, exacerbated during the reign of Henry VIII by the fact that his two great ministers were themselves rela-tively low-born. Although both Thomas Wolsey and Thomas Cromwell ultimately acquired the estates and titles that gave them an entrée to the world of aristocratic privilege, neither enjoyed the personal connections or clientage that would lubricate relations with the ancient nobility.[8] Accordingly they were more at ease with the gentry, whom they came to prefer as prospective rulers of the counties partly because they were not intimidated by them and partly because they recognized that gentry governance might incur both fewer political risks and lower financial costs than did aristocratic patronage. In any case, reliable magnates were few and far between, and in the absence of a dominant nobleman, the crown had to grant office directly to gentlemen, who might be persuaded to serve the king where they had once served the local magnate, creating a royal affinity in the localities.

On the face of it, the crown might have chosen to exploit one or more of several professional offices for the purpose of governing the localities. The sheriff, who had long been nominally responsible for co-ordinating the judicial, military and financial administration of the county, was one such appointment, but since the shrievalty was held for one year only, its holder could guarantee neither continuity nor consistency. Another possibility was the coronership, an office originally created in the twelfth century as a counter-weight to the authority of the sheriff (a balance reflected in the fact that coroners were appointed for life) and granted responsibility for the pleas of the crown.[9] By the fifteenth century, however, the power of each of these offices was vestigial and over the course of the sixteenth their powers were gradually to be side-lined by the bolstering of the authority of two other medieval offices: those of the itinerant judiciary and the county magistracy.

As early as the thirteenth century, the crown had recognized the desirability of sending royal judges out from Westminster into the localities to try felons and hear civil pleas in the county towns of provincial England. By the sixteenth century the Justices in Eyre and their successors the Justices of Assize were riding out twice a year in pairs, each of them perambulating one of the six assize circuits (into which English counties were grouped) in spring and autumn. These visits, as we shall see, came to enjoy political as well as judicial significance, but they were too infrequent in and of themselves to allow the judges to leave an enduring political imprint of royal policy in the provinces.

The Tudors' preferred alternative was, therefore, to place increasing reliance on the county magistrates or justices of the peace (JPs), an office that had enjoyed a gradual rise to prominence since its foundation in the fourteenth century. From 1363, JPs had been required to meet four times a year in each county on the bench at quarter-sessions where they would handle the routine administrative and judicial business of county government. In 1461, the shrievalty was required to surrender its most significant judicial powers to the magistracy. From the mid-sixteenth century, the crown built on these developments both by using assize judges as intermediaries between the central government and the county benches, especially through the use of circuit and assize charges delivered by the lord keeper to the judges and in turn by judges to county magistrates; and by increasing the powers of the JPs themselves. So confident was Thomas Cromwell in particular that magistrates rather than magnates might prove to be more reliable agents of the regime in the localities that those areas of the realm which had not previously been subject to the authority of JPs, especially the shires of the principality of Wales, had commissions of the peace issued for them from the 1530s. By the Elizabethan period, magistrates were meeting in small groups in each hundred or wapentake of several counties at 'petty' sessions every six weeks; exercising very significant summary powers acting singly or in pairs out-of-sessions;[10] and (most importantly of all) administering the 'stacks' of penal statutes for which Tudor legislation made them responsible.[11] Even though the terms of the commission of the peace were changed in 1590 to ensure that felonies (capital crimes) could be tried only by royal judges at assizes rather than by county magistrates at quarter-sessions, the powers and responsibilities of JPs had been substantially augmented by the end of the sixteenth century.

Magistrates were appointed at the crown's pleasure by virtue of a commission of the peace issued for each county by the monarch in consultation with the lord keeper. Their numbers could be reduced or augmented by the simple expedient of issuing a new commission that dropped names from, or added names to, the list of appointments. Magistrates could, therefore, never be sure that they were appointed for life and lived in constant fear of the shame of being put from the commission. More significantly still, the office carried with it no salary (its only recompense being the fees which magistrates' clerks were due for the drawing up of legal documents), and those who received it were expected to regard the commission itself as sufficient reward and recognition of their local standing and influence.[12] There was, correspondingly, enormous pressure on, and competition among, the gentry to serve on the bench and both inclusion in the commission and promotion to a higher order of precedence within it might be treasured as a marker of increased prestige and reputation. The whole system depended on an ethos of participation according to which those with local influence felt obliged not only to recognize but also to fulfil their duty to serve the crown. From the early sixteenth century, moreover, the crown was deliberately engineering the county commissions in order to grant local influence to the 'king's servants'. Not only were local landowners and JPs sworn to the king's affinity, therefore, but courtiers and trusted members of the royal household were conversely 'placed' strategically in the commissions of the peace.[13] The intention, not always realized, was to create an identity of membership between the king's affinity within a given county and the commission of the peace. The problem, of course, was that the crown's territorial power extended nowhere near far enough to make this goal achievable, and the vast majority of magistrates served not because they were king's men but because the king recognized that the localities could not be governed without them, or men like them.

Thus is was that several thousands of gentlemen, esquires, knights and minor peers voluntarily undertook the onerous responsibilities of justice and administration required by the king's commission of the peace: drawing up warrants and indictments for felony, riot and misdemeanour; taking examinations and depositions from those who were accused of, or were witnesses to, crime; policing breaches of the peace through the system of recognizances and sureties; co-ordinating and supervising the administration of the Poor Laws; apprehending and interrogating vagrants; regulating contracts of service, apprenticeship and employment under the labour statutes; licensing alehouses and monitoring the conduct of those who both ran and frequented them; dispensing justice collectively on the quarter-sessions bench and individually in the parlours of their country seats. The gentry carried out all these duties alongside the social and economic responsibilities customarily expected of landlords: administering their estates; summoning manorial courts, exercising hospitality, maintaining the 'theatre of the great', presiding over the countryside as paragons of paternalism.[14]

In the late fifteenth century, a dozen or two magistrates might serve in each county commission, and in each case a smaller knot of more dedicated and reliable men would usually prove more conscientious and active than their colleagues, a tendency reflected in the rhetoric adopted by successive lord keepers of the great seal who castigated the majority of 'slow-bellied' magistrates who slept like 'idle drones' while a dedicated but small swarm of 'busy bees' did most of the work on the bench. As the burden of local government increased, however, the crown realized that the county commissions had to be increased in size, an impulse that was characteristic of the 1520s and 1530s and the 1590s in particular. It was equally common, however, for the crown to assert its authority by *purging* the magistracy: picking, choosing and dismissing its local agents in the light of their record of achievement and, increasingly, with special reference to their religious affiliations. It is axiomatic, therefore, that the lord keeper was anxious to create and maintain an effective network of surveillance through which assize judges, and occasionally even paid informers, might provide an adequate flow of information on the conduct of particular magistrates. Purges, which had only limited effect under Wolsey and Cromwell, became increasingly effective under Elizabeth, and are the ultimate proof that by the end of the Tudor period, central government had the whip hand in its relationship with provincial elites. As a seller of patronage in a seller's market, the crown was able to dictate the terms of service.

The ethos of royal service was not, however, restricted exclusively to the gentry. In *De Republica Anglorum*, published in 1583, the humanist civil lawyer Sir Thomas Smith famously described the social structure of the English commonwealth in terms of four ranks of men, descending from the gentry at its apex to day-labourers at its base. Simultaneously, however, he noted the more fundamental distinction between 'them that bear office, and them that bear none'. In this way, Smith transformed his own four-class social hierarchy into a binary, indeed adversarial, model of political participation. The threshold of access to office-holding was, he nevertheless argued, relatively low. Smith noted that, next to the gentry, yeomen had 'the greatest charge and doing in the commonwealth' and conceded that in villages even 'such low and base persons' as 'poore husbandmen', 'copiholders' and 'artificers' (among others) 'be commonly made Churchwardens, alecunners, and manie times Constables, which office touch more the commonwealth'.[15] Smith's list of the considerable public responsibilities exercised by the middling sort included 'administration in judgements', 'correction of defaults', 'election of offices', 'appointing and collection of tributes and subsidies' and 'making lawes'. Thus even in the formal tradition of political thought, the widespread participation of men of middling status was recognized as a significant structural characteristic of the English state. It seems likely that only a minority of rural villages could even claim a resident squire, let alone a magistrate, in the Elizabethan period, ensuring that only the yeomen – the 'plebeian', 'vulgare and common sorte of people' of whom the heraldic purist Sir John Ferne was so dismissive in 1586; the 'midle people, betweene Cottagers and gentlemen' of whom George Tooke wrote so approvingly in 1635 – were present to run their local affairs. Rural governance in particular therefore became increasingly reliant on men of middling rather than gentle status.[16]

This is not to say that participation was uncircumscribed. The most obvious criteria of exclusion were those of wealth and gender. Service in county, hundred and parish was invariably limited by qualifications of property, and even female heads of household who owned property of sufficient value were prevented from being empanelled among the 'twelve good men and true' who made up the criminal trial juries at assizes and quarter sessions. The patriarchal nature of local government was also reflected in the constitution of parish meetings, where the bishops' faculties which stipulated the rules and regulations of vestry attendance and participation began in the late sixteenth century to adopt a generic formula as justification for the circumscription of participation in parish affairs. While the number and *quorum* of vestrymen might therefore vary from parish to parish, the impulse behind the creation of these 'select vestries' was a general desire to exclude the poorer sort of people who had no stake in the running of communal affairs. In Ealing (Middlesex), for instance, parish meetings had allegedly been characterized by 'much disorder', both in 'taxing men indiscretely by the consent of the inferior sort of people' and 'in disorderly placing of many in the church contrary to their rank and degree'. At Isleworth (Middlesex), audits had apparently been undermined by the dissent of the 'evil disposed and others of the inferior and meaner sorte of the parishioners'. At Twickenham (Surrey), such dissent had been all the more significant because 'the meaner and inferior sort of the multitude were so far the greater in number'. At Enfield (Middlesex), the formula referred to 'the great confusion and disorder at the church meetings by reason of the ignorance and weakness in judgement of matters of that nature by some of the parishioners that resort thither'. The result was 'great disquietness and hindrance to the good proceedings which they desire should be in their parish'. At Chigwell (Essex), the admitting of 'the parishioners of all sorts' to their church meetings had created confusion and disorder since so many of them were 'ignorant or weak in judgement and others were not so readie to yield to that which the better sort of the parishioners would determine and agree upon as they should be'. Business could not therefore be dispatched without much 'difficulty and trouble'.[17] Just as county governance became dominated by the leading gentry, therefore, power in the parishes increasingly became consolidated in the hands of self-selecting groups of chief inhabitants, whose self-image was, as in the Wiltshire parish of Swallowfield, that of 'men of discretion, good Credett, honest Myndes & Christian lyke behaviour one towards another'.[18]

By the end of the sixteenth century therefore, the governance of rural England had come largely to depend upon the active participation of a body of male property-holders of noble, more especially of gentle, and even of middling status who, through their skilful management of county quarter-sessions and parish vestries, bore rule on behalf of the crown. To what end did they exercise authority in the governance of county and parish alike? To answer this question requires a more detailed look at the responsibilities and obligations of the various offices to which magnates, gentlemen and yeomen were appointed.

Chains of Command: The Exercise of Authority in the Localities

The most significant institutional innovation in Tudor local government was the creation of the lieutenancy, an office designed to improve defence and security. Lord lieutenancies were first introduced for groups of counties in 1550 when the paroxysm of disorder with which southern and central England had been seized during the 'commotion tyme' of 1549 necessitated special measures to deal with popular unrest. As was so often the case with institutional reform in sixteenth-century

England, the experiment proved short-lived and only sporadically successful. By the 1560s, the military governance of the counties had devolved back onto the militia levies co-ordinated by the JPs (which had become common during the war-torn 1540s), who were for this purpose constituted in each county into commissioners for musters under the terms of a statute of 1558. The demands of renewed war had by the 1580s placed too great a strain on this system, however, and the lieutenancies were reintroduced as a permanent element within the office-holding structure, the crown usually granting the commission to trusted courtiers with a power base in the county concerned, such as the Stanleys in Lancashire and Cheshire or the Talbots in Derbyshire, or less commonly appointing an outsider who had a seat on the privy council, as in the case of Lord Hunsdon in Norfolk in 1585.[19] As we shall see, however, the deliberate augmentation of their powers ensured that by the late sixteenth century lords lieutenant were not merely military commanders of the county militia but also supervisors of a very wide range of administrative activity in county government. Indeed, their political role in county government was more significant than their military responsibilities, since most of the work of marshalling the trained bands was carried out by deputy lieutenants, who were primarily drawn from the ranks of the gentry.

If lord lieutenants came to exercise one kind of supervision over the magistracy, another was exercised by the judges of assize. The periodic presence in the localities of the itinerant judiciary, who arrived biannually to deliver the county gaols, was intended to assume the 'awful remoteness of a divine visitation'.[20] Contemporaries were very familiar with the idea that the assize circuit was a channel of communication between central government and local elites. The judges were the eyes 'fixed in the king's sceptre' and carried the 'two glasses or mirrors of the State': the representation of 'the graces and care of the king to the people', and the presentation of the 'distastes and griefs of the people' to the king.[21] Even so, the crown was concerned that these channels should be impersonal, untainted by the networks of patronage and association that might divert the flow of information or pervert the course of justice. The crown therefore repeatedly shuffled the judicial partnerships on the assize circuits in order to prevent the evolution of too cosy a relationship between over-familiar judges and complacent county benches. County assizes were therefore a form of political theatre, in which judges formally met the magistrates in a ceremonial atmosphere where a strict order of precedence and honour was maintained.[22] Part of the judges' responsibility was to intimidate and flatter the county elite into performing the crown's wishes, but they were also required to upbraid the county freeholders who made up the grand and criminal trial juries, among whom they exhorted conscientious performance of solemn judicial responsibility and to whom they gave detailed charges of the statutes which the crown expected to see enforced. The 'gentlemen' of grand jury (the title was usually honorific, temporarily granted to those yeomen who were empanelled), the judges argued, were the conscience of the county community in whom the 'trust of the country' was invested. Trial jurors were the 'eyes of the country', chosen as 'men of conscience and uprightness'.[23] Every time judge and jury came face to face, the judicial priorities of the state and the local community were rearticulated.

If the sensory functions of county government were exercised by judge and jury, its motor functions were provided by the magistrates themselves. Numerous case studies of the political dynamics of local society have revealed the ways in which 'country gentlemen commissioned by the king' not only responded to, but themselves shaped, the demands of government: resisting the appointment of provost marshals to round up vagrants as prohibitively expensive; raising constitutional doubts about the legality of control of the grain markets under the royal prerogative; delaying the construction of county bridewells pleading the recalcitrance of taxpayers and the corruption of their masters; neglecting the enforcement of the poor laws on the grounds that householders would rather exercise traditional habits of charity and hospitality than suffer compulsory assessments. There is now a substantial scholarly literature on county government in Tudor England, much of it written up from gentry papers and concerned largely, though not quite exclusively, with the politics of the upper tiers of county society. Whether or not the principal agents of local administration – deputy-lieutenants, sheriffs and magistrates – constituted an independent-minded 'county community', perhaps even a self-conscious gentry republic, has been a matter of considerable debate, but all those who have studied their activities are ultimately concerned with the effectiveness of self-government provided by county elites on behalf of the crown Among others, Penry Williams, Anthony Fletcher and Steven Gunn have undertaken the unenviable task of synthesizing this enormous range of work, an enterprise particularly complicated by the widely-differing agenda of 'county studies'. The historiographical consensus appears to be that the most reliable index of the efficiency of county government is the effectiveness of policy enforcement. Fletcher accordingly concluded that government in the provinces was untidy, and often inconsistent, but that it was, in the last analysis, coherent. The story of its development, he argued, was that of 'the growing pretensions of the state'.[24] Its symbol was the lengthening agenda facing county benches. Magistrates were increasingly over-burdened with responsibilities. As early as 1581 the Kentish antiquarian and JP William Lambarde was worried that magistrates' backs would break under the pressure of bearing 'so many, not loads, but stacks of statutes'. By 1603, no fewer than 309 statutes imposed responsibilities on justices: and 176 (57 per cent) of these had been passed since 1485.[25] Keeping abreast of legislative requirements was evidently very difficult, since although the 'printed statute book' was sent out to the localities, so many of the channels of communication about parliamentary initiatives were informal, through reports to corporations, private correspondence, and newsletters. In 1614, one lawyer MP commented that 'few' magistrates 'knew fifty' of the requisite statutes, and in the late 1620s the author of a revision of the magistrates' handbooks by Lambarde and Dalton was worried by his own inability to discover which pieces of legislation they discussed were still active.[26] In the context of this heavy and uncertain burden, it is hardly surprising that county benches regarded periodic threats from the privy council or the assize judges as 'stabs in the back'.[27] Surveying the enthusiasm with which magistrates generally exercised their authority, Fletcher takes a relatively optimistic view. In emphasizing the firm grip of local elites on the whip of government, however, he contests the assumptions of historians of council and court such as Williams and Gunn who prefer to see central government calling the shots. In Fletcher's opinion, magistrates themselves decided if, and how quickly, central directives should be implemented. Policies that rested on consensus were enforced, but only at a pace with which local governors were comfortable. Policies that they found dubious, or that aroused violent opposition, were quietly obstructed.[28] It has, furthermore, recently been suggested that even where magistrates proved compliant or persuadable, the critical factor determining the effectiveness with which any policy might be enforced was not the initiatives taken by the JPs, but the co-operation of churchwardens, constables and overseers of the poor across thousands of parishes who together comprised the bottom line of early modern government.[29]

The parish, no less than the county commission of the peace, was therefore subject to the Tudor 'increase of governance'. This process was obviously supervised by magistrates, but even the legislators themselves recognized that the parish was the one organization with sufficient local presence and administrative machinery to deal with collective responsibilities. Thus a unit that had been developed to deal with the agricultural problems of the local peasantry became appropriated for a much wider series of purposes. Having to a very large extent functioned outside the state system, the parish now changed its character, becoming to an unprecedented extent a local expression of state power. The laws for which parish officers now assumed responsibility are well known: the appointment of surveyors to co-ordinate the repair of local roads by an act of 1555; the collective provision and maintenance of weapons under the militia statue of 1558; and most significantly the matrix of discretionary powers for the relief and regulation of the poor under a series of acts codified in 1598 and 1601.[30] These legislative initiatives were, however, only the beginning of the governmental process, and were reinforced by a continuous stream of orders in council. Parish officers regularly received exhaustive sets of articles, some issued directly by the itinerant justices of assize, others on the initiative of magistrates. By the early seventeenth century, therefore, the relatively autonomous medieval parish had become incorporated within a national system of provincial governance. This trend seems to have reached its apogee during the 1630s when magistrates in several counties were informing the privy council that petty sessions were attended by 'all [the] officers and chief inhabitants' of all parishes.[31]

Circuits of Authority: The Relationship between Crown and the Peripheries

Four circuits of authority in particular improved the effectiveness of the centre in communicating its priorities to the localities over the course of the sixteenth century: the lieutenancy; commissions of various kinds; Star Chamber and circuit charges; and articles of inquiry. As we have seen, commissions of lieutenancy, issued for the mustering of the county militia and the levying of militia rates in the early 1550s, ultimately became a regular feature of Elizabethan county government. By 1585, the lords lieutenant had also taken on civilian responsibilities, including the maintenance of law and order, the management of food supplies, the collection of forced loans, the detection of recusants and the enforcement of economic regulations, and had become so institutionalized that three or four deputies were normally appointed in most counties. Since the commissioners were few enough in number to feel truly responsible for carrying out government regulations, they 'formed a close and valuable link between central government and the shires'.[32] The increasing authority of lords lieutenant paradoxically added greatly to their unpopularity, especially where they were perceived to encroach on the jurisdiction of county quarter-sessions.

Protests were most marked in the shires of the south and east where tax and military burdens fell heaviest in the 1590s. The patterns of conflict created by the emergence of the lieutenancy varied: while there was provincial resistance in Suffolk, factional strife in Wiltshire, and uneasy compromise in Northamptonshire, the sharpest divisions among a county elite occurred in Norfolk.[33] It is nonetheless remarkable that the crown allowed the lieutenancies to lapse during the 1590s, despite invasion threats and the demands of continental warfare. Sixteen lieutenancy commissions were left unfilled for as long as three years, seven for as long as ten years, and in all thirteen were vacant by 1603.[34] For the next thirty years, therefore, the military governance of most counties devolved upon deputy lieutenants and provosts-marshal. When they faced their first real test, 'billeting, succouring, and preserving order among the beaten, sick, demoralised, poorly clad, ill-disciplined, hungry and miserable remnants who survived battle, disease, and the rigours of a hard voyage' during the continental expeditions of the 1620s, their failure proved to be 'constitutionally significant, institutionally destructive and politically dangerous'.[35] By the mid-1620s, the lieutenancy had nonetheless 'become fully integrated into the fabric of society', with both lieutenants and their deputies seeing themselves 'as part of a locally-oriented political and social order' beset by 'rate-payers' awe and irritation at the regime's persistent efforts to tap the nation's resources'.[36]

The lieutenancy, however, was only one manifestation of the Tudor regime's predisposition to delegate authority. Indeed, the 'enforcement of royal orders was, more than anything else, government by commission', a tradition which can be traced back at least to the fourteenth century.[37] These executive and investigatory agencies ranged from permanent institutions to ad hoc inquiries. While commissions of the peace, fusing together political and judicial power, were a continuous part of government, commissions of array and muster were issued only in conditions of war, rebellion or alarm, and subsidy commissions were necessary only when parliament had authorized grants of money. By the late sixteenth century, however, specialized local commissions had been created for the execution of specific policies: for causes ecclesiastical; for restraining the export of grain; for sewers; for charitable uses; for concealed lands.[38] The increasing tendency of the central law courts to refer legal actions to special commissions (for taking evidence and for settling cases by mediation), rather than to full-scale hearing and judgement at Westminster Hall, is particularly striking. In enlisting the judgement, influence and practical morality of responsible laymen in the administration of prerogative justice and especially of prerogative equity, commissions symbolize the importance of arbitration as a technique of Tudor judicial administration.[39] While early-sixteenth-century commissions had given special authority to members of the royal household, Elizabethan commissions were very much in the hands of local landowners. In many cases, however, the system depended upon the energies and abilities of the middling sort who served on juries for the purposes of social and political investigation and the presentment and trial of offences. Without the co-operation of these relatively humble men, 'the agencies of the state were ineffective'; and 'that co-operation, often grudging and partial, had to be won, for it could not be assumed'. Commissions were peculiarly English both in their flexibility and in their rather curious central–local relationships, and they gave the early modern state a palpability and presence in the localities that it could not otherwise have enjoyed. In short, the widespread use of commissions is symptomatic of 'the steady growth of state intervention in national life'.[40]

Two further techniques were similarly intended to win, or at least to police, the co-operation of local officers. First, from the second decade of the sixteenth century, Thomas Wolsey was assiduous in using the court of Star Chamber as a forum for disciplining corrupt or negligent magistrates with the sanctions of prerogative justice. Wolsey instructed the crown lawyers to bring informations against JPs suspected of fraud, extortion or embracery, and actively encouraged those who felt aggrieved by the treatment they had received at the magistracy to issue private bills of complaint against them in the court.[41] Well into the seventeenth century, magistrates might find themselves called upon to justify their actions in this way, and where they were unable to do so convincingly, they were liable for swingeing fines.[42] Wolsey and his successors were evidently aware that an exemplary summons to attend the court might, in and of itself, jolt county benches out of their complacency or independent-mindedness. Indeed, Wolsey also pioneered the practice of summoning the judges and sheriffs to Westminster to hear the lord chancellor or the lord keeper deliver the Star Chamber address (or 'charge') and to renew their oaths of loyalty.[43]

The Star Chamber charge gradually evolved into a model of juristic oratory designed to bind the circuit judges into collective responsibility and to reinforce the principle of delegated authority. Used by Lord Keeper Bacon in 1561 to instruct assize judges to report the names of negligent magistrates, and in 1565 to urge the commendation of 'bees' and the purging of 'drones', early Elizabethan charges generally diagnosed traditional economic diseases, publicised existing legislation, and encouraged magistrates to execute the law. The practice fell into abeyance in about 1570, only to be reintroduced as part of a reorganization of the circuit system 'considering the present scarcity' in 1595. Thereafter charges were consistently used in periods of acute governmental anxiety, especially in the critical period 1595–1602 (when seven charges were issued) and after 1625. As the lord keeper's address was echoed and embellished by the judges in the political theatre of the assizes, the circuit charge became a 'potent vehicle for propaganda' through which conciliar pressure could be indirectly maintained on magistrates and magnates alike. Given the presence of the grand jury, moreover, the charge was also intended for the edification of a wider public.[44] Although 'most charges after 1615 were set-pieces devoted largely to eloquent analyses of the role of the assize judges in the structure of prerogative rule, and general exhortations to encourage religious harmony, good order and diligence in local office', surviving charges by later lord keepers may still be read as 'a barometer of official emphases and preoccupations'.[45] The likely impact of charges in the localities has, however, proved controversial. Although 'the judge's skilful blend of flattery and admonition, delivered in the august surroundings of court ceremonial and thronging countrymen', might plausibly be 'an inspiring experience', judges probably 'knew too little of the localities they rode to involve themselves in the details of local administration and politics'. Even the judiciary itself recognized the limitations of its role: the judges might be the 'eyes of the state', but they in turn needed to see by the eyes of others, especially the justices of the peace. More confidence can therefore be expressed in the conscientiousness of judges 'in publicising though less certainly in implementing royal judicial policy'.[46]

Second, the insistence that the petty constables of individual parishes and townships themselves submit regular written replies to specifically enumerated 'articles of inquiry' issued by the judges was a practice adapted from the church courts. Articles were first introduced by Chief Justice Sir John Popham on the home circuit in 1598, and central government used them as guides for magistrates regularly thereafter.[47] By the mid-1610s, however, precepts listing the articles were sent out by the assize judges directly to the high constables of the hundreds and were communicated by them in turn to petty constables. In this respect, their political significance lies in the attempt to secure the regular presentment of offenders without troubling either magistrates or informers. In effect, the judges were liasing directly with middling parish officers at the expense of the gentry.[48] In the early years, the content of the articles varied considerably. From 1615, however, a standard, but sweeping, set of precepts was employed on most circuits and continued in use into the eighteenth century: constables were to enquire into and report on the numbers of felons, vagrants and recusants; the decay of tillage; alehouses, engrossing, forestalling and brewing; the relief of the poor; the sufficiency of parish officers; the regulation of wages; the erection of cottages; drunkenness, whoredom and incontinency; apprenticeships; purveyance; and infringements of the game laws. Articles came to be 'of absolutely critical importance where an increase of governance was desired', and the results in Essex and Lancashire were 'spectacular', with parish officers scurrying to enforce both economic regulation and public morality.[49] It is especially striking that the intensive use of both circuit charges and articles should date from the mid-1590s, when the privy council developed an itchy trigger finger, its anxieties intensified by the intersecting crises of war, dearth, vagrancy and theft.

Conclusion: Self-Government at the King's Command

The counties of Tudor England can certainly be said to have experienced an increase of governance. The 'presencing' of royal authority in the shires of England and Wales was, as we have seen, achieved with very little in the way of institutional innovation and at very little expense. The powers of the magistracy were certainly augmented, both in the geographical sense by the granting of commission of the peace to Welsh counties in the 1530s and in the jurisdictional sense by the growing number of duties for which statutes made them responsible, especially in the final quarter of the century. The North of England, where in the early 1520s, Lord Dacre had once exercised authority almost as an uncrowned king, was tamed to the extent that by the time of the 1569 rising of the northern earls the cry that the northern marches knew 'no prince save a Percy' was merely empty rhetoric.[50] In both the North and in Wales, moreover, where the crown felt that further supervision was necessary, the Tudors' preferred intermediaries with the magistracy were not local magnates, or at least not noblemen who acted in isolation. Where local lords were granted office, they were usually commissioned in conjunction with a council of clerical administrators, as was the case in the Council in the Marches of Wales and the Council of the North (and briefly the Council in the West). In these cases, regional councils of this kind were less independent power-bases for local aristocrats than fora for the exercise of delegated royal authority. In the wake of the failed Northern Risings of 1536–7, moreover, the powers of the Council in the North were augmented in order that it could dispense prerogative justice in the northern shires on the model of the court of Star Chamber. Although at first sight the creation of the lieutenancy in the aftermath of the 1549 risings might seem to be a reinforcement of aristocratic power, the effective military governance of the shires paradoxically lay in the hands of their deputies, who were gentlemen rather than magnates. If there was 'a Tudor revolution in government', it seems, it is more easily identified as the long-term social process of incorporating gentry elites into the governance of the shires and middling men into the governance of the parishes than as the overnight bureaucratic achievement of institutional innovation at Whitehall.

If the counties of England could not be, indeed were not, governed by the nobility without the help of the gentry, then the gentry also perforce had subordinates on whom they had to rely. Historians of Tudor England are rapidly coming to terms with the social depth of governance, a process which engaged the active participation of thousands of men of relatively humble status as grand and trial jurors, parish officers and commissioners of various kinds. These men were, as Patrick Collinson has noted, not simply subjects of the crown but citizens of a commonwealth that depended for its very survival on their sense of civic duty. For Collinson, the implications of this insight are profound: the recognition that 'citizens were concealed within subjects' entails a further characterization of the Tudor regime as a 'monarchical republic' in which traditions of popular participation sat somewhat uneasily alongside the sovereign authority of the crown.[51] It has been the achievement of the 'new political history' of Tudor England to recognize that the 'points of contact' within the polity were not, as Geoffrey Elton thought, confined to privy council, Court and parliament, but were also to be found in gentry parlours, grand jury chambers and parish vestries throughout the realm. The processes of negotiation involved in the tailoring of royal policy to meet the needs and interests at play in this enlarged political society were complex and often protracted. On the one hand, the crown might bring to bear its powers of political and judicial coercion, sending out authoritative royal commissions to the shires to secure immediate compliance with its wishes. Yet just as often the crown was reluctant to insist, and although such reluctance often created space for passive resistance and even for outright political dissent, the more subtle approach often proved to be more rewarding. One of the implications of that delightfully ambiguous phrases, 'self-government at the king's command' was that exhortation might be just as effective a governmental technique as coercion.[52]

NOTES

1. Gunn, *Early Tudor Government*, p. 12.
2. Hindle, *The State and Social Change*, p. ix.
3. Smith, *County and Court*, pp. 157–200.
4. MacCulloch, *Suffolk and the Tudors*, pp. 192–219.
5. Eales, 'The rise of ideological politics'; cf. Clark, *English Provincial Society*, pp. 111–48.
6. Cust, 'Honour and politics'; Cogswell, *Home Divisions*, pp. 68–107.
7. This phrase was used as a book title by A. B. White.
8. Guy, 'Thomas Wolsey, Thomas Cromwell'.
9. Williams, *The Tudor Regime*, p. 407.
10. Youngs, 'Towards petty sessions,' and Fletcher, *Reform in the Provinces*, pp. 123–35; Hindle, *The State and Social Change*, pp. 94–115.
11. Slack, 'Poverty and social regulation'.
12. Fletcher, 'Honour, reputation and local office-holding'.

13. Guy, 'Thomas Wolsey, Thomas Cromwell', pp. 54–5.

14. Thompson, *Customs in Common*, pp. 45–6.

15. Smith, *De Republica Anglorum*, pp. 65, 74, 76–7.

16. Fletcher and MacCulloch, *Tudor Rebellions*, p. 117; Cooper, 'Ideas of gentility'; Peltonen, *Classical Humanism and Republicanism*, pp. 293–6; Hindle, *The State and Social Change*, pp. 204–30.

17. Hindle, 'The political culture of the middling sort', pp. 131–2.

18. Hindle, 'Hierarchy and community', p. 851.

19. Smith, *County and Court*, p. 50.

20. Cockburn, *A History of English Assizes*, p. 3.

21. Spedding, *The Letters and Life of Francis Bacon*, VI, p. 211.

22. Cockburn, *A History of English Assizes*, pp. 153–87.

23. Hindle, *The State and Social Change*, p. 117.

24. Williams, *The Tudor Regime*; Gunn, *Early Tudor Government*; Fletcher, *Reform in the Provinces*, quotation from p. 372.

25. Lambarde, *Eirenarcha*, p. 38; Fletcher, *Reform in the Provinces*, p. 3.

26. Hirst, *Authority and Conflict*, p. 44; Russell, *Parliament and English Politics*, p. 70 n.2.

27. Fletcher, *Reform in the Provinces*, p. 356.

28. Ibid.

29. Hindle, *The State and Social Change*, p. 12.

30. Kümin, *The Shaping of a Community*, pp. 222–54; Hindle, *The State and Social Change*, pp. 204–30.

31. Hindle, *The State and Social Change*, p. 216.

32. Williams, *The Tudor Regime*, p. 417.

33. MacCulloch, *Suffolk and the Tudors*, pp. 258–82; Wall, 'Faction in local politics'; Goring and Wake, *Northamptonshire Lieutenancy Papers*, pp. xx–xxxi; Smith, *County and Court*, pp. 229–46.

34. Guy, 'Introduction: the 1590s', p. 5; Levy Peck, 'Peers, patronage and the politics of history', pp. 93–4.

35. Barnes, 'Deputies not principals', pp. 60–1.

36. Stater, *Noble Government*, p. 12; Cogswell, *Home Divisions*, p. 3.

37. Williams, *The Tudor Regime*, pp. 410–19.

38. Manning, 'The making of a Protestant aristocracy'; Slack, 'Dearth and social policy'; Holmes, 'Statutory interpretation'; Jones, *History of the Law of Charity*, pp. 16–56; and Kitching, 'The quest for concealed lands', pp. 63–78.

39. Dawson, 'The privy council and private law', pp. 424–5; Hindle, *The State and Social Change*, pp. 94–115.

40. Williams, *The Tudor Regime*, pp. 418, 420.

41. Guy, *The Cardinal's Court*, pp. 51–78.

42. Hindle, *The State and Social Change*, pp. 71–8.

43. Scarisbrick, 'Cardinal Wolsey and the commonweal', pp. 45–67.

44. Baildon (ed.), *Les Reportes del Cases in Camera Stellata*, p. 20; Knafla, *Law and Politics*, p. 146; Cockburn, *A History of English Assizes*, pp. 7, 161–2.

45. Cockburn, *A History of English Assizes*, p. 184; Sharpe, *The Personal Rule of Charles I*, pp. 425–7.

46. Fletcher, *Reform in the Provinces*, pp. 48–9; Sharpe, 'Culture, politics and the English Civil War', pp. 309–10; Sharpe, *The Personal Rule of Charles I*, p. 430; Lake, 'Constitutional consensus and Puritan opposition', p. 812; Cockburn, *A History of English Assizes*, p. 185.

47. Scott, 'The journal of Roger Wilbraham', p. 20.

48. Quintrell (ed.), *Proceedings of the Lancashire Justices of the Peace*, pp. 4, 171–7, 192–3; Beresford, 'The common informer'.
49. Cockburn, *A History of English Assizes*, pp. 116–17; Fletcher, *Reform in the Provinces*, p. 137; Wrightson, 'Two concepts of order', pp. 38–41.
50. Ellis, 'A Border baron and the Tudor state'; James, 'The concept of order and the Northern Rising'.
51. Collinson, '*De Republica Anglorum*', p. 19.
52. Hindle, 'Dearth, fasting and alms'.

BIBLIOGRAPHY

Baildon, W. P., ed., *Les Reportes del Cases in Camera Stellata, 1593 to 1609, from the Original MS of John Hawarde* (London, 1893).

Barnes, T. G., 'Deputies not principals, lieutenants not captains: the institutional failure of the lieutenancy in the 1620s', in M. C. Fissel, ed., *War and Government in Britain, 1598–1650* (Manchester, 1991), pp. 58–86.

Beresford, M., 'The common informer, the penal statutes and economic regulation', *Economic History Review*, 2nd series, X, 2 (1957), 221–37.

Clark, P., *English Provincial Society from the Reformation to the Revolution: Religion, Politics and Society in Kent, 1500–1640* (Hassocks, 1977).

Cockburn, J. S., *A History of English Assizes 1558–1714* (Cambridge, 1972).

Cogswell, T., *Home Divisions: Aristocracy, the State and Provincial Conflict* (Manchester, 1998).

Collinson, P., '*De Republica Anglorum* or history with the politics put back', reprinted in P. Collinson, *Elizabethans* (London, 2003), pp. 1–30.

Cooper, J. P., 'Ideas of gentility in early modern England', reprinted in J. P. Cooper, *Land, Men and Beliefs: Studies in Early Modern History* (London, 1983), pp. 65–72.

Cust, R., 'Honour and politics in early Stuart England: the case of Beaumont *v.* Hastings', *Past and Present*, 149 (November 1995), pp. 57–94.

Dawson, J. P., 'The privy council and private law in the Tudor and early Stuart periods: parts I and II', *Michigan Law Review*, XLVIII, 4 (1950), 392–428, 627–56.

Eales, J., 'The rise of ideological politics in Kent, 1558–1640', in M. Zell, ed., *Early Modern Kent, 1540–1640* (Woodbridge, 2000), pp. 279–313.

Ellis, S. G., 'A Border baron and the Tudor state: the rise and fall of Lord Dacre of the North', *Historical Journal*, XXXV, 2 (1992), 253–77.

Fletcher, A., 'Honour, reputation and local office-holding in Elizabethan and early Stuart England', in A. Fletcher and J. Stevenson, eds, *Order and Disorder in Early Modern England* (Cambridge, 1985), pp. 92–115.

Fletcher, A., *Reform in the Provinces: The Government of Stuart England* (New Haven, 1986).

Fletcher, A., and MacCulloch, D., *Tudor Rebellions* (4th edition, Harlow, 1997).

Goring, J., and Wake, J., eds, *Northamptonshire Lieutenancy Papers, 1580–1614* (Northampton, 1975).

Gunn, S. J., *Early Tudor Government, 1485–1558* (Basingstoke, 1995).

Guy, J., *The Cardinal's Court: The Impact of Thomas Wolsey in Star Chamber* (Hassocks, 1977).

Guy, J., 'Introduction: the 1590s, the second reign of Elizabeth I', in J. Guy, ed., *The Reign of Elizabeth I: Court and Culture in the Last Decade* (Cambridge, 1995), pp. 1–19.

Guy, J., 'Thomas Wolsey, Thomas Cromwell and the reform of Henrician government', in Diarmaid MacCulloch, ed., *The Reign of Henry VIII: Politics, Policy and Piety* (Basingstoke, 1995), pp. 35–57.

Hindle, S., 'Dearth, fasting and alms: the campaign for general hospitality in late Elizabethan England', *Past and Present*, 172 (August 2001), 44–86.

Hindle, S., 'Hierarchy and community in the Elizabethan parish: the Swallowfield articles of 1596', *Historical Journal*, XLII, 3 (1999), 835–51.

Hindle, S., 'The political culture of the middling sort in English rural communities, *c*.1550–1700', in T. Harris, ed., *The Politics of the Excluded, 1500–1850* (Basingstoke, 2001), pp. 125–52.

Hindle, S., *The State and Social Change in Early Modern England, 1550–1640* (Basingstoke, 2000).

Hirst, D., *Authority and Conflict, 1603–58* (London, 1986).

Holmes, C., 'Statutory interpretation in the early seventeenth century: the courts, the council and the commissioners of sewers', in J. A. Guy and H. G. Beale, eds, *Law and Social Change in British History: Papers Presented to the British Legal History Conference, 14–17 July 1981* (London, 1984), pp. 107–17.

James, M., 'The concept of order and the Northern Rising', reprinted in James, *Society, Politics and Culture: Studies in Early Modern England* (Cambridge, 1986), pp. 270–307.

Jones, G., *History of the Law of Charity, 1532–1827* (Cambridge, 1969).

Kitching, C. J., 'The quest for concealed lands', *Transactions of the Royal Historical Society*, 4th series, XXIV (1974), 63–78.

Knafla, L., *Law and Politics in Jacobean England: The Tracts of Lord Chancellor Ellesmere* (Cambridge, 1977).

Kümin, B., *The Shaping of a Community: The Rise and Reformation of the English Parish, c.1400–1560* (Aldershot, 1996).

Lake, P., 'Constitutional consensus and puritan opposition in the 1620s: Thomas Scott and the Spanish match', *Historical Journal*, XXV, 4 (1982), 805–25.

Lambarde, W., *Eirenarcha: Or, Of the Office of the Justice of the Peace* (London, 1583).

MacCulloch, D., *Suffolk and the Tudors: Politics and Religion in an English County* (Oxford, 1986).

Manning, R. B., 'The making of a Protestant aristocracy: the ecclesiastical commissioners of the diocese of Chester, 1550–98', *Bulletin of the Institute of Historical Research*, XLIX (1976), 60–79.

Peck, L. Levy, 'Peers, patronage and the politics of history', in J. Guy, ed., *The Reign of Elizabeth I: Court and Culture in the Last Decade* (Cambridge, 1995), pp. 87–108.

Peltonen, M., *Classical Humanism and Republicanism in English Political Thought, 1570–1640* (Cambridge, 1995).

Quintrell, B. W., ed., *Proceedings of the Lancashire Justices of the Peace at the Sheriff's Table During the Assizes Week, 1578–1694* (Lancashire and Cheshire, 1981).

Russell, C., *Parliament and English Politics, 1621–29* (Oxford, 1979).

Scarisbrick, J. J., 'Cardinal Wolsey and the Commonweal', in E. W. Ives, R. J. Knecht and J. J. Scarisbrick, eds, *Wealth and Power in Tudor England: Essays Presented to S. T. Bindoff* (London, 1978), pp. 45–67.

Scott, H. S., ed., 'The journal of Roger Wilbraham', Camden Miscellany, 10, Camden 3rd series, 4 (1902).

Sharpe, K., 'Culture, politics and the English civil war', reprinted in Sharpe, *Politics and Ideas in Early Stuart England* (London, 1989), pp. 279–316.

Sharpe, K., *The Personal Rule of Charles I* (New Haven, 1992).

Slack, P., 'Dearth and social policy in early modern England', *Social History of Medicine*, 5, 1 (1992), 1–17.

Slack, P., 'Poverty and social regulation in Elizabethan England', in C. Haigh, ed., *The Reign of Elizabeth I* (London, 1984), pp. 221–42.

Smith, A. H., *County and Court: Government and Politics in Norfolk, 1558–1603* (Oxford, 1974).

Smith, T., *De Republica Anglorum,* ed. M. Dewar (Cambridge, 1982).

Spedding, J., ed., *The Letters and Life of Francis Bacon* (7 vols, London, 1861–74).

Stater, V., *Noble Government: The Stuart Lord Lieutenancy and the Transformation of English Politics* (Athens, GA, 1994).

Thompson, E., *Customs in Common* (London, 1991).

Wall, A., 'Faction in local politics, 1580–1620: struggles for supremacy in Wiltshire', *Wiltshire Archaeological Magazine,* LXXII–LXXIII (1980), 119–34.

White, A. B., *Self-government at the King's Command: A Study in the Beginnings of English Democracy* (Minneapolis, 1933).

Williams, P., *The Tudor Regime* (Oxford, 1979).

Wrightson, K., 'Two concepts of order: justices, constables and jurymen in seventeenth-century England', in J. Brewer and J. Styles, eds, *An Ungovernable People: The English and Their Law in the Seventeenth and Eighteenth Centuries* (London, 1980), pp. 21–46.

Youngs, F. A., 'Towards petty sessions: Tudor JPs and divisions of counties', in DeLloyd J. Guth and J. W. McKenna, eds, *Tudor Rule and Revolution: Essays for G. R. Elton from His American Friends* (Cambridge, 1982), pp. 201–16.

FURTHER READING

G. W. Bernard, *War, Taxation and Rebellion in Early Tudor England* (1986); and (ed.), *The Tudor Nobility* (1992).

Michael J. Braddick, *State Formation in Early Modern England, c.1550–1700* (2000).

M. L. Bush, *The Government Policy of Protector Somerset* (1975).

J. S. Cockburn (ed.), *Calendar of Assize Records: Home Circuit Indictments, Elizabeth I and James I: Introduction* (1985), pp. 1–134.

J. S. Cockburn and T. A. Green (eds), *Twelve Good Men and True: The English Criminal Trial Jury, 1200–1800* (1988).

G. R. Elton, 'Tudor government: the points of contact', reprinted in Elton, *Studies in Tudor and Stuart Politics and Government,* vol. III: *Papers and Reviews* (1983), pp. 3–57.

T. A. Green, *Verdict According to Conscience: Perspectives on the English Criminal Trial Jury* (1985).

Joel Hurstfield, 'County government: Wiltshire, c.1530–1660' (1957), reprinted in Joel Hurstfield, *Freedom, Corruption and Government in Elizabethan England* (1973), pp. 236–93.

R. R. Reid, *The King's Council in the North* (1912).

G. S. Thomson, *The Lords Lieutenants in the Sixteenth Century* (1923).

Keith Wrightson, 'The politics of the parish in early modern England', in Paul Griffiths, Adam Fox and Steve Hindle (eds), *The Experience of Authority in Early Modern England* (1996), pp. 10–46.

CHAPTER SEVEN

Town and City Government

CATHERINE F. PATTERSON

Towns and cities held only a minority – perhaps 5 to 10 per cent – of the population in the British Isles during the Tudor period. Yet urban places lay at the centre of much of the dynamic change occurring in the sixteenth century. Population rise, economic tensions, and increasing mobility (both geographical and social) resulted in larger numbers of people moving off the land and into towns in search of employment. Religious reformation introduced new divisions into civic life and significantly altered many traditional expressions of civic unity and governance. At the same time, central government placed increasing demands on urban officials, requiring, above all, that good order be kept, despite forces of disorder in their midst. The Tudor era presented major challenges to the men who ruled the towns. It is perhaps surprising that, by and large, town and city governments lived up to the challenges that confronted them.

Interest in towns and their governments remained largely the preserve of anti-quarians and local historians until the late twentieth century, when the rise of the new social and economic history brought urban studies into focus. The early modern town became an important area of scholarly enquiry, as Peter Clark and Paul Slack's path-breaking work in the mid-1970s set an agenda for research into urban life. Drawing out themes of crisis and order, Clark and Slack and others stressed economic and social change in towns, analysing how rapidly increasing population, dramatic inflation, and shifting social boundaries affected urban communities. Towns teetered on the brink of chaos, and urban government became increasingly oligarchic to keep disorder at bay. While much of this work has stood the test of time, more recent studies of towns have moved beyond economic topics and a 'crisis' model to broader discussion of urban life. Robert Tittler's work has analysed how religious, political, and economic shifts in the early modern period shaped urban culture. The religious reformation and the economic restructuring of the sixteenth century helped transform the patterns of civic government, the symbolism of urban authority, and relations among townsmen and between townsmen and other authorities. Research into urban history in the last thirty years has clearly demonstrated the importance of urban government in the larger polities of England, Wales, and Scotland in this period of change.[1]

This chapter will explore the nature of urban government in Tudor Britain and how it met the challenges of the day. It will focus on provincial cities and towns, with only occasional reference to London, which – given its size, complexity, and uniqueness in Britain's urban hierarchy – is given separate treatment elsewhere (chapter 20 of this volume). England, with its larger and more numerous towns and cities, will command the greatest attention, but Wales and Scotland are included, as well. Urban government in Ireland has been little studied for the sixteenth century and will not feature significantly in this essay. Leaders of urban government throughout the British Isles, like their counterparts in the gentry who dominated county government, strove to promote and maintain order and stability in their communities. Not simply unsophisticated provincials, urban governors could be savvy operators who tried, with some success, to maintain the traditions of peaceful self-government within borough boundaries, while aligning themselves with the powers beyond town walls, as well.

Towns and Town Government

All 800 or so towns in the British Isles shared certain basic characteristics: they had an economic base in commerce, trade or industry; they had denser populations than in the countryside; they had some apparatus of government at least partially separate from the surrounding rural hinterlands; and they had some influence on those hinterlands outside their own boundaries. Beyond those basic similarities, however, urban communities displayed a tremendous range in size, organization and importance, reflected in wide variations of civic government and local autonomy. By modern standards, many of the towns and cities of the period were not very 'urban' at all. The word is applied to London, a true metropolis and an urban place by any standard, but it also is used to describe a small market town with only a few hundred inhabitants. Even a town of a few thousand residents like Leicester had arable fields just outside the town centre and a portion of the population employed in husbandry. England had a handful of provincial capitals – York, Norwich, Bristol and Exeter, for instance – with populations in the range of 10–20,000. It had a larger number of county towns, whose populations figured in the thousands, while many more were small market towns with several hundred souls. Scotland had four 'great towns' – Edinburgh, Aberdeen, Perth, and Dundee – which had quite sophisticated economies but only modest populations that never approached that of the English metropolis. Most burghs had only several hundred residents. Welsh towns generally had quite small populations, as well. Such variations in size and function not surprisingly had an impact on the complexity and authority of civic government.

The majority of towns throughout the British Isles were small market centres with populations under 1,000. In England, most of these – at least at the beginning of the Tudor period – were seigneurial boroughs, in which a lord of the manor had a great deal of influence over the workings of borough government. The structures of government in manorial boroughs grew out of the court leet; the lord of the manor or his bailiff exercised final authority and often determined who would serve in borough offices and what powers they held. The degree to which manorial lords or their bailiffs exercised their authority depended upon local circumstances; some manorial boroughs experienced little interference from their lords and largely governed themselves, while others remained subordinate to manorial authority. This subordination was not directly related to size or importance. A moderately large and important borough like Bury St Edmunds remained almost completely under the thumb of its ecclesiastical overlord, the abbot, until the time of the dissolution of the monasteries. In the cathedral city of Peterborough, the dean and chapter of the cathedral still held 'the principal power of government and managing the affairs of the city' in the 1630s.[2] Many Welsh boroughs, most of which had been founded by the conquering English in the Middle Ages, remained historically tied to their manorial lords and subject to the lord's authority.

Almost all urban government emerged from a manorial context, but over the course of time many towns developed institutions of self-government and gained charters granting liberties and some measure of autonomy. A lord of the manor might hold nominal rights in the borough, but in practice this meant that he was owed certain financial dues but had little say in borough business. More significant county towns and provincial capitals had engaged in this push for self-government for centuries, establishing specific privileges and liberties by charter throughout the middle ages. By the time the Tudors attained the throne, cities like Norwich, York and Bristol could claim to have been largely autonomous since time immemorial, answering only to royal authority. In between the dependent seigneurial borough and the provincial capital lay an array of towns with powers varying across the entire spectrum. Many, if not most, would attempt to increase their autonomy in the Tudor period. Significant numbers of towns sought royal ratification of their privileges through charters of incorporation, issued by the crown. A select group of Welsh boroughs also benefited from this constitutional development, as the 1536 Act of Union with Wales placed them on an equal legal footing with English boroughs; several received the parliamentary franchise and gained royal charters of incorporation.

While English and Welsh boroughs varied widely in terms of legal rights and constitutional status, Scottish burghs were more clearly defined. By the sixteenth century, a Scottish burgh could hold one of three legal statuses. Royal burghs held their rights directly from the crown, as tenants-in-chief to the monarch. They held self-governing authority under the crown and enjoyed special trade privileges that only the monarch could confer. The Scottish parliament recognized their status, and they by right were members of the Convention of Royal Burghs, through which as a group they could address king and parliament directly. Burghs of barony and burghs of regality both held their rights by charter from noble or ecclesiastical lords by licence from the crown, with burghs of regality having slightly greater rights. In 1500, about one-third of Scotland's towns were royal burghs, while two-thirds were burghs of barony and regality. The latter half of the sixteenth century saw the foundation of a number of dependent, seigneurial burghs, often established by local lairds for their own purposes. Scotland's leading cities, such as Edinburgh and Aberdeen, were royal burghs, but a town's legal status was not necessarily directly related to its size or importance.

The clarity in legal status of Scotland's burghs was never fully realized in England and Wales, but over the course of the sixteenth century urban constitutions became better defined. The Tudor period saw a dramatic rise in the number of royal charters of incorporation. Almost all boroughs had, over the course of centuries, accumulated customary privileges and developed institutions of self-government, either despite or with the tacit consent of the lord of the manor. But especially in the years after 1540, town governors sought royal guarantees of borough liberties. Crown charters validated and strengthened customary rights, gave specific liberties and privileges to the freemen of a borough, and delineated the powers of government that the ruling body of the corporation could exercise. The details of these chartered privileges were anything but uniform, but most incorporations followed a few basic outlines. The corporate body became, in essence, an individual and could engage in economic or legal activities, for instance to buy and sell land, to hold land inalienably in mortmain, or to sue and be sued. Charters usually confirmed a borough's right to hold fairs or markets, as well. They also guaranteed administrative, judicial and governmental authority, delineating the governing bodies, officers and courts of the corporation. Incorporated boroughs could hold various courts, often gaining a court of record over which borough officials presided in the king's name and from which county officials were specifically excluded. The extent of this exclusion from borough government varied from charter to charter, but royal incorporation certainly bolstered the authority of civic leaders to govern their people.

As noted above, some major cities had obtained such guarantees long since, but during the Tudor period incorporation was becoming the norm, as towns of very modest size and importance obtained charters. A trickle of incorporations began as early as the reign of Henry VII, but the gush only came after 1540, in the wake of the Reformation and the land transfers associated with it. From 1485 to 1540, the crown granted thirteen incorporations; from 1540 to 1603, it granted 116 incorporations or re-incorporations.[3] Both town and crown had reasons to promote this trend. Royal authority in England and in Scotland increased its grasp on local government at every level during the sixteenth century; forming direct ties with growing urban communities helped assure stable, loyal government in the localities. In a time of political and economic instability, it was particularly important for the crown to have reliable and accountable officials at the local level. From a town's point of view, a charter confirmed important legal rights and strengthened local autonomy, especially regarding manorial lords. Charters of incorporation increasingly formed the basis for urban government in the sixteenth century, binding local officials to royal authority and spelling out the particulars of civic governing institutions.

Institutions of Government

All town government started with the freemen. In any town or city, it was not the residents in general, but only the freemen of the borough who had the right to participate in decision-making and exercise authority. Freemen were those men (and occasionally women – usually widows) who had obtained the freedom of the borough through apprenticeship, inheritance or purchase. In effect, freemen were citizens; they held economic and political rights in the borough. They could buy, sell and keep shop; they could take apprentices; and they could take part in the governing institutions of the town. The Tudor period saw some erosion of the freemen's full participation in civic government, but nevertheless only those who were freemen had the right to participate at all. This was true in all incorporated boroughs, and in many unincorporated ones, as well.

The freemen served as the basis of urban government, but towns were far from democratic. Townsmen by definition did not fit within the traditional hierarchy of landed wealth that predominated in this period, but they did subscribe to hierarchical principles, which were reflected in urban governing bodies. Practices varied from place to place, but every town had a chief officer or officers and a council, made up of some of the 'discreeter' and 'more fit' part of the freemen, that carried out the executive and legislative activities of civic government. In most chartered towns in England and Wales the mayor served as chief civic officer; in some, a bailiff, or even two bailiffs, as at Great Yarmouth, filled this role. The chief officer of a manorial borough was generally a bailiff who was responsible to the lord of the manor, although some boroughs had acquired significant control over this office. Mayors were generally elected in the autumn on one-year, non-renewable terms, and the freemen of the town usually had some role in their choice, though not invariably a free vote. Schemes in which the freemen chose from among predetermined candidates were not uncommon. The mayor presided over all civic business, attending to the proper running of the town's markets; holding various courts – both trading courts like the court of pie powder and judicial courts like the court of record; leading the town council in its administration of local government; and representing the town in its dealings with external authorities. As one contemporary commentator put it, a good mayor is one who has 'loved her [the town], her honor, her peace, her profit.'[4]

The wide-ranging duties of the mayor made his job a demanding one. The men who held it had to be responsive both to the needs of the local community and to the demands of central government. They had to be willing and able to divide their time and attention between the public business of the town and their own private businesses. In addition, holders of the office frequently bore a significant financial burden, spending personal wealth to cover public costs. During the sixteenth century, most towns experienced some financial difficulties, and it was expected that governing officials would open their own purses on behalf of the town. For these reasons, as well as the hierarchical ideas that influenced office-holding and authority, mayors came from among the wealthier and more respectable townsmen, those who had already served in civic government for some years. The office was burdensome enough that some attempted to avoid serving, but in most towns those who shirked their duty incurred heavy monetary penalties, and service was more common than its avoidance.

Assisting the mayor in civic government was a town council whose name varied from place to place – the Assembly in Chester, the Chamber in Exeter – but whose functions were consistent among both corporate and unincorporated towns. In most towns it was made up of two councils, a smaller, more senior council of aldermen (from among whom the mayor was almost always chosen) and a larger junior common council. Frequently, the junior council was twice the size of the senior council, and these bodies were often referred to by their numbers: the Twelve and Twenty-four, or the Twenty-four and Forty-eight. These councils made by-laws, oversaw town finances, levied local rates, and carried out all the business of civic government. Members of these assemblies were expected to appear in their honorary gowns of office (typically black for common councillors and red for aldermen) at meetings and other ceremonial occasions. Wealth, reputation, and standing in the community usually determined admission to the inner circles of civic government; connection to the leadership of religious guilds (before the Reformation) and craft fellowships also often played a role. Selection to the council generally occurred through co-optation rather than election, with a life-time appointment. Movement from the junior council to the senior council and ultimately to the mayoralty followed a regular pattern of seniority called the *cursus honorum*. When an alderman died or resigned, his fellows filled his place with a senior member of the common council. His spot was then filled by the co-optation of a reputable, up-and-coming freeman, who would himself follow the *cursus honorum* up through the levels of civic government. In most towns in England and Wales, the freemen at large had little role in the selection of these town councils. Central government promoted this pattern, viewing it as more controllable and therefore more effective at maintaining order.

In addition to the mayor and council, most towns also had an array of appointed officials ranging from prominent legal advisers to keepers of the town's pigs. An incorporated borough invariably had a town clerk who kept the borough's records, and a recorder, who served as the town's chief legal official. Usually professional lawyers, recorders often had local roots or connections, but they operated in a wider sphere and many had appointments in the central courts. The corporate charter typically named the recorder as JP of the borough, but he was not expected to be permanently resident in the town or present at all town council meetings. Recorders spent much of their time in London and Westminster, carrying out their own business and defending the interests of the town at court. Increasingly across the Tudor period – and especially under the early Stuarts – towns also chose high stewards, members of the upper gentry or nobility whose honorary position served to cultivate patronage and to promote local interests among the powerful. In addition to such prominent men, towns usually employed a variety of lesser officials: a mace-bearer or sword-bearer, who carried the symbols of civic authority before the mayor, and any number of even more humble servants who cleaned streets, kept poor-houses, and maintained a town gaol. All of these offices, whether humble or noble, were designed to add to the dignity, prosperity and order of a town.

The governing institutions of Scotland's burghs followed a similar pattern to those of England and Wales, with some differences in terminology and organization. In Scotland, the governing body generally consisted of a provost, a bailie or bailies, and a council. In towns that were not royal burghs, local lords serving as provosts wielded tremendous influence in burgh government; even in royal burghs, a noble provost could have significant clout. Burgh government in Scotland, as in England, was largely self-perpetuating; new councillors were co-opted from among the burgesses and officers were chosen from among the councillors. In Edinburgh, the sitting council met each Michaelmas to choose its successor, then the new and former councils together selected the provost, four bailies, a treasurer, and the dean of the guild merchant.[5] Typically, the wealthy merchants dominated civic government, though craftsmen and lawyers played a significant role in some burghs.

Throughout the British Isles, finances played a central role in town government. Most boroughs, whether incorporated or not, had a common fund to support public business. In England and Wales, the push to become incorporated often rose in part from borough leaders' desire for specific legal guarantees over town finances. Incorporated boroughs had the explicit right to own, buy and sell land; to levy rates on the inhabitants; and to keep corporate accounts. As a legal entity, a corporation could also defend itself and its property at law. Property ownership and civic finances loomed particularly large in the Tudor era, given the tremendous turnover in land ownership from ecclesiastical to secular landlords, stemming from the Reformation. Many towns took advantage of this fluid land market to purchase neighbouring monastic properties or to buy up the fee farm of the land on which the borough sat. Newly purchased lands were often leased out for income, which added to the public purse. While the size of civic budgets, and the amounts of revenue-generating land that towns owned, varied widely, all towns used what finances they did have to cover a broad range of expenses incurred by local government. These included everything from basic services and infrastructure to pursuing lawsuits to building new town halls, all of which will be discussed more fully below.

Overseeing civic finances formed an important element of local governance. Day-to-day administration lay in the hands of officers, chosen from among the councillors, who saw to the public accounts. In most English towns, these were the chamberlains, though some larger towns and cities had a more extensive group of chamberlains and treasurers. Chamberlains, usually two in number, served terms of one or sometimes two years; the office of chamberlain stood as an important step along the *cursus honorum*. Most men who held this position were tradesmen and merchants with some business expertise, but they were not professional accountants hired by the town. Not surprisingly, inconsistent accounting abounded. Over-spending the budget occurred regularly in some boroughs, and most town govern-ments experienced financial difficulties in the sixteenth century. Maintaining solvency proved difficult, as inflation, economic dislocation, and increasing demands from central government severely stretched civic finances. Major projects, such as the build-ing of a new town hall, usually required towns to engage in creative financing, using a combination of public funds and private money loaned by wealthy townsmen or landed neighbours. Indeed, 'creative accounting' – including such things as raiding the poor relief accounts to fund other civic projects – was not unknown in this period. Finances were central to civic government, but they could also be a source of con-flict, both within city councils and between governors and governed.

In addition to financial and administrative functions, town governments also had judicial responsibilities. As places of dense population, significant mobility and com-mercial enterprise, towns were bound to experience conflict and crime which had to be contained by local officials. Mayors and bailiffs of boroughs, incorporated or not, had long been holding market courts, designed to assure the orderliness and fairness of trade in their town and thus making the market more attractive. As civic govern-ment became more sophisticated, urban leaders seeking to gain more responsibility and more control over their citizens worked to obtain greater judicial powers. One important privilege usually guaranteed in a charter of incorporation for English and Welsh boroughs was the right to hold a court of record in the town, thus limiting the authority of county JPs in borough business. This gave town leaders greater authority over the residents by allowing the trial of minor offences within the borough. The mayor, some of the aldermen, and often the recorder served as JPs of the court; as officers of the crown, they could bring petty criminals and wrongdoers to justice more swiftly and effectively. The scope of borough courts varied. Some towns had the right only to hold petty sessions. At the other end of the spectrum, a few important towns and cities gained the status of counties in themselves, holding quarter-sessions like the shires. Many towns kept their own gaols, to house those who fell foul of local justice. In the Tudor period, towns increasingly sought charters which granted the greatest degree of legal jurisdiction, providing civic leaders with more authority over the community, but also adding to the stature of civic government as the sole locus of royal authority in the town.

All the institutions of civic government – executive, administrative, financial and judicial – developed gradually over the course of centuries for the purpose of maintaining order in towns and enhancing the self-government of the townsmen. In many ways, the flurry of royal chartering that occurred after 1540 simply reinforced a set of structures that had worked effectively, if informally, for some time. Whether incorporated or not, a borough's governing institutions provided structure for the economic and political life of the townsmen, and the patterns of authority that emerged in the Tudor and Stuart period would stand largely unchanged until the era of municipal reform in the nineteenth century.

Civic Government and Citizens

The institutions of civic government developed to provide self-governance and a degree of autonomy to urban communities. As will be seen more fully below, this did not mean that town government was simply inward-focused. But the main brief of urban government was to see to the good order and prosperity of a town. Given the significant political, religious, economic and social transformations occurring in the sixteenth century, it is not surprising that this period saw changes in the ways that government related to citizens in towns and cities. While town leaders continued to cultivate some traditional aspects of civic culture and a sense of community among citizens, they also distanced themselves from the freemanry, narrowing and consolidating authority in their own hands.

A focus on the growth of oligarchy has dominated historical discussion of borough government. Sidney and Beatrice Webb, writing in the early twentieth century, saw the consolidation of power among urban elites as a negative development of the Tudor and Stuart periods. In medieval boroughs, the freemen often had a significant voice in local government, including the selection of the mayor and council. By the fifteenth, and especially the sixteenth, centuries, authority had become more concentrated in the hands of the magisterial body, to the detriment of the freemen as a whole. Possibilities for corruption abounded, as narrow cliques of wealthy men had the opportunity to wield authority for their own gain. This theme has been echoed over the decades by many historians. The influential work of Clark and Slack in the 1970s tended to reinforce the notion of division and alienation between civic elites and commoners, though for somewhat different reasons. The 'crisis' mentality of urban leaders in the face of serious economic and social tensions encouraged them to expand their own authority so as to be able to control the citizens; this pattern was approved and reinforced by a central government that demanded the maintenance of order.[6] Power was concentrated in the hands of a few men, and complaints by the freemen went unheeded.

Few historians would dispute that authority in towns rested with a relatively small group of men selected from among the wealthier, more respectable townsmen. Merchants dominated civic government in many towns; in some Scottish burghs, they held authority almost to the exclusion of craftsmen. It is also clear that over the course of the sixteenth century, urban government tended to narrow, while in some closed corporations the freemen lost their official voice in civic affairs. This narrowing caused friction between freemen and civic leaders in a number of towns, as citizens resisted their loss of input in decision-making. When the civic leaders of Totnes gained a charter of incorporation late in Elizabeth's reign that largely excluded freemen from participation, the freemen organized themselves sufficiently to persuade the crown to issue a writ of *quo warranto* against the newly chartered corporation. (With *quo warranto*, the crown asked 'by what warrant' an individual or body held rights or privileges, forcing the defendant to prove the rights in question.) Nevertheless, in the end the crown upheld the new, more restrictive charter.[7] Urban government in the sixteenth century did not encourage broad participation of the citizenry.

Recent interpretations have moved away from a focus on the negative aspects of oligarchy and its growth, however. Questions have been raised as to what 'oligarchy' really means, and the extent to which it dominated town government. Detailed studies of the personnel of borough corporations have shown the rarity of long-lasting family dynasties that hoarded power in particular communities. The frequency of early death, migration and business failure made it very difficult for family 'dynasties' to keep a lock on government. Most towns seem to have experienced a significant turnover in the elite governing circles and a regular influx of new men.[8] Nevertheless, it is true that certain types of people – that is, men of greater wealth and status – generally held power in towns and cities, and historians have looked afresh at the social and political reasons that made concentration of authority attractive.

Just as wealth and reputation were determinants of authority in rural society, so they were in towns, as well. Those men supposed to have greater resources, both in monetary terms and in terms of experience, political savvy, and possibly education, were thought to be better able to do the work of government. It would also potentially damage the honour and reputation of the town to have 'mean' men in positions of authority. Townsmen as a whole already suffered from an inferiority complex in their status in relation to the landed elite; they did not wish to compound this by having the lowly serving in civic government. In addition, given that urban rulers usually had to spend their own money on civic causes, it made practical sense that the better-off merchants and tradesmen served in those positions. Civic elites were expected to help pay for the ceremonies and feasts associated with town culture, and they also regularly bore substantial parts of the costs of obtaining charters, defending lawsuits, and other local business. Poorer artisans might (and did) complain of exclusion, but they were also not in a position to bear the expense of public service.

The increasing strength and reach of central government also reinforced the concentration of authority. The steadily growing responsibility placed on local government by the crown made the delegation of authority to a smaller group of (presumably) able men attractive, from the perspective of the locality as well as the crown. The increase in incorporations during the sixteenth century solidified this trend, as the crown named 'small knots of reliable men' to govern these newly incorporated boroughs. Robert Tittler has noted that the narrowing of urban constitutions in England and Wales followed a clear progression, with a first big wave of incorporation in the years following 1540, and a second wave of reincorporation – which generally strengthened existing authorities and weakened freemen's participation – occurring in the years following 1590.[9] The crown first granted basic autonomy to urban government, then continued to promote ever-stronger local authority as time progressed.

All of this calls into question what the concentration of authority in urban government really meant for townsmen. The chipping away of freemen's participation certainly caused friction and could open urban government to corruption. The men who governed the towns ruled with their own interests in mind, and the needs of the populace could go unheeded. But the argument for alienation seems to have been overstated. Closed corporations did exist, but most towns retained some venues for limited popular participation. Towns like Norwich and Great Yarmouth had constitutions that allowed for significant input from the freemen in the choice of town councillors and other civic officers. In Exeter, a city that had a quite closed constitution, the freemen retained a residual voice in mayoral elections, choosing the mayor from pre-selected candidates. Many small towns, especially unincorporated boroughs, continued earlier patterns of freeman participation. In Scotland, urban unrest led to the representation in civic government of not just merchants but also craftsmen in some burghs. Edinburgh's redrafted constitution of 1583 opened burgh government more widely to members of the crafts, a pattern that was followed in other burghs, as well.[10]

Urban leaders throughout the British Isles needed the co-operation of the citizenry to govern, and there were practical opportunities for interaction between different levels of civic society. Below the level of government delineated in corporate charters were a variety of 'officers' ranging from collectors for the poor to churchwardens to constables that gave an important role to more middling sorts of townsmen. The craft and trade guilds (whose strength, coherence and relationship to civic government varied significantly from town to town) provided another venue for more popular participation. In Scottish burghs, men of middling rank held minor, but still important, responsibilities in government such as deacons on kirk sessions or as constables.[11] It would have been difficult (and probably dangerous) for urban leaders to ignore their fellow townsmen entirely.

It must also be remembered that civic government used its authority in large part to provide services to the residents and thus maintain order in the locality, something demanded by the crown that also might benefit the populace. Parliament passed reams of economic regulatory legislation, 'stacks of statutes' by one account, that local authorities had to enforce upon their residents. But beyond these national legislative imperatives, town governments were expected to provide for the safety, health and prosperity of their communities. Street improvements, bridge repair, improvement of harbours or quays, upkeep of walls (where there were walls), and maintenance of defences came within its purview. So did sanitation and public health, as town government regulated dunghills, took steps to prevent fire, provided rudimentary sewerage, and guarded against plague and disease. Many towns also provided sources of fresh water for their citizens, building and maintaining public conduits which brought water into the centre of town. These amenities benefited the community as a whole and provided a sense of common purpose for townsmen.

Provision of these services was not altruistic, of course. Intense concern for the disruptive potential of the increasing – and increasingly poor – urban population forced town governors to develop programmes and policies to both relieve and control humbler townsmen. With so many of the poor flooding to towns seeking economic betterment, civic governments were at the leading edge of poor-relief policy, developing extensive programmes to respond to local needs. Such programmes generally involved both monetary relief for the 'deserving poor' like widows and orphans and more coercive programs such as workhouses and houses of correction for those identified as vagrants or the 'idle poor'. They also often included the purchase of supplies of grain for distribution to poorer townsmen in hard times. Typically initiated by and responsible to the governing body of a town, urban poor-relief programmes managed through parish institutions gave parish officers a stake in borough government and contributed to the increasingly secularized role played by the parish by the end of the sixteenth century. In England, the experiments in poor relief developed in places like London and Norwich and Ipswich would eventually become part of the national system of poor relief institutionalized in parliamentary statute. While not fully sympathetic to the plight of the poor by modern standards, these innovative programmes did offer some succour to the poorest residents, demonstrating the sense of responsibility urban government had toward its own citizens and fulfilling central government's mandate to preserve order.

The sense of urban identity displayed through civic culture provided another arena for common ground between governors and governed. For townsmen of all sorts, the honour of the town and the symbols of civic authority were important parts of urban life. Civic processions and festivals, often connected to religious guilds or local patron saints, celebrated the town and reinforced communal ideals. Even after the Reformation, as Alexandra Johnston describes in chapter 24 of this volume, many towns maintained civic celebrations. Chester's midsummer celebrations were still being held in the seventeenth century, although their content and symbolism changed with the times.[12] As Protestantism came to replace Catholicism by the later sixteenth century, many urban communities established lectureships, in which civic government appointed town preachers to provide public sermons. No doubt, in towns that had a strong godly magistracy, religion was used as a means of social control over a less enthusiastic populace, particularly during the hard times of the 1590s. But while religion could be a source of contention, it could also provide a platform for communal activity. Many towns also held civic celebrations directly in connection with civic government and elections; election dinners were common, and newly elected officials sometimes 'owed' a breakfast or dinner to the freemen. The festive aspects of town life helped strengthen notions of common identity and civic order.

Symbolic use of material objects could do the same. The sword or mace that was usually carried before the mayor in his official business represented the dignity and honour of the town and generally garnered respect from all quarters of urban society. When these symbols of civic dignity came under threat, it was not only a town's leadership that felt aggrieved. Town halls, which many towns built or rebuilt in the sixteenth century, could also stand as manifest symbols of civic dignity, local authority and the local economy, as well. Language of civic government often stressed themes of brotherhood, corporate unity, harmony and peace, even if reality did not always live up to the flights of rhetoric. Muriel McClendon has argued that in Norwich, with its considerable potential for divisions among the citizens based on religion, the city's leadership intentionally constrained divisive language and actions so as to preserve civic amity.[13] Historians have sometimes emphasized the loss of communal culture and the divisions this loss engendered, but celebrations, symbols and language continued to play a critical role in town life in the sixteenth century.

   The extent of community solidarity and submission to urban authorities should not be over-stated. The rhetoric of consensus could hide real division. Town records contain plenty of examples of civic governors using their position to benefit their own pocketbooks, for instance obtaining leases of town properties at favourable rates – the 'sweetheart deals' of the day. Freemen could and did protest about these arrangements, as they protested about the narrowing of governing authority and the sometimes heavy hand of urban government. Cries of 'A turd in the teeth of the mayor!' rang out in more than one town in the sixteenth century. Such bold attacks on the dignity and authority of civic leaders were not, however, a frequent occurrence in the sixteenth century. When they did occur, they rarely denounced hierarchy or authority as a whole, but rather insulted individual mayors or aldermen. Serious civic unrest was a rarity. For all the economic, social and religious tensions present in sixteenth-century towns, urban communities remained generally peaceful and urban government proved remarkably resilient.

Town and Nation

Civic government's complex connection with its own citizens is mirrored by its multifaceted relationship with individuals and authorities beyond borough boundaries. Town and city government contained inherent tensions between impulses toward local autonomy and the practical necessity of interacting with central authority and neighboring gentry. If 'oligarchy' is the word that has often framed historians' discussions of the inner workings of civic government, then 'independence' is perhaps the word that has most shaped their treatment of relations between towns and other authorities. Civic government is portrayed as struggling to free itself from the domination of ecclesiastical, gentle or noble landlords through royal incorporation, greater control of borough properties, and a tighter grip on parliamentary representation and local office-holding. Sir John Neale, writing specifically about parliamentary patronage, called towns that chose their own residents as MPs 'meritorious' and 'among the elite'; those that accepted nominees from outside the borough, whether local gentry or – most egregiously – 'foreigners' with no connection to the locality, 'fell from grace'.[14] Many town studies, focused on borough autonomy, saw little connection between civic government and the authorities of the wider realm.

   While towns' desire for greater self-control is clear, framing the discussion in polarized terms perhaps misleads. Urban government was an integral and increasingly integrated part of the polity of England and Wales, as town and crown crafted a closer relationship through royal charters of incorporation. Borough officials, whether operating under a charter or not, had a significant responsibility to carry out royal orders and parliamentary statutes (of which there were a rapidly increasing number) within their boundaries, thus carrying out the wishes of the crown. In a time of changing religious policies, central government enforced religious uniformity through local institutions, providing another venue for royal intervention into borough business. The crown also placed greater monetary demands on local government, requiring more by way of military support and taxation. As the crown strengthened its grip over the provinces generally, town government had more and more to resort to institutions of royal government – the privy council, the central courts, regional councils – to accomplish local business. This integration can be seen even more clearly in Scotland, where the development of the institution of the

Convention of Royal Burghs gave cities a defined role in the constitution and a corporate voice in the Scottish parliament.[15] While not eager to admit crown officials into borough business, town leaders understood that they were part of a larger polity and not islands of self-government in the sixteenth century.

This increased interaction with central government also made town leaders find new ways to interact with other local and regional authorities, whether neighbouring gentry or powerful courtiers. As much as town governments tried to free themselves from the authority of manor lords and even county JPs, they also knew the value of connection to powerful men in gaining their own local ends. Litigation pursued in the central courts – against rival towns or litigious gentry – required not only a good lawyer but often also a 'friend' to pave the way for a positive outcome. Suits made before the privy council had a better chance for success if a patron helped to oil the wheels of bureaucracy. Urban governments actively cultivated patronage in the Tudor period as a means to strengthen their own positions within the polity.

One of the most important suits a town might make was a request for a charter of incorporation. Such suits required the outlay of considerable sums of money and typically had the backing of some man of prestige. It is not surprising, then, that the period which saw a rise in litigation by towns and of charters of incorporation also saw the increasing usage and formalization of the offices of recorder and high steward. Tewkesbury named Robert Dudley, earl of Leicester, the town's high steward when he helped the borough obtain its charter in 1574; Newcastle-under-Lyme did the same for the second earl of Essex in 1590. These officials were expected to protect civic interests in the courts and at Court. Without them, civic business could go badly awry. Throughout the sixteenth century, the city of Salisbury, despite numerous attempts, failed to achieve royal incorporation but instead remained under the authority of the bishops of Salisbury. The bishops were implacably opposed to the borough's incorporation, and even the town's choice of Sir Francis Walsingham as high steward in 1590 could not overcome episcopal hostility.[16] Civic leaders often had to rely on gentle and noble connections to achieve their ends.

Patterns of carefully cultivated relations between towns and gentlemen can be seen throughout the British Isles. The city of Chester, a provincial capital with privileges of self-government extending back centuries, had close relations with various noble and gentle neighbours, going so far as to choose members of the Stanley family (earls of Derby) as aldermen of the city. Many towns gave honorary freedom to friendly gentlemen in hopes of gaining useful patronage connections; with the same idea in mind, almost all towns offered hospitality and sometimes gifts to gentry and nobles who visited their communities. Towns with the parliamentary franchise often selected gentlemen as their members of parliament explicitly for reasons of influence and patronage. In Scotland, burghs might have very close relations with the noblemen who served as their provosts. The burgh of Peebles relied on the neighbouring noble family, the Hays of Yester, to defend the townsmen in the law courts and the royal court against encroachment by local lairds on burgh lands. In times of danger, the burgh sent its charters to Yester for safekeeping.[17] The level of closeness between towns and gentle and noble 'friends' varied a great deal from place to place – Chester was much more likely to invite gentry participation than was, for instance, Exeter. And such relationships were always delicately balanced. Towns wanted assistance, but they did not want domination. The men of Peebles dutifully elected the Hays of

Yester as provosts year after year, but they would not grant them the office in life-rent. Townsmen shrewdly understood the necessity of cultivating such connections to carry out civic government and accomplish local business, but they attempted to protect their own interests, as well.

Civic leaders may have felt an especially keen need for advocacy in the sixteenth century, given the dramatic economic and religious changes witnessed in the period. Town governors had to contend with internal pressures from their own growing populations, attempts to regain lost claims on the part of manorial lords, and the demands of the crown to enforce order and carry out royal policy. The Reformation, with its complicated emergence in the various parts of the British Isles, added new divisions into the social and political fabric which local officials found difficult to mend. If a town's government failed to meet the expectations of royal authority, it could be vulnerable to serious correction. A town with a royal charter might, for instance, be threatened with the revocation of that charter. This was not an idle threat, as the leaders of Maidstone discovered in 1554. Several of their number, apparent Protestants, were implicated in Wyatt's rebellion, resulting in *quo warranto* proceedings and ultimately the dissolution of the corporation for a period of time. Chartered corporations were at the mercy of the power that created them. Scotland's burghs also came under close scrutiny by royal officials in the changeable and intrigue-laden religious politics of the sixteenth century. While royal burghs, at least, gained a measure of mutual strength through the institution of the Convention of Royal Burghs, they paid a disproportionate amount of national taxation and they were open to intervention by royal government as well as by noble patrons. Throughout the sixteenth century, particularly at times of political tensions such as royal minorities and the Reformation crisis, the Scottish crown took direct action in urban government.[18]

Despite their vulnerability to royal power, towns on the whole benefited from their changed relationship with central authority in the sixteenth century. While *quo warranto* proceedings and charter revocation did occur, they were highly unusual. For most English and Welsh towns, the strengthened bond with royal government broadened the authority of civic leaders. In Wales, closer ties to royal authority had the immediate effect of making many towns, which had been almost exclusively English-dominated since their founding in the middle ages, open to the majority Welsh population. In Scotland, relations between the crown and the royal burghs varied over the course of the sixteenth century, but it is perhaps telling that no rebellion or conspiracy (of which there were many) had any significant urban support.[19] Towns throughout Britain might resent the intrusion of royal authority into borough business, but they also knew that the benefits of the self-government they enjoyed rested to a great extent on the power of the crown. While town authorities fretted about the possibility of direct intervention, royal government seemingly had little interest in taking an active, permanent role in managing urban affairs in the sixteenth century.

Conclusion

Royal government in London and in Edinburgh took a keen, though not always direct, interest in the doings of the towns. Authorities, from kings to county JPs to civic magistrates, feared the possibility of urban uprising, given the unstable economic, social and religious backdrop of the sixteenth century. The crowns of England

and Scotland empowered the governors of many towns, making them part of royal government, bolstering their authority over their fellow inhabitants, and making them responsible for the peace and order of their communities. Wealthy merchants and tradesmen strengthened their grip on most aspects of civic government, a change that led to some friction and tension. The erosion of the freemen's voice in many towns caused conflict, as a smaller number of prominent men came to dominate civic politics. Town governors used the power they had to enforce order strenuously, in some cases using the rhetoric of godly reformation to clamp down on unruly behaviour among the populace. Spurred on by the crown, civic magistrates knew that failure to keep order on their part would result in serious consequences, as royal government demanded obedience. But urban government had to preserve a delicate balance, to be responsive to the crown and to neighbouring elites, while also retaining strong ties to the civic culture that bound governors to governed in the towns. The changing circumstances of the sixteenth century did not destroy the sense of communal identity that had been part of urban life for centuries. Belief in the dignity of the town and the protection of its privileges was shared by town-dwellers across the economic spectrum. The patterns of government reinforced by royal charter were not created by these instruments but rather developed over the centuries. Town and city government in Tudor Britain remained resilient because civic leaders linked themselves to increasingly powerful royal government, learned to become savvy operators in the networks of patronage that connected the politically powerful, and capitalized on notions of civic identity and political culture to bind themselves to their fellow-townsmen. As a result, urban government weathered the storms of the sixteenth century, emerging stronger than before.

NOTES

1. Clark and Slack, *Crisis and Order in English Towns*; Clark and Slack, *English Towns in Transition*; Tittler, *Architecture and Power*; Tittler, *Reformation and the Towns*; Tittler, *Townspeople and Nation*.
2. Public Record Office (PRO), London, PC2/48, p. 332.
3. Tittler, *Reformation and the Towns*, pp. 88, 345–6.
4. Norfolk Record Office, The Book of Francis Parlett, f. 6v.
5. Lynch, *Edinburgh and the Reformation*, p. 15.
6. Sidney and Beatrice Webb, *The Manor and the Borough* (1908; reprinted 1963), ch. 6; Clark and Slack, *English Towns in Transition*, pp. 128–9.
7. Roberts, 'Parliamentary representation of Devon and Dorset, pp. 228–9; PRO, KB21/2/fols 59, 101v.
8. Rigby, 'Urban "oligarchy" in late medieval England'; Rigby and Ewan, 'Government, Power and Authority'; Evans, 'The decline of oligarchy in seventeenth-century Norwich'.
9. Tittler, *Reformation and the Towns*, pp. 161, 188.
10. MacCaffrey, *Exeter*, ch. 2; Evans, *Seventeenth-Century Norwich*, p. 26; Lynch, *Early Modern Town in Scotland*, p. 13.
11. Lynch, *Early Modern Town in Scotland*, p. 16.
12. Tittler, *Townspeople and Nation*, ch. 6.
13. McClendon, *The Quiet Reformation*.
14. Neale, *The Elizabethan House of Commons*, pp. 162–9.
15. Lynch, 'The Crown and the burghs', p. 62.

16. Patterson, *Urban Patronage in Early Modern England*, pp. 172, 175.
17. Lynch, *Early Modern Town in Scotland*, pp. 20–1.
18. Clark and Murfin, *The History of Maidstone*, p. 57; Lynch, 'The Crown and the burghs', p. 60.
19. Lynch, 'The Crown and the burghs', p. 62.

BIBLIOGRAPHY

Clark, Peter and Murfin, Lyn, *The History of Maidstone: The Making of a Modern County Town* (Stroud, 1995).

Clark, Peter and Slack, Paul, eds, *Crisis and Order in English Towns, 1500–1700* (London, 1972).

Clark, Peter and Slack, Paul, *English Towns in Transition, 1500–1700* (Oxford, 1976).

Evans, John T., 'The decline of oligarchy in seventeenth-century Norwich', *Journal of British Studies*, 14 (1974), 46–76.

Evans, John T., *Seventeenth-Century Norwich: Politics, Religion and Government, 1620–1690* (Oxford, 1979).

Lynch, Michael, "The Crown and the burghs 1500–1625' in M. Lynch, ed., *The Early Modern Town in Scotland* (London, 1987).

Lynch, Michael, ed., *The Early Modern Town in Scotland* (London, 1987).

Lynch, Michael, *Edinburgh and the Reformation* (Edinburgh, 1981).

MacCaffrey, Wallace, *Exeter, 1540–1640* (Cambridge, MA, 1958).

McClendon, Muriel, *The Quiet Reformation: Magistrates and the Emergence of Protestantism in Tudor Norwich* (Stanford, 1999).

Neale, John E., *The Elizabethan House of Commons* (London, 1949).

Patterson, Catherine, *Urban Patronage in Early Modern England: Corporate Boroughs, the Landed Elite, and the Crown 1580–1640* (Stanford, 1999).

Rigby, Stephen, 'Urban "oligarchy" in late medieval England', in J. A. F. Thomson, ed., *Towns and Townspeople in the Fifteenth Century* (Gloucester, 1988), pp. 62–86.

Rigby, S. H. and Ewan E., 'Government, power and authority 1300–1540', in D. M. Palliser, ed., *The Cambridge Urban History of Britain*, vol. I, *600–1540* (Cambridge, 2000).

Roberts, John, 'Parliamentary representation of Devon and Dorset, 1559–1601' (MA thesis, University of London, 1958).

Tittler, Robert, *Architecture and Power: The Town Hall and the English Urban Community c. 1500–1640* (Oxford, 1991).

Tittler, Robert, *The Reformation and the Towns in England: Politics and Political Culture, c. 1540–1640* (Oxford, 1998).

Tittler, Robert, *Townspeople and Nation: English Urban Experiences 1540–1640* (Stanford, 2001).

Webb, Sidney and Webb, Beatrice, *English Local Government*, vol. 2, *The Manor and the Borough* (Hamden, CT, 1963).

FURTHER READING

Ian Adams, *The Making of Urban Scotland* (1978).

Jonathan Barry (ed.), *The Tudor and Stuart Town, 1530–1688* (1990).

Robert Bearman (ed.), *The History of an English Borough: Stratford-upon-Avon 1196–1996* (1997).

Peter Borsay and Lindsay Proudfoot (eds), *Provincial Towns in Early Modern England and Ireland: Change, Convergence, and Divergence* (2002).

Peter Clark (ed.), *The Cambridge Urban History of Britain*, vol. II, *1540–1840* (2000).

Alan Dyer, *Decline and Growth in English Towns, 1400–1640* (1991).

R. A. Griffiths (ed.), *The Boroughs of Medieval Wales* (1978).

Laquita Higgs, *Godliness and Governance in Tudor Colchester* (1998).

Sybil Jack, *Towns in Tudor and Stuart Britain* (1996).

Keith Kissack, *Monmouth: The Making of a County Town* (1975).

Graham Mayhew, *Tudor Rye* (1987).

David Palliser, *Tudor York* (1979).

D. M. Palliser (ed.), *The Cambridge Urban History of Britain*, vol. I: *600–1540* (2000).

David Harris Sacks, *The Widening Gate: Bristol and the Atlantic Economy, 1450–1700* (1991).

W. S. K. Thomas, *The History of Swansea: From Rover Settlement to the Restoration* (1990).

J. A. F. Thomson (ed.), *Towns and Townspeople in the Fifteenth Century* (1988).

Chapter Eight

Centre and Periphery in the Tudor State

Steven G. Ellis

What exactly do we mean by 'English history' in the sixteenth century? The short answer is that English history is about the kingdom of England, the rise of the English nation, and the development of an English nation-state under England's ruling dynasty, the Tudors. No doubt from the seat of royal government in London, such questions about kingdom, nation and state may have seemed much of a muchness: country, people and culture were all the same; they were all English. Yet further consideration of Tudor concepts of Englishness shows that they encapsulated three different sets of ideas with overlapping definitions: they referred to the king's subjects, the English, living mainly in England, Ireland and Wales and distinguishable from other peoples by customs and culture; to that part of Britain settled by the English before 1066, the kingdom of England; and to such things as English culture, law and government. It is a measure of the monarchy's success in moulding a concept of Englishness that neither its own officials nor modern historians have shown much appreciation of these differences. Other peoples inhabiting the British Isles, however, were keenly aware of them. The Scots described the language spoken in lowland Scotland (and, in effect, in much of northern England too) as Scots. In the other language of Scotland and also of Ireland, Gaelic, the English/Scots language was called *Béarla*, or *Gaillbhéarla*, '(foreign) speech, dialect', the language of the *Gaill*, 'foreigners', who lived in other parts of the archipelago, particularly *Saxain*, 'England'. Thus in Gaelic three different words were employed for three different aspects of Englishness; and the distinction between England as a geographical entity (*Lloegr*) and an Englishman and his language (*Saes, Saesneg*) was also replicated in Welsh.

The conventional assumptions of modern historians about the character of the Tudor state are well captured by two leading Tudor historians of the last generation, Sir Geoffrey Elton and Joel Hurstfield. In the Preface to his *Policy and Police*, Elton remarked that he wanted to 'investigate the normal processes of government', and to see how 'the changes of that time impinged on the nation', in 'what may be called the normal setting of government action'. Accordingly, he had 'omitted from the study the highly special case of the northern rebellions (1536–1537) and the case, special for different reasons, of the dependencies of Ireland and Calais'.[1] For reasons which are not entirely clear he did, however, include evidence from Wales. Indeed, studies like the Tudor volume of the *Agrarian History of England and Wales*, edited by Joan Thirsk (1967), sometimes included Wales in a predominantly English study. The Tudors did, after all, have Welsh origins. It could hardly be denied, moreover, that the Tudor North was part of English history. *The Historical Association Book of the Tudors*, edited by Hurstfield in 1973, duly included a whole essay on the Council of the North. Yet the book's index discloses just the one reference to 'Wales, lawlessness of' and two to 'Ireland, war with' and 'Catholicism' there.[2] Given that the Tudor North, Calais, Ireland and Wales together comprised around half of the state's geographical area, this seems somewhat unbalanced. Certainly, in these territories on the margins of English royal power, where its officials were confronted with other peoples and other cultures, the conventional assumption that this was an English state for an English people seemed much less in accordance with political and cultural realities.

Tudor historians have been equally slow to address developments in the Tudor monarchy in terms of a process of state formation which may be compared with those of other Renaissance monarchies in continental Europe. Even so, the Tudor period marked a clear transition between two quite different phases of state formation, between the Anglo-French dual monarchy which had effectively collapsed with the loss of the major French possessions in 1449–53 and the British multiple monarchy which was established by the accession of James VI of Scotland to the English crown in 1603. The late-medieval monarchy had been an extremely diverse patchwork of lordships, duchies, towns and kingdoms, with five or six separate blocs of territory separated by land or sea, and many marches to patrol and defend; but the monarchy's emerging administrative capital, London, was conveniently sited for the defence of these far-flung possessions. After the loss of the continental possessions, however, the centre of gravity of the English state shifted further north and west. The new British multiple monarchy established in 1603 was a much more compact block of territory – three contiguous kingdoms in an archipelago, with no military frontiers – but London's location in the extreme south-east was an obvious disadvantage. In Tudor times, the state's territorial components did in fact remain comparatively stable, but the Tudor drive towards centralization and administrative uniformity brought about a quite radical reshaping of its essential character – by broadly the same methods as were employed by rulers of similar conglomerate states all over early modern Europe. In this sphere too, however, we need to look beyond the boundaries of early Tudor England in order to appreciate the extent of the changes.

When Henry Tudor became king in 1485, he assumed control of a disparate group of territories annexed piecemeal to the English crown over the previous four centuries. South of the monarchy's core territory of lowland England lay Calais, plus the Channel Isles, the remnants of England's French possessions. To the north and west lay a much more extensive group of peripheral territories, the product of intermittent attempts by medieval kings to realize their claim to dominion throughout the British Isles. Wales was divided between the principality established by Edward I in 1283 and approximately 130 marcher lordships in the east which had previously marked a military frontier with native Welsh princes. The far north of England constituted another frontier zone with the still independent kingdom of the Scots; and the English lordship of Ireland was likewise a predominantly marcher region forming a military frontier with Gaelic Ireland. By 1603, however, Calais had gone: all of Wales had been shired along English lines and incorporated into a new kingdom of England and Wales. English rule had likewise been extended throughout Gaelic Ireland which, together with the English parts, now formed a second Tudor kingdom of Ireland. And even before 1603, the advent of better relations with Scotland had greatly reduced the problems of defending the Tudor north. Governmentally, too, the administration of these regions had been transformed: in all three cases early Tudor rule there was characterized by the prevalence of feudal liberties and special quasi-military institutions in which various forms of march law operated alongside English common law. Yet, beginning in the 1530s, almost all the liberties were reduced to shire ground and by 1603 the operation of English law and royal government had been greatly extended. None of these changes had much impact on Tudor subjects living in lowland England, even though to those living elsewhere they were truly revolutionary. Thus, only by viewing the changes holistically, in terms of a pattern of state formation, can their magnitude be appreciated: to reduce the Tudor state to Tudor England is to marginalize them.

A further distinction between core and periphery which the Tudors were unable to do much about was the traditional geographical divide between the English lowlands and the British upland zone. The general character and quality of the land ensured that the territories of the British upland zone were distinguished by more dispersed patterns of settlement, contrasting social structures, and different patterns of landholding. Culturally too, these territories exhibited sharp contrasts from the English lowlands. Medieval English colonization in Wales and Ireland had led to the establishment of smaller 'Englishries' in what were conquest lordships; but half the British Isles was still predominantly Celtic-speaking in 1500, and in general medieval expansion had brought other non-English peoples under English rule. The 'mere Irish' and the 'mere Welsh' were treated as serfs by royal courts and disabled at law, and there were two other predominantly Celtic-speaking territories, the Isle of Man and western Cornwall. The Channel Isles and Calais included French subjects of the crown, and the English far north included significant Scottish minorities, aliens by birth but many of them 'sworn English'. Altogether, contemporaries numbered five distinct nations (English, French, Irish, Welsh and Cornish) among the king's subjects. From the 1530s, however, English law was extended to the Irish and Welsh, and this, combined with the cultural impact of the Tudor Reformation, ensured that outside the English heartland the English language was steadily gaining ground by 1603 at the expense of indigenous Celtic languages.

Overall, the Tudor territories and peoples were a good deal more diverse than conventional histories of 'Tudor England' have implied. It is of course true that the Tudor population was heavily concentrated in lowland England; and the bias of the surviving sources also reflects the more intensive character of royal government in this region. Much less has survived of the records relating to the devolved administrations established for Ireland, Wales and the English North, and cases from these regions were less likely to come before the central courts on appeal. Yet, perhaps the most fundamental reason why historians have been so slow to offer a holistic account of the Tudor monarchy as a problem of state formation is historiographical, the tenaciously nation-based character of so much history-writing in the British Isles. In the Tudor case, the effect was to hive off events relating to Ireland and, to a lesser extent,

Wales for separate consideration by other national historiographies. And once the Tudor monarchy was reduced to Tudor England, the far north of England, as the one remaining Tudor borderland, could indeed be marginalized as the exception to 'the normal setting of government action'. Essentially, however, the division of the archipelago into separate grand narratives about the rise of four nations reflects the influence of a form of modernization theory. It is not a division which would have been obvious to the king's subjects in these regions, much less to the Tudors themselves. This kind of 'English history', for instance, excludes at the outset those English who had settled outside England, in Ireland or Wales, and whose descendants were not therefore destined to remain English. Instead, their activities are discussed in the context of 'Irish history' and 'Welsh history' (both of which examine relations between English and Celtic peoples in those countries), because their descendants would later on be classed as Irish or Welsh. In turn, however, Irish history excludes at the outset those Irish (or *Gaedhil*) who lived outside the national territory, in Scotland, and so would later on be seen as Scots.

Thus, what is actually being studied in this kind of nationalist history is English, Irish or Welsh people 'in the making', not people who in the past – in 1500, for instance – saw themselves, or were identified by others, as 'English', 'Irish' or 'Welsh'. Given the composite character of the modern British state, the teleological nature of this historiography is, to say the least, surprising. In the case of Ireland, its historiography had a more obvious political edge to it: for nationally minded historians, the erection around the English Pale of a continuous national frontier between Irish and English in the later fifteenth century was uncomfortably reminiscent of the modern frontier and the two Irish states following partition in 1921. Thus, the modern relabelling of the two nations as 'Gaelic Irish' and 'Anglo-Irish' seems to reflect a political imperative in the Irish Free State to invest both native and settler alike with an Irish identity so as to develop a common front against the Unionists. And in so far as the early Tudor frontier figured at all in the literature, it was not as a frontier of separation – which was how English and Scottish historians have most commonly depicted the Anglo-Scottish frontier – but as a zone of interaction and convergence. Much ink was spilled on charting the 'gaelicization' of the 'Anglo-Irish'; but the reverse side of the coin, Ireland's heroic resistance to the Tudors, contrasted markedly with the allegedly peaceful assimilation of metropolitan values in the north of England. This contrast is neatly epitomized in the different depictions of the ruling magnates on whom the early Tudors relied to administer these outlying territories. The Percy earls of Northumberland were the archetypal 'overmighty subject' who resisted the extension to the backward and feudal north of that strong uniform and centralized government which was 'essential to the growth of national unity'.[3] So their eclipse was 'a good thing'. Though every bit as over-mighty, the Fitzgerald earls of Kildare, as exemplars of 'the blended race', had championed 'home rule' against the English. So their destruction was 'a bad thing'.[4] In short, the different agendas of the national historiographies have tended to inhibit the development of the kind of holistic or comparative approaches and perspectives needed to study the wider pattern of Tudor state formation, particularly the sort of interaction between an English core and a Celtic periphery which was central to this process.

Successive English monarchs were of course conscious of their God-given duty to provide for the good rule and defence of these predominantly marcher regions to the north and west of the English lowlands, even though events in continental Europe were much more important to them. Yet, unlike their Yorkist predecessors, the Tudors had little personal knowledge of the geography and peoples of the British upland zone. Henry VII knew Wales well from his youth and upbringing, but the later Tudor monarchs never ventured much beyond York or the Welsh marches, and none of the Tudors ever visited Ireland. In Tudor times, therefore, these borderlands were increasingly seen through lowland English eyes. There were, of course, significant differences in terms of society and government between the three Tudor borderlands: strictly, Wales was no longer a frontier society following the Edwardian conquest, but it still had many of the attributes of one; the marches between English Ireland and the innumerable petty Gaelic chieftaincies were fluid and shifting; and unlike the other two, northern England was not really a conquest lordship with a still partly Celtic population – its frontier was comparatively stable – but the threat from the Scottish monarchy was far more formidable. Yet what were most apparent to Tudor eyes about these territories were the departures from lowland English norms: these were predominantly upland regions with compact lordships, powerful marcher lords, few towns, and a more turbulent marcher society.

Tudor perceptions of a common border problem were reflected, for instance, in the regular practice of shuffling between the three borderlands those soldier-administrators who had experience of governing the one march. The duke of Norfolk spent long periods on the Anglo-Scottish borders after his service as governor of Ireland (1520–2); and one of his northern captains, Leonard Musgrave, constable of Penrith, twice returned to Ireland, where he was killed in 1534. More fundamentally, perceptions of a common problem also informed the vocabulary used to describe the borders. Ever since the twelfth century, the English had been in the habit of distinguishing between Europe's different nations on grounds of material culture. They denigrated their Celtic neighbours as lazy, bestial and barbarous. High culture, allegedly, was associated with economic development – chiefly towns, commerce and cereal-based agriculture, along the lines of the society which had developed in lowland England. Yet where the land was uncultivated, so also were the people: hence the traditional distinction between 'civility' and 'savagery' by which, supposedly, the English were distinguished from the neighbouring pastoral peoples of the Celtic fringe living in idleness and brutality in their woods and bogs.

The clearest instance of this was the description by English officials of Ireland's political boundaries. The area inhabited by 'the king's loyal English lieges' was 'the land of peace', the area around Dublin where conditions most closely resembled lowland England which, under the early Tudors, was renamed 'the English Pale'. In 'the English marches' surrounding 'the land of peace' lived 'border surnames' like the Welshmen who, through contact with the natives, had 'degenerated' from English ways and become 'English rebels'. (The border surnames of the Irish and Scottish frontiers were kinship groups who banded together for mutual protection.) Beyond them lay 'the land of war' inhabited by 'the wild Irish', 'the king's Irish enemies'. Irishness, it was believed, was like a disease which undermined the constitution of the body politic: Richard Stanyhurst believed the Palesmen were formerly so 'addicted to all ciuilitie' and insulated 'from barbarous sauagenesse, as their only mother tongue was English'. But then, with the Irish language and customs 'free denizened in the English pale', 'this canker tooke suche deepe roote, as the body that before was whole and sounde, was by little and little festered, and in maner wholy putrified'.[5] Conversely, natives who adopted English ways were seen to 'grow civil', or 'become English' – the two terms were interchangeable! Thus, in effect 'Englishness', 'civility' and 'peace' were synonyms: so also were 'Irishness', 'savagery' and 'war'. In 1560, Archbishop Parker warned Secretary Cecil that if bishops were not soon appointed to northern sees, the region would become 'too much Irish and savage'.[6] The same vocabulary about 'civility', 'degeneracy' and 'savagery' also informed Tudor comments about conditions in Wales and the English North. Archbishop Cranmer dismissed the northern surnames as 'a certain sort of barbarous and savage people' ignorant of 'farming and the good arts of peace'.[7] Essentially, English officials saw these frontier regions as a bulwark of civilization against the barbarian hordes. Particular farming customs, notably transhumance or booleying which was practised by the northern surnames and in parts of Ireland, were also held to betray the nomadic nature of these peoples, and the Tudors speculated on the Scythian origins of the Irish. In short, the dynamic of the Tudor state might properly be described as one of core and periphery: the Tudors identified a range of common problems in regard to the borderlands to which, on the whole, they responded by trying different permutations on tried and tested methods of royal government in what we should now call a pattern of state formation. Scottish officials had similar ideas about civility and savagery: they castigated Gaelic as 'one of the cheif and principal causis of the continewance of barbaritie and incivilitie' in the Highlands and Islands,[8] and also denounced 'the vicked inclinatioun of the disorderit subiectis inhabitantis' both there and 'on sum pairtis of the bordouris'.[9] Yet, as we shall see, the Tudor monarchy had more resources to put these ideas into practice in regard to frontier administration, and they also exercised a profound influence on perceptions of English identity.

In many ways, traditional Tudor history seems rather like a history of the core with the periphery left out. The preoccupation with developments in lowland England automatically skews the perceived pattern of interaction between centre and locality in favour of the one region where conditions were uniquely favourable to centralized royal government, so presenting the Tudor state as comparatively efficient and successful. In reality, a much fairer test of the regime was how it performed in those territories which lay further from the centre of royal authority. The inherited administrative structures for the government of this predominantly upland zone reflected the patterns of land usage and the earlier feudal settlement of these regions, which in turn shaped the structures of society. In all three cases, the land had for purposes of defence mostly been parcelled out into large lordships or baronies; and often the explicitly military character of this feudal settlement had also been recognized by grants of special liberty jurisdictions which conferred regalian rights on the lord of the liberty, subtracting the lordship from the normal mechanism of shire government in the region. The classic example of this practice were the Welsh marcher lordships, but in the far north of England there were the liberties of Hexham, Tynedale and Redesdale, plus the palatinate of Durham and its northern enclaves known as North Durham, while early Tudor Ireland had similar liberty jurisdictions in Wexford, Kerry, Kildare and Tipperary, plus parts of Co. Dublin. In consequence, early Tudor society in these regions was dominated by great regional magnates such as Lord Dacre of the North in the west marches towards Scotland, the earl of Kildare in the southern marches of Ireland's English Pale, and the earl of Worcester in the Welsh marches. In Cumberland, for instance, only two crown tenants under baronial rank held as much as half a knight's fee. Thus, there were very few substantial gentry able to challenge Dacre influence. Lord Dacre was indeed among the ten wealthiest peers, but more important in marcher society was *manraed*, the military service owing from tenants and gentry supporters, not income *per se*. Marcher lords whose incomes were quite modest by lowland English standards – the earl of Ormond, worth just £260 annually, or even Lord Ogle, at £200 a year – were more powerful than their nominal incomes might suggest. Dacre's three great Cumberland baronies of Gilsland, Greystoke and Burgh-by-Sands formed a relatively compact lordship, worth £650 a year in 1525, with an extensive *manraed*.

In these circumstances, the traditional method of ruling these outlying territories was reliance on these marcher lords to supply the military muscle as ruling magnates, supplemented by regional councils in the North, Ireland, and Wales to co-ordinate administration. Under the early Tudors, for instance, Lord Dacre was the natural choice as warden of the west marches, Northumberland for the east and middle marches; Kildare as governor of Ireland; and the duke of Buckingham, the earl of Worcester, and Sir Rhys ap Thomas for offices in south Wales. The pervading influence of marcher lords and the scarcity of substantial gentry families also shaped the character of local government in these regions. The system of local government as it had developed in the English lowlands presupposed the existence of a substantial pool of wealthy gentry to serve the leading offices of sheriff, escheator and coroner, and above all to staff the peace commissions on which an increasing weight of business was heaped by the Tudors. Moreover, if lowland conditions were normative, we need to consider more carefully whether Tudor reform strategies from the 1530s (as analysed below) were not vitiated from the outset by the allegedly exceptional conditions encountered in the upland zone. Was it possible to govern a large upland shire 300 miles from London by the same structures as had been developed for a small lowland county like Bedfordshire? Earlier English kings had thought not, but then they knew what these upland regions were really like. Scottish kings continued to rely on the nobles to maintain peace and justice within their own lordships. At least occasionally they also visited these outlying parts on royal progresses. The Borders were far more accessible from Edinburgh than from London: James IV, for instance, conducted 'the raid of Eskdale' in August 1504 – significantly, in the company of the English warden, Lord Dacre – hanging thieves to restore order on the borders where there was 'greit misreule';[10] he also visited the Isles twice and, exceptionally, could speak Gaelic.

The economic base of the upland zone was much poorer than that of the lowland zone: not only were administrative units there (parishes and manors, hundreds and baronies, shires) generally much larger than in the lowlands, but the pool of county gentry available to discharge the major offices was far smaller. Many of the marcher gentry were essentially professional soldiers: they kept horsemen for defence (and during truce or peace, these might turn their hand to other, less acceptable activities), but their lands were often worth less than £10 a year – the income of a yeoman. The liberty of Tynedale, Northumberland, was coterminous with the manor of Wark, a wild stretch of territory some twenty-seven miles by seventeen covering 183,000 acres, but the only substantial gentry families there were Ridley of Willimontswick and Heron of Chipchase, both worth 100 marks a year. Further up the valley, there was only one tower house (the normal gentry residence in the marches) at Hesleyside, belonging to the head of the Charlton surname. Redesdale and Hexhamshire nearby had no major gentry families resident at all. Altogether, only 118 gentry lived in Northumberland in 1528 – by lowland standards a remarkably small number, but not untypical of large upland shires elsewhere – of whom just half had the £20 a year in land which was the statutory minimum for a JP, and few had much legal knowledge. The peace commissions for these upland shires were thus noticeably smaller than for other English counties, often less than a dozen JPs, many of whom were non-resident; and their work suffered accordingly. In 1526, it was claimed that there were so few justices in Northumberland, particularly of the quorum, that quarter-sessions had not been kept for a long time.

In any case, particularly before the reforms of the 1530s, quarter-sessions were not a universal feature of English local government: instead, sessions were held once or twice a year by the king's justices visiting the shires, as in much of Ireland and the principality of Wales, or by the lord's officers in feudal liberties. In the Welsh marches, when the introduction of quarter-sessions was proposed in 1536, the president, Bishop Rowland Lee, opposed this, arguing that the natives were not ready for English-style self-government. 'There are very few Welsh in Wales above Brecknock who have £10 in land', he declared sternly, 'and their discretion is less than their land.'[11] Wales had to be excluded from the requirement that JPs have an annual landed income of £20; but even then the clause in the Act of 1542/3 specifying that the lord chancellor should appoint just eight JPs and a *custos rotulorum* for each Welsh county underlined the difficulties in poor upland regions of finding sufficient and substantial gentry to serve on the English-style commissions. Others were equally mistrustful of the Welsh gentry as 'bearers of thieves and misruled persons'.[12]

The overriding aim of royal government in these regions was not the ministering of justice to the punishment of wickedness and vice, but the more basic one of defending the king's subjects from enemies and rebels. Only in the northern and Irish marches was there an actual ongoing threat of invasion, but all three regions suffered from continual depredations by thieves and border reivers. Thus, military matters were a far more important aspect of local government among the turbulent marchers than in the increasingly peaceful lowlands. Northern sheriffs, for instance, had sometimes to lead the *posse comitatus* against the border surnames as well as against Scottish reivers. In Ireland the work of the peace commissions was still chiefly military: until the 1550s the keepers of the peace might or might not have power as justices to determine indictments. Thus, there was an increasingly obvious gap in performance between Tudor rule there and in the turbulent borderlands. As the character of royal government intensified and Tudor expectations of its leading officials rose, so the machinery of local government came under increasing strain. In the 1530s, the renewed concern for internal security which accompanied the Reformation crisis precipitated more radical measures for administrative reform.

Tudor perceptions of a common border problem were again underlined in May 1534 when Henry VIII replaced Kildare as governor of Ireland, dismissed Dacre as warden of the west marches, and appointed Bishop Rowland Lee as the new president of the council in the marches of Wales. In the ensuing reorganizations, it was the arrangements for Wales and the Marches which most neatly encapsulated the shift in Tudor attitudes to the borderlands. Hitherto, a conservative attitude to landed property rights, the needs of defence, and sheer administrative inertia had dissuaded the regime from more radical change. Fearing further Yorkist conspiracies, Henry VII had extended the previous policy of pruning subventions to the ruling magnates governing Ireland and the far north: this obviated any threat from private armies raised at crown expense. Yet it also placed the burden of defence more squarely on local shoulders, so reducing the number of nobles who were able and willing to undertake this type of quasi-military office – a point underlined by Henry VIII's unsuccessful experiments in the 1520s with the earls of Cumberland, Westmorland and Ormond. Moreover, some magnates who were able and willing (the fifth earl of Northumberland, the third duke of Buckingham) were plainly not trusted. Henry VII also had the liberty of Tynedale incorporated into Northumberland in 1495. In the 1530s, however, piecemeal tinkering with the inherited system as and when opportunity arose gave place to more sweeping changes which betrayed a settled distrust of this type of ruling magnate and a new confidence in the ability of English common law and shire government to work a reformation of society.

The so-called Welsh Act of Union (1536–43) abolished the previous distinction between the Marches and the principality of Wales, incorporating both into a new kingdom of England and Wales. It extended English common law throughout Wales, introduced quarter-sessions and the normal structures and officers of English local government, and granted to the 'mere Welsh' the same rights as Englishmen. The marcher lordships were abolished (as also Welsh law, and pleadings in Welsh), seven new shires were created (one of which was added to England), and a few other districts with their Welsh communities were added to existing English shires, so in effect extending England further into Wales. By this blanket imposition of English law and government, it was somehow expected that 'Welsh rudeness would soon be framed to English civility'.[13] A Shrewsbury chronicle duly credited Bishop Lee with having 'brought Wales into civility before he died',[14] and English officials were convinced that this kind of doctrinaire policy really could train the natives to civility. Yet the underlying problem in Wales was the fragmentation of authority and absentee lordship which encouraged crime and the harbouring of thieves by local gentry and hindered efforts to stamp out lawlessness. Wales had no military frontier to defend, was closer to the centre of power, and the marcher lordships there were both an anachronism and increasingly administered (on behalf of the crown and other mainly absentee lords) by native Welsh gentry who saw in English-style self-government confirmation of their *de facto* position. In Wales, moreover, not only were the Tudors seen as Welsh, but the Tudors also took care to conciliate this new ruling elite through the ecclesiastical settlement – initially by grants of monastic land to the gentry, and then by commissioning Welsh translations of the Book of Common Prayer and Bible so as to facilitate religious services in Welsh. Under Elizabeth, moreover, thirteen of the sixteen bishops appointed to Welsh sees were Welshmen, an unprecedented proportion. Overall, Tudor reform in Wales removed the legal disabilities on the native Welsh, promoted Welsh culture through the status accorded to Welsh as a literary language for the church, and advanced the idea of Wales as a single territorial entity. For these benefits, the loss of Welsh law and the removal of particular Welshries into England was perhaps not too high a price to pay.

By contrast, attempts to 'civilize' the northern and Irish marches by a reform strategy which combined centralization, administrative uniformity and cultural imperialism ran up against more intractable problems. The basic difficulty was the overriding need for defence. All over Europe, princes relied on territorial magnates to raise troops, maintain order, and co-ordinate border defence: in the sixteenth century, moreover, the more powerful monarchies also built up standing armies for this purpose. Henry VIII's ousting from office of Tudor magnates like Dacre in the 1530s thus cut across accepted practice and deprived the administration of a cheap means of border defence. Queen Elizabeth likewise excluded the northern magnates from border office, and even refused to appoint her kinsman, the earl of Ormond, as governor of Ireland, although he was the obvious candidate. The Tudors then compounded their difficulties by their reluctance to maintain standing garrisons for border defence.

As historians have noted, Tudor reform certainly brought about a vast expansion of crown land in these regions. In Northumberland, for instance, the Percy inheritance, Tynemouth and Hexham priories, and Redesdale and Hexhamshire (acquired by 'exchange') greatly increased the royal estates. The 1536 statute strengthened crown control over feudal franchises there, with Redesdale and later Hexhamshire being incorporated into Northumberland, so opening up the region to royal government. Yet the most obvious result was a crisis of lordship and a 'decay of the borders'. Within two years of Dacre's banishment to Yorkshire, a rebel proclamation in Cumberland roundly asserted that the 'rulers of this country do not defend us against the Scots'.[15] In the west marches, however, the underlying structure of power was less disturbed: Dacre survived and was restored as warden in 1549. Things were quite otherwise in the east and middle marches, where the Tudors had long sought to undermine Percy rule. The fourth earl (d. 1489) had been able to raise 1,000 spearmen there, but allegedly the sixth earl (d. 1537) could only raise 100. By 1550, the Percy castles of Alnwick, Warkworth, Prudhoe and Langley, now in the king's hands, were reportedly 'much in decay . . . to the ruin and destruction of the country'.[16] The Marches were further weakened by the failure of other major landowners to reside there: excluded from major office, they had less need of border service from their tenants, and so raised rents and entry-fines in response to inflation. By 1543, the county was unable to defend itself.

Initially, the main beneficiaries of this decay of the Borders were the northern surnames whose activities became virtually uncontrollable. The muster returns for Northumberland in 1538 numbered 6,375 able men, of whom 2,913 were equipped with horse and harness. Of these, all 391 of the Tynedale 'thieves' had horse and harness, as did 185 (about 40 per cent) of the Redesdale 'thieves'. In other words, the English surnames were a formidable force, the military equivalent of all but the most powerful Gaelic chieftaincies in Ireland: in wartime, their troops were a substantial addition to English military might. (They disposed about 20 per cent of the shire's highly prized mounted spearmen.) Yet in truce or peace they turned their hand to other pursuits, notably reiving and robbery in the Northumberland and Durham lowlands. In 1559, Sir Ralph Sadler with twenty years' experience of the frontier reported, after another war with Scotland, that he had never known it 'in such disorder': 'for now the officer spoyleth the thefe' without bringing him to trial, 'the thefe robbeth the trew man', and true men paid blackmail to thieves. During the last war, he asserted, English borderers had even paid blackmail to Scots, a development 'which I never harde of before'.[17] And in the traditional cross-border reiving, even the English surnames eventually lost out: for instance, the number of horsemen which the Tynedale surnames could muster had dwindled to 134 by 1580 and to only 21 by 1595. Another indication of this military collapse was the successive surveys recording the decay of border service: the 1584 returns, for instance, showed that of 1,522 Northumberland tenancies which owed border service in 1535/6, only 200 were still furnished for service fifty years later. At a time of rising population, increasing stretches of the march were waste.

Rather than strengthen defences, however, Queen Elizabeth chose to mend relations with the Scottish Court. The establishment of Protestant regimes in both countries in 1558–60 meant that, in the ensuing age of religious wars, the two states now saw each other as natural allies. The 'long peace' and increased co-operation thus reduced frontier defence to the threat from the border surnames, but Elizabeth was now more concerned about the solidly Catholic northern nobility as the defence of God's elect nation against popery began to replace civility versus savagery in the rhetoric of Englishness.

The religious question eventually became even more important in regard to the Irish frontier. Kildare's opposition to his dismissal in May 1534 had led to a major rebellion which took fourteen months and cost £40,000 to suppress. In the revolt's aftermath, the forfeiture of the Kildare estates and then the dissolution of the monasteries and the resumption of lands belonging to English absentees again swelled crown lands in the region, much as in the English North: landed revenues climbed spectacularly from IR£400 per annum in 1534 to IR£3,100 annually by 1537. Yet the earl's destruction and associated aspects of Tudor reform also disrupted traditional power structures, undermining the system of alliances and fortifications by which the English Pale had previously been defended. Gaelic chiefs exploited the resultant power vacuum to encroach on the English marches. For instance, without a resident lord to defend them, Kildare's Irish estates, worth IR£1,585 annually before the revolt, never yielded more than IR£895 per annum to the crown. By 1542, the nominal value of crown lands, based on valuations made before the revolt or the dissolution, had reached IR£7,450 a year, but many of them were now waste or uninhabited. Less than half this total was actually leviable. Thus, just as in the English North, Tudor reform had precipitated a similar crisis of lordship and decay of the border regions in English Ireland.

Appointing an English-born deputy and other key officials to a remodelled council did nothing to address these problems. The king was forced to maintain a permanent garrison, in order to keep order. Yet, since the increased costs of the new governor and garrison far outstripped the additional revenues from Kildare and the church, Ireland now became an increasing drain on English finances. This deficit the king was very reluctant to accept as the price of increased control and security. An attempt to balance the books by reducing the garrison and cutting its pay failed when the two leading Ulster chiefs, O'Neill and O'Donnell, combined to invade the Pale, thus underlining the administration's weakness. Reinforcements were rushed in and the government attempted instead a much more ambitious solution to the lordship's problems. Essentially, the initiative now known to modern historians as 'surrender and regrant' was an Irish adaptation of Henry VIII's Welsh policy. As with Wales, Tudor reform aimed to address Ireland's political fragmentation by incorporating the Gaelic chieftaincies, with the English lordship, into a new political entity: but, instead of union with England, this was to be accomplished by making Ireland into a separate Tudor kingdom. Gaelic chiefs would be induced to recognize English sovereignty in return for feudal charters confirming the lands they occupied, with the clansmen in turn receiving fixed estates by a process of subinfeudation. The Gaelic lordships would be shired as English counties, and rather than being Irish enemies, 'the mere Irish' would enjoy the same legal status as freeborn Englishmen, with protection at common law for their lands and goods. Thereby, the island's medieval partition and the military frontier would be abolished.

This plan to create a second centralized Tudor kingdom, English in culture, law and government, was an extremely ambitious undertaking. Wales had taken seven years just to assimilate administratively into England. Ireland was four times as large, and around two-thirds of the island was part of an independent Gaelic entity extending into Scotland whose peoples had no natural ties with the Tudors. Yet, of all the Tudor initiatives for Ireland, 'surrender and regrant' most nearly matched ultimate aims and available resources, providing for a gradual extension of English rule with Gaelic co-operation. Initial progress was quite promising. Two major chiefs, O'Neill and O'Brien, and Burke, one of the 'degenerate English', were created earls of Tyrone, Thomond and Clanrickard respectively; MacGillapatrick became Lord Fitzpatrick of Upper Ossory; and the co-operation of the estranged earl of Desmond was also secured. For the Gaelic lords, the initiative offered security against expropriation by the Tudors, while English modes of inheritance and fixed estates, replacing the uncertain Gaelic system, stabilized the chief's authority over his clansmen. For the local English, Tudor reform held fewer attractions than in Wales because they were already English subjects, not 'mere Irish', but it nonetheless held out the prospect of lucrative leases of ex-monastic land and provincial office in an extended administration.

Yet the process of assimilation was extremely complicated: it was not until 1557, for instance, that the shiring of two Gaelic lordships, Leix and Offaly, as Queen's County and King's County respectively, was completed, and then only in very different circumstances. One reason for this was the level of resources which Henry VIII was prepared to commit to Ireland: he was far more interested in acquiring new territory by war with France (where, altogether, the capture of Boulogne (1544) cost c.£1.6 m) than in adventures in the bogs of Ireland. After 1547, however, the Edwardian regime was prepared to pay for results and experimented with plantation in a bid to force the pace. The English garrison was quadrupled; and when a rising in Leix and Offaly by the O'Mores and O'Connors allowed the confiscation of their lordships, the Pale could be extended by colonization. Yet the emphasis on coercion and colonization soon proved counter-productive. Anglo-Gaelic relations plummeted, and the ensuing guerrilla warfare against the newly established colony and Forts Governor and Protector in the midlands quickly frustrated hopes that plantation rents would cover defence costs. The annual deficit snowballed from £4,700 to £35,000, whereupon the government reverted to more conciliatory methods so as to reduce costs.

Essentially, the various initiatives of the mid-Tudor period lacked coherence and consistency. Surrender and regrant addressed the need to regularize relations between the Tudor state and autonomous Gaelic warlords and lordships, but this kind of rolling programme did not directly tackle the problem of defence in an extremely militarized society. Thus, the newly created Tudor peers with their compact lordships resembled the marcher lords and lordships of the British upland zone far more than the intended model of Tudor service nobles with more scattered holdings. Even so, some Gaelic chiefs saw in the new arrangements a means of securing outside support against rival factions within the ruling clan, as in the O'Brien lordship of Thomond, thus providing the basis of a stable settlement: the English-educated and Protestant fourth earl of Thomond eventually became president of Munster. Yet, more often, the rigidities of primogeniture could not cope with the fluctuating power struggle within the ruling clan and between Gaelic lordships more generally, so that in Tyrone, for instance, chiefs appointed by Gaelic custom (Shane O'Neill, Turlough Luineach O'Neill) ousted the earl's designated successor by English law. From the 1560s, the government tried to curb the enhanced authority of Gaelic chiefs under surrender and regrant by establishing individual clansmen as tenants-in-chief, instead of mesne tenants, in the hope of fostering an independent landed gentry within the lordship; but this subversion of the chief's power over his clansmen was fiercely resisted.

The introduction of English plantations aimed to tackle two related problems which had been thrown up by surrender and regrant, but plantations in turn introduced new complications. Model colonies of Englishmen would supposedly train the natives to civility while acting as military strongpoints against the growing threat of foreign invasion. In Scotland, James VI had similar ideas (equally unworkable), dividing Gaeldom there into two sorts, the one barbarous 'yet mixed with some shewe of civilitie'; 'the other, that dwelleth in the Iles, and are all utterly barbares, without any sort or shew of civilitie': for the latter, he recommended 'planting colonies among them of answerable inlands subjects' to 'reforme and civilize the best inclined among them, rooting out or transporting the barbarous and stubborne sort, and planting civilitie in their roomes'.[18] Yet colonies established on expropriated land proved a very disruptive influence in local society. Leix-Offaly, moreover, aimed to extend English influence into the Gaelic midlands, but its location beyond the standing defences of the English Pale also made it very awkward to defend. For their part, the colonists were far more interested in establishing themselves as landed gentry than in promoting the benefits of English civility among the natives. In the longer term, too, reliance on New English settlers to operate the system of English local government which replaced Gaelic law and lordship also subverted the government's good intentions: small groups of English newcomers had no interest in sharing office and power with the more numerous Gaelic landowners and had every reason to maintain that the latter were not yet ready for self-government. Thus, in practice, the autocratic Gaelic system gave place to a new system of colonial exploitation which could only be maintained by the standing army on which Tudor rule in Ireland came increasingly to depend. Behind all this, however, lay the basic fact that it was quite impossible to govern a predominantly pastoral lineage-based society by the blanket imposition of administrative structures gradually built up over centuries to govern the quite different society of agricultural villages and market towns in lowland England.

The result was growing resistance – in the 1560s the so-called revolt of Shane O'Neill, and military resistance to plantations in the midlands and, later, east Ulster – to which the government responded by increased coercion. Under Elizabeth, a small standing army of at least 1,500 men (frequently much larger) backed by numerous commissions of martial law (at least 259 issued in Elizabeth's first two decades) was seen as essential to maintain order. In turn, the Palesmen were alienated by the government's efforts to shift the burden of maintaining the army onto the English Pale by extending the incidence of purveyance. From 1569–70, moreover, regional councils were established for Connaught and Munster to extend the reach of the administration: these likewise had power of martial law, backed by small garrisons to overawe local opposition, and were financed by appropriating the billeting rights of Gaelic chiefs and imposing composition monies in lieu. Thus, increasingly, government was financed by a system of military taxation which ensured that, until the mid-1590s, English subventions were generally kept below £30,000 per annum, notwithstanding inflation. Yet, there was a heavy price to pay in terms of a gradual erosion of political consensus in English Ireland and an insidious transformation in the overall character of Tudor rule which became increasingly absolutist. From 1568, unrest and rebellion among the Englishry became increasingly common and by 1580 Gaelic and English movements of political opposition that were originally separate had begun to coalesce. By that date, too, religious differences had become far more important.

Seen from the borderlands, the Tudor Reformation was a religious manifestation of the same policies of centralization, uniformity and cultural imperialism as had characterized Tudor reform since the 1530s. Most obviously, this development was reflected in the intrusive character of successive royal injunctions and the Acts of Supremacy and Uniformity which were enacted by parliaments in which the borderlands remained seriously under-represented. Moreover, since the Reformation involved a shift from a visual presentation of Christianity to a bibliocentric one, its enforcement created major problems in the upland zone where parishes were larger and poorer, towns were fewer, and levels of literacy lower. For Celtic-speaking regions, however, the introduction of prayer books and bibles in English also amounted to a policy of cultural imperialism against the indigenous cultures of these regions. In the event, the New Testament and the Book of Common Prayer were soon translated into Welsh (by 1567), but Gaelic translations did not come until much later (1603 and 1608 respectively), and Cornish translations not at all. Moreover, the need to operate through two languages further dissipated the government's reforming energies and the ensuing religious divisions exacerbated its difficulties in consolidating Tudor rule. In Wales, where the local gentry profited substantially from leases of ex-monastic land, the effects were not too serious. In Ireland, however, where in the longer term soldiers and settlers from England were the chief beneficiaries, the government soon ran into difficulties over the enforcement of religious uniformity. Initially, Gaelic chiefs had made no difficulty about accepting Henry VIII as Supreme Head of the Church of Ireland, but as Anglo-Gaelic relations plummeted chiefs like Shane O'Neill began to canvass support from Catholic Europe to defend their lordships against English heresy. Concurrently, religious dissidents among the Old English, such as James Fitzmaurice, also intrigued against Elizabeth.

Increasingly, religious movements were coalescing with political dissent, so that resistance became more general, ideological and entrenched, sparking distinct phases of rebellion of growing intensity – in the south and west (1568–73), in Leinster and Munster (1579–83), and in Ulster (the Nine Years War, 1594–1603). Initially, revolts in English Ireland had generally followed the mainland pattern of political demonstrations within a context of overall obedience, by contrast with the localized Gaelic 'wars of independence'. The Butler rising and the earl of Thomond's rebellion in 1569–70 were Irish echoes of the political intrigues surrounding Norfolk, but the

Fitzmaurice rebellion also included a pronounced religious dimension. By the second phase, it had become difficult to disentangle political and religious grievances. For instance, the earl of Desmond's grievances were predominantly political, but his cousin, Fitzmaurice, led a Catholic crusade supported by the papal legate, Dr Nicholas Sander, and a few Italian troops. In 1580 this crusade spread to the Pale with Viscount Baltinglass's Catholic rising, supported by the O'Byrne chief in Gaelic Leinster, whose motives, however, were more political; and of those Pale merchants and gentry implicated in the rising, many were fervent Catholics, but others had been alienated from government by the growing New English hold on local office. Finally, in the 1590s, the earl of Tyrone, of Gaelic stock but raised in the English Pale, adapted Fitzmaurice's commonwealth rhetoric to develop a new faith-and-fatherland ideology with which to appeal for Catholic Old English support. Overall, therefore, Tudor reform achieved a distinctly odd result in Ireland. In effect, military conquest created a second Tudor kingdom, but it also alienated the local Englishry and left a bitter legacy of racial and sectarian animosity, with an administration controlled by a colonial elite of New English adventurers dependent on a standing army to maintain authority. As English senses of identity were increasingly shaped by Protestant perceptions of England as God's elect nation, so the Englishness of the Catholic Old English of Ireland was increasingly impugned. Concurrently, in opposition to the Tudor state and Protestant New English settlers, the spread of new senses of Irish identity based on faith and fatherland helped both to drive a wedge in medieval Gaeldom between Catholic Irish and Protestant Scots, and also to dissolve traditional differences between Gaelic and Old English communities in Ireland. Irish and English identity in the modern sense were thus very much an unwitting product of Tudor state formation.

So how should we assess the overall impact of Tudor rule? By 1603, the Tudors had consolidated monarchical power in the upland zone, so achieving a long-term goal of successive English monarchs. This had been accomplished by breaking down local autonomy and extending royal authority through a strategy of political centralization, administrative uniformity, and cultural imperialism. In short, the Tudors had simply imposed on the borderlands the norms and values of the region with which they were most familiar, lowland England. At one level, then, the Tudors had – in a typical piece of early modern state-building – reorganized an extremely diverse patchwork of marcher lordships with different legal systems and administrative structures, the remnants of England's medieval empire, into a much more compact block of territory all governed by English law and administration. The completion of the Tudor conquest of Ireland and the Union of the Crowns with Scotland thus created a multiple monarchy of three contiguous kingdoms in one archipelago and also spelled the end of the military frontiers whose rule and defence had caused such problems for the Tudors. The Anglo-Scottish borders were shortly renamed the middle shires and English local government was extended throughout Ireland. In lowland England, the political nation which had suffered almost none of the inconveniences of this policy – was indeed scarcely affected by these sweeping changes apart from having to pay for them – might very well, like the Tudors themselves, have seen the events of 1603 as a vindication of Tudor reform.

It is unclear at what point, if at all, Tudor monarchs and officials were able to visualize the establishment of this post-1603 British multiple monarchy without military frontiers. Yet even if the neglect of the borders was eventually conscious policy, based on far-sighted planning, this was hardly likely to impress the long-suffering inhabitants of the Tudor borderlands who had been so sacrificed on the altar of Tudor state formation. The fact remains that, in the far north and in English Ireland, the Tudors had manifestly failed to discharge even the most basic duties of early modern monarchy in maintaining good rule and defending their subjects from enemies and rebels. In Ireland, they had conquered new territories, but their new subjects there had been thoroughly alienated from Tudor rule by systematic coercion and the accompanying wholesale proscription of Gaelic law and custom as evil and barbarous.

In the longer term, moreover, the manner of Tudor expansion and centralization was to exert deep-seated pressures on the political stability of the new British state. In effect, Tudor centralization had reshaped power structures to create a monarchy which was something of a hybrid between an English nation-state and a more typical multinational composite state of the early modern period. For instance, behind the English appearance and institutions of the kingdom of Ireland (central courts and parliament, Church of Ireland, shires and sheriffs) lay a predominantly Catholic and Gaelic-speaking population ruled from London through a small group of New English soldier-settlers. In Wales and the English North, tensions between centre and periphery were less overt: these regions were at least represented in the English parliament, with twenty-nine and sixteen MPs respectively in 1601 in a lower house of 462. The dismantling of the military frontiers did of course eliminate one major problem, but only by creating another – the relationship between the English monarchy and Scotland which, as an independent monarchy in its own right, could not be governed by the kind of strategies devised for Ireland and Wales. Initially, King James's experience of Scotland's more fragmented power structures, decentralized administration and cultural pluralism helped to mitigate the rigours of the Tudor system. Yet given the differences of geography and problems of communication in a pre-industrial society, continuing attempts to centralize power and to replicate elsewhere conditions in the south-east corner of the archipelago soon ran into trouble.

NOTES

1. Elton, *Policy and Police*, pp vii, viii.
2. Hurstfield (ed.), *Historical Association Book of the Tudors*, pp 224, 227.
3. Reid, 'Rebellion of the earls', pp 176, 201.
4. Curtis, *Medieval Ireland*, pp 309–75.
5. Stanyhurst, 'Description of Irelande', pp 13, 14.
6. Ellis, *Tudor Frontiers*, p. 68.
7. MacCulloch, *Cranmer*, p. 178.
8. Macinnes, *Clanship, Commerce and the House of Stuart*, p. 76.
9. Goodare, *State and Society in Early Modern Scotland*, p. 254.
10. Nicholson, *Scotland*, p. 568.
11. Williams, *Wales and the Act of Union*, p. 20.
12. Ibid.
13. Roberts, 'Tudor Wales, national identity and the British inheritance', p. 14.
14. Williams, *Wales and the Act of Union*, p. 18.
15. Ellis, *Tudor Frontiers*, p. 240.
16. Ellis, 'Civilizing Northumberland', p. 119.

17.   Ellis, *Tudor Frontiers*, p. 120.
18.   Goodare, *State and Society in Early Modern Scotland*, p. 264.

BIBLIOGRAPHY

Curtis, Edmund, *A History of Medieval Ireland from 1086 to 1513* (2nd edition, London, 1938).
Ellis, S. G., 'Civilizing Northumberland: representations of Englishness in the Tudor state', in *Journal of Historical Sociology*, xii (1999), 103–27.
Ellis, S. G., *Tudor Frontiers and Noble Power: The Making of the British State* (Oxford, 1995).
Elton, G. R., *Policy and Police: The Enforcement of the Reformation in the Age of Thomas Cromwell* (Cambridge, 1972).
Goodare, Julian, *State and Society in Early Modern Scotland* (Oxford, 1999).
Hurstfield, Joel, ed., *The Historical Association Book of the Tudors* (London, 1973).
MacCulloch, Diarmaid, *Thomas Cranmer: A Life* (New Haven, 1999).
Macinnes, A. I., *Clanship, Commerce and the House of Stuart, 1603–1788* (East Linton, 1996).
Nicholson, Ranald, *Scotland: the Later Middle Ages* (Edinburgh, 1974).
Reid, R. R., 'The rebellion of the earls, 1569', *Transactions of the Royal Historical Society* 2nd ser. (1906), 171–203.
Roberts, Peter, 'Tudor Wales, national identity and the British inheritance', in Brendan Bradshaw and Peter Roberts, eds, *British Consciousness and Identity: The Making of Britain, 1533–1707* (Cambridge, 1998), pp. 8–42.
Stanyhurst, Richard, 'The description of Irelande', in *Holinshed's Irish Chronicle*, ed. Liam Miller and Eileen Power (Dublin, 1979).
Williams, Glanmor, *Wales and the Act of Union* (Bangor, 1992).

FURTHER READING

Brendan Bradshaw, *The Irish Constitutional Revolution of the Sixteenth Century* (1979).
Ciaran Brady, *The Chief Governors: The Rise and Fall of Reform Government in Tudor Ireland* (1994).
M. L. Bush, 'The problem of the far north: a study of the crisis of 1537 and its consequences', *Northern History*, vi (1971), 40–63.
R. R. Davies, *The First English Empire: Power and Identities in the British Isles 1093–1343* (2000).
S. G. Ellis, *Ireland in the Age of the Tudors, 1447–1603: English Expansion and the End of Gaelic Rule* (1998); and *Reform and Revival: English Government in Ireland, 1470–1534* (1986).
S. G. Ellis and Sarah Barber (eds), *Conquest and Union: Fashioning a British State 1485–1725* (1995).
Andrew Hadfield, 'Briton and Scythian: Tudor representations of Irish origins', *Irish Historical Studies*, xxviii (1992–3), 390–408.
Mervyn James, *Society, Politics and Culture: Studies in Early Modern England* (1986).
A. I. Macinnes and Jane Ohlmeyer (ed.), *The Stuart Kingdoms in the Seventeenth Century: Awkward Neighbours* (2002).
C. J. Neville, *Violence, Custom and Law: The Anglo-Scottish Border Lands in the Later Middle Ages* (1998).
Robert Newton, 'The decay of the borders: Tudor Northumberland in transition', in C. W. Chalklin and M. A. Havinden (eds), *Rural Change and Urban Growth 1500–1800: Essays in English Medieval History in Honour of W. G. Hoskins* (1974), pp. 2–31.

Daniel Power and Naomi Standen (eds), *Frontiers in Question: Eurasian Borderlands, 700–1700* (1999).

Joan Thirsk (ed.), *The Agrarian History of England and Wales*, vol. IV, *1500–1640* (1967).

S. J. Watts, *From Border to Middle Shire: Northumberland 1586–1625* (1975).

Glanmor Williams, *Recovery, Reorientation and Reformation: Wales c.1415–1642* (1987).

Jenny Wormald, *Court, Kirk, and Community: Scotland 1470–1625* (1981).

CHAPTER NINE

Politics and Government of Scotland

JENNY WORMALD

No historian nurtured in the politics and government of sixteenth-century England can ever quite believe in sixteenth-century Scotland. Nor, indeed, could sixteenth-century Englishmen. Especially in view of the recent, fifteenth-century, past, it became axiomatic among English historians that the way forward to a civilized and governed society was greater central control, with the balance between royal and aristocratic power moving decisively towards the former. Yet sixteenth-century Scotland, with a population roughly one-fifth of that of England, had as many peers. Justice was, essentially, the king's justice. Yet only in the sixteenth century was Scotland acquiring a centralized supreme civil court, and it would not have a central criminal court until the late seventeenth; criminal justice was presided over by the justice-general, a hereditary office held by the mighty aristocratic family of the Campbells, earls of Argyll. Moreover, the justice of the bloodfeud, surely the epitome of a violent and bloody society, was alive, well and flourishing. And while the institutions of government might share the same names as their English counterparts – parliament, council, exchequer – in practice they were so constitutionally ramshackle as hardly to deserve comparison. Small wonder, then, when in 1603 a Scottish king inherited the throne of England, his new English subjects were horrified and could only devoutly hope that he would forget his Scottish past, and turn to English ways of governing. For Scotland was, by definition, uncivilized and ill-governed.

A major source of tension throughout James VI and I's English rule was that the king did not agree with them, even although he did on occasion have sharp things to say about the Scots, those 'men not of the best temper', that in itself gives grounds for pause; the king of Scotland and England was, after all, in a position to know. But there is a wider issue here. The underlying question is what constitutes successful government. We have lived for a very long time under the shadow of the Westminster parliament as the 'mother of parliaments' and of the vast historiography of English government. This in itself has led to the almost inevitable assumption that the English model has always necessarily been the most effective one, with the corollary that Scotland, which did not follow it, was therefore badly governed. In particular the power of the early modern Scottish aristocracy has been regarded by English historians, and also Scottish ones, themselves perhaps much too persuaded by the superiority of English government, as a threat to, rather than bastion of, royal authority; there still linger on the remnants of the belief that James VI's successful kingship of Scotland lay entirely in his ability to survive against his overmighty aristocracy.

It is, however, possible to take a very different approach. No doubt Scottish government could, by English standards, be described as undeveloped and backward. But the real question is whether these standards had any actual relevance to Scotland at all, whether, in other words, the Scots retained a style of government which was very different because it worked, and even worked remarkably well. Simpler and often amazingly casual it certainly was; but do we have to continue to fall into the trap of thinking that greater complexity automatically means better government?

The beginning of the 'Tudor' period immediately opens up reasons to regard the second approach as the more valid. In England in 1485, in Scotland in 1488, there was a crisis of kingship. But what a difference in scale. Richard III's defeat and death at Bosworth was the last major act in the dynastic drama of the Wars of the Roses, and the last change of dynasty, in the person of Henry Tudor, a man with virtually no claim to the throne at all. James III's defeat and death at Sauchieburn was likewise the violent overthrow of a king. But there the comparison ends. James III, exponent of a kingship which was unacceptably arbitrary, fell foul of a sufficiently powerful section of the political nation; attempts at negotiation failed, and the issue was resolved on the battlefield. To avoid the distraction created by the pervasive influence of English historiography, it is worth pointing out that this is not simply a demonstration of the excessive violence of Scottish politics; the score of kings who died by violence in the fifteenth century is England four, Scotland two – and the score of usurpations England six, Scotland nil. What matters is what James III's fate tells us about expectations of Scottish kingship. Like his grandfather James I before him in 1437, James died because he abused his power and ultimately the only resolution was the bloody one. Both kings were succeeded by their sons.

It is, of course, impossible to quantify precisely the difference between a political nation which might challenge individual kings but consistently maintained loyalty to the ruling house and one which not only challenged individuals but repeatedly changed dynasties. But it is equally impossible to ignore the much greater stability of the first, compared to the second. One only has to contrast the strenuous propaganda of the Tudors, in literature, imagery and architecture, to demonstrate their right to the crown and the blessings of peace and dynastic security they brought to a disturbed and demoralized kingdom – the latter, as it turned out after 1547, deeply ironic – with the absence of any such need in Scotland, which concentrated far more on its place as a truly important European kingdom. The first was defensive, the second – if somewhat exaggerated – supremely confident.

The contrast between 1485 and 1488 is, however, far more than the question of dynastic stability, or otherwise. It is one of the keys to the remarkable history of early modern Scottish kingship. Whether in the lamentable reign of Henry VI or the minorities of Edward V and Edward VI, England appears to have found it impossible to cope with the absence of an effective adult ruler, and the French experience after the death of Henri II in 1559 was hardly much better. Scotland, where every ruler came to the throne as a minor between 1406 and 1625 – a record unrivalled in Europe – did learn to cope. Thirty-eight years of minority in the fifteenth century were bad enough, fifty in the sixteenth even more dire, and to these fifty can be added the dismal and dithering six years of the adult reign of Mary Queen of Scots. In such circumstances, Scotland offers the unique spectacle of a kingdom where personal kingship simply could not be consistently exercised, and yet the government of the kingdom was somehow maintained without the extremes of factional struggles seen in mid-sixteenth century England or late-sixteenth-century France. The strong identification of the kingdom with Stewart kingship, that kingship which was the focal point of Scottish identity, whatever the age of the king, does much to explain why Scotland could be so significantly out of line with the accepted norms of Western European kingship – and survive. And kingship as the focal point was reinforced by two remarkable pieces of underpinning. First, from a very early date, the Scots removed doubts over the legitimate succession to the throne, with the entails of 1281, 1284, 1318 and 1371 – the first three made because of a paucity of male heirs, the fourth when Robert Stewart succeeded his childless uncle David Bruce. Dynastic disputes, while not wholly impossible, were therefore carefully guarded against. Second, individual Scottish kings might succeed as children, but the Scottish king never died. As early as 1214, Alexander II was inaugurated as king at Scone, before presiding over the burial of his father, William the Lyon, at the abbey of Arbroath. And from 1329, the new king's reign began on the day of the death of his predecessor, a practice anticipating that of England by 154 years. In both cases, these events were politically rather than constitutionally motivated, most occurring at times when the Scots were vulnerable to threat from their powerful southern neighbour England. Nevertheless, despite the vagaries of minorities and the personalities of individual monarchs, the Scots found very basic and practical ways of emphasizing the solidarity and permanent existence of their personal monarchy.

This does not, of course, mean that Scottish kingship was no more than a focal point. Interrupted it might be; but personal kingship, when exercised, was strong kingship indeed, for the sixteenth century witnessed three kings of exceptional ability, James IV (1488–1513), James V (1513–42) and James VI (1567–1625). These were men who utterly understood the art of kingship, both in their political skills and in their brilliant instinct for a distinguished Court culture, something which even Mary, in this if in nothing else, shared with them. And it was not kingship which could be ignored. Scotland was one of the two countries with whom Henry VII sought a marriage alliance, the other being Spain. Henry VIII loathed James IV because he presided over a more dazzling Court than Henry could create in his early years, and went on to be beaten by James V in the international marriage market, while Elizabeth spent a great deal of time raging at James VI because of his refusal to be ruled by her, while paying him a virtually annual pension in an attempt to ensure that Scottish politics would not undermine English ones.

In the second half of the sixteenth century, the fact that the Scots joined the English in breaking with Rome and the increasing probability that the determinedly childless Elizabeth would be succeeded by a Stewart monarch have focused attention on relations between England and Scotland as the primary theme of the period. This has to an extent distorted the view of the politics of the first half of the century. For then the Scots were not mainly concerned with England; James IV did not dwell on the fact that as long as Henry VIII was childless, he, by virtue of his wife Margaret Tudor, was heir presumptive to the English throne.

Why, after all, should early Tudor England have been of particular importance to Stewart Scotland? Anglo-Scottish friendship of the twelfth and thirteenth centuries had been violently ended when Edward I used the Scottish succession crisis of 1290 to impose his alleged overlordship of Scotland; and from then Scotland and England were almost constantly at war until the 1350s. Thereafter, there was much less fighting, but no restoration of friendship. As late as the 1540s, the English were the 'auld inemie'. Friends lay abroad, in Europe, the main one being France, with whom the Scots had entered into an alliance in 1296 which would be consistently renewed up until the mid-sixteenth century. The excessive ambitions of Edward I and his grandson Edward III towards Scotland had very far-reaching results. Scotland discovered that she could survive very well despite bad relations with her nearest neighbour, and indeed benefit from ignoring that neighbour and looking to Europe; and this her kings capitalized on, adding to their prestige by their strenuously European stance. When the great theologian and historian John Mair published his *History of Greater Britain* in 1521, arguing for the advantages of closer ties with England, his was a very lone voice. He was on surer ground when he talked of the excessive pride of the Scots, that pride derived from their place as a European monarchy, compared to the insularity of the English.

One king had made an effort to move Anglo-Scottish relations on to a less hostile plane. In 1474, James III made a peace treaty with Edward IV, the first treaty as opposed to temporary truce, and accompanied this with a series of marriage proposals between the two royal houses, none of which came to anything. It was not a popular policy. It was in this decade, and very possibly in response to royal policy that Blind Hary produced *The Wallace*, the second of the great epic poems on the Wars of Independence. And in the first parliament of James IV in 1488, part of its justification for the attack on James III was that the king had been guilty of 'the inbringing of Inglissmen to the perpetuale subieccione of the realme'. So traditional attitudes were restated. In contrast to his father, James IV now offered protection to the Yorkists defeated at the battle of Stoke in 1487. In 1495–7 he went further, taking up the cause of Perkin Warbeck and providing him not only with an aristocratic Scottish bride but an army which twice he himself led into northern England. The mission failed; there was no rallying in England to the Yorkist cause. Instead the idea of Anglo-Scottish peace became once again a diplomatic issue. But this time the initiative came not from a Scottish king out of line with the priorities of Scottish foreign politics, but from an English one, seeing the need, in the interests of English security, to try to shift these priorities. The outcome was the treaty of 'Perpetual Peace' in 1502 – 'perpetual' in fact being eleven years – and the marriage of James and Margaret Tudor in 1503.

A change of direction in Anglo-Scottish relations in this period did not, however, signal a fundamental shift in foreign relations. The success of the Scottish monarchy against the odds cannot be understood without reference to its assertion of its place in international politics. For there followed on from its attitude to Europe and England the same pride and high morale of Scottish merchants, scholars flocking into the European universities, clerics with far more contact with Rome than the English had. There was indeed a gulf between Scottish perceptions of the importance of the kingdom and the reality of that importance. But what matters, in the context of the remarkably successful kingdom that was sixteenth-century Scotland, was how

Scotland viewed the matter. Thus James IV took Warbeck up as a way to make Scottish presence felt not only in England, but in Spain (with whom Henry VII was in alliance) – earning himself enthusiastic plaudits in a letter from the Spanish ambassador in Scotland, Pedro d'Ayala, to Ferdinand and Isabella – while at the same time continuing diplomatic relations with France. It worked. The Scottish king, in the eyes of his subjects, was a king of international importance; and that importance was demonstrated visually, for there he is, included among the leading monarchs of Europe, in the twelve kings portrayed in Durer's triumphal arch designed for Emperor Maximilian. This was high-prestige kingship; and that, of course, fed in to the king's prestige and authority at home.

Despite the fact that James's reign ended with the bloody carnage of Flodden in 1513, followed by the lengthy minority of James V, the same trick was repeated in the 1530s. James used to brilliant effect Henry VIII's break with Rome, making himself the most attractive of all Scottish kings in the international marriage market, in his dealings with both the papacy and the emperor Charles V. Once again, a Scottish king, using as his bargaining counter his efforts to resist pressure from his uncle, Henry VIII, was not only able to extract vast amounts of money from the papacy but could portray himself as a major player among European monarchs. And he got what he really wanted: marriage with the daughter of François I, Madeleine, despite the French king's attempts to fob him off with a lesser French bride in the interests of his own diplomatic manipulations; and then, when Madeleine died within months of the wedding, a second marriage to a member of one of the mightiest aristocratic houses of Europe, Mary of Guise.

The sheer panache and flair of these two kings go a very long way towards explaining the power of the Scottish monarchy, despite the repeated setbacks of the minorities. Both had a confidence in their kingship which far outweighed the fears and worries of Henry VII, having to establish his dynasty's control of the English kingdom, and the neurotically bombastic efforts of Henry VIII, seeking in his dealings with Scotland and France to recreate himself as Edward I or Henry V, in a desperate attempt to obscure the fact that, with the final loss of the Hundred Years War in 1453, England had become, like Scotland, a small offshore European kingdom. The Scots simply had longer experience of dealing with this, and they did so in a way which emphasized their place in Europe in contrast to the English obsession with the importance of being English. The effects can be seen in the a very revealing contrast between the assurance of the Scottish monarchy and the agonizing of the English over the succession – that James V died leaving a daughter only a week old to succeed him, to no particular concern other than the inevitable and brief factional struggle at the centre as to who would act as regent, while Henry VIII embarked on a course of matrimonial divorce and execution in order to ensure a male heir.

Their subjects did not, of course, view their monarchy with pride only because of its international relations. Both James IV and V provided plenty of evidence of impressive kingship at home. Both enhanced the image of the monarchy by their extensive building. At Stirling James IV created the vast and magnificent great hall and a four-towered gatehouse modelled on a Roman triumphal arch, embellished the facade of Edinburgh castle with three great oriel windows, and began the building of the palace of Holyrood. His son extended the building at Holyrood, constructing the massive double tower and new west front, which were incorporated into the reconstruction of the palace in Charles II's reign. Linlithgow was given a new heraldic gatehouse and large and elaborately sculpted fountain. The Fifeshire hunting-lodge of Falkland, already extended by James II and James IV, was transformed into a palace of great elegance and beauty, with its classical columns and sculpted medallions. Above all, there was the glorious new palace block in Stirling castle. Again, the exterior is classical, adorned with statues representing the ancient deities, the virtues, and modern humans, including James V himself. Internally, the palace is the one surviving building in the British Isles showing the new design of Court building in both England and Scotland, which departed from the great hall, replacing it with parallel rooms for the king and the queen, each having a guard hall, a presence chamber and a bedchamber; royalty had withdrawn into privy apartments, making itself less immediately accessible than in the more public life of the great hall, and thus fundamentally altering the nature of Court politics, because accessibility to the king was now much more controlled. On the ceilings of the presence chambers were the great carved wooden roundels, the Stirling Heads, displaying allegorical imagery and human faces, including members of the Court. Their only parallel are the heads in the Wawel palace in Krakow; but there, heads and necks jut straight down out of the ceiling to somewhat sinister effect, compared to the gentler and more attractive impact of the heads within the great roundels in Stirling.

For all this, James used James Hamilton of Finnart, his master of works, himself the designer of his own innovative castle of Craignethan, and masons from Scotland, France and Flanders. His second wife, Mary of Guise, with no doubt some wifely tact, claimed to have seen nothing finer than the Scottish palaces outside the Loire valley. But it was not just tact. Both James IV and James V put on a dazzling display of majesty, for visitors from abroad and subjects at home. Between their reigns was another royal minority. That was by now a familiar interruption of adult rule. It mattered much less to the continuing authority of the monarchy than a royal style which made that monarchy highly prestigious.

Exactly the same point can be made about what went on within the walls of their buildings, the brilliance of their Courts. After 1509, indeed, when Anglo-Scottish relations worsened with the accession of the bellicose Henry VIII, himself eager to impress Europe with his own Court, one element in the rivalry between the two kings was that Henry had nothing to match the smaller Court to the north. Not until the 1520s and 1530s would he have his own circle of Court poets to match those of James IV; initially all that was on offer was the old-fashioned and bad-tempered John Skelton, useful for writing anti-French and anti-Scottish diatribes but appreciated for little else. The great Court poet was the Scottish William Dunbar, a poet of European stature and great range, from wit and satire to religious verse. He has left us a compelling picture of James's Court, with its scholars, rhetoricians and philosophers, its artists, musicians and merry singers, and those 'shoulderaris and schoveris that hes no schame', that brilliant description of the archetypal courtier. And it was Dunbar and his fellow-poet Gavin Kennedy whose great 'flyting' of 1507, that fast, furious, scurrilous verse quarrel, gives us an insight into one way in which the court was entertained. Poor Henry, trying to stage it in 1514, could only put up Skelton and a courtier, one Christopher Garnesche, who was no poet at all.

Even during the minority of James V, literary and musical culture did not lapse. Gavin Douglas, bishop of Dunkeld, produced his *Eneados*, the first translation of

Virgil's *Aeneid* in the British Isles; and Robert Carver wrote one of his superbly lovely masses for the Chapel Royal at Stirling in 1520. And it flowered again during James's majority, when the literary talent of the Court was dominated by the courtier and diplomat Sir David Lindsay of the Mount. Like Dunbar, his writings provide us with a whole range of insights into early-sixteenth-century Scotland, but with one great difference. Lindsay was well aware of the religious divisions now tearing Christendom. One of his masterpieces, the *Satyre of the Thrie Estaitis*, includes the highly witty and brilliant attack on the leading clergy; at the performance at Court in 1540, James V, it has been claimed, threatened to send the bishops off to his uncle Henry VIII, if they would not reform themselves. That was not good hearing for the bishops. What was not good hearing for the Court, revealed in a delightful little thumbnail sketch by the contemporary musician Thomas Wode, was James's insistence in joining in the singing in a harsh and raucous voice.

Up until James's death in December 1542, then, the dominant note struck by Scotland and its monarchy was one of confidence and achievement. Yet as in 1513, so in 1542: an impressive reign ended in the disaster of a defeat by the English, this time at Solway Moss. The king was not present, and the carnage was much less than at Flodden. But James died soon after; his two sons were already dead, and his heir not only the youngest of all Scottish monarchs – aged one week – but a girl.

Like previous minorities, Mary's was complicated by the presence of the queen-mother, Mary of Guise, with her legal rights as guardian of her child. Her rivals for power were the leading Catholic churchman, Cardinal David Beaton of St Andrews, the man believed to have held the dead king's hand to trace his signature on his will (a suspicion very similar to that surrounding Henry VIII's will in 1547), and the heir presumptive to the crown, James earl of Arran, at that stage going through a wavering Protestant phase, who, being closest to the throne, was appointed as governor. This was not just internal political faction fighting at the centre. This was a new era, an era of religious and diplomatic faction fighting. Whatever his criticisms of it, James V had strenuously upheld the Catholic church, as exemplified only one year earlier in the acts of the 1541 parliament, which emphasized reform, not reformation; and his foreign policy had been grounded on the old alliance with France rather than any new friendship with England. The year 1543 witnessed a reversal of both.

Knox prematurely saw, in this year, with the cartloads of bibles being sent up from England, the advance of Protestant reform. Henry VIII, recreating the ambition of his predecessor Edward I, saw his opportunity to annex Scotland to England by marrying his son Edward to the infant Scottish queen. It might have worked; the treaty of Greenwich, which accepted the marriage with optimistic provisions for preserving Scotland's independence, came close to acceptance in July 1543. It failed primarily because Henry, with astonishing pigheadedness, overplayed his hand, insisting, despite solid Scottish refusal, that Mary should immediately be sent south to England. When in 1544 he began the brutal assaults on southern Scotland known as the Rough Wooing, all he did, like Protector Somerset after him, was to ensure that the way forward for Scotland was not what it had seemed in 1543. Henry might manage to knock out one leading opponent of that way forward, by arranging the murder of Cardinal Beaton in 1546, but that had little effect compared to his vicious demonstration to the Scots that England remained the 'auld inemie'. Somerset, fighting with perhaps more genuinely missionary zeal than Henry, did no better. In

September 1547 he won a stunning victory at Pinkie, which was no doubt good for morale, but for nothing else. His attempts to woo the Scots into a union in which England would not dominate were not believed; and he had no better answer than Edward I to controlling Scotland – his vastly expensive Scottish policy only built up problems for his government of England, and had much to do with his downfall in October 1549. Meanwhile, the Scots who had refused to allow Mary to go to England in 1543 now sent her off to France for her safety in 1548. Nothing, it seemed – despite the presence of an emerging Protestant party in Scotland – had changed.

Nor did it appear to do so in the 1550s. In 1554, the highly intelligent Mary of Guise ousted the weak and vacillating Arran from the regency. Her policy was naturally pro-French and pro-Catholic, her ambition the marriage of her daughter to Henry II's son, the dauphin Francis; and with a Catholic England to the south under Mary Tudor, replacing the Protestant regime of Edward VI, there was even less hope for Scottish Protestants, with nowhere to turn for support. And indeed it is by no means clear, after the experiences of the 1540s, that we can simply make the apparently obvious assumption that Scottish Protestants saw alliance with even a Protestant England as the answer to their problems. That would be to take too narrow a view of the matter, ignoring other things which mattered much: their European tradition, their independent vision of themselves. It is a revealing fact that the marriage of Mary Queen of Scots to the dauphin was not only sought by her mother but supported by the leading Scottish Protestants, her bastard half-brother Lord James Stewart and others. In other words, Scottish Protestants were thinking out their own way forward, a way which maintained the Auld Alliance but with a curious twist. For their support for alliance with Catholic France can surely be explained only in terms of their hope that their queen, when married, would stay in France – as indeed she clearly would have done had her husband not died in December 1560 – leaving them to pursue their cause at home. They were, in effect, drawing on their long-established role during minority or, in this case, absentee monarchy. The difference from the past was that this time the stakes were very much higher. But in coping with that, they turned to something very traditional indeed: the making of bonds.

As has been pointed out, the relationship between a relatively non-centralizing crown and the localities meant that local politics were still personal politics, very much dominated by the aristocracy and gentry, and heavily dependent on ties of kinship and lordship. Since the 1440s, relationships between lords and their followers had been written down, as bonds of manrent (allegiance) and maintenance (protection); likewise, men of social status had recorded their common enterprises in bonds and contracts of friendship. The first two were normally made for life, or in perpetuity; this was generally the case with the third, but these might also relate only to a specific purpose. The intention of the written bonds was to bring the parties to them under the same obligations as those which bound members of kin-groups, obligations which in the case of kinsmen naturally remained unwritten; men specifically agreed to act as kinsmen to one another, to give loyalty, service and counsel, in return for counsel and protection, and the settling of feud and dispute. Because of the nature of the sixteenth-century monarchy, these bonds lived on until the end of the sixteenth century, as a record of local power structures, and of the informal nature of local control which sat easily and effectively with the more formal local and royal judicial institutions. Indeed, a lord or head of kin sorting out the disputes of their followers, bringing to an end feud between them, might well be more effective simply because of being personal and immediate than the slower workings of the courts. Dramatically, in the 1550s, this longstanding practice was raised to a new and ideological level. In December 1557, five Protestant nobles made the first Band of the Lords of the Congregation. Their cause was the cause of God; their feud was with the Scottish Catholics, the regent, Mary of Guise, and her French councillors and soldiers in Scotland.

It was a brave and desperate effort by these men – Lord James Stewart, the earls of Argyll, Glencairn and Morton, Archibald Lord Lorne and John Erskine of Dun – to break out of the stalemate in which the protestants were trapped. With much more intelligence than her fellow-ruler in England, Mary Tudor, Mary of Guise did not persecute Protestants; she left them alone. They were not, therefore, provided with a cause to identify with; they had to create it themselves, try to unite Scottish Protestants in a common purpose, as the congregation of God. In late 1557, their chances seemed remote. But the movement was growing. Less than two years later, in May 1559, there was a second, much more general Band, representing the congregations of the west country, Fife, Dundee, Perth, Angus and the Mearns, and Montrose. By that time, Mary Tudor was dead, and the non-Catholic Elizabeth on the throne. But she had only been there for seven months, and had not yet shown any willingness to back the Protestant party in Scotland. Much more to the point was the growth of Protestantism spearheaded by the magnates and lairds of the localities, and the town authorities. And much more relevant to the condition of Scottish Protestantism in the first half of 1559 than Elizabeth of England was the making of peace between the great Catholic powers, France and Spain, by the treaty of Cateau-Cambrésis in April, and the subsequent threat by Henry II that he would now take action against the heretics not only of his own kingdom, but of his daughter-in-law's kingdom of Scotland.

The stalemate was ended. The period between May 1559 and August 1560 witnessed a certain amount of sword rattling and iconoclasm; Edinburgh suffered rapid changes of regime, and the regent and the Lords of the Congregation battled for control, which was finally established by the Lords in April 1560. The Scottish Protestants were by now in close contact with William Cecil who persuaded his reluctant queen to offer armed assistance in February 1560, and much more decisively between March and July. But even more decisive was the death of Mary of Guise in June 1560, against the backdrop of the weakness of the French monarchy after Henry II's death in 1559 and internal divisions within France, which lessened its ability to support the regent. Yet it is a most instructive comment on the nature of Scottish politics that Lord James and Argyll, two leading members of the Lords of the Congregation who had unconstitutionally 'suspended' her from office the previous October, were there with her, showing their respect for this most able opponent, at her deathbed.

In July, by the Treaty of Edinburgh, both French and English troops withdrew from Scotland, and the scene was set for the Reformation parliament of August. Like its continental counterparts, the Scottish parliament was a meeting of the three estates. There were no shire elections, James I's attempt in 1428 to introduce them, on the English model, having been entirely ineffective. Attendance, other than by the burgh representatives, came mainly from the aristocracy, temporal and ecclesiastical, and the Lords of Parliament, a peerage title created in the mid-fifteenth century which gave the beneficiaries the right to individual summons. It was therefore a comparatively small body, but, given its composition, a very powerful one. On the whole, lairds did not attend, unlike the English gentry, no doubt for the very good reason that taxation had not yet become regular; thus, whereas it was to the financial benefit of the English gentry that they should turn up in order to consent to taxation which they would pay, it was to the financial disadvantage of the Scottish lairds to spend the money on travel to and lodgings in Edinburgh. That was forgotten in August 1560, when religious reform became the burning issue. Over 100 lairds flooded into parliament, claiming their right to be there under the terms of the 1428 Act. This only demonstrates typical Scottish indifference to and muddled thinking about matters constitutional; the shire election act restricted their presence, and they should have appealed to the Act of 1426, which enjoined all crown tenants to attend parliament. That is the kind of point which would have had relevance in England. In Scotland, all the concentration was on political reality, and political reality gave them their place.

This was not the only difference between the Scottish and English parliaments. The English Reformation parliament sat for seven years. The Scottish Reformation parliament lasted a mere three weeks, issuing a confession of faith, an impressive and moving statement of the Calvinist faith, and passing only three acts. Yet the Confession and these three acts created a reformation as thoroughly and decisively as – perhaps even more so than – Henry VIII's parliament and indeed those of Mary and Elizabeth. The mass was made illegal; the authority of the pope was abolished; and all acts taking the old church under the protection of the state were annulled. There were indeed many details to be filled in, many problems to be resolved over the coming years. But the Scottish parliament concentrated entirely on the fundamental issue. That in itself is a compelling reminder of the difference between Scottish and English political attitudes. Small wonder, then, that after 1603 James VI and I, well aware of the need to impose control on his Scottish parliament, would still complain more bitterly about the way in which his English parliament, interpreting more correctly the fact that the word meant, in effect, talking-shop, would delay action in the cause of the relentless need to debate; how things should be done appeared to the king with Scottish experience to matter more than getting them done.

Religious division and the international situation meant that the years leading up to 1560 saw minority, or what by now might be called absentee, government on a dramatic and wholly novel scale, a scale which has indeed been called rebellion or even revolution. A religious revolution there certainly was. But can one talk even of political rebellion? Mary's hysterical reaction in France to the Reformation parliament was distinctly muted by her refusal to return to her kingdom of Scotland to deal with the dissidents. Not until 1567, when she was embroiled in the final stages of her own political crisis in Scotland, did she actually ratify its acts, but after her initial outburst, she never challenged them. Rather, she left her government of Scotland in the hands of those 'rebels' the Protestants who had dominated parliament and dominated her privy council; and within a matter of months, after the death of her husband, it was the leading Protestants with whom she discussed her return to Scotland, rather than with the leading Catholics, John Leslie bishop of Ross and George Gordon earl of Huntly, the earl who hoped that she would come to Aberdeen in the north-east, his area of influence, and allow him to spearhead a counter-reformation. A monarch who sits back and allows political and religious opponents to control events in her kingdom is certainly a remarkable phenomenon, but her actions undoubtedly make it difficult to categorize the events of 1560 in terms of what is usually understood by 'rebellion'. In any case, there was a huge religious change in 1560, but no attempt whatsoever to alter the political structure. God's cause came first. But no one challenged the queen's authority or right to rule.

The history of the reformed kirk, indeed, owes virtually nothing to the fact that in its early years, a Catholic queen sat on the throne; the Catholic queen even helped to finance it. In her Protestant son's reign, its aspirations would certainly have an effect on Scottish politics. But during Mary's personal rule, 1561–7, its good fortune was that her futile obsession with being recognized as Elizabeth's heir meant that apart from a brief period after her marriage to Henry Lord Darnley in 1565 she never challenged it. And if she was a religious non-event, she was equally a political non-event, at least for the first four years of her reign. She stirred up a little trouble in the north by giving her half-brother Lord James the earldom of Moray, which was claimed by the Gordons of Huntly; in 1562, Huntly embarked on a short-lived and unsuccessful rebellion which ended with his death at the battle of Corrichie. She had a frustrating time trying to find a second husband. Unlike the much-wooed Elizabeth, she was turned down in 1561–2 by the French and the Spanish, and her pro-English policy only resulted in the farce of negotiations for a marriage with Elizabeth's favourite, Robert Dudley earl of Leicester, negotiations which none of the three parties involved intended to succeed. Finally, and disastrously, she acquired a husband, when Henry Lord Darnley, son of the earl of Lennox, came to Scotland from England in 1565. He succumbed to measles, and she promptly succumbed to him.

In the long term, there was of course much more to be said for Mary's policy than Elizabeth's; she was prepared to fulfil that fundamental royal duty of providing an heir. More immediately, it was her choice which was catastrophic. Personally, Darnley was weak, vain and drunken. Politically, a marriage into the Lennox family plunged Scotland into two years of kaleidoscopic factionalism. Favour to the Lennox Stewarts and the queen's unilateral declaration of Darnley as king, without parliamentary approval, pushed Moray into rebellion in the summer of 1565, the 'Chaseabout Raid' which Mary won. Her greater favour to Catholics might last only a few weeks, but created further instability. And her wholly ill-judged favour to her Italian musician and secretary, David Rizzio, was all too readily a matter of scandal, and made her foolish husband an easy prey to the blandishments of Moray and his associates, who promised him the crown matrimonial in a bond which explicitly involved him in Rizzio's murder. The unfortunate Rizzio was the ultimate scapegoat for another exceptional aspect of Mary's reign, the division between her largely Protestant council, whose composition she had taken little part in determining, and her household, with its strong component of French servants. Mary of Guise's French followers had been deeply unpopular. Mary, showing more interest in chamber than council, chose to carry on the pattern. It did not greatly matter while she did not challenge the political control exercised by Moray and William Maitland of Lethington, her immensely able secretary of state. After the Darnley marriage, it became a considerable problem; and poor Rizzio was murdered in March 1566.

There was then another switch of alliances. With unusual skill, Mary detached Darnley from the Protestant lords, but went on to join her fortunes to these lords, allowing Moray back from exile. Her greater triumph was to give birth to a son, the future James VI and I, in June 1566. But that was for the future. The present involved a powerful group which even included that individualistic rogue elephant, James Hepburn earl of Bothwell, who now focused on the need to eradicate the irresponsible and politically highly embarrassing Darnley, who was murdered in February 1567.

What matters, in this overblown murder mystery which is the Scottish equivalent to the Princes in the Tower, is not whether Mary was involved – could she not have been? – but what happened next. She lost whatever small political judgement she had, had herself abducted by Bothwell, married him, and ensured her downfall, enforced abdication and imprisonment in Lochleven castle in the summer of 1567. These two years have given her a quite undeserved interest for historians, if a rather better one for the Scottish tourist industry. What is much more important is what they and their aftermath tell us about the Scottish political nation. The first useless Stewart monarch since 1406 forced a political crisis and then another inevitably lengthy minority on that nation. The habit of upholding the monarchy at is weakest point came back into play; so did the habit of respect for the legitimate ruler. Within months of her abdication, when she had alienated all support, there developed a group who, having had a breathing space from having to deal with her directly, began to react against her deposition. She escaped from Lochleven in 1568, and got enough support to fight her half-brother at Langside in 1568. But she lost, and fled to England, thus making herself a nineteen-year problem for Elizabeth, as opposed to seven for the more fortunate Scots.

The clash, however, between a Scottish political tradition going back for almost three centuries which owed nothing to polite fantasies about evil counsellors but rather made demands on and criticisms of the king entirely explicit, and that even longer tradition which consciously upheld the rights of the king by legitimate descent, now came into sharp and immediate focus because of the crisis caused by Mary, and led to a further five years of civil war between 'Queen's Men' and 'King's Men', in which two of James VI's four regents died by violence. That war came to an end in 1573, with the success of the 'King's Men'. Yet in all this we are considering a mere eight years, 1565–73, years exaggerated out of proportion because of their dramatic quality. Thereafter, normality returned: another minority, like Mary's own, made more complex than those of the past because of the new problem of the Reformation and the enhanced complexity of international relations.

James's minority lasted for some ten years after the end of the civil war. Its highlight came in 1578, when his fourth regent, the tough and unpopular James earl of Morton was brought down, and the king over-optimistically announced that he was now capable of rule. Yet only one year later he made a progress from Stirling, where he had been brought up, to his capital of Edinburgh, which showed that he, or his advisers, had a shrewd instinct for an impressive display of royalty; and he went on to recreate a Court culture centred round a circle of brilliant Court poets which in part followed on his mother's own ability in this field, but, because this time it was not all too brief, was more of a reminder of the dazzling Courts of James IV and V. Scotland once again had an impressive king; the backhanded compliments to that dissimulating 'false Scots urchin', as English ambassadors and Elizabeth herself described him when he was fifteen, are a testimony to a political skill which would restore the prestige of the monarchy and ensure that there was now a monarch in Scotland who renewed the belief in the importance of Scottish kingship in its European context, rather than one whose fixation was the English succession.

James's kingship was, however, kingship with a profound difference. For most of the century, the Scots had survived the problems of minority, the crises of the 1540s and 1550s and the drama of Mary, because of their distinctive political mix of strong monarchy and strong local autonomy. After 1603, when James inherited the English throne, that mix would do much to ensure the success of his absentee kingship. But by that time, the balance had changed. New factors had come into play which did much to alter Scottish political life. James himself, in his great political tracts written in 1598–9, *The Trew Law of Free Monarchies* and *Basilikon Doron*, entered with enthusiasm into the late-sixteenth-century European debate about the nature of kingship and the source of royal authority, and naturally came down decisively in favour of divine right rather than contractual monarchy. But his rule was always infinitely more pragmatic, based on political reality rather than ideology, and it was not the king who was primarily responsible for the developments of his reign. Rather, his reign witnessed the flowering of seeds sown well before the 1580s and 1590s.

There was, to begin with, a pressing need to complete the unfinished business begun in the parliament of 1560. That lairds could simply turn up in considerable numbers when it seemed good to them to do so brought a new and potentially dangerous element into central politics, especially when central politics were complicated by religious divisions. They were indeed showing a new awareness of the 'centre', but with the threatening twist that far from central government imposing greater control on the localities, the localities were asserting their right to impose on the 'centre'. Religion had been the motivating force in 1560. To that was added the introduction of regular taxation after 1581, another compelling reason for the demand of the lairds to have a voice. Thus in 1587 the composition of parliament was for the first time strictly defined, by the shire election Act which revived the dead Act of 1428; now the shires as well as the burghs would send elected representatives. It took time to become effective, but the new political mood was evident enough; the purely political events of 1560 and the financial exactions of the crown were forcing the Scots to do something very novel and think constitutionally. But this was not the only way in which the need for control of the post-Reformation parliament was made very evident. The detailed work of drafting legislation was done by a small committee, elected by the three estates, the Lords of the Articles. After 1560, and increasingly during James's personal rule, the government sought to intrude onto that committee unelected officers of state on whom it could hopefully rely to push its views. James went further, in trying to prevent contentious business coming to parliament at all. By an act of 1594, four members of each estate were to meet twenty days before the full parliament assembled, to examine petitions and articles, and eradicate 'frivolous' matters. Only the king was exempt; he could introduce business at any time.

Yet his own concern with parliamentary management had an extra dimension. Although the doctrine of king-in-parliament was not articulated, James, in the interests of restoring his own prestige and authority, so damaged by the scandals surrounding his mother, enhanced that of parliament. In the 1580s, it was parliament which was used to legislate against defamation of the king's ancestors, parliament which banned the works of Mary's most vicious detractor, George Buchanan, parliament who would now put on a visual display to impress the king's subjects when its members wore the robes designed by the king in 1587 and again in 1606 for its solemn procession through the streets of Edinburgh for its opening. Where James IV had shown distinct wariness of parliament, summoning only three after 1494, James VI picked up on James V's greater use of it, and took it much further. It was not always successful, from the crown's point of view. The religious legislation of 1584, for example, which sought to increase royal control over the kirk was overturned in 1592 by his presbyterian opponents. But in its own way that only underlined the point that a powerful king needed a powerful parliament, to cope with the new problems created by the demands of the kirk, and the altered balance between centre and locality. From the king's point of view, its power was essential – provided it was harnessed.

More generally, in Scotland as in England, there was a decisive shift away from the clerical to the secular in the king's government. In Scotland it can be traced back to the 1530s. It was strengthened in 1584, when the kirk pulled its ministers out of service to the state, insisting on their purely clerical role. But it derived from the aspirations of an increasingly literate laity; lairds who had formerly been content with their power and influence in the localities now wanted a place not only in parliament but in the king's government. The demand for place never reached the grotesque dimensions of late-sixteenth and early-seventeenth-century England, although the development of the role of the master of requests is a clear indication of what was happening; and James's government was markedly more aristocratic than Elizabeth's, for it was aristocrats as well as lairds who replaced churchmen in the high offices of state. But the English Cecils were paralleled by the Scottish Maitlands, the two brothers William of Lethington and John of Thirlestane, respectively secretaries of state to Mary and James, and in the latter case also chancellor; they were the notably successful sons of a more typical example of the ambitious literary laird, Richard Maitland of Lethington, poet and privy councillor.

To this general trend can be added one very distinctive group: the lay lawyers. It is just about possible, indeed, to talk about a legal profession by the end of the sixteenth century, though one still very much restricted to Edinburgh. From 1579, the senators of the college of justice – the Court of Session – were increasingly attacking amateur justice; to merit appointment, judges had now to demonstrate their legal training. And it was not only a matter of the courts. The first Act to attack the long-established justice of the feud – private arbitration and settlement of civil dispute, murder on one side and murder on both – came in 1598. It was only partially successful. The lawyers seized control of cases of unilateral murder; the king backed those who argued for the traditional method of dealing with the others. Yet the presence of the lawyers, with their dual careers in law and central government, and their new insistence on greater professionalism, greater definition, exemplifies in a more focused and dramatic way than anything else the changing nature of Scottish government.

But it was not all new. Much remained traditional. The parliament of 1587, much exercised by the need for stronger royal justice, saw the solution to the particular problems of the borders and highlands in something with a very long history, the making of bonds, when it enacted that under the General Band landlords and clan chiefs were to be responsible, under financial penalty, for the good behaviour of their followers. The king himself saw the value of the bond in the settlement of feud and, as the 1598 Act shows, was much less worried than his new breed of lawyers about personal and private justice. And even in this new age of definition, much remained undefined. A distinguished group of academic lawyers at the end of the century, Thomas Craig of Riccarton, John Skene of Curriehill, were turning their attention to an attempt to rationalize that huge legal jumble, the Auld Lawes, and to sorting out the superiority of parliamentary statute. Yet the privy council retained remarkably wide powers, legislative, fiscal and judicial as well as administrative. Political circumstances, religious tensions and lay aspirations were having an inevitable impact; they created the voice of the future. For the present, late-sixteenth-century Scotland still retained a great deal of its pragmatic muddle, its concentration on what actually worked as opposed to concern with how it should work. And for all his theorizing, that was the approach taken by king James.

For the king was a master of pragmatic politics. The old idea that his main political problem was an overmighty aristocracy, nourished in excessive power because of the repeated interruptions of adult royal rule, is visibly exaggerated. James could criticize his aristocracy, but he believed in and relied on them, the 'arms and executors' of his laws, as he described them. Before 1603, any magnate willing to do the job found a place in central government. After 1603, one of his solutions to kingship from England was to give, with a lavish hand, earldoms to those lairds who had served him well, become prominent in his government and were now raised to the aristocracy to give them the prestige to run things in his absence. In the 1580s and 1590s, his real problem was with the powerful presbyterian wing of the kirk, the antiepiscopal 'Melvillians', under their leader Andrew Melville. Their denial of his authority in the kirk was far more threatening than any problem posed by any individual magnate. It was the Melvillians, as well as his own interest in the European debate, who provoked his political theory, the royal answer to their claim that in Christ's kirk the king was but a member. In the second half of the 1580s and the 1590s, the king, despite many setbacks, worked steadily to build up moderate support, especially in the highest court of the kirk, the general assembly, to reintroduce bishops, first in the parliamentary arena where they mattered much to him, and then, from 1610, in a full-scale diocesan role. The political solution to the problem of a kirk which sought to restrict royal control was an intensely practical one: a hybrid, in which the king's bishops worked with and alongside the hierarchy of Calvinist courts, from national to local. It was highly effective. Meanwhile, the king pursued the traditional role of his predecessors, as a monarch of European importance – and in the 1590s sat back and waited, if, like her English subjects, for a frustratingly long time, for Elizabeth to die.

Sixteenth-century Scotland does not follow the obvious rules for success. It was small, comparatively poor, geographically remote, decentralized; and its political system was and remained haphazard, despite the visible changes of the 1580s and 1590s. Yet for all that, and for all the political vicissitudes of the period, it was indeed a success. Unlike England, it had no legacy of failure in European war and dynastic disturbance at home to shake off. Its determination to be a prominent European kingdom was a source of high morale. So also, as English morale steadily declined in the 1590s, was its future, when a Scottish, not an English, king would at last resolve another long-term English failure, the uniting of the crowns of Scotland and England.

BIBLIOGRAPHY AND FURTHER READING

Cameron, J., *James V: The Personal Rule, 1528–1542* (East Linton, 1998).

Cowan, I. B., *The Scottish Reformation: Church and Society in Sixteenth-Century Scotland* (London, 1982).

Dawson, J. E. A., *The Politics of Religion in the Age of Mary Queen of Scots: The Earl of Argyll and the Struggle for Britain and Ireland* (Cambridge, 2002).

Donaldson, G., *All the Queen's Men: Power and Politics in Mary Stewart's Scotland* (London, 1983).

Donaldson, G., *Scotland: James V–VII* (Edinburgh, 1978).

Donaldson, G., *The Scottish Reformation* (Cambridge, 1960).

Goodare, J., *State and Society in Early Modern Scotland* (Oxford, 1999).

Lee, M. Jr, *Great Britain's Solomon* (Urbana, 1990).

Lee, M., Jr, *John Maitland of Thirlestane and the Foundation of the Stewart Despotism in Scotland* (Princetown, 1959).

Lynch, M., *Edinburgh and the Reformation* (Edinburgh, 1981).

Lynch, M., ed., *Mary Stewart: Queen in Three Kingdoms* (Oxford, 1988).

Lynch, M., *Scotland: a New History* (London, 1991).

Macdonald, A. R., *The Jacobean Kirk, 1567–1625: Sovereignty, Polity and Liturgy* (Aldershot, 1998).

Macdougall, N., *James IV* (Edinburgh, 1989).

Macdougall, N., ed., *Church, Politics and Society: Scotland 1408–1929* (Edinburgh, 1983).

Mason, R. A., *Kingship and Commonweal: Political Thought in Renaissance and Reformation Scotland* (East Linton, 1998).

Mason, R. A., ed., *Scotland and England, 1286–1815* (Edinburgh, 1987).

Merriman, M., *The Rough Wooings: Mary Queen of Scots, 1542–1551* (East Linton, 2000).

Wormald, J., *Court, Kirk and Community: Scotland 1470–1625* (London, 1981).

Wormald, J., *Mary Queen of Scots: Politics, Passion and a Kingdom Lost* (London, 2001).

CHAPTER TEN

Anglo-Scottish Relations: Security and Succession

JANE E. A. DAWSON

And for that oure equall rycht to both the Crownes mon neidis affect us with as equall cair to boith thair weillis and that being now joyned togidder under ane head, as they haif bene of long tyme past in ane religioun, ane language, and ane commoun habitatioun of ane Ile, disjonit fra the great Continent of the world, our princelie cair mon be extendit to sie thame joyne and coalesce togidder in a sinceir and perfyte unioun.[1]

Introduction

James VI and I, writing to his Scottish privy council on 12 January 1604, dwelt on the twin themes of his lawful succession to the crown of England and the welfare and security of his two realms, and looked forward to 'a sinceir and perfyte unioun'. Less than a year earlier his smooth accession to the English throne finally removed the two dominant problems of Anglo-Scottish relations, the security of the British mainland and the English succession question. With a Stewart succeeding the last Tudor monarch in 1603, the possibility of war between the two dynasties vanished and the security threat of independent countries sharing the British mainland disappeared. For most of the sixteenth century, the question of the succession to the throne had loomed like a spectre over relations between the two countries, generating great anxiety and fear for the English and their rulers. The continued fragility of the Tudor dynasty had ensured that only one life stood between the English throne and a Scottish claimant. As Elizabeth adamantly refused to name her successor, uncertainty persisted right up to her death. Throughout the period these vital issues of security and succession had dominated Anglo-Scottish relations, bringing together its two separate levels: diplomatic interchanges between the Tudor and Stewart sovereigns; and the everyday contacts between the peoples of England and Scotland.

Instead of recounting recent diplomatic history, James chose to highlight three types of relations between the English and the Scots based upon religion, language and culture, and geographical proximity. From the triumphal perspective of 1603, he was able to characterize previous Anglo-Scottish relations as a gradual growing together of the two countries which he fervently hoped would speedily culminate in a 'unity of love' and the creation of a new kingdom of 'Greater Britain'. His selective view of the past and his plans for the future were far too sanguine. James had not dwelt upon the diplomatic interchanges of the previous hundred years because they had brought more hostility and warfare than alliance and peace. He would not have acknowledged that every one of his royal predecessors since 1488 had met their deaths as a direct or indirect result of their dealings with England. On the one hand, tangling with the English had proved an extremely dangerous occupation for the Stewart dynasty of Scotland, and would bring new hazards in the seventeenth century. On the other hand, it had undoubtedly been a rewarding dynastic ploy because in 1603 a Stewart inherited the two Tudor kingdoms of England and Ireland.

In the world of early modern international relations, such a dynastic strategy was readily appreciated by the rulers of other multiple monarchies in Europe. They understood that a union of the crowns had been achieved peacefully by a combination of marriage alliance and patient diplomacy over several generations instead of by costly conquest and warfare. The French royal family of Valois and, most spectacularly, the Habsburgs of Austria and Spain had enlarged their lands in just such a manner. For these rulers the interests of the royal dynasty and those of the territories they ruled were inseparable and foreign relations meant first and foremost the relationships created between fellow sovereigns. The attitudes of subjects were not afforded great weight nor were their representatives normally consulted on foreign policy, as Elizabeth I on several occasions was at pains to remind the English parliament.

In a literal sense the Stewart triumph of 1603 had signalled the end to diplomatic relations between the English and Scottish monarchs for the simple reason that they were now one and the same. In his royal person, and that of his heirs, James VI and I embodied the joining of the two monarchies. His failure to persuade his multiple kingdoms to unite more closely was caused in part by the past tensions created by having two levels of Anglo-Scottish relations. Although two sovereigns had become one, the two peoples manifestly had not. Even at the level of diplomatic interchange, the succession question had been solved by default rather than by the normal channels of international relations; friendship, alliance or negotiation. This left a difficult legacy for the British Isles and the origins of many of the problems faced by the Stewart rulers of seventeenth-century Britain can be traced back to the complexities of the relationship between England and Scotland during the Tudor period.

Among the three factors James VI had chosen to describe Anglo-Scottish relations, the geography was crucial. Sharing one island had been a fact of life for as long as the kingdoms of England and Scotland had existed. There were two borders running between the countries: the first along the land frontier from Berwick to Carlisle: the second stretching invisibly through the North Channel between Ulster and the western coast of Scotland, and in their different ways they presented security threats. English attempts to conquer its northern neighbour had provoked the Wars of Independence, thereby creating a legacy of 'hereditarie hatred' between the Scots and the English. Mutual antipathy had developed an acute consciousness of being separate and focused attention specifically upon that land border between the countries. Its very existence had profoundly affected both kingdoms by creating a military frontier and a militarized hinterland: the Borders were viewed by Scots and English alike as a region socially and culturally set apart from the rest of their countries. Though militarized, the borderlands were not well fortified by the standards of sixteenth-century warfare; raiding was endemic and full-scale incursions a permanent possibility, creating deep and justified fears concerning invasion. The English did not seriously expect a Scottish attempt at direct conquest but worried instead that their 'postern gate' was wide open should a French army, or even one from Spain, use Scotland as an operational base to enter the Tudor state. By contrast, the Scots actually faced an English invading and occupying army marching through its 'front door' in the 1540s. An abiding hostility between the two peoples was the main consequence of being able easily to cross the land border from one country to the other.

The other, sea frontier between the Tudor state and the kingdom of Scotland had not become deeply entrenched in Anglo-Scottish consciousness and mythology. Although in London and Edinburgh this second border was out of view and frequently out of mind, it was of vital importance to the political dynamics of the British Isles. By linking Scotland and Ireland the sea frontier brought the third kingdom into the equation and ensured that Anglo-Scottish relations always possessed a British dimension. The short sea-crossing kept the north of Ireland in permanent and close contact with Scotland and carried trade and migrants between the two countries; and, sharing the same language, the Gaels of Scotland and Ireland were united by a profound social and cultural bond. These longstanding links were given a new significance in the sixteenth century when the Tudor state sought to extend its control over the whole of the island of Ireland. The English government's increasing intervention in Ulster raised its awareness and its concern about Scottish settlement and influence there and placed the Irish activities of the Scottish clans firmly on the agenda of Anglo-Scottish negotiations. Adding Ireland, the second kingdom within the Tudor state, complicated diplomatic contacts between London and Edinburgh. In addition to having to take account of Dublin, further confusions were created: the Scottish Highlands and Irish Gaeldom followed their own independent policies with neither the Tudor nor the Stewart rulers maintaining complete control over their Gaelic subjects. Instead of a simple bilateral relationship, Anglo-Scottish relations could revolve around three, four or even five separate points of contact, with the interconnected nature of the politics within the Atlantic archipelago ensuring that some form of 'British' dimension was permanently present. The permeable Irish frontier between the Tudor state and Scotland introduced the dynamics of the 'British context' into Anglo-Scottish relations and in the long run produced more complex problems than the high-profile land border.

During the Tudor period, Anglo-Scottish relations could not be divorced from the wider arena of European diplomacy. From 1296 Scotland's Auld Alliance with France had created the eternal triangle between France, England and Scotland, turning the Anglo-Scottish border into a permanent second front during the periodic warfare between France and England. England's traditional allies, Spain and the Low Countries, were engaged in a Europe-wide power struggle with France. By the middle of the century these international alignments took on a new significance for the British Isles. Both the emperor Charles V, who ruled Spain and the Netherlands, and his rival King Francis I of France concluded that gaining control over the British mainland might be enough decisively to tip the balance of power in their favour. The possibilities for direct intervention in the British Isles markedly increased since neither England nor Scotland possessed an adult male monarch. In the first round of the struggle, France secured control over the marriage and person of Mary Queen of

Scots, and proceeded to invest heavily in Scotland. The Habsburgs subsequently countered this French success by establishing themselves in England through the marriage of Mary Tudor to Philip of Spain. Having effectively cancelled each other out on the British mainland and running out of resources for their European conflict, the Habsburgs and the Valois were seeking peace by the end of the 1550s. The Treaty of Câteau-Cambrésis of 1559 allowed both France and Spain to turn to more pressing domestic concerns, thereby reducing their direct interest in British affairs. In the short term this gave space and opportunity for the British diplomatic revolution of 1559–60 that made England and Scotland allies.

The traditional pattern of international relations had been broken and was to prove incapable of restoration. For the remainder of the century France was embroiled in civil and religious wars whilst Spain initially turned its attention to the Mediterranean and was later preoccupied with the Dutch revolt. At the close of the century, international alignments had been reversed: the centuries-old Franco-Scottish alliance had been abandoned, the English were friends with their old enemies, the Scots, and at war with their erstwhile ally, Spain. Looking back in 1589 William Cecil, Lord Burghley, commented wryly to the earl of Shrewsbury,

> My Lord, the state of the world is marvellously changed when we true Englishmen have cause, for our own quietness, to wish good success to a French King and a King of Scots; and yet they both differ, one from the other, in profession of religion. But seeing both are enemies to our enemies we have cause to join with them in their actions against our enemies.[2]

During the second half of the sixteenth century, the confessional dimension transformed European diplomacy in general, and Anglo-Scottish relations in particular. The fracturing of the unity of medieval Christendom introduced an ideological element into European politics, as increasingly Protestant and Catholic countries aligned themselves in mutually antagonistic camps. Within the diplomatic world the dynastic interests of sovereigns were forced to compete with confessional considerations. In the British mainland the fear of a grand Roman Catholic conspiracy to destroy all European Protestants was widespread by the final quarter of the century. For many English and Scots the belief that the island of Britain was a divinely protected bastion of Protestantism upholding the faith against the forces of the Antichrist was vindicated by the Spanish Armada's defeat. Such an interpretation of international relations put great pressure upon the English and Scottish monarchs to conduct their foreign policies within this exclusively confessional framework and it altered many of the calculations concerning the security of the British Isles.

The religious factor had also turned Anglo-Scottish relations on their head when the Scottish Reformation succeeded with English help. A shared Protestantism provided the crucial foundation for that diplomatic revolution of 1559–60, changing enemies into friends and helping to keep them at peace until 1603. Occupying the same side of the confessional divide had become an essential ingredient in the security of the British mainland by the end of the century. This new attitude ensured that James's Protestant credentials were a necessary prerequisite to his succession, without which his claim to the English throne would have faced insurmountable opposition.

Since 1560 it had been assumed that the two countries were united by a common faith and this helped change the attitude of the English and the Scots towards each other. The fundamental bond of religion was capable of overcoming some of the hostility that had existed by altering the attitudes of individuals. When in January 1560 William Douglas of Lochleven had recognized the English fleet sailing across the Firth of Forth to rescue the Scottish Protestants, he felt able to forgive the 'auld enemy' for killing his father at the battle of Pinkie. A shared faith did not obscure the fact that Scottish and English church organizations had developed differently so that by the end of the Tudor period the distinctive natures of the Church of England and the Scottish Kirk had each become entwined within their respective national identities.

Protestantism also reinforced and increased the cultural links brought about by the shared language of Lowland Scotland and England. Though accents and vocabulary were noticeably different, it was a major advantage for the Scots and English to be mutually comprehensible. This linguistic coming together increased the division within Scotland between the Gaelic and Scots speakers. By the end of the century, a recognizable Protestant and anglophone culture had developed within the English-reading parts of the British Isles. It had been nurtured by the common pool of ideas and attitudes carried in the books and pamphlets that circulated freely in Britain and by the general standardization encouraged by employing a common language of print. These similar cultural and religious outlooks offered one slow and painstaking way of surmounting and replacing the traditional hostility between the peoples of England and Scotland.

James' classification highlighted the general framework within which Anglo-Scottish relations existed, but the three factors of geography, religion and language do not offer a guide to the diplomatic story. The record of diplomatic contacts over the sixteenth century underlines the failure to secure long-term alliances that were firmly based upon the mutual interests of the two countries. The diplomatic switches between the two poles of alliance and of warfare may be illustrated by examining four episodes, 1503–13; 1544–9; 1559–60; and 1586–8. Each provides a key turning-point in Anglo-Scottish relations and demonstrates the dominance of the issues of security and succession.

The Thistle and the Rose, 1503–13

During the early modern period international relations were essentially relationships between the sovereigns of the different European countries. Their personal and dynastic nature made it natural for marriages to be one of the chief means of making alliances and the status and level of the marriage gave an indication of the relative diplomatic standings of the countries and the priorities of their rulers' foreign policies. When Henry VII first mooted a marriage to James IV in 1493 the English king suggested as a prospective bride the daughter of the countess of Wiltshire. Her relatively lowly status indicated that at this point Henry was not over-anxious to secure a Scottish alliance. Henry's valuation of peace with Scotland changed as a result of the threat to English security posed by James' aggressive policies. Nine years later Henry offered his own daughter Margaret to the Scottish king. The Treaty of Perpetual Peace signed between the two countries signalled a serious attempt to end the long-running hostility between Scotland and England, with a threat of excommunication by the pope should either party break the treaty. On 8 August 1503

Margaret and James were married with great pomp and pageant at Holyrood Palace. By that ceremony the Scottish king gained a claim to the English throne for his future children. Of greater immediate relevance, given the vulnerable state of the Tudor dynasty, was that James, as Margaret's husband, also acquired a claim for himself. The death of Arthur, Henry VII's elder son, meant the young prince Henry's life was all that stood between England and a civil war where rival claimants, possibly including the Scottish king, fought for control. This was merely the first episode in a permanent Tudor dynastic fragility that generated the continuous English preoccupation with the succession which formed the backdrop to Anglo-Scottish relations for the remainder of the century.

Although the marital union of the Scottish Thistle and the English Rose offered a magnificent subject for literary celebration and for spectacle, it could not overnight transform the diplomatic realities. Once the priorities of foreign policy changed, the brittle peace ushered in by the marriage was soon broken. When Henry VIII succeeded his father in 1509 he was intent upon attacking France. James, aware of the implications of England's martial policy, rearmed Scotland against possible attack. In 1512 Scotland explicitly renewed its alliance with France, seeking this traditional remedy to maintain its security. During his speech to parliament in January of that year, Henry VIII had resurrected English claims to sovereignty over Scotland, reviving memories of the Hundred Years War and Wars of Independence. As it seemed plain that England had reverted to a hostile stance, James decided to summon his lieges to war and take the initiative. Their enthusiasm to take up arms against the traditional enemy was vividly expressed in a Gaelic incitement to battle addressed to the second earl of Argyll. This poem also revealed the clear sense of solidarity between Scottish and Irish Gaels who were seen to be fighting against a common enemy, the English.

'To fight the Saxons is right
no rising followed by flight;
edge of sword, point of spear,
let us ply them with good cheer.

Against Saxons I say to you,
lest they rule our country too;
fight roughly; like the Irish Gael,
we will have no English Pale'.[3]

Having marched into England and taken Norham castle, the Scottish army met the English forces at Flodden field, where James along with the flower of the Scottish nobility and commons were killed. Being neighbours and kin had not prevented the fighting between the Scottish and English sovereigns, though even in the midst of war, the personal and dynastic aspects of foreign relations remained present. The English queen, Catherine of Aragon, wrote a letter of condolence to her sister-in-law, the Scottish queen, deeply regretting the loss of Margaret Tudor's husband, James, the enemy of Catherine's husband, Henry VIII.

Although the devastating military defeat inflicted upon Scotland in 1513 left the country with a royal minority and a huge gap in its governing class, the English king did not seize this opportunity to attempt the conquest of his northern neighbour. At this stage, Henry VIII was far more concerned with achieving personal glory on the battlefield across the English Channel campaigning against the French. The English lost interest in Scotland once the security of the British mainland was guaranteed, preferring to pursue a policy of containment by destabilizing Scottish politics to prevent any future threat developing. The rapprochement between the two countries heralded by the marriage alliance had been short-lived. In response to renewed Anglo-French warfare, the traditional hostility of the English and the Scots was effortlessly resumed. In each case, once a security threat had been identified, it triggered warlike policies. The Treaty of Perpetual Peace had not delivered what its grandiloquent title had promised. For an Anglo-Scottish alliance to last, the traditional foreign policy alignments for both England and Scotland needed to be changed. Henry VII and James IV had been prepared to contemplate this and experiment with the security and other benefits to be gained, but Henry VIII, with his old-fashioned foreign-policy aims, was not. The consequences of the marriage of the Thistle and the Rose had a much longer life than the alliance itself, for by introducing the Stewart dynasty into the English line of succession, Anglo-Scottish relations were transformed.

'Our Lass and Your Lad'

The combination of a marriage alliance and warfare was once more at the centre of Anglo-Scottish relations in the final years of Henry VIII's reign. Another decisive English victory over the Scots on the battlefield of Solway Moss in 1542 precipitated the death of James V leaving Scotland with a royal minority, the week-old baby girl, Mary, now queen of Scots. The prospect of a royal heiress whose marriage would in the long run secure the kingdom of Scotland for her spouse created an intense struggle for power between England and France and their respective supporters inside Scotland. Initially, when the Treaty of Greenwich was signed in 1543, it appeared as if negotiation had secured the prize for England. With Edward Tudor as the groom and Mary Stewart the bride, such a marriage would eventually bring a dynastic union between the two countries. England would solve its security problem by gaining control over the entire British mainland and, if the marriage were fruitful, the Tudor dynasty would be secured for another generation.

For the Scots the handicap of having an heiress as their sovereign gave them a very different attitude to the proposed marriage. They assumed that in the long run the kingdom of Scotland would be absorbed into the Tudor state and the English would gain by the peaceful route of a marriage alliance what they had failed to win by force of arms. As Sir Adam Otterburn of Redhill wryly remarked, the English would have displayed much less enthusiasm for the match, 'If your lad was a lass, and our lass a lad'.[4] With most Scots continuing to regard the English as their ancient enemies there was considerable opposition to the treaty. The Englishman Sir Ralph Sadler reported 'there is not so little a boy but he will hurl stones against it, and the wives will handle their distaffs, and the commons universally will rather die'.[5] When the anglophile party that had negotiated the Treaty of Greenwich lost power, Scotland speedily reverted to its French alliance. A marriage for the infant queen of Scots, this time to Francis, the dauphin or heir to the French throne, was also part of this agreement. At that point the direct and immediate threat to Scotland's security from south of the border overrode the more distant prospect of absorption into the territories of the French crown.

In response to losing the marriage-alliance struggle, England embarked upon a series of military campaigns between 1544 and 1549, known as the Rough Wooing, amounting to a sustained and concerted attempt to conquer Scotland and impose union. The high level of commitment and the intensity of England's military effort were made possible by the financial windfall received by the crown following the dissolution of the monasteries and it gave the English their best chance of success since the Wars of Independence. At the battle of Pinkie in 1547 a Scottish army suffered a serious defeat on the battlefield and in the following two years English troops were able to occupy and garrison the country as far north as Broughty Ferry on the Tay estuary. The levels of destruction and dislocation within Scotland were massive, but brought the English no closer to achieving their goal of conquest.

The depressing conclusion to be drawn by the English government at the end of the 1540s was that even making Scotland its top priority and pouring resources into the campaigns, it was not capable of conquering the northern kingdom by force of arms. Securing the country was beyond its grasp because however many times it defeated Scottish troops on the battlefield and even with the co-operation of a significant minority of Scots, long-term control could not be sustained. Persuasion fared little better, for with English soldiers pillaging their way through the Scottish Lowlands, the propaganda campaign waged by Protector Somerset setting out the benefits of a complete union between the two countries struck a particularly hollow note. When writing a letter to his brother the earl of Huntly, held prisoner in England after Pinkie, Alexander Gordon summed up the situation: the English 'gane nocht the rycht way to mak unuon off thyr twa realmis. Gyf thay thynk to hawe hartlynes, thay suld traist ws moir tendyrly'.[6]

One of the chief causes of the English failure was the willingness of the French king, Henri II, to give substantial support to his Scottish allies. Securing Scotland was a key step in the Franco-British strategy of the 1540s and 1550s implemented through Mary of Guise, the dowager queen of Scotland, whose long-term dynastic aim was for her daughter to rule the entire British mainland. For the English, the prospect of a French-dominated Scotland that would eventually be absorbed into the Valois territories, massively increased the security threat from the northern kingdom. From a secure Scottish base, France had a variety of options: it could attack the north of England across the land border or the western coast via Ireland or undermine the Tudor state by stirring up rebellion in Ireland. With Mary Queen of Scots, possessing a substantial claim within the English succession, it was even more alarming to the English to realize that their 'postern gate' was wide open. The twin problems of security and succession had merged into a single issue that completely overshadowed Anglo-Scottish relations.

'The Best Worldly Felicitie'

With the death in November 1558 of Mary Tudor, the Scottish queen's claim to the English throne became a matter of pressing importance, with the succession issue spreading from Anglo-Scottish relations into European power politics and developing into an immediate security crisis. According to the Roman Catholic view-point, Elizabeth was illegitimate and therefore not entitled to inherit, making Mary Queen of Scots the rightful queen of England. Henri II of France pointedly reminded the English ambassador of his daughter-in-law's rights when they dined from plates bearing the English royal arms alongside those of France and Scotland. The direct Franco-Scottish threat was the gravest problem confronting the new Elizabethan regime. To counter it they were willing to go to war, but in a radical break from the past England chose instead to ally with the Scots.

For their part a significant group of Scots were willing to welcome the English with open arms because the Protestants had rebelled against the regent, Mary of Guise, in order to procure religious change. In the summer of 1559 they actively sought English military aid to defeat the regent's experienced French troops, using the fear of French domination of Scotland to persuade Elizabeth to send assistance and to gather domestic support. After much persuasion from William Cecil, the English queen agreed and immediately dispatched a fleet. It battled up the North Sea coast in mid-winter to arrive off the Fife coast in time to prevent the Scots Protestants losing one of their main bases at St Andrews. In the spring of 1560 an English army marched unopposed into Scotland and besieged the fort at Leith where the regent's troops were based. The death of Mary of Guise ended the military campaigning and allowed a peace treaty to be negotiated in Edinburgh in July 1560 arranging for foreign troops to leave Scotland. The signatories of the treaty were Elizabeth of England and Francis and Mary, king and queen of France and Scotland, though formal 'Concessions' were included for the Scottish 'Lords of the Congregation' who were now governing in Edinburgh. Because the Lords did not possess any formal diplomatic standing, this Anglo-Scottish triumph lacked the public face of a formal alliance and was therefore twice as vulnerable in the future to political change.

The Scots were impressed by the willingness of the English army to leave their country once the French threat had been removed because it suggested that a new era in Anglo-Scottish relations had dawned. During this phase of co-operation the language employed by both parties was replete with idealism about the new 'amity' between the two kingdoms that had the potential to transform Anglo-Scottish relations and unite the two peoples. In the summer of 1559 William Cecil wrote, 'The best worldly felicitie that Scotland can have is either to contynew in a perpetuall peace with the kingdom of Ingland or to be made one Monarchie with England as they both make but one Ile devided from the rest of the world'.[7] In his memo Cecil fused the separate concepts of an alliance and a union based upon shared geography, language and culture and cemented together by a common religious affiliation; the same ingredients highlighted half a century later by James VI and I. Such a strong and unifying friendship presupposed that the fear of French domination of the British mainland and a shared Protestantism would provide sufficient common ground to overcome centuries of hostility between the two peoples. Cecil was prepared to go much further in his political planning, envisaging a 'British policy' in which the governments of England and Scotland would pursue the joint aim of securing a peaceful, united and Protestant British Isles.

The second and far less obvious aspect of the diplomatic revolution of 1559–60 was the willingness to include Ireland within these new prospects for the British mainland. During the previous fifty years the English had repeatedly complained to the Scottish monarch about the activities of Scots in Ireland, in particular the Scottish settlement within Antrim and the influx of Scottish mercenaries to fight for the Irish Gaelic chiefs. In an unprecedented move, the English were prepared in 1560 to reverse that policy and employ Scottish troops to subdue the north of Ireland and bring it under direct English governmental control. Though this joint 'British policy' did not last, the Irish dimension persisted as a permanent and increasingly important element within Anglo-Scottish relations.

Only a year after the heady idealism of the summer of 1560, the Scottish situation had altered dramatically with Mary Queen of Scots returning to her native country to rule in person after the death of Francis II. Far from disrupting the new peace, this initially opened the way for a more conventional method of regularizing good relations between the two neighbouring kingdoms. In her foreign policy Mary's primary aim was to secure recognition as the heir to the English throne and she was prepared to use her own marriage to further that cause. This raised in an acute form the dilemma that Elizabeth faced for the rest of her reign: a formal alliance with Scotland could readily be concluded, but at a price she would not contemplate. Because the English queen would never allow the succession question to be resolved during her lifetime, this left permanent unfinished business on the agenda of Anglo-Scottish relations. It transpired that the English queen, by fortune rather than her political judgement, was allowed to consume the benefits of peace with Scotland without having to cut the succession cake.

It was Mary's bad judgement allied with her worse fortune that lifted Elizabeth off the succession hook. In July 1565 Mary Queen of Scots married her second husband, Henry Lord Darnley, who himself possessed a claim to the English throne. The ensuing British crisis produced an unsuccessful rebellion in Scotland and a complete breakdown in diplomatic relations bringing England and Scotland to the brink of war. The tangles produced by Elizabeth's stance on the succession issue reintroduced the security threat of a hostile Scotland. On this occasion, William Cecil and the English privy council judged the danger to queen and country to be less immediate than it had been in 1560 and advised against sending military support to the Scottish rebels, their former allies. Such advice, readily accepted by Elizabeth, was an admission that the long-term benefits of Anglo-Scottish amity and a joint British policy would be sacrificed to the immediate needs of English security as defined by the succession question. The major consequences of this decision within Anglo-Scottish relations were felt not on the British mainland but in Ireland, where they had a profound effect upon the conquest and subjugation of that kingdom.

'A Daingerous Precedent for All Princes'

Further dramatic changes in Scotland decisively swung the diplomatic advantage within Anglo-Scottish relations in England's favour. The murder of Darnley ultimately led to Mary's downfall and her forced abdication. Regent Moray and his successors, who were exercising power in the name of the young king James, found themselves heavily dependent upon English support to maintain their own position against those fellow countrymen who continued to uphold Mary. Although professing neutrality in the civil wars, English money and troops aided the king's party. The

Elizabethan regime was given the luxury of intervening in Scottish domestic politics with impunity and as a consequence treated Scotland like a satellite kingdom. The return of the policy of the 1540s of paying English pensions to bolster an anglophile party did nothing to enhance English opinions of the Scottish ruling elite. It fed the myth of the unprincipled, avaricious Scottish noble on the make which became such a potent image after 1603.

The English grip over Scotland had been immeasurably strengthened by the disastrous decision made by Mary Queen of Scots in May 1568. Following her escape from Lochleven castle and the subsequent defeat of her forces at the battle of Langside, Mary fled into England. Instead of receiving the assistance in her restoration she had expected from a cousin and fellow monarch, for the remainder of her life the Scottish queen was confined as a guest of Her Majesty Queen Elizabeth. Being in firm control of Mary's person presented the English with an invaluable bargaining counter in their dealings with all parties in Scotland and permitted the Elizabethan regime to pose as the arbiter of the affairs of the whole British mainland. Their assumption of jurisdiction was publicly demonstrated by Mary's first trial when she faced an English judicial panel, though charged with a crime committed within the kingdom of Scotland. These proceedings gave an indication to the Scots of the value which the English placed upon Scotland's sovereign status and were prophetic of the legalistic means eventually used to eliminate Mary. They also signalled that Mary's presence was being treated by the English regime as part of the domestic succession problem, instead of as a central issue within Anglo-Scottish diplomacy. Viewed from this myopic perspective, the Scottish queen represented an enormous headache for which Elizabeth's advisers could find no simple cure.

As the years of Mary's imprisonment in England stretched out, Elizabeth and her council, blinded by their obsession with Mary's claim to the English throne, nearly forgot they were harbouring the exiled or deposed queen of Scots. In many respects this suited the Scots who had finally brought their civil wars to an end in 1573. With a male ruler approaching adulthood and taking an increasing part in active government, Scotland's semi-satellite status was disappearing. King James did not repeat his mother's mistake of making the goal of the English succession the sole focus of his foreign policy. He was much more adept at the diplomatic game and, following in the footsteps of his predecessors, James IV and James V, utilized his European alliances to give him extra manoeuvrability within Anglo-Scottish relations. As part of this strategy James sought his Protestant bride across the North Sea in Denmark and not in the southern kingdom.

By the mid-1580s England was feeling increasingly beset as Elizabeth's belated intervention in the Dutch revolt brought open war with Spain. The security of the British Isles in general and the mainland in particular gained even greater significance. To ensure England's 'postern gate' was locked and bolted, relations with Scotland were placed on a formal footing when a defensive alliance was concluded in 1586 in the Treaty of Berwick. As part of the bargain, James VI gained a substantial subsidy from the notoriously parsimonious Elizabeth. The signing of the alliance led Elizabeth's chief ministers, Lord Burghley and Sir Francis Walsingham, to conclude they could move directly against Mary Queen of Scots. They wanted to eliminate the chief Roman Catholic claimant, who had become the focus of Spanish-backed intrigues to place her on the English throne. Although the twin themes of succession and security were paramount, they had been divorced from the Anglo-Scottish setting. The very public judicial prelude and justification for Mary's death were of great advantage within an English context and in the long term helped untangle the succession issue by firmly separating James' claims from those of his mother.

However, from an international-relations perspective, the manner of Mary's trial and execution had major drawbacks. Elizabeth's ministers miscalculated because they assumed incorrectly that they did not have to be over-concerned about James' reaction. In fact, Mary's death badly soured Anglo-Scottish relations and nearly broke apart the defensive league between the two countries. As James had warned during the trial process, the execution of one who had been a reigning queen set 'a daingerous precedent for all princes', because it was 'sa repugnant to [the] immediat supremicie granted be God to soverayne princes'.[8] In addition to undermining the special status of all monarchs, for James and his subjects his mother's public execution insulted his personal and royal honour and the reputation of his kingdom. The Scots demanded satisfaction to avenge the death and wipe out the insult and in the Scottish parliament held in August 1587, 'concerynyng the revenge of his majesteis motheris deithe. . . . the haill lordis of parliament sitting on thair knees, vowit that thay wald revenge the same to the uttermaist'.[9] During this tense time much of the language James employed in his diplomatic exchanges reflected the widespread assumption that alliances between countries were agreements or bonds between individual monarchs which, in Scottish parlance, entailed 'keeping kindness' or a kin relationship with one another. This included respect and honour between the parties in addition to mutual obligations and reciprocal acts of friendship. The manner in which the English had dealt with Mary Queen of Scots, as much as the outcome, suggested the relationship between the English and the Scots fell well short of 'kindness'.

In the following year facing the Spanish Armada did produce some sense of combined purpose throughout the mainland of Britain. The main security threat was directed against England but, if the Armada had achieved its purpose and had landed Spanish troops on the mainland, Scotland's position would have been precarious. The subsequent sense of divine deliverance when the Spanish fleet was scattered was not confined to England, and it was the Scottish monarch who rushed into print on the subject. He spoke of 'this Ile oppugnit by ye natiounis about, haiteris of ye holie word' and compared the scattering of the Armada to the flight of the Old Testament Philistines when God had blown on the tree tops, 'hes he nocht in lyke maner by brangling with his michtie wind thair timmer castellis scattered and shaken them a sunder to ye wrak of ane greit part and confusioun of the haill'.[10] Such an apocalyptic reading of the events of 1588 did not prevent James from continuing to remain in diplomatic contact with his fellow monarch, Philip II of Spain. During the 1590s when the English were at war with the Spanish, this caused some tension in Anglo-Scottish relations.

That final decade of Elizabeth's reign also witnessed the Nine Years' War, the greatest crisis the Tudors faced. Scotland's continuing involvement across the North Channel guaranteed that from the beginning when the earl of Tyronne took Ulster into rebellion, the crisis became a lively issue within Anglo-Scottish relations. However, the lack of a strong alliance between England and Scotland in the closing years of the sixteenth century removed the possibility of any joint British policy in Ireland. The English and Scottish monarchs continued to pursue widely different strategies in Ulster. The landing of the Spanish army in the south of Ireland during the final stages of the Nine Years' War demonstrated that the security threat to England from the north had been completely overshadowed by the fear of invasion from the west across the Irish Sea: Ireland had replaced Scotland as the 'postern gate' into England. This was largely the result of the confessional divide within the Tudor state, where, whilst Protestantism struggled to make much impact within Ireland, England and Wales projected an increasingly self-conscious Protestant identity that could be shared with Scotland. The ensuing sense of confessional solidarity throughout the British mainland was of major significance, but it was no substitute for an alliance between the sovereign states of Scotland and England.

Conclusion

'What God hath conioyned then, let no man separate. I am the Husband, and all the whole Isle is my Lawfull wife'.[11]

The demise of the Tudor dynasty in 1603 transformed Anglo-Scottish relations. The King of Scotland peacefully acquired two new kingdoms, thereby bringing the entire British Isles under the rule of a single sovereign and removing the security threat of having independent polities occupying the same mainland. The relatively smooth transition heralding the new reign had given the English the inestimable benefit of solving their succession problem without plunging their country into civil war. By placing their king on the English throne, the Scots had won a victory over their neighbours which they would not otherwise have gained. These were considerable achievements, though as James explained in 1604 to his Scottish councillors and at his first meeting with the English parliament, he had no intention of stopping there, but was pressing for a 'perfect' union of the crowns.

James' analysis of past relations and his hopes for the future foundered because of the manner in which he had come to the present situation. This was not a triumph for Anglo-Scottish diplomacy; his succession had not been negotiated or even formally discussed. Equally, it had not flowed from a joint British policy pursued by the governments of England and Scotland. It had happened because a dynastic strategy had been fortunate to pay off in the long run. Though the marriage of James IV and Margaret Tudor was deliberately ignored a hundred years later in the English proclamation of James VI's accession, it had provided the precondition of a Stewart claim in blood to the throne of England. For much of the sixteenth century that place in the succession had proved a stumbling block to good diplomatic relations between the sovereigns of the two countries. As regards the other level of Anglo-Scottish relations between the peoples of England and Scotland, the traditional hostility remained and was entrenched within their respective national identities. The measure of integration achieved in the religious, cultural and linguistic spheres failed to dissipate this deep-rooted antagonism. Judged in these terms, neither the dealings between the monarchs of England and Scotland nor those between their subjects could be regarded as a story of success or as a high road to union. The image of King James riding south in triumphal progress through two peaceful kingdoms obscures as much as it reveals about the winding paths of Anglo-Scottish relations during the sixteenth century.

NOTES

1. 12 January 1604, Burton, *RPC*, VI, p. 596.
2. 27 May 1589, cited in Read, *Lord Burghley*, p. 456.
3. Cited in Thomson, *Introduction to Gaelic Poetry*, p. 31.
4. Cited in Merriman, *Rough Wooings*, p. 124.
5. Cited in Donaldson, 'Foundations of Anglo-Scottish union', p. 139.
6. 18 January 1547/8: Cameron, *Scottish Correspondence of Mary of Lorraine*, pp. 213–14.
7. 31 August 1559. 'A memoriall of certain pointes meete for restoring the Realme of Scotland to the Auncient Weale', printed in Alford, *The Early Elizabethan Polity*, Appendix 1, p. 223.
8. Cited in Doran, ' "Revenge her foul and most unnatural murder?" ', p. 595.
9. Cited in Goodare, 'James VI's English subsidy', p. 124.
10. Quotations from *Ane Fruitfull Meditatioun on Revelation, 20, 7–10* [1588] and *Meditation on 1 Chronicles, 15, 25–9* cited in Burns, *True Law*, pp. 259–60.
11. James VI and I's speech to the English Parliament, 19 March 1604,' cited in Burns, *True Law*, p. 262.

BIBLIOGRAPHY

Alford, S., *The Early Elizabethan Polity: William Cecil and the British Succession Crisis 1558–1569* (Cambridge, 1998).

Burns, J. H., *The True Law of Kingship: Concepts of Monarchy in Early Modern Scotland* (Oxford, 1996).

Burton, J. H. et al., eds, *Register of the Privy Council of Scotland* (*RPC*) (38 vols, Edinburgh, 1877–).

Cameron, A. I., ed., *The Scottish Correspondence of Mary of Lorraine, 1543–60* (Edinburgh, 1927).

Donaldson, G,. 'Foundations of Anglo-Scottish union', in G. Donaldson, *Scottish Church History* (Edinburgh, 1985).

Doran, S., ' "Revenge her foul and most unnatural murder?": the impact of Mary Stewart's execution on Anglo-Scottish relations', *History*, 85 (2000), 589–612.

Goodare, J., 'James VI's English subsidy', in J. Goodare and M. Lynch, eds, *The Reign of James VI* (East Linton, 2000).

Merriman, M., *The Rough Wooings: Mary Queen of Scots, 1542–1551* (East Linton, 2000).

Read, C., *Lord Burghley and Queen Elizabeth* (London, 1960).

Thomson, D., *An Introduction to Gaelic Poetry* (2nd edition, Edinburgh, 1989).

FURTHER READING

Most general books covering the Tudors or the Stewart monarchs discuss Anglo-Scottish relations as part of their chapters on foreign policy or within a domestic or British setting. A general British approach can be found in P. Collinson, ed., *The Short Oxford History of the British Isles: The Sixteenth Century* (2002). Susan Doran gives a brief survey of the foreign policy setting in *England and Europe in the Sixteenth Century* (1999) and *Elizabeth I and Foreign Policy* (2000) and Norman Macdougall provides the Franco-Scottish angle in *An Antidote to the English: The Auld Alliance 1295–1560* (2001). An earlier interpretation can be seen in the detailed biographies of Cecil by Conyers Read, *Mr Secretary Cecil and Queen Elizabeth* (1955) and *Lord Burghley and Queen Elizabeth* (1960). Gordon Donaldson outlines the 'Foundations of Anglo-Scottish union' in his volume of essays, *Scottish Church History* (1985), pp. 137–63 and the opposite perspective is given trenchant treatment in W. Ferguson, *Scotland's Relations with England: A Survey to 1707* (1977).

Gervase Phillips, *The Anglo-Scots Wars 1513–50* (1999) covers the military side of Anglo-Scottish relations to the mid-century and the 1540s are excellently treated by Marcus Merriman, *The Rough Wooings: Mary, Queen of Scots, 1542–1551* (2000), whilst Franco-British strategy can be followed in P. Ritchie, *Mary of Guise in Scotland* (2002). The 1559–60 crisis is discussed in S. Alford, *The Early Elizabethan Polity: William Cecil and the British Succession Crisis 1558–1569* (1998) and J. E. A. Dawson, *The Politics of Religion in the Age of Mary Queen of Scots* (2002). The impact of the execution of Mary Queen of Scots upon Anglo-Scottish relations has been traced by S. Doran, '"Revenge her foul and most unnatural murder?": the impact of Mary Stewart's execution on Anglo-Scottish relations', *History*, 85 (2000), pp. 589–612, and Julian Goodare discusses 'James VI's English subsidy' in *The Reign of James VI* ed. J. Goodare and M. Lynch (2000).

CHAPTER ELEVEN

Britain and the Wider World

DAVID POTTER

Historians have naturally been inclined to highlight how much changed in the stance of the kingdoms of the British Isles *vis-à-vis* their neighbours in the course of the Tudor era. R. B. Wernham, for instance, suggested that the reign of Henry VIII saw the final phase of England as a continental military power (the fall of Calais in 1558 symbolized this) and a shifting of the emphasis to the oceanic and world-wide role of England in the reign of Elizabeth. There is a core of truth in this but it does obscure the many continuities that contemporaries would have felt with their immediate past. The Elizabethan period in some ways carried on many of the themes of dynastic warfare of the reign of Henry VIII and indeed, as will be shown below, militarization was an important element of Elizabethan society. The norms of chivalric warfare loomed no less dominant in the mind of the militarily active nobility under Elizabeth than they had under Henry VIII.

The British Isles were not, of course, a single entity in their relations with the rest of the world during the sixteenth century. They remained, as they had been for centuries, divided between hostile polities which naturally used foreign alliances against each other. For the Scots, the Auld Alliance with France remained a corner-stone of security until the 1560s, and for England the longstanding alliance with the inheritor of the Burgundian Netherlands – now the king of Spain – remained equally valid. But things were changing. Early Tudor England inherited the pretensions of the Plantagenets to power in France and continued to behave, with difficulty, as a major military power; the internal consolidation of the early Tudors sought to bring Ireland (marginally) and Wales (more successfully) under central influence and reflected the increasing economic, social and cultural predominance of England within the archipelago. There was nothing particularly new in this but the changes altered the balance of military and political power within Britain. The relations between Britain and the rest of the world in the Elizabethan era were thus shaped by the tensions created by this unequal balance of power within the islands.

Projects for a union with Scotland were active from the 1540s but these provoked serious opposition. English influence in Ireland had withered in the fifteenth century just at the time it became a serious threat to English security. Its instability invited radical plans to 'colonize' it and provoked increasingly strenuous resistance. Next, the onset of the Reformation from the 1530s shaped the way foreign relations were understood and introduced another kind of conflict within the kingdoms of the British Isles. So relations with Scotland were shaped by the pushing of a Protestant Reformation there with English support in the 1560s and the problem of Ireland was aggravated by the religious gulf between an English-dominated Dublin government and the rest of the country. Finally, the precariousness of the succession to the throne in England was bound to have significant impact on foreign relations; this underlay much of Henry VIII's matrimonial problems. Intermarriage between dynasties meant that, for countries without rules which excluded it, foreign succession became a real possibility. For the first decade of her reign, it was assumed that Elizabeth I would marry a foreign prince, but the dangers of this were obvious from the experience of Mary I. The longer Elizabeth left the issue in suspense, so did the significance of the claims of others, above all those of the Scottish Stewarts, grow.

At the start of the period, Henry VII is often thought to have been catapulted onto the English throne by French money and military muscle. This has been exaggerated in that Tudor had to borrow much of the money for his enterprise and was fortunate that a corps of battle-hardened infantry from the wars in Flanders were available for hire. Be that as it may, his successful coup illustrates the depth of weakness to which England had sunk in 1485. Henry felt the need to mount an expedition to France in 1492 which is often dismissed as a public-relations operation designed to emphasize his right to rule (he advanced the claims of his predecessors to Normandy and Gascony). It is true that the expedition was brief and concluded by a financial arrangement whereby the king of France agreed to resume the payment of a pension to England (which the kings of England always affected to call a 'tribute'). There were, though, sound diplomatic reasons connected with the dangerous French acquisition of Brittany (Henry's old protector). Though the Hundred Years War with France is usually given the terminal date of 1453 by historians, its after-shocks went rumbling on for another century. The Treaty of Boulogne (1492) was, curiously, the first true 'perpetual' peace treaty between Engand and France since the unimplemented Treaty of Bretigny in 1360. It pointed the way to further 'treaties of perpetual peace' between the two countries, such as that of 1527.

It is usually suggested that the political and economic link-up with the house of Burgundy constituted the major element of continuity throughout this period. There is of course no doubt that the Netherlands was England's major trading partner, indeed an essential outlet for the wool trade, or that Henry VII was concerned to establish the terms of this in his great trade treaty with the Low Countries, the Magnus Intercursus (1496). However, Burgundy had proved an unreliable political ally since its abandonment of England in 1435 and had complicated the civil wars by its close alignment with the Yorkist cause. Neither Charles the Bold nor Maximilian did much to help English military enterprise in 1475 and 1492. What shifted the ground was the emergence in the 1490s (largely for fortuitous reasons) of the dynastic link between the Habsburg Netherlands and Spain on the one hand and England and Spain on the other. The marriage alliances so coveted by Henry VII in quest of international acceptance for his dynasty therefore aligned England with an emerging Habsburg dynastic complex (which was to take full shape only after the death of Ferdinand of Aragon in 1516 and the accession in Spain of Charles V).

Henry was also increasingly involved in negotiations with Italy, given the centrality of the peninsula in international relations by the end of the fifteenth century. To some extent this reflected the important links between Italian banking and trading houses and England that were well established by the earlier fifteenth century but also the fact that the nascent 'system' (if it can be called that) of continuous diplomacy had its roots in Italy.

After 1492, Henry VII maintained a wary peace with Charles VIII and Louis XII (which did not preclude some unlikely marriage negotiations) and moved more closely into the Habsburg-Burgundian-Spanish orbit. Relations with Scotland remained tense throughout the 1490s because of Perkin Warbeck's activities and, indeed, the anchoring of Scottish policy in reliance on France was more deeply entrenched by growing French cultural influence north of the border. So, when Henry VIII decided in 1512 to return to the path of war with France he precipitated a Scottish invasion that led to the disaster of Flodden and the death of James IV. For his part, Henry's victory over the French at the battle of the Spurs was a minor skirmish but one which enabled him to magnify it for his prestige and also acquire two isolated French fortresses in Burgundian territory, Thérouanne and Tournai (the 'ungracious dogholes' referred to in a parliamentary speech of 1521 attributed to Thomas Cromwell).

Though Henry VIII waged war in France in 1512–13, 1522–5 and 1543–6 it would be a mistake to think that his reign was dominated by a return to traditional campaigning against France or that enmity to France remained the determining feature of English policy. In fact, relations with France were close in 1519–20 and then again from the late 1520s to the middle 1530s (partly for reasons connected with the king's marriage problems). There developed a degree of what has been called 'competitive emulation' between Francis I and Henry VIII, two monarchs very much of an age (they died within a few months of each other), both of whom saw themselves as exponents of chivalric kingship, both of whom set out to magnify their respective monarchies by great building and art patronage, eager in particular to show off their buildings to their respective ambassadors.

French cultural influence in England was strong despite the inherited and very real hostility to the French which had been a product of the wars of the fifteenth century. Tudor Englishmen were by no means the cultural isolationists they have been portrayed to be, but English was virtually unspoken beyond the Channel and, with the rise of the vernacular discourse, European languages became necessary alongside Latin for communication. The gentlemen appointed to attend on the French marshal d'Esquerdes after the treaty of 1492 had to be given interpreters. Cardinal Wolsey's knowledge of the French language was poor and he did most of his negotiating in Latin, the traditional vehicle for English diplomats in the late middle ages. John Palsgrave, though, published the first systematic French grammar in 1530 and then in 1576 Claude de Sainliens, an exiled Protestant, produced a widely-read handbook for learning French called *The French Littleton*, the precursor of Randall Cotgrave's great *Dictionarie* of 1611. Certainly by the middle of the sixteenth century, French was the channel through which much of the vernacular literature of the Continent came into England and a foreign visitor in 1550 observed that at Court the French language was commonly spoken. In 1550 William Thomas had published the first Italian grammar in English. Travellers abroad (who had a translation of Thurler's *The*

Traveller from 1575) were eager for information and this was now supplied by works such as John Eliot's *Survay or Topographical Description of France* (1592), to be followed by the more famous *View of Fraunce* by the schoolmaster Robert Dallington in 1604, written in 1598 (two years after his *Survey* of Tuscany, published 1605). The Master of the Revels Edmond Tyllney was from the 1560s compiling his vast *Topographical Descriptions* and drawing them together in the 1590s; these, though never published, were widely known in the scholarly world. Privately, minor diplomats such as Robert Beale and Sir John Smith compiled collections of papers on the history and customs of European countries.

In addition to all this, translations of foreign literature and polemics into English, though still controlled, saw a significant rise in the Elizabethan period. There was, for instance, a vast appetite for translations from the French on history, religious polemics and literature, to say nothing of the widely read and accomplished translations of Bodin, Montaigne and du Bartas. There is also no doubt that there was a hunger for information on the religious conflicts in France that saw the beginnings of proper printed news-reporting from the Continent.

Italy was the other major source of influence on Englishmen drawn by the revival of classical learning and culture and Italian travel was frequent in the mid-century decades. William Thomas, traveller, scholar and political tightrope walker who ended up on the block, brought out the influential *Historie of Italie* in 1549. His fellow-traveller, the diplomat Sir Philip Hoby (d.1558) was a friend of Titian and Aretino, while his brother Sir Thomas (d.1566) – whose *Courtyer* (1561) made Castiglione widely available to Englishmen – travelled in Italy, part of the time with Peter Whitehorne, translator of Machiavelli in the *Arte of Warre* (1562). Elizabeth had no formal diplomatic representation in Italy after 1559 and, though travelling in Italy remained possible, from about 1570 to the 1590s it was very much more difficult because of the religious climate. An anti-Italian perspective was provided by Ascham in *The Scholemaster* (1570) that 'ye see what manners and doctrine our Englishe men fetch out of Italy.' His loathing for 'Englishe men Italianated' (taking the proverb *inglese italianato e un diavolo incarnato*) stemmed from a suspicion that Italy was a source of impiety and paganism.[1] Contact with it also risked the taint of heresy. Some of the accounts that were published in the 1590s were made by men like Edward Webbe who had done time as galley slaves but this did not deter travellers such as Fynes Moryson from visiting Italy in his journeys around Europe between 1591 and 1597: 'From my tender youth I had a great desire to see forraine Countries. And having once begun this course I could not see any man without emulation and a kind of vertuous envy, who had seene more Cities, Kingdomes and Provinces, or more Courts of Princes, Kings and Emperours, then myselfe';[2] or military men like Sir Roger Williams with 'griedy desires to travaile and see strange warres.'[3] Italy was a major cultural influence, the Italian code of honour excercising a particular fascination on the young English gentlemen in Italy. Webbe recorded in 1590 that he had seen the earl of Oxford at Palermo in the 1570s issue an open challenge to tournament 'in the defence of his prince and country.'[4]

In the earlier sixteenth century, the genesis of the ambassadorial system already meant that more and more gentlemen had to be sought who were 'mete to serve' the king abroad beyond the traditional clerics who had usually served this purpose in the past. This involved a degree of travel and experience. Though we cannot yet

talk of a 'diplomatic service' in the reign of Henry VIII, the ground had been prepared for the emergence in the reign of Elizabeth of a body of diplomatically trained
gentlemen who were in touch with the main streams of European culture.

Cardinal Wolsey, the architect of much of English policy in the period 1509–30
(though always within the king's ultimate control), was one of the most active English
politicians abroad in the century and stood at the crossroads of such developments,
a clerical diplomat who was fully at home in the diplomatic dealings between Renaissance princes. At the beginning of the century, though England may have been relatively weak and peripheral, Wolsey was able to maximize the impact of England
diplomatically. In 1519, for instance, he sought to make of England a partner in an
improbable scheme for universal peace which presupposed an equal distribution of
power between Henry VIII, Francis I and Charles V. There is serious doubt, *pace*
Scarisbrick, that this was ever meant as a serious system of conflict resolution but it
does betray the over-ambitious scope of Wolsey's thinking. What the 1519 treaty
system did do was to allow Wolsey to pose as an international mediator between
France and the emperor and shift English alliances towards the latter when necessary
in 1521–2. What rapidly became apparent was that English military power was marginal to the main geo-political and dynastic conflicts on the Continent, the English
invasion of 1523 a costly failure. Neither Wolsey nor Henry should be pigeon-holed
as 'peace-maker' or 'war-monger' as some historians have tended to do. Both were
opportunists who saw different possibilities at different times but Henry was a
monarch who insisted that his 'honour' was always maintained in the twists and turns
of diplomatic dealings. This was not always possible. Nor was public opinion a completely neutral matter. Foreign policy was very much part of the royal prerogative
but had to operate within the bounds of the possible. When Henry, and consequently
most of his advisers, were keen to exploit the catastrophic defeat of France at Pavia
in 1525 it proved impossible to do so since the taxpayers revolted. In the context,
honourable terms offered by the French regent were welcome.

The 'King's Great Matter', his need for an annulment and the moves towards a
break with Rome that this precipitated, at first brought relations with France closer
and Henry saw Francis I as a fellow-monarch who could bring pressure to bear on
the pope. Cardinal Wolsey had failed to obtain the necessary papal agreement by
1529 and was ruthlessly disposed of. The Anglo-French meeting at Boulogne in
1532, though not as sumptuous as that of the Field of Cloth of Gold in 1520, had
a very serious political purpose. As Henry moved further towards a complete break
with Rome, he even sought to draw Francis into a similar course, which was politely
rejected on the grounds that it was impossible for the king of France. This highlights
the great chasm which the Reformation introduced into English relations with the
Continent from the 1530s onwards. Though Henry never thought of himself as anything other than Catholic, his action in rejecting papal authority could only, in the
context of the continental Reformation, be seen as favourable towards heresy. While
it is certainly the case that heresy did not prevent the rulers of France from entertaining close relations with German princes and with England in the decades after
the 1520s, it certainly introduced a complication in that alliances with heretical rulers
were difficult to defend publicly. This pointed the way towards a more ideological
attitude with respect to foreign policy in the years after 1560.

The break with Rome also led English policy towards a period of unusually close
relations with the German Protestant princes (in this Henry was to some extent in

competition with France). Thomas Cromwell saw alliance with the Protestants as an answer to isolation in the late 1530s (with France and the emperor, unusually, in alliance or at least truce with each other) and though the fall of Cromwell is supposed to have led to a Catholic reaction, negotiations with the German princes continued. This was not least because the German princes to some extent controlled the supply of mercenaries – *landsknechts* and *reiters* – who were considered by the 1540s one of the keys to success on the battlefield. For their part, the German Protestants were eager to ensure peace between their two most useful potential allies against the emperor, France and England. After the establishment of the Reformation in Germany, the power of the German princes *vis-à-vis* the Habsburgs had become a major component in the calculations of English policy. The negotiations with the League of Schmalkalden were not just an aberration of Cromwell's in the late 1530s. The new diplomats who had come to the fore in the later years of Edward VI – Richard Morrison, Philip Hoby, Roger Ascham – argued that one way of escaping from the invidious dependence upon either France or the emperor was to seek alliances with the German princes and Scandinavian monarchs. As the monarchia of Charles V was transformed into the Spanish monarchia and the empire of the Vienna Habsburgs, the Protestant princes continued to be credible counterweights.

In the later 1560s, the idea of a Protestant alliance involving England and the German and Scandinavian powers was very much a live one but it was the refocusing of English commercial interests that proved more significant. The quest for new 'vents' for English wool had started seriously with the glut of the Antwerp market in 1550. The establishment of the Muscovy Company in 1553 (typically with substantial investment by gentlemen-courtiers) had been seen as one answer to this and prefigured substantial English interest in the Baltic trade under Elizabeth and attempts to establish diplomatic relations with Ivan IV's Muscovy. With the deterioration of relations with Brussels, in 1564 the Merchant Adventurers transferred their staple to Emden in north Germany. There was still much attachment to Antwerp – costs of transport to it were cheap and it usually guaranteed good relations with the Low Countries – but the deteriorating security of the Netherlands led to a more lasting agreement with Hamburg in 1567. This was much more successful and the trend was confirmed by the Spanish sack of Antwerp in 1575. By the end of the century, too, English shipping was much more evident in the Mediterranean.

The unusually long peace between England and France cooled in the late 1530s and collapsed in 1543. There has been much debate about whether this was because of Henry VIII's undoubted interest in controlling Scotland or whether the root cause was the king's desire in his old age to return to the path of his Plantagenet ancestors. Whatever the reason, a pre-emptive strike against Scotland in 1541–2 certainly prepared the way for war with France as did the treaty with the emperor Charles V in February 1543. The dissolution of the monasteries had placed at the disposal of the crown resources which enabled it (until the large-scale sell-off of monastic lands) to use the wealth acquired for military purposes. Despite reluctance to fight on the part of Francis I, this led to a declaration of war against France in June 1543 and the beginning of renewed English military intervention on the Continent. The high point came with the joint campaign with the emperor in the summer of 1544 which culminated in Henry's personal campaign and the capture of Boulogne in 1544. Though Henry undoubtedly regarded this as a vindication of his military power, it had the effect of crippling the English crown for the rest of the 1540s and played a major part in the growing interrelated political and economic crisis of the mid-Tudor years. Charles V had been eager to come to terms in September 1544, leaving his English ally in the lurch. Francis I refused to make peace with Henry unless the latter gave up Boulogne. The fact that Henry managed to hold onto the town despite determined French efforts condemned England to debilitating and costly war until eventually the two sides made peace in (June 1546) under the common threat of renewed Habsburg power. Henry was to hold on to Boulogne for the time being.

The problem for England was the escalating cost of Henry's acquisitions which, with the costs of continuing wars with Scotland, came near to bankrupting the crown by the end of the 1540s. At a time when normal peacetime revenues stood at around £160,000 per annum the total cost of the wars from 1542–50 was £3.5 m, of which £1.34 m was accounted for by the siege and occupation of Boulogne. In addition, Henry VIII's death in January 1547 and the inception of the Somerset protectorate began a period in which the rapid move to a more radical Protestant settlement at home led to internal divisions and external problems. This was not at first apparent as Somerset's able generalship enabled him to triumph in Scotland militarily and impose a degree of control on the Lowlands. The problem was that Scotland was an essential component of French diplomatic calculations and France could not allow it to pass under English control. There gradually emerged on the part of the new French king, Henri II, a pretension to a protectorate over Scotland that merged by the late 1550s into a vague notion of hegemony over the British Isles that also involved some interference in the affairs of Ireland and support for anti-English lords there. The immediate problem for England was French intervention in Scotland in 1548–9 which further drained English resources and led to the collapse of the protectorate and loss of Boulogne (March 1550) amidst faction-fighting and recriminations.

While the extent of English weakness in the mid-Tudor years has to some extent been exaggerated (it has been suggested that all the regimes of the period were to an extent dependent on either the Habsburgs or the French) it is nevertheless the case that the period was seen at the time as one of great dangers and external threats. Boulogne was abandoned in March 1550, the intervention in Scotland liquidated in 1551, Calais lost in 1558. Yet the period was also a fruitful one in which a much wider strand of public opinion began to participate in the formulation of English views of the Continent. This was partly because of the minority of Edward VI, during which it became much more possible for advisers such as William Paget to speak brutally frankly to the Protector. It was also partly because of the emergence of a new generation of humanist-trained envoys – such as the Hoby brothers and Richard Morrison – who took it upon themselves to range widely in their reflections on foreign affairs, often pushing a 'Protestant' view in foreign policy. The process, though, went further. Humanists such as Ascham certainly took it upon themselves to reflect on foreign policy but more unofficial 'projectors' like Thomas Barnaby sought to influence government policy by lengthy policy papers. Finally, the increasingly strident religious divide of the mid-century stimulated the production of pamphlets and books on the issue of the influence of Spain in English affairs under Mary that testifies to a fairly sophisticated participation of public opinion.

Thus, by the accession of Elizabeth strong opinions had been generated on foreign affairs which to some extent operated independently of government policy. The older statesmen inherited by Elizabeth were commonly deeply anti-French and looked back to the old idea of an alliance with 'Burgundy' even though the reality of that entity had completely changed. William Paget in February 1559 wrote of 'the Necessite of Friendship with the House of Burgundy . . . the naturall enmity betwene us and Fraunce.'[5] Nicholas Wotton, a diplomat both knowledgeable of France and experienced in its culture, wrote in January 1559 of 'the auncient, immortall hatredde they beare unto us.'[6] Hostility to France and the idea of using the alliance of Spain against her were commonplace in the first two years of the reign. Throckmorton could argue for seizing the opportunity of Henri II's death to recover Calais 'and of the commodite offered to sende now to the king of Spayne as well to entre in amitie and straight league with hym and also be in hand with hym for the recovery of Calleys.'[7]

In the 1560s, though, the experiences of English Protestant activists in the 1550s were amplified by a developing phobia about Spain which in the course of the reign partly displaced the old hostility to France. The latter, during its civil wars, could not pose a threat and provided scope for alliance with co-religionists, so attitudes to it became more ambivalent. As for Spain, hispanophobia was built up by the legend of Spanish treachery in the course of Hawkins's expeditions to the West Indies in the 1560s. In 1568 vice-admiral Champernown wrote, at the time of the seizure of the Spanish gold, 'I am of the mind that anything taken from that wicked nation is necessary and profitable to our commonweal.'[8] Anti-Spanish sentiment was nourished by the circulation of Las Casas's work on the conquest of the Indies (translated 1583) and the Spanish Inquisition emerged as the measure of Spanish tyranny. While Drake's chaplain claimed that they spread 'the poisonous infection of Popery wherever they went', Raleigh in *The Last Fight of the Revenge* (1591) could argue how 'irreligiously they cover their greedy and ambitious pretenses with that veil of piety.'[9] No Protestant state was safe from them, though the kings of Spain claimed even Catholic realms as though they were 'the natural heirs of all the world'.

Such views meshed into the view of foreign affairs as part of God's will and providence which had been accumulating, as has been said, since the tentative move towards Reformation in the 1530s and the radicalization of the 1550s. The pressures on Elizabethan policy were shaped by the fact that since the establishment of the Reformation on the Continent it had become impossible to ignore a prince's religion in the conventional calculations of power politics, no matter how worldly the ultimate objectives. By the start of Elizabeth's reign the cause of international Protestantism was a major imperative in the thinking of political Puritanism represented by Leicester and Walsingham. This has tended, under the influence of Conyers Read's studies, to be regarded as a kind of 'lunatic fringe', too radical and too impractical. Simon Adams has argued that it was no more so than the old-fashioned 'Habsburg-Burgundian' view. In 1559/1560 Throckmorton anchored the role of religion in the making of foreign policy when he wrote 'now when the general design is to exterminate all nations dissenting with them in religion . . . what shall become of us, when the like professors with us shall be destroyed in Flanders and France?'[10] In 1568, Coligny's agent wrote to Throckmorton that 'nous sommes membres d'un mesme corps.'[11] William Stubbs, in his attack on the Queen's marriage to Anjou and the French Catholics in 1579 said: 'we have the Lord's right hand on our side and all the hearts and hands of those of our religion.' The cause of the Protestant leader Henry of Navarre was described by the muster-master John Stubbes as 'God's cause' and fighting in his interest 'an honour'.[12] While Leicester rose to importance in foreign affairs by seizing on the Protestant cause in the mid-1560s, by the mid-1570s his and Walsingham's influence, Adams argues, stood at parity with Cecil's. Nevertheless, what he sees as Elizabeth's strictly *realpolitik* view constantly undermined international Calvinism, not least in the Netherlands.

The outbreak of civil wars in France and the Netherlands proved the touchstone for English policy after 1560. A degree of freedom of action was conferred by the reversal of the unfavourable conditions that prevailed through the mid-Tudor period. To some extent this was fortuitous. Despite the overwhelming fear of foreign domination that was in the air by the end of the 1550s, the sudden death of Henri II in July 1559 provided an opportunity, which William Cecil clearly saw and persuaded Elizabeth of, to reverse French domination in Scotland. This was done by 1560 and, though Scotland remained a danger throughout the reign, the Elizabethan regime managed – just – to preserve a favourable regime north of the border. Intervention in the French civil war in 1562 – partly motivated by lingering desires to use it in order to recover Calais – was less successful but pointed the way to later English military involvement.

Despite the failure of 1562–3, England could not remain disengaged. The civil wars interlinked with religion that broke out in France and the Netherlands in the 1560s and 1570s were the main foreign problems that England had to confront. It is often said that Elizabeth was hostile to the idea of rebellion against lawful sovereigns but those conflicts were too threatening to English interests to be ignored. In France, while Elizabeth had some sympathy for the attempts of Catherine de Medici to maintain peace, the prospect of Guise domination of the government that arose during the false peace of 1568 and again after the Massacre of Saint Bartholomew in 1572 inevitably presented severe dangers. The envoys to France, such as Henry Norris, actively fed fears by stressing the Guise threat and the opportunities of civil war. Norris's despatches pushed a strong line in the war of 1568–9: the cardinal of Lorraine was 'your cruel enemy',[13] the royal government was disarrayed and the new wave of religious violence directed against the Protestants was 'so extreme as the very Papists, in whome remaineth any spark of piety, doth abhor to hear the same.'[14] He generally talked up the prospects of the Huguenots despite their defeats, underlined the dangers of their overthrow and even suggested in the third civil war that there was an opportunity to gain control of La Rochelle in place of Calais. Practical help, however, remained limited. A report sent to Coligny from Paris in March 1569 claimed that Elizabeth had sent 20,000 *écus* to the duke of Zweibrucken for the mercenaries he was leading to the help of Condé and Coligny, though whether this made much difference is doubtful. In 1568, with the Huguenot cause under pressure, the Merchant Adventurers supplied munitions to La Rochelle in exchange for its produce and in 1570 offers of money were again made to Coligny. The peace of Saint-Germain (1570), ostensibly advantageous to the Protestants, was seen by Norris as posing the danger of French action elsewhere, possibly in Scotland, but he finally concluded that the peace was fragile 'the very same causes yet remaining, we may presume of the like effects.'[15]

It could be argued that underhand help to rebels in France and the Low Countries was normal *realpolitik* in the period and that Elizabeth just wished to promote strife though short of direct intervention. However, she showed her usual caution. After 1570 she reverted to her instinct to try to build on the peace in France by bringing it into an alliance against Spain. Cecil argued the dangers of this in August

1571 but the Treaty of Blois was concluded in 1572, before the St Bartholomew's Day massacre. Again, in the fourth civil war that followed the massacre, supplies and money were secretly sent to La Rochelle.

Involvement in the Spanish-dominated Netherlands also concerned economic and religious policy. Philip II was hostile to Elizabeth's religious stance but in the early years more concerned that England should not drift into the French orbit. Hence, he resisted any papal condemnation of Elizabeth until 1570. As France weakened, his attitude was modified and Granvelle, his representative in the Low Countries, imposed a trade embargo on English cloth at the end of 1563. This began a long period of serious economic conflict. The internal conflict in the Netherlands worsened with the 1565 *Compromise of the Nobility* and the popular iconoclasm of 1566. Alva's arrival in August 1567 with 10,000 Spanish veterans transformed the whole situation since it gave Spain real military muscle in the north. The dangers of a war with Spain prevented active English help to William of Orange's invasion of 1568 but the effective arrest at Plymouth and Southampton in December of the £80,000 loan from Genoese bankers being transported to Alva's army led to another trade embargo on both sides. The motives of the action remain shrouded in controversy but there is no doubt that it made life more difficult for Alva while he was further outraged by the covert protection offered in England to the Dutch pirates known as the 'Sea Beggars'. Their expulsion from the south-east ports of England in March 1572, whatever its motives, had the effect of precipitating a new crisis in the Netherlands with their seizure of Brille.

Thereafter, events in France and the Netherlands became closely intertwined, with plans from Coligny in France and Orange in Germany to carve up the Netherlands with English help. The Massacre of Saint Bartholomew put paid to this for a while but the idea was to resurface after 1579. In retrospect it looked to Camden (*Annals* for 1577) that Elizabeth held a strong hand: 'Thus sate she as an heriocal princess and Umpire betwixt the *Spaniards*, the *French* and the Estates . . . And true it was that one hath written, that France and Spain are as it were the Scales in the Balance of Europe, and England the Tongue and Holder of the Balance.'[16] Was she really in a position to wield the balance of power in Europe? Wernham's view is that Elizabeth aimed essentially 'to get the Spanish army out of the Netherlands without letting the French in.' Charles Wilson argued that Elizabeth's instinctive fear of rebellion led her to discount the Dutch rebels and there was a traditional reason for fearing French ambitions in the southern Low Countries. Wilson's analysis of what he saw as half-hearted and bungled intervention, echoed Raleigh's remark the Elizabeth 'did everything by halves'.[17] He denies that English interests may have been best served by maintaining the Habsburg regime in the Low Countries in its traditional form as a bulwark to France. A traditionalist remote-control form of Spanish authority in the Low Countries was no longer on offer and the logic of events had taken the rebellion too far. In Elizabeth's and Burleigh's defence, it should be said that taking on a war with Spain was a massive and dangerous commitment, so it is hardly surprising that they sought to delay it as long as possible; Dutch interests were not necessarily identical with those of England, though the protagonists of the Protestant cause would have argued otherwise.

In any case, what this debate neglects is the fact that, though England did not intervene directly until 1585, its military potential was partly at the disposal of the rebels long before that. From the first major expedition to Zeeland in 1572, English volunteer troops under Thomas Morgan, Edward Chester, Sir John Norris (who took 1,700 men to the Low Countries in 1578) and many others were crossing the sea quietly or with tacit government approval to fight in the cause of the rebels, recruited through personal connections and affinities of Protestant nobles and gentry, eventually paid for by the estates-general. Participants in these 'voluntary wars', far from being the 'scum of the earth', were, as John Smythe asserted in *Certain Discourses Military*, for 'the greater part young gentlemen, and in a greater part of yeomen and yeomen's sons . . . desirous, of a gallantness of mind, to adventure themselves and see the wars. . . . being the very flower of England.'[18]

Oceanic exploration and colonization have always provided one of the main strands for the heroic narrative of Elizabethan England. Wernham argued that the keynote of the Elizabethan period was the seeking of an oceanic role, to solve the problems of the loss of a continental empire by making England politically as well as geographically an island and relying primarily on naval force for defence. All this to some extent neglects the fact that England had started its exploration of the Atlantic in the fifteenth century, though it is certainly the case that state patronage for oceanic exploration waned after the 1490s. Was there a conscious choice? It is clearly the case that the decades from 1560 to 1600 saw the focus of English power shift towards the Atlantic and the Caribbean as word of the wonder and mystery of the New World spread and English traders and seamen gradually realized that the Spanish colonial empire – apparently so all-powerful – was a source of plunder and profit. Yet the English colonial and oceanic empire was begun haphazardly and without much planning and many in power, such as Cecil, were distrustful of the trend. Most European states of the period did not have the administrative structures to allow them to create empires and England, like them, shifted to an oceanic focus very largely under a partnership between the crown and commercial interests. Elizabeth I, as usual, acted as an unpredictable mistress, sometimes encouraging the developments, at others clearly deeply sceptical of their value.

It is easy to find evidence that attitudes to naval power were shifting by the start of Elizabeth's reign. Nicholas Throckmorton, pondering the dangers faced by England in 1559–60, argued that 'youe shulde arme to the sea forthwythe . . . yt ys nowysse to be sufferyd, that eyther the Frenchemen shall vanquyshe the Scots that now faver your relygion, or that you suffer any suche numbir of the Frenche there to lande.' A year later, he was more emphatic: 'bend your force, credytt and devise to maintain and encrease your navy . . . yt is the flower of Englandis garlande.'[19]

The role of sea power under Sir William Winter in blockading the French in Leith and so bringing matters in Scotland to a successful conclusion is well known. In fact, the navy had been in a process of overhaul since the later reign of Henry VIII. Without these changes, as David Loades has shown, the naval successes of the Elizabethan era would have been impossible. The fleet performed well in the French war of 1557–9 and by 1560 there was a standing fleet with institutionalized administration, provided with regular funds to support an effective nucleus. The failure at Le Havre was obviously a military and diplomatic rather than naval one. With the fall of Calais and the emergence of an insular defensive strategy under Cecil's aegis, it was bound to play a central part in both defence and attack. The navy had long held a defensive role. In 1535 the duke of Norfolk had remarked blusteringly to Chapuys that 'it was a good thing for a king of England to be provided with such vessels to inspire awe in those who wished to attack him and he thought with these two and four or five in the river before them, they could fight the whole world.'[20] The Spanish ambassador in 1569 reported that 'they expect to be able to repel any attack by means of their fleet' and in 1571 Cecil described the fleet as 'the wall of England.'[21] In 1577 John Dee called for a 'Petty Navy Royal' of a least 60 well-equipped ships so that no country 'can have such liberty, for Invasion, or their mutuall Conspiracies, or Ayds, any way'[22] while Richard Hakluyt in 1584 called for a 'new navy of mighty, new strong ships . . . to offend or defend.'[23] In fact, from the early 1560s the main focus for the development of English naval power was a series of quasi-private-enterprise operations, with royal ships periodically hired out to consortia of traders and courtiers in search of profit overseas; this was the naval equivalent of the way in which, in military expeditions, royal troops could to switch to serve as private soldiers of fortune and vice versa. In practice there was no strict demarcation between the public and the private even though there was a regime of royal commissions and licences for state military and naval activity. The pursuit of profit from such expeditions led the queen and some of her advisers to think, erroneously, that naval war could pay for itself. Nothing was further from the truth but the spectacular early profits certainly gave cause for optimism.

The consortia of the 1560s were in part continuing in the privateering tradition (privateers were essentially pirates with the royal authorization of letters of marque or reprisal). It is obvious that west-country gentry families like the Killigrews were at one and the same time pirates and royal servants and increasingly in the Elizabethan period served a useful political purpose. Piracy flourished, directed against the French, the Spanish Netherlands and the Scots. There was co-operation with the Huguenot pirates of La Rochelle from 1568 and, of course, sheltering of the Dutch Sea Beggars.

In this context, the line between legitimate ventures and pillage was vague. In 1561 royal ships were loaned for a voyage to Africa in return for a share of the profits; more substantially, a great ship was loaned for Hawkins' expedition to Hispaniola in 1564 which was backed by the queen, Leicester, Pembroke, Lord Admiral Clinton, Winter and a group of London merchants. This was the precursor to royal investment in Hawkins's slaving voyage of 1567 which led to the disaster of San Juan d'Ulloa. The voyages of the 1570s (there were thirteen between 1570 and 1577), as a result of this misadventure, were more obviously piratical rather than 'trading' ventures and, in the case of Francis Drake's activities, all the more profitable.

The idea of a 'Brytish Impire' was taken up by the astrologer Dr John Dee in his *Perfect Art of Navigation* (1577) and given the connotation of overseas colonies. He tried to persuade an apparently fascinated queen in several meetings between 1577 and 1580 and, though his ideas were too scholarly and impractical, the idea of colonies was in the air. It found a ready response in the political nation amplified by the success of Richard Hakluyt the younger's *Principal Navigations . . . of the English People* (1589, revised 1598). Sir Humphrey Gilbert in 1577 had set forth (with the proviso no doubt welcome to the queen of allowing her to disavow anything done in her name) the classic arguments for colonization: annoying the enemy, economic opportunities and planting true religion. In a number of persuasive discourses between 1582 and 1585 the Hakluyts added the dimension of ridding the realm of idle vagabonds. It is often assumed that Hakluyt's aim to find in colonies a 'safe and sure place to receive people . . . that are forced to flee for the truth of God's word'[24] applied only to godly Protestants. In fact, Catholics, too, were looking westward for refuge. In 1568 Sir Thomas Gerard had offered to plant English Catholics in Ulster and in 1582 he joined Sir George Peckham in approaching Gilbert with the idea of finding a refuge in America for Catholics under pressure in England. This received some official approval but foundered with the problems of the first colonies.

The establishment of colonies was the field of promoters and, as with the great voyages, there was a mixture of public and private enterprise which displayed a wide range of objectives and methods. The earliest promoters, however, were gentlemen-courtiers who saw themselves as *conquistadores*, though the fact that they were late-comers to the New World limited their scope of conquest. The numbers involved were small; of a dozen Elizabethan colonizing projects, nine sent out expeditions with about 4,600 sailors at a cost of about £75,000 in all. Thomas Stukely and Richard Grenville in 1562–4 learned of the possibility of golden cities from Huguenot adventurers Jean Ribault and Villegaignon. But it was in 1574 that the first signifi-cant proposals emerged for the establishment of colonies in the New World to chal-lenge Spanish hegemony. Elizabeth refused to license these but was more receptive to Drake's proposal in 1577 to penetrate the Straits of Magellan and explore the Pacific coast of America. Drake and his fellow projectors obtained strong Court backing for what developed into the first English circumnavigation, contact with the Spice Islands of the East Indies and a phenomenal loot of £150,000 by the time of his triumphant return in September 1580. The knighting of Sir Francis on board his own ship symbolized firstly the fact that, although Elizabeth was ambiguous about such operations, she was highly susceptible to the mystique and profit of naval success, and secondly that the royal-navy and private-enterprise operations were inextricably intertwined.

Throughout these voyages, the idea of developing English settlements on the coast of North America remained active. Gilbert's plans from 1578 to 1583 involved the establishment of fiefdoms with tenants for himself and his family – very much on Old World lines – but his ideas were taken over by his half-brother Sir Walter Raleigh on his death and led to the first serious attempt to establish such a colony in the form of the Roanoke enterprise in the land to be named Virginia. Grenville left the first 108 colonists at Roanoke in 1585. It was refounded in 1587 but had disappeared mysteriously by 1590. The reasons are fairly obvious; demands of the war with Spain prevented regular supply-voyages, the settlers were unsuited to co-operating with the native inhabitants or working the land. No more than 250 men in all were involved and financing of the enterprise was beyond the resources of the promoters; nor were the returns as yet promising. Raleigh, after all, in his account of his 1596 voyage, *The Discovery of Guiana*, was to remark 'where there is store of gold, it is in effect needless to remember other commodities.'[25] Roanoke, though, pointed the way and justified further colonization.

The vast expenditure on sea and land from the 1580s led to what has been called 'the militarisation of the Elizabethan state.'[26] The acquisition of Portuguese sea-power by Spain in 1580 and the subsequent defeat of the French attempt to counter this (Terceira, July 1583) brought full-scale naval confrontation between England and Spain closer. The Treaty of Nonsuch with the Dutch States (August 1585) inau-gurated a period of war in all but name that was sharpened by the issue of letters of marque to English merchants whose goods had been confiscated in Spain. Drake was commissioned as admiral to lead a fleet in retaliation but with very wide discretion and organized, along the lines of Hawkins's in the 1560s, a private venture with large-scale royal investment both in cash and ships. The first appearance of a serious hostile war fleet in the ill-fortified West Indies resulted in the plunder of San Domingo in Hispaniola in January 1586, and Cartagena in February. Drake returned in July via the struggling Roanoke colony bearing the comparatively modest profit of £67,000. The damage to Spanish prestige was more significant than the concrete achievements of the voyage as its fame spread throughout Europe.

Thereafter, English fleets were constantly in the planning stage or on active operations against Spain and the year 1586 saw Philip II's decision to deal finally with the problem by launching his great Armada (talked about as far back as 1574). Royal expenditure on new warships soared as the English were well aware of the emerging threat. Drake was commissioned in March 1587, with another public-private fleet, to head off the preparations for the Armada by a pre-emptive attack. Despite Elizabeth's hesitations, Drake got away before his orders were countermanded and made for Cadiz where he effectively destroyed the assembling fleet. Having achieved domination of the sea-lanes for a while he was able to return with the plunder of a great Spanish treasure-ship that justified his shareholders' investment and so disrupted Spanish preparations that the Armada had to be delayed until 1588.

The campaign of 1588 was the first great oceanic campaign of modern times, fought on a titanic scale in terms of numbers of ships, armament and time-scale. The English fleet was in action for eight months without interruption with nearly 200 ships. Innovations in tactics such as the line-ahead attack harried Medina Sidonia up the Channel, and artillery played a major part. The fire-ship attack at Calais on the night of 7 August, though not an innovation, was daring and decisive; the Spanish fleet finally broke up and had to 'cut and run', abandoning the risky plan to transport Parma's army. Though the aftermath, in terms of the failure to destroy the whole Spanish fleet as well as the eventual loss of many English seamen to plague, was an anti-climax the triumph was not diminished and was naturally seen as providential divine intervention.

The Armada was of course not the end of the war – it was more like its opening salvo – and fleets had rapidly to be refitted. The amphibious expedition to Lisbon in 1589, lacking much local support, achieved little except to 'annoy' the king of Spain and the focus of English strategy turned, under tighter royal control, to the naval blockade of the Spanish coast, a more profitable long-term objective. As the threat of a Spanish counter-blow grew, new raids were staged on the Caribbean in 1594–5 (which saw the deaths of Frobisher and Drake) but the greatest achievement was the amphibious attack on Cadiz in June–July 1596, almost a textbook case of effective strategy and tactics which cost the Spanish monarchy dear in material and prestige losses. Thereafter, the naval struggle ran out of steam. Philip II's counter-blow of 1597 failed through adverse weather rather than English defences and the Azores raid under Essex was a costly failure. Privateering continued and the navy managed to counter Spanish intervention in Ireland.

The tension between the limited aims of Elizabeth (national security, maintaining a rough balance between France and Spain) and those of her advisers who saw the defeat of Spanish power at sea and in the Netherlands as the main priority became apparent during the military campaigns that began in the Netherlands in 1585 and were continued in France and Ireland in the 1590s. The Netherlands campaigns of 1585–7 have traditionally been discounted as ineffective but English soldiers performed well in small engagements; the ferocious Anglo-Dutch defence of Sluys in the summer of 1587 earned Parma's respect. Leicester's expedition was undermined by inadequate numbers, poor supply and unclear objectives. Though the queen did not grudge money for war when necessary she wanted to concentrate on the defence of her cautionary towns. Her local commanders, though, under pressure from the States-General, were drawn into wider struggles.

Then, with the collapse of Henri III's position in 1589 and the near triumph of a Catholic League under Spanish patronage, it became necessary to intervene in France to bolster the position of Henry of Navarre and keep the Channel coast clear of enemies. In spring 1591 John Norris was sent to Brittany (where Spanish forces were backing up the League) with 3,400 men, and Sir Roger Williams to Dieppe with 600. It was the need to cover Dieppe that produced the idea of sending an army to join Henri IV in besieging Leaguer Rouen. The army sent to Normandy under Essex (1591–2) revealed the usual weaknesses of English military organization – insufficient numbers and poor co-ordination with French allies. Parma relieved the city in April 1592. Yet the English were among the best infantry at the disposal of Henry of Navarre. His conversion in 1593 and the collapse of the Catholic League made further English intervention pointless and from 1594, England again disengaged from military action in France. While Wernham has argued that English military enterprise largely ceased after that (giving place to naval activity), in fact substantial numbers of men were paid by the States-General and served at Turnhout (1597) and Nieuwpoort (1600) and in the siege of Ostend from 1601.

Ireland remained a running sore for Elizabethan England and began to take the place of Scotland as the potentially disastrous 'back door' through which enemies could attack. This was exacerbated by the development of the notion of Ireland as a 'colony' that needed both pacification and settlement. This saw unprecedented cruelty, barbarity and bitterness from the 1570s and was bound to provoke savage rebellion which in turn sucked in more English military effort and led the Irish to turn abroad for help. The French were no longer in a position to help, but Fitzmaurice secured part of a force of Italians and Spaniards paid for by Pope Gregory XIII in 1579, which landed at Smerwick and sparked off a series of revolts until it was finally crushed. This was a severe warning. Ireland, though a problem, had hitherto been relatively easy for English troops to dominate. From the 1580s onwards it became increasingly a graveyard for English military effort. When the much more serious revolt of Tyrone in Ulster began in 1594 the rebels sought actively to bring in Spanish troops by offering Philip II the kingdom of Ireland and Tyrone had at his disposal Irish troops – the famous 'wild geese' – trained in the modern style by extensive service abroad. Tyrone was able to wear down successive attempts to defeat him, tying down some 17,000 men at the height of the crisis. This came with the Spanish landing at Kinsale in 1601, which should have given Tyrone the strength to face Lord Deputy Mountjoy in the field. Spain like France before it, though, saw Ireland only as a useful diversion and sent insufficient numbers of men. Mountjoy was thus able to defeat the rebellion piecemeal and bring Tyrone to negotiate, vindicating English arms, as Fissel has put it, 'at a time when guerilla warfare had instilled self-doubt' in English commanders.[27]

Whatever the extent of the disagreements over foreign policies and whatever motivations we might ascribe to them, the international scene in which England was placed changed significantly between 1485 and 1603. At the start of that period, England was a small and weakened country prey to its neighbours' ambitions. This had been to some extent reversed by the self-confident handling of foreign policy by Henry VIII and Wolsey but the basic weaknesses became apparent again in the mid-Tudor years. In the Elizabethan era the dangers of foreign conquest and domination were still seen as very real. However, although England remained small in terms of population, the islands of Great Britain had become measurably closer to the prospect of a real union. France had collapsed (temporarily) as the major European power, while Spain had supplanted her but was bogged down in military and financial problems. English economic and political horizons had expanded to the four corners of the globe and a new degree of self-confidence was generated; Charles Merbury wrote in 1581 that 'It is no small comfort unto an English Gentleman, finding him self in a far country, when he may boldly shew his face.'[28] England was undoubtedly now a formidable naval power in a era in which that would be increasingly significant, and had acquired serious and up-to-date military clout. While participating fully in the European cultural scene, England as a Protestant nation was increasingly led to see itself as specially chosen by God and had taken decisive steps towards a new identity. It was thus that it entered the new era of the Union of Crowns in 1603.

NOTES

1. Ascham, *English Works*, pp. 229, 233–4; Raab, *English Face of Machiavelli*.
2. Moryson, Introduction.
3. Evans, *Works of Sir Roger Williams*, xvii.
4. Edward Webbe, *Rare and Most Wonderful Things* (1590), quoted in Chaney, *The Evolution of the Grand Tour*, pp. 10–11.
5. Paget to Cecil, 28 February 1559, Haynes, *Collection of State Papers*, pp. 208–9 (*Cal.Hatfield* I, 151).
6. 9 January, 1559, Forbes, *Public Transactions*, I, p. 18.
7. Forbes, *Public Transactions*, I, p. 158.
8. MacCaffrey, *Shaping*, p. 191.
9. Maltby, *Black Legend*; Raleigh, *Selected Prose and Poetry*, p. 85.
10. Adams, 'Protestant cause,' p. 428. Haynes, *Collection of State Papers*, pp. 471–2.
11. Chastellier to Throckmorton, La Rochelle, 4 September 1568, SP70/102, fo.33.
12. Adams, 'Protestant cause', pp. 121–2.
13. Norris to the queen, 11 August 1570, SP70/113, fo.115.
14. Norris to Cecil, 25 September 29 October 1568, SP70/102, fo.67, /103, fo.92.
15. Norris to the queen, 31 August 1570, SP70/113, fo.185.
16. Camden, *Annals*, p. 223.
17. Wernham, 'English policy', pp. 30–2; Wilson, *Queen Elizabeth and the Revolt of the Netherlands*, pp. 128–30.
18. Smythe, *Discourses Military*, p. 26.

19. 18 July 1559, Forbes, *Public Transactions*, I, p. 165; to Cecil, 28 April 1560, Forbes, *Public Transactions*, I, p. 416.
20. *Letters and Papers of Henry VIII*, 48, p. 16.
21. Spanish despatch of 31 May/1 June 1569; Haynes, *Collection of State Papers Span. 1568–70*, p. 157; *Calendar of State Papers Foreign (CSPF)* 1569–71, p. 513.
22. Dee, *Arte of Navigation*, p. 3.
23. Wright and Fowler, *English Colonization*, pp. 24–5.
24. Ibid., p. 25.
25. Raleigh, *Selected Prose and Poetry*, p. 103.
26. Nolan, 'The militarisation of the Elizabethan State'.
27. Fissel, *English Warfare*, 235.
28. Charles Merbury, *A Briefe Discourse of Royall Monarchie* (1581), quoted in Sherman, *John Dee*, p. 150.

BIBLIOGRAPHY

Adams, S., 'The Protestant cause: religious alliance with the West European Calvinist communities as a political issue in England, 1585–1630' (D.Phil. thesis, Oxford university, 1973).

Ascham, Roger., *English Works*, ed. W. A. Wright (Cambridge, 1904).

Calendar of State Papers Foreign, Reign of Elizabeth, ed. J. Stevenson et al. (23 vols, London 1863–1950).

Camden, William. *Annals* (London, 1688).

Chaney, E., *The Evolution of the Grand Tour* (London, 1998).

Dee, John. *The Perfect Arte of Navigation* (London, 1577).

Evans, J. X., ed., *The Works of Sir Roger Williams*, (Oxford, 1972).

Fissel, M. C., *English Warfare 1511–1642* (London and New York, 2001).

Forbes, Patrick, *A Full View of the Public Transactions in the Reign of Elizabeth* (2 vols, London, 1740–1).

Haynes, Samuel. ed. *Collection of State papers . . . Left by William Cecil, Lord Burghley* (2 vols, London, 1740–59).

Letters and Papers, Foreign and Domestic, of Henry VIII, 1509–47, ed. J. S. Btewer, J. Gairdner and R. H. Brodie (21 vols, London, 1862–1932).

MacCaffrey, W., *The Shaping of the Elizabethan Regime* (London, 1969).

Maltby, W. S., *The Black Legend in England: the Development of Anti-Spanish Sentiment, 1558–1660* (Durham, NC, 1971).

Moryson, Fynes. *An Itinerary Containing his Ten Years' Travel* (4 vols, Glasgow, 1907–8), 'Introduction'.

Nolan, J., 'The militarisation of the Elizabethan state', *Journal of Military History*, 58 (1994), 391–420.

Raab, Felix. *The English Face of Machiavelli: a Changing Interpretation, 1500–1700* (London and Toronto, 1964).

Raleigh, Sir Walter. *Selected Prose and Poetry*, ed. A. M. Latham (London, 1965).

Sherman, W. H., *John Dee: The Politics of Reading and Writing in the English Renaissance* (Amherst, 1995).

Smythe, Sir John, *Certain Discourses Military*, ed. J. R. Hale (Ithaca, NY, 1964).

Wernham, R. B., 'English policy and the revolt of the Netherlands', in J. S. Bromley and E. H. Kossmann, eds, *Britain and the Netherlands* (London, 1960), pp. 29–40.

Wilson, C., *Queen Elizabeth and the Revolt of the Netherlands* (London, 1970).

Wright, L. B., and Fowler E. E. eds, *English Colonization of North America* (London, 1968).

FURTHER READING

S. Adams, 'Eliza enthroned? The Court and politics', in C. Haigh (ed.), *The Reign of Elizabeth I* (1984), pp. 55–78; and 'Favourites and factions at the Elizabethan Court', in R. Asch and A. M. Birke (eds), *Princes, Patronage and the Nobility* (1991), pp. 265–87.

E. Bonner, 'The French reactions to the rough wooings of Mary Queen of Scots'; and 'The *politique* of Henri II: de facto French rule in Scotland', *Journal of the Sydney Society for Scottish History* 6 and 7 (1998, 1999).

M. L. Bush, *The Government Policy of Protector Somerset* (1975).

P. S. Crowson, *Tudor Foreign Policy* (1973).

J. M. Currin, 'Pro expensis Ambassatorum: Diplomacy and financial administration in the reign of Henry VII', *English Historical Review*, 108 (1993), 589–609; 'Henry VII and the treaty of Redon (1489): Plantagenet ambitions and early Tudor foreign policy', *History*, 81 (1996), pp. 343–58; and 'Persuasions of peace: the Luxembourg-Marigny-Gaguin embassy and the state of Anglo-French relations, 1489–90, *English Historical Review*, 113 (1998), 882–904.

C. S. L. Davies, 'England and the French war', in J. Loach and R. Tittler (eds), *The Mid-Tudor Polity, c.1540–1560* (1980), pp. 159–85; ' "Roy de France et Roy d'Angleterre": the English claims to France 1453–1558', in *L'Angleterre et les pays bourguignons*, Centre européen d'Etudes bourguignonnes, 35 (1995); and 'Richard III, Brittany and Henry Tudor, 1483–1485', *Nottingham Medieval Studies*, 37 (1993), 110–26.

J. E. A. Dawson, 'William Cecil and the British dimension of early Elizabethan foreign policy', *History*, 74 (1989), 196–216.

S. Doran, *Elizabeth I and Foreign Policy, 1558–1603* (2000); *England and Europe 1485–1603* (1986, rev. 1996); and *Monarchy and Matrimony: The Courtships of Elizabeth* (1996).

D. Dunlop, 'The politics of peacekeeping: Anglo-Scottish relations from 1503 to 1511', *Renaissance Studies*, 8 (1994), 138–61.

C. Giry-Deloison, 'Le personnel diplomatique au début di XVIe siècle: l'exemple des relations franco-anglaises de l'avènement de Henry VII au camp du drap d'or (1485–1520)', *Journal des Savants*, July–September 1987, 205–53; 'Henry VII et la Bretagne', in J. Kehervé (ed.), *Bretagne Terre d'Europe* (1992), pp. 223–42; 'Money and early Tudor diplomacy: the English pensioners of the French kings (1475–1547)', *Medieval History*, 3 (1993), 128–46; 'La diplomatie anglaise 1485–1603', in L. Bély and I. Rochefort (eds), *L'invention de la diplomatie. Moyen-Age – Temps Modernes* (Paris, 1998); and (ed.), *François Ier et Henri VIII, Deux Princes de la Renaissance (1515–1547)* (n.d.).

D. Grummitt (ed.), *The English Experience in France, c.1450–1558: War, Diplomacy and Cultural Exchange*, (2002).

S. J. Gunn, 'The French Wars of Henry VIII', in J. Black, ed., *The Origins of War in Early Modern Europe* (Edinburgh, 1987), pp. 28–51; and 'Wolsey's foreign policy and the domestic crisis of 1527–8', in S. J. Gunn and P. G. Lindley (eds), *Cardinal Wolsey: Church, State and Art* (1991), pp. 149–77.

P. Gwynn, *The King's Cardinal: The Rise and Fall of Thomas Wolsey* (London, 1990); and 'Wolsey's foreign policy: the conferences at Calais and Bruges reconsidered', *Historical Journal*, 23 (1980), 755–72.

D. M. Head, 'Henry VIII's Scottish policy', *Scottish Historical Review*, 61 (1982), 1–24.

M. K. Jones, 'The myth of 1485: did France really put Henry Tudor on the throne?', in D. Grummitt (ed.), *The English Experience in France, c.1450–1558: War, Diplomacy and Cultural Exchange*, (Aldershot, 2002), pp. 85–105.

N. Jones, 'Elizabeth's first year: the conception and birth of the Elizabethan political world', in C. Haigh (ed.), *The Reign of Elizabeth I* (London, 1984), pp. 27–54.

W. R. D. Jones, *The Mid-Tudor Crisis, 1539–1563* (1973).

E. Kouri, *England and the Attempt to Form a Protestant Alliance in the Late 1560s: A Case Study in European Diplomacy* (Helsinki, 1985).

H. Lloyd, *The Rouen Campaign, 1590–92* (Oxford, 1973).

M. A. Lyons, *Franco-Irish Relations, 1500–1610* (2003).

D. Loades, *The Mid-Tudor Crisis, 1545–1565* (London, 1992); *The Tudor Navy: an Administrative, Political and Military History* (Aldershot, 1992); and *England's Maritime Empire: Seapower, Commerce and Policy* (Harlow, 2000).

W. MacCaffrey, *The Shaping of the Elizabethan Regime: Elizabethan Politics 1558–72* (London, 1969); 'The Anjou match and the making of Elizabethan foreign policy', in P. Clark et al. (eds), *The English Commonwealth, 1547–1640* (Leicester, 1979), pp. 59–75; *Queen Elizabeth and the Making of Policy* (Princeton, 1981); *Elizabeth I* (London, 1993); and 'The Newhaven Expeditions, 1562–63', *Historical Journal* 1 (1997).

R. McEntegart, *Henry VIII, the League of Schmalkalden and the English Reformation* (Boydell, 2002).

C. Martin and G. Parker, *The Spanish Armada* (London, 1988).

M. Merriman, *The Rough Wooings: Mary Queen of Scots 1542–51* (Edinburgh, 2000).

D. Potter, 'The duc de Guise and the fall of Calais', *English Historical Review*, 98 (1983), 481–512; 'The Treaty of Boulogne and European diplomacy', *Bulletin of the Institute of Historical Research*, 55 (1982), 50–65; 'French intrigue in Ireland during the reign of Henri II, 1547–59', *International History Review*, 5 (1983), 159–80; 'Foreign policy', in D. MacCulloch, *The Reign of Henry VIII* (1995), pp. 101–33; 'Anglo-French relations 1500: the aftermath of the Hundred Years War', *Franco-British Studies*, 28 (1999), 41–66; and 'Mid-Tudor foreign policy and diplomacy 1547–1563', in S. Doran and G. Richardson (eds), *Tudor England and its Neighbors* (Basingstoke, 2004).

D. Quinn, *England and the Discovery of America, 1481–1620* (1974).

C. Read, *Mister Secretary Cecil and Queen Elizabeth* (1955); *Lord Burleigh and Queen Elizabeth* (London, 1960); and *Mister Secretary Walsingham and the Policy of Queen Elizabeth* (3 vols 1923).

N. M. Sutherland, *The Massacre of Saint Bartholomew and the European Conflict, 1559–72* (London, 1973); 'The origins of Queen Elizabeth's relations with the Huguenots, 1559–62', *Proceedings of the Huguenot Society of London*, 20 (1958–64), 626–48; *Princes, Politics and Religion* (London, 1984); and 'The foreign policy of Queen Elizabeth, the Sea Beggars and the capture of Brill, 1572', in her *Princes, Politics and Religion*.

G. Richardson, *Renaissance Monarchy: The Reigns of Henry VIII, Francis I and Charles V* (2002).

M. J. Rodriguez-Salgado and S. Adams (eds), *England, Spain and the Gran Armada, 1585–1604* (1991).

J. Russell, *The Field of Cloth of Gold: Men and Manners in 1520* (1969); *Peacemaking in the Renaissance* (1986); and *Diplomats at Work: Three Renaissance Studies* (1992).

J. Scarisbrick, *Henry VIII* (1968).

D. Trim, ' "Fin de siècle": the English soldier's experience at the end of the sixteenth century', *Military and Naval History Journal*, 10 (1999), 1–13; 'The foundation-stone of the British army? The Normandy campaign of 1562', *Journal of the Society for Army Historical Research*, 77 (1999), 71–87; and 'The "Secret War" of Elizabeth I: England and the Huguenots during the early Wars of Religion, 1562–77', *Proceedings of the Huguenot Society of London*, 27, ii (1999), 189–99.

R. B. Wernham, *Before the Armada: The Emergence of the English Nation, 1485–1588* (1972); *After the Armada* (1984); *The Making of Elizabethan Foreign Policy, 1558–1603* (1980); and *The Return of the Armadas* (1994).

PART II

Belief

INTRODUCTION

In assembling the articles in this volume we were influenced by the contours of existing historiography and by our perception of the directions in which scholarship on the British Isles is currently moving. For most of the post-Reformation era, British Reformation histories were a set of competing triumphalist narratives written by denominational proponents. Whiggish Protestant self-certainty dominated the establishments, battling with romantic nostalgia and real Catholic martyrologies for the title of 'true' Reformation histories. However, in the last half of the twentieth century, historians turned away from these apologetics and became interested in the social history of the Reformation, using anthropological and religious-studies models to open new questions about how the reformations were experienced. Theological discussions declined and the process of reform took centre stage for scholars of English and Scottish Reformation history.

This style of historical interpretation came at the reformations from above and below, arguing about whether the reforms had been embraced by a population already anticlerical and inclined to accept the Protestant message, or if those reforms had been imposed from above. A. G. Dickens and G. R. Elton dominated these debates until Eamon Duffy, J. J. Scarisbrick and Christopher Haigh settled the issue by demonstrating that in England, at least, the majority of the population was Catholic and probably would have remained so if the reforms had not been forced upon them. Similar arguments have been made about Scotland, but not about Ireland.

Of late a new trend has emerged, as the secular implications of the Reformation have begun to interest scholars. The destruction of the physical and cultural world of late-medieval Catholicism brought about economic, social and political changes of sometimes monumental proportions in the communities that absorbed them. The disappearance of a great abbey like that of Reading, forced the entire reorganization of the community, restructured its government, and created a local depression, with attendant knock-on effects. All of which had to be dealt with in the context of a spiritual identity crisis, in which people were trying to survive emotionally as well as economically.

Much of the current study of religion in the sixteenth century is consumed by questions concerning the causes, processes and impacts of the national reformations, rather than a comparative perspective on the way the Reformation occurred in the various locales. The dominance of regional narratives has restricted most conversations about the Reformation to a single political context. Thus, although the Scots, the Welsh, the Irish and the English were all part of Catholic Christendom before the massive changes in the mid-sixteenth century, their post-Reformation stories usually become local, and often with a nationalist spin. This is natural, in that local political systems conditioned the imposition of reform. However, as our essays make clear, the making of Scottish, Irish, Welsh and English identities was linked to the larger worlds of the Isles and the Continent.

The essays in this section reflect the current state of the historiography, as well as suggesting some questions that might nuance the national conversations about the Reformation. Because English historians have spent so much time elaborating the political process of Reformation, we did not ask for an article which would review the political evolution of the reforms, focusing instead on cultural impacts. Ben McRee was given the challenging task of creating a baseline for pre-Reformation religious culture, in keeping with current historiographical perceptions of the strength of habitual Catholicism in the British Isles before the reforms began to be imposed.

Peter Cunich, in portraying the process and impacts of the dissolutions of monasteries and chantries, opens up a vitally important comparative perspective on this massive change in British religious cultures. The English and Welsh dissolutions were clearly the result of political decisions. The thorough destruction of monasteries and chantries in England and Wales was not, however, matched in Ireland, where legislation dissolving the chantries was not passed and the machinery of government was weaker. In Scotland, with its very different Reformation, there was no dissolution. Monasticism, rather than being extinguished by royal authority, died a slow, natural death in the face of public enthusiasm for the Calvinist reforms. The fact that Scottish monasticism declined without repression suggests that historians of the English Reformation need to think about what happened to medieval English Catholicism. Would it have continued as it was without the suppressions, or was its decline already occurring in the 1530s in ways that would have led to its natural death?

Michael Graham shows that the Scots showed little inclination toward Protestantism before the mid-century. Perhaps this was because the king of Scotland already had broad control of the Scottish church after the Indult of 1487. Profiting from it, the Scottish laity had the use of much church property and did not need the expedients used by Henry VIII to seize it. Lacking the incentive to embrace the reforms provided in England, the troubled politics of Scotland in the 1540s and 1550s may explain more about the religious alteration than theological inclinations of the Scots. If Mary Queen of Scots had not come to the throne as a newborn, and if she had not been widowed, things might have turned out differently, since there would have been no French occupation of Scotland. This may explain why although the Scottish parliament enacted the Reformation as a 'popular' act, the Scottish religious settlement was so different from the English Elizabethan settlement.

In England, Ireland and Scotland formal religious settlements were created by political processes and imposed by royal authority. Each settlement created a framework for a religion more than a thorough Reformation. In England and Scotland, as Norman Jones and Michael Graham explain, the religious settlements did eventually create new national religious identities. The Elizabethan settlement of 1559, ironically, became the vehicle for a resurgence of Welsh language and identity, while in Ireland the settlement failed. Although none of the reformations lived up to the expectations of the evangelicals who prayed for them, they did cause enormous cultural changes in the British Isles.

Among other things, the creation of established state religions gave rise to religious dissent. William Sheils and Peter Kaufman explore the cultures of those who did not settle easily into the new state churches. In the case of English Catholics, debates have swirled around the question of whether the Elizabethan recusant movement was a continuation of medieval Catholic belief, or the creation of post-Tridentine missionary priests. Sheils adds a welcome corrective by adding the Scottish experience into the picture, as well as exploring the importance of church papists. The history of Catholic recusants suggests to us that further exploration of how the Catholic and the non-Catholic communities co-operated would be useful.

Kaufman, on the other hand, looks at the emergence of Protestant dissent. If there were many Catholics, there were also many Protestants. Certainly, by the 1580s England, Scotland and Wales had Protestant majorities, but they did not all see eye to eye. One effect of the years of Henrician and Edwardian attempts to undermine Catholicism was the creation of a Protestant community in England, if not so clearly in Wales or Ireland. Galvanized by Marian persecution, many of them entered Elizabeth's reign with a deep commitment to a reformed ecclesiology and an evangelical theology that sat uneasily within the Tudor church. These Tudor Protestants, turning into Puritans and Separatists, often looked longingly toward the reformed kirk of Scotland as their preferred, Presbyterian model of church governance. Like the Catholic recusants, these dissenters were creating a culture on the periphery of, and existing because of, the established church.

Of course, the various British reformations were local variants on the wider European phenomena of religious upheaval. The English style of reformation was distinctive, using the Book of Common Prayer as its vehicle and more closely related to North German Lutheranism than anything else. It did not please English Calvinists, who much preferred the Calvinist forms that became entrenched in Scotland by the late sixteenth century. In neither the English nor the Scottish cases do we see the pattern of confessionalization – a religious variant of state formation – noted by scholars in Switzerland, Germany and elsewhere. The unstable Scottish religious establishment, the hiccuping English reforms and Elizabeth's broad-church approach, and the imperfect Tudor control of Ireland all made the reformations more a process of cultural transformation than of political state formation.[1]

All of the contributors in this volume recognize the cultural importance of religion. Although politics remain at the heart of the causation for religious changes, those changes created new majority and minority cultures and fashioned new national identities throughout the British Isles.

NOTE

1. See Patrick Collinson's reflection on this in his 'Comment on Eamon Duffy's Neale Lecture and the Colloquium', in Nicholas Tyacke, ed., *England's Long Reformation 1500–1800. The Neale Colloquium in British History* (Cambridge 1998), pp. 78–80.

CHAPTER TWELVE

Traditional Religion

BEN R. MCREE

At one time the religious landscape of late medieval England was drawn in bleak colours. Men and women, it was thought, attended services they did not understand and participated in rites that had become hollow through meaningless repetition. Occasional splashes of colour provided by pockets of Lollardy or the enthusiasm of mystics and recluses were lost in the general dullness of a religion of habit. Such a dark assessment is no longer tenable. Our view of traditional religion has been transformed during recent years by the work of scholars who have focused attention on a variety of topics, but particularly on the parish as a centre of religious life. There, they have discovered a lively faith with a rich liturgy, a strong emphasis on community, and a deeply felt yearning for the sacred. In this revisionist effort no writer has been more influential than Eamon Duffy. Indeed, the use of the term 'traditional' to describe the religion of the period preceding the Reformation comes from his work. In *The Stripping of the Altars* he rejected the commonly used label 'popular religion', arguing that it assumed a false dichotomy between the beliefs and practices of the elite on the one hand and of ordinary Christians on the other.[1] In its place he proposed the term 'traditional religion', which he used to describe the beliefs and practices of all men and women of orthodox faith. The term has the additional advantage of recognizing the ties that linked the religion of this period to that of earlier centuries. The term does have its drawbacks, however. To some it might suggest stasis, when in fact this was a period of considerable creativity and change. And, as Christopher Marsh has noted, the term 'traditional' can become confusing when carried forward into the Reformation years.[2]

Duffy and others have drawn their information from a variety of sources, making use of churchwardens' accounts, saints' lives, the liturgy, religious primers and books of hours, and church-building and decorating schemes. The last, which includes painting, windows, statues, candles, woodwork and altars and their furnishings, has proven especially rich. Much of the evidence has been drawn from East Anglia and from the south-western counties. Surviving evidence for other regions, including Scotland, is thin. For Ireland, Samantha Meigs has recently made extensive use of Gaelic chronicles and bardic literature both to accentuate the unique role played by the educated elite in Irish religious life and to compensate for the lack of more conventional sources. Although many of the standard sources have long been familiar to historians, the information they are now yielding is new. The change is not the result of a new theoretical framework. Indeed, historians working in this area have employed a wide range of approaches, including straightforward narrative, quantitative analysis, and more theoretically coloured discussions of gender and texts. What, then, has allowed revisionist views to emerge? In part, it is the result of considering various sources together rather than in isolation, looking at the art that adorned the walls of the church together with the wills made by the parishioners and the accounts that recorded the administration of parish property, for example. But it is also the result of looking at religious life from the point of view of the parishioners themselves, asking what they experienced, what their priorities were, and how they expressed their religious convictions. As a result, passive parishioners have become, in revisionist accounts, active worshippers who played an important role in shaping their religious environment. There is, of course, a danger in over-playing such evidence and romanticizing the late-medieval past. If it is wrong to see the faith of the late fifteenth and early sixteenth centuries as a hollow one, surely it is equally inaccurate to see it as the foundation of an idyllic world where shared beliefs and religious practices fostered harmonious communities in which equality was the governing principle and strife was effectively banished.

What has become then of the evidence of lay disaffection from a late-medieval church rife with abuses? The short answer is that the evidence has not disappeared, and some may still find it persuasive. This was, after all, a period in which clergymen often hired vicars to serve the parishes to which they had been appointed and often held multiple appointments simultaneously – practices known as non-residence and pluralism. The parish clergy, as a result, was less well paid and less well trained than it might have been. This was also a period of disputes between priests and their parishioners over tithes, mortuary payments and other financial dues, disputes that could result in bitter and protracted conflicts. Revisionists have responded to this sort of evidence in two ways. First, they have argued that abuses had long existed and that the late-medieval situation was no different from that of earlier centuries. The situation may, in fact, have been improving, as reform efforts began to take effect. Parishioners were, in any case, accustomed through long experience to distinguishing between the quality of their clergy and the elements of their faith. They may have believed the message even if they had their doubts about the messengers. Second, recent work has set beside the evidence of corruption and strife a great deal of new evidence of continuing lay faith in traditional institutions and practices – of prayers to saints, masses for the welfare of souls in purgatory, and donations for decorating or expanding parish churches. The new material has not displaced signs of corruption and disaffection, but it has raised questions about its significance and about the laity's readiness for religious change.

Perhaps the most important element in the reinterpretation of parish religion has been the detailed recreation of ceremonies and services as parishioners might have experienced them in their local churches. Here the work of Duffy has been crucial. His accounts help to evoke the richness of the medieval liturgy and have gone a long way toward helping modern readers to imagine medieval services. What follows is an overview of some of those services, as he and other scholars have described them. The most important service, without a doubt, was the weekly High Mass. All parishioners were required to attend this service, though how many did is, of course, unknown. Parishioners gathered in the nave of the church, separated from the chancel – where the high altar stood – by the rood screen, a divider constructed of wood or stone and decorated with images of saints. Candles supplied by parish groups or through bequests would have illuminated some of the images on the screen. Suspended above the screen was the crucifix or rood. Beyond the screen was the chancel, visible through the upper part of the screen. The stone high altar where the mass took place would have been located there. In most churches additional altars would have been located to either side, decorated with images, candles and objects donated by parishioners. Medieval churches generally lacked pews, though many had a simple form of seating in the form of benches. It was customary for men and women to occupy different parts of the nave, women usually on the north side and men on the south. Alternatively, men might be in front and women at the back. Pews began to appear more frequently in the fifteenth century, and, by the Tudor era, it would have been unusual for a church not to have some seating for parishioners. In the sixteenth century the advent of family pews began to break down the division between men and women.

The priest, dressed in his vestments, began the service by blessing salt and water and leading a clerical procession around the church, sprinkling the altars with holy water as they went. He then moved to the chancel, where he recited the Confiteor, read the scripture lesson, called for prayers for the living and the dead, received offerings, and prepared the bread and wine for consecration. All but the call for prayers was spoken in Latin. This did not mean that parishioners were uninvolved in or uninformed about the actions taken by the priest, however. Most would have said private prayers, such as the Pater Noster, during the service. Devotional aids containing appropriate prayers for different parts of the service and meditations linked to the actions of the priest proliferated during the fifteenth century, providing a more nuanced program of private worship for those who could read. Here, for example, is what the *Lay Folks' Mass Book* instructed its readers to do as the most solemn moment in the mass approached:

> 'Make sure you are saying Our Father until he [the priest] is making a cross over the chalice: then the time of sacring is near. People usually ring a little bell; then you shall pay reverence to Jesus Christ's own presence, which may loose all baleful bonds. Kneeling, hold up both your hands, and so behold the elevation: for that is he whom Judas kissed, and who thereafter was scourged and put on the rood, and there shed his blood for mankind, and died, and rose, and went to Heaven, and yet shall come to judge us all – each man according to his deeds: the same is he whom you look upon.'

At that point the worshipper was to recite an elevation prayer. The *Lay Folks' Mass Book* instructed readers to follow their own inspiration, 'each man in his best manner.'[3] John Mirk's *Instructions for Parish Priests* suggested a prayer beginning with these lines:

> Ihesu Lord, welcome thow be,
> In forme of bred as I the se;
> Ihesu! For thy holy name,
> Schelde me to day fro synne & schame.[4]

Such texts suggest the sense of wonder that could accompany the moment of elevation, as Jesus himself became present on the altar of the parish church. Sometimes that wonder could be overwhelming, as in the case of Margery Kempe, a fifteenth-century woman who, much to the irritation of her fellow congregants, was often reduced to wailing at the sight of the host, or, somewhat less dramatically, by parishioners who moved from altar to altar within a large church, hoping to glimpse as many hosts as possible. Such fascination led one historian to describe the 'cultic element of the devotion to the Host' as 'perhaps the strongest aspect of lay piety of the time.'[5] It has also led some modern writers into raptures of their own. Here is Duffy's moving but perhaps overly enthusiastic description of the moment:

> Christ himself, immolated on the altar of the cross, became present on the altar of the parish church, body, soul, and divinity, and his blood flowed once again, to nourish and renew Church and world. As kneeling congregations raised their eyes to see the Host held high above the priest's head at the sacring, they were transported to Calvary itself, and gathered not only into the passion and resurrection of Christ, but into the full sweep of salvation history as a whole.[6]

In the last part of the mass the power of the divine made manifest on the altar was harnessed to heal social rifts among the parishioners and promote a sense of community. The primary vehicle for this was the paxbred – a tablet inscribed with a sacred image. Before taking communion, the priest kissed the *corporas*, which held the consecrated bread, the chalice, which held the wine, and finally the paxbred, which a clerk then passed to the congregation. In order of status, each kissed the tablet before passing it to the next parishioner. At the conclusion of the service, in another gesture of peace, a loaf of bread, supplied by one of the parish households and blessed by the priest, was cut up and divided among the parishioners. Both the sharing of responsibility for the loaf and the sharing of the bread itself emphasized the bonds that tied parishioners together. But the need for precedence in both the passing of the paxbred and the distribution of bread from the holy loaf could work against that end, provoking argument, and even violence, as some took offence at their place in the sequence. Duffy relates the story of Joanna Dyaca, who in 1494 threw the paxbred to the ground, breaking it, because another woman had been allowed to kiss it before her, as well as the story of John Browne, who in 1522 smashed the paxbred over the head of the clerk who had handed it to him because the clerk had given the tablet first to another parishioner.[7] Such incidents were not the norm, but they do reveal the ways in which liturgical customs could heighten tensions rather than reducing them. That did not change the symbolic importance of the practice, however, which presented to the assembled parishioners an ideal of social harmony rooted in weekly services they attended with their neighbours.

The way in which the mass was conducted called attention to the division between clergy and laity. The priest occupied a secluded space during the service, spoke an unfamiliar language, and dressed in distinctive clothing. He alone had the power to transform bread and wine, and he alone took communion on a regular basis. He also heard parishioners' confessions and granted (or denied) absolution, a requirement for communion. The priest's special status could breed tensions with the laity, although documented complaints are rare. Those that did surface often focused on a clergyman's failure to perform the very duties that set him apart – saying mass or baptizing newborns, for example – rather than objections to his distinctive powers.[8] Even so, critics of late-medieval religion have long felt that the distance between clergy and laity had the effect of turning parishioners into passive spectators, unable to participate fully in their faith.

Historians of traditional religion have recently sought to address this issue, arguing that medieval parishioners were neither passive nor disinterested. Eamon Duffy has provided the fullest statement of this revisionist view. He has pointed out that in contrast to the High Mass, daily Low Masses were celebrated in the nave at side altars or at altars in front of the rood screen. At those services no screen separated laity from clergy. He added that through their donations, the laity could and did control the content of these masses, specifying particular prayers or readings. Even on Sunday during the High Mass, the congregation was more involved in the service than often thought, according to Duffy. He described the rood screen less as a barrier than a frame that enhanced the sacred quality of what took place beyond it. The screen was, in fact, solid only to waist level. Above that height, it took the form of unglazed windows that served as 'a frame for the liturgical drama.' Nor was the lower section always solid. In some churches it was pierced by 'elevation squints,' small peep holes that allowed those kneeling in front of it 'to pass visually into the sanctuary.'[9] All of this evidence suggests that the laity may have been separated from the clergy, but they were not alienated from their faith.

Feast-day ceremonies provided opportunities for the laity to participate even more actively in religious life. At Candlemas in February, for example, parishioners customarily processed to the church carrying candles, which were then blessed by the priest and offered to the church. A procession also took place at Rogationtide, five weeks after Easter, when parishioners carried bells and banners around the boundaries of their parish, ceremonially defining their territory and driving evil spirits out of it (and presumably into the next parish!). But perhaps the best-known medieval processions took place in late May or June on the feast of Corpus Christi. These were most fully realized in larger towns and cities, where they featured local citizens, usually organized according to craft affiliation and wearing the colourful liveries of their guilds, marching with the clergy to the church where a special mass was celebrated. In Edinburgh musicians led the column as it made its way through the city.[10] In some places play cycles depicting the life of Christ and other stories taken from the Bible were added as well.

The most elaborate ceremonies were reserved for the Easter season. In these observances the potential for participation in the liturgy by parishioners was most fully and dramatically realized. On Palm Sunday one or two clergymen carried the consecrated host into the churchyard, where they joined parishioners in a procession into the church, re-enacting Jesus's entry into Jerusalem. They halted before the rood screen, where a veil, which had covered the crucifix throughout Lent, was lifted and mass was celebrated. On the following Thursday, Maundy Thursday, all the altars in the church were stripped of their coverings and decorations and ritually washed with water and wine. On Good Friday the parishioners crept barefoot to a cross brought into the chancel for the purpose, and kissed it. Later, that cross, together with a consecrated host, was 'buried' in the Easter sepulchre, usually a wooden frame temporarily installed along the north wall of the church. The sepulchre was covered with cloths depicting the crucifixion and resurrection, and surrounded by candles. Some parishes had more permanent stone sepulchres built into the wall, often as part of a donor's tomb. Members of the congregation kept watch before the sepulchre during the night on Friday and throughout the day and night on Saturday. Early Sunday morning the cross and host were triumphantly removed, completing the re-enactment of the resurrection.

On such occasions the liturgy became a drama, with parishioners joining the action, and the church itself becoming a stage for sacred performance. It seems fitting then that parishioners played a major part in decorating that stage, donating windows, paintings, statues, paintings, crosses, cloths, candles and other items to their churches. Late medieval wills are filled with such benefactions, which could be as simple and inexpensive as a candle for a particular altar, or as elaborate as the bequest of Thomas Goisman, an alderman of Hull, for the construction of a device to raise and lower angels over the altar during the mass.[11] The rood screen itself, far from being resented as a barrier separating parishioners from the holy, attracted numerous donations for pious adornment, including images of saints painted on the solid lower section and candles burning on the beam above. Guilds and more informal organizations such as 'stores' also contributed images, candles and other decorations for the screen.[12]

Historians have offered a number of explanations for the intensity of lay interest in church decoration. Part of the appeal was the scope they offered for the expression of individual devotional preferences. Through his or her will, a parishioner could choose to honour particular saints or altars in a public way. Some testators also took advantage of the opportunity to place personal possessions in sacred spaces where they could be in contact with the holy. A pillow might become a book-rest. A wedding ring might adorn a statue. Sheets, towels, and prized pieces of clothing might be used to make altar cloths, placing the most personal and intimate of possessions at the physical heart of the worship service. There must have been an element of ostentation in some gifts as well; certainly one's ability and willingness to contribute to the adornment of the parish church could be a mark of status. The fact that such donations would have been seen weekly by friends and neighbours and remembered annually in the reading of the bede roll, a list of men and women who had made gifts to the local church, would not have been lost on donors.[13] Clearly those with the most to give could do this most impressively, so it was merchants in towns and cities and members of the gentry in the countryside who most often underwrote statuary, stained glass and elaborate wall tombs. Such worldly motives have to be balanced against the role that gifts played in calling forth prayers for their donors' souls. Indeed, where donors' motives are explicit, it is the desire for prayers that is mentioned, prayers that donors believed would hasten their journey through purgatory. But that does not mean that concerns for status did not also figure in donors' plans as well. Indeed, it might be argued that prominent display by men and women of means was both a religious and social obligation, and that those who wanted to maintain their place in society had to fulfil that obligation or face a loss of status.

Purgatory looms large in all accounts of late-medieval religion. Parishioners believed that virtually everyone's soul was destined for purgatory after death, only the unregenerate and unbelieving going to hell and only the saintly directly to heaven. Souls in purgatory would eventually enter heaven, but only after a period of painful cleansing. Time spent in purgatory was dependent upon the quality of one's life –

both the number and type of sins committed and good works performed. Works completed on one's behalf *after* death could also reduce time spent in purgatory. The most common strategy was to endow masses to be said after one's death, a practice that remained popular through the 1520s. The wealthy and powerful left instructions and funds for thousands of masses to be performed shortly after death. One archbishop of Canterbury provided, for example, for 15,000 masses on his death.[14] Less spectacular provision could be made through the establishment of chantries – endowments that supported a priest saying a daily mass for the donor's soul for a specified period. Such establishments did not come cheaply, with the annual salary of a priest typically £5–6, and most chantries were of limited duration, ranging from a few months to a few years. Those with sufficient wealth might endow perpetual chantries (chaplainries in Scotland), which were intended to continue until the end of time, or collegiate churches employing a number of priests. Testators of more modest means might choose to fund a trental – thirty masses performed in thirty days. Also popular was the Trental of St Gregory, or 'pope trental,' which called for the thirty masses to be celebrated on specified feast days spread over the course of a year.

Critics of the late-medieval intercessory system, both then and now, have argued that it put salvation up for sale, giving unfair advantage to the wealthy and smacking of simony. They have also complained that it exploited parishioners' fear for its success.[15] In this view, men and women who heard about the suffering of those in purgatory in sermons and popular stories, and saw those sufferings depicted in paintings, invested in the church's system of salvation in a frantic attempt to shorten the sufferings that would inevitably follow their exit from this world. The cynicism of literary characters such as Chaucer's Pardoner would seem to reinforce this notion. Clive Burgess has offered a strong counter to those views, which he attributes to Protestant prejudice and academic discomfort with strongly held beliefs. He has argued that the belief in purgatory and the intercessory system that accompanied it was essentially optimistic, promising salvation to the truly penitent, no matter how many sins they had on their consciences, while offering people of all ranks a practical way to mitigate their suffering. As to the inequalities of wealth and their influence on an individual's ability to fund masses and chantries, he pointed out that requiem masses benefited all the souls in purgatory, not just those for whom they were celebrated, and called attention to the widely held presumption that greater wealth entailed greater obligation. Indeed, Burgess posited a 'circular flow' in which the wealthy traded alms for the prayers of the spiritually better-off poor.[16] The chantries funded by the wealthy also benefited the parish community in a more worldy way by supporting additional priests who could help with services, especially at busy times such as Easter. As Marsh and others have pointed out, however, the system was open to abuse by clergy who were willing to exploit parishioners' fears to extract gifts. The extent to which that happened is impossible to gauge. It is at the very least worth remembering that clergy played an important role in encouraging donations, affording ample opportunity to remind parishioners of both the benefits to be gained and the penalties to be avoided.

The cult of the saints, soon to come under attack by reformers, remained popular during the early Tudor period. Saints were regarded as holy helpers who could provide aid to worthy supplicants, particularly those who found themselves in distress. The sailor trapped on a ship foundering at sea, the mother whose child had fallen ill, or the traveller frightened by a thunderstorm might all have recourse to the saints. Less dramatically, perhaps, aid might be sought in securing a bountiful harvest, finding a missing spoon or remedying a toothache. Men and women sought saintly assistance through prayer, but prayer was often supplemented by pilgrimages and by contributions of candles or coins to the altars dedicated to saints. Although the great medieval pilgrimage sites, such as Canterbury, seem to have declined in popularity by the fifteenth century, pilgrimage itself remained a desirable way to seek the assistance of a saint as pilgrims turned to a variety of local shrines, such as those at Tain in Scotland, Trim in Ireland, and Walsingham in England. Some followed the custom of bending a coin – typically a silver penny – as a sign of an intention to make a donation to the altar of a saint. There was a notion of contract behind such practices, with an expectation of help accompanying the intent to honour the saint, and parishioners felt justified in withdrawing their veneration when saints did not fulfil their part of the bargain. Such attitudes suggest something of the highly personal, homely character of such relationships. In Ireland the personal link extended to kinship, with supplicants seeking protection from saints associated with their clans, a development facilitated by the emergence of a distinct genre of bardic literature – the saintly genealogy.

Saints to which religious guilds (popular organizations that will be described more fully below) were dedicated provide one indication of the relative popularity of various saints. Easily the most popular cult was that of the Virgin Mary. Katherine French recorded fifty-three parish guilds dedicated to Mary in the diocese of Bath and Wells alone between 1298 and 1548; the next most popular dedications (a tie between St Katherine and the Holy Trinity) had only eleven. Recent surveys of guilds in Yorkshire and East Anglia affirm Mary's pre-eminence. The popularity of other saints as patrons of guilds varied by county, but the Holy Trinity, Corpus Christi, St Katherine and St John the Baptist had widespread appeal. The evidence of wills and rood-screen imagery suggests that early Christian martyrs were particular favourites during the late fifteenth and early sixteenth centuries. St Erasmus, martyred during the reign of Diocletian, was one of these, as were a group of women who defended their faith and their virginity at the cost of their lives during the same period. The most popular of these 'virgin martyrs' were St Katherine, St Margaret and St Barbara, but there were others as well.

The members of one group in early Tudor England did not share such confidence in masses and saints or such affection for images and shrines. These were the Lollards, adherents of ideas put forth in the fourteenth century by John Wyclif. Although the writings of the Oxford theologian and priest had been condemned by the church, they took root in the decades that followed among small groups scattered through the midlands and southern parts of the country. The identities of those brought to trial for heresy suggest that Lollardy appealed more to men than to women, more to those who lived in towns and cities than in the countryside, and more to those of humble or middling status than to elites. There were always exceptions, of course, such as Alice Rowley of Coventry, a prominent figure among the Lollards of that city and the widow of one of the city's leading citizens.[17]

Lollards held a number of beliefs that placed them at odds with the church and with their neighbours. They looked to scripture as the sole source of religious truth and encouraged adherents to read it in their native tongue. Indeed, one of the surest – though not infallible – signs of Lollardy was possession of an English bible. They did not believe in transubstantiation, maintaining that the bread and wine used during the mass remained just that. They denied that the clergy had any special powers conferred by ordination. The true priesthood, they believed, was distinguished by virtuous living and effective teaching. They decried the cult of the saints, and with it pilgrimages, images and prayers for the dead. Suspected Lollards were pursued sporadically by church authorities, and those whose beliefs were found to be heretical were compelled to abjure and do penance or face death. There were waves of trials in various English dioceses in the 1420s and 1460s, and from the 1480s to the 1520s. Heresy cases were few in Scotland, where they were concentrated in the first half of the fifteenth century, and entirely absent in Ireland during the same period. Despite the attempts of authorities to drive it out of existence, Lollardy persisted throughout the fifteenth and early sixteenth centuries, finally merging with Lutheranism during the 1530s and after.

The significance of the Lollards remains a matter of dispute. They are dismissed by some as cranky misfits without a coherent theology or significant numbers, while others have seen them as important forerunners of Protestantism, introducing some of the central ideas of the later reformers and signifying a wide but silent dissatisfaction with the church. The most influential recent work has favoured the latter view, emphasizing the continuity and coherence of Lollard ideas and communities.[18] There may even have been links between centres of Lollardy in the sixteenth century and Baptist and Quaker activity in the seventeenth, suggesting local persistence of nonconformist views beyond the Reformation.[19]

Notwithstanding the Lollard experience, the vast majority of men and women remained solidly within the confines of orthodoxy. Nowhere is that more evident than in the prevalence of religious guilds – voluntary lay associations of men and women devoted to particular cults – during the late fifteenth and early sixteenth centuries. These popular organizations were dedicated to saints or aspects of the sacred (Corpus Christi, the Holy Cross, the Holy Trinity, for example) and held processions and worship services on their feast days. They often provided images of their patron saint for the local church, as well as candles and altar decorations. English guilds, unlike many of their continental counterparts, were almost always parish-based and often enrolled women as well as men as members. Guilds were closely involved in the intercessory system, typically providing a set number of masses for the souls of members who died and requiring all members to attend the funeral and offer prayers. In the early 1980s, J. J. Scarisbrick cited the proliferation of guilds during the early Tudor period as a sign of the continuing appeal of traditional religion to English men and women right up to the Reformation.[20] Work done since that time has confirmed the religious traditionalism of the guilds and documented their continuing popularity in communities of all sizes. In Cambridgeshire, for example, one recent study found signs of guild activity in 73 per cent of the towns and villages in the county.[21] More than 40 per cent of the guilds identified made their first appearance only after 1500. David Crouch found that guilds remained popular with Yorkshire testators until the 1530s; and although the frequency of bequests fell after the break with Rome, support did not disappear entirely.[22] Many communities had multiple foundations. A study of East Anglian guilds reported thirteen and fourteen guilds respectively in the Norfolk

market towns of Wymondham and Swaffham.[23] Not all of those guilds operated at
the same time, but a number did, and some residents belonged to more than one.

Guilds engaged in a variety of corporate undertakings that illustrate the way in
which conviviality was combined with religious observance in the late Middle Ages.
Most sponsored a mass in honour of their patron saint, which all members were
obliged to attend. Some guilds had their own chapels within the church where those
services might be held. Many fraternities held a procession as well, some of which
could be quite elaborate. In Beverley, the guild of St Helen recalled the role of its
patron saint in the discovery of the cross by featuring a man carrying a cross and
another a spade at the head of the column, followed by a boy dressed as St Helen.[24]
In Norwich, members of the Guild of St George paraded through the city on horseback while other members playing the parts of St George and the dragon fought a
spirited combat. A guild might also sponsor a feast on the same day. Some of these
could be quite elaborate, with music, minstrels and an abundance of food. In Bishop's
Lynn, later King's Lynn, for example, the Corpus Christi Guild purchased mackerel,
herring, whelks, chickens, capons, doves, geese, marrowbones, pigs, crab, beef, lamb
and veal for two feasts in 1444.[25] At other times of year guild members gathered at
meetings, often held quarterly, and at funerals. Attendance at the burial of a fellow
'brother' or 'sister' and an offering for his or her soul was an almost universal requirement of guild membership and a palpable manifestation of the fraternity they
espoused. Many guilds also promised charitable assistance to members who had fallen
on hard times or made loans of cash or stock to members.

Some guilds formed close ties with local governments, or served as surrogate
governments in communities that lacked the right to self-government. They could
be particularly useful in the latter case because they had clearly identified leaders,
financial resources that they could tap for community projects, a forum for
decision-making, and the means to discipline unruly members.[26] In communities with
chartered rights to self-government, guilds provided ceremony, adjudicated disputes,
and helped to define the path through civic office. In Coventry, for example, those
with political aspirations joined the Corpus Christi Guild early in their public careers,
graduating to the more prestigious Holy Trinity Guild when their fortunes flourished. In Norwich, the union of city government and the Guild of St George followed two decades of civic disturbances and was part of the effort to preserve the
recently restored peace.

If the proliferation of guilds demonstrates the extent of lay initiative in religious
matters, the duties of the churchwardens illustrate the depth of lay responsibility for
worship. Parishioners were responsible for the upkeep of the nave of their churches
(the chancel falling under the priest's care) and for providing liturgical equipment.
They also had to respond to episcopal inquiries concerning the state of parish religious life – the physical condition of the church itself, the provision of the sacraments, the behaviour of the priest – during periodic visitations. All this required
organization, leading to the emergence of the churchwarden as an important figure
in parochial life. Over time the responsibilities of churchwardens grew, so that by the
sixteenth century they had to administer parish property, raise money for building
projects – the repair of the roof, the construction of a tower, or the purchase of a
bell, for example – purchase material and hire workers, represent the parish in the
courts, both lay and ecclesiastical, and oversee myriad bequests made to the church

by parishioners. Most parishes had two churchwardens, chosen in one fashion or another by the parishioners, with tenure of office varying widely. In a study of church-wardens in the diocese of Bath and Wells, Katherine French found that wardens in some parishes served two-year terms, staggered so that there was always a senior and a junior warden. Other parishes elected two new wardens each year. In Nettlecombe, Somerset, the office rotated regularly among thirty families, with widows taking their families' appointed places in the cycle when necessary.[27] In his study of ten English parishes, Beat Kümin found that churchwardens usually came from the middle ranks of society. The wealthiest parishioners rarely served, and those on the lower end of the social scale were similarly unlikely to be chosen.[28]

One of the principal tasks of the churchwardens was to raise the money necessary to carry out their responsibilities, and they employed a variety of means to accom-plish that goal. The most important sources were rents, collections from parishioners and entertainments. Rents gathered from property bequeathed to parishes predom-inated in urban areas, and could comprise 80 per cent or more of the income used for maintaining the nave and discharging parishioners' other obligations. Property rent contributed much less in rural parishes, where the absence of burgage tenure and the prevalence of agricultural land made it a less reliable source of income. Rural parishes relied much more heavily on collections and entertainments for their funding. Collections often paid, for example, for recurring expenses, such as Christmas and Easter candles. Special collections might be made to purchase new ornaments and to fund building projects, such as Tintinhull (Somerset)'s addition to its bell tower.[29] The extent to which collections were voluntary and the means used to gather them remain unclear. In some cases, however, they were combined with entertainments in a festive approach to fundraising. That was the case with Christ-mastime 'hogling' in which collectors went from door to door, combining requests for money with songs and good cheer, and with Hocktide games in which young men and women of the parish took turns capturing and holding one another for ransom.[30] Many rural communities depended on church ales for a large portion of their funds. Such ales were typically held in the spring and summer and could bring in substantial amounts of money. Scholars have suggested that the method used to raise money may have had an effect on the tenor of parish life, with rent-collecting urban churchwardens able to tackle the job without much involvement from their fellow parishioners while rural wardens depended on more direct involvement of the entire parish, perhaps producing a stronger sense of community.[31] Whatever methods parishes used to raise the funds necessary to discharge their responsibilities, the sums gathered were apparently increasing in the late fifteenth and early sixteenth centuries, suggesting a strong lay commitment to parish life.

The picture of traditional religion that has emerged from recent research has emphasized enthusiastic lay involvement in religious services, capable and creative management of parish resources, and strong affective ties between parishioners and the saints whose images adorned their churches. In this context the collapse of the medieval church appears neither longed-for nor inevitable, a conclusion with impor-tant implications for understanding the changes to come. Strong attachment to tra-ditional beliefs and practices, together with the desire to maintain a degree of local autonomy in parish affairs, would surely pose a formidable challenge to religious reformers in the 1530s and after.

NOTES

1. Duffy, *The Stripping of the Altars*, p. 2.
2. Marsh, *Popular Religion in Sixteenth-Century England*, p. 7.
3. Swanson, *Church and Society in Late Medieval England*, p. 88.
4. Duffy, *The Stripping of the Altars*, p. 117.
5. Swanson, *Church and Society in Late Medieval England*, p. 276.
6. Duffy, *The Stripping of the Altars*, p. 91.
7. Duffy, *The Stripping of the Altars*, pp. 126–27.
8. Swanson, 'Problems of the priesthood', p. 861, and Cowan, 'Church and society', p. 113.
9. Duffy, *The Stripping of the Altars*, p. 112.
10. Cowan, 'Church and society', p. 118.
11. Rubin, *Corpus Christi*, p. 62. Goisman's bequest is also mentioned by Duffy, *The Stripping of the Altars*, p. 96.
12. Stores were devotional funds created and maintained by parishioners. See Duffy, *Voices of Morebath*, pp. 24–32.
13. The annual reading of the bede roll was intended to call forth prayers from parishioners for the souls of the church's benefactors.
14. Archbishop Courtenay: Swanson, *Church and Society in Late Medieval England*, p. 298.
15. A view articulated in Marsh, *Popular Religion in Sixteenth-Century England*, pp. 53–4.
16. Burgess, 'A fond thing vainly invented', p. 69.
17. McSheffrey, *Gender and Heresy*, pp. 123–4.
18. Hudson, *The Premature Reformation*; and McSheffrey, *Gender and Heresy*.
19. Margaret Spufford, *The World of Rural Dissenters*, pp. 23–40.
20. Scarisbrick, *The Reformation and the English People*, ch. 2.
21. Bainbridge, *Gilds in the Medieval Countryside*, p. 33.
22. Crouch, *Piety, Fraternity, and Power*, pp. 46–52.
23. Farnhill, *Guilds and the Parish Community in Late Medieval East Anglia*, pp. 91, 119–22.
24. PRO, Guild Returns, C.47/46/446.
25. King's Lynn, Guildhall, Records of Religious Guilds, Gd.26.
26. For example: A. G. Rosser, 'The town and guild of Lichfield in the late middle ages'.
27. French, *People of the Parish*, pp. 76–84.
28. Kümin, *The Shaping of a Community*, pp. 32–8.
29. French, *People of the Parish*, p. 115.
30. Ibid., pp. 116–17, 127.
31. French, *People of the Parish*, pp. 114, 134, 136, 137.

BIBLIOGRAPHY

Bainbridge, Virginia, *Gilds in the Medieval Countryside: Social and Religious Change in Cambridgeshire c.1350–1558* (Woodbridge, 1996).

Burgess, Clive, 'A fond thing vainly invented: an essay on purgatory and pious motive in later medieval England', in S. J. Wright (ed.), *Parish, Church and People: Local Studies in Lay Religion, 1350–1750* (London, 1988).

Cowan, Ian B., 'Church and society', in Jennifer M. Brown (ed.) *Scottish Society in the Fifteenth Century* (New York, 1977).

Crouch, David J. F., *Piety, Fraternity, and Power: Religious Gilds in Late Medieval Yorkshire, 1389–1547* (Woodbridge, 2000).

Duffy, Eamon, *The Stripping of the Altars: Traditional Religion in England, c.1400–c.1580* (New Haven, 1992).

Duffy, Eamon, *The Voices of Morebath: Reformation and Rebellion in an English Village* (New Haven, 2001).

Farnhill, Ken, *Guilds and the Parish Community in Late Medieval East Anglia* (Woodbridge and Rochester, NY, 2001).

French, Katherine, *People of the Parish: Community Life in a Late Medieval Diocese* (Philadelphia, 2001).

Hudson, Anne, *The Premature Reformation: Wycliffite Texts and Lollard History* (Oxford, 1988).

Kümin, Beat A., *The Shaping of a Community: The Rise and Reformation of the English Parish, c.1400–1560* (Aldershot, 1996).

McSheffrey, Shannon, *Gender and Heresy: Women and Men in Lollard Communities, 1420–1530* (Philadelphia, 1995).

Marsh, Christopher, *Popular Religion in Sixteenth-Century England: Holding Their Peace* (New York, 1998).

Meigs, Samantha A., *The Reformations in Ireland: Tradition and Confessionalism, 1400–1690* (New York, 1997).

Rosser, A. G., 'The town and guild of Lichfield in the late middle ages', *Transactions of the South Staffordshire Archaeological and Historical Society*, 27(1987), 39–47.

Rubin, Miri, *Corpus Christi* (Cambridge, 1991).

Scarisbrick, J. J., *The Reformation and the English People* (Oxford, 1984).

Spufford, Margaret, ed., *The World of Rural Dissenters, 1520–1725* (Cambridge, 1995).

Swanson, R. N., *Church and Society in Late Medieval England* (Oxford, 1989).

Swanson, R. N., 'Problems of the priesthood in pre-Reformation England', *English Historical Review*, 105(1990), 845–69.

FURTHER READING

A. D. M. Barrell, *Medieval Scotland* (2000).

Andrew D. Brown, *Popular Piety in Late Medieval England. The Diocese of Salisbury, 1250–1550* (1995).

Clive Burgess, 'London Parishioners in Times of Change: St Andrew Hubbard, Eastcheap, c1450–1570', *Journal of Ecclesiastical History*, 53 (2002), 38–63; and 'Shaping the parish: St Mary at Hill, London, in the Fifteenth Century', in *The Cloister and the World: Essays in Medieval History in Honour of Barbara Harvey*, ed. John Blair and Brian Golding (1996).

Ian B. Cowan, *The Scottish Reformation: Church and Society in Sixteenth Century Scotland* (1982).

Eamon Duffy, 'The parish, piety, and patronage in late medieval East Anglia: the evidence of rood screens', in *The Parish in English Life, 1400–1600*, ed. Katherine L. French, Gary G. Gibbs and Beat A. Kümin (1997).

Ronald Hutton, *The Rise and Fall of Merry England* (1994).

Anthony Lynch, 'Religion in late medieval Ireland', *Archivium Hibernicum*, 36 (1981), 1–15.

Ben R. McRee, 'Religious gilds and civic order: the case of Norwich in the late middle ages', *Speculum*, 67 (1992), 69–97.

Peter Marshall, *The Catholic Priesthood and the English Reformation* (1994).

Gervase Rosser, 'Communities of parish and guild in the late middle ages', in *Parish, Church and People: Local Studies in Lay Religion, 1350–1750*, ed. S. J. Wright. (1988).

Robert Whiting, *The Blind Devotion of the People: Popular Religion and the English Reformation* (1989).

Jenny Wormald, *Court, Kirk, and Community: Scotland 1470–1625* (1981).

CHAPTER THIRTEEN

The Dissolutions and their Aftermath

PETER CUNICH

The dissolution of the monasteries (1536–40) has long been recognized as one of the principal distinguishing features of the English Reformation under Henry VIII. The later dissolution of the chantries (1545–8) is less well known but over recent years its enormous importance in the reform of parish life during the reign of Edward VI has been widely acknowledged. In Ireland, the suppression of monasticism under the Tudors was a long drawn-out process which was pursued as a major element in the policy of extending English colonial rule, but the Irish chantries survived virtually unscathed until much later in the sixteenth century. In Scotland, chantries and other intercessory institutions were one of the immediate targets of Calvinist reformers after 1560, but monasticism was allowed to die a slow death in the second half of the century rather than being subjected to the more immediate suppression which had been achieved in England. In this sense the dissolution movement in the British Isles was not a unified process but rather a series of distinctive movements set in train by princes and politicians who had markedly different religious beliefs and secular goals. The British Isles was therefore no different from the Continent in the variety of ways in which religious institutions were treated during the Protestant Reformation. Moreover, as in many other parts of northern Europe, the Catholic beliefs underpinning monastic and intercessory institutions were no longer openly tolerated anywhere in Britain by the end of the sixteenth century.

Monastic and chantry foundations were two of the most distinctive features of the medieval religious landscape in the British Isles. A range of religious orders for men and women had been established since the missions of St Patrick to Ireland (AD 405) and St Augustine of Canterbury in England (AD 597). Early monastic communities were later joined by various orders of canons regular, Cistercians and Carthusians, mendicant friars and several other religious orders. Wealthy patrons endowed these religious foundations with lands and buildings which were given to provide for both the physical needs of the religious and the spiritual needs of the patrons. In return for endowments, religious communities bound themselves to the perpetual celebration of masses for the souls of founders and their families. Monasteries also attracted smaller donations from the less wealthy in return for intercessory services of a more limited nature, ranging from elaborate perpetual chantries within their conventual churches to shorter-lived endowments for obits. Later in the middle ages, the desire for intercessory prayer spread throughout the church and newer types of intercessory institutions were established in parish churches as parishioners sought to secure their paths to heaven. Collegiate churches, chantry chapels, urban guilds and fraternities, rood lights, obits, trentals, and various other small-scale intercessory arrangements were placed within the parish community and put under the trusteeship of vicars, churchwardens and other lay feoffees. By the end of the middle ages a complex web of intercessory institutions within the monastic, cathedral and parochial churches of the British Isles provided an unending stream of prayers and masses for the dead.

Both monasteries and chantries therefore owed their endowments to the church's theology of purgatory which taught that the souls of the faithful departed were puri-fied of earthly sin during an intermediate stage of existence between the moment of death and the entry of the soul into eternal life. It was believed that purification of the individual soul was achieved primarily through punishment, but the church also taught that intercessory prayer, often directed through particular saints or the Virgin Mary, and masses offered by the living could hasten the soul's progress to heavenly bliss. This belief in purgatory and the efficacy of prayers for the remission of sin had existed within the church from the earliest times. The essential elements of the doc-trine were approved at the Council of Lyon (1274), but it was not until the Council of Florence (1439) that a fully formed dogma of purgatory was finally adopted in the West. By this time over a thousand monasteries, nunneries and friaries, and many thousands of intercessory institutions had been established in the British Isles. Of course, the religious life of a monk, nun or friar involved more than just the recital of intercessory prayers. The regular life (under a religious rule) was an alternative form of Christian living which had existed since ancient times and which demanded a very different lifestyle from that of the laity or even the secular clergy. By the end of the middle ages the religious life in its various forms had developed a distinctive spiritual, liturgical and physical presence within the English, Irish and Scottish churches.

In common with the rest of Protestant Europe, virtually all these institutions were swept away during the course of the sixteenth century. While Martin Luther, who was himself an Augustinian friar, did not insist on the suppression of religious orders as part of his reform movement, both he and John Calvin were very definite in their rejection of the doctrine of purgatory. They also objected to intercessory prayer, teaching that salvation depended solely on the faith of individuals and could not be achieved through the prayers of priests or the intercession of saints. This rejection of the whole structure of intercessory prayer and the doctrine underpinning it made the continuation of chantry and other intercessory institutions within European and British churches virtually impossible. The desire to dissolve religious houses and appropriate their endowments for the use of the state was, however, normally a policy demanded by secular authorities rather than the reformers themselves. This was cer-tainly the case as the Reformation unfolded across different parts of the British Isles.

In examining the dissolution process it is therefore necessary to distinguish between the different aims of those who were involved in policy formulation. In Scot-land, the last of the major countries of Europe to adopt the reform, the dissolutions were the fruit of Calvinist influence with very little state action until the crown annexation of monastic lands in 1587. The dissolutions in Scotland have therefore always been regarded as a purely religious manifestation of the wider Calvinist reform movement. In England, Wales and Ireland, the state was much more involved in the process and therefore the interpretation of the dissolutions has veered more towards a political explanation. It was the Reformation parliament in England that enacted the legislation dissolving the monasteries in 1536 and 1539, and in Ireland similar legislation was passed in 1537 and 1539. Again in the mid-1540s it was parliament which suppressed the chantries in England and Wales, but similar legislation was never enacted in Ireland so the chantries there escaped dissolution. Traditionally, therefore, both the English and the Irish dissolutions have been interpreted within a 'Whiggish' framework of modern British history. The dissolutions were considered to be part of a larger process by which the English crown was able to rid its dominions of superstitious popish institutions and practices, allowing the development of an enlightened national religion, a liberal constitution and the full flowering of parliamentary democracy. But this interpretation of the dissolutions has not gone uncontested.

The traditional interpretation of the English dissolution painted a dark picture of monasteries as dens of 'manifest sin, vicious, carnal, and abominable living' which were ripe for reform or destruction.[1] It was not until the publication of Cardinal Gasquet's *Henry VIII and the English Monasteries* (1888–9) that this view was seriously challenged, but since then there have been many studies demonstrating that the monasteries were not as uniformly corrupt nor had they reached such an advanced stage of terminal decline as earlier accounts had taken for granted. There are still many critics of the monastic life in late medieval Britain, but the main focus of research on the dissolution of the English monasteries has shifted significantly away from earlier concerns with regular discipline and communal piety. While there is now convincing evidence to suggest that Cardinal Wolsey was planning to undertake a major reform of the religious orders in England around the time of his fall, it also seems certain that a loose coalition of courtiers and government officials were at the same time demanding a substantial disendowment of the entire English church.[2] It is therefore now widely accepted that the dissolution in England was ultimately more concerned with the expropriation of monastic lands and wealth than with wider reformist or political motivations. In Ireland too it has been shown by Brendan Bradshaw and others that there was no uniformity of regular observance in the monasteries on the eve of the dissolution and that financial motivations were an important component in policy-making. But Henry VIII's principal motivation for suppressing the religious orders in Ireland seems on balance to have been more political than financial. The dissolution was aimed at consolidating the crown's landholdings and therefore its political grip on the Pale and the other Anglo-Irish areas under its control, while later suppressions outside these areas extended the crown's dominion over large parts of Gaelic Ireland. In the cases of England, Wales and Ireland, then, the dissolution of the monasteries was not primarily motivated by a desire for religious reform as was clearly the case in Scotland.

Recent times have also witnessed a revolutionary change in the interpretation of the religious culture that existed in the parishes of pre-Reformation England, Wales and Ireland. 'Revisionist' scholars such as Eamon Duffy and Jack Scarisbrick have demonstrated the underlying strengths and flexibility of early Tudor religion. The late-medieval English parish was the principal interface between the church militant and the church triumphant and considerable resources continued to be lavished upon the paraphernalia of Catholic belief and worship until after Elizabeth's religious settlement was enforced. Perpetual chantries, guilds and fraternities, or the more temporary obits and trentals favoured by the majority of testators, constituted potent spiritual resources in every parish. They were suppressed only with great difficulty in England and Wales and not at all in Ireland. Historians are now less comfortable with derogatory traditional assertions about the 'superstitious' nature of practices associated with intercessory prayer, nor is it any longer possible to ascribe purely religious motivations to those responsible for the chantry legislation of 1545 and 1547. The dissolution of the English and Welsh chantries was in fact motivated as much by a financial need for 'the relief of the King's Majesty's charges and expenses which do daily grow and increase' as the putting down of 'superstition and errors in Christian religion'.[3] In evaluating the motives for the dissolution of the chantries it is therefore necessary to balance the reforming desires of Edward VI's Protestant advisers with the serious financial situation faced by the crown in the mid-1540s.

The processes involved in dissolving monastic houses and chantries across three separate kingdoms cannot therefore be treated as a single movement. Even in England the dissolutions were not part of a planned or carefully co-ordinated attack on medieval religious institutions. The processes of dissolution in England, Ireland and Scotland will be considered separately in this chapter while a more comparative approach will be taken in assessing the results of the three different processes.

The Dissolutions in England and Wales

England and Wales accounted for more than 60 per cent of the religious houses in the British Isles and it was the first of the three kingdoms to start dismantling the structures of medieval monasticism. The dissolution process involved the suppression or surrender of approximately 800 communities of monks, canons regular, nuns and friars from many different orders, and the number of religious displaced has been variously estimated at between eight and ten thousand people. There was nothing new in the idea of suppressing religious houses and diverting their endowments for other purposes. In earlier centuries English kings had used this expedient as a way of supplementing crown revenue or endowing new religious foundations. Edward III and Henry V in particular had confiscated the endowments of 'alien' priories to finance the English armies during the Hundred Years' War. During the early sixteenth century Lady Margaret Beaufort secured the dissolution of St John's Hospital in Cambridge to make way for the foundation of her university college in 1511, and in the 1520s Cardinal Wolsey was able to procure a papal licence to suppress thirty smaller houses to provide endowments for his collegiate foundations at Oxford and Ipswich. These previous dissolutions had been limited programmes, however, and did not in any way prefigure the wholesale expropriation of monastic lands that took place in the 1530s.

From the late 1520s there were rumours of a planned large-scale attack on church endowments, but the monasteries were not singled out for special attention until 1535. Thomas Cromwell commissioned a visitation of monastic houses using his authority as the king's vicegerent (vicar-general) in spiritual matters and visitation commissioners were dispatched in the summer of 1535 to enforce the acquiescence of the religious orders to Henry VIII's break with Rome and the alteration of the succession. A year earlier each religious community had been required to sign the oath of supremacy so this new visitation aimed at obtaining an even fuller submission to the royal will. A comprehensive set of injunctions drafted by Cromwell sought to reinforce traditional monastic observances, but he also insisted on introducing some new rules into the English cloisters and these proved to be unpopular. No one below the age of twenty-four was to be professed, and members of religious houses were encouraged to denounce their fellow religious who failed to observe the injunctions. These injunctions were applied uniformly across the country irrespective of the order or type of house being visited by Cromwell's commissioners, men who were completely inexperienced at conducting such visitations. The main commissioners, Drs Richard Layton and Thomas Legh, were efficient but totally lacking in any sympathy for the regular life, and their subordinates John ap Rice and John Tregonwell were no better qualified for the job. Nor did the commissioners spend much time in any of the houses they visited because a tight schedule had been arranged to make sure the visitation was accomplished as quickly as possible. These were not, therefore, proper canonical visitations but rather an attempt by the state to impose its will upon a large and, until that time, relatively independent sector of the English church.

The 1535 visitation also had other, more sinister aims. The commissioners were charged with collecting statistical data concerning each house, ranging from the annual revenues and number of religious in each community, to the identity of founders and patrons. The level of religious observance and the incidence of 'superstition' within the individual communities was to be assessed according to a questionnaire containing seventy-four 'articles' to be administered to all the religious and a further twelve questions to be addressed specifically to nuns. Such an exhaustive questioning could not have been achieved in the time available to the commissioners, however, and it seems likely that they focused instead on serious moral failings, attempting to uncover as much scandal as possible. They were particularly keen to unearth sexual lapses whether real or imagined. Their salacious reports were assembled into a digest known as the *Compendium Compertorum* and it was this document, or one abstracted from it, which was to convince scandalized members of the House of Commons that widespread immorality existed within the 'lesser' religious houses. While modern historians agree that these visitation records are an exaggerated and unreliable source for making a balanced assessment of monastic morality on the eve of the dissolution, Cromwell was nevertheless able to use such evidence to secure a potent propaganda victory. From the time of its compilation and for centuries afterwards this so-called 'Black Book' was treated as a true picture of pre-Reformation monasticism in England and Wales.

At the same time that Cromwell's visitation was progressing, a separate set of commissions had been issued for assessing clerical income so that the new tax of first fruits and tenths could be more effectively imposed upon the English church. Commissioners were therefore criss-crossing the countryside during 1535 collecting financial data on the religious houses. This data was eventually brought together with information on other church livings to form the *Valor Ecclesiasticus*. The *Valor* played an extremely important role in the first wave of dissolutions. Once Cromwell had convinced parliament that the religious orders were in serious need of reform and that the worst offenders were the 'lesser' houses valued at under £200 per annum, these monasteries were singled out for suppression under the first dissolution Act passed early in 1536 (27 Henry VIII, c.28). The court of Augmentations, a new revenue department completely separate from the Exchequer, was set up under its own Act (27 Henry VIII, c.27) to receive and administer the ex-monastic lands, and suppression commissioners were dispatched throughout the country to negotiate the surrenders. The first suppressions began in the summer of 1536 and were completed by early 1537. At this stage only the superiors of suppressed houses were granted pensions while the rank-and-file monks and nuns were given the option either to transfer to another house or else accept a dispensation from their vows and return to secular life. Some houses marked down for suppression by the 1536 Act were exempted from suppression upon payment of large fines and continued to exist until later in the 1530s, but in many parts of the country this first wave of dissolutions was extremely unpopular and added significantly to a more general sense of unease at the wider religious changes which were occurring at that time.

The progress of the dissolution commissioners in Lincolnshire and Yorkshire provided a focus for discontent among the people of the North and during the later part of 1536 several rebel armies assembled in a revolt which became known as the Pilgrimage of Grace. One of the many demands of the rebels was that the dissolved monasteries should be restored. The crown made a number of concessions in pacifying these mobs, but the restoration of dissolved monasteries was not to be one of them. A second rebellion by Sir Francis Bigod in Yorkshire early in 1537 was put down brutally and all concessions were revoked. Many religious houses had been involved in the two rebellions and their fate was swiftly decided. Several were suppressed on account of the attainder of their heads, and more than thirty monks were executed for their part in the revolts.[4] More importantly, the abbot of Furness, a large Cistercian monastery, was induced to surrender his house to the crown in return for a pension and a reprieve. This first voluntary surrender of a 'greater' abbey was to provide the crown with a convenient model for future attacks on the hundreds of monastic establishments which remained standing after the suppressions of 1536 and 1537. In fact, it seems that there was no general plan of suppression until after the surrender of Furness. Henry VIII and Cromwell were quick to take advantage of this new development, however, and began to apply pressure to religious superiors to surrender their houses voluntarily. The majority of monastic houses dissolved between 1537 and 1540 came into the hands of the crown in this manner and a new Act was passed in 1539 (31 Henry VIII, c.13) to confirm the king's title to their endowments.

It took some time for monastic communities to start surrendering their houses freely, and most of the wealthier houses resisted dissolution for as long as they could, so voluntary surrenders did not reach a peak until 1539 and early 1540. In the meantime, the crown set about destroying shrines and confiscating their treasures as part of a wider attack on the cult of relics and saints, and many of the larger monastic houses were forced to relinquish the shrines and relics of their founders and patron saints. At the same time, a commission was appointed in 1538 to dissolve the 200 houses of mendicant friars (Dominicans, Franciscans, Augustinians and Carmelites). It seems likely that many monastic communities simply lost their nerve at this juncture and decided to surrender on the best possible terms before being forced into such a course of action under less attractive conditions. But still many of the princi-pal monastic houses in the country resisted the coercion of Cromwell and his disso-lution commissioners and it was not until late 1539 with the attainder and execution of the abbots of Glastonbury, Reading and Colchester that resistance crumbled. The greatest monastic houses in the country surrendered one after another in early 1540 and finally, in May of that year, the order of St John of Jerusalem (the Hospitallers) was dissolved. Throughout this later part of the dissolution the crown granted gen-erous pensions to both heads and members of the monastic houses, and it was only the mendicants who were expelled from their cloisters without pensions.

In a period of less than four years, then, the entire structure of medieval monas-ticism in England and Wales was destroyed and thousands of ex-religious expelled from their cloisters. This attack on one of the most prominent institutions of the traditional church had a threefold impact on lay society. First it removed a time-honoured alternative to the secular clerical life within the church, and this was most profoundly felt by women who lost the only institution within the medieval church which had offered them any real degree of empowerment. Second, with the destruc-tion of the great shrines in the monastic and other churches an important focus of intercession was removed and consequently the central position of saints and inter-cessory prayer through them was undermined. Third, in addition to removing from the religious landscape the monastic intercessory institutions which had played so prominent a role in traditional religion, the dissolution also resulted in the loss of countless other chantry foundations which had been endowed by laymen and women within monastic churches. This was to be just the beginning of the assault on inter-cessory institutions, however, for later in Henry VIII's reign further legislation was passed which attacked other ecclesiastical institutions that had been left unscathed by the dissolution of the monasteries.

The wealth generated for the royal coffers by the dissolution of the monasteries proved to be a boon to the crown. It was not long, therefore, before Henry VIII and his ministers again began focusing their gaze on the English church in search of resources which might be plundered for the use of the state. The chantries were prob-ably singled out as being the least likely of the remaining church endowments to be fiercely protected from crown appropriation. In December 1545 parliament duly passed a Chantries Act (37 Henry VIII, c.4) which authorized the king to dissolve chantries and use their revenues to assist in defraying the 'inestimable expenses' of foreign wars and the fortification of England's coasts. The Act was a purely financial expedient and contained no theological pronouncement against purgatory or inter-cessory institutions, but it still met with considerable resistance in the Commons. While this Act authorized the king to issue commissions to dissolve all chantries, col-leges, hospitals, free chapels, religious fraternities and guilds, very few suppressions were undertaken before the king died in January 1547, so this first stage in dissolv-ing the chantries brought relatively little profit to the crown.

The second Chantries Act (1 Edward VI, c.14) was an entirely different under-taking, however, and brought about the dissolution of all intercessory institutions in England and Wales. This piece of legislation was once again partially a financial expe-dient to defray the enormous military expenses of Edward VI's initial year as king, but more importantly it was the first move by Edward and his Protestant ministers to undermine the Catholic foundations of the English church. The Act therefore began with a robust denial of the doctrine of purgatory and intercessory prayers for the dead, together with an explanation of the need to dissolve the chantries in order to free England from 'superstition and errors in Christian religion'. To achieve this end all intercessory institutions within the realm were to be dissolved and annexed to the crown on Easter Day 1548. The legislation had a stormy passage through parliament, however, requiring the reading of four different bills and a scaling down of the types of institutions which fell within its purview. The second Chantries Act was not passed until the very end of the parliamentary session and only after the insertion of several saving clauses protecting university colleges and chantry endowments in Coventry and King's Lynn. Despite the unpopularity of the legislation in both houses of parliament the implementation of the statute raised little commotion and virtually no resistance when the Augmentations commissioners set about dissolving the chantries in the weeks after Easter 1548. With their usual efficiency the Augmentations men quickly dissolved the 2,374 perpetual chantries and many thousands of other intercessory endowments in churches up and down the country, holding great clearance sales of chantry goods and arranging pensions for all chantry priests who were eligible for compensation. The remarkable ease with which the chantries were swept away no doubt emboldened the Protestant reformers around the king and paved the way for a series of reforms which were implemented in the next few years of his short reign. There were other results too, and these will be discussed below.

The Dissolution in Ireland

As lord and (after 1541) king of Ireland, Henry VIII attempted to implement a programme of monastic suppressions similar to that which had been stage-managed by Cromwell in England and Wales. Unfortunately the situation in his Irish kingdom was very different from that which existed in England. Henry's ability to impose his will upon Ireland was seriously limited: he exercised full dominion over only a relatively small geographical area of what was essentially a frontier colony, and his royal servants were generally inferior to those who managed royal affairs in England. Ireland boasted nearly 400 religious houses scattered across both 'English' and 'Gaelic' parts of the country. Like their English equivalents, they had been endowed with substantial tracts of land. Around 200 of these houses belonged to the mendicant orders, more than a quarter of which had adopted the observant reform introduced from Europe during the fifteenth century. This wave of reform gave the mendicant orders considerable lay support. In contrast, by the early sixteenth century the 'monastic' orders in Ireland had degenerated into a parlous state of observance. Most of the wealthier houses were inhabited by largely secularized landholding communities of monks and a great many of the other houses lay in ruins. The Irish gentry nevertheless had their own vested interests in the abbeys and feared that Cromwell and the new English settlers were intent on upsetting the local status quo through the appropriation and redistribution of monastic lands. Therefore when an attempt was made to introduce a dissolution bill into the Irish parliament in 1536 it was strongly resisted and did not finally become law until October 1537, and then in a much diluted form. Only thirteen of the smaller and more isolated monasteries within the lordship were dissolved in this first stage of the Irish dissolution.

The second stage commenced when the friaries began to be dissolved in 1538. A more general programme of suppression throughout the lordship was then initiated in 1539. The ex-religious were awarded state pensions during the rush of dissolutions in 1539–40, but these suppressions were limited to those areas under crown control and a number of remote communities were able to escape the clutches of the royal commissioners. From 1541 until the end of Henry VIII's reign the pace of suppressions was slow but relentless as the lord deputy, Sir Anthony St Leger, gradually extended the crown's jurisdiction and persuaded some Gaelic lords to assist him in implementing the dissolution policy. By 1547 most of the religious houses in the earldoms of Ulster and Desmond had been suppressed, and the majority of houses in the Gaelic lordships extending west from the Pale to Galway had likewise been absorbed into the crown estate. Despite this rapid advance of crown control in Ireland, by the time of Henry VIII's death only one-half of the Irish religious houses had been dissolved. The rest of the Irish monasteries were not finally suppressed until Elizabeth's reign when the entire island was brought under English control. Unlike the dissolution in England, however, the Irish dissolution was never completed. Numerous communities survived into the seventeenth century and the mendicant friars in particular continued to be an influential element of Irish religious life.

The Irish dissolutions also differed from the process in England and Wales in that legislation dissolving chantries was never introduced into the Irish parliament, so belief and practice within the Irish church with regard to purgatory and intercessory prayers for the dead underwent little major change until the reign of Elizabeth. This did not mean that all chantries survived intact. Large numbers of chantries had been established in monastic churches and these were swept away as the monasteries were progressively dissolved. But the collegiate churches which had been endowed by the Irish aristocracy, the numerous intercessory foundations in parish churches, and the urban guilds and fraternities in the large towns continued to exist well into the seventeenth century, although often in a far less openly Catholic form. This meant that important elements of medieval religious belief continued to be supported by institutional structures within the Irish church and this in turn was one of the factors which arrested the spread of Protestantism in Ireland. Despite attempts by later governments to undermine belief in purgatory and the efficacy of intercessory prayer these observances continued to be one of the defining features of Irish religious devotion and one which it proved virtually impossible to eradicate in later centuries.

The Dissolution in Scotland

In the kingdom of Scotland there was no state-sponsored attempt to reform the church in the 1530s and 1540s as there had been in England and Ireland, so the monasteries did not come under attack until 1560 when a more wide-ranging reform of the Scottish church occurred. There were barely a hundred religious houses in Scotland at the end of the middle ages and these were generally in a state of serious decline by the mid-sixteenth century. Many houses had become extinct, numerous others were already subject to a high level of interference from laymen who coveted their financial resources, and the practice of appointing 'commendatory' lay superiors had become common. James V resisted the temptation to treat the Scottish monasteries in the same way that his uncle Henry VIII had dealt with those in

England, but he nevertheless used them as an important source of revenue and royal patronage. In 1531 he obtained a papal licence to tax the monasteries in order to establish a college of justice and his abuse of monastic patronage ultimately included the appointment of three of his illegitimate children as commendatory abbots in five of the most important abbeys in the kingdom. Numerous houses were forced to alienate their endowments to pay ruinously expensive royal taxes and many others lost control of their lands to commendators who established hereditary claims to monastic resources. In this way the monasteries slowly lost their influence in Scottish society and after James V's death in 1542 they appear to have gone into a period of headlong decline during which many houses fell into utter decay, both physically and morally.

Even though there were sporadic attacks on a number of friaries after the death of James V, the dissolution of the Scottish monasteries did not happen formally until the Reformation parliament of August 1560. In the twelve months leading up to the proscription of Catholicism several houses were destroyed by armed mobs and their communities scattered, including the important houses of Dunfermline, St Andrews, Scone, Holyrood, Kelso and Melrose. A number of friaries in urban locations had also been attacked. Some abbots and commendators joined the Lords of the Congregation, and a few monastic communities supported the Protestant cause, but others held quietly to their Catholicism and waited to see what would happen next. After the initial turmoil of 1559–60 most religious communities simply continued to inhabit their monasteries as the government made no formal attempt to dissolve religious houses or appropriate monastic endowments. The majority of communities did however cease to perform the old Catholic choir office and the distinctive liturgies of their monastic profession. Many ex-religious even opted to serve the kirk. There appears to have been little hostility towards the ex-religious after 1560 and the majority seem to have lived out their lives in relatively secure retirement, continuing to receive a portion of the income of their houses tax free until death. Many ex-religious were still living unmolested in their monastic homes until the early 1600s. Unlike the English and Irish dissolutions, then, the Scottish state did not initially seek to appropriate monastic endowments in their entirety. A standard one-third tax was applied instead which was uniform throughout the Scottish church. It was not until the Act of 1587 that the monasteries were formally annexed to the crown but by that time much of their property had long been irredeemably alienated to lay feuars and very little ex-monastic land ultimately came to the crown. In this way the landed wealth of the Scottish monasteries was converted into lay lordships by stealth with only marginal benefit to the crown. In Scotland the monasteries can be said to have simply withered away rather than having suffered the far more active suppression which occurred in England, Wales and Ireland.

The Scottish intercessory institutions were another matter, however. They came under fierce attack during the reform process because they represented one of the most 'superstitious' of Catholic practices. It is not clear whether chantry foundations played as important a role in the Scottish church as they did in England or Ireland, but it is known that there had been considerable growth in these institutions in the century before the reformation. Collegiate chapels were established in large numbers during the fifteenth and early sixteenth centuries and religious guilds appear to have performed a central role in the creation of corporate identity within urban communities. These and all other intercessory institutions were formally abolished in 1560 when the Catholic doctrines of purgatory and intercession were outlawed. The prebendal endowments of collegiate churches were diverted for the support of students in 1567 but the other revenues of the chantry foundations appear to have been applied mostly to parochial or charitable uses with one-third of income reserved as a tax to the crown. Little research has been done on the demise of the Scottish chantries, but what little evidence there is suggests that there was some resistance to the change, especially among urban craft guilds which in some areas continued to celebrate their patronal feast days with processions and other traditional Catholic practices.[5] Such survivals were eliminated by the late 1570s, however, and all trace of the old institutions which owed their existence to a belief in purgatory or the efficacy of masses and saintly intercession disappeared. The dissolution of intercessory institutions was therefore central to the wider process of reformation in Scotland.

The Aftermath of the Dissolutions

The dissolution of religious houses and intercessory institutions across the British Isles were clearly acts of lasting significance in the longer-term reform of religion in the three kingdoms, but the impact of these changes was uneven. The dissolutions ultimately led to the abandonment of the religious life as an acceptable alternative mode of Christian living and the almost complete denial of belief in purgatory and the efficacy of intercessory prayers for the dead. It is true that these developments were felt more acutely in England and Scotland, but even in Ireland, where chantries were never outlawed and many monastic communities continued to exist well into the seventeenth century, these institutions were nevertheless seriously weakened. Perhaps the most obvious result of the dissolutions was a sudden superabundance of idle clergy who had been expelled from their cloisters and chantry livings, but the sixteenth-century man-on-the-street must also have been acutely aware of the rising tide of iconoclasm which was engulfing his world. This iconoclasm was apparent everywhere. Hundreds of monastic buildings which had once been among the wonders of the medieval built environment now lay ruined. The policy of obliterating all memory of and monuments to monasticism was not carried to the same extremes in Ireland and Scotland but in England the monastic ruins eventually came to be recognized as a major blot on the Protestant conscience. The sense of loss which many Englishmen felt when contemplating these ruins ultimately fostered a feeling of nostalgia for a world which had been irretrievably lost.[6] This would eventually become an important element in the growth of antiquarian and historical activities in the seventeenth and later centuries, but it should also be remembered that the dissolution of the monasteries and the propaganda generated by it were responsible for creating a prejudice against all forms of 'monkery' which is still evident in many sectors of British society today.

It has been argued by A. G. Dickens that the dissolution of the chantries 'impinged far more obviously and directly upon the spiritual and social life of the English people' than did the suppression of the monasteries. This was particularly so in the towns and cities where chantries, guilds and fraternities had become a much more prominent feature of the urban religious landscape than monasteries had ever been.[7] Eamon Duffy considers the disappearance of the intercessory structures of the parish to have been nothing short of a disaster for lay religious life, sundering forever that nexus between the living and the dead upon which the medieval parish community had been built. The sudden abolition of belief in purgatory and intercessory prayer, the downgrading of patron saints as intercessors between man and God, and the effective casting out forever of deceased loved ones into 'collective anonymity' must have had a disturbing impact upon both individual parishioners and the whole fabric of parish life.[8] A great spiritual void was left at the heart of the parish which took several decades to fill with the new Protestant doctrines of justification, predestination and salvation. The suppression of the chantries was both a harbinger of further religious change during the later years of Edward VI's reign and a vitally important break with the past which made attempts by Mary Tudor to revive Catholicism all the more difficult to achieve. The disappearance of guilds and fraternities, which had acted as a 'social cement' in the towns, perhaps also led to a weakening of traditional forms of corporate identity and urban solidarity, helping to usher in a new type of secularized urban community which became the norm across England. Fraternity houses, guild-halls, alms houses and chapels had all been potent symbols of urban pride in towns great and small across the country. Once they were closed and their goods dispersed a feeling of despair settled upon many urban communities. In Scotland there are well-attested examples of guilds which attempted to retain their traditional Catholic practices, so it seems likely that the loss of chantry institutions had a similar impact on urban culture in the North. In Ireland the weakening of the traditional role of guilds took longer to accomplish, but by the end of the century they were becoming far less overtly Catholic and oriented more towards secular activities as Anglicanism established itself more firmly in the major urban areas.

In addition to these rather intangible roles in urban society, the chantries had been important providers of social services that the monasteries had also supplied until their dissolution. Chantry chaplains often acted as schoolmasters in small parish schools while many monasteries conducted more ambitious educational enterprises within their cloisters. The dissolution effectively brought an end to all these schools. Although Edward VI endowed a small number of grammar schools to replace the hundreds of humbler institutions which he and his father had closed there is still considerable debate as to whether a handful of new grammar schools represented a viable replacement for hundreds of less formally constituted parish and monastic schools. The dissolutions had a similar but less crushing impact on elementary education in Ireland, while in Scotland schools continued to be funded from parish resources. Some of the ex-monastic lands in England were eventually used to endow new cathedrals which often had schools attached to them, while Henry VIII established two new university colleges at Oxford and Cambridge, but even these splendid new foundations failed to replace the seventeen religious houses which had previously provided higher educational opportunities for a large number of young men in Oxford and Cambridge, nor did they make amends for the dispersal of countless ancient monastic libraries. In fact, the dissolutions were probably the main reason for a serious decline in the English universities in mid-century as the clerical job market became flooded with ex-religious and ex-chantry chaplains seeking preferment within a much-reduced church. The dissolutions had no impact on the provision of higher education in Ireland (where there were no universities) but in Scotland a portion of the resources of the chantries was used to support university students. Much research is still needed into the impact of the dissolutions on education, but current opinion seems to indicate that the dissolutions were the cause of a diminution of educational provision across the British Isles.

Another area where the dissolutions had a marked negative impact was in the provision of poor relief. Monastic and chantry almsgiving has traditionally been criticized for being too indiscriminate and of little help to the 'honest poor', but more recent studies have revealed that the monasteries in particular were providing a much more effective means of poor relief than was available elsewhere in late-medieval society. Neil Rushton has demonstrated that the 7–8 per cent of monastic income which was devoted to poor relief (approximately £10–12,000 per annum in England and Wales) was far greater than all other sources of secular-controlled charity in the period 1540–1614, and that the need for poor relief was increasing sharply just as the dissolutions occurred.[9] The chantries also provided significant (though as yet uncalculated) levels of poor relief and their disappearance in the 1540s exacerbated an already dire problem in the towns and cities of Tudor England. Other institutional structures providing a range of social services which had developed under the supervision of monasteries and chantries over the centuries were similarly lost at the time of the dissolutions. The repair of roads, bridges, sluices and seabanks, the provision of midwifery services, and even the maintenance of municipal water supplies had been under the control of monasteries and chantries across England and it would be some time before all these functions were fully adopted by secular corporations.

Most of the impacts of the dissolutions which have been discussed above were felt primarily at the parish level. Such local manifestations of religious change take on a larger significance when considered together as part of the wider reform movement, and there are other effects of the dissolutions that are best assessed at the national level. In England one of the most important of these developments was the establishment of the court of Augmentations, the government administrative agency which managed the former endowments of the monasteries and chantry institutions. Beginning as a secondary revenue court in 1536, the Augmentations soon overshadowed even the Exchequer to become the English state's principal organ of financial administration by 1540, a leading position which it retained until the final dissolution of the court of Augmentations in 1554. The new sources of income from landed estates and the sale of ex-monastic and ex-chantry lands completely revolutionized state finance in England and allowed Henry VIII and Edward VI to expand crown expenditure on an enormous scale, particularly in waging major wars against France and Scotland which would not have been possible on the pre-dissolution income of the English crown.[10] These recurrent revenues continued to be the principal source of the crown's regular income until the death of Edward VI and beyond. This notion of a 'fiscal revolution' in England during the 1530s and 1540s is still a topic of vigorous debate, but it is now generally agreed that the dissolutions were the most successful of the numerous attacks on the patrimony of the English church and allowed Henry VIII and his successors to live like true Renaissance princes. Perhaps even more significant is the fact that the administrative practices of the Augmentations were ultimately adopted by the reformed Exchequer in 1554 and continued to be the mainstay of the English crown's administration of land revenue until the early nineteenth century.

The Scottish and Irish dissolutions did not bring the same level of financial reward to the state as that in England. In Scotland, the returns were meagre. The one-third tax on all ecclesiastical revenues certainly gave the crown a source of income which it had never enjoyed before, but the profits from ex-monastic lands were relatively small owing to earlier alienations of property to lay feuars. In Ireland, most of the ex-monastic lands were very quickly granted to crown servants and members of the Anglo-Irish elite in an attempt to win their support for the further extension of English political jurisdiction. So while ex-monastic lands played an important role in the gradual conquest of Ireland, they did not assist in reducing the colonial government's ballooning debt.[11] In England the alienation of ex-monastic and ex-chantry lands during the 1540s was on a massive scale: the crown received £812,000 from land sales during Henry VIII's reign and at least another £314,000 before the accession of Queen Mary. A redistribution of landed wealth on such a scale had not been seen since the Norman Conquest. Of ex-monastic lands valued at around £102,100 per annum which were alienated by Henry VIII during the 1540s approximately one-quarter were used to establish new cathedral chapters and colleges or to augment pre-existing ecclesiastical foundations. The remaining lands were sold or in some cases granted as rewards for service to members of the peerage, royal household and civil service (44 per cent), the gentry (15 per cent), and merchants (13 per cent).[12] In this way the endowments of the monasteries and chantries provided an important pool of patronage for the use of the crown, but contrary to some accounts of social change in Tudor England, no new gentry class was formed as a result of the dissolutions. Rather, the existing peerage and gentry classes were further consolidated. This process of land redistribution did not occur in Scotland because the monastic lands had already been alienated to feuars long before the dissolution occurred, but the effect was the same – the ruling elite acquired impressive additions to their landed inheritance for little pecuniary loss.

If the dissolutions did not bring a revolution in landholding they were nevertheless responsible for a social revolution of another kind. As many as 20,000 ex-religious were expelled from their cloisters and were forced by circumstances beyond their control to reconstruct their lives in a world which they had forsaken when entering religion. This transition was in some cases eagerly anticipated, particularly by religious who had lost their vocations or had embraced the continental religious reform, or who simply looked forward to generous pensions and good prospects in the secular church. But in other cases it was a personal disaster of enormous proportions, especially for women who faced the prospect of returning to a male-dominated lay society in which they would play subservient roles with only meagre pensions to sustain them. In Scotland the life of the ex-religious was relatively stress free because of the barely noticeable change to their daily routines, but elsewhere in the British Isles the transformation from regular to either secular or lay life was profound and unwelcome. Unpensioned friars found it difficult to secure preferment in a glutted clerical job market, and the thousands of predominantly elderly chantry priests were similarly cast adrift with little role to play in the formal church. Some married, others became converts to evangelical Protestantism, many of the old and infirm simply died destitute, while the great majority blended back into the secular world from which they had originally come. Very little serious research has yet been attempted on this personal dimension of life as an ex-religious or ex-chantry priest, but it seems likely that the impact of the dissolutions on the personnel of the suppressed institutions was as varied as were the individuals who inhabited their walls.[13] It should also be noted that some ex-religious attempted to sustain a form of communal religious life in the years immediately after the dissolutions, and this was particularly successful in Ireland where many of today's religious communities can trace their descent from pre-Reformation monasteries. Several religious houses were refounded under Queen Mary in England, but it was not until the seventeenth century that English, Irish and Scottish men and women were once again entering religion in large numbers in houses which were specially founded on the Continent for this purpose.

The impact of the dissolutions on the three kingdoms of the British Isles can therefore be assessed at many different levels. 'Reform' of belief and practice brought purely religious and cultural changes; a fundamental revolution in land ownership resulted in wide-ranging social, economic and political upheavals; while individual men and women had their worlds turned upside down during the 1530s and 1540s. Monasteries and intercessory prayer were pivotal features of medieval religion in Britain and it is axiomatic that the traditional church was seriously undermined by the removal of these institutions. Unlike other religious changes that were to be hotly contested or even to some extent later reversed, the dissolutions were final and irreversible. The suppression of monasteries and chantries therefore left an empty space at the heart of British religious experience which was gradually filled by other institutions, beliefs and practices. Such modifications of traditional belief and practice took a long time to evolve but they had been largely achieved by the end of the Tudor period. Monasteries, purgatory and intercessory prayer thereafter became distinguishing marks of a foreign religion which had no place in the British Isles. In the meantime, the dissolutions had had an equally important secular impact on England, Ireland and Scotland which would likewise be felt far beyond the end of the sixteenth century.

NOTES

1. 27 Henry VIII, c. 28.
2. Hoyle, 'The origins of the dissolution of the monasteries', pp. 284–9.
3. 1 Edward VI, c. 14.
4. Shaw, 'The religious orders in the Northern Risings', pp. 104–5.
5. Todd, *The Culture of Protestantism in Early Modern Scotland*, pp. 186–7.
6. Aston, 'English ruins and English history', pp. 231–5.
7. Dickens, *The English Reformation*, pp. 240–2.
8. Duffy, *The Stripping of the Altars*, pp. 454, 494.
9. Rushton, 'Monastic charitable provision in Tudor England', pp. 9–11, 16.
10. A full discussion of state finance in England during this period can be found in Cunich, 'Revolution and crisis in English state finance', especially pp. 122–32.
11. Lennon, *Sixteenth-Century Ireland*, pp. 160–2, 172–4.
12. The exact figures for Edward VI's reign have not yet been calculated precisely, but seem likely to follow the same basic pattern.
13. For a preliminary discussion of this issue see Cunich, 'The ex-religious in post-dissolution society'.

BIBLIOGRAPHY

Aston, Margaret, 'English ruins and English history: the Dissolution and the sense of the past', *Journal of the Warburg and Courtauld Institutes*, 36 (1973) 231–55.

Brendan Bradshaw, *The Dissolution of the Religious Orders in Ireland under Henry VIII* (1974) is the only comprehensive account of the dissolution in Ireland.

Cunich, Peter, 'The ex-religious in post-dissolution society: symptoms of post-traumatic stress disorder?', in James G. Clark, ed., *The Religious Orders in Pre-Reformation England* (Woodbridge, 2002).

Cunich, Peter, 'Revolution and crisis in English state finance, 1534–47', in Mark Ormrod, Margaret Bonney and Richard Bonney, eds, *Crises, Revolutions and Self-sustained Growth: Essays in European Fiscal History, 1130–1830* (Stamford, 1999), pp. 110–37.

Dickens, A. G., *The English Reformation* (2nd edition, London, 1989).

Duffy, Eamon, *The Stripping of the Altars: Traditional Religion in England, c.1400–c.1580* (New Haven and London, 1992).

Hoyle, Richard, 'The origins of the dissolution of the monasteries', *Historical Journal*, 38 (1995), 275–305.

Lennon, Colm, *Sixteenth-Century Ireland: The Incomplete Conquest* (Dublin, 1994).

Rushton, Neil, 'Monastic charitable provision in Tudor England: quantifying and qualifying poor relief in the early sixteenth century', *Continuity and Change*, 16 (2001), 9–44.

Scarisbrick, J. *The Reformation and the English People* (Oxford, 1984).

Shaw, A. N., 'The involvement of the religious orders in the Northern Risings of 1536/7: compulsion or desire?', *Downside Review*, 117 (1999).

Todd, Margo, *The Culture of Protestantism in Early Modern Scotland* (New Haven and London, 2002).

FURTHER READING

Ian B. Cowan and David E. Easson, *Medieval Religious Houses, Scotland* (2nd edition, 1976): a listing of medieval religious houses in Scotland with a comprehensive bibliography.

Claire Cross and Noreen Vickers, *Monks, Friars and Nuns in Sixteenth Century Yorkshire* (1995) lists the religious of the Yorkshire monastic houses and traces their whereabouts after the dissolution.

Peter Cunich, 'The dissolution of the chantries', in *The Reformation in English Towns, 1500–1640*, ed. Patrick Collinson and John Craig (1998) gives an overview of the dissolution of the chantries and its impact in England.

Mark Dilworth, *Scottish Monasteries in the Late Middle Ages* (1995) provides a brief but informative account of the Scottish monasteries on the eve of the dissolution.

Thomas S. Flynn, *The Irish Dominicans 1536–1641* (1993): a comprehensive study of the Irish Dominicans and their place in Irish society before and after the dissolution.

Aubrey Gwynn and R. N. Hadcock, *Mediaeval Religious Houses, Ireland* (1970): a listing of medieval religious houses in Ireland with a comprehensive bibliography.

W. G. Hoskins, *The Age of Plunder: King Henry's England, 1500–1547* (1976): an account of the dissolution of the monasteries which emphasizes the financial motivations of Henry VIII.

David Knowles, *The Religious Orders in England*, vol. 3, *The Tudor Age* (1959) is still the definitive treatment of the English dissolution although some of the themes have recently been challenged by younger scholars.

David Knowles and R. Neville Hadcock, *Medieval Religious Houses, England and Wales* (2nd edition, 1994): a listing of medieval religious houses in England and Wales with a comprehensive bibliography.

Alan Kreider, *English Chantries: The Road to Dissolution* (1979) is the best account of the chantries immediately before the dissolution, but contains little treatment of the impact of the 1547 legislation.

Colm Lennon, 'The chantries in the Irish Reformation: the case of St Anne's Guild, Dublin, 1550–1630', in *Religion, Conflict and Coexistence in Ireland,* ed. R. V. Comerford, Mary Cullen, J. R. Hill and Colm Lennon (1990): an important study illustrating the changing role of intercessory institutions in post-reformation Ireland.

Walter C. Richardson, *History of the Court of Augmentations, 1536–1554* (1961): the definitive study of the administration of the ex-monastic lands in England and Wales.

G. W. O. Woodward, *The Dissolution of the Monasteries* (1966): an older but still useful overview of the dissolution of the monasteries in England and Wales.

Joyce Youings, *The Dissolution of the Monasteries* (1971): contains an excellent selection of primary documents.

CHAPTER FOURTEEN

Religious Settlements

NORMAN JONES

The years 1559–60 saw the "settlement" of religion in the British Isles. In England the Acts of Supremacy and Uniformity ended legal Catholic worship in June of 1559. The Irish parliament approved the same acts, with some special Irish provisions, early in 1560. The parliament of Scotland declared the confession of faith professed by the Protestants within the realm of Scotland to be wholesome and sound doctrine, grounded upon the infallible truth of God's word in August of 1560. On paper all three kingdoms had become Protestant. But the official acts of parliaments were just the beginning of the long road to national churches. In England and Scotland, the journey to a national Protestant culture was successful; in Ireland it failed.

The reasons for success or failure of the Reformation in these kingdoms are complex, but in each one the officially imposed change of religion had profound effects. Whether succeeding or failing, these changes in religion provoked changes in national cultures. Of course, for the people in Westminster, Dublin and Edinburgh in 1560 it was not immediately a question of cultural change, it was one of religious and political survival. There were enemies within and without who did not want to see the Reformation take root. Worse, none of these settlements had clearly established procedures, theologies or clergies. The churches, especially in Ireland and Scotland, were desperately poor, and even the English church, though wealthier, was the target of what Matthew Parker, then master of Corpus Christi College, Cambridge, and later archbishop of Canterbury, called 'gaping wolves' intent on gobbling up as much church property as possible.

Just as essentially, the Protestant establishments were dependent on political support, making Reformation a political game which, as the subjects of the Tudors knew too well, might change its rules at any time. The extent and effectiveness of Protestantization was, therefore, a coefficient of the political will, the efficiency of enforcement, structures of local government, fiscal concerns, the quality and commitment of ecclesiastical administrators and clergy, the tools made available to speed conversion, the organization of external interventions (such as the Jesuits), and the levels of local co-operation. Complicating all of these variables is the issue of who stood to gain or lose power and wealth through reformation. Certainly, reformations everywhere rose or fell according to levels of ideological commitment filtered through balances of power and the lure of redistributed ecclesiastical property. These complex factors explain why the process varied so wildly by geography and political arrangements.

The most obvious things these reformation settlements share is their political nature. In England, Wales and Ireland the Elizabethan settlement was imposed by parliamentary statute and royal proclamations, enforced by officers of the crown. The decisions of the worthies sent to the Westminster parliament met with general acceptance in England and Wales, but that apparent religious conformity was made possible by the ways in which the local elites were allowed to negotiate the speed and depth of the imposition of the new religion. As Michael Braddick has observed, 'the promotion of true religion was perceived to be of crucial importance ideologically but in practice it proved impossible to achieve. . . . The government did not control the means by which this might . . . have been done.'[1] Because of the inability of the crown's enforcement machinery to achieve complete uniformity, communities and institutions reinvented and secularized their identities slowly over several decades, allowing generational attrition to slowly displace old-fashioned notions and behaviors.

Even if the Tudor state had possessed better tools than voluntary magistrates, neither the church nor the crown was prepared to make a thorough reformation. As Puritans were soon pointing out, the continuation of the forms of the medieval church, including its courts and many of its personnel, made a clean break impossible. Moreover, the failure of the Elizabethan ecclesiastical leadership to secure parliamentary passage of new articles of religion and church discipline slowed reform, as did Elizabeth's deep reluctance to actually enforce the law against those who did not conform. Until the Northern Rebellion in late 1569 and the bull of excommunication that arrived in early 1570, Elizabeth was content to let Reformation sink slowly into the political fabric.

The Dublin parliament passed the Irish Acts of Uniformity and Supremacy, modelled on the English ones, with a few slight modifications to bring them into line with existing Irish law. However, in Ireland there could be no hope of a general enforcement of the Act of Uniformity. Within the Pale and the royal towns, governmental authority was sufficient to ensure conformity, but any further imposition depended on the extension of royal authority to places where it did not easily run. Most of the sitting Irish bishops conformed to the Elizabethan settlement and so did their clergy. In contrast, the Marian English bishops had all, except one, refused to accept the supremacy. Importantly, the English *Book of Common Prayer* could not be understood by most of the people in Ireland. A proviso in the Irish Act of Uniformity permitted Latin to continue in use as a liturgical language in those parishes whose people did not speak English.

In Scotland, the Reformation was the work of the Lords of the Congregation, allied with the English, in opposition to the French and the crown of Scotland. Their reformation was not, therefore, tied to the concept of royal supremacy. It came from the 'people', or, in the Calvinist terms preferred by John Knox, the 'lesser magistrates'. Consequently, enforcement of the *Book of Common Order* depended heavily on local magnates and burgh councils. The early Jacobean kirk itself, drawing on its Genevan theology, saw itself as apart from and sometimes superior to secular governments of all kinds, demanding that even the king admit that he was a subject in Christ's kingdom. Confusingly, the Scots, while setting up a presbyterian system, did not abolish their bishops, leaving them as a counter to the growing kirk.

The enforcement of settlements of religion everywhere depended on the ways in which local governments and ecclesiastical leaders were empowered and staffed to carry out the new laws, and on the ability and willingness of the ecclesiastical establishment to use the new liturgies and instruct the people in the new formulations of faith.

The Tudor state was reconstituted, if not revolutionized, in the 1530s by Cromwell's restructuring of regional governments. Peripheral government was removed from the hands of the great lords who had dominated Ireland, the North and Wales in the late middle ages. By handing government over to the local elites, the new Henrician system sought to enhance royal power by ensuring co-operation, but it was still limited in its ability to enforce reformation. Those same local gentlemen who responded so enthusiastically to their new power became the arbiters of the speed and method of the Reformation in England and Wales. This is especially obvious in Wales, where the Act of Union of 1543 gave the Welsh legal equality with English people, seats in the Westminster parliament, and the English legal system. All of these changes benefited the Welsh elite, and so did the Reformation. The Welsh were granted what amounted to home rule, of a sixteenth-century sort.

The willingness of elite families to protect the Reformation was increased by the profits it brought them. Across England and Wales monastic and chantry properties enriched the local elites, who showed little interest in defending their religious uses. After the resistance put up by their representatives in parliament to the Marian restoration of Catholicism until the pope guaranteed their possession of former ecclesiastical property, the Elizabethan settlement must have come as a great relief to the magisterial classes. Even Catholic peers who resisted the Uniformity seemed inclined to support the royal supremacy for fiscal reasons.

The Elizabethan style of enforcement depended upon local co-operation and did very little to alienate local authorities. Even in 1564, when the bishops were ordered to survey the justices of the peace to find out which were enemies of the Reformation, the privy council did not purge the resisters they identified. The reality of Tudor government was that the monarch could only do what the local magistrates agreed to do, which gave the local magistrates a great deal of breadth in interpretation and imposition. Parishes, guilds, towns, colleges and cathedrals had varying degrees of reformation according to the nature of the compromises made by their leadership. But in each of them, the compromises were quickly hardening into custom by the 1580s. By then a new set of definitions, religious and therefore political, were at work, driven by the need for order generated by rising Protestant and Catholic dissent.

The rule of thumb applied by the Elizabethan council required that a magistrate maintain order in his community. That good order included acceptance of the religious change, but not a passionate embrace of that change. As lord keeper Nicholas Bacon, speaking on behalf of the queen at the close of parliament in 1559, said, the national goal was civil tranquillity in the face of dangerous social and religious currents. The MPs were sent home with instructions to avoid all manner of frays and riots through swift justice, to 'appease all brabblings and controversies', and to draw the nation together in a single religion.[2]

In another 1559 speech, this time in the Star Chamber before those who had 'charge and governance' of the counties through the lesser courts, Bacon said: 'my Lords [of the privy council] would wish you to flee and eschew chiefly and above all the rest . . . all manner of factions and sects, and specially such as concern religion, for these are the most deadly enemies that may be to unity and concord.'[3]

Lord keeper Bacon, his queen, his fellow-councillors, and all other leaders, local as well as national, were faced with a national crisis in 1559, brought on by plague, food shortages, war, and religious strife.[4] Their response was to seek order, to stress neighbourliness and external obedience, and to encourage peaceful conformity, unifying the nation through a national church. Although Protestantism was being reimposed, it was being done with a gentleness that stressed conformity over theology, allowing space for local institutions to find their own ways to local religious peace.

The Elizabethan settlement, then, was a political response to the fracturing, bruising nastiness of the 1550s. By 1559 people had learned to sort their neighbours into religious camps. Attaching labels, they were focusing their hatreds and fears on the 'others' among them. It was this divided society that Elizabeth set out to protect from internecine conflict. As the queen herself put it in one of her private prayers published in 1563:

> O my God, God of all power and mercy, govern all Thy people by Thy most holy Spirit, so that they may religiously worship Thee, excellent Prince and only Power, with true service; and may quietly be subject unto me, their queen on earth, by Thy ordinance; and may in obedience to Thee live together in mutual peace and concord. . . . God of peace and concord, who hast chosen me Thy handmaid to be over Thy people that I may preserve them in Thy peace, be present and rule me with the Spirit of Thy wisdom, that according to Thy will I may defend a Christian peace with all peoples.[5]

The *Book of Common Prayer* (1549, revised in 1552 and 1559) was a perfect answer to this problem, embodying an emphasis on the imitation of the sacrifice of Christ that moved the congregants to conceive their lives in terms of service. A very effective tool for education, its creation showed that Archbishop Thomas Cranmer, its primary author, appreciated that reform would only truly come when habits and hearts changed. Polemic was not the foundation of a reformed Christian lifestyle.[6] Coupled with the homilies, which instructed their hearers in the essentials of their faith, the *Book of Common Prayer* assured that people knew their Bible in context, heard it explained, and understood their duty.

Like water dripping on hard stone, the words of the liturgy were to bore into the hearts and minds of the congregants. The goal was to create automatic religion, an internalized set of responses that guided the individual in his or her duty. When it worked, it worked through patient repetition. Thus, by the middle of Elizabeth's reign prayer-book worship had become natural and right to many because it was the habit of the communities in which they were raised. By the 1580s the pattern of worship enforced by law in 1559 had penetrated to the grass roots.[7]

The most politically valuable thing about the Prayer Book was that it imposed structure, not ideology. To people slowly becoming accustomed to the changes forced by the Reformation, it permitted local interpretation, and, to a remarkable extent, local adaptation of the liturgy. It did not put the congregants who had no religious zeal to a test.[8] Attend, listen and conform were the orders from on high, but over time attending and listening became habit and habit informed faith.

Of course, despite pious intentions, the *Book of Common Prayer* only worked when people could understand it. The Protestant zeal for worship in the common tongue had produced it, but there were many in the Tudor realm who found it just as incomprehensible as the Latin mass. Ironically, the first translation of the *Book of Common Prayer* into another language was in 1560, when a Latin version appeared. For use in academic communities, where Latin was spoken by all, it was used as a substitute for the English book in Ireland, in communities that did not speak English. It was clear to many that the Cornish, Welsh and Irish needed their own liturgies, but only the Welsh got one in Elizabeth's reign.

Acting under pressure from the Welsh bishops, parliament passed a statute in 1563 ordering the translation of the liturgy and the Bible into Welsh, lest the people of Wales remain in 'even more darkness' than in the 'time of papistry'. If they were able to read the Bible and say common prayers, the Act reasoned, the Welsh would know God's promises to the elect, love and fear him, and be obedient subjects.[9] Printed in 1567, along with the New Testament, the translation provided worship in Welsh for the first time, quickly gaining popularity. The full Welsh Bible, translated by William Morgan, was published in 1588, making it possible for Welsh Protestants to worship and read in their tongue.

The popular success of worship in Welsh underscores the importance of the absence of a translation into Irish. Poorly staffed and poverty-ridden, the established church in Ireland lacked the basic tools of evangelization. In England and Wales the repetition of the lessons in the Prayer Book slowly drummed Protestant theology into the people. In Ireland, Protestant worship in Latin continued, with the result that many Irish speakers assumed that the Elizabethan settlement was a variant of Catholicism.[10]

The first Protestant form of worship available to the Irish came from Scotland, where the Gaelic translation of the Scot's *Book of Common Order, Foirrm na n-Urrnuidheadh*, was published by John Carswell, bishop of the Isles, in 1568. Its availability in Northern Ireland cut across the attempt of the Tudor authorities to wean Ulster away from Scotland. It was not until 1571 that a Gaelic translation of the catechism of the English *Book of Common Prayer* and Archbishop Parker's Twelve Articles of religion appeared. The Irish New Testament did not see print until 1603; the Prayer Book not until 1608. Ironically, the English church, though moving at a snail's pace, was far ahead of the Catholics in producing Gaelic materials for the Irish.

The Scots provided tools for the religious education of their people in the reformed religion by adopting John Knox's *Book of Common Order* in 1562, adding Calvin's *Catechism* and William Tyndale's translation of the Bible to their core texts. However, unlike the Tudor prayer book, *Order* was not a liturgy. Created by Knox as an alternative to the Prayer Book of Edward VI, its adherents liked it because it specifically rejected the forms of worship in the Edwardian service. Providing for ecclesiastical discipline and articles of faith, the *Common Order* had its greatest impact through its catechism and metrical psalms. Scots imbibed their Protestantism through rote-catechizing and enthusiastically singing psalms to popular tunes.

The book was quickly translated into Gaelic, though Michael Lynch observes that the translation, which used learned Gaelic, probably had little impact on the ordinary Gaels.[11] The translation of 1568 was the last attempt of the kirk to provide printed works in Gaelic until the 1630s.

Knox's book did have the great advantage of defining the articles of faith and providing a disciplinary structure. The Tudor establishment did not define its beliefs officially until the Thirty-Nine Articles were approved by parliament in 1571. Elizabeth's bishops had prepared legislation to enact articles of faith and a Protestant code of discipline in 1563, but Elizabeth stopped their passage, wary of interference with her prerogative. One suspects that her reluctance to allow definition arose from her political sense that articles of faith and a new religious discipline could be very divisive. However, once she was excommunicated by the pope in 1570, she became more willing to have the articles of faith enacted. Her clergy, however, never got a new code of discipline. There were several parliamentary attempts to reform discipline, especially that contained in the Edwardian *Reformatio Legum Ecclesiasticarum*, but royal and lay resistance stopped them.

With the ruling Tudor elite more interested in concord and profits than in religious zeal, the crown left it to the clergy to actually educate the laity in the new religion. In the best of all possible worlds, the servants of the church would have been educated, wise, zealous and well-supported, but that was not the case. Everywhere in the British Isles the poverty of the churches, the shortage of clergy – let alone educated, Protestant, preaching clergy – and the impropriation of ecclesiastical livings by laymen constituted a sea anchor that dragged on the advance of the Reformation. Ironically, that slowing made it possible for the change to sink in without causing an explosion.

Everywhere, the new Protestant religious establishments had to depend for clergy primarily on men who had already conformed to several other religious settlements. Many incumbents had been Catholic priests for years before becoming ministers. Some of them were former monks or chantry priests, who, made redundant by the Reformation, supported themselves by becoming parish clergy. Their commitment to any theological model was doubtful, since most had learned the most important lesson about Tudor religion – wait a few minutes and it will change. Men of their ilk could not be expected to provide enthusiastic leadership for this latest dispensation, and many could be expected to enact the least amount of change possible. The archetype of this sort of Elizabethan parish priest/minister is Sir Christopher Trychay, vicar of Morebath, Devon, who served from August 1520 until May 1574.[12]

The Elizabethan bishops knew they had to remedy this situation, but there were very few men interested in ordination. Most churches could not pay enough to attract the university-educated preachers needed to advance the cause. Even in London churches readers were appointed because properly qualified ministers could not be found. Unable to administer the sacraments or preach, the reader was limited to reading prayers and homilies. In the poorer reaches of the realm the problem was even worse. In 1560 Archbishop Parker could not find anyone willing to take an Irish living, though all church leaders agreed on the necessity of sending educated men there to preach the Word. In Wales the poverty of livings was such that educated Welshmen were drawn into English livings, rather than returning to Wales to preach in their native tongue. In the North there were similar problems. Archbishop Parker told William Cecil that Elizabeth's refusal to spend money on the church created the real danger that the people there 'should be too much Irish and savage', losing their quiet and civility.[13] In Scotland the shortage of ministers was met with the same expedient. Readers were created, charged with leading services without preaching.

The clerical shortage was partially caused and compounded by the way in which ecclesiastical property was held. Thanks to the dissolutions and English property law, Elizabethan bishops had few chances to put good ministers into pulpits. The right of appointment lay with the improprietors (laymen) who owned the churches, and, if they were cheap, or lazy, or Catholic, or Puritan, the bishop had few tools to improve the spiritual services provided by a living. In England, over 40 per cent of church livings were impropriated, with the proportion rising to over 60 per cent in Ireland.

In 1586 Puritans assembled a 'View of the state of the church', listing the positions, names, incomes and attributes of rectors and vicars across the land. After asking about the morals of the incumbent, they asked two other questions: Who made him a minister? and Who is the patron? They knew that the quality of the clergy was often proportional to the quality of the patron's nominations. Thus when Mr Waddam Tanner nominated one who was 'lately a serving man and simple fellow', who never preached, to look after a thousand souls, he was not advancing the cause of religion in Cornwall. And what good did the 700 people in Wen derive from their pluralist vicar, appointed in the long-ago reign of Henry VIII? He was decried as 'a massman, a grazier, ignorant, his curates unlearned. A great taker of bargains, non resident in both charges.'[14]

Impropriations combined with the legal title of incumbency to make serious reform wait until the deaths of the mid-Tudor clergy made jobs available for the better-educated, Protestant men coming out of the universities. In England at least, the shortage began to ease by the middle of Elizabeth's reign, and the educational quality of the clergy began to rise. Of course, these new ministers were young men like Richard Greenham, vicar of Dry Drayton from 1570, whose education had occurred in the 1560s, and who had scant memory of Catholic worship, let alone sentimental attachment to it. For Greenham's generation 'papists' were an alien, enemy specie.[15]

This was a frustrating problem for bishops bent on teaching their flocks to be Protestant, but it was a political good. By protecting the property interests of the owners of advowsons and benefices, the crown got their co-operation in enforcing conformity and keeping the peace, while their biddable clergy, where they existed, showed little enthusiasm for wholesale change.

While English elites were attracted to the Reformation by the spoils, the break-up of the old church in Ireland did not have that attraction to most of the Irish and Anglo-Irish elites. Much of the monastic property in the Pale was distributed to English administrators and the New English colonists, with the political purpose of establishing dependable crown servants in the country. Much of the rest went to established Anglo-Irish families, who used it to build up and rationalize their existing estates. These established families disapproved of the colonists and, although the annexation of the properties allowed the establishment of these colonists, the colonists were not embraced by the establishment. A rift grew between the two landowning gentries in the Pale, who, by the 1560s, were at loggerheads with one another. Increasingly, the Old English identified with the Irish.

In the areas outside of direct royal control, Irish magnates such as the Desmonds controlled the distribution of the spoils of the church, if they bothered to take them. The weaknesses of Tudor control in the west of Ireland meant that changes in religion were largely ignored, but even in the Pale the aristocracy kept their own priests.

In Scotland the situation was similar, in that church property was in lay hands, but it had been acquired by different means. The Scottish law before the Reformation allowed feuing, or feu-farming, a form of heritable feudal tenancy. It was widespread in Scotland by the late fifteenth century, when James IV began putting crown lands into feu. In the sixteenth century feuing became common on church lands, too, as the church, suffering from James V's massive taxation and the depredation of the English army in the 1540s, covered its expenses by converting old leases into feu. It was a quick way to raise money through entry fines and renegotiated rents, but the heritable nature of the feu permanently transferred large amounts of church land into lay hands. Naturally, much of the land came under the control of the lairds, and many tenants were displaced, but it created a class uninterested in re-endowing the church in Scotland. As in England, the Scottish parliaments ended up leaving this land in the hands of the laity.

Scotland had also found ways to appropriate monastic wealth without the Tudor method of dissolution. Commendators, lay people who managed the property of monasteries, were drawing the revenues of religious houses without performing any religious duties. Often recruited from the local nobility, by the early sixteenth century they were common across Scotland. One result was that in Scotland, unlike England, powerful people had a vested interest in not allowing the seizure of the monastic properties by the crown. Consequently, monasticism in Scotland died a slow death, with the monks often sharing their properties with commendators who were slowly converting them into lordships. At the Cistercian abbey of Dundrennan, for instance, the dwindling group of brothers shared the premises with their commendator, Edward Maxwell, son of Lord Herres, from 1562 until 1598. In 1606 it became a secular lordship.[16]

By act of parliament in 1567 the Scottish church was officially granted the tithes, or teinds, that had always been collected.[17] However, it was never successful in collecting them. Although the general assembly protested, it was not until 1587 that James VI and John Maitland of Thirlestane addressed their concerns, but they did so by annexing them. The whole teinds of Scotland belonged to either the crown, the lords of erection, called titulars, the original founding patron, feuars from the church, or institutions that held church property, the clergy being given only a right to a third of their benefices. Technically, the third was reserved to the crown to provide for the support of ministers, but it was never sufficient, or efficiently distributed. One of the effects of the annexation was the sharp increase of the power of the king over the kirk.

The annexations were a round in the struggle for control of the church that included the 'Black Acts' of 1584. These asserted royal authority over the church generally and required the recognition of bishops, giving James VI powers over his church comparable to those of Elizabeth. Although James backed down in the 'Golden Acts' of 1592, granting presbyteries power over bishops, the Acts of the 1580s established the supremacy of the crown of Scotland over the kirk.

None of these Scottish arrangements boded well for the church, no matter what its theology, and the problem of poor livings would not be properly addressed until the creation of the Teinds Commission in 1617. But, like the English redistribution of property, it had the effect of creating loyalty to the reformed church among its beneficiaries. Moreover, in Scotland the kirk sessions (parochial disciplinary courts made up of the minister, deacons and elders) and the increased lay control of property meant that the property-owning classes were more empowered than ever.

The shortage of clergy, let alone Protestant clergy, and the increasing poverty of the churches in the three kingdoms left reformation highly dependent on the willingness of local elites to embrace and enforce the religious settlements of 1559–60.

Given the barriers to successful reformation, we must ask how the peoples of England, Scotland, Wales and Ireland became 'confessionalized', acquiring a collective religious identity. Beginning with the willingness of the majority to conform to the new religious settlement, time and occasional intervention nudged the cultures along. Given that most Tudor magistrates agreed with Elizabeth that their job was to maintain order and concord, a steady, gentle pressure to conform slowly produced results.

The process of 'confessionalization', the mental and institutional consolidation of each of the Christian creeds after the Reformation into a set of semi-stable ecclesiastical complexes with corresponding dogmas, constitutions and religious-moral modes of behaviour, which created new, Protestant identities, was political and generational in Britain. Religion could not be separated from politics in the sixteenth century because it was part and parcel of governance. As Julian Goodare has observed, 'all governmental authorities were concerned about religion, if for no other reason than that it was seen as the basis of their own authority. . . . there was a single network of authority encompassing both civil and religious institutions in fruitful cooperation.'[18]

Goodare's comment was made about Scotland, but it mirrors studies of Wales by Peter Roberts, of Ireland by Brendan Bradshaw, Steven Ellis and Samantha Meigs, and of England by Michael Braddick and myself. As Bradshaw suggests in his comparative study of Wales and Ireland, one of the deciding factors in local responses to the Reformation was the way the Tudor revolution in government was applied in the two Celtic borderlands. In Wales, it brought the Welsh political recognition and autonomy, the revolutions in church and state working symbiotically 'as tailored in each case to suit the predilections of a patriotic and conservatively minded local elite to whom the Tudor regime chose to entrust the implementation of both. . . .' In Ireland the twin revolutions caused the alienation of both the Irish and Anglo-Irish communities. Tudor attempts to break up the power of septs (ancestral clans) and to create a new colonial elite, marked by the creation of Ireland as a separate kingdom in 1542, created a dynamic that allowed the missionaries of the Counter-Reformation to play on an Irish sense of national culture, identifying Protestantism with Englishness. In much of Europe this process was achieved as much through civil war and the Inquisition as through conversion. In England, Scotland and Wales, the religious settlements sat uneasily on the culture for a couple of generations, slowly becoming absorbed until by the end of the sixteenth century they could all be called Protestant nations. For the Irish, the picture was different, in part because the Irish came to identify Protestantism with the colonizing English.

The politics of the religious settlements were played out by local leaders in all sorts of institutions. In the boroughs of England, Ireland and Scotland local governments controlled the disciplinary tempo. Once people had, by statutory fiat, become Protestant, it was left to local secular and ecclesiastical governors to make them act like Protestants. Traditional, but 'superstitious', practices had to be halted, and moral reforms, often connected with a 'reformation of manners', implemented. But the intensity of this discipline was modulated by the aldermen, mayors, churchwardens, elders and other officials on the ground. In most places the first results were mixed. Community leaders showed themselves reluctant to act against their neighbours, and the pace of change reflected the preferences of these local enforcers. Michael Graham has demonstrated that Scottish burghs formed and used kirk sessions according to the nature of local politics – so that the Aberdeen kirk session, when the burgh government finally got around to forming one in 1574, was led by a Catholic, and five of its thirteen members were known enemies of the Reformation. Similar patterns are visible in English towns like Lincoln, where the common council did not bother about enforcing church attendance until 1572, though it had been required since 1559. Muriel McClendon's study of Norwich demonstrates that its civic leaders bent over backwards to ignore religious division, showing little taste for enforcement.

Those living through the Reformation absorbed it through all institutions, not just the church, as the communities reinvented their identities in response to official interventions. Thus the leaders of local institutions of all kinds were consciously involved in the adaptation of their communities until, late in the century, they settled into new habits of communal identity and purpose.

Generational tensions and forced institutional adaptation prompted cultural adaptations, reorienting English culture, secularizing its institutions and teaching the English people, of all religious inclinations, a new anthropology that fitted the emerging demand for religious allegiance based on conscience. Much of this change was mediated through the local authority of organizations that governed people's lives, such as town governments, trade guilds and colleges.

The Reformation presented institutions of every type with two problems. They were forced to make decisions that involved their corporate incomes and identities. In turn, these decisions reflected their second problem, finding ways in which they as organizations could negotiate the growing ideological differences amongst members while achieving their organizational ends. The adaptive choices they made reshaped them into post-Reformation cultural forms.

As we look at institutions such as town governments, livery companies and schools we can see phases of adjustment. First, of course, are the formal responses to the legally imposed changes. But removing an altar or hiring a preacher was only the beginning. There followed changes not legally mandated. Commemorations of benefactors, funeral customs and other ways of celebrating identity and status altered slowly but steadily, evolving into new customs. The language in which people spoke about their daily business changed, too, as did the weight they gave to various civil and religious practices. The speed of the changes was often dictated by the governing structures of institutions. In places like livery companies, where older men dominated and direct intervention was unlikely, things changed slowly. In places like university colleges, the fairly rapid turnover of fellows and official intrusion hurried the process. Towns had to conform officially, yet they scrabbled to protect community resources in inventive ways. Sometimes a local settlement emerged when tensions burst like a religious abscess, forcing local leaders to seek ways to find peace; sometimes the adjustments crept in on little cats' feet as customs fell out of use and were replaced with actions and understandings more modern.

An example of the 'slow' reformation through conformity and generational adaptation is the history of the London livery companies. All of them conformed to each change of the official religion, but each of them adapted in its own way. The London Pewterers' Company records show that they had an active corporate religious life before the Reformation, maintaining an altar where their parish priest celebrated their Lady Day dirge and requiem mass for the departed members of the Company. In 1549 they lost their altar and the Lady Day ceremonies ended, so they switched to a communion celebrated by a priest, a clerk and some singers. By 1553 the expenses for this simple service were noted as 'for all necessaries as hath been accustomed in times past'.

This custom ended in the reign of reign of Mary. In 1554 their mass and dirge began again, and by 1555 they were back to the full ceremony as practised in 1548. *Mutatis mutandi*, on Lady Day, 25 March 1559, the Pewterers had already returned to Protestant services, even though parliament had not yet settled the form of Elizabethan religion. The term 'Lady Day' disappears from their records in 1560, the entries simply referring to 'our feast day'.

The Pewterers administered obits for departed members, like most companies. The wills of their departed members bound them to have masses said for their souls, and provided bequests to pay for them. The Pewterers carried out those wills as best they could throughout the Reformation, but they had to adapt to changing circumstances. They stopped their obit for Lawrence Ashlyn, their largest, in 1548, when all chantries and bequests for obits were seized by the crown, but they faithfully carried out all the other terms of his will. In 1555 they began providing the obits again, having bought back the property seized by Edward VI that paid for them. In 1559 they stopped Ashlyn's obits again, returning to scrupulous observance of all the rest of the terms of his will.

The Ashlyn obit entry for 1561/2 indicates the political correctness of the Pewterers. That year the word 'obit' in the entry was crossed out and the word 'bequest' written in. 'Bequest' established the Company's opinion that they were bound to carry out the terms of Ashlyn's will, in so far as it was legal, and so they scrupulously observed all the acceptable provisions. Unable to have mass said on his behalf, they took the money for the obit and spent it on an annual dinner in Ashlyn's memory. These annual dinners in honour of Master Ashlyn continued far into the next century.[19]

The Pewterers made the change from religious guild to secular company deliberately, although they seem to have been more zealous than some in their willingness to abandon their old religious life. They continued to honour the intentions of their benefactors by converting what had been requiem masses and gifts to bedesmen into a commemoration feast. This seems to have been a nearly universal pattern, in that the City companies interpreted the gifts of benefactors to be binding, even if they could not continue the masses for their souls.

Other companies followed a similar pattern. The Grocers, dominated by elderly men until the 1570s, conformed like the others in 1559, using similar half-way measures. Only in 1567 did they dispose of their altar clothes and vestments.[20] By the mid 1570s the younger men, much more reformed in sentiment, were demanding a more thorough revamping of company custom. In 1575, under pressure, the court of Assistants had the old, superstitious hearse-cloth unpicked, replacing its old symbols with new, secular ones. In subsequent years the feast of their patron, St Antholin, slowly turned into a commemoration of the founding of the company. The Grocers, like the other guildsmen, slowly removed the Catholic elements of their customs without abandoning their social value of those customs. Transmogrification was not the same as sudden abolition.

As the City companies were recasting their customs they, like all other organizations which sought benefactions, reinvented the purposes and memorialization of benefactions. Robert Tittler and Ian Archer have demonstrated that the Protestant benefactor, bereft of prayers for his soul, was still remembered as a good man or woman. In hall after hall portraits, in paint or glass, memorialized the great donors and leaders, creating a secular genealogy to replace the connection to the saints. At the same time, a rising tide of historical enthusiasm created a new collective memory for organizations, one that discounted the religious connection and celebrated the communal virtues. These were, as Robert Tittler remarks, all moves, taken in the post-Reformation confusion, to 'inspire the harmonious interaction of the community's members, to sustain a common purpose, to legitimize the contemporary political order.'[21]

Towns and other institutions had to look after their fiscal well-being, too. Thus, many struggled to recover and redirect revenues that had been going to their monasteries and chantries, modifying their communal identities along the way. In Liverpool, for instance, the community had taxed itself, in the early 1540s, to hire a priest to sing prick-song and play the organ, as well as to say mass daily in the early morning for the comfort of labouring people. In 1551 the town, trying to protect itself from the depredations of the dissolution of the chantries, took all the church goods into its custody, including things like the cow whose milk had paid for the lights before the rood altar. Over the next fifteen years they kept adapting. The Carpenters' Guild, for instance, took the value of the three tapers they had kept burning in honour of the Holy Trinity and spent it on alms to the poor. The town put in a communion table in 1559, and their priest said one last mass and ran off to the Continent. By 1562 the town had taken responsibility for seeing to it that moneys formerly spent on the chantry of St Nicholas were being spent on the school that had been attached to it. The mayor was now officially charged with seeing to it that divine service was read three days each week in the chapel of St Nicholas.[22] In twenty years the town's leaders had redirected their communal religious expressions into new paths and, as in towns all over England and Scotland, they took greater responsibility for their own worship and instruction.

The wardens, aldermen, assistants and other officers who pragmatically adapted established customs to fit the new times may not have been much concerned with theology. Certainly, they were putting their organizations' needs before the demands of overly sensitive consciences. Consequently, they were much abused by the theologically committed, who were attempting to impose on their society theologically informed paradigms.

If these pragmatic adaptations are the rule for most institutions and families in the period, they were not for some, most notably the universities. If the nature of magistracy and aristocracy made it difficult to force rapid reform in many institutions, the universities were in the opposite situation. They were closely watched by chancellors and episcopal visitors alike, so that each change in religion was marked by a purge of the universities.

Oxford and Cambridge, nursing mothers of all Tudor theologians, were subjected to visitations of some harshness in the reigns of Edward VI and Mary. Edwardian visitors made the scholars take an oath that required them to believe that whatever was not proven by the word of God was not necessary for men. A year later, Marian visitors required them to swear that the Catholic church cannot err in matters of faith. Bishop Gardiner ordered the vice-chancellor of Cambridge: 'none shall be admitted to give voice or receive degrees, but such only as have openly in the congregation house detested particularly and by articles the heresies lately spread in this realm and professed by articles the Catholic doctrine now received and subscribed the same with their hands . . .'[23]

By the 1570s the curricula and even the structures of the universities were being overhauled to guarantee that colleges could not serve as havens of dissenters and to ensure that graduates were prepared to teach the correct doctrine. In 1579 Oxford revised its old statute *Contra Hereticam Pravitatem* and listed books suitable to extirpate every heresy and inform young men of true piety. Catechesis was conducted primarily in college. Graces were sometimes refused to suspected papists. At the same time, catechists were required to be appointed in every college, and no one was to be a tutor unless he was found 'esse sufficienter in catechismo instructos.'[24] However, even in the universities there was scrupulous observance of college statutes, allowing each college to control elections to the fellowship and to vary, to some degree, the ways in which Reformation was carried out.

The Scottish universities underwent similar reforms. As in Oxford, where the Edwardian statutes required that all references to Peter Lombard's *Sentences* were to be construed as meaning 'scripture', the Scots abandoned the schoolmen and pursued strictly biblical exegesis. At Glasgow university a minister was appointed principal, and at King's College the principal and many of the teachers were removed for Catholicism and for teaching logic. Glasgow was refounded in 1577 and its new principal, Andrew Melville, modernized the curriculum, introducing theology and abasing philosophy. Melville went on to help with similar reforms at Aberdeen and St Andrews.

Of course Ireland, lacking a university, also lacked the university-trained men needed to preach reform there.

Thanks to this combination of intervention, new leadership and new structures, by the 1580s, most of the educated elites of Tudor and Stewart Britain were getting a Protestant outlook on theology and life. As they left the universities they took their views with them into pulpits and parishes, preaching to people who were increasingly seeing papists as national enemies. If nothing else they were learning whom to hate, forming their identities around who they were not as much as around who they were.

The Reformation settlements worked in England, Wales and Scotland for structural reasons as much as religious reasons. In these regions local political elites who valued quiet and took seriously their duty to ensure order, saw to it that the law was honoured, if not exactly obeyed. The inability of central authorities and religious leaders to create absolute uniformity allowed local leaders to shape reformations that worked for their locales. Their control of church property and advowsons worked to the same effect, permitting them some control over which clergy served their churches, and ensuring that they were hostile to any settlement that threatened their property in ecclesiastical benefices and land.

Their churches were weakened by a shortage of clergy, by their poverty, and by their lack of tools for conversion. This meant that no matter how much their leaders dreamed of a wholesale conversion through the Word, they could not expect one. In many places the pace of reform was slowed to a walk by the lack of ministers and books. Stopgaps, like the appointment of readers, may have helped, but they could not deliver the evangelical promise as they wished. However, like the independence of the magistracy, this may have made the transition to a Protestant culture easier. The sheer ignorance of the people, as well as the ignorance of many parish priests, benefited the state's desire for order.

Slowly, with the help of extra governmental institutions as well as the magistracy, England, Scotland and Wales acquired Protestant instincts. Until the 1580s the religious settlements were unsettled and uncertain, but by the middle of that decade their cultures had turned a corner into Protestantism. Old Catholics were dying, the generations were changing, and education and enforcement were bringing the young to the Protestant world-view.

The process failed in Ireland for many of the same reasons it succeeded elsewhere. Local politics and linguistic barriers militated against integration into Protestant culture, just as they helped in Wales. The Welsh got the tools and teachers they needed, the Irish did not get them. With too few preachers, the Irish Protestant establishment had little to work with. 'Common' prayer was still in a foreign tongue, either Latin or English, and English was the language of colonial government, just as Protestantism was increasingly seen as the religion of the evil English.

The study of confessionalization in the British Isles is still in its youth, and before we are certain how all these processes come together it will be necessary to do many more studies. This is especially true for Ireland, Scotland and Wales, but even English historiography needs much more exploration of the process in the later sixteenth century.

NOTES

1. Braddick, *State Formation*, p. 291.
2. Hartley, *Parliaments of Elizabeth I*, I, p. 51.
3. Henry E. Huntington Library, El 2579, fo.15.
4. Jones, *Birth of the Elizabethan Age*, pp. 4–16.
5. Marcus et al., *Elizabeth I. Collected Works*, pp. 138–9.
6. Brooks, *Thomas Cranmer's Doctrine*, pp. 112–13.
7. Maltby, *Prayer Book and People*, p. 15.
8. Booty, *The Book of Common Prayer 1559*, pp. 372–3.
9. 5 Eliz. I, c. 28.1.
10. Meigs, *The Reformations in Ireland*, pp. 67–8.
11. Lynch, 'Religious life', p. 512.
12. Duffy, *Voices of Morebath*.
13. Bruce, *Correspondence of Matthew Parker*, p. 123.
14. Peel, *The Seconde Parte of a Register*, pp. 100, 104.
15. Jones, *English Reformation*, p. 95.
16. Ewart, *Dundrennan Abbey*, pp. 85–6.
17. *Acts of the Parliaments of Scotland*, II, 607 a [1560]; c. 6, III, 37 [1567].
18. Goodare, *State and Society in Early Modern Scotland*, p. 173.
19. London Guildhall Library, 11588/1, fo. 188. LGL, 7086/2, 8v; 126v; fo. 176; 195v; 118v, 126v; 187, 232v; 247v; 247v; 7086/3 fo. 328v. 7112, fo. 40.

20. Ibid., MS 11588/1, fols. 175v.
21. Tittler, *The Reformation and the Towns*, p. 272; Ian Archer, 'The art and acts of memorialization', pp. 89–116.
22. Twemlow, *Liverpool Town Books*, 3, 23, 32, 109, 120, 129, 130, 196, 411–15.
23. Lamb, *Manuscript Library of Corpus Christi College*, 170 (spelling modernised).
24. Gibson, *Statuta Antiqua*, 416.

BIBLIOGRAPHY

The Acts of the Parliaments of Scotland (London, 1816).
Archer, Ian, 'The art and acts of memorialization in early modern London', in J. F. Meritt, *Imagining Early Modern London: Perceptions and Portrayals of the City from Stow to Strype, 1598–1720* (Cambridge, 2001), pp. 89–116.
Booty, John, ed., *The Book of Common Prayer 1559: The Elizabethan Prayer Book* (Washington, DC, 1976).
Braddick, Michael J., *State Formation in Early Modern England c. 1550–1700* (Cambridge, 2000).
Brooks, Peter Newman, *Thomas Cranmer's Doctrine of the Eucharist* (2nd edition, Basingstoke, 1992).
Bruce, John, ed., *Correspondence of Matthew Parker* (Cambridge, 1853).
Duffy, Eamon, *The Voices of Morebath: Reformation and Rebellion in an English Village* (New Haven, 2001).
Ewart, Gordon, *Scottish Archaeological Internet Reports 1: Dundrennan Abbey: Archaeological Investigation Within the South Range of a Cistercian House in Kirkcudbrightshire (Dumfries & Galloway), Scotland* (The Society of Antiquaries of Scotland, 2001), pp. 85–6; also online at http://www.britarch.ac.uk/sair/sair1.html.
Gibson, Strickland, ed., *Statuta Antiqua Universitatis Oxoniensis* (Oxford, 1931).
Goodare, Julian, *State and Society in Early Modern Scotland* (Oxford, 1999).
Graham, Michael F., 'Conflict and sacred space in Reformation Scotland', *Albion*, 33 (2001), 371–87.
Hartley, T. E., *Proceedings in the Parliaments of Elizabeth I* (Leicester, 1981).
Jones, Norman, *The Birth of the Elizabethan Age* (Oxford, 1995).
Jones, Norman, *The English Reformation. Religion and Cultural Adaptation* (Oxford, 2002).
Lamb, John, ed., *Collection of Original Documents from the Manuscript Library of Corpus Christi College, Illustrative of the History of the University of Cambridge, 1500–1572* (London: 1838).
Lynch, Michael, 'Religious life', in M. Lynch, ed., *The Oxford Companion to Scottish History* (Oxford, 2001).
McClendon, Muriel C., *The Quiet Reformation: Magistrates and the Emergence of Protestantism in Tudor Norwich* (Stanford, 1999).
Maltby, Judith, *Prayer Book and People in Elizabethan and Early Stuart England* (Cambridge, 1998).
Marcus, Leah, Jane Mueller and Mary Beth Rose, eds, *Elizabeth I: Collected Works* (Chicago, 2000).
Meigs, Samantha A., *The Reformations in Ireland: Tradition and Confessionalism, 1400–1690* (Basingstoke and New York, 1997).
Peel, Albert, ed., *The Seconde Parte of a Register* (Cambridge, 1915).
Tittler, Robert, *The Reformation and the Towns* (Oxford, 1998).

Twemlow, J. A., ed., *Liverpool Town Books: Proceedings of Assemblies, Common Councils, Portmoot Courts, etc., 1550–1862*, vol. I, *1550–1571* (London, 1918).

FURTHER READING

Brendan Bradshaw, 'The English Reformation and identity formation in Ireland and Wales', in Brendan Bradshaw and Peter Roberts (eds), *British Consciousness and Identity: The Making of Britain, 1533–1707* (1998), pp. 43–111.

Brendan Bradshaw, 'The Tudor Reformation in Wales and Ireland: The Origins of the British Problem', in Brendan Bradshaw and John Morrill (eds), *The British Problem, c. 1534–1707* (1996), pp. 39–65.

Marc Caball, 'Faith, culture and sovereignty: Irish nationality and its development, 1558–1625', in Brendan Bradshaw and Peter Roberts (eds) *British Consciousness and Identity: The Making of Britain, 1533–1707* (1998), pp. 112–39.

Steven G. Ellis, *Ireland in the Age of the Tudors 1447–1603: English Expansion and the End of Gaelic Rule* (1995).

Michael Graham, *The Uses of Reform: 'Godly Discipline' and Popular Behavior in Scotland and Beyond, 1560–1610* (1996).

Christopher Haigh, *The English Reformations: Religion, Politics, and Society Under the Tudors* (1997).

Steve Hindle, *The State and Social Change in Early Modern England, 1550–1640* (2000).

Michael Lynch, *Edinburgh and the Reformation* (1981).

Roger A. Mason (ed.), *John Knox and the British Reformations* (1998).

Glanmour Williams, *Renewal and Reformation: Wales c. 1415–1642* (1993).

CHAPTER FIFTEEN

Catholics and Recusants

WILLIAM SHEILS

It cannot be denied that, after 1560, Catholics in all parts of the British Isles found themselves living at odds with the religious policies of their governments, and embroiled in the mutual hostility and suspicion which the great European divisions between Catholic and Protestant generated at that time. This informed the policies adopted both by their own leaders, national and international, and the governments of England and Scotland, where the increasing anti-popery of the governing classes, founded on the identification of the pope as Anti-Christ and the evidence of Catholic plots against the regimes involving foreign, usually Spanish, intervention, effectively outlawed Catholicism in a series of legislative measures. This legislation, which was designed to force individuals to come within the confines of a uniform confessional state, but which was often couched in language which suggested a reactive response to Catholic aggression, was important in that it established the formal framework within which Catholics led their lives. How it influenced their less formal relations with their Protestant neighbours or the internal history of Catholics in England and Wales, Scotland and Ireland has been the subject of much debate, and forms the basis of this chapter.

Although the English Act of Uniformity of 1559 required men and women to attend church on pain of a 12d. fine, it made no mention of the Mass. This was targeted in the Act of 1563 which made anyone found attending mass liable to a fine of 100 marks, and those priests who said mass, or the laity who procured it, liable to the death penalty. This legislation was essentially a declaration of Protestant commitment in parliament and remained pretty much a dead letter until the later 1570s, by which time Elizabeth was under increasing pressure to act against her Catholic subjects. The year 1563 also marked the ending of the Council of Trent which was unequivocal in its condemnation of those attending Protestant services, but its decisions were not published widely in Britain and uncertainty about the legality of attending services which differed in language but retained much of the form of traditional worship was widespread among conservatives, clergy and laity alike. This changed in 1570 with the publication of the bull, *Regnans in Excelsis*, in which Pope Pius V excommunicated Elizabeth and absolved her subjects from obedience to her.

The loyalty of Catholics, already suspect following the rebellion of the Northern Earls in 1569 and further compromised by the Ridolfi Plot of 1571, which sought to replace Elizabeth with her Catholic cousin, Mary Queen of Scots, was thereafter publicly questioned simply on the grounds of their faith. Both the leaders of the rebellion and the Duke of Norfolk were executed for their involvement in these events, but the government's actions were directed principally against their political activities rather than their religious faith.

In 1574 the first Englishmen trained as priests in seminaries on the Continent arrived in England with the intention of reconciling the nation to Catholicism, and on 30 November 1577 Cuthbert Mayne, the first of them to be put to death under the legislation of 1563, was executed at Launceston in Cornwall. These seminary priests grew in numbers, with over a hundred returning by 1580, when they were joined by the Jesuits, through the mission of two former Oxford dons, Edmund Campion and Robert Persons, directed from Rome. Their public challenge to the establishment, expressed in their pamphleteering and willingness to engage in disputation, represented a more aggressive clerical stance than had been the case hitherto, further polarizing attitudes. The activities of Campion and Persons, and the growing numbers of foreign-trained priests active in England finally forced Elizabeth to acquiesce in parliament's demands to adopt a more vigorous policy against her Catholic subjects, expressed in the Act of 1581, which equated the activities of priests with treason and imposed the monthly fine of £20, directed against the leading Catholic laity, on those refusing to attend their parish church. The execution of Campion in that year, and the continued presence of Mary Queen of Scots, as the heir apparent of Elizabeth, led to a period of turmoil among English Catholics, which saw some of them embroiled in plots in 1583 and 1585 with papal, Spanish, and even French involvement. In 1585 parliament passed more stringent laws against Catholics, declaring that any priest found in England and Wales was, *ipso facto*, guilty of treason, and threatening the death penalty to any lay person found guilty of harbouring priests. Although there was some subsequent legislation, this Act represented the culmination of Elizabethan legislation against Catholics. But plots continued; the Babington plot of 1586 finally persuaded the queen to accede to parliamentary pressure and allow the execution of her cousin, Mary, the following year, whilst the abortive Armada invasion of 1588 did little to dispel fears among the establishment of Catholic involvement with foreign powers. Exaggerated as these fears were in popular imagination, and exploited as they were by the government, they were not without foundation; when, in the wake of the first Jesuit mission, 103 Catholic laymen were asked if they would support a papally sanctioned invasion, almost half declared that they would. By the 1590s, however, these ambitions had shifted and, although radical political solutions had not been abandoned completely, the hopes of most English Catholics were placed in finding a place within the English state following the legitimate succession from north of the border.

If the presence in England of Mary Queen of Scots complicated the position of English Catholics in the middle years of Elizabeth's reign, her presence in Scotland during the early stages of its Reformation, and that of prominent Catholic noblemen such as the earl of Huntly, did much to protect the position of Scottish Catholics in the years following 1560. Mary's flight from Scotland in 1567 heralded a period of official persecution of priests, some of whom were executed for saying the Mass, and the requirement of all clergy to subscribe to the new kirk's confession of faith from 1573. Legislation was one thing, implementation another, and a number of clergy from the old religious orders such as the Dominicans, as well as the new Jesuits, were able to avoid the full rigour of the law, which was largely imposed through the kirk sessions, where Catholics faced excommunication, an ecclesiastical penalty with greater social consequences in reformed Scotland than in England. The legal framework within which Scottish Catholics lived their lives owed more to reformed ecclesiastical discipline on the Genevan model than to parliamentary legislation, though the latter was employed to exact punishment on the more serious offenders. The general assembly of the kirk denounced the Council of Trent in 1592 and sought to equate Catholicism with sedition, but it was the religious crimes of heresy and witchcraft which were more frequently laid at the doors of Catholics. Thus, although Scotland shared with England the same sense of threat from Spanish and papal 'machinations' and also had emigré clergy wanting to return to reconcile the faithful, the secular judicial penalties facing Scottish Catholics were not as rigorously employed as those against their English co-religionists. This was not surprising perhaps in a sparsely populated land with a young king who seemed to delight in the cut and thrust of doctrinal debate, even to the point of engaging in a disputation on the Mass with the Jesuit James Gordon in 1585.

The papacy had always taken a close interest in Ireland and actively promoted Tridentine reforms in the 1560s whilst still attempting some accommodation with the Elizabethan regime, but native Irish opposition to English rule was exploited by the Fitzgeralds in 1569 when a petition was presented to Philip II, which professed Ireland's loyalty to the Holy See and invited Philip to place a kinsman on the 'Irish throne'. Continental Catholic powers continued to think of Ireland as a possible route to overthrow the English state, and various attempted landings were made, even as late as 1601 when Irish Gaeldom, under the O'Neills, was in the midst of rebellion. The government was able to deal with the rebellions, but could make no inroads into traditional Irish Catholicism, or even to combat the growing impact of the Catholic Reformation, brought chiefly by Jesuit and Franciscan missionaries, among the Irish governing classes in both town and country. Government policy adopted two strategies: the first being containment, through a loyal Catholic professional and office-holding class, and the second, towards the end of the reign, the building of a Protestant presence through plantation, intellectually in the foundation of Trinity College, Dublin, in 1592, and personally through encouraging plantations of English settlers, firstly in Munster and later in Ulster, in return for grants of land.

The political and legal frameworks within which Catholics operated in the differing nations of Britain owed much to the international situation and to the character of the Protestant churches and regimes under which they lived, and we can see the ways in which legislation and its enforcement reflected those realities. The ways in which Catholics were able to negotiate their way through these situations also depended on their internal structure and organization, social and devotional, and it is to these that we now turn.

The publication of John Bossy's study of *The English Catholic Community* in 1975 challenged the traditionally dominant interpretation of post-Reformation English Catholicism as the surviving remnant of medieval Catholicism, and re-interpreted its history as that of an essentially new religion introduced to England and Wales after 1570 by priests trained in the priorities of the Catholic reformation (the counter-Reformation) on the Continent which had little or no connection with the pre-Reformation English church. Bossy's book has stimulated its own critiques, which rest their cases on three main issues, the first two of which are related. These essentially address the question of continuity and are associated particularly with the work of Christopher Haigh and Eamon Duffy. Using rather different sources both suggest that there was far greater continuity than Bossy allowed for between the pre-Reformation church and the Catholicism of the 1570s and that traditional religion provided a powerful devotional reserve among large sectors of the population on which the seminary priests could draw in their missionary activity. To this argument for continuity we might add the work of Patrick McGrath and others, who emphasize the religious vitality of the restored Catholic church under Mary and the important role of the Marian clergy in providing the sacraments and services to the people in the early years of Elizabeth's reign and into the 1580s. Both of these arguments stress the survival of traditional Catholicism in the critical years between 1520 and 1580 as crucial to the subsequent history of the post-Reformation Catholic community. Another critique, not based on chronology but on the character of Elizabethan Catholicism, is based on the work of Alexandra Walsham. Bossy defined the community he studied as comprising those in 'habitual, though . . . not necessarily very frequent, resort to the services of a priest', and suggested that it numbered about 40,000 in 1603, about half of whom were strict recusants, that is to say those who would have nothing to do with the established church. Bossy regarded this figure as a mark of substantial missionary success.[1] By defining his community in this way Bossy, in common with many contemporary clerical observers, may have taken a rather restricted view of those who considered themselves Catholic, over-emphasizing the role of recusants at the expense of the church papists, but Walsham's work has demonstrated that, alongside these recusants there was a large body of 'church papists', probably greater than Bossy estimated. These were Catholics who, for a variety of social reasons, self-interested and altruistic, sought to remain in touch with the wider community among whom they lived and, in order to do so, retained some contact with the services and worship of the established church. They were an important – perhaps numerically the larger – element in English and Welsh Catholicism at the end of Elizabeth's reign, for Walsham quotes an informed observer writing in 1601 who claimed that three out of four Catholics at that time were 'papists of state' and only a quarter of them recusant.[2] On this analysis English Catholics at the end of Elizabeth's reign were both more numerous and a more religiously diffuse body, perhaps with more time for the traditional religion of Duffy, than either Bossy or the Jesuits allowed.

It comes as no surprise to find that both these views on the chronology and character of post-Reformation Catholicism had their origins in contemporary observation, within traditions which one might describe as lay and clerical. The lay tradition emphasized survival, cogently expressed in the words of Cecilia Stonor in 1584 who recalled that she was 'born in such a time when the Holy Mass was in great reverence, and brought up in the same faith'. For her and for many other Catholic gentry in this period, such as the Blundells of Little Crosby in Cheshire, their pre-Reformation heritage was an essential part of their sense of identity in a rapidly

changing and, to them, often hostile world, and it continued to influence a particular strand of English lay Catholicism down to the twentieth century.[3] This contrasted
with the views of many of the priests who, as they saw it, brought the faith back to
England from the continent, describing themselves as 'missioners'. But to them, the
faith they brought was a revitalized religion, markedly different from both the piety
of the medieval church and that being preached by the Protestant clergy. In their
public pronouncements men like the Jesuit superior Henry Garnet were openly critical of the equivocations, as they saw them, with which the Marian clergy had misled
the laity before the arrival of the mission, and from the middle of Elizabeth's reign
they maintained that recusancy was the only theologically acceptable course for a
Catholic. To this end, in 1593 Garnet published the declaration against schismatics
originally issued by the Council of Trent in 1562, but previously suppressed in
England because of papal diplomatic overtures to Elizabeth in the 1560s and in
recognition of the political difficulties of English and Welsh lay Catholics thereafter.[4]

The case for continuity has been based on questions of geography, personnel and
the survival of devotional practice. Haigh, looking at the distribution of Catholics at
the end of Elizabeth's reign, was struck by their concentration in the northern and
western regions where testamentary evidence from the early sixteenth century suggests that attachment to traditional devotions, especially to Mary and the saints, was
strongest. It was these regions also which witnessed risings in defence of traditional
religion, among other things, in 1535 and in 1549, when government policy brought
gentry, priests and people together in defence of the monasteries and of the Latin
Mass. The alliances were uneasy and the risings abortive, but it is no surprise to note
that in the Yorkshire dales the churchwardens at Masham did not divest themselves
of their traditional ornaments and vestments until 1595, or that today's visitor can
still see the rood screens of the dissolved abbeys of Jervaulx and Easby doing service
in the nearby parish churches of Aysgarth and Wensley. Similar screens survive in
many churches in East Anglia and in Devon, where Duffy's work on the tiny parish
of Morebath demonstrates both the vigour and tenacity of traditional piety. That
vigour and tenacity owed much to the personality of the vicar, Christopher Trychay,
whose ministry from the 1520s to the 1570s has been eloquently chronicled by Duffy.

Trychay reminds us that many clergy active in the early Elizabethan church had
been ordained as Catholic priests; in the diocese of Lincoln over 40 per cent of those
working in 1576 had been ordained before 1559. Some of these, like the vicar of
Bonnington in Lincolnshire in 1580, continued to hold to Catholic doctrine such as
auricular confession and the seven sacraments, but most, although dismissed by more
radical Protestant clergy as 'old monks and friars and old popish priests' responsible
for the slowness of reform, ultimately led their congregations to the Reformation, as
did Trychay.[5] It was not from these conservative careers that the argument from continuity derived, but from those of the deprived Marian priests, who left their parishes
at the beginning of Elizabeth's reign to continue a clandestine ministry. By 1564
such priests were active in the dioceses of Lichfield, Hereford, Worcester and
Peterborough, and in 1567 an enquiry in the diocese of Chester uncovered at least
seventeen Marian priests operating through a circuit of gentry houses in south-west
Lancashire. Some of these, like William Tresham, former vice-chancellor of Oxford,
were learned men who had played a leading part in the Marian church before embark-
ing on a roving ministry 'secretly and in corners' among the gentry, but others were

humble curates, like the seven priests from Blackburn deanery in Lancashire who continued to provide masses for the people of the region in 1571.[6] These examples demonstrate that this generation of clergy, whose efforts were dismissed by Protestant and Catholic reformers alike, played a significant bridging role between the Marian church and the mission, and continued to do so after 1574. Not being subject to the severe penalties of those priests ordained abroad the Marian priests had a greater degree of freedom in pursuing their ministry, although later in the reign they shared the sufferings of the missionaries, thirty of them dying in gaol. This led Professor Scarisbrick to the view that these men 'laid the foundations of the Catholic mission', and this is certainly true in the practical sense, for it was a Lancastrian Marian priest, William Allen, who established the seminary at Douai charged with training priests for the conversion of England.[7] Before looking at the work of the mission itself, however, we need to examine the third evidential basis for continuity, devotional practice.

Eamon Duffy's study of traditional religion, *The Stripping of the Altars*, demonstrated the continuing strength which many late-medieval devotional forms had within English religion, both official and unofficial, on the eve of Elizabeth's accession. The continuing use of church ales, bell tolling, processions and pageants among the people, both in towns and to rural shrines like St Winifred's Well, and the preservation or concealment of vestments and ornaments of Catholic worship in many localities into the 1570s and beyond has been used by him and others to demonstrate the vigour of 'popular religion' at this time. This accords with Professor Scarisbrick's view that 'on the whole, English men and women did not want the Reformation and most of them were slow to accept it when it came', and regional studies have revealed what can best be described as cultural conflicts between Protestant local regimes and their preachers on the one hand and local defenders of traditional values on the other in counties as disparate as Durham, Suffolk and Sussex, and towns as dispersed as Newcastle upon Tyne, Shrewsbury and Banbury into the 1580s and beyond. Traditional religion in its devotional and cultural manifestations, if not in its fully doctrinal sense, was alive and well in many parts of England and Wales when the missionary priests first landed.[8]

The argument for continuity, viewed in the light of this material, is a strong one: the distribution of Elizabethan Catholics reflected those areas with the strongest attachment to traditional forms in the early sixteenth century; a large number of Marian priests, having left the Church at Elizabeth's accession, continued a roving or domestic ministry among Catholic families and communities; and many of the cultural manifestations of the 'old religion' enjoyed continuing popularity despite government hostility. The question posed by Bossy's model, however, relates to the relevance of these survivals to the character of Catholicism as envisaged by the missionary priests and the Jesuits in the years following 1574. The mission to England was part of the Catholic reformation, and was conceived by exiled clergy in the years immediately after the Council of Trent. Its primary purpose was to contend with the Protestant regime and restore England and Wales to the Catholic church, but to a Catholic church which was itself undergoing a renewal that redefined its pastoral objectives and engaged with a missionary impulse. Both these developments were relevant to the English mission, as it came to be called, so that the religion which the missionaries brought with them to England was very different from that of the English and Welsh Catholics they found there. For Bossy the survival of 'traditional' religion had little or no significance to the mission, which made little attempt to engage with it, and whilst the geographical distribution was of interest it had more to do with the sociology of religion, that is to say with the patterns of religious activity which operate in pastoral upland regions as opposed to lowland arable ones, than with the activities of the priests. On the question of the Marian priests most scholars would consider that Bossy tends to underestimate their contribution: the church of Mary's reign has recently been brought out of the shadow caused by the burnings and has been shown to have been more in touch with developments on the Continent than was previously thought.[9] The religion of English Catholics in the 1570s was not as out of touch as the newly arrived missionaries claimed, but the Marian priests were an ageing group who, without the exiles, could not sustain the ministry or the sacraments to the faithful beyond a generation or so. On Bossy's analysis therefore these three arguments for survival were irrelevant (traditional religion), at best a holding operation (Marian priests), or neutral (geography).

Haigh has challenged the last of these, arguing that ignoring the geographical distribution of the Catholic laity, and especially its non-gentry elements, led to a fundamental misdirection of strategy, passing up a 'real chance of setting up a separate, popular catholic church in the western and northern regions'. Priests were not placed where the people were, but drifted to London or to the houses of the southern gentry in which they served as domestic chaplains, turning English Catholicism into what he castigates as 'a seigneurially structured minority'. Though he modified his argument later, this was, for Haigh, a policy doomed to failure; one which resulted in decline rather than revival as Catholic gentry gradually conformed under the political pressures of the regime or withdrew into 'a separate recusant community' marked by a distinctive regime of domestic piety, as expressed by the households of the Meynells in Yorkshire or the Bedingfields in Norfolk.[10] Haigh's analysis is driven by what he considers to be the undue attention given to the gentry by Catholic historians, and it is true that on the Recusant Roll for 1592, in which gentry Catholics were likely to figure more than those of lesser status, they are in a minority of almost two to one. Although the non-gentry figure is conflated by the 339 listed for Lancashire, it remains the case that in ten of the twelve counties with more than thirty recusants listed, the non-gentry recusants outnumber the gentry ones. It is clear that more attention needs to be given to them, but in making that point Haigh overestimates the opportunities for a popular Catholicism which, outside of Lancashire, Derbyshire and the upland regions of Yorkshire and Durham, were limited. He also underestimates the impact on the wider community of a priest working in a gentry household; the mission did not stop at the gatehouse and many clergy used the shelter of a country house such as Braddocks, the home of the Wiseman family near Saffron Walden in Essex, from where John Gerard conducted a ministry among the gentry and farming community of Suffolk and Essex between 1591 and 1594.[11] The strategy was not as misguided as Haigh suggests; not only did it adapt to the socio-political realities of Elizabethan England, but it also accorded with the aims of the mission, to produce a devout, disciplined and theologically well-informed laity. Recusant religion, like that of its Protestant counterpart, puritanism, was a religion of the godly rather than a religion of the people and, as such, the household was its natural environment.

That strategy was formed in the seminaries, first at Douai and subsequently also at Rome, and it is noteworthy that English Catholics were, *faut de mieux*, the first post-Tridentine Catholics to be served by a priesthood trained in that quintessential Tridentine institution, the seminary. That, in itself, is indicative of a break with the past. In the early years of the mission, before 1580, there was little formal organiza-tion of the mission and priests generally led a peripatetic existence, operating chiefly among known sympathizers in their native region. In this respect their ministry was not dissimilar to that of the Marian priests. A synod of 1581 changed this. A decla-ration against attendance at church services was aimed at the sort of accommodation which the Marian priests had tolerated, and established greater organization and control of the mission at the continental end, largely through the activities of the Jesuit Robert Persons. As government activity against Catholics intensified during the 1580s a clerical network, organized by the Jesuits and based on safe houses in London and the South and Midlands, emerged, as did differences among the priests. These focused on two issues, ecclesiastical discipline and church papistry, both of which touched on the fundamental nature of the mission. Was its purpose regime-change, the conversion of England, as public statements, polemical and pastoral declared? Or was it a mission to English Catholics, supporting them in their religion and helping them to survive in a hostile political environment, as much casuistical writing suggested?

To take the question of church papistry first: Haigh and Bossy are in agreement in seeing this as a failure of the mission, but for different reasons. Clearly the clergy had no time for the practice and constantly inveighed against it, especially the Jesuits, who referred to such people as 'schismatics'. As such they are largely written out of Bossy's account of English Catholicism, which in his terms was an essentially recu-sant community, growing in numbers and living alongside but having no close contact with its Protestant neighbours beyond the social courtesies. For Haigh church papistry was the first step on the road to what later became known as Anglicanism, and an inevitable symptom of decline. What Alex Walsham's work has done, however, is to demonstrate the vigour and ingenuity of church papists in holding on to their religious beliefs while maintaining a foothold in political society, especially important in those areas of the country, such as the diocese of Durham, where priestly pres-ence was limited. This was often done by the husband conforming, as did John Dyneley, the mayor of York in 1577, while his wife remained recusant. In such cir-cumstances a 'husband's concentration on protecting the family resources and repu-tation could both enable and necessitate his wife's more energetic role in safeguarding its spiritual integrity'. In this way conformable Catholics, like the Herefordshire lawyer Ambrose Griffith, who 'though he goeth to the church, yet he runneth the Jesuites' or the Yorkshire gentry family of Meynell, continued to provide support for the priests and for their recusant co-religionists, even at the end of Elizabeth's reign. To judge by the admissions registers to the English college at Rome, church papist parents produced many priests for the mission, even if their clerical sons came to denigrate their parents' stance. Church papists, therefore, had a key role to play in securing the future of the wider Catholic community in this period, and it was the sons of church-papist families who acted as servants to the priests imprisoned in Wisbech Castle in the late 1590s.[12]

Mention of Wisbech Castle brings us to the question of ecclesiastical discipline, for it was among the priests imprisoned there that the first major disagreement about the organization of the English mission took place in the years following 1588. By that date the experience of the early missioners, and the failure of plots and international intervention against an increasingly settled government, had brought a reconsideration of the purposes of the mission among some clergy, and consolidation of the existing Catholic community rather than a national campaign of conversion emerged as an alternative strategy. The disagreements between the priests imprisoned in the castle arose over church papistry, which some priests accepted as a pastoral necessity if Catholicism was to survive. Furthermore, many of these were secular seminary priests who objected to the authority claimed by the Jesuit William Weston over the mission. The seculars sought the establishment of normal ecclesiastical discipline through the appointment of a bishop for England, a move which, because it implied a restored hierarchy and characterized English Catholicism as a normal province within the universal church rather than as a mission field, appealed to those who stressed the argument for continuity. Such a governing structure would have reduced the power of the Jesuits, who were most actively committed to the idea of the mission and to uncompromising recusancy, in public at least. The dispute was referred to Rome and in 1598 a secular, George Blackwell, was given authority, with the novel and ambiguous title of 'archpriest', and ordered to work closely with the Jesuits. This was an unsatisfactory compromise which left the question of ecclesiastical discipline unsettled and failed to heal the split within the clerical leadership, and further appeals were sent to Rome on behalf of the seculars, who were subsequently known as the 'appellants'. This group became increasingly identified with a policy designed to try and find a space for Catholics within the Protestant nation, and in 1602 Blackwell's commission was revised so that he reported directly to Rome, bypassing the Jesuits, and operated with an advisory group of three seculars. In 1603, shortly before Elizabeth's death, the appellants proffered a Protestation of Allegiance to the queen in the hopes of obtaining some relief for their co-religionists, but which was also designed to sideline the Jesuits and assert their own authority over the gentry.[13]

Thus by the end of the reign the organizational structure of the Catholic church in England and Wales remained a contentious issue. This was a sign of success, in that the community had grown large enough, numbering about 40,000 in 1603 according to Bossy's estimate, and probably nearer double that if 'church papists' were included, to require a more structured management. But it was also a sign of internal tension: many priests no longer saw the original aims of the mission to convert the nation as the guiding principle of their ministry, but rather thought of themselves as ministering to a settled nonconforming church, most of whose members wanted to live in peace with their neighbours. These tensions resulted from experience in the field, one aspect of which was persecution. Persecution was disruptive to the mission; between 1568 and 1603 189 Catholics were executed, of which 125 were priests, most of them seminarians trained at Douai, though it was the execution of the Jesuit Edmund Campion in 1581 which caused the widest stir, nationally and internationally. The loss of so many priests undoubtedly diminished the pastoral impact of the mission, but it also influenced its character, as accounts of the executions of Catholics became a polemical tool, not only in linking the martyrs, as they were designated, to those, like Thomas More, who had suffered under Henry VIII, but also in shoring up the faithful in the face of oppression. Persecution also became a polemical issue in the internal politics of Elizabethan Catholicism, especially when the laity were involved, and to demonstrate this we might turn to the case of the York tradesman's wife, Margaret Clitherow, pressed to death in 1586 for harbouring priests and refusing to recognize the jurisdiction of the court.

Margaret spent some time in the household of the Catholic lawyer Thomas Vavasour which, in the ears after 1558 drew on the surviving traditions of late-medieval urban piety to sustain a domestic, or neighbourhood, piety centred on the Mass whilst keeping in touch with the 'new springs of Catholic piety on the Continent'. It was there that Margaret probably met the seminary priest John Mush, who became her confessor and, ultimately, her martyrologist. Mush's account of the life and death of Margaret Clitherow circulated in manuscript within Catholic circles in the 1580s and 1590s, but whilst its message of sacrifice for the faith was clear, the context was much less so. The account of Margaret's trial and execution was typical of the genre, but Mush prefaced this with an account of her life and character in which her high devotional standards were depicted as divisive within the York community and her own family. The message which Mush wished readers to take from this was that total commitment to the faith, recusancy, was the only acceptable course, but in contrasting Margaret's actions with those of her less committed neighbours, he also revealed the range of responses within the Catholic community, and the tensions within that community which might result from the presence of an over-zealous piety. The microcosm of the York community in the 1580s, therefore, can be used to illustrate the diversity that existed within Catholicism nationally, and the case of Margaret Clitherow demonstrates how persecution could be deployed by the clergy to prioritize one particular view of the community and the mission.[14]

This case also reminds us of the role of the laity within the community, and of the fact that this was not confined to the gentry. Port towns, such as Whitby, Lowestoft and Rye were important points of entry for priests, and inns and innkeepers in towns such as Chester and Sherburn in Elmet, as well as in the capital, provided temporary rest for priests on the road. Like York, some towns had recognizable Catholic communities, such as Bury St Edmunds in the 1570s, Newcastle as late as the 1590s, but above all London, around the embassies and at the Inns of Court in particular.[15] Of course many London Catholics were only temporary residents there, visiting on business or for study, before returning to their country estates. These gentry families were crucial to the survival of the mission and, with the priests, have dominated its historiography, to the extent that John Bossy has subtitled his study of the years between 1660 and 1770 as 'The Age of the Gentry'. What role did the gentry play under Elizabeth?

Inevitably, in the early years of the reign, the regime had to depend on Catholic gentry for the maintenance of local government in many parts of the realm. The magisterial benches of most counties included many Catholics in the 1560s and early 1570s, and it was only in the early 1580s that even in counties like Suffolk, with a strong and vigorous Protestant gentry, Catholics were removed from office and 'withdrew into their own recusant community'. In other counties some Catholics remained within the governing elite for longer; in Sussex the Caryll family, closely linked to the Catholic earl of Arundel, provide a good example. Edward Caryll was sheriff of Sussex in 1571, despite not taking the oath of supremacy, was linked by marriage to most Catholic families in the county and was named as a recusant by Bishop Curteys in 1577. In the early 1580s the bishop held discussions with him and he began to conform, but he was involved in the fall-out from the Throgmorton Plot of 1583, imprisoned, and removed from the magistracy in 1587, only to be restored in 1591, remaining as a member until the end of the reign, and being knighted by James I in 1603. His daughter was a nun, his son kept a priest as chaplain, and two of his houses had priest-holes in them, but this did not prevent him playing an important part in county affairs throughout the reign. In the north of England, where Catholic gentry were so numerous that it was difficult to exclude them entirely from local government, examples such as this could be multiplied, and Yorkshire, with 254 such families in 1604, was a prime example. Even Burghley's son, as president of the Council in the North at the end of the reign, could do little to stem the growth of recusancy; in the West Riding the number of armigerous families with recusant connections grew from seventy-one in 1580–2 to 130 in 1603–4, and included a relative of Cardinal Allen, Sir William Mallory, a member of the Council in the North from 1577 to 1602, MP for Yorkshire in 1585, sheriff in 1592 and a JP throughout his adult life. Other families such as the Yorkes of Kirby and the Inglebys of Ripley continued in local office despite having recusant members. Catholics were also prominent among North Riding JPs, a leading member being Henry Cholmley of Whitby. He had a recusant wife and, in the 1590s, their home was a well-known stopping point for newly arrived priests, who were kitted out and clothed at their expense before moving on. In contrast to these, other Yorkshire families were excluded from office and suffered financially for their faith: Thomas Meynell of North Kilvington had two-thirds of his estate seized in 1596 and was imprisoned by the High Commission, and it is this experience, of financial hardship and social exclusion, which has characterized the historiography of the catholic gentry.[16]

A classic example of this comes from Northamptonshire in the person of Sir Thomas Tresham. From a family which had profited from sales of former monastic lands, Thomas succeeded his grandfather, a member of Mary Tudor's privy council, in 1559. The family's known traditional views and close association with the Marian regime did not prevent Thomas filling local office on reaching his majority in 1565 and, having been active in county administration, he was knighted in 1575, by which time he had consolidated his inheritance through enclosure. The arrival of the mission, and in particular the Jesuits in 1580, changed all this: Thomas was imprisoned on suspicion of harbouring Edmund Campion, and thereafter spent many years in prison or under the threat of prison. His political career was finished and his fortune diminished by recusancy fines, which he paid in full for the rest of the reign, a total over £8,000. He maintained a traditional mode of hospitality, keeping a household of over fifty servants, many of whom were related to him, within which was practised the piety of the Catholic reformation. His triangular lodge at Rushton, embellished with Catholic iconography, was erected during the 1590s in devotion to the Trinity, and another unfinished building at Lyveden was decorated with motifs of the Passion; his home was a regular stop for neighbouring Catholic gentlemen, the round of devotion being maintained by the priests he sheltered there; and his younger brother gave up a career at Court, fleeing to France in 1582 and ending up as an officer in the Spanish army in the Netherlands. At his death in 1605 Tresham had managed to protect his family fortune by astute estate management and through a careful distancing of himself from plots and intrigue; he established his house as a centre for loyal recusancy, formulating the gentry's proposed declaration of loyalty to Elizabeth presented at the end of her reign, only to have all his efforts dissipated by his son's involvement in the Gunpowder Plot later that year.[17]

Tresham's story could be mirrored, in less dramatic ways perhaps, among families throughout the country, and his brother's experience reminds us that, however much recusants withdrew from wider English society, they did not do so from Europe. One of Burghley's spies listed 300 English Catholics known to be living in Paris in the early 1580s, and families regularly sent their sons and daughters to be educated abroad, some to become priests and nuns, though few could emulate the achievement of Francis and Katherine Bedingfield of Redlington in Suffolk who, in the early seventeenth century, sent ten daughters to be professed as nuns, five of them becoming heads of religious communities stretching from York to Munich.[18]

If the importance of the gentry to recusancy has long been recognized, the contribution of ordinary Catholics has only recently been acknowledged. Of course many of these lived under the protection and within the households of gentry families, as the dispersal of Catholics in Yorkshire in 1604 reveals, but in parts of Lancashire and other upland regions the people played an important role in the survival of Catholicism. If the farming communities of the Blackburn deanery owed their Catholicism to the Marian clergy in the early years of the reign, it was they who provided support and protection to the missioners in the 1580s and 1590s, and this was also true of those parishes on the northern edge of the North York moors, in some of which Catholics comprised a significant proportion of the population. In these communities it was not the household chaplain but the roving minister who brought the sacraments, which were, in consequence, less certain. Often going for long periods without a priest, they used devotions such as the rosary and other traditional prayers to sustain themselves, and in that regard their religious practices differed from those of their social superiors, incorporating more 'traditional' elements than the aspirations of the clergy allowed. Their social practices differed too for, whereas religion often became a social barrier between Catholic gentry and their Protestant neighbours, among the people this was less common, faced as they were with a shared need to maintain economic life and keep parochial institutions functioning. The Catholicism of the people was not just a pale imitation of that practised by their betters, but one which, though it rarely transcended the immediate locality, demonstrated the ability of Catholicism to adapt to widely differing social contexts.[19]

Catholicism in Elizabethan England and Wales was a much more diverse phenomenon than the polemical claims of the clergy allowed, though their view was central to it. It was a new church, that is to say, a post-Reformation one, though it built on earlier foundations and employed those rhetorically to proclaim its identity. It included a wide range of opinions, on political loyalty as well as on the legality of attending Protestant churches, which divided the community from time to time. Recusants stood at one extreme and church papists at the other, with many families containing both, and by 1600 there was division within the clergy on this issue also. Among the gentry political exclusion led some Catholics to turn inwards, as evidenced by marriage patterns, to a distinctive Catholic social world, but in many places contact with Protestant neighbours and the machinery of the state was maintained. Indeed, individuals crossed and re-crossed confessional boundaries to the frustration of priests and ministers on both sides, and a vigorous polemical debate about conversion arose towards the end of the reign.[20] Elizabethan Catholics were different from their neighbours, and those differences were marked, and remarked upon by contemporaries, but they also had much in common, not least a concern with domestic piety, and separation was never as complete as the authorities wished and some earlier historians assumed.

Ireland was also part of the Elizabethan dominion and, as such, is dealt with more fully elsewhere. The precarious position of Protestantism within Ireland has already been noted, and during the 1550s and 1560s reforming Catholic bishops, such as William Walsh of Meath, did much to revive the traditional religion of Ireland, setting up Mass centres, tightening marriage law, and strengthening episcopal administration in line with Trent. The religious orders continued, especially in the West, where the Franciscans established a school of philosophy in the early seventeenth century, and the North, where twenty friaries and monasteries were said to be functioning in 1594. In Dublin itself the corporation was firmly Catholic for most of the reign and traditional civic institutions, such as the medieval guild of St Anne, came through the Reformation undisturbed, to be revived in the 1590s as a major source of civic power whose members were mostly Catholic, and often related to priests. Many of the Dublin corporation educated their children in colleges on the Continent, and they produced skilled controversialists like the Jesuit Henry Fitzsimon, a Gaelic scholar and lecturer at Louvain, who returned to Dublin in 1598. Men like Fitzsimon were trained in the Tridentine church, but retained a close sympathy with the supernatural world of traditional Irish religion, bringing relics into the countryside and acknowledging miraculous cures brought about by *agnus dei* medals. Another member of the urban elite, this time from Waterford, was Luke Wadding, bishop of Ferns in the early seventeenth century, who grew up in a household whose domestic piety centred around daily recital of the breviary, the psalms, the litany and the office of the dead. He and his Jesuit cousins testify to the success of the Catholic reformation among the Irish governing classes by the 1620s. Unlike their English co-religionists, Irish Catholics belonged to a recognizable, alternative national church, albeit a fugitive one, with bishops, priors, and centres of learning, which existed alongside that established by law and which, also unlike England, commanded the loyalty of the majority of the population. In most parts of Ireland the Reformation of the later sixteenth century was brought not by Protestant preachers, but by Catholic priests, and one recent commentator has described Ulster as emerging as 'a model missionary province of the Tridentine Church'.[21]

In Scotland the situation could not have been more different. Between 1549 and 1559, under Archbishop Hamilton, the Scottish church was among the first to introduce Tridentine reforms, with a stress on preaching and catechizing, but when the Reformation came in 1560 the church lacked the leadership to combat Knox. Hamilton continued his ministry after deprivation, but others went into exile, chief among them James Beaton, archbishop of Glasgow. With his aristocratic connections Beaton represented continuity with the pre-Reformation church as it entered a new era; he actively supported Scots clergy abroad, especially in France where he held many livings, and he founded the Scots college at Rome in 1600, but his vision was essentially a nostalgic one. He saw the kirk as a temporary disruption prior to the restoration of Catholicism and did not provide the leadership that William Allen did for English Catholics abroad. In consequence the Scottish mission was less well organized and many potential leaders looked to careers in Europe rather than to the mission at home, among them the celebrated Jesuit John Hay who, between 1572 and 1608, taught at Vilnius in Lithuania, and at Bordeaux, Paris, Tournon, Lyon and Pont-a-Mousson in France.[22]

This did not mean that Scottish Catholicism was of no account. Aristocratic support provided cover for clergy and even for bishops, in some areas; Jesuit missionaries, supported by the Huntly family, sustained the faithful in Aberdeenshire, the Maxwell family kept Dumfries Catholic and the Kennedys were influential in Ayrshire. In both Edinburgh and Glasgow Catholic burgesses remained part of the governing elites into the 1570s, and papistical magistrates were recorded at Perth as late as 1591, but by then they were fighting a rearguard action. Individual priests continued to minister to Catholic congregations and in some places, such as the diocese of Dunkeld, they existed in sufficient numbers to have more than just local influence, but by the end of the reign Catholic activity was chiefly to be found in the highland, Gaelic-speaking regions to the north and west. These parts had never been evangelized effectively by the reformers and so, in the early 1600s, they provided fertile territory for the religious orders, especially the Dominicans and Franciscans. The process here was, in Tridentine terms, essentially one of 'christianization', and conflict arose not between missioners and Protestants but between the priests and a laity still strongly attached to their holy places and their local Celtic saints. In the words of one reporting back to Rome in the early seventeenth century, 'these people are neither Catholic nor heretical, since they detest Protestantism' and their ignorance in matters of religion was put down to the lack of priests. It was in these regions, in many respects peripheral to the emerging Scottish state, that the Catholic reformation was to have most success.[23]

The contrasting experiences of Catholicism in Britain suggest that survivalism was not enough to ensure continuing vitality, even where the pre-Reformation church was vigorous. It did survive in most of Ireland, and those parts of the other three countries where Protestant evangelization had been absent or made little headway, and these regions proved fertile ground for missionaries in the years after 1590. But those missionaries had to be sustained, in their seminaries and in their ministries, by a committed gentry or an urban elite, whose members often lived in areas where the Reformation had taken root and who had to strike some accommodation with both their Protestant neighbours and rulers. The compromises they made sometimes brought them into conflict with their priests but, without them, the mission would have been impossible and the Catholic Reformation would not have been brought to Britain.

NOTES

1. Bossy, *The English Catholic Community*, pp. 193–5.
2. Walsham, *Church Papists*, p. 76.
3. Quoted in Haigh, 'The continuity of Catholicism', 37; Woolf, 'Little Crosby and the horizons of early modern historical culture', and see Mathew, *Catholicism in England*.
4. Walsham, *Church Papists*, p. 47.
5. Haigh, *English Reformations*, esp. pp. 143–9, 174–5, 247; E. Duffy, *The Stripping of the Altars*, esp. pp. 157–83; E. Duffy, *The Voices of Morebath*.

6. Haigh, 'The Church of England, the Catholics and the people', pp. 200–1; McGrath, 'Elizabethan Catholicism: a reconsideration'.

7. Scarisbrick, *The Reformation and the English People*, pp. 141–5; Bossy, *English Catholic Community*, pp. 12–18.

8. Scarisbrick, *Reformation and the English People*, p. 1; James, *Family, Lineage and Civil Society*, pp. 137–46; MacCulloch, *Suffolk and the Tudors*, pp. 192–214; Manning, *Religion and Society in Elizabethan Sussex*, pp. 238–53; for survival of traditional festivals see the volumes of *Records of Early English Drama* (Toronto, 1976–).

9. Duffy, *Stripping of the Altars*, pp. 524–64; Haigh, *English Reformations*, pp. 203–18.

10. Haigh, 'The Church of England, Catholics and the people', pp. 200–1; Haigh, 'From monopoly to minority', 129–47 esp. 145–7, but see also his recent review article, 'Catholicism in early modern England', 481–94; Aveling, *The Papers of the Meynell family*; Pollen, 'The Bedingfield Papers'.

11. Rowlands, *Catholics of Parish and Town*, pp. 10–35, esp. p. 18; Caraman, *The Hunted Priest*, pp. 50–3.

12. Walsham, *Church Papists*, pp. 78, 80–1; Kenny, *The Responsa Scholarum*.

13. Bossy, *English Catholic Community*, pp. 35–48.

14. Dillon, *The Construction of Martyrdom*, pp. 89–100, 277–322; Rex, 'Thomas Vavasour MD', 436–54.

15. Rowlands, *Parish and Town*, p. 16; MacCulloch, *Suffolk*, pp. 210–12; de Parmiter, *Elizabeth I and Catholic Recusancy*.

16. Manning, *Sussex*, pp. 250–2; Aveling, 'The Catholic recusants of the West Riding of Yorkshire, 210–14; Cliffe, *The Yorkshire Gentry*, pp. 206, 230, 240–3, 375.

17. Finch, *Five Northamptonshire Families*, pp. 75–94; Bossy, *English Catholic Community*, pp. 37–9.

18. Pollen, 'Bedingfield papers', pedigree.

19. Rowlands, *Parish and Town*, pp. 10–36, 113–20; Sheils, 'Catholics and their neighbours in a rural community', 109–33.

20. Questier, *Conversion, Politics and Religion in England*, esp. pp. 40–75.

21. Mullett, *Catholics in Britain and Ireland*, pp. 55–64; Gillespie, *Devoted People*, pp. 90, 162; Lennon, 'The rise of recusancy among the Dublin patricians', Meigs, *The Reformations in Ireland*, pp. 57–76.

22. Mullett, *Catholics in Britain*, pp. 33–54; Sanderson, 'Catholic recusancy in Scotland', 84–96.

23. Cowan, *The Scottish Reformation*, pp. 165–81.

BIBLIOGRAPHY

Aveling, Hugh, 'The Catholic recusants of the West Riding of Yorkshire, 1558–1790', *Transactions of the Leeds Philosophical and Literary Society*, 10 (1963), 210–14.

Aveling, Hugh, ed., *The Papers of the Meynell family* (Catholic Record Society 56, London, 1964), pp. ix–112.

Bossy, John, *The English Catholic Community 1570–1850* (London, 1975).

Caraman, P., ed., *The Hunted Priest: The Autobiography of John Gerard* (London, 1959).

Cliffe, J. T., *The Yorkshire Gentry from the Reformation to the Civil War* (London, 1969).

Cowan, Ian, *The Scottish Reformation: Church and Society in Sixteenth-Century Scotland* (London, 1981).

de Parmiter, G., *Elizabeth I and Catholic Recusancy at the Inns of Court* (London, 1976).

Dillon, A., *The Construction of Martyrdom in the English Catholic Community 1535–1603* (Aldershot, 2002).

Duffy, Eamon, *The Stripping of the Altars: Traditional Religion in England* (New Haven, 1992).

Duffy, Eamon, *The Voices of Morebath: Reformation and Rebellion in an English Village* (New Haven, 2000).

Finch, M. E., *Five Northamptonshire Families* (Northampton, 1956).

Gillespie, R., *Devoted People: Belief and Religion in Early Modern Ireland* (Manchester, 1997).

Haigh, Christopher, 'Catholicism in early modern England: Bossy and beyond', *Historical Journal*, 45 (2002), 481–94.

Haigh, Christopher, 'The Church of England, the Catholics and the people', in C. Haigh, ed., *The Reign of Elizabeth I* (London, 1984), pp. 195–220.

Haigh, Christopher, 'The continuity of Catholicism in the English Reformation', *Past and Present*, 93 (November 1981), 37–69.

Haigh, Christopher, *English Reformations, Religion, Politics and Society under the Tudors* (Oxford, 1993).

Haigh, Christopher, 'From monopoly to minority: Catholicism in early modern England', *Transactions of the Royal Historical Society* 5th series, 31 (1981), pp. 129–47.

James, M. E., *Family, Lineage and Civil Society: A History of Society, Politics and Culture in the Durham Region 1500–1640* (Oxford, 1976).

Kenny, A., ed., *The Responsa Scholarum of the English College, Rome, 1598–1621* (Catholic Record Society 54, London, 1962).

Lennon, Colm, 'The rise of recusancy among the Dublin patricians, 1580–1613', in W. J. Sheils and D. Wood, eds, *The Churches, Ireland and the Irish* (Oxford, 1989), pp. 123–32.

MacCulloch, Diarmaid, *Suffolk and the Tudors: Politics and Religion in an English County 1500–1600* (Oxford, 1986).

McGrath, P., 'Elizabethan Catholicism: a reconsideration', *Journal of Ecclesiastical History*, 35 (1984), 414–28.

Manning, R. B., *Religion and Society in Elizabethan Sussex* (Leicester, 1969).

Mathew, D., *Catholicism in England: The Portrait of a Minority, its Culture and Tradition* (London, 1936).

Meigs, S. A., *The Reformations in Ireland: Tradition and Confessionalism, 1400–1690* (Basingstoke, 1997).

Mullett, M. M., *Catholics in Britain and Ireland, 1558–1829* (London, 2000).

Pollen, J. H., ed., 'The Bedingfield Papers', in *Miscellanea*, 6 (Catholic Record Society, London, 1909).

Questier, M., *Conversion, Politics and Religion in England, 1580–1625* (Cambridge, 1996).

Records of Early English Drama (21 vols, Toronto, 1976–).

Rex, Richard, 'Thomas Vavasour MD', *Recusant History*, 20 (1991), 436–54.

Rowlands, M., ed., *Catholics of Parish and Town 1558–1778* (London and Wolverhampton, 1999), pp. 10–35.

Sanderson, M. H. B., 'Catholic recusancy in Scotland in the sixteenth century', *Innes Review*, 21 (1970), 84–96.

Scarisbrick, J. J., *The Reformation and the English People* (Oxford 1984).

Sheils, W. J., 'Catholics and their neighbours in a rural community: Egton chapelry 1590–1780', *Northern History*, 41 (1999), 109–33.

Walsham, Alexandra, *Church Papists: Catholics, Conformity and Confessional Polemic in Early Modern England* (Woodbridge, 1999).

Woolf, Daniel, 'Little Crosby and the horizons of early modern historical culture', in D. R. Kelley and D. H. Sacks, *The Historical Imagination in Early Modern Britain: History, Rhetoric and Fiction 1500–1800* (Cambridge, 1997), pp. 93–132.

FURTHER READING

Both English and Scottish Catholics have journals dedicated to their histories – *Recusant History* and the *Innes Review* respectively – and the Catholic Record Society has published several editions of records relevant to the period, as well as some monographs. The modern history of English Catholicism dates from the publication of John Bossy's *The English Catholic Community 1570–1850* (1975), and a valuable survey of the subsequent debates and the British context is contained in M. Mullett, *Catholics in Britain and Ireland 1558–1829* (1998). The argument for continuity was first made by J. J. Scarisbrick, in *The Reformation and the English People* (1984) and more vigorously by C. Haigh in *English Reformations: Religion, Politics and Society under the Tudors* (1993) and an important series of articles, most of which are cited in his recent review article, 'Catholicism in early modern England: Bossy and beyond', *Historical Journal*, 45 (2002), 481–94. The vigour of traditional religion into the later sixteenth century has been eloquently demonstrated by E. Duffy, *The Stripping of the Altars: Traditional Religion in England, c1400–1600* (1992), and the role of the Marian clergy by Patrick McGrath, 'Elizabethan Catholicism: a reconsideration', *Journal of Ecclesiastical History*, 35 (1984), 414–28, and further articles in *Recusant History*. A. Walsham, *Church Papists: Catholics, Conformity and Confessional Polemic in Early Modern England* (1993) looks at those who occupied the space between recusancy and conformity, and M. Questier, *Conversion, Politics and Religion in England 1580–1625* (1996) on those who crossed those boundaries. Martyrdom is the focus of A. Dillon, *The Construction of Martyrdom in the English Catholic Community 1535–1603* (2002), and T. McCoog has examined the Persons/Campion mission in 'The English Jesuit mission and the French match, 1579–1581', *Catholic Historical Review*, 87 (2001), pp. 185–213. Catholicism among the gentry has been treated in many regional studies, the most important of which have been referred to in the footnotes, and non-gentry Catholics have been the subject of M. Rowlands (ed.), *Catholics of Parish and Town 1558–1778* (London, 1999). A. Shell, *Catholicism, Controversy, and the English Literary Imagination, 1558–1660* (1999) addresses an important cultural aspect of the story not dealt with in the chapter.

Scottish Catholicism in the years after the Reformation awaits its modern historian, but I. Cowan, *The Scottish Reformation: Church and Society in Sixteenth-Century Scotland* (1981), provides some overview and M. Lynch, *Edinburgh and the Reformation* (1981) an excellent case study. Irish Catholics have aroused more recent historical interest and among a number of good studies, R. Gillespie, *Devoted People: Belief and Religion in Early Modern Ireland* (1997) and S. Meigs, *The Reformations in Ireland: Tradition and Confessionalism, 1400–1690* (1997) provide excellent introductions.

CHAPTER SIXTEEN

The Protestant Opposition to Elizabethan Religious Reform

PETER IVER KAUFMAN

Plumage, call and habitat were long thought to distinguish the Protestant opposition from other late-Tudor religious reformers. Historians spotted them plainly attired in their pulpits complaining that elaborate clerical vestments were Roman and retrograde. Members of the opposition were also heard to call for more rapid reform, to prefer sermon to sacrament, to commend voluntary forms of religious association along with a piety that their critics construed as obsessive austerity, and increasingly to hoot against episcopacy. And historians found them flocking to Cambridge or favouring London, Essex and Kent, and nesting where previous religious dissidents thrived. Some elements of this composite still seem judicious. The whole, however, is too tidy to survive the accumulation of detail over the last half century, particularly the evidence of regional variation and data illustrating discrepancies between what opposition preachers censured or countenanced and what ordinary auditors accepted, accommodated or rejected. No single chapter can do justice to the heterogeneity of Elizabethan Protestant dissent. The chronicle that follows records the protests that developed from impatience with the prescribed reforms during the early 1560s – before the term 'puritan' applied – and developed into experiments with alternative polities in the early 1570s and, thereafter, into intense preoccupations with personal regeneration as Puritans of the 1580s and 1590s became avid connoisseurs of spiritual conflict. We conclude with a look at parts of the Protestant opposition that evangelized and organized differently and to different ends.

Edmund Grindal had resigned himself to a lengthy period of exile and had just started to learn German in late 1558, when he heard that Queen Mary had died. He and a few hundred other Protestant refugees on the Continent prepared to repatriate. Some returned with unrealistically high expectations. They figured that the reforms they liked before they left – reforms approved by King Edward's Protectors and parliaments – were stalled or suspended rather than reversed by his half-sister's government. They trusted an army of articulate preachers would soon be recruited to resume progress in even the most remote parishes. And they assumed the new queen and regime would lend immediate, complete and vital support to the evangelization of the realm. They were wrong on all counts.

Their optimism was based less on their knowledge of lay sentiment and of their new sovereign's religious sensibilities than on their faith in the power of the Word. The shortage of reformed preachers at first seemed surmountable. Learned lay lectors could read passages of the sacred texts at worship. Ordinary people might read the gospels or hear their peers read them. John Jewel returned from exile to defend the English laity's right to have bibles 'in their own tongue'; laymen, liberated from conditions Catholics purportedly set on their salvation, would get from their sacred texts far more than a glimpse of what God required of them, their congregations and their kingdom. And all would be well. Yet the government, more cautious reformers, and Jewel himself, as time passed, were not so certain. They feared that proles were prone to excess, 'giddy', fond of the old church's unreformed devotions, 'vulgar' in more than tongue. The queen and her new bishops came to endorse more modest changes than many of the bishops, Jewel of Salisbury and Grindal of London among them, hoped to implement as late as 1563. The 'establishment' planned to keep reform orderly and religion uniform rather than 'nulliform'.[1]

As an exile in the 1550s, James Pilkington admired the reformed religious settlements in Geneva and Frankfurt. As bishop of Durham in 1564, he told Robert Dudley, earl of Leicester, that lasting reform in England depended on making the differences between 'papistry' and Protestantism as clear as they had been on the Continent. Jewel agreed. Commoners 'know not whither to turn them', he observed; 'they know neither what to leave nor what they should receive'. Pilkington, Jewel, Grindal and the other dissidents-turned-diocesans increasingly realized that there was no quick fix. Too few reformed pastors served too many parishioners, still mystified at mid-decade by the changes in regime and religion over the previous twenty years.[2]

That problem was widely acknowledged, and Elizabeth's bishops grew weary being reminded of it. They became impatient with the continuing agitation for further reform and discouraged their clerical colleagues who wanted to steer English churches into channels cut by Swiss reformers. For their part, dissidents looked to simplify worship, loathed the loose-fitting clerical gowns called surplices, and favoured composing parish consistories to oversee reformed discipline locally and, later, eliminating episcopacy. To Archbishop Matthew Parker and his suffragans, what the still loyal opposition liked or loathed was irrelevant alongside what the queen and her council preferred. The government wanted to discourage 'diversitie, varietye, [and] singularitie', and by 1566, Parker obliged, requiring conformity in clerical attire and worship. He got less support from Court than he expected yet prevailed on his bishops to enforce his rules, his *Advertisements*. Dissidents, now turned nonconformists, promised to listen to reason, yet they claimed, with the next breath, that no reasonable person would defend their archbishop's regulations and none would dare try to distinguish the customs and costumes prescribed in the *Advertisements* from the Jewish practices that Jesus repudiated and from Catholic practices continental Protestants scorned.

Thomas Lever signed the nonconformists' remonstrance. Returning from exile years before, he travelled widely preaching around the realm before he settled as town preacher and archdeacon of Coventry. He was as anxious as Jewel about the common people 'know[ing] not whither to turn', yet his concern led him to a conclusion unlike that (and not at all liked by) the queen's new bishops. Lever fretted that the retention of 'popish' attire and ritual in reformed churches was sure to confuse the laity, that the old clerical wardrobe led laymen to anticipate a reunion with Rome. The opposition elsewhere echoed Lever's concern. Percival Wiburn, William Whittingham, Christopher Goodman and John Knox, 'to the end that we might rather goe forward to perfection than backwarde', opposed wearing prescribed vestments and assured that their careers would stall well shy of episcopacy. Several had already distanced themselves from 'the establishment'. Thomas Sampson refused to be made bishop. Miles Coverdale declined reappointment to his see at Exeter. And there seems to be something irresistible about Patrick Collinson's observation that 'the failure or reluctance of many of the most forward Protestants to land high ecclesiastical positions was an important factor in the formation of the puritan mentality, and specifically of the anti-prelatical, even presbyterian temper of the party'. Lay support was not wanting. Dissidents enjoyed the patronage of the earls of Leicester, Huntingdon, Bedford and Warwick. Partisans at court included former exiles such as Francis Knollys. They favoured 'forward' preaching, but well-placed, influential laity had to learn, for the most part, to avoid the line of fire. They appreciated the opposition's impatience for further reforms yet would also have understood Grindal's choice to become bishop and 'not to desert our churches for the sake of a few ceremonies'.[3]

Clerical dissidents were not as generous. Protests against Parker's regulations branded the bishops who endorsed and enforced them, including Grindal, as turncoats. The required vestments were resented as 'garments dedicated to idolatry', as 'implements and trappings of Antichriste'. A 'Griefe' complained 'rudelye and trulye' that Jewel was 'contented . . . with a corrupt manner of the service of God'. The aggrieved said they had attended ordinations where he borrowed benedictions from the old, unreformed churches, exhorting priests to receive the Holy Spirit as though they, and no lay person, might be so blessed and 'graced'. The opposition insisted that bishops' wardrobes and words widened the chasm between clergy and laity opened by the Catholics that the best reformers were trying to close. That Elizabeth's officials failed to rank among those 'best reformers' was clear to nonconformists after 1566. That year, the queen torpedoed the reform initiatives introduced in parliament, showed she opposed further changes in the church, and showed as well that she had her new bishops in tow. Dissidents were left to remonstrate or 'grieve' and claim the right to pick and choose which of Parker's and the Prayer Book's prescriptions were worth observing. Parker, for his part, thought it tragically necessary to deprive them of their pulpits when there was such 'a scarcytie of teachers', yet he figured that it was necessary to discipline the dissidents. Pilkington also regretted the casualties. The war over what to wear would have been eminently forgettable, a teapot tempest, he said, were it not for their disobedience. No doubt, the spectacle of the self-styled 'best' (or godly) and their bishops exchanging insults 'rejoyceth the adversaryes of reformed religion', Pilkington gathered, imagining how it thrilled Catholics abroad to see the reformed church in England 'stop the mouths of so many grave and learned and godly zealous preachers'.[4]

But 'stop the mouths' they must, Parker advised his bishops; 'the willfulness of some men' recklessly endangered the church. They were uncompromising. 'They will offer themselves to lose all . . . rather than they will condescend' and conform. At one sitting in London in late March 1566, he and Grindal suspended three dozen preachers and warned they would lose their livings if they did not resign themselves to the Prayer Book and prescribed clerical apparel. Parker knew that the universities where preachers were trained would be hard to bring in line. 'The wiser sort' there had 'strange' notions about authority and reform. Andrew Perne, master of Peterhouse, Cambridge, from 1554, called them 'wise in their conceits'. Henry Howard who attended their debates with John Whitgift during the early 1570s, suggested they were driven by 'the desire of innovating' and not by a 'zeal to further or advance religion'. William Fulke was 'frivolous'. He led protests from Cambridge pulpits against the surplice in the 1560s and afterward agitated for broadly participatory parish regimes.[5]

Parker, Perne, Howard and others were obviously unsettled by the opposition at the colleges, notably at Magdalen and Christ Church, Oxford, and at Trinity, St John's and Christ's, Cambridge. Friendship circles formed around the likes of Fulke, Thomas Cartwright and Lawrence Chaderton. Their conversations and camaraderie appealed to students training for the ministry and attracted pastors from East Anglia to Cambridge conferences. Thomas Sampson, James Calfhill and Lawrence Humphrey influentially expressed reservations at Oxford about the Prayer Book and Parker's *Advertisements*. Cambridge, though, was more closely identified with puritan dissent, and Parker was powerless to halt its spread to his own college, Corpus Christi, particularly after Cartwright's now famous, though lost lectures on early Christian polity. By late 1570, the lecturer and Lady Margaret professor of divinity had been expelled from the university for having advocated parity in the ministry and for comparing unfavourably the condition of the reformed church in England to that of the first Christians' congregations described in the early chapters of the Acts of the Apostles. Cartwrightean dissidents blamed Parker, from their perspective, 'the pope of Lambeth', and John Whitgift who, as vice-chancellor and, after 1583, from Lambeth as well, hounded the controversial Cartwright. To the end of Elizabeth's reign, however, authorities were unable to clear the colleges of Cantabridgean and modified Cartwrightean puritanism.

Into the 1570s, opposition elsewhere still held out hope for church authorities, hope that they might be moved to make a final, strenuous and successful effort to have the queen and council reform worship, wardrobe and discipline more comprehensively and then – for unanimity was an aim of all parties – to collapse with their critics in contented exhaustion. Historians are surely correct to maintain that the parliament of 1571 changed such expectations for many, if not most, of those who later contributed substantially to puritan petitions and proposals. Dissidents introduced measures into the Lower House only to see them fail. To the more radical reformers, failure signalled the impossibility of accommodating both episcopacy and consistory, that is, the unlikelihood of implementing local autonomy with episcopal supervision. Bishops had balked. They would have pastors uniformly subscribe to all the articles specified in the queen's settlement of religion, for otherwise it settled nothing, save a few commonly agreed doctrinal formulations. Circumstance made dissent of any sort seem subversive. Rome had only recently (1570) excommunicated Elizabeth. Her council required conformity, reproved 'singularitie', and approved when bishops directed convocations of their clergy to make the distribution and renewal of licences to preach contingent on unconditional subscription, tantamount to the nonconformists' unconditional surrender. Thomas Wilcox and John Field, just down from Oxford, Edward Dering and others fresh from Cambridge, and former

Marian exiles, including Thomas Lever and Christopher Goodman, refused to give much ground. Some offered to cease carping at conformists if they themselves could continue *sans* surplice in their pulpits, but bishops were unwilling to sanction a selective obedience and thus to normalize what looked to them like insubordination. Another tack and tone seemed to Field and Wilcox to promise better results.

They prepared an *Admonition to Parliament* in 1572 when it became known that members would soon assemble to contemplate the government's responses to prominent Catholics' recent conspiracies. Yet Field and Wilcox held off publishing their document, perhaps fearing the offensive tone would divide Protestant dissenters, as it eventually did. Few if any among them would have denied that deprived nonconformists had legitimate grievances. How many – if any – however would have agreed that grievances absolved the aggrieved, Field and Wilcox, in this instance, from a charge of tactless and irresponsible intimidation? Besides, there were still chances that parliament might decide to have the penalties for nonconformity in its Act of Uniformity apply exclusively to papists still in the realm. But by late spring the queen intervened. She halted the deliberations aimed at amending and enacting further reform bills and instructed parliament to sift no measure until her clergy approved it. Leading dissidents were disheartened. By summer the *Admonition* was circulating. It complained of the concentration of power in the church and accused bishops of exercising an authority over the ministry that the local congregations once possessed. And it complained, predictably, about the customs of the current, partially reformed churches of England – interrogation and crossing at baptism, baptismal fonts, private communions, and, of course, surplices – that resembled corruptions of the unreformed churches of Rome. Ostensibly admonishing parliament, Field and Wilcox were also assuring their partisans that the government and its bishops were politically, although not altogether effectively, subverting reform, defeating radicalism, and – only temporarily – keeping their realm from restoring the purity of the primitive Christian churches.

Authorities worried that those assurances were being well and widely received. Yet – conveniently, for them – the more moderate dissidents recoiled from the radicals' rhetoric. With Cartwright back from Geneva and engaged in a pamphlet punch-up with Whitgift, the circulation of admonition literature was hardly likely to plummet. Nonetheless, Cartwright put the opposition's case more temperately than did Field who added to the *Admonition* a *View of Popish Abuses remaining in the English Church*, the language of which was particularly offensive. Conformists composed their Prayer Book and Parker his *Advertisements* from 'a popish dunghill'. The government and its bishops, preferring scripted homilies to spirited sprawling sermons, were 'corrupt and strange to maintain an unlearned and readyng ministerie'. The supposedly reformed liturgy of the realm's reputedly reformed church was 'full of childishe and superstitious toys'. The outcome of it all: 'no edification . . . but confusion'. Diocesan administration 'spoils the pastor of his lawful jurisdiction'; the 'filthie court[s] of pettie pope[s]', especially those of 'the pope of Lambeth' were embarrassments. Surviving exiles on the episcopal bench, Grindal, Cox, Horne and Sandys, *inter alia*, struck by the dissidents' wholesale repudiation, must have despaired of containing such radical sentiments within the national church. Martyrologist John Foxe flinched on reading the *Admonition* and *View* and became increasingly irenic, as did Thomas Norton, the Puritans' chief strategist in the parliaments of 1571 and

1572, who might once have been Field's duelling second. Edward Dering, defending, elected to be succinct rather than scalding. Asked if he believed the Reformation had introduced 'right ministry' into the realm, he responded that, 'if by right ministry is meant the order which the apostles instituted, this is not right'.[6]

Into the 1570s, the radical dissidents' focus shifted from liturgy to polity. Their line was that godly magistrates must 'plant' a 'right' and godly ministry in every church in England. That came to mean parish consistories staffed by elders (usually current and former lay churchwardens along with the pastor), considerable local autonomy, informal congresses of clerical presbyters (pastors), and, later, regular regional synodical activity. Percival Wiburn, under the earl of Leicester's protection, looked to reform Northamptonshire on that model before the first *Admonition* was issued. Norwich ministers launched a similar experiment by mid-decade. Field's clerical conferences attracted recent university graduates assigned their first livings in London. And subsequent conferences or 'classes', mostly in south-east and central England, co-ordinated devotion and discipline, occasionally across diocesan boundaries, leaving little for the bishops and thinking less of them.

Whitgift, answering Cartwright, conjured a terrifying world without bishops, a world of 'sects and schisms', 'insolency' and 'factiousness'. He borrowed liberally from Cyprian, a third-century bishop of Carthage known to have consoled Cornelius, his episcopal colleague in Rome, provoked by dissidents' 'presumptuous disdain' as Parker and his suffragans were provoked long afterward in England. Cyprian reminded the pope of the importance of episcopacy. Without bishops, 'compound[ing] contentions', 'redress [ing] heresies, schisms, factions', seeing that all 'which be under [them] do their duty', there could be no unity and accountability in the church. Protestant opposition boasted celebrity endorsements as well. The dissidents pointed to Theodore Beza, who replied earlier and angrily on learning that English bishops granted dispensations to pluralists. Beza, Calvin's successor in Geneva, and other continental reformers who seemed to be prospering without episcopacy, braced the English opposition's argument that the very existence of bishops signalled 'a manifest falling away from Christ'. Scripture, though, was an even more welcome source. To Cartwright, it revealed that the church and ministry could and should be 'brought to perfection without bishops'. Whitgift's rejoinder was that God countenanced far more than was written in the New Testament. Magistrates and bishops in every age were encouraged to improvise, specifically, to distribute authority and demand conformity as occasion and the preservation of order required. The opposition, arguing for the omni-sufficiency of scripture, showed an insufficient grasp of both the Bible and present circumstance, according to Whitgift; the dissidents, that is, exaggerated the importance of the sacred text's silences and understated the importance of order. Their case against episcopacy acquired a sinister and broadly subversive colouring as well, for it could be used against Christian magistrates as well as bishops. It was difficult to find New Testament precedents for Parker, yet equally hard to find them for Elizabeth.

The dissidents typically answered that no political disloyalty was intended; they looked to scripture to learn about godly congregations not to discover alternatives to the present political settlement. The Bible, they claimed, censured unpreaching prelates, for there were no examples in the New Testament of diocesan executives without local pastoral responsibilities. A second *Admonition* to parliament, probably written by Christopher Goodman while Field and Wilcox were in prison, saw no need for such officials. Local congregations could arrange things splendidly when leaders chose 'to be directed by the course of the scriptures . . . following the generall rules of the scripture for order.' That way, Cartwright promised elsewhere, reformed Christians in the sixteenth century should behave as had the earliest Christians, 'so plentifullie endued with the spirit of God'. Each English congregation conforming to the biblical model would conform to all the others, establishing the uniformity the queen so desired. William Fulke foresaw a rather less tidy result. He was satisfied that the Acts of the Apostles proved the earliest Christian authorities tolerated variation and thereby suggested that local variability in Tudor East Anglia and, for that matter, all through the realm, was permissible. Cartwright and Goodman, though, were more ambitious. They would give the government the uniformity that it wanted and get their perfected reform as well because 'the examples of all the apostles in all the churches in all purer times' argued, as far as they could tell, emphatically and incontrovertibly for lay discretion and for local autonomy.[7]

Whereas Fulke, Cartwright, Goodman and others, trying to get a 'godly reformation' restarted, disagreed on the preliminary and provisional desirability of certain variations, they agreed that the government was neglecting, at the realm's peril, the need for more aggressive and sweeping reformist initiatives. Preaching in London, for instance, got bolder as the Protestant opposition's 'sense of apocalyptic crisis grew in the 1570s'. Protestantism in France, Flanders and Holland was under fire and at risk, and the most ardent and outspoken reformers on the queen's council and at Paul's Cross urged her to assist their continental colleagues. Sermons also implored her to continue with the reform of the realm, to do away with idolatry and episcopacy, and, a few dared to suggest, to endorse a more broadly participatory parish regime. Spurts of such presbyterian and populist sentiment, shards of argument, and perceptions of possibility may not have amounted to a formidable, radical religious movement, yet enough now survives to question Edwin Sandys' insistence, as bishop of London in 1574, that dissidents were not accomplishing much (*non multum efficiunt*). He must have overlooked, at least, that Field and Wilcox, released from prison, were tireless. Their conference of ministers in London looked like a presbyterian classis. Colleagues came from as far as Northamptonshire and Norwich. The conference or classis provided the English congregation in Antwerp with a pastor, Walter Travers, sent there to receive a presbyterian ordination that was illicit at home. Similar synodical assemblies developed into the 1580s, by which time Travers had returned to draft the opposition's influential *Book of Discipline*, a self-styled order or technology (that is, a pattern for fully reformed churches), and later, after Field's death, to assume leadership of the London conference.[8]

But the government was unrelenting. By 1576, it prevailed on the queen's bishops to suppress protests at prophesying by discontinuing the exercises themselves. Prophecies had been held on market days to provide pastors in the vicinity with in-service training, yet the public sermons that preceded clerical seminars sometimes doubled as rants about the current state or stasis of the realm's religious settlement, although it became terribly dangerous to 'impugne any parte of the government ecclesiasticall received'. John Aylmer gathered that the trouble ordinarily started when younger ministers groused about their seniors, but the complaining was contagious, he warned; the rabble were quickly infected. Richard Curteys, bishop of

Chichester, scolded his critics for putting their protests – 'manye ill wordes' about diocesan officials – before 'the changeable people'. And, even after suppression, Aylmer was so wary of prophesying that, as bishop of London, he ordered a preacher arrested simply 'for touchynge that which they call exercise'. Aylmer was also among those who, later at Lambeth, reminded the Protestant opposition that the Genevan discipline they tried to smuggle into English parishes was intolerant of the kind of dissent they and their preachers at prophecies practised. Yet the dissidents continued to oppose what they called England's papistical Prayer Book, to disclose the poor quality of a ministry 'greatly unprovided' with sermons, Travers noticed, and to lament the prevailing indiscipline. Sandys, archbishop of York in 1581 and asked to answer the Protestant opposition, thought all of the above – the talk about popery, preaching and indiscipline – was cover for the radicals' campaign 'to bring patronage to the people'.[9]

Yet their attitudes towards 'the people' were more complicated than Sandys realized. They were aware that parishioners of the middling sort had long made and implemented parish policy. As churchwardens, they collected and disbursed revenues. Occasionally, they referred decisions on appropriations to their peers. For example, the funds sent for the relief of prisoners in the 1570s had been 'agreyd by the consent of the parish' at St John the Baptist, Bristol. In the same city, wardens at Christchurch mentioned that they consulted the congregation before advancing their stipendiary priest one-third of his annual salary. Wardens themselves were elected and sometimes impeached by panels of parishioners. Dissidents interested in consistorial and presbyterian alternatives to present parish arrangements planned to build on such responsible and responsive lay leadership, yet they worried as well that many commoners who filled reformed parishes were partly reformed. And nothing expresses the opposition's anxieties and ambivalence better than George Gifford's inventive *Countrie Divinitie*, billed when first published in 1581 as 'a briefe discourse of certain points of the religion which is among the common sort of Christians'. Gifford's protagonist Zelotes demands more of his lay interlocutor than outward conformity. He would have Atheos understand reformed doctrine and subscribe enthusiastically to reformed discipline. But he failed, and by leaving Atheos indifferent and unmoved at the end, in effect, Gifford suggested the opposition's expectations were unrealistic, a view probably shared by Aylmer, the bishop of London who ordained him in 1578. Gifford's other opinions, though, were closer to those of Cartwright and Fulke, whom he doubtlessly heard at Cambridge, than to those of the queen's bishops. Before settling in the parish of Maldon, formerly the site of one of Essex's many prophesyings, he was as unhappy with the progress of reform as was his Zelotes, and the two knew exactly whom to blame for the greatest number of Christians in the realm being

as farre from God as they were even in the blindest time of poperie. . . . This I find, that in the best and most religious townes generally, the greatest part have verie little zeale. This I find, that where there is one of these townes which are forward, there be five which are not, because they want teaching. This further I know by experience, that those which are the willing ones and as it were the dayly hearers for a long time are verie raw when they bee examined. Then judge you what is in the rest which are verie seldome taught. . . . And yet there be idle bellies which are not ashamed with open mouth to crie that lesse preaching would serve and that there is knowledge enough among the people, when the poore people doe not understand so much as the Lord's Praier. Unlesse they would hold them still in poperie, they can be no more ignorant.[10]

Authorities suppressing the prophecies figured 'lesse preaching would serve'. To Gifford, that was unthinkable. Yet he was soon called to account for preaching outside his parish without his fellow-pastor's invitation and slightly later deprived of his position for non-conformity.

Gifford persisted elsewhere, convinced of what his Zelotes claimed, namely, that the godly must either correct or answer for their neighbours' naive faith that, God's mercy being immense, they will be forgiven their trespasses if only they observe most of the ten commandments and occasionally go to church. Zealots of the realm, therefore, preached and persevered to correct that misapprehension. They could not stand idly by and watch their countrymen head to perdition, Gifford explained; the Protestant opposition ought to confront misinformed laymen as well as the officials of the established church who misled them. Yet Atheos unflatteringly spoke of dissidents who assumed responsibility for the salvation of entire parishes. They were prurient, tightly buttoned, 'troublesome fellowes', he said, and the parishes were better off without such meddlesome souls. The churches were better served with 'smooth tales in the pulpit garnished with some merry story'. Gifford's Zelotes and England's Puritans launched themselves at that preference, finding it necessary to cause a commotion, to make 'a stir and hurley burley' to awaken indolent Christians and alert a drowsy, partly reformed kingdom to impending peril. Elizabeth and Whitgift, archbishop of Canterbury from 1583, wanted less noise.

What they heard from some quarters into the 1580s and the 1590s was a somewhat different sound. The dissidents increasingly tried to preach up storms in the souls of the faithful. It was as if, without meaning to, the Protestant opposition distracted attention from what radical reformers perceived to be imperfections in the settled church's liturgy and polity. They aimed more deliberately at the target George Gifford had posted in his *Countrie Divinitie*, the lackadaisical laity. One might say today they took perfection 'off the table' and conceived of their parishioners' time on the planet as a period of probation and an opportunity or occasion for self-reproach. The objective was to awaken the reprobate and remorseful to the immense mercy of God, to how little they deserved it, and to how assured of it and grateful for it they ought to be. Repentance was prerequisite. The Puritans' preaching was designed to touch off parishioners' remorse, repentance and re-dedication; their prayers were supposed to express both.

Prayers 'stirre up our selves'. Nicholas Bownde memorably commended the 'stirring'. He complained first of his parishioners in Suffolk and Norfolk who prayed too perfunctorily and lethargically. Prayers 'flowe from [them] like a still streame', showing hearts and consciences 'senseless and dead like lake[s] . . . without motion'. The complacency of Atheos comes to mind, and it is likely that Gifford was still preaching against it in nearby Essex. Bownde proffered a remedy to religious indifference. 'Our hearts must be working like a great ocean sea that sometimes cometh with great billowes so that it bringeth up things that are at the bottom of it'. 'Great billowes' disturb sins sedimented beneath the sinners' calm and complacence. Surges of remorse result, and from remorse and repentance come Christians' assurance of their election.[11]

Assurance of election meant certainty of salvation. Dissidents preached to 'stirre up' despair and prayer so that souls so afflicted and agitated would know both the proximate and the final or purposive causes of their anguish. Sins, ingratitude and guilt obviously prompted their ordeals and were proximate or efficient causes. But the final cause was God's love. Souls that were untroubled were probably unloved and unelect. Such souls were lost. The despair of the elect assured them of their election, for they came to know that God cared enough to send the very worst.

From the 1580s to his death a year before Elizabeth's, William Perkins preached to move Christians to what he called 'a holy desperation'. He was known for 'mak[ing] his hearers' hearts fall down'. He shamed them and, at Cambridge, taught the next generation of dissident preachers to shame and thus save their parishioners. 'He would pronounce the word 'damne' with such emphasis [it] left a doleful echo in auditors' ears a good while after', historian Thomas Fuller wrote decades later, by which time the route from remorse to rededication was remembered as characteristic of the pastoral theology of the Protestant opposition. Pilgrim to Massachusetts John Winthrop recalled Perkins spurring him to repentance. Melanchologist Robert Burton commended his depressing yet soterially hygienic sermons. Perkins himself credited God. The 'holy desperation' that inspired auditors to repent was God's doing, he averred, for no natural force could create introspective, hyper-reflective, sincerely sorrowful pietists from partly reformed Christians who 'partly will and partly abhorre that which is evil'. William Fulke said much the same, specifically that the subtle subsurface work of God's spirit complemented the ministry of God's word. Spirit and sermon directed Christians to 'looke downeward to [them]selves', empathically to appreciate the agony of King David and that of the apostle Paul and to know first-hand how 'the most excellent servants of God may fall into fits and pangs of despair' only to rise again with greater confidence in their election and assurance of God's mercy.[12]

Puritan preacher John Downhame composed one of the more compendious guides to godliness published in late Elizabethan and early Jacobean London. Downame distinguished between Protestants' 'fits and pangs of despair' and Catholics' ascetic practices. Catholics fasted to retaliate against their unruly flesh and, he alleged, failed to find the enemy within. But Protestants'

> spirituall and inward exercise is nothing else but a serious humiliation of our soules before God joined with fervent prayer and unfained repentance. . . . [I]n this humiliation we are to expresse our sorrow and grief of heart by our lamentations and wofull complaints, bewailing our wretched condition both in respect of sinne and punishment and bemoaning our miserie before the Lord as a fit subject whereon hee may exercise his abundant and rich mercies in pardoning our sinnes and removing our punishments.[13]

Presumably, this 'bewailing' sounded safer to Whitgift and Elizabeth than 'the noise' of Puritans railing against the liturgy and polity of their established church. Some dissident preachers, however, reported that parishioners were unhappy with those harping on their sins from the pulpit. Henry Smith, whose sermons were legend in Cambridge and, later, London, puzzled over 'the people's little profiting' from reformers' 'painefull preaching'. He concluded England was under a curse. Parishioners seemed resolved to defer 'downeward lookes' by turning a deaf ear to Puritans' accusations. Still, 'the serious humiliation of [their] souls' was so important for their salvation that Smith persevered. The immediate effects of his sermons – 'preparatives', he called them – might seem negligible, but he thought it unwise to discontinue treatment. Perkins, Downame and Smith had not conspicuously opposed the established church's arrangements for liturgy and polity. Their often unwelcome efforts to shake up the complacent and, from their perspective, unconverted, to 'oppose' them, as it were, secure their place among those historians now call 'hot Protestants' and a place on the roster of the Protestant opposition. Arguably, they negotiated the opposition's 'inward turn'.[14]

As just suggested, however, the churches were not often eager to turn with them. Unresponsive parishioners were nostalgic for what their more radical preachers denied them. Many were fond of the Prayer Book piety, particularly of the kneeling, bowing and signing with the cross that dissidents despised. We cannot calculate with any certainty how many reformed parishioners mourned the loss of those vestments that their more fearless or reckless preachers did without, yet we know that the Protestant opposition's demystification of the liturgy did not invariably sell well. Christopher Haigh argues now, with considerable cogency, that 'consumer resistance' 'contained and domesticated' the reformation of the realm. Perhaps, as Gifford's Atheos would certainly agree, the Puritans' moral standards were too high. Perhaps the soul-searching and self-discovery demanded by dissident evangelists were altogether unappealing. Perhaps a regular, taxing confrontation with the prospect of damnation simply was too a high a price to pay for a chance at assurance of election.[15]

Or perhaps the dissident preaching ministry never achieved sufficient traction to convert the realm to its causes: the simplification of worship, redistribution of religious authority, and promotion of self-lacerating assessments ('downeward looks' or 'inward turns'). Government and diocesan authorities in 1567, 1576 and 1583 strenuously campaigned to silence the most outspoken and uncompromising evangelists. The number of resident preaching ministries increased during Elizabeth's decades, yet, save for London and East Anglia, the increase was rather unimpressive. It was not for want of the Puritans trying, however; into the 1580s, the opposition struggled to overcome resistance from its consumers, bishops, and queen.

They were 'young ministers of these our times grow[n] madd', Edwin Sandys growled, 'greene and light heades', according to others. Agitators initially targeted the problem of pluralism. 'Griefes' were filed with parliament in 1581, protesting patrons who yoked parishes and provided one pastor for several. Sandys claimed the coupling was necessary to compose attractive salaries for capable candidates. But the dissidents objected that little regular preaching resulted and that parishioners 'perish for want of food'; 'the want of teaching destroyeth souls'. Dudley Fenner, curate in Kent, looked forward to a time when 'no man need goe above five myle to have a sermon' and saw nothing seditious or malicious in labouring to make that happen. Told that he and like-minded preachers were 'persuaders of rebellion' conspiring to preach nonconformity, alternative polity and disrespect for authority, Fenner countered that, quite the contrary, 'rebellion is avoyded' and 'poperie is rooted out' when preaching fires lively discussion of the terms of the current religious settlement. Should officials be obstacles, preachers ought to defy them. Young and 'greene' they might be, another adversary of pluralism conceded, yet 'God hath not tyed himselfe unto . . . yeares, but where it pleaseth him to reveale . . . one poore man bringing reason and authoritie out of the holie scripture is more to be esteemed thenne ten thousande bishoppes'.[16]

That 'one poore man', in this application, doubtlessly referred to the puritan preacher. To assure his presence in every pulpit dissidents increasingly suspected by the 1580s that they would have to work around the queen's bishops and reprise suggestions for participatory parish regimes. Fenner, for example, proposed that elders be appointed in every parish to consult parishioners, sift candidates for the ministry, and then choose the best. But parish involvement of that sort struck bishops as the kind of levelling that would only breed discontent, rivalries and factions, causing sloppy scenes (rather than encouraging serious deliberation) that would surely embarrass the churches' leadership. Proposals for participatory parish regimes convinced church officials of the Left's 'slide into anabaptistry'. They accused dissidents of wanting to 'make every man a controller', of promoting a levelling so comprehensive and extraordinary that it would not only destroy the local church but corrupt family life, a levelling so severe that thereafter 'none maie obey other'. Fenner was accused of being 'an English anabaptist' and left for the continent. Gifford was said to have been 'a ringleader of the rest' in 1584 and, as mentioned, was suspended from preaching. Whitgift was proceeding at full tilt from the very beginning of his pontificate in Canterbury 'to throw downe the preachers', either, as one complained, by 'procuring matters of complaint against them' or by summoning them to show cause why their nonconformity ought not be punished. Later criticized for having compelled self-incrimination, the proceedings were effective at the time. Still, deprived dissidents occasionally had the good fortune to find and fill endowed lectureships and to get employment as schoolmasters where they continued to claim that their objective was instruction rather than insurrection. Their explanation at the time was emblematic of the Protestant opposition's enduring insistence that nonconformity to the partly reformed church of England was not the same as disrespect for its supreme governor, the queen, and was justifiable, inasmuch as it enabled the opposition to conform to the more fully reformed international community of reformed churches. Dissidents realized, however, that Whitgift and other influential adversaries, 'favourers of the Romish religion', said one, were outmanoeuvering them.[17]

Dissidents appealed to parliament. They filed the results of surveys that showed the deplorable condition of the ministry throughout the realm, specifically the dearth of preachers in local parishes. The Puritans all but gave up efforts to persuade their bishops and peers in the convocation of clergy. Indeed, they charged the bishops with 'thrusting' upon local churches indifferent pluralists, many of whom were sitting in Convocation's lower house. Dissidents, therefore, turned for relief to the lower house of parliament where presbyterian members, Peter Wentworth, Job Throckmorton and others, pressed the case in 1584. Two years later, a *Lamentable Complaint of the Commonaltie* directly solicited the government to cover the costs of 'plant[ing a] holie ministrie in every place' in the kingdom, to 'plant' or seed seminaries, and to augment parish budgets to have the supply meet the purported demand for preaching. The *Complaint* assumed that most lay and ecclesiastical patrons would resist. '[T]he leprosie of spoyling of the church hath pearced [their] bones and marrow so deep that it cannot be washed away by any good law'. Minor adjustments would not improve the ministry as long as patrons nominated their favourites: 'the only way and remedie is to restore presentations to the church'. The opposition promised that their 'only remedie', lay participation and local choice, would be perfectly safe, because 'many skillful and vigilant eyes' in every parish would maintain order and prohibit anarchy and faction. But the queen stopped deliberations in parliament before members voted. Although the dissident preachers, petitioners and presbyterian members trusted parishioners were watchful, honest, irenic and eager for instruction, experience taught the queen, her councillors and their bishops that the laity was listless, on the whole, incurious, and sometimes wilfully ignorant – more like Gifford's Atheos than his Zelotes. Somewhat paradoxically, however, authorities also thought the laity were easily misled and potentially subversive. Christopher Hatton carried the counter-attack for the Court. By 1587, the Puritans' critics were in command. Parliamentary discussion of the Puritans' petitions and complaints was adjourned indefinitely. As Peter Lake now says, 'the royal will was trumps'.[18]

The rejection of the opposition's plans for the liturgy, polity and preaching of the realm's churches drove it to rhetorical excesses, which demonstrated dissidents' inability to stay on message. Seven Marprelate treatises flailed at the 'impudencie of [the] proude fooles' who were preventing the Protestant opposition from furthering reform. Moderates were distressed by the violence of their friends' denunciations and declarations, while the alleged 'fooles' pilloried all Puritans for Marprelate's irreverence. Cartwright was put in prison along with other dissidents for 'practising the discipline', for attending what might now seem 'harmless professional associations of clergymen', but what looked then to be direct challenges to the authority of Elizabeth's officials. Arguably, by 1589, while the Marprelate tracts were circulating, with Field and Fenner dead and Cartwright evasive, 'the great cause of church government' was abandoned. Commenting on 'the nastiness of the nineties', Patrick Collinson attributed the coming political irrelevance of agitation for religious reform ('English Presbyterianism had begun a long decline') to the success of an anti-Marprelate backlash. Puritan preachers still urged patrons and parishioners to turn inward, 'look downeward', and discover the seriousness of their sins and shame as well as the immense mercy of the God that forgave them. But puritanism as the 'movement' for further liturgical, institutional reform, which had moved to the centre of the Protestant opposition from the early 1570s, moved underground.[19]

Related dissenting 'movements' earlier moved to secession. In 1567, when the bishop of London suspended several pastors for their unwillingness to wear prescribed vestments and conform to other practices of their realm's recently re-reformed church, over one hundred commoners rented the Plumbers' Hall, worshipped there without benefit of authorized clergy, and defended their *de facto* declaration of independence to commissioners appointed to investigate. The proles at Plumbers' Hall specifically objected to kneeling and crossing in the Prayer Book's liturgy. They complained of the continual use of clerical vestments, which, along with the objectionable gestures, seemed to them more Roman than right. They wanted to worship as had the earliest Christians. And when one commissioner asked how laymen with little learning could be expected to design a discipline similar to that of the first Christians and 'according to the Word of God', William White and Robert Hawkin answered that the commoners at Plumbers' Hall were perfectly competent to draw lessons from scripture. The two took offence at the commissioner's condescension. He was as smug as the Catholics to presume that only one church, his church, could or should judge 'the Word of God'. But Grindal, then bishop, taking the commissioner's side, remarked that for arrogance, none surpassed White and Hawkin. We know nothing of what became of them, though the silence suggests that persistent, reckless defiance was unlikely. Nonetheless, the congregation at Plumbers' Hall was perhaps only the most conspicuous of many that, for a time, 'made assemblies, using prayers and preachings, yea ministering of the sacraments', and practising lay, local autonomy in defiance of Elizabethan authorities.[20]

As did those assembled in Norwich by Robert Browne and Robert Harrison nearly fifteen years later. Browne, studying for the ministry in Cambridge during the 1570s, was 'soare grieved', he said, by the slow pace of church reform. His autobiographical account also suggests that he was bent on transferring power over local parishes from bishops and other diocesan administrators to 'the whole people guided bei elders and the forwardest'. He went from door to door looking for the 'forwardest', presuming that their smouldering discontent with current church discipline would give them away. But the householders in Cambridge disappointed him. By 1579 he renewed his acquaintance with Harrison, an old college friend whom he serenaded with criticism of Elizabethan religious authorities, and returned with him to Norwich. Local authorities there understood the significance of what the two were doing. The magistrates were jealous of their influence over the church as well as protective of their bishop's. They told the pair 'to be carefull of their proceeding', sure, however, that Browne and Harrison would not comply. Their 'proceeding' was to devolve power over the ministry to the congregation, and it must be a matter of speculation whether they, like John Penry and other dissidents ten years later, might have been executed for their trouble. For Browne instructed his partisans from prison to prepare to leave the realm. Scotland by then had accommodated a presbyterian polity, yet Browne and Harrison figured the far side of the Tweed was unsafe, 'seeing it framed itself . . . to please England toe much'. Instead, they fled to the Netherlands, cursing moderates, the 'somewhat conformable', for devising 'tolerations, mitigations, and other trim distinctions' to keep bishops at bay and to appease ordinary people who might otherwise have pressed for a more thorough reformation of polity and discipline. England weathered its most serious bout with Elizabethan separatism, thanks, in part, to the prudence of those moderates, and better than Browne weathered his subsequent struggles for and with lay, local autonomy. He was expelled from his congregation after quarrelling with Harrison and returned to England and conformity.[21]

The urge to conform, at least outwardly, was encouraged in other instances by many moderates who aimed to contain nonconformity gently. Perhaps the best example was the effort to kill the Familists with kindness – specifically, to limit their evangelizing without vigorously punishing their evangelists. The English Family of Love, during the 1560s, 1570s and 1580s, was a loose federation of fellowships. Members might pass as mystics today. At the time they looked to their critics like Catholics or Anabaptists, and they looked on Hendrick Niclaes, accused of Anabaptism in Emden, Antwerp and Rotterdam, as their founder. Itinerant *illuminati* kept the fellowships or 'parlour associations' aware of each other's views and news. They and other Familists, though, were discreet, usually careful not to attract the authorities' attention. But when they did, well-placed partisans, such as courtier Robert Dorrington in 1580, coached them how to behave before government and diocesan commissioners. Yet, as noted, some officials, while appreciating that the Family was genuinely controversial, were not persuaded that it was subversive. John Aylmer, bishop of London, and Andrew Perne, dean of Ely, distinguished themselves from the impatience character-istic of Protestant dissidents at the time ('fierce persuaders'), agreed to examine Familists' beliefs, and played down differences between them and those of their con-formist Protestant neighbours. Aylmer, Perne and other moderates continued to see reformation as gradual and to disavow the intense antagonisms that had come to be the defining feature of Protestant dissidence during the 1580s and 1590s. To them ('moderate persuaders'), accommodation promised re-absorption. Meaning to shed new light on the Familists, Christopher Marsh has also put a case that lodges neatly here as a conclusion. The more militant dissidents at 'the puritan pole' of the religious spectrum, he says, often drove their enemies to extremes and made polarity a reality. The Familists who eventually 'faded back into the church' attest the success of an alter-native, kinder, gentler approach. But, of course, that 'puritan pole' persists, as does 'fierce persuasion', and, in the next century, attests its failure.[22]

NOTES

1. See Nicholas Bacon's later remarks on 'nulliformity': BL, Harley MS 36, 298r–299r.
2. BL, Lansdowne MS 7, 212r and Ayre, *Works of John Jewel*, 2, pp. 983–4.
3. Robinson, *Zurich Letters*, 1, pp. 84–5 and Collinson, *Puritan Movement*, pp. 45–55, on 'the beginnings of a party'.
4. BL, Additional MS 48064, 173v–174r and Bodleian, Selden Supra MS 44, 48v–52r, for the anonymous 'Griefe' against Jewel.
5. Bruce, *Correspondence of Parker*, p. 264; BL, Lansdowne MS 8, 146r and LPL, MS 2002, 19, for Parker and Perne respectively on 'the wiser sort'; and BL, Cotton Titus MS C VI, 19v, for Howard on Fulke.
6. Bodleian, Selden Supra MS 44, 32r. *A View of Popish Abuses* is printed along with the Admonitions and related correspondence in Frere and Douglas, *Puritan Manifestoes*.
7. Ayre, *Works of Whitgift*, 2, pp. 97–8, 193, for Whitgift; Frere and Douglas, *Puritan Man-ifestoes*, pp. 95–7, for Goodman; Cambridge University, CCCC MS 340, 171–72 and Ayre, *Works of Whitgift*, 1, pp. 296–300, for Cartwright; and BL Cotton Titus MS C VI, 21v–22r, for Fulke.
8. Collinson, *Puritan Movement*, pp. 233–4, 295–302; for 'apocalyptic crisis', Brigden, *New Worlds*, pp. 239–43.
9. BL Lansdowne MS 30B, 203v–204r; Travers, *Answere*, p. 216; Dr Williams Library, Morrice MS B.2, 103v, for 'the government ecclesiasticall received'; Curteys, *Two Sermons*, F7r–F8v; and BL Additional MS 29546, p. 57 and BL Cotton Titus MS B VII, 18v, for Aylmer's remarks.
10. Gifford, *Briefe Discourse*, pp. 68–70 and, for what follows, pp. 51–5, 77–8. For the wardens and congregational consent, see Bristol Record Office, P/StJB/ChW/ 1(b)I, 25r; P/Xch/ChW/1(a), 264r; and London, Guildhall MS 2590/1, 25.
11. Bownde, *Medicines*, pp. 130–43 and Linaker, *Comfortable Treatise*, pp. 13–14, 34–5, 43–7.
12. Perkins, 'Foundation' in *Workes*, 1, pp. 78–9; 'Treatise tending' in *Workes*, 1, pp. 372–3, pp. 408–9; and 'Treatise of imaginations', in *Workes*, 2, pp. 466–7. For 'doleful echoes' and Perkins's effectiveness, see Fuller, *Holy and Profane State*, pp. 90–2. Also see Fulke, *Text*, C6v and, for 'fits', Dent, *The Plaine Man's Pathe-way*, pp. 242–4.

13. Downhame, *Guide to Godlynesse*, p. 673.
14. Smith, *Works of Smith*, 2, pp. 59–61, pp. 84–6.
15. Haigh, 'Taming of the Reformation'.
16. *Dialogue Concerning Strife*, pp. 21–4. For Fenner, CCCC, MS 121, 142 and Fenner, *Counter-Poyson*, p. 68; for Sandys's criticism, Bodleian, Tanner MS 79, 152v.
17. *Dialogue Concerning Strife*, 6v–7r; For Whitgift's charges against Gifford, see BL, Lansdowne MS 42, 105r; for Fenner, BL, Harleian MS 6879, 127v and Fenner's *Sacra Theologia*, 121r.
18. Lake and Questier, *Antichrist's Lewd Hat*, p. 488; 'Lamentable Complaint', in *Register*, pp. 206–10, 218–23, 242–3.
19. See Collinson, 'Ecclesiastical Vitriol', pp. 150–70 and Collinson, *Puritan Movement*, pp. 415–16, 432–3. For 'impudencie', see 'Hay Ane Worke for Cooper' (1589), in *Marprelate Tracts*, 23.
20. Nicholson, *Remains of Grindal*, pp. 202–14.
21. Peel and Carlson, *Writings of Harrison and Browne*, pp. 334–5, 340–1, 399–405, and 477–8; BL, Lansdowne MS 33, 167r; and Brachlow, *Communion of Saints*, pp. 174–6.
22. Marsh, 'Piety and persuasion', pp. 148–57. For Dorrington, see Marsh, *Family of Love*, pp. 260–4.

BIBLIOGRAPHY

Ayre, John, *Works of John Jewel*, vol. 2 (Cambridge, 1854).
Ayre, John, *Works of John Whitgift* (3 vols, Cambridge, 1851–3).
Bownde, Nicholas, *Medicines for the Plague* (London, 1604).
Brachlow, Stephen, *The Communion of the Saints: Radical Puritan and Separatist Ecclesiology, 1570–1625* (Oxford, 1988).
Brigden, Susan, *New Worlds, Lost Worlds: The Rule of the Tudors, 1485–1603* (New York, 2000).
Bruce, John, ed., *Correspondence of Matthew Parker* (Cambridge, 1853).
Collinson, Patrick, 'Ecclesiastical vitriol: religious satire in the 1590s and the invention of Puritanism', in John Guy, ed., *The Reign of Elizabeth I: Court and Culture in the Last Decade* (Cambridge, 1995).
Collinson, Patrick, *The Elizabethan Puritan Movement* (Berkeley, 1976).
Curteys, Richard, *Two Sermons* (London, 1576).
Dent, Arthur, *The Plaine Man's Pathe-way to Heaven* (London, 1601).
Dialogue Concerning Strife in Our Churche (London, 1584: STC 6801).
Downhame, John, *Guide to Godlynesse or a Treatise of a Christian Life* (London, 1629).
Fenner, Dudley, *Counter-Poyson* (London, 1584).
Fenner, Dudley, *Sacra Theologia sive Veritas quae est Secundum Pietatem* (London, 1586: STC 10773.5).
Frere, W. H. and Douglas, C. E., eds, *Puritan Manifestoes* (New York, 1972).
Fulke, William, *The Text of the New Testament of Jesus Christ Translated out of the Vulgar Latine by the Papists* (London, 1589).
Fuller, Thomas, *The Holy State and the Profane State*, ed. Maximilian Graff Walten (New York, 1938).
Gifford, George, *A Briefe Discourse of Certaine Points of the Religion which is among the Common Sort of Christians, which may bee termed the Countrie Divinitie, with a Manifest Confutation of same* (London, 1581).
Haigh, Christopher, 'The taming of the Reformation: preachers, pastors, and parishioners in Elizabethan and Early Stuart England', *History* 85 (2000), 572–588.

Lake, Peter and Questier, Michael, *The Antichrist's Lewd Hat: Protestants, Papists, and Players in Post-Reformation England* (New Haven, 2002).

'Lamentable Complaint of the Commonaltie', in *A Parte of the Register* (Middleburg, 1593: STC 104000).

Linaker, Robert, *A Comfortable Treatise for the Relief of such as are Afflicted in Conscience* (London, 1595).

Marprelate Tracts (facsimile ed., Menston, 1970).

Marsh, Christopher, *The Family of Love in English Society, 1550–1630* (Cambridge, 1994).

Marsh, Christopher, 'Piety and persuasion in Elizabethan England: the Church of England meets the Family of Love', in Nicholas Tyacke, ed., *England's Long Reformation, 1500–1800* (London, 1998).

Nicholson, William, ed. *Remains of Edmund Grindal* (Cambridge, 1843).

Peel, A. and Carlson, I. H., eds, *The Writings of Robert Harrison and Robert Browne* (London, 1953).

Perkins, William, 'The foundation of the Christian religion', in *Workes of that Famous and Worthy Minister of Christ in the University of Cambridge, Mr. William Perkins*, vol. 1 (London, 1616).

Perkins, William, 'A treatise of Man's imaginations', in *Workes of that Famous and Worthy Minister of Christ in the University of Cambridge, Mr. William Perkins*, vol. 2 (London, 1617).

Perkins, William, 'A treatise tending unto a declaration whether a man be in the estate of damnation or in the estate of grace', in *Workes of that Famous and Worthy Minister of Christ in the University of Cambridge, Mr. William Perkins*, vol. 1 (London, 1616).

Robinson, Hastings, ed., *Zurich Letters*, vol. 1 (London, 1842).

Travers, Walter, *An Answere to a Supplicatorie Epistle of G. T. for the Pretended Catholiques* (London, 1583).

Smith, Henry, *Works of Henry Smith*, vol. 2 (Edinburgh, 1867).

FURTHER READING

Patrick Collinson's *Elizabethan Puritan Movement* (1967) is indispensable for the when, where, who and how of Protestant dissent; his subsequent studies are elegant, informed and invariably informative. His biography of the leading establishment dissident, *Archbishop Grindal, 1519–1583* (1979), rakes the intrigue and issues that animated the 1560s and early 1570s into a compelling narrative, but for the regime's early arrangements, Norman Jones's *Faith by Statute: Parliament and the Settlement of Religion* (1982) is now the go-to volume, and his *Birth of the Elizabethan Age: England in the 1560s* (1993) sets the settlement and its unsettling consequences in context.

Peter Lake's *Anglicans and Puritans? Presbyterianism and English Conformist Thought from Whitgift to Hooker* (1988) is as good a guide to Thomas Cartwright's dissent as we now have. Lake's justly influential *Moderate Puritanism and the Elizabethan Church* (1982) revisits a few reportedly radical dissenters and finds them leaning to the Right. Stephen Brachlow, *The Communion of Saints: Radical Puritan and Separatist Ecclesiology, 1570–1625* (1988) catches others leaning Left. Studies of pastors – Kenneth L. Parker and Eric J. Carlson, *Practical Divinity: The Works and Life of Reverend Richard Greenham* (1998) and a forthcoming book by Scott McGinnis on George Gifford – illustrate how difficult it is to apply the terms 'puritan,' 'moderate,' 'radical,' or 'retrograde,' to some of the most prolific, articulate persons in the pulpits. Studies of parish elites and social control – notably Keith Wrightson and David Levine, *Piety and Poverty in an English Village* (2nd edition 1995) – suggest sifting disciplinary measures may be a useful way to plot the trajectories of dissent in different regions and to test the influence of the parishioners' residual Catholicism, emphasized in Christopher Haigh's provocative 'Taming of the Reformation: preachers, pastors, and parishioners in Elizabethan and early Stuart England', *History*, 85 (2000), 572–88. Evidence for the local effects of Protestant dissent is presented to excellent effect in Robert Tittler's *Reformation and the Towns in England: Politics and Political Culture, 1540–1640* (1998), as in John Craig's *Reformation, Politics, and Polemics: The Growth of Protestantism in East Anglian Market Towns, 1500–1610* (2001).

Two recent narratives enable readers to compare the period and problems here, in 'The Protestant opposition', to the full range of Tudor religious reforms: Felicity Heal's *Reformation in Britain and Ireland* (2003) and Norman Jones's *English Reformation: Religion and Cultural Adaptation* (2002). Some of the finest, more narrowly conceived studies conveniently reside in two relatively new collections: *England's Long Reformation, 1500–1800*, ed. Nicholas Tyacke, (1998) and *Belief and Practice in Reformation England*, ed. Susan Wabuda and Caroline Litzenberger, (1998).

CHAPTER SEVENTEEN

The Scottish Reformation

MICHAEL GRAHAM

The inclusion of a chapter on the Scottish Reformation in what has been titled a *Companion to Tudor Britain* raises issues of scholarly as well as political hegemony, seeing as Scotland, unlike England, Wales and Ireland, was never a Tudor kingdom, principality or lordship. At the time of its reformation, Scotland was ruled by the Stewart dynasty which would, in less than half a century, unite all the British Isles (at least nominally) under one crown. But this essay also offers the opportunity for comparison and the assessment of influences. Certainly, neither British kingdom existed in a vacuum, and the issues of dynastic politics raised by the succession to the Scottish throne of a two-week-old princess (Mary Queen of Scots) in 1542 placed many cards (including those of religion) on the table between the two. In the years that followed (except for a brief respite in 1553–8), Protestant England would seek to convert Catholic Scotland, and then after that conversion (in official terms, at least) two Protestant kingdoms would at times try to shape each other in their own images, a competition which only really eased with the revolutions of 1688–9, well beyond the chronological scope of this volume.

The comparisons were obvious to contemporaries. Offering advice on ecclesiastical politics to his son and putative successor at the end of the sixteenth century, King James VI of Scotland lamented that the Scottish Reformation had been 'maid be populaire tumulte and rebellion and not proceeding from the princes ordare as it did in Englande.'[1] In this statement the king, whose relations with some of the leading ministers of the Scots kirk had grown increasingly contentious in the mid-1590s, was laying the basis for his criticisms of what he viewed as ministerial pretensions, but in so doing was also making a useful, if very simplified, comparison of the English and Scottish reformations. That of Henry VIII and his successors had been, it seemed, to James, a 'top-down' affair. The Scottish Reformation had been something else. More than a decade earlier Patrick Adamson, James's controversial choice as archbishop of St Andrews, made a liturgical comparison between the two reformations while seeking to reassure dissident Scots ministers of their king's Calvinist credentials. Elizabeth of England, wrote Adamson, 'hath continued the reformatioun of King Edward, wherin the kirk is burthened with sindrie ceremoneis and injunctions,

wherunto their clergie is astricted, wherewith his Hienesse [James] hath not burthened his realme.'[2] The ministers in question (James Lawson and Walter Balcan-
quhal of Edinburgh) were not convinced, but the general point was correct: the
reformed liturgy which evolved in Scotland was much less ceremonial than that practised south of the border, and would remain so despite the post-1603 attempts of
James and his son Charles to fancy it up. Further, the governing structures which
developed within the Scottish reformed kirk would prove to be, despite royal efforts
to use the office of bishop (particularly after 1600), much less authoritarian, and open
to broader participation by both laymen and parish ministers, than those in England.
Presbyterianism, even if mixed with episcopacy, did tend to limit royal authority over
ecclesiastical affairs. But if James VI was correct that the Scottish Reformation had
been the result of 'populaire tumulte and rebellion', what had been the sources of
the tumult? Was it really a grassroots movement? The evidence for such a claim (which
has been made by others since the king weighed in on the subject) is thin. Nevertheless, it is clear that the prince was rarely in firm control.

The Pre-Reformation Church and Dissent

While the impetus for the English Reformation stemmed at least in part from a crown
which resented Roman interference and landowning classes (including the crown)
which had their eyes on church properties, none of these factors was of much importance in Scotland. Roman influence had largely been shoved aside with the Indult of
1487, an agreement under which the pope promised to allow eight months after the
death of any major benefice holder (bishops, abbots, priors, etc.) to allow the king
of Scots to nominate someone for the post. The pope would then confirm the royal
appointee while the crown collected any revenues accrued to the benefice during the
vacancy. Except for a six-year lapse from 1513–19, the Indult kept the Scottish crown
in firm control of leading ecclesiastical appointments, and allowed it in effect to tax
such appointments, right up to the Reformation. In 1535 Pope Paul III even broadened the Indult by giving the king up to a full year to collect the revenues and offer
a nominee. Thus Scots monarchs were able to use the high offices of the church to
reward important followers or, as in the notorious case of James V (r. 1513–42) to
set up comfortable livings for illegitimate sons. Given that England was severing its
ties with Rome during the last decade of James V's reign, the papacy was unlikely to
raise a fuss about what appears to modern eyes as such an abusive practice; it was a
small price to pay for the continued allegiance of Britain's northern kingdom.

Scotland's leading families also enjoyed ecclesiastical perks. The sons of noble or
substantial gentry families were often imposed on monasteries as abbots, priors or
commendators. In many cases, these leading families had endowed the monasteries
in the first place, and their family ties with the heads of religious houses could help
them disendow them later. The process of disendowment was accelerated by the
common practice of feuing in the early sixteenth century. Those who administered
church property, often facing increased taxation from the crown, would hand lands
over to feuars in exchange for a hefty lump-sum payment followed by annual feu
duties. These reverse mortgages (for this is in effect what they were) would transfer
control of lands from the church to those who had ready cash. The price inflation of
the sixteenth century (and after) ensured that the feu duties themselves would

become insignificant over time. Such arrangements, whether the result of 'sweetheart deals' between ecclesiastical officials and their relatives, or simple financial desperation on the part of hard-pressed clerics, spurred a silent revolution in landholding akin to the dissolution of the English monasteries. But unlike the latter, it did not require a reformation as a justifying impulse.

While the religious houses faced financial pressures, Scotland's parochial structure was truly impoverished. The revenues of many of the kingdom's 1,000 or so parishes (serving a population of just under a million) had been diverted to non-local ecclesiastical institutions such as monasteries, universities or cathedrals. What was left over was often insufficient to attract even minimally qualified resident clergy. Those who did take up posts (often several at a time, to cobble together a living wage) were sufficiently underpaid that bribes must have always been a significant temptation. Historians are well-advised not to take at face value reformers' criticisms of the corruptions of the late-medieval church, but its financial situation certainly left it vulnerable, despite the hard work and undoubted sincerity of many of its clergy.

But to what extent was Scotland's version of late medieval Catholicism losing souls as well as money? As in England, there are historians of the Scottish Reformation who see it as the culmination of a grassroots movement (perhaps taking their cue from James VI's suspicions, noted above), while others have seen little evidence that believers were unsatisfied with traditional ways. The opinions offered often depend on the region of the kingdom under consideration. King James IV did sit in on a group trial of about thirty 'lollards' from Kyle (central Ayrshire, south and west of Glasgow) in 1494. Charged with advocating clerical marriage and the priesthood of all believers (women as well as men), denying papal authority, transubstantiation and the usefulness of prayers for the dead, all were acquitted. John Knox, whose *History of the Reformation in Scotland* is the only source for their trial (none of the relevant records have survived, although he appears to have had access to some), certainly placed them in a tradition of grassroots Scottish Protestantism, and others have followed his lead. But Knox, who was writing many decades later, was hardly nonpartisan; he wrote that the survival of the trial records until his day, at least, showed 'how mercifully God hath looked upon this realm, retaining within it some spunk of his light, even in the time of greatest darkness.'[3] In fact, the evidence for Scottish lollardy is far scantier than that for the English version. However, the fact that Ayrshire did later accept the Reformation before most other regions is suggestive of some sort of enduring dissenting tradition. Angus and the Mearns (north of Dundee) also displayed reformist sympathies relatively early. David Straiton, who refused to pay teinds (tithes), leading to a charge of heresy and his eventual incineration in Edinburgh in 1534, was an example from that region. Straiton had read from the New Testament with John Erskine, laird of Dun, who became a leading patron of reform. The long-lived Dun went on to play host to John Knox in 1555, helped author the *Book of Discipline* (1560) and, despite his non-clerical status, served as a superintendent in the early reformed kirk after 1560.

Scotland also had a prominent 'Lutheran' martyr – Patrick Hamilton, commendator of Fearn Abbey, who studied on the Continent (Paris, possibly Louvain and later Marburg), meeting Luther and Melanchthon and writing a devotional work, which circulated under the title 'Patrick's Places'. In 1528, at the instigation of James Beaton, archbishop of St Andrews, he was tried and convicted at St Andrews for his open affirmation of Lutheran beliefs, and burned at the stake. The perceived threat of Lutheranism is also evident in a 1525 act of the Scottish parliament banning the importation of Lutheran books.

But Patrick Hamilton and John Erskine of Dun were both lairds closely related to noblemen. Indeed, Hamilton's connections (which had 'earned' him the lucrative commendatorship to finance his studies in the first place) make his execution particularly remarkable. Even some of the lollards of Kyle were said to have been 'great familiars' of the king, which Knox thought contributed to their acquittal. The shortage of evidence for the persecution of people from the lower (and thus much more vulnerable) orders suggests that, in the main, Scotland's reformation was hatched in the homes of lairds (substantial landowners below the rank of nobility) and wealthy merchants, with the aid of clergy or dissenting academics, not in the fields or in the streets of its burghs.[4] Outside of a handful of early martyrdoms or near-martyrdoms, its early history is largely a political history, and the two largest early factors were pressure from its southern neighbour and the succession of the infant queen Mary in December 1542.

Dynastic Ambitions, Protestant Reform and the British Kingdoms

The inauguration of this royal minority (succession before adulthood was becoming the rule, rather than the exception, for the sixteenth-century Stewarts), came on the heels of the defeat of a Scots army by the English at Solway Moss. Henry VIII now saw the opportunity to extend Tudor power over all of Britain with a marriage between his son Edward and the seemingly very vulnerable queen of Scots. The dowager queen of Scotland – Mary of Guise – and her ally Cardinal David Beaton, archbishop of St Andrews and nephew of Patrick Hamilton's nemesis, preferred the idea of a French match based on the anti-English 'Auld Alliance' between Scotland and France. But in the short term, the governorship of Scotland fell upon James, 2nd earl of Arran. Arran headed the house of Hamilton, and stood next in line for the throne due to his descent from James III's sister. Although Arran was forced to accept Beaton as chancellor, he quickly showed a preference for the related policies of amity with England and support for Protestantism. Scots noblemen and lairds taken prisoner at Solway began to return home with English pensions, turning them into the 'assured Scots' (although some proved willing to double-dip by taking French pensions as well). One, Lord Maxwell, helped introduce a bill which parliament approved in March 1543, legalizing the possession of vernacular scripture. Arran himself began to question the existence of purgatory and the legitimacy of papal authority. Reformist Scots clergy such as the Dominican John Rough and the Zwinglian George Wishart (most recently in exile in England) were given licence to preach.

Indeed, if Arran had possessed half of Mary of Guise's political acumen, we might date the Scottish Reformation to 1542–3 rather than 1560. But he didn't. Territorial magnates such as the 4th earl of Argyll, who controlled the western Highlands and Islands, and the 4th earl of Huntly, the major power in the north-east, opposed the growing power of the Hamiltons and the English, and iconoclastic riots in Perth and Dundee offended traditional religious sensibilities. Cardinal Beaton and the queen-mother worked hard to spike negotiations for the English match, and by the end of 1543, the mini-reformation known thereafter as 'Arran's Godly Fit' was over. A new parliament rejected the English marriage and forced the vernacular Bible back underground. In early September, Arran publicly recanted in the Franciscan church in Stirling, and the heavy-handed tactics pursued by the English in the aftermath (the so-called 'Rough Wooing' – invasions in 1544, 1545 and 1547 which devastated southern Scotland) convinced many that Arran's heresies had been political as well as religious. In 1548 the young queen was shipped off to France for her education and eventual marriage (to the dauphin François, son of Henri II). Arran, who retained the governorship, was rewarded for his pains with the French dukedom of Châtelherault. Ironically, Cardinal Beaton did not fare so well.

George Wishart did not regard his preaching mission as ending with Beaton's reassertion of traditional policies. He continued to draw crowds to sermons, both indoors and out, in and around Edinburgh, Montrose and Dundee in the east, and Ayr in the west. Among those who became his followers and ardent admirers was the Catholic priest and notary John Knox. But in December 1545 Wishart was arrested south of Edinburgh by the earl of Bothwell, acting on orders of Cardinal Beaton. After a period of confinement in Edinburgh, he was shipped off to St Andrews, where he was convicted of heresy and burned at the stake at the beginning of March. Knox's hagiographical account of Wishart's suffering and death, written more than a decade later, can be read in the context of John Foxe's descriptions of the burnings of Latimer and Ridley, with Beaton, seconded by Gavin Dunbar, archbishop of Glasgow, cast as Herod and Pontius Pilate.[5] Conveniently for the resolution of the story, the villain came to an untidy end shortly thereafter.

Beaton had certainly earned enemies, some of them for his suppression of protestant dissent, although most of them for more clearly political or familial reasons. On 29 May 1546, three months after Wishart's demise, a group numbering between sixteen and thirty-four (accounts vary), and led by several Fife lairds who despised the archbishop for reasons related to local politics, broke into the archepiscopal castle in St Andrews, murdered Beaton and hanged his body from the tower. They then hunkered down in the tower, hoping for English aid.[6] It never came, but the efforts of Arran's government to recapture the castle were desultory at best. The 'Castilians' as they came to be known, were joined by others, including John Rough and Knox, who arrived in the spring of 1547 and became a kind of house preacher to them. This marked the beginning of the public ministry of Knox who, more than any other figure, has seemed to personify the Scottish Reformation. His role has certainly been exaggerated, due mostly to the fact that he wrote the major account of the early phases of the movement, and he was not shy in his self-presentation. But he would not star in the story for a few years yet; with French aid, Arran's government finally retook St Andrews Castle in July 1547. In the aftermath, Knox (and several others) would spend time as French galley slaves. Knox would then serve in the Edwardian English church followed by exile in Frankfurt and then Geneva during the reign of Mary Tudor. His residence in the latter city (along with the Englishman Christopher Goodman, who would later take up a ministerial post in St Andrews), certainly helped put a Calvinist stamp on the Scottish Reformation.

In the meantime, Mary of Guise was able gradually to reassert herself and solidify the French alliance. She was careful to placate the Hamiltons, using the church, in traditional Scottish fashion, as a source of largesse for important families. Arran's illegitimate half-brother John Hamilton succeeded Beaton as archbishop of St Andrews, while another half-brother, James Hamilton, succeeded Dunbar in Glasgow. However politicized his appointment, John Hamilton was no idle time-server. From the see of St Andrews, he pursued a policy of moderate Catholic reform, calling three church councils, (1549, 1552 and 1559), aimed at improving the behaviour and educational standards of the clergy. In 1552, he published a vernacular catechism, which fudged controversial issues such as justification by faith, and neglected to mention the pope. The death of Edward VI in 1553 removed Protestant evangelization from the English agenda, and Mary was formally made regent for her daughter, still resident in France, in 1554. Scotland's Catholic reformation seemed well under way. But, as happened in 1542–3, the dynastic interests of more powerful neighbours (and now, Stewart aspirations to the English throne), would prevent the situation from becoming (or remaining) too settled.

The End of the Auld Alliance and the Politics of Reformation

In the eyes of many Scots, the advantage of the Auld Alliance was that it protected Scotland from becoming a mere province of its more powerful southern neighbour. But the alliance carried a clear danger when it was solidified by a royal marriage of a young Scots queen who was herself growing up in France. In such a context, it did not seem like an arrangement between sovereign kingdoms (albeit one weaker). Rather, by the late 1550s, it looked to some as though Mary of Guise, with her reliance on French advisers and French arms, was turning Scotland into a French province. Members of the Scots nobility, like those of other European kingdoms, felt that high office and influence were theirs by birthright. This was looking less like the case in the government led by this regent, however sharp her political skills. Those who resented the situation found natural allies among those who favoured Protestant reform; in some cases they were the same people.

Members of the nobility had often formalized alliances with each other and among their followers through the instrument of the bond, which pledged its swearers (in writing) to unity in the face of perceived enemies. Since Scotland was a society lacking strong central institutions, bonds of manrent were often the glue which sustained civil peace, although they could also perpetuate bloodfeuds.[7] But in what can be seen as the birth of the Scots covenanting tradition, a small faction of noblemen in 1557 bound themselves together for a different purpose. Led by the earl of Argyll and his eldest son Lord Lorne, and including the earl of Morton, they pledged themselves 'to mentene sett forwarde and establische the MAIST BLISSED WORDE OF GOD, and his Congregatioune, and . . . lawboure, at oure possibilitie, to haif faithfull ministeres purelie and trewlie to minister Christes Evangell and Sacramentes to his Peopill.' In fact, Mary of Guise had been fairly tolerant of religious dissent (and this may be why this bond of the 'Lords of the Congregation' garnered so few signatures), but she had made it clear that fundamental change in the religious settlement was not subject to negotiation.[8]

But the reformers got a political boost when Mary Tudor died in 1558, succeeded by her half-sister Elizabeth. This placed Protestantism back on the English agenda, raising once again the possibility of foreign aid. From the English perspective, intervention almost became necessary, due to the fact that the queen of Scots immediately began styling herself 'queen of England'; Catholic powers had not accepted the legitimacy of the marriage of Elizabeth's parents, so for them, Mary Stewart was the rightful heir, due to her legitimate descent from Margaret Tudor, daughter of Henry VII. This revived association of England and Protestantism also forced Mary of Guise to take a harsher line with religious dissent. Support for the Lords of the Congregation grew, although their followers clearly remained a minority; in the summer of 1559 Mary of Guise shrewdly proposed a religious plebiscite for Edinburgh, calculating that Catholicism would win. The reform party declined her offer, opining that divine truth should not be subject to voting. But it appears that underground 'privy kirks' had been functioning in Edinburgh and other cities, and this helps to explain the speedy emergence of (barebones) Calvinist church structures in burghs such as Perth and Dundee once the tide shifted.[9] Knox also returned to his native kingdom at this time, although he had to bypass England due to Elizabeth's ire over his untimely and impolitic publication of the *First Blast Against the Monstrous Regiment of Women*, which had been aimed at the Maries of England and Scotland. Knox was preceded in his return by John Willock, a former Dominican from Ayr who had served in the Edwardian English church and also spent time in Emden, another Calvinist centre on the continent. Both would become important figures in the early Scottish Reformation, as would Goodman (although he wouldn't stay long), and John Winram, sub-prior of St Andrews who had debated Knox in 1547, but who now joined the reformers.

But this was not strictly a confessional debate. After the burgh councils of Perth, Dundee and Ayr voted in favour of reformation in the spring of 1559 (and a Knox sermon in Perth inspired a riot against the town's friaries and the Charterhouse, home to Carthusian monks) the Lords of the Congregation fielded an army near Perth at the end of May. A brief truce was reached with the regent, but it broke down amid mutual recriminations as soon as it became clear that she intended to recatholicize the burgh. So the Lords mustered an even larger force at St Andrews, and that town also joined the ranks of the reformed camp, marking the change with a Knox sermon. From there, the rebels went on a military offensive. They recaptured Perth, secured Stirling and marched on Edinburgh. They attacked wealthy symbols of the church such as the abbey of Scone, and removed images from churches in the burghs they captured, including those of the capital. The regent withdrew to the nearby port of Leith and awaited French reinforcements, which arrived at summer's end. The sudden death of the French king Henri II in July meant that Mary Queen of Scots was now queen consort of France as well, and Scots affairs loomed even larger on the French royal agenda. Now the Lords of the Congregation seemed to be losing support and, unsurprisingly, the defection to their camp of Châtelherault (the former governor Arran) and his son did little to enhance their strength. The Catholic mass was restored in Edinburgh in November. But soon England became directly involved in Scots affairs, and that would change the situation.

Queen Elizabeth was wary of seeming to support rebels against their sovereign, but William Cecil saw in the struggle gripping Scotland the opportunity for a diplomatic revolution which might break the Auld Alliance once and for all. Leading figures among the Lords of the Congregation such as the 5th earl of Argyll (the former Lord Lorne who had succeeded to his father's title in 1558) and Lord James Stewart (future earl of Moray and illegitimate half-brother of the queen of Scots) saw little hope of ultimate success without English aid, and began seeking it in the summer of 1559. In February 1560, English and Scots representatives met at Berwick-upon-Tweed. Lord James Stewart and William Maitland of Lethington (the latter had previously helped prepare the terms in Westminster) on the Scots side and the Duke of Norfolk on the English side agreed that the English would provide military assistance for a short period in order to help the Scots preserve their traditional sovereignty against French encroachment. Significantly, the terms also promised that Argyll would assist the English in pacifying Ulster, suggesting that Cecil and Argyll had a grand 'British' Protestant strategy in mind.[10]

With the agreement expected, an English fleet had already been dispatched, and it went a long way toward turning the tide once again in the Congregation's direction. Even conservative Aberdeen now offered token support to the Congregation. In addition, an English army crossed the border in April. But the most critical factor in the rebel victory was the death of the regent in June 1560. Mary of Guise had earned the respect even of her opponents, but with growing religious divisions in France, others serving her daughter did not want to commit more French resources to continuing the dead regent's policies. In July, French and English representatives (now including Cecil himself) concluded a treaty ostensibly aimed at removing foreign influence from Scotland. Certainly, the absent Mary would remain queen, but all foreign troops would withdraw save two French garrisons. A council, drawn from the Lords of the Congregation and others appointed by Mary and François as monarchs, would govern Scotland in the monarchs' names. The agreement called for the summoning of a Scots parliament, which met in August. This body was expressly forbidden from legislating on matters of religion, but this proviso would be ignored.

The parliament of 1560 was also somewhat radical in its make-up. For the first time, lairds below the status of 'lords of parliament' participated, making it more broadly representative. It endorsed a reformed confession of faith, outlawed papal authority, the Mass and Catholic baptism. The 'Scots Confession', authored by a committee of six which included Knox, Willock and Winram, made congregational discipline the third mark – after preaching and proper administration of the sacraments – of the true church.[11] This placed it in a vanguard of Calvinist confessions which included the French reformed confession of 1559 and the Belgic confession of 1561, and the emphasis on discipline and the reformation of manners which it introduced would be critical in the cultural transformation of Scotland ushered in by the Reformation. The initial blueprint for this congregational discipline in the Scots context would come in a 'book of discipline' drawn up several months later which never received parliamentary approval (due mainly to its claims on the revenues of the old church to support the new), but which was nevertheless partially implemented.[12] The organ of congregational discipline would be the kirk session (Scotland's version of the Calvinist consistory), including the parish minister, lay elders and deacons. Such sessions had begun to function openly in Perth, Dundee and St Andrews in 1559. Now they started springing up elsewhere, although it would be decades before many parishes would see them.[13]

While the actions of parliament with regard to religion had technically been illegal, there was little the absentee monarchs could do. Three of the old bishops went along with the changes and served, with varying degrees of enthusiasm and efficiency, in the reformed kirk. The others did not, and continued to enjoy their revenues unmolested. There was little dramatic upheaval and few, if any, martyrs. Rather than facing a frontal assault (as it did in England in the 1530s), Catholicism simply began to wither away. While a reformation had been accomplished in a political sense, the real work of reformation – winning over and indoctrinating the population to a new belief system – had only begun. Scotland might have continued indefinitely in the odd position of being a Protestant (or protestantizing) country with absentee Catholic monarchs if François II had not suddenly died of an ear infection in December 1560. His widow Mary, despite her thoroughly francophone upbringing and outlook, had no great desire to remain as a fifth wheel in the French court now that Guise power was on the wane. Her return to Scotland in August 1561 was bound to bring some matters to a head.

The Return of the Queen and the Planting of the Reformed Kirk

While Mary Stewart appears as just another Jezebel in John Knox's partisan rendition of the Scottish Reformation, she deserves much more credit. She consciously chose a *politique* course, which helped stabilize a very unsettled situation and of course displeased extremists on both sides. When an emissary from the Catholic 4th earl of Huntly invited her to land in Aberdeen instead of Leith, offering an army to re-establish the old religion by force, she declined, opting instead to follow the advice of her half-brother Lord James, a leading figure in the Lords of the Congregation. Huntly's simmering resentment over the queen's refusal to use him as an ally, coupled with her reliance on a younger generation of Protestant advisers, led him into a botched rebellion during a royal progress to Aberdeen and the surrounding country in 1562. Huntly died shortly after his army was routed at Corrichie. Mary's grant to Lord James of the title earl of Moray, which carried significant lands and prestige in the north, had been the last straw, and indeed it was the new earl of Moray who led the army which defeated Huntly. Lord James had travelled to France to advise his half-sister even before her return to Scotland, convincing her of the loyalty of most of her Protestant subjects. She took his advice not to meddle in the religious settlement, as long as she could practise Catholicism in the royal residence of Holyrood. This exception for the queen's court was controversial; Lord James had to guard the door of the chapel when the first mass was performed for the royal entourage, and Knox preached the following Sunday that 'one Mass . . . was more fearful to him than if ten thousand armed enemies were landed in any part of the realm, of purpose to suppress the whole religion.'[14] But cooler heads prevailed.

Knox's aggressive intolerance may have been a reflection of insecurity due to the popularity of the Mass and, by extension, Catholicism in general. Of course, resident courts often set the style for local elites, but contemporary (and probably a bit exaggerated) estimates claimed that 9,000 people attended Easter mass at Holyrood in 1566 and over 12,000 in 1567.[15] It is hard to accept these as literally true (the population of Edinburgh itself was only 10–12,000), but they do reflect a perception that Catholic ceremonies could still draw large numbers. They also show that reformed Protestantism still had a long way to go before it would become the dominant religious outlook of the kingdom.

Queen Mary would give it space to do so; in 1562 she agreed to a funding scheme known as the Thirds of Benefices which left two-thirds of the revenues of the old church in the hands of whoever currently controlled them, but divided the remaining third between the crown and the reformed kirk, to pay for ministerial stipends. To Knox, this meant 'two parts freely given to the Devil, and the third must be divided betwix God and the Devil,' but it was more funding than the landowners who had refused to endorse the *Book of Discipline* had been willing to offer.[16] In fact, it was the last concerted effort to ensure funding for the reformed kirk until Charles I's controversial revocation scheme, introduced in 1625. Also, as a Catholic, Mary lacked interest or qualifications to govern the reformed kirk, leaving it largely free to develop its own structure of local kirk sessions, regional synods and the general assembly, which met twice a year at the national level. Kirk sessions and the general assembly would be mixed bodies of ministers and laymen, although over time ministers (and particularly those of Edinburgh, the Lothians and Fife) would come to dominate the kirk's leadership. The *Book of Discipline* also envisaged the office of superintendent, an official who would handle some of the administrative functions of a bishop by visiting parishes, auditing accounts, convening synods, and so on, all within a particular region. Several superintendents (John Winram, John Willock and John Erskine of Dun were three) were appointed, but the office fell into abeyance in the early 1570s. The kirk's accustomed habit of governing itself would later become controversial when Scotland had a 'godly' (i.e. Protestant) ruler.

Scotland would find itself with such a ruler as the result of a series of political crises ushered in by Mary's choice of a husband in 1565. Religion would be an issue, but the factional politics of the Scottish court are more critical in explaining what happened. As a result, these crises lie mostly outside the scope of this chapter. Suffice to say that Mary's choice of Henry Stewart, Lord Darnley, a handsome, generically Protestant anglicized Scot who also carried some Tudor blood in his veins pleased nobody – not the earl of Moray (Darnley's family, the Lennox Stewarts, would now seek to muscle their way back into Scottish politics), not the Hamiltons (any royal marriage that did not include them would further remove them from the succession), not Elizabeth of England (she was angry at the uniting of two claims to her throne) and, finally, not Mary herself (after the initial infatuation wore off, it became clear that Darnley was an arrogant cad of limited intelligence whose only real contribution would be the siring of the future James VI). In the short run (1565), Moray, the Hamiltons and Argyll went into rebellion. In the middle run (1566), Darnley would spearhead the murder of Mary's private Italian secretary, David Riccio. In the longer run (1567), Darnley himself would be murdered in a mysterious plot (or plots) which may have involved most of the leading political figures in the kingdom, including the queen herself. As all students of British history and afficionados of historical romance know, after another ill-advised marriage, this one to the earl of Bothwell, leading suspect in Darnley's murder, Mary was deposed and defeated by a faction headed by the earl of Moray, and, in 1568, driven into exile in England, where she would remain until her execution nineteen years later. Her *politique* strategy had come completely unglued when mixed with a 'British' marriage. The relative unimportance of religion in these matters is underscored by the compositions of the parties which vied for control of the kingdom in the civil war (1567–73) which followed; while the faction around the infant James was solidly Protestant, the party which supported the queen was a Protestant-Catholic mixture, including Argyll, one of the original signatories of the Band of the Congregation.

Reforming Scottish Society

While the civil war ground on (most intensely in and around Edinburgh) and after, ministers, often assisted by 'godly' laymen, got down to the long and often unwelcome (to many members of their congregations) task of recasting Scottish culture along reformed lines. The early reformed clergy were themselves a mixed bag. Many were former Catholic priests (about a quarter of the old clergy served in the new kirk) who made some superficial changes in their practices but continued many of the traditional rituals, in collusion with their congregations or the lairds who dominated rural parishes. The educational qualifications of many in this first generation were not up to the standards being promulgated by the leadership of the kirk; some were given the title of 'reader' or 'exhorter' rather than minister because they were not regarded as qualified to preach sermons or minister the two Calvinist sacraments, baptism and communion. Some ignored these limitations and continued to baptize (at least) anyway, with their congregations probably ignorant of their apparent demotions. Given the prevalence of infant mortality, belief in the salvific power of baptism continued, and lay people were eager to get it quickly for their children, regardless of what the new official doctrines said. Of course the shortage of qualified men (and stipends to pay them) meant that a reader (if that) was all many parishes, particularly those outside major burghs, were going to see for some time. As late as the mid-1570s, only a quarter of Scots parishes had their own minister. There were additional challenges in the *Gaidhealtachd*, the Highland and Island regions to the north and west of the kingdom where sermons or readings would have to be in Gaelic if they were to be comprehensible to most of the population. These zones were then home to a much higher proportion of the Scots population (perhaps a third) than they are today, and the absence of surviving kirk-session records (in either language) from the Highlands and Islands for the period under consideration has led many historians (including this writer) to conclude that the reformed kirk made little headway there until later.[17]

The going would be hard in some non-Gaelic regions as well. The northerly burgh of Aberdeen provides a good example. William Gordon, pre-Reformation bishop of Aberdeen and relative of the earls of Huntly, never conformed to the reformed kirk, and remained resident in Old Aberdeen (just north of the burgh) until his death in 1577. Aberdeen's government was dominated by the Menzies family, Gordon clients who remained Catholic, despite the fact that several of them served on the burgh's kirk session. Indeed, the first couple of kirk-sessions erected in Aberdeen were Potemkin facades, set up in response to outside pressures in 1562 and 1568. The session did not become permanent until the queen's party was finally defeated at the national level in 1573, and even then it did not much trouble Catholics about their beliefs and practices, except briefly during a 1574 visit by the earl of Morton, then regent of the kingdom, accompanied by the Scottish privy council and the English ambassador.[18] Morton also saw to the removal of the organ and choir stalls from the burgh church. When Aberdeen's kirk session turned its attention to congregational discipline, it was mostly worried about fornication and irregular marriage, issues on which conservative Catholics and reformed Protestants (particularly those of means who sat as elders on the session) could agree. And rather than forcing offenders (male as well as female) to perform public repentance, as was common in more fully reformed burghs such as St Andrews, Perth or Edinburgh, Aberdeen's elders in the 1570s were happy to collect fines instead. Certainly, Aberdeen was not typical (it also resisted the National Covenant in 1638). But neither was Dundee, the 'Geneva of Scotland'. Rather than a single, national movement, Scotland experienced a myriad of local reformations, each one progressing at its own pace according to a logic dictated by local needs and outside pressures.

Over time, kirk sessions (where they existed)[19] would concern themselves with broader cultural issues such as the celebration of Christmas, the practice of witchcraft, pilgrimages to wells or other holy sites, sabbath-breach, gaming, slander, interpersonal violence and even golf. But unlike sexual discipline (which usually involved naming the fathers of illegitimate children, thus helping to ensure support for those who might otherwise become a burden on the parish) these other attempts at behavioural modification were slow to gain acceptance. Sexual indiscretions made up the majority (55 per cent) of the cases of individual misbehaviour handled by kirk sessions in the first half-century of the Scottish Reformation. Walter Younger, a craftsman in St Andrews, may well have spoken for many others when he allegedly told his craft brethren in 1574 that 'he [was] ane yowng man and saw Zuilday [Christmas] kepit halyday, and . . . thetyme may cum that he may see the like yit,' but the elders of the local kirk session forced him to sit in the stool of public repentance during a sermon for this dissent against the cultural revolution of reformed Protestantism, and his countrymen in more remote areas would receive similar messages in the decades which followed.[20] Some kirk sessions would use the jougs (an iron brace similar to the stocks) in tandem with the penitent stool, and/or force offenders to wear special clothing and make public apologies to the congregation. Communion, ideally celebrated four times a year, could only be received by those in possession of tokens, and tokens would only be given to those in good standing with the session. In a more positive pedagogical vein, some sessions would come to require that couples demonstrate that they could recite the Lord's Prayer and Ten Commandments before they would be allowed to marry. Those seeking the roots of Anglo-American puritanism would be well advised to take a close look at the workings of Scottish social discipline in the last decades of the sixteenth century.

Ecclesiastical Politics and the Revival of the Episcopate

One institutional change which helped the disciplinary apparatus function more comprehensively and encouraged more local co-operation within the ministry was the erection of presbyteries, first introduced in 1581, suspended by government order in 1584, and then revived permanently in 1586. Indeed, it is only in the 1580s and after that the reformed kirk of Scotland can properly be called 'presbyterian'. Presbyteries provided an intermediate tier of clerical oversight and professional fellowship, between the level of the local kirk session and the regional synod. At first, they included some lay elders as well as the ministers of all the parishes (typically 15–25) in a district. But, since most of their business was theological rather than disciplinary (recent graduates seeking entrance into the ministry would be tested on their scriptural interpretation) and travel to meetings might take some time, lay elders seem to have stopped attending early on, only to return in the covenanting years of the late 1630s. As with kirk-sessions, it took several decades for presbyteries to spread throughout the kingdom, but they covered the Lowlands (at least) by 1600. The presbytery was proposed, although not explicitly by name, in the *Second Book of Discipline*, a refinement and expansion of the earlier book of 1560, drafted in the late 1570s by a committee which included Andrew Melville, a minister and theology professor (in Glasgow and then St Andrews) who had studied with Pierre Ramus in Paris in the 1560s and then moved on to Theodore Beza's Geneva before returning to Scotland in 1574.[21] In addition to recommending the creation of the 'common eldership' (or presbytery), the *Second Book* provided a blueprint for a more clerically dominated reformed kirk. Its proposals, for an educated clergy policing the general population as well as its own ranks, fiercely independent of any civil magistrate (including the king), were the programme favoured by many members of the second generation of reformed clergy, particularly those active around Edinburgh and in Fife, close enough to attend general assembly meetings regularly.

These 'Melvillians', as some have called them, came into conflict with royal policies on several occasions in the quarter-century or so after 1580 (Andrew Melville himself was sent into permanent exile in 1606). While recent scholarship has suggested that the extent of these conflicts, and the prominence of Melville as a leader of a definable party, have been exaggerated,[22] there certainly were disagreements. These centred on efforts by the crown to carve out a role in governing the kirk, on the extent to which speech from the pulpit was subject to royal regulation, and on how prominent Catholics ought to be treated.

Episcopacy had never been abolished in Scotland. As stated earlier, three Catholic bishops joined the reformers. Starting in 1572, the government led by James Douglas, earl of Morton, sought to incorporate the office of bishop into the reformed kirk and state (the latter is significant because of the traditional role of church officials in the Scottish parliament). Several bishops were appointed (including Morton's kinsman John Douglas, named to the archepiscopal see of St Andrews). But the general assembly, which had become used to governing the kirk with relatively little outside interference during the reign of Mary Queen of Scots, was soon chafing at what seemed to some to be unwanted meddling. The relation of the office of reformed bishop to the office of superintendent, used in the 1560s, was unclear, and the bishops appointed by Morton's administration were regularly censured by the general assembly for lack of diligence. The appointment of Patrick Adamson to the see of St Andrews in 1576 provided the crown with a ready ally, and critics of episcopacy with a prominent target (he held the position until his death in 1592, although he embraced presbyterianism – clearly under duress – in 1591). These problems simmered into the 1580s, as the young king began to govern more in his own name (Morton's regency officially ended in 1578, but the king would continue to use a series of powerful advisers for most of the following decade). Disagreement over how the kirk ought to be governed led to the suspension of presbyteries and the exile to England of several prominent ministers (including Andrew Melville and his nephew James) in 1584. In England, they came into contact with leading English presbyterians such as John Field and Walter Travers, but the fall of the regime led by James Stewart, earl of Arran, brought the exiles back and led to the revival of the presbyteries in 1586.[23] There would be no new episcopal appointees for a while, but from the king's perspective, the problem remained that the general assembly as it had developed left him little official role in the kirk, and if there were going to be no bishops he would be left without a reliable clerical estate in parliament.

Further, some in the general assembly were so determined to limit the king's ecclesiastical role that they seemed far too willing to condone seditious preaching. This was demonstrated most dramatically in the case of David Black, minister of St Andrews, who was summoned to Falkland Palace in 1595 for allegedly impugning the memory of Mary Queen of Scots in a sermon. The following year, he was called before the privy council for another sermon, in which he was said to have labelled all kings as offspring of the devil and suggested that Elizabeth of England was an atheist. On both occasions, Black and his supporters insisted that only the courts of the reformed kirk had any jurisdiction in the matter, and on the second occasion, the leadership of the general assembly spearheaded a campaign of support through the presbyteries which might have gained as many as 400 ministerial signatures.[24] In the end, the council banished Black north of the Tay, and the king's determination to bring the kirk under some form of control was renewed.

Another controversial issue was the treatment of prominent Catholics, particularly the 6th earl of Huntly. Huntly, along with several other noblemen, had been implicated in intrigues with the king of Spain in 1592, and he was also involved in the feud-related slaughter that year of the 'bonnie' but ineffectual earl of Moray. The following September, Huntly and the others were excommunicated by the synod of Fife, with James Melville presiding. But Huntly was a friend of the king, who pardoned him in defiance of the kirk. This confrontation dragged on for several years before James finally persuaded a general assembly called at Dundee in 1597 to lift the sentence against Huntly. To many ministers, this open toleration of a Catholic (and one involved in treason) was an abomination; to James the kirk was meddling in high affairs of state and dictating to him whom he could associate with. As with the controversy over Black, James emerged determined to find ways to manage the kirk. This he did by establishing the precedent that the king alone could determine the time and place of general assembly meetings (meetings north of the Tay, such as that at Dundee, would be easier for clergy from the more conservative north to attend), and by reviving the office of bishop, with the first new appointments coming in 1600. This last pill, bitter to more determined presbyterians, would be sugared by the fact that those chosen to episcopal posts now tended to be men of impressive credentials as preachers and administrators. After 1603, general assemblies met only sporadically, and by 1608 the absent king had ensured that bishops would serve as permanent moderators of presbyteries within their dioceses.

Conclusion

The reformed kirk of Scotland was in a new period of transition when James VI succeeded to the English throne in 1603. It was, and would remain, presbyterian at the local and district level, but higher up it was becoming a hybrid, with bishops serving as agents of royal policy both within the kirk and in the Scottish parliament. Several of them were able and effective in both spheres, and helped push changes in liturgy – such as the Five Articles of Perth (1618) – which were favoured by the king, but resisted by many ministers. Their political influence would be resented by the nobility, to whom this new professionalized clerical administration was not closely connected by blood, as the pre-Reformation bishops had been. As is well known, their place in the kirk and in the Scottish state would be a major point of contention in the late 1630s.

In the parishes, the work of Calvinist acculturation was well under way – but far from complete – when the king took up his southern inheritance. At this level, far removed from the controversies of ecclesiastical politics, Scots culture was being fundamentally transformed. This, in the long run, would be the most significant aspect of the Scottish Reformation, for better or worse. It would be felt by those who still clung to Christmas and other traditional celebrations, by those who preferred fishing, golf or other outlets to the attendance at Sunday preaching, by those inclined to rough speech or violent assault, by those practising informal marriage and, most keenly, by those, especially women, who practised folk medicine or behaved in other ways which might bring them under suspicion of diabolism. Those who claimed to look out for His interests were certain that the God of Reformed Scotland was a jealous master, and quite a lot would be done in His name in seventeenth-century Scotland.

NOTES

1. James VI, *Basilikon Doron*, vol. 1, p. 74.
2. Calderwood, *History of the Kirk*, vol. 4, p. 90.
3. Knox, *History of the Reformation*, vol. 1, pp. 8–10; Sanderson, *Ayrshire and the Reformation*, pp. 36–45.
4. Much of the evidence for Scottish Protestantism before 1560 is cited in Kirk, *Patterns of Reform*, pp. 3–15. In fairness, I should point out that Dr Kirk sees a much stronger pre-1560 reform movement than I do.
5. Knox, *History of the Reformation*, vol. 1, pp. 68–74.
6. For Beaton's murder, the siege of the castle and its aftermath, with a particular focus on the role of John Knox, see Edington, 'Knox and the Castilians'.
7. Wormald, *Lords and Men*; Brown, *Bloodfeud in Scotland*.
8. Donaldson, *Scottish Historical Documents*, pp. 116–17. Jane Dawson has recently argued that the last extant signature on the bond is that of John Erskine, the future earl of Mar and not John Erskine of Dun, as was previously believed. See Dawson, *Politics of Religion*, p. 24 n.52.
9. Lynch, *Edinburgh and the Reformation*, pp. 31–2, 37–9, 76, 83–5; Kirk, *Patterns of Reform*, pp. 1–15.
10. Dawson, *Politics of Religion*, pp. 1–2, 100–3. This strategy was abandoned by both parties in 1565.
11. Henderson, *Scots Confession*, p. 75.
12. Cameron, *First Book of Discipline*.
13. For the fitful but (in the end) very significant progress of discipline, see Graham, *Uses of Reform*.
14. Knox, *History of the Reformation*, vol. 2, p. 12.
15. Lynch, *Edinburgh and the Reformation*, p. 188; and 'John Knox, Minister of Edinburgh', p. 262.
16. Knox, *History of the Reformation*, vol. 2, p. 29.

17. For dissenting views, see Kirk, *Patterns of Reform*, pp. 449–87 and Dawson, 'Calvinism in the *Gaidhealtachd*', pp. 231–53.
18. White, 'Regent Morton's Visitation'.
19. As late as 1596, the general assembly felt compelled to remind ministers that they were expected to set up sessions in their parishes. See Thomson, *Acts and Proceedings*, vol. 3, p. 865.
20. Fleming, *Register of the Minister, Elders and Deacons of the Christian Congregation of St Andrews*, vol. 1, pp. 389–90.
21. Kirk, *Second Book of Discipline*.
22. MacDonald, *Jacobean Kirk*.
23. Donaldson, *Scottish Church History*, pp. 178–90.
24. Graham, *Uses of Reform*, pp. 209–10; MacDonald, *Jacobean Kirk*, pp. 66–8.

BIBLIOGRAPHY

Brown, Keith, *Bloodfeud in Scotland, 1573–1625: Violence, Justice and Politics in an Early Modern Society* (Edinburgh, 1986).
Calderwood, David, *The History of the Kirk of Scotland by Mr. David Calderwood*, ed. T. Thomson (8 vols, Edinburgh, 1842–9).
Cameron, James, ed., *The First Book of Discipline* (Edinburgh, 1972).
Dawson, Jane E. A., 'Calvinism in the *Gaidhealtachd* in Scotland', in A. Pettegree, A. Duke and G. Lewis, eds, *Calvinism in Europe, 1540–1620* (Cambridge, 1994), pp. 231–53.
Dawson, Jane E. A., *The Politics of Religion in the Age of Mary, Queen of Scots: The Earl of Argyll and the Struggle for Britain and Ireland* (Cambridge, 2002).
Donaldson, Gordon, *Scottish Church History* (Edinburgh, 1985).
Donaldson, Gordon, ed., *Scottish Historical Documents* (Edinburgh, 1970), pp. 116–17.
Edington, Carol, 'Knox and the Castilians: a crucible of reforming opinion?', in Roger Mason, ed., *John Knox and the British Reformations* (Aldershot, 1998), pp. 29–50.
Fleming, D. Hay, ed., *Register of the Minister, Elders and Deacons of the Christian Congregation of St Andrews 1559–1600* (2 vols, Edinburgh, 1889–90).
Graham, Michael, *The Uses of Reform: 'Godly Discipline' and Popular Behavior in Scotland and Beyond, 1560–1610* (Leiden, 1996).
Henderson, G. D., ed., *The Scots Confession, 1560 and the Negative Confession, 1581* (Edinburgh, 1937).
James VI, *The Basilikon Doron of King James VI*, ed. J. Craigie (2 vols, Edinburgh, 1944–50).
Kirk, James, *Patterns of Reform: Continuity and Change in the Reformation Kirk* (Edinburgh, 1989).
Kirk, James, ed., *The Second Book of Discipline* (Edinburgh, 1980).
Knox, John, *John Knox's History of the Reformation in Scotland*, ed. W. C. Dickinson (2 vols, London, 1949).
Lynch, Michael, *Edinburgh and the Reformation* (Edinburgh, 1981).
Lynch, Michael, 'John Knox, minister of Edinburgh and commissioner of the kirk', in Roger Mason, ed., *John Knox and the British Reformations* (Aldershot, 1998), pp. 242–63.
MacDonald, Alan, *The Jacobean Kirk, 1567–1625: Sovereignty, Polity and Liturgy* (Aldershot, 1998).
Sanderson, Margaret H. B., *Ayrshire and the Reformation: People and Change, 1490–1600* (East Linton, 1997).
Thomson, Thomas, ed., *Acts and Proceedings of the General Assemblies of the Kirk of Scotland* (3 vols, Edinburgh, 1839–45).

White, Allan, 'The regent Morton's visitation: the Reformation of Aberdeen, 1574', in A. A. MacDonald, Michael Lynch and Ian Cowan, eds, *The Renaissance in Scotland* (Leiden, 1994), pp. 246–63.

Wormald, Jenny, *Lords and Men in Scotland: Bonds of Manrent, 1442–1603* (Edinburgh, 1985).

FURTHER READING

Frank Bardgett, *Scotland Reformed: The Reformation in Angus and the Mearns* (1989). A good early regional study of the Scottish Reformation, particularly strong on the role played by lairds and other local notables.

Keith Brown, *Bloodfeud in Scotland, 1573–1625: Violence, Justice and Politics in an Early Modern Society* (1986). A thorough examination of one of the more controversial aspects of early modern Scottish culture, and one which Protestant ideology certainly influenced.

David Calderwood, *The History of the Kirk of Scotland by Mr. David Calderwood*, ed. T. Thomson (8 vols, 1842–9). Calderwood, who wrote in the midst of seventeenth-century controversies over the intentions of early reformers, cannot be trusted entirely, but the bulk of this work makes it an essential resource for the history of the Scottish Reformation.

Ian Cowan, *The Scottish Reformation* (1982) updated, but did not replace, Gordon Donaldson's work of the same title. Cowan is particularly strong in his awareness of the regional variations in the Scottish Reformation.

Jane E. A. Dawson, *The Politics of Religion in the Age of Mary, Queen of Scots: The Earl of Argyll and the Struggle for Britain and Ireland* (2002). A recent study of a major figure in the era of the Scottish Reformation which is stronger on politics and diplomacy than on religious issues.

Gordon Donaldson, *The Scottish Reformation* (1960) is still the essential starting point for any student interested in the subject.

Gordon Donaldson, *All The Queen's Men: Power and Politics in Mary Stewart's Scotland* (1983). A detailed study of the factionalism of the mid-to-late sixteenth century which stresses the importance of family and patronage ties over those of religion.

Gordon Donaldson, *Scottish Church History* (1985) is a collection of Donaldson's most important (and widely cited) essays on the Scottish Reformation.

Linda Dunbar, *Reforming the Scottish Church: John Winram (c. 1492–1582) and the Example of Fife* (2002) examines the career of one of Scotland's reformers and assesses his impact on an important region.

Walter Roland Foster, *The Church Before the Covenants: The Church of Scotland 1596–1638* (1975) examines key institutional issues such as provision to the ministry, finance, the revival of bishoprics, etc.

Julian Goodare (ed.), *The Scottish Witch-hunt in Context* (2002) provides the results of the most recent research into the Scottish witch-hunt, which coincided with the Reformation and cannot be understood without reference to it.

Michael Graham, *The Uses of Reform: 'Godly Discipline' and Popular Behavior in Scotland and Beyond, 1560–1610* (1996) studies the impact of the Reformation on several urban and rural communities through the lens of social discipline (morals control).

James Kirk, *Patterns of Reform: Continuity and Change in the Reformation Kirk* (1989). Kirk has written several important essays on aspects of the Scottish Reformation, and this volume collects them together. His general thesis is that Scotland's Reformation was both popular and Calvinist from the start.

John Knox, *John Knox's History of the Reformation in Scotland*, ed. W. C. Dickinson (2 vols, 1949). Like Calderwood (who used him as a source), Knox cannot be trusted entirely, particularly in the starring role he wrote for himself in this drama. But this *History* cannot be ignored, either. It has had a huge impact on our perception of the period, and is our only source for some of its events.

Christina Larner, *Enemies of God: The Witch-hunt in Scotland* (1981). Not about the Reformation *per se*, this book is nevertheless critical to understanding the culture of Reformation-era Scotland, particular since clergy and pious laymen were at times active witch-hunters.

Michael Lynch, *Edinburgh and the Reformation* (1981) is a revisionist view of the history of the Reformation in Scotland's capital, suggesting that the reform programme was not particularly popular at first, but that a popular Protestantism was emerging by the 1580s.

Alan MacDonald, *The Jacobean Kirk, 1567–1625: Sovereignty, Polity and Liturgy* (1998) takes a primarily narrative approach to analyzing the Reformed Kirk as an institution. Revisionist in its tendency to stress consensus rather than controversy, particularly in the discussions of the role of episcopacy.

Roger Mason (ed.), *John Knox and the British Reformations* (1998). Proceedings from a 1997 conference which examine various aspects of the career and ideas of Scotland's most famous (or infamous) reformer.

David Mullan, *Episcopacy in Scotland: The History of an Idea, 1560–1638* (1986). Episcopacy proved to be one of the most controversial issues in the Scottish Reformation, and the question was not really settled in Scotland until 1690. This book studies the issue during the early, formative period.

David Mullan, *Scottish Puritanism, 1590–1638* (2000). A tremendously detailed study of the 'puritan' world-view as it developed in Scotland, which suggests minimal Arminian influence up to 1638.

Margaret H. B. Sanderson, *Ayrshire and the Reformation: People and Change, 1490–1600* (1997). Study of a region in which there was some history of Lollardy before the Reformation. Regards Protestantism as a grassroots movement.

Thomas Thomson (ed.), *Acts and Proceedings of the General Assemblies of the Kirk of Scotland* (3 vols, 1839–45). Sometimes called the *Book of the Universal Kirk*, or *BUK*, this is all that remains of the official proceedings of the general assemblies during the era of the Scottish Reformation.

Margo Todd, *The Culture of Protestantism in Early Modern Scotland* (2002) delineates an emergent Protestant 'culture' in the Reformation era. This work is very strong on describing that culture, less so on analysing the process which gave birth to it. Contains valuable photographic material.

Arthur Williamson, *Scottish National Consciousness in the Age of James VI* (1979). A brilliant book which is about a lot more than its title suggests. In general, it is a study of the impact of the Reformation on Scotland's intellectual culture.

PART III

People and Groups

Introduction

The tendency of people to live in communities is as old as organized society itself. Aristotle saw that the family constituted the primary building block of all societies, and he worked upwards from there to extol the importance of social groupings which were increasingly large and complex. Along with the need for security, the imperative for social and economic interaction has been the prime motivator for such comings together, indeed for the formation of most sorts of communities.

A discussion of this issue might take many forms, as (with rare exceptions) single individuals always belonged to several groups, many of them arranged in concentric patterns. The town butcher belonged to his family, both immediate and extended, but also probably to his parish, his fraternity or religious guild prior to the Reformation, his craft guild, the town's freemanry and perhaps one of its governing councils, the town in a broader sense, the hundred, the county, the nation and so forth. Both the butcher and his wife also belonged to gender groups. Many activities were exclusively reserved for either men or women, and even group activities, such as worship, were experienced differently by each gender. Recent scholarship has begun exploring the gendered nature of those roles, with the roles of women, as we see in Anne Laurence's essay (chapter 22), being given particular prominence.

In designing this volume, we have decided to approach groups of this sort by emphasizing the economic and social environments in which they formed and operated: whether rural or urban and, if urban, whether town, city or metropolis. We have tipped the balance slightly to the urban side of the rural/urban equation because that configuration more accurately reflects the relative balance of recent scholarship. The resurgence of interest in urban society from the mid-1970s forward has made it the more pressing area of historiographical concern. Though scholarship on agrarian issues has a lengthier pedigree, our understanding of it has changed somewhat less in recent decades than has our understanding of urban history.

Notwithstanding that admitted bias in what follows, Richard Hoyle provides an excellent summary of recent work in addressing the agrarian economy of the era. His essay makes a useful point of comparison with what Alan Dyer, Joseph Ward and Robert Tittler have to say about the economy and society of the urban world. Dyer's description of the urban economy in general provides a succinct summary of the quite considerable scholarship devoted to that subject over the past generation. Joseph Ward addresses the complexities of London's groupings by attending succinctly to its governing structure as well as its economic and social role as Britain's one true metropolis. Robert Tittler summarizes current work on urban society in general, and especially considers the interaction of individual people and the groups to which they belonged. Anne Laurence's essay summarizes recent scholarship on the role of women in the British Isles, providing especially useful insights into the Scottish and Irish as well as the English scene.

A last word must be said about the uneven distribution of scholarship devoted to the different parts of the British Isles. Save for Anne Laurence, whose subject has justifiably enjoyed something of a privileged position in recent scholarship, our authors have been constrained by the vast preponderance of scholarly attention paid to the English scene as opposed to the rest of the British Isles. Again it would appear that historians of Ireland, Scotland and Wales – far fewer in number to begin with – have been preoccupied with questions regarding political traditions and both ethnic and national identities. Their English counter-parts, who have inherited a much deeper historiography on questions of politics and identity, have felt freer to address social, economic and other more current issues. We have tried to right that imbalance as best we can in view of current scholarship, and also at least implicitly to suggest where the scholarly catching-up must be done.

CHAPTER EIGHTEEN

Rural Economy and Society

R. W. HOYLE

The very extent of the British Isles means that there was no one rural economy in the sixteenth and seventeenth centuries but several, each adapted to the local geography. In the lowland south and east of the islands, the prevailing crops were wheat and barley, sown in rotation, often integrated into farming systems with sheep. In large parts of central England, arable cultivation had substantially disappeared by 1600 and the economy was based on sheep and (increasingly) cattle-rearing. The west and north of England, Wales and much of lowland Scotland had an economy based on hardier grains with a shorter growing season – barley, oats – which were more dependable where the climate was unreliable and prone to be wet and cold, and on cattle and sheep. In Gaelic Ireland (that part of Ireland in which the forms and habits of Anglo-Norman government and settlement had been lost), the economy was based on oats, cattle and butter. There the land was lightly populated, settlement was shifting and transhumance widely practised.

These economies, ranging from sophisticated commercial agriculture to shifting subsistence cultivation, do not simply reflect the schoolboy checklist of altitude, rainfall and temperature but an equally basic geographical factor. Taken as a whole, the British Isles lay on the edges of Europe. The south-east of England was best placed to trade with the economic powerhouses of late medieval Europe – the Low Countries, the Rhineland and northern Italy – and so it is no coincidence that the English capital (which was also its largest city, major port, prime capital market and leading industrial centre) was located on a river estuary facing the Low Countries. Not only was corn occasionally shipped over the southern North Sea (either to the Low Countries or, in times of desperate need, imported into England), but large (and growing) quantities of finished and semi-finished cloth were sent from England's eastern and southern ports into Europe. The Atlantic-facing side of the British Isles was locationally disadvantaged, and would remain so until the development of the Atlantic economy.

It was the ease of access into the European markets for textiles which made the rural economy of the south-east into much more than an agrarian economy: it was the relative density of population, whether in London, towns generally or in the countryside itself, which made agriculture here orientated towards production for sale. The western and northern parts of Britain were not without commercial contacts with Europe. That cloth from Westmorland was supplied to the Continent through Southampton at the beginning of the sixteenth century has long been commented upon. As we shall see, the Scots had well-established export trades with France, the Baltic and Scandinavia. But the broad case remains true. Europe, and European demand, made south-eastern England more populous and its agriculture more commercially orientated than any other part of the British Isles.

The further one moves outside this core, the smaller the stimulus agriculture received. This had other implications for the economy. There is no doubt that the English countryside was entirely monetarized by the twelfth century. It is true that some rents and notably tithes were still gathered in kind but the English thought instinctively in coin. In Ireland beyond the Pale and in the highlands of Scotland, the payment of rent in the form of grain, animals or even hospitality was entirely normal at the beginning of the sixteenth century and had by no means disappeared at the beginning of the seventeenth. To English eyes, rents in commodities were archaic. Their policy in Ireland was to convert them into fixed money rents, with disastrous consequences for those who received them. That landlords in the north and west of the British Isles still received rents in commodities rather than money may reflect not a preference but a necessity: it reflects the weakly developed urban sector and, in turn, the lack of integration of these peripheral areas into the larger trading system. The only major town in Ireland was Dublin, and whilst it may have been the sixth largest British town, its market stimulus cannot have reached far. Within Ireland as a whole, there was a lack of commercial (as opposed to subsistence) production even at the end of the century. This is reflected in the products it traded with England. It must be admitted that in 1559/60 some 26,556 yards of cloth were imported through Bristol from Irish ports, but an expatriate writer in 1585 held that 'this realm [Ireland] hath not any other working of cloth than frieze or blanketing, which is of very small quality and excepting Waterford and Kilkenny [is found] in few other places'.[1] The more typical Irish exports into England were unprocessed or part-processed primary products: hides, wool, tallow (a by-product of a pastoral economy), fish, timber and linen yarn, to be woven in the textile industry about Manchester. There may also have been an unknown quality of grain. Likewise, Scots exports were largely products which had undergone only the basic value-added processing. In the 1560s and 1570s they exported enormous numbers of hides into the Baltic – in the 1560s and 1570s over a million a year – and cloth and salt to Sweden, in return for timber, iron ore and, in some years, Baltic grain. They exported fish, skins, hides, coarse cloth and wool to France in return for salt, wine and manufactured goods. Only towards the end of the century did Anglo-Scottish trade really begin: it was a gibe made at the time of the unification of the crowns that all the Scots had to offer in the way of trade was poor quality fish and worse cloth.

I

From this prologue, it is possible to disentangle some of the themes of this essay. It is impossible to discuss the rural economy without reference to population, towns and markets, nor it possible to consider the British rural economy as though it were a single entity. Moreover, no one would attempt to discuss it as an unchanging or undynamic economic regime.

Let us begin with population. For England we have reliable estimates from the 1540s onwards: for Scotland we have little more than an impressionistic sense of the direction of change. (Irish population movements follow a completely different trajectory.)

Before the modern growth of population which began after 1750, the number of the English is known to have moved within broad limits.[2] After a long period of growth, it has been estimated that English population c.1300 lay at about 5–6 million persons. By the middle of the fifteenth century an oppressive disease regime, possibly coupled with late age at marriage (and so low marital fertility) had reduced it to two million or, on some estimates, even less. For whatever reason, this trend was reversed in the late fifteenth or early sixteenth century. An estimate of 2.3 million based on the tax records of 1524–5 is compatible with the figure computed for 1541 from parish register data of 2.774 million; by 1600 the computed figure is 4.1 million. Growth was not completely linear: there was a major famine and epidemic (of influenza) in the mid- and late 1550s which may have reduced the national population by as much as 20 per cent. But the rate of growth before this reverse was historically very high – 0.8–1.0 per cent per annum – diminishing in the second half of the century. The great increase progressively ran out of steam in the seventeenth century. English population peaked at 5.3 million in the 1650s, and then remained static at about 4.9 million until the early eighteenth century. The startling consequence of these figures is that it was certainly the early seventeenth century before English population reached the levels of c.1300: it may have been after 1750 before it exceeded it.

What is immediately clear is that population numbers broadly doubled in the sixteenth century. Contemporary comment in the first half of the century often referred to the shortage of people: by the 1580s and 1590s comment was directed at the consequences of their superabundance. In part this was because the growth in population was not even but resulted in a much higher proportion of the national population living in towns.[3] The best estimate of the size of the urban population in c.1520 suggests that about 125,000 people or 5 per cent of the national population lived in towns of 5,000 people or more, of whom perhaps 55 per cent were resident in London. By 1600 this had risen to about 8 per cent (335,000 out of a population of 4.1m) of whom 200,000 (say 60 per cent of the urban and 5 per cent of the national population) lived in London. Estimates have also been prepared of the proportion of the national population engaged in non-agricultural pursuits (and so dependent on markets for their foodstuffs). In 1520 this has been placed at about 24 per cent, in 1600 30 per cent. But this non-agricultural sector was not simply urban: at the two dates about 20 per cent and 24 per cent respectively of the rural population were not engaged in agricultural production. The growth in people resulted in stronger growth in the urban rather than the rural sectors: it also produced an increase in the proportion engaged in rural trade and manufacture. Whilst the growth in absolute numbers and the increase in the proportion of the population dependent upon the market for foodstuffs offered great opportunities for farmers, it also created a range of social problems which we will consider later in this essay.

This account has – so far – ignored what may be taken to be the key issue. Why did population grow so fast in the sixteenth century but slow down (and finally go into stasis) in the seventeenth? There is no easy answer to the first of these questions. As we saw, population was already growing before we have the earliest parish register data. Indeed, it seems likely that the pivotal half-century between 1470 and 1520 will, for want of data, always remain one of the least understood periods in English demographic history. It is possible that renewed population growth reflects an alleviation in the mortality regime of the fifteenth century but is perhaps more likely that there was some alteration in the marriage regime. It has been suggested that it was a characteristic of the market for labour in the fifteenth century that a relatively prosperous urban sector employed large numbers of young women as domestic servants. Service was incompatible with marriage, so the character of the employment opportunities available acted to delay marriage and so reduce the number of births to each married woman. By analogy with late-seventeenth-century conditions, a prevalence of domestic service might also be connected with a high level of lifelong celibacy, again a factor contributing to a low gross reproduction rate. And so it has been suggested that the growth of population, whenever it began, may indicate changes in the pattern of employment in the urban sector which made marriage easier to achieve. Whilst this is demographically plausible, it must be acknowledged that this hypothesis is based on a reading of the fifteenth-century urban economy which has never been universally accepted.[4]

It is easier to explain why population ceased to grow. Whilst population near to doubled, there was no similar increase in the number of employment opportunities. The depopulation of those parts of the countryside where arable communities had been converted into pastoral sheep ranches was not reversed. Equally the process whereby several tenements had been brought together to make one when the demand for land had been low in the fifteenth century was not reversed in the sixteenth. Population flowed from arable communities – the fielden – to pastoral and woodland areas – the arden – where there were opportunities for the building of houses on waste land.[5] It is possible that these cottages had de facto rights to graze on the commons of the villages in which they were situated and that these rights formed a major part of the livelihood of the cottagers, which they supplemented by employment in textiles and other crafts. Most however had little or no land attached to them, a situation which a statute of 1589 tried to remedy by insisting that each new cottage had four acres of land. As some communities were open to migrants where others were not, the social and cultural experience of arden and fielden communities (or 'cheese' and 'chalk') increasingly differed, with the arable communities tending to be dominated by landlords where pastoral ones were prone to be more populous, less well-disciplined and plagued by the poor.[6]

Pastoral communities, with their large numbers of artisans, were notably vulnerable to economic downturns. They were reliant on the market not only for their food, but for the sale of the fruits of their labours. Rises in food prices arising out of harvest shortfalls (years of what contemporaries called 'dearth'), by forcing people to devote a larger proportion of their income to food, reduced the market for manufactured goods (such as textiles) and thereby produced unemployment amongst textile workers. Moreover, the reduction in spending power produced by higher grain prices may also have limited the market for higher quality, protein-based foodstuffs – meat, butter, cheese – as men and women tried to keep away hunger with bread, pottage and ale. And so it has been suggested that specialist pastoral farmers saw their markets collapse in years of high grain prices. It is significant that the two north Essex vil-lages where the 'present dearth of grain hath caused a great and lamentable cry of the poor there inhabiting' in January 1595 were described as 'pasture towns . . . and little or no tillage used by them'.[7] We must suppose that they relied on others for their grain but in this difficult year had no money to spend. It was not only single villages which were vulnerable in this way, but extensive areas of the north and west of England.

Superficially, the pattern of poor harvest years in the sixteenth century can be read as showing that population had grown too far and that a Malthusian positive check – famine – had been invoked to scythe population back down to a sustainable level. If we take the years of worst crisis after 1550 (as indicated by the movement of prices), we find they tend to bunch together at the end of the century: 1551, 1555, 1556, 1562, 1586, 1595, 1596, 1597. Certainly 1586–8 and the years of the mid-1590s were desperate in the north of England, but the parish register evidence also shows instances of crisis mortality in counties as far south as Essex, Kent and Suffolk (although not in eastern England or the east midlands).[8] The actions taken by gov-ernment to alleviate crisis were, by the end of the sixteenth century, very familiar. Commissions were established in the dearth year of 1527 and given instructions to carry out local censuses of corn, to ensure that the stocks they discovered were brought to the market in an orderly fashion without profiteering, and to regulate the activities of middlemen. Similar orders were reissued in the dearth years 1549–50, 1550–1 and again in 1556–7. In 1586–7 they were codified and reissued as *Orders desired by the especial commandment of Her Majesty for the relief and stay of the present dearth of corn within this realm*. This book of dearth orders was then reissued again in 1594 and 1595, 1608, 1622 and (for the last time) 1630.

Activism by magistrates at times of dearth was one of the unspoken contracts between rulers and ruled. It may be doubted whether the *Orders* made the difference between life and death, but by ordering that grain was to be sold in the open market, that the poor were to be helped by giving them a right of pre-emption in the market place (and farmers were exhorted to sell to them at less than market rates at the farm gate out of charity), even instructing that work was to be found for the poor, it showed a concern for their predicament. In fact some of the orders may have worked against the interest of the poor. Attempts to limit the amount of grain expended in brewing probably derived them of a key element in their diet, whilst the determination to have grain 'exposed' for sale in the open market disrupted the networks of badgers who sold grain door to door. Local attempts to maintain supplies and morale could all too easily be disrupted by instructions from the privy council to move grain to London: the sight of foodstuffs being carried out of reach provoked occasional disturbances, as in April 1586 when a number of barques carrying grain down the River Severn were boarded by crowds and their contents rifled. The rioters, it was reported by the Gloucestershire JPs, were unable to buy food because they had been laid off by clothiers: 'so great was their necessity . . . that . . . they were driven to feed their children with oats, docks and roots of nettles with such other things as they could come by'.[9] The fear of disturbances in London always preoccupied the privy council and so the maintenance of food supplies there at the cost of additional hunger in the countryside was seen as an acceptable trade.

Localized peaks in mortality are obvious in parish registers. Less obvious are the other signs of distress: a rise in illegitimacy as marriages were delayed, an increase in petty criminality as people thieved to eat; or in the numbers who took to the roads looking for urban charity: what cannot be recovered is the suffering of men and women reduced to famine foods.[10] But years of distress like these were caused less by too many mouths than by a sudden downturn in the supply of food caused by harvest failure, itself the result of unusual and adverse weather.

One cannot see harvest crisis (or disease mortality) determining the slowing of late-sixteenth-century population growth. What brought about the downturn in growth was an insidious fall in real wages prompted by the tendency of labour supply to outrun demand. Real wages fell by about 60 per cent between 1500 and 1600. In turn this meant that people had to wait longer to marry: but it is the discovery of Wrigley and Schofield that the crucial determinant of population growth was not age at marriage but the proportion marrying. Of those born between 1556 and 1571 (and so of marrying age from say 1580–1600), about one in 20 was still unmarried at the age of 40. Of those born in 1576–86 it was three in 20: of those born between 1591 and 1616 (so looking to marry in the 1620s), it was between four and five in 20. The consequences be seen in the gross reproduction rate estimated by Wrigley and Schofield. This gives us the average number of *female* births to women aged between 15 and 44 who survived through the full thirty-year period. For women born in the mid-sixteenth century, it stood at about 2.8: by the end of the century it had reached 2.4 and by the middle of the seventeenth century it had reached 2.0.[11] This then is a Malthusian prudential check: it controlled population by delaying or denying marriage.

II

Whilst there were years of high prices (and in some locations genuine distress) at the end of the sixteenth and beginning of the seventeenth century, English farming seems to have been capable of sustaining, at a reasonable level, a population which was double that of around 1520. How was this done?

In truth, we do not really know. There is little evidence of technical innovation in the sixteenth century. The area under arable cultivation was increased through the enclosure of waste; but it was also diminished by arable being converted to pasture and so it is not obvious that the area under bread crops expanded significantly. Once farmers were confident of a market for their produce, they may have raised outputs by adjusting the management of their farms, by increasing sowing rates, manuring their ground more heavily and ploughing more thoroughly to eradicate weeds (and committing more labour to weeding standing crops). On the other hand, it has also been suggested that the expansion on to marginal land – whether upland or heath – and the proliferation of squatter holdings may have diminished agricultural productivity on some measures.[12]

Enclosure is a convenient portmanteau word within which is included a whole range of processes.[13] (That enclosure implied different things in different places is indicated by the 1536 and other statutes against depopulating enclosure which only applied to the midland counties.) It includes the consolidation of arable land held as strips in common fields as well as the enclosure of waste land (heath, fen, moorland) and the abolition of common rights, whether exercised over arable or over waste. When waste was enclosed, land which had been used in a relatively unintensive fashion for grazing came to be used more intensively, perhaps even as arable; but the enclosure of waste was often about securing control over land, whether contested between communities, or between landlords and tenants or between the larger farmers and commoners (including the cottagers mentioned earlier). But where arable was enclosed in the fifteenth and sixteenth centuries, the outcome, particularly in midland England, was its conversion from arable to pasture with a consequent loss of employment and so rural depopulation. Enclosure of this sort often went hand in hand with engrossment (where farms were merged into larger units): contemporaries sometimes muddled engrossment with enclosure and certainly talked of them as twin evils.

Because of the implication that enclosure equalled conversion to pasture and so depopulation, it was illegal throughout the sixteenth century except for a short period after 1593, the key statute being one of 1515, 'for avoiding [preventing] of the pulling down of towns', which was reinforced in a number of occasions. Enforcement was a different matter. Government attention was intermittent: indeed, a blind eye was turned except on those occasions when it was politic to be seen to be enforcing the statutes. The normal method was to establish county commissions to investigate enclosure. Those identified might then be prosecuted. This was done by Cardinal Wolsey in 1517 and 1518, and whilst an older generation of historians held that this was for show, we now know that at least 264 legal actions followed the commissions and that in some cases litigation dragged on into the 1530s. What the crown sought was the rebuilding of houses and the restoration of land to arable. Further commissions were launched in 1548 and 1549, prompted by the high prices of these years and again in 1565. In 1607 rioting directed at recent enclosures in the east midlands prompted a revival of the enclosure commissions, backed by prosecutions in Star Chamber. Hand in hand with statutes against enclosure was legislation to try and limit the number of sheep. A statute of 1534 attempted to deter enclosure and conversion by limiting the number of sheep which an individual could keep: a further statute of 1549 tried to make sheep farming less profitable by instituting a tax on sheep but this was repealed within a matter of months.

It will be suggested later that the disturbances of 1549 made landlords (and the government) very cautious of agrarian change which might alienate and provoke the peasantry. There may be something of the same in enclosure: but by 1593 any caution that there might have been had been dispelled by a succession of good harvests and the whole body of anti-enclosure legislation was repealed. It has been suggested that the progress of enclosure accelerated in the early 1590s but it is a moot point whether this was because enclosure was newly permissible or because it was a reaction to low grain prices.

Depopulating enclosure was a regional phenomena. It occurred in areas which suffered the twin disadvantages of heavy soils but a limited local market stimulus: where access to London was difficult, the depopulation of the countryside further reduced local demand. But legislating against enclosure was like damming a stream with pebbles: the economic logic of the situation, which pointed towards enclosure and conversion, could not be restrained by legislation. For contemporaries living in these areas, and particularly those who suffered empty stomachs in years of high prices, the spread of hedges and fences over tilled ground was symbolic not of inevitable economic progress but of private profit being placed over the public good. The hungry and deluded men in the villages to the north of Oxford who talked of rebellion in November 1596 lived in a landscape which had been incrementally enclosed over their lives. Their recruiting ground included Begbroke, enclosed in the early 1590s, the landlord of which had 'most pitifully defaced the said village and undone his poor tenants by hedging and ditching and enclosing . . . and by unreasonable raising of his rents from sixteen nobles [£5 6s. 8d.] a year unto £100 and upwards' which necessitated enclosing all but five of the sixteen yardlands there.[14] This experience was replicated elsewhere in the south and east midlands in the last quarter of the sixteenth century and the years immediately following. Whilst government was impotent to restrain these economic changes, there is a plausible connection to be drawn between this failed rebellion in Oxfordshire and the re-enactment of enclosure legislation the following year.

So we have a paradox. The population grew overall and the urban population inched upwards as a proportion of the whole. But whilst Malthusian preventive checks – which we see operating through the rising age and declining rate of marriage – probably came into play, there was no general crisis, and the food supply was sufficiently strong that low arable prices, higher wool and animal prices, and locational disadvantage encouraged large areas of arable to be converted into pasture.

III

One of the basic contradictions of the sixteenth-century countryside is that as population rose and both the demand for land and the opportunity to sell produce increased, rents seem to have remained relatively flat. In fact access to land became increasingly restricted. There was no reconversion of grassland laid down in the fifteenth century (indeed the process continued throughout the sixteenth). Within many arable communities the number of holdings diminished as they were engrossed, price pressure making small holdings uneconomic. Whilst there was probably a continuing demand for small tenements, there was no livelihood to be made out of subsistence farming in an increasingly market-orientated and commercial world. From the tenants' point of view, the best profits were to be made out of increasingly large arable holdings, often held by copyhold, or low-labour-input extensive sheep and cattle farming on leaseholds. Neither option served to reward landlords with the sorts of rent rises they might have expected. They had an added urgency to increase rents because of inflation. Throughout the century there was a slow increase in prices, but monetary inflation, caused by the reduction in the precious-metal content of the currency between 1544 and 1552, around halved the purchasing power of money. Both population pressure and inflation should have stimulated landlords to increase rents, but their ability to do so was limited by a number of factors, both institutional (the character of tenure) and social.

We can approach this by a consideration of rent and tenure. Money, rather than labour or produce rents, were normal and often took the form of an entry fine paid by an incoming tenant and an annual rent paid by the same tenant. Tenure, which is the relationship between lord and tenant, was informed by ideas of custom and contract and was regulated by law: tenants had recourse to the courts to defend their position against their lords. Tenures came in four broad types. At one extreme there was freehold in which the freeholder had as near a right of absolute possession as the law allowed whilst paying a fixed and notional rent. At the other extreme were tenants who held on annual contracts, whose rents varied from year to year: these were tenants 'on the rack' (that is tenants stretched as far as they could be). But the majority of farmers held by either forms of contractual tenancy or customary tenancy. Contractual tenancies – leaseholds – were negotiated for a fixed period of time in an open market. The lord could accept the best rent he could secure: he was under no obligation to his previous tenant.

In customary tenancies however, the tenants held according to the custom of the manor. The most familiar types of customary tenure are copyhold of inheritance, found in eastern England, and tenant right, found throughout the northern counties.[15] Custom accorded tenants holding by these tenures a series of rights over their land which were inimical to their lords – the right to a fixed *annual* rent, a right of sale, a right of inheritance and increasingly the right to sublet – all of which could be protected by the courts. Lords were not opposed to such rights at the beginning of the sixteenth century when inheritance ensured a supply of tenants at a time when the demand for land was flat and the possibility of raising rents limited. Indeed, a few lords can be found creating estates of inheritance at this time. But custom prevented lords raising the *rents* of these properties although they might be able to raise the level of the *entry fines*: but the rule was that the entry fine could not be so large as to defeat the right of inheritance.

The implication of these differing tenures for landlords is plain enough. Lords with leaseholds could take advantage of the rising demand for land and – in time – overcome the worst effects of inflation. Lords with customary tenants had an asset which yielded less and less over time. Particularly after the mid-century inflation, there was an imperative for lords to convert customary tenancies into leaseholds with market rents. Unfortunately for them, copyhold could not simply be abrogated in the sixteenth century: tenants clung to it (for obvious reasons) and their claims of custom were frequently supported by the courts. In the north-west of England, tenants who claimed to hold by tenant right were involved in a violent confrontation with their lords during the autumn of 1536 (the existence of which has been masked by the Pilgrimage of Grace) during which they attempted to secure their lords' acceptance of their claims of inheritance and sale. They were unsuccessful: but where disputes continued, the equity courts showed themselves to be willing to treat the tenants' claims as valid by the end of the 1540s.[16] This was not, by any means, the end of disputes between lords and tenants. Lords continued, throughout the sixteenth century, to try and prove that their tenants' estates were flawed and that they were entitled to substitute leases or raise fines to market levels. The thirty or so years after 1570 seem to have been a notable period for litigation between lords and tenants over the latter's tenurial status: by this time the disadvantages of having customary tenants was all too obvious to lords.[17]

By the end of the 1540s there was an appreciation that rents were increasing: the phenomenon was commented on equally in *The Common Weal of This Realm of England* (1549) attributed to Sir Thomas Smith and in the petitions sent to the privy council in the camping season in the summer of 1549: these frightened government so much that it promised (temporarily) to return rents to the levels of 1509. It had no more a means to do that than to ban enclosure and conversion.[18]

But after 1549, there seems to have been a positive discouragement of rent-raising for a generation, with a particular example being set by the management of the crown's own estate. It became fashionable to praise lords such as Burghley who did not raise their rents. ('He did never raise his rents, nor displace his tenants. But as the rent went when he bought the lands, so the tenants still held them. And, as I know, some of his tenants paid him but £20 for a thing worth £200'.) Conversely when the earl of Shrewsbury tried to issue new leases at enhanced rents of his lands in Glossopdale (Derbyshire) in the late 1570s, the tenants were able to blacken his name and he was condemned for his greed by everyone from the queen downwards.[19] It seems likely that the generation who lived through 1549 appreciated only too keenly the dangers of disorder provoked by revanchist landlordism and therefore set their faces against it. This same view pervaded the equity courts who were ready, throughout the latter part of the century, to rule against landlords. A combination of social pressures and legal thinking thereby made it difficult for landlords to claw back the income they had lost through inflation (never mind increase rents in line with the demand for land).

So how did they survive? One can identify a number of strategies. Some weathered the crisis by taking advantage of the considerable acreages of ex-monastic lands available for sale to extend their estates. Some copyhold of recent origin was voided ('demesne copyholds') and transferred to the leasehold sector, and where tenure permitted, many raised entry fines. Sponsoring enclosure, which served to extend the rent-paying area, was another strategy. We have already met the practice of taking land in hand – bitterly complained about in East Anglia in 1549 and 1553 – and identified as an option by the author of the *Common Weal*:

> And for that we cannot so do [raise rents] of our lands that is already in the hands of other men, many of us are forced to keep part of their own possessions or to purchase some farm of other mens lands and to store it up with sheep or other cattle, to help make up the decay of their revenues and to maintain with old estate with all.[20]

It is likely that it was only in the last quarter of the century that rents began to return to market levels. Two reasons can be offered for this. One was that a new generation of landowners had no compunction about treating their tenants ruthlessly: they understood that it was their survival which was at stake. This needed to be done carefully to avoid bad publicity at court or tenant appeals to the courts. The ninth earl of Northumberland persuaded his tenants to accept cheap leases in place of their copies at the beginning of the 1590s, and then hit them for the full economic rent when these leases came up for renewal about 1610. Then there was also the application to land management of a new technology – land surveying – and the development of the surveyor as a sort of company doctor, to be sent into under-performing estates to set them right. Surveying and the making of measured maps developed in the middle of the century as a military building technology. From about 1575 measured maps were made, but the key element was the measurement of land itself.

Landlords could now know exactly what their tenants held (rather than having to rely on the tenants' self-description), and, as a part of the surveyor's job was to value land, the landlord could now move to adjust rents in line with values.[21]

How far landlords had managed to claw back the value of their lands by 1603 is uncertain. What can be seen is that England was now bifurcated by tenancy, with large areas held by customary tenures (where rents were fixed and entry fines, if flexible, offered only small compensation) and others by leasehold which allowed for the upward adjustment of rents. That the process might not have proceeded very far at all is suggested by figures calculated by D. C. Coleman from those presented by Lawrence Stone in his *Crisis of the Aristocracy* (1965).[22] Coleman showed how on Stone's figures, the average value of a manor (in constant prices) was £40 in 1559, but only £43 in 1602. By 1640 it had reached £94. Whilst these figures make no allowance for entry fines, they suggest that landowners received little benefit from the rising demand for land before the end of the century and imply that it was only after that period that they recovered some of the real value of their lands. Moreover, as the rents of a manor in 1559 were almost certainly the same as in 1540 (before inflation set in), landowners, manor by manor, were substantially poorer in real terms in 1603 than they had been in 1540. Although the idea has been much contested, the idea of a crisis in the landowning class in the latter part of Elizabeth's reign should not occasion any surprise.

IV

We have already seen how growing population did not reverse the medieval contraction of arable agriculture and depopulation which continued throughout the sixteenth century. In the same way the repopulating of the countryside was not accompanied by any reversal of the engrossing of tenements which had taken place in the 150 years after 1348. On the contrary: the creation and elaboration of already large holdings throughout the sixteenth century appears to have been every bit as unstoppable a process as enclosure. Of course, like enclosure, engrossment proceeded at different speeds in different regions. The result was that by the end of the century there had emerged a relatively small but still significant number of large farmers whose fortunes were based on land which, a generation or two before, had been held by a number of much smaller yeomen. These men were the beneficiaries of the collapse of seigniorial control over land, for the profits of their farming now supported their higher standard of living. William Harrison, discussing Essex rural society in the 1570s, commented on the new-found prosperity of farmers. They had cash reserves; their houses had chimneys; people slept on mattresses and pillows rather than straw pallets and mats and ate from pewter plates using metal cutlery, where in living memory wooden platters and spoons had commonly been in use.[23]

This new prosperity was unevenly distributed. It has become a commonplace of the recent literature that villages pulled apart over the sixteenth century as the economic, social and cultural distance between the richer landholding inhabitants on the one hand and wage-earners and the poor on the other increased. Care must be taken not to over-stress the scale of these changes, as has sometimes been done as a result of the influential accounts of a limited number of southern villages. In the recent account of the Devon moorland village of Morebath, Eamon Duffy is able to show the whole range of ritual within the pre-Reformation village in which every element (including the women and the village's youths) had a role. Much of this turned on parochial sociability to generate funds for the beautification of the church.[24] Whilst the arrangements here may have been unusually elaborate, they make the point that the pre-Reformation church sponsored a whole range of communal activities (from which it expected to profit financially) which had completely disappeared by the end of the century. For this reason the impact of the Reformation on the countryside has been seen as one of cultural (and certainly social) impoverishment. Moreover, the remnants of those social activities – church ales, football, piping and the like – increasingly came to be inherited by the youths of the village community and were frowned upon – if not actively prosecuted – by the 'sober' inhabitants of the villages. In part their anxiety was to maintain sexual morality. It is plain, for instance, that by the end of Elizabeth's reign the churchwardens of some Essex villages were counting the months between marriage and the birth of the eldest child and prosecuting newly wed couples guilty of pre-marital sex. Youth activities which may have been a cover for licentiousness were repressed: but equally drunkenness amongst adult men was no longer acceptable, nor were communal occasions centred around the consumption of ale. Alehouses, the haunt of the poor, which supplied them with drink and ready-cooked food and were the means by which widows made a living, were increasingly the object of suspicion. They came to be licensed by magistrates, their numbers reduced and, one may assume, their management placed in men's hands. Another aspect of the 'reformation of manners' was a struggle to control space and time. The use of the churchyard for profane reasons – whether it was football, grazing animals or parochial fairs – was increasingly forbidden. Popular recreations were no longer condoned on Sunday which was redefined (by those enthusiasts loosely called Puritans) as a day for religious observance and contemplation.

The redefinition of what was – and was not – acceptable behaviour continued into the seventeenth century. The punishment of illegitimacy, drunkenness and Sabbath sports proceeded with greater enthusiasm in some localities than others – many of the leading instances come from Essex – and could be divisive. In Lancashire the struggle to suppress Sunday sports divided the county elite along religious lines, but even though James I and later Charles I later issued permissive declarations permitting recreations on the Sabbath, the general direction of change, towards greater social regulation and intolerance of moral nonconformity, was plain.[25]

The treatment of the old was more problematic. Their numbers probably grew over the sixteenth century and the assumption that widows in particular could support themselves by a mixture of casual work, alehouse-keeping, gleaning, woodgathering and charity became increasingly insupportable. The perceived inadequacy of these informal arrangements had two outcomes. The first is that the increased reluctance to support elderly women through charity contributed to the rash of witchcraft accusations of the later sixteenth and early seventeenth centuries. The classic thesis advanced by Sir Keith Thomas and Alan Macfarlane starts with the premise that contemporaries understood that there were within their communities individuals who could inflict damage on them through cursing and spells. When misfortune occurred, whether the relatively trivial (milk curdling in an unusual way), the economically damaging (the death of cattle), the mystery illness or the death of a family member, it was logical to look for explanation to individuals who might have cursed family members. Older women, who had reason for revenge because they had been denied charity, were an obvious source of suspicion.

The second is the development of formal systems of poor law. The statutes of 1597–8 and 1601 – which extended to the countryside arrangements which had developed in towns and a few southern English villages over the previous thirty or forty years – were an attempt to root the poor in their home villages. They, rather than the towns to which the poor were prone to migrate, were made responsible for provision for their poor. Relief was to be provided through the twin strategies of putting the poor to work on parish-provided stocks or giving them weekly doles raised through the levying of parochial rates on property. Begging was permitted only if licensed (with the assumption that it would cease). The system was to be put into effect locally by new parochial officers, the Overseers of the Poor, and supervised by the JPs. Of course, the speed with which these arrangements were implemented varied enormously from region to region. In some areas the magistracy continued to maintain that charity was adequate (as in south Lancashire in 1624). It has recently been shown that there was no uniform system of parochial poor relief in Warwickshire in the 1630s and this was probably true of many counties until the 1650s.[26]

V

We must recognize that there was one crucial difference between the English experience and that of Scotland and Ireland: war. The consequences of war in Ireland we will treat in a moment, but we should note that lowland and eastern Scotland sustained major damage from the English after they invaded in 1543. There were then periods of civil disturbance in the years between 1567 and 1573. (Keith Brown has calculated there were military campaigns of one sort or another in twenty-four out of the thirty-six years between 1559 and 1594.[27]) Little has been written about the impact of war on Scottish society, but in one respect it had a major effect. This was in feu farming, the granting of the freehold of land to either investors or tenants for a fixed rent as a way of realizing capital. This had been encouraged during the fifteenth century and continued through the early sixteenth: but there is some evidence that the damage inflicted by English military incursions on Scottish abbeys in the 1540s encouraged the practice. Likewise, later feu charters justify the need to raise money by feuing by reference to the costs of the crisis of 1558–60 and civil war of the mid-1560s.[28]

War apart, the usual assumption is that Scottish population history broadly followed the trajectory of English growth. The difficulty lies in confirming that this is so: the Scots lack good parish registers before the seventeenth century. Scottish population history is therefore hedged around with cautious caveats. The best estimates of Scottish population place it at about 0.5–0.7 million in 1500. Thereafter there is certainly evidence of growth. In the Lowlands there is the subdivision of townships and an apparent expansion of the agrarian landscape; in the Highlands outmigration, both seasonal migration into the Lowlands or to Ulster, and life-cycle migration into Europe as mercenaries. Population growth also suffered the same sort of reverses due to famine as that in northern England: this is hardly surprising for, as we shall see, the agrarian economy broadly mirrored that of the northern counties. There was a drift into towns: the best estimate is that Edinburgh held 1.1 per cent of the national population in 1560 but 2.7 per cent in 1639: towns of 2,000 inhabitants contained 2.5 per cent of the population in 1560 and 11.7 per cent in 1639.[29]

Agriculture in the Lowlands took place within an infield-outfield system. Infields were subdivided arable fields on the best land which were cropped continuously. They therefore received the maximum quantity of manure from cattle. Individual parts of outfields might be cropped for two or three successive years, and then allowed to come back into heart through a long period under grass. Infields tended to be sown with a cold-tolerant variety of barley called Bere and outfields with oats. This was a poor, low-yield agriculture designed to match both the lack of demand and the disadvantages of climate and location. The Highland economy was based on cattle. There was a general shortage of arable and it was this limitation which forced the outflow of population.

The two agrarian zones in sixteenth-century Scotland were not merely economic adaptations to landscape and location. They were also political zones, reflecting the divide between the Lowlands governed from Edinburgh and the Highlands dominated by clans, and cultural and linguistic zones (between Scots- and Gaelic-speaking populations). The same distinctions can be found in sixteenth-century Ireland. At the beginning of the sixteenth century there was a small enclave around Dublin (the Pale) under the control of the English government, a larger area in the south-east of Ireland under magnates like the earls of Ormond of Kilkenny, loosely aligned to the Pale government; and a much larger area in the west and north of Ireland, over which the Pale government had little control, which again was dominated by unstable and shifting clans. A well-known description of Ireland dating from 1515 divided Ireland between some sixty Gaelic Irish and thirty gaelicized Anglo-Irish lordships. The former were based around kinship groups or 'septs': political power was therefore widely dispersed amongst the members of the ruling family who elected their lord. Lordship was not hereditary but depended on the lord's ability to command not only his own family but also other subsidiary lords within his area of control. The ability to collect rent was directly based on the exercise of this power, Gaelic society having no familiarity with the tenurial contract. Lords levied rents of cattle and other produce ('coigne and livery') and demanded work services from their tenants.

The English saw Gaelic society as backward rather than adapted to the landscape. In this they brought to bear on Ireland a prejudice which is also seen displayed in England towards the inhabitants of woodland and fen economies: that pastoral agriculture was lazy and unproductive. English policy towards the native Irish after 1536 swung wildly between attempts to extend the influence of the Pale government over the island by a process of legal and cultural assimilation, and attempts at conquest. In the first, the individual Gaelic lords were invited to adopt English customs in return for an English title and recognition of their land title in English law. This, the policy of 'surrender and regrant', was launched in 1540 (with an antecedent in 1538) but had run out of steam by 1543, to be revived on a number occasions subsequently. It is one of the great might-have-beens of Irish history, but its significance for us is that the process entailed the Gaelic lords not only receiving English titles (so the MacGiollapadraigs of Upper Ossory became the barons Fitzpatrick) but them undertaking to accept 'cultural anglicization'. They would eschew Gaelic dress and the Gaelic language, but they also undertook to adopt English habits of sedentary arable agriculture, building houses after the English mode.[30] Later attempts to assimilate the Gaelic lords included forcing them to establish English-style tenurial relationships with their tenants, and converting arbitrary exactions in cattle into money rents. The ambition to bring about a cultural transformation of agriculture was obvious. No opportunity was passed over: when the MacGiollapadraigs/Fitzpatricks took a lease of monastic lands in 1573–4, they were instructed to settle them with English tenants. It must be questioned whether these methods brought about any transformation of Irish rural society: the most recent view is that the Irish lords were quite capable of paying lip-service to these demands whilst making only the most limited and grudging changes on the ground.

The alternative was the seizure of land and its colonization by English (or, after 1603, Scots) tenants. This was first done in King's and Queen's counties (the modern Leix and Offaly) in the mid-1550s to establish a quasi-military buffer against the Irish. Plantation was undertaken most notably in the mid-1580s after the suppression of the Desmond revolt and the confiscation of the lands of the earldom and its supporters. A number of schematic plans survive showing projected settlements: they were to be centred around a church and mill, with a variety of holdings – freehold and tenanted – of different sizes.[31] Villages were fundamental to this concept of a society which was expected to operate at much higher level of economic activity than the Irish. The implementation of these schemes proved to be difficult. The lands available for settlement in Munster were not contiguous blocks but widely scattered. The number of settlers there by 1598 – probably about 4,000 and, mostly drawn from the west country – fell far short of the promoters' aspirations: moreover, the first generation of settlers were unable to make a success of the arable economy the projectors wished to see established. Instead they adopted Irish practices of cattle-ranching as the means to make a living.[32]

The movement of English tenants into south-west Ireland may well be a reflection of the land hunger of the English. But inward migration was necessary for another reason. The war in Munster between 1579 and 1583 had left the countryside depopulated. Economic warfare and starvation were used by the English to secure military dominance. Hence, when we hear of Irish vagrants in English towns in the latter part of Elizabeth's reign, they are as likely to be English-speaking refugees from war as betterment migrants. Ireland was lightly populated: but late-sixteenth-century war destroyed swathes of the native Irish economy and left the way open for colonization.

VI

Development in the British rural economy in the sixteenth century can be seen to have been uneven. Population growth and market opportunity drove change in England and to a lesser extent Scotland. War and population decline were the tools of the mission to anglicize Ireland. England in general and the South-east in particular certainly became more prosperous, aided by the inability of many landowners to extract economic rents from their tenants. And throughout England land became concentrated in the hands of the few: landlessness became a problem in rural communities. Whether these same problems impinged on Scotland before the seventeenth century remains to be seen. There is then the paradox of how attempts were being made to introduce the ideal agrarian economy – the market-orientated, corn-growing economy of the English fielden counties – into Ireland at a time when that same economy was being found unviable within midland England.

Of course, many of the trends and tendencies outlined here only worked themselves out in the new century. From the perspective of the English economic and social historian, the tide turns in the decades immediately after the Restoration: for Scots historians, this is the moment when traces of improvement begin to be seen in the Scots economy. History is seamless and continuing: it knows no word counts and only historians end with a full stop.

NOTES

1. PRO, SP63/116 no. 18.
2. All accounts of English population movements are now reliant on Wrigley and Schofield, *Population History of England, 1541–1871* from which the following figures are derived. For essays making this often technical work more accessible, see Houston, *Population History of England and Ireland*, and Smith, 'Geographical aspects'.
3. The following figures are based on the estimates of Sir Tony Wrigley, most conveniently found in Glennie, 'Industry and towns'.
4. Bailey, 'Demographic decline' summarizes the debate.
5. Outhwaite, 'Progress and backwardness', p. 10, offers examples of this.
6. The fielden/arden divide underlies much recent writing but 'arable' and 'pastoral' communities with their pure characteristics should be seen as opposite poles, with many intermediate positions between them. For a helpful summary, Davie, 'Chalk and cheese?'.
7. Emmison, *Elizabethan Life*, p. 184.
8. Wrigley and Schofield, *Population History*, appendix 10.
9. Sharpe, *In Contempt of All Authority*, p. 15. Oats were horse provender and not normally consumed by people in lowland England.
10. For some indications of these less obvious problems, Sharpe, 'Social strain and social dislocation'.
11. Wrigley and Schofield, *Population History*, tables 7.28, 7.15.
12. Outhwaite, 'Progress and backwardness', pp. 7–8.
13. The fullest account of government attitudes to enclosure and engrossing is Thirsk, 'Enclosing and engrossing'. For Wolsey's commissions, see Scarisbrick, 'Cardinal Wolsey and the Common Weal'.
14. Walter, 'A "rising of the people"?', p. 116.
15. Copyhold for lives, found throughout western England, conveys none of the security of a customary tenure and ought not to be considered as one: it is actually a system of leasehold.
16. Hoyle, *The Pilgrimage of Grace*, ch. 8; Hoyle and Winchester, 'A lost source'; paper in preparation on the Wharton estates by Hoyle.
17. For this, see Hoyle, 'Tenurial change in England'.
18. Smith [attrib.], *A Discourse of the Common Weal*, pp. 38–9; Shagan, 'Protector Somerset and the 1549 rebellions'.
19. Peck (ed.), *Desiderata Curiosa*, I, p. 43; Kershaw, 'Duty and power in the Elizabethan aristocracy'.
20. Hoyle, 'Agrarian agitation'; Lamond, *Discourse of the Common Weal*, p. 20.
21. Percy, ed. Harrison, *Advice to his Son by Henry Percy, Ninth Earl of Northumberland*, pp. 82–3 (although whether he did as he claimed remains to be established); Harvey, 'Estate surveyors and the spread of the scale-map in England'.

22. Coleman, 'The "gentry" controversy', p. 174.
23. Harrison, *The Description of England*, pp. 200–4.
24. Duffy, *The Voices of Morebath.*
25. The most recent summary of the large literature on the Reformation of Manners is Hindle, *State and Social Change* chapter 7.
26. Again, the best recent account is Hindle, *State and Social Change*, chapters 6, 8.
27. Brown, 'Aristocratic finances'.
28. Sanderson, *Scottish Rural Society.*
29. Whyte, *Scotland Before the Industrial Revolution*, table 10.2.
30. Edwards, 'Collaboration without anglicisation'.
31. For an example Canny, *Making Ireland British*, p. 131.
32. MacCarthy-Morrogh, *The Munster Plantation*, p. 118.

BIBLIOGRAPHY

Bailey, Mark, 'Demographic decline in late medieval England: some thoughts on recent research', *Economic History Review*, 49 (1996), 1–19.

Brown, K. M., 'Aristocratic finances and the origins of the Scottish revolution', *English Historical Review*, 104 (1989), 46–87.

Canny, N., *Making Ireland British, 1580–1650* (Oxford, 2001).

Coleman, D. C., 'The "gentry" controversy and the aristocracy in crisis, 1558–1641', *History*, 51 (1966), 165–78.

Davie, N., 'Chalk and cheese? "Fielden" and "Forest" communities in early modern England', *Journal of Historical Sociology*, 4 (1991), 1–31.

Duffy, E., *The Voices of Morebath: Reformation and Rebellion in an English Village* (London, 2001).

Edwards, D., 'Collaboration without anglicisation: the MacGiollapadraig lordship and Tudor Reform', in P. J. Duffy, D. Edwards and E. Fitzpatrick, eds, *Gaelic Ireland: Land, Lordship and settlement, c.1250–c.1650* (Dublin, 2001), pp. 77–97.

Emmison, F. G., *Elizabethan Life: Home, Work and Land* (Chelmsford, 1976).

Glennie, P. D., 'Industry and towns, 1500–1730', in R. A. Dodgshon and R. A. Butlin, eds, *An Historical Geography of England and Wales* (2nd edition, London, 1990), 199–222.

Harrison, W., *The Description of England: The Classic Contemporary Account of Tudor Social Life*, ed. Georges Edelen (Ithaca, NY, 1968).

Harvey, P. D. A., 'Estate surveyors and the spread of the scale-map in England, 1550–80', *Landscape History*, 15 (1993), 37–49.

Hindle, S., *The State and Social Change in Early Modern England, 1550–1640* (Basingstoke, 2000).

Houston, R. A., *The Population History of Britain and Ireland, 1500–1750* (Basingstoke, 1992).

Hoyle, R. W., 'Agrarian agitation in mid-sixteenth century Norfolk: a petition of 1553', *Historical Journal*, 44 (2001), 223–38.

Hoyle, R. W. and Winchester, A. J. L., 'A lost source for the rising of 1536 in north-west England', *English Historical Review*, 118 (2003), 120–9.

Hoyle, R. W., *The Pilgrimage of Grace and the Politics of the 1530s* (Oxford, 2001).

Hoyle, R. W., 'Tenurial litigation in England, 1540–1640: the evidence of the Chancery decrees' (in preparation).

Kershaw, S., 'Duty and power in the Elizabethan aristocracy: George, earl of Shrewsbury, the Glossopdale dispute and the council', in G. W. Bernard, ed., *The Tudor Nobility* (Manchester, 1992), pp. 266–95.

MacCarthy-Morrogh, M., *The Munster Plantation. English Migration to Southern Ireland, 1583–1641* (Oxford, 1987).

Macfarlane, Alan, *Witchcraft in Tudor and Stuart England: A Regional and Comparative Study* (London, 1970).

Outhwaite, R. B., 'Progress and backwardness in English agriculture, 1500–1650', *Economic History Review*, 39 (1986), 1–18.

Peck F. (ed.), *Desiderata Curiosa* (2 vols, London, 1732).

Percy, H., earl of Northumberland, *Advice to his Son by Henry Percy, Ninth Earl of Northumberland* (1609), ed. G. B. Harrison (London, 1930).

Sanderson, M. H. B., *Scottish Rural Society in the Sixteenth Century* (Edinburgh, 1982).

Scairsbrick, J. J., 'Cardinal Wolsey and the Common Weal', in E. W. Ives, R. J. Knecht and J. J. Scarisbrick, eds, *Wealth and Power in Tudor England* (London, 1978), pp. 45–67.

Shagan, E. H., 'Protector Somerset and the 1549 rebellions: new sources and perspectives', *English Historical Review*, 114 (1999), 34–63.

Sharpe, B., *In Contempt of All Authority: Rural Artisans and Riot in the West of England, 1586–1660* (London, 1980).

Sharpe, J. A., 'Social strain and social dislocation, 1585–1603', in J. Guy, ed., *The Reign of Elizabeth I: Court and Culture in the Last Decade* (Cambridge, 1995).

Smith, R. M., 'Geographical aspects of population change in England, 1500–1730', in R. A. Dodgshon and R. A. Butlin, eds, *An Historical Geography of England and Wales* (2nd edition, London, 1990).

Smith, Sir Thomas [attrib.], *A Discourse of the Common Weal of this Realm of England*, ed. E. Lamond (Cambridge, 1929).

Thirsk, J., 'Enclosing and engrossing', in J. Thirsk, ed., *The Agrarian History of England and Wales*, vol. IV, *1500–1640* (Cambridge, 1967).

Thomas, K., *Religion and the Decline of Magic: Studies in Popular Beliefs in Sixteenth- and Seventeenth-Century England* (London, 1971).

Walter, J., 'A "rising of the people"? The Oxfordshire rising of 1596', *Past and Present*, 107 (1985), 90–143.

Whyte, I. D., *Scotland before the Industrial Revolution: An Economic and Social History c.1050–c.1750* (London, 1995).

Wrigley, E. A. and Schofield, R. S., *The Population History of England, 1541–1871: A Reconstruction* (London, 1981).

FURTHER READING

B. M. S. Campbell and M. Overton, 'A new perspective on medieval and early modern agriculture: six centuries of Norfolk farming, c.1250–c.1850', *Past and Present*, 141 (1993), 38–105.

R. Gillespie, 'Explorers, exploiters and entrepreneurs: early modern Ireland and its context, 1500–1700', in B. J. Graham and L. J. Proudfoot (eds), *An Historical Geography of Ireland* (1993).

J. Goodacre, *The Transformation of a Peasant Economy. Townspeople and Villagers in the Lutterworth Area, 1500–1700* (1994).

D. G. Hey, *An English Rural Community. Myddle* [Shropshire] *under the Tudors and Stuarts* (1974).

S. Hindle, 'Custom, festival and protest in early modern England: the Little Budworth Wakes, St Peter's Day, 1596', *Rural History*, 6 (1995), 155–78.

R. W. Hoyle, *The Estates of the English Crown, 1558–1640* (1992).

E. Kerridge, *Agrarian Problems in the Sixteenth Century and After* (1969).

A. McRae, *God Speed the Plough: The Representation of Agrarian England, 1500–1660* (1996).

C. Moreton, *The Townshends and Their World: Gentry, Law and Land in Norfolk, c.1450–1551* (1992).

M. O'Dowd, 'Gaelic economy and society', in C. Brady and R. Gillespie (eds), *Natives and Newcomers: The Making of Irish Colonial Society, 1534–1641* (1986), 120–47.

M. Overton, *Agricultural Revolutions in England: The Transformation of the Agrarian Economy, 1500–1850* (1996).

M. Overton and B. M. S. Campbell, 'Norfolk livestock farming, 1250–1740: a comparative study of manorial accounts and probate inventories', *Journal of Historical Geography*, 18 (1992).

D. M. Palliser, 'Tawney's century: brave new world or Malthusian trap?', *Economic History Review*, 35 (1982), 339–53.

J. Sharpe, *Instruments of Darkness: Witchcraft in England, 1550–1750* (1996).

M. Spufford, *Contrasting Communities: English Villagers in the Sixteenth and Seventeenth Centuries* (1974).

L. Stone, *The Crisis of the Aristocracy* (1965), chapter 6.

J. Thirsk (ed.) *The Agrarian History of England and Wales*, vol. IV, *1500–1640* (1967); and *The Rural Economy of England* (1984: collected essays).

J. Walter, 'The social economy of dearth in early modern England', in J. Walter and R. S. Schofield (eds), *Famine, Disease and the Social Order in Early Modern Society* (1989).

J. Whittle, *The Development of Agrarian Capitalism: Land and Labour in Norfolk, 1440–1580* (2000).

K. Wrightson, *Earthly Necessities: Economic Lives in Early Modern Britain* (2000).

K. Wrightson and D. Levine, *Poverty and Piety in an English Village: Terling* [Essex], *1525–1700* (1979).

CHAPTER NINETEEN

The Urban Economy

ALAN DYER

The towns of Tudor Britain may be understood in terms of a hierarchy in each of the three kingdoms. At the top in England and Wales lay London, so much bigger than any other town, and so dominant over the economy, that it must be placed in a category of its own, a position which was greatly strengthened during the course of the sixteenth century. Edinburgh possessed something of this distinction in Scotland, but to a much lesser degree, but in Ireland Dublin was scarcely beginning to have such a role in an urban network which was still very immature. Below the English metropolis lay at least five large regional centres which co-ordinated the wider life of extensive districts, though it seems overly ambitious to call them provincial capitals when England had no provinces of a distinctly administrative kind to compare with the ancient provinces of a country like France. These towns – Norwich in East Anglia, York and Newcastle in the North, Bristol and Exeter in the South-West – articulated regional economies by acting as industrial centres, shipping exports and providing specialized shopping facilities or social amenities where smaller towns could not satisfy such sophisticated demands. Such towns were larger than their neighbours, but rarely dramatically so: the regional economy, and with it the need for a dominant regional centre, was not yet well developed. Often their role was based on being a port, and it is significant that where there was no dominant port, as in north-western England and Wales or central southern England, or where trade could not be funnelled through a port of any kind, as in land-locked midland England, there was no prominent regional centre, and we might think of the functions of such a centre as being split between several towns in so far as the economy in those areas could be thought to possess a clearly defined regional identity at all.

Below these greater towns lay the vast majority of the urban stock, which we may term greater or lesser market towns. The larger ones might have some administrative role as county capitals – Shrewsbury, Taunton, Derby – or a distinctive manufacture which could supply more distant markets or a larger rural market area because it lay in the centre of an especially fertile district or at the confluence of major roads or navigable rivers, but they were in essence merely a modestly overgrown version of the ubiquitous small market town with which the British Isles, and especially England, was generously stocked by comparison with many European countries.[1]

The Tudor economies of the British Isles were essentially agricultural: in the countryside lay the productive heartland, where not only foodstuffs and raw materials were raised but also much industrial activity took place. Consequently the bulk of the population lived in rural areas, leaving the towns, despite their undoubted antiquity and value, with a relatively small share of the total population. Exactly how modest that proportion was depends on how one defines a town. If for England and Wales one counts only settlements with more than 5,000 inhabitants, then in 1500 perhaps 5 per cent of the population was urban, and in 1600 maybe eight; if one then includes every small town, even when occupied by less than a thousand people, then possibly 15 to 20 per cent was urban in 1500 and 20 to 25 in 1600 – there must be a degree of guesswork involved in estimating the size of the many smaller market centres at these dates. In Scotland, and especially Ireland, these levels would be significantly lower. It would be difficult to guess at whether the urban share of total wealth or production was greater or less than its share of the population, but this approach may unfairly belittle the role of the towns, for their contribution to the whole economy was vital in supplying the main locus for the exchange of goods and services: increasingly, agriculture depended on the market, which lay in towns.

In the modern economy, larger towns are primarily centres of industrial activity, but in the sixteenth century they were chiefly commercial, that is, concerned with the provision and exchange of goods and services. Industrial production there certainly was in towns, but it frequently involved the finishing of complex processes begun in the countryside and was usually of a small-scale handicraft nature. Administration was a modest activity in Britain, since bureaucracies were so small, with what little there was in England and Wales concentrated in London; the county capitals were devoid of much permanent activity, and only came to life on the occasions when courts of assize or quarter-sessions met for a few days in the year; Warwick, Stafford or Lancaster might have been the formal centres of their shires but this factor alone did not make them very big or prosperous. In Scotland, the lack of a city with London's economic dominance meant that the economy of Edinburgh owed more to governmental activity, but the seat of courts and parliament still did not make too great a contribution to urban growth. The church had a separate governing structure, but that too was relatively modest, though when diocesan centres were also county capitals (which was usually the case – consider Lincoln, Durham, Salisbury, Gloucester, Canterbury) the combined influence could be more substantial. Whether lay or ecclesiastical, administration provided a useful node around which other, more effective economic activities could congregate, and so helped to decide which settlements became towns, and raised some to an enhanced status, but it rarely provided the prime *raison d'être* of any town.

Thus the principal features of urban economies in the Tudor period were their concentration on commerce and the provision of small-scale goods and services. Most demands were met locally from local resources and by local traders, and this factor was a major cause of the proliferation of trades in small towns. Instead of the concentration of large-scale production in limited numbers of distant centres characteristic of the industrial revolution and beyond, in this period most needs were supplied by businesses which lay in every street, such as shoemakers or bakers. The majority of towns of medium and small size were not dominated by any one activity. One can see five broad categories of business. Firstly there were distributive traders, those who mainly sold goods which had been imported from abroad or another region. They were often the wealthiest trades, and included mercers, who sold fine fabrics, the grocers who dealt in imported commodities such as sugar and spices, and the drapers who supplied textiles made in Britain, whether woollen or linen. Apothecaries dispensed drugs, stationers stocked paper and similar goods and ironmongers sold metal objects of all kinds. Often one of these trades would absorb some of the others to provide a shop rather like a modern department store, the mercer being involved here most usually. The second category is the largest both in numbers of trades and of men involved; here the business was concerned with both making goods by some sort of craft and retailing them, perhaps with some additional stock acquired from elsewhere. Leather was made and then manufactured into a wide variety of goods; wood was the raw material for another range of trades, and metals, iron, pewter, brass, lead and copper were the basis of another group. Wool was converted into textiles by a very complex series of interconnected trades – this point will be expanded below. A specialized sub-group supplied food and drink – bakers, brewers and fishmongers.

The third division supplied services. Tailors were common here, working on cloth which the customer had usually bought elsewhere, while the barber was often combined with the surgeon, both deploying a razor to cut or bleed. Innkeepers became more important as travel and leisure demands expanded. The fourth category were building workers, since the sixteenth century saw in many towns a major programme of building and rebuilding in which medieval structures were modernized with the addition of chimneys, upper floors and glass windows. The fifth group covered the professions, practitioners rising in status and numbers – doctors, clergy and lawyers. Only large towns could themselves provide a majority of customers for all these traders; for most towns, supplying a rural market was their central activity, which was after all where the majority of the population, and of the wealth of the country, lay. We might add to these activities those which could only be found in a minority of specialized towns; chief among these were the merchants who ran wholesale trades, chiefly concerned with overseas commerce and concentrated in the major ports, and the sailors, harbour workers and fishermen to be found along the coast.

The Market Town

Most Tudor towns were mere market towns, that is, their economies centred chiefly on their weekly market. The 644 markets which are recorded in 1588 in England and Wales lay spread over the country in a relatively uniform network, so that most countrymen could walk to one, do their business and return home in one long day; but they were more thickly distributed in southern England, where they were on average about seven or eight miles apart, and more sparsely set in upland Wales and the north of England where there might be twelve, fifteen or more miles between them.[2] But this principle did not invariably apply, and there were counties in the south, such as Sussex and Hampshire, with relatively few markets and others in the north and west, such as Lancashire and Pembrokeshire, with relatively many. This structure had been established in the middle ages and had by the sixteenth century been slimmed down to be confined to settlements which, however small, mostly had a basically urban character; the system existed in essence to service an agricultural economy which was beginning to become commercialized in the middle ages and became increasingly market-orientated during the later sixteenth and seventeenth centuries. In consequence the prosperity and numbers of market towns was growing slowly after – say – 1560, though probably numbers did not significantly rise until after 1600, when market-orientated agriculture spread more strongly into the backward west and north, and the scale of the process began to speed up notably.

All of this was the creation of an economy in which subsistence farming, which sought primarily to feed the farmer's own household, was being replaced by a commercial agriculture, which aimed to make cash by producing surpluses to sell on the open market. Sixteenth-century population growth led to rocketing prices for food and rich rewards for those able to sell it. This encouraged local and regional specialization, as each area concentrated on doing what it did best, importing what it then lacked; this process led in turn to long-distance trade in foodstuffs from which the market towns were ideally placed to profit. The supply of food to London was the earliest manifestation of this process, and we find the market town of Hemel Hempstead in Hertfordshire being founded, partly on a greenfield site, in 1539 and flourishing by channelling corn to the capital.[3] Barley was grown in the warmer, drier south-east, turned to malt (in towns), and taken over many miles to the north and west to brew beer, while cattle were raised in the wetter west, sold in border towns such as Shrewsbury and Hereford and driven to be fattened in pastures nearer London. Cheshire cheese was sold in fairs in midland towns and taken on to the London consumer. So the vigorous, comprehensive market-centre network in England was the result of a long process of economic modernization which depended on the commercialization of a relatively advanced and productive agricultural system. Such a state of affairs did not exist in Scotland and Ireland in the middle ages and did not begin to develop to any great degree until the seventeenth century, when both countries saw a wave of market creation which we ought to compare with the high middle ages in England – and with the same high level of failure and of 'market villages' rather than towns; consequently in the sixteenth century outside England and Wales the market town system still remained very imperfectly developed.[4]

Markets were held on one weekday in smaller towns and on two or three in larger ones, and at these gatherings much of the commercial activity of the urban economy was concentrated. To the countryman they provided the main opportunity to buy and sell agricultural produce of all kinds, in bulk and in person, and to access the range of goods and services which the town had to offer – butcher's meat, cloth, grocery or the services of the barber or tailor would all be available. Town traders depended heavily on this rural demand, which greatly enlarged the pool of likely customers beyond the modest confines of the urban community itself. Country people patronized the inns and alehouses, for their visits were partly social; large inns around marketplaces were essential features of town centres. For the townsmen the market provided food and raw materials, not just corn and livestock but the bread and meat they became, for most foodstuffs were retailed by town traders from market stalls rather than their own premises. Traders drew their raw materials from the market – skins were bought by tanners, and the consequent leather was bought in turn by shoemakers. Not all town traders had stalls, for every shop became an extension of the marketplace and most shop business was done on market days. The shop was in any case beginning to develop its modern character, with displays of goods but not yet a window display, and then only in the case of the more pretentious retailers.

The economies of market towns were often circumscribed by the limitations of their localities; they could do little to prosper beyond the modest opportunities offered by the trading potential of their market regions, and if those districts were relatively poor, as was true of – say – Northumberland, then that poverty subverted the towns at their centres. However, extra prosperity was brought to market towns by a number of factors. Traffic on the major roads, especially the arterial routes leading to London, provided a steady stream of travellers who required frequent servicing in an era when covering twenty miles a day was a good record: Ware in Hertfordshire or Faversham on the route to Dover are good examples. The development of specialist trades enlarged the market for commodities far beyond the modest limits of the marketplace. Pewter was made in Wigan and taken over a wide area; Walsall specialized in the metal components for horse harness, Wolverhampton came to rely on locks and keys and Sheffield on knives; many towns supplied leather to distant markets; Stratford-on-Avon made malt which was taken over a hundred miles to the north and west. By these means, extra prosperity was brought into these places, but good communications were crucial in taking the specialized product to the consumer, and the lack of good roads was a permanent problem for many inland towns.

Fairs were held much less frequently than markets, rarely more than six times per year and often only twice, though they might last for several days. While markets dealt with local produce available for much of the year and often in relatively small quantities, the essence of the fair was that it was concerned with regional and inter-regional trade, often concerning goods which were available for a limited season and in large or wholesale quantities, such as wool, cheese or hops. Most large fairs were necessarily urban, but they could be held in open country for the exchange of farm stock. The great days of the medieval international fairs were over, but Stourbridge fair, held outside Cambridge, and Bartholomew fair in London survived as major events in the commercial calendar; Stourbridge, held in the autumn, dealt in wool and cloth, salt-fish, horses, hops and many other commodities, articulating the wholesale trade of much of East Anglia and the east midlands. Fairs brought a rush of trading opportunities to the towns which hosted them: Nottingham acted as the commercial hub of the eastern midlands in part because London wholesalers used its Lenten fair to bring goods by boat via the sea and the navigable Trent to supply shopkeepers in the surrounding region, and Bristol's January fair had a similar function, even drawing in merchants from Ireland. Fairs could specialize in particular goods – Yarmouth for herrings, Newbury for cherries, Atherstone or Yarm for cheese, Tavistock for geese, Coventry's Crock Fair and York's Dish Fair for kitchenware and Norwich's Rush Fair for light wicks. All this activity brought a tide of customers to urban shops and inns, enlarged by the influx of local people who regarded fairs as an entertainment and social event without much commercial significance. When most of the local population, and many of the region's tradespeople could be found in one centre at one time, debts were paid, deals struck, and employees hired.

London

London was so much bigger than any other town that its economy demands separate treatment – economic factors are the main reason why London was probably four times the size of the largest English provincial city (Norwich) in 1500, and perhaps ten times in 1600, with the gap yawning ever wider in the following century. Perhaps one could argue that London's economy was in essence a version of that of the regional centre (Bristol, Norwich) writ large, but there were aspects of the metropolitan economy which were so much more developed that they were different, in kind as well as degree, from that of any other town in the British Isles. Although Edinburgh could be seen as a similar political capital, and it came to absorb more than half of Scotland's overseas trade, it did not dominate in the same way, its population of up to 20,000 in 1600 being greater than that of any English provincial city but only double that of its nearest Scottish rival, Aberdeen.[5] Dublin should be seen as a colonial political centre, without any commercial dominance, though its estimated 15,000 inhabitants in 1600 already marked it out as Ireland's largest town.[6] London's economic power lay in the piling up of function on function, most of them inter-related; the two most important functions are aptly summarized as 'the Court and the Port'.[7]

It was, most important of all, much the greatest port in the British Isles. Between the early and middle years of the sixteenth century its share of English cloth exports rose from over 60 per cent to a dominating 80 to 90 per cent, and this commodity comprised most of the country's exports.[8] London's commercial pre-eminence over the country's foreign trade was cemented by the contruction of the Royal Exchange in 1566–8 as a centre for financial dealing. At this stage England's foreign trade was centred on Antwerp, the hub of European commerce, and London's domination is partly explained by its geographical proximity to the Low Countries.[9] Most imports came from the same source, cloth merchants naturally loading return cargoes in Antwerp. London finished the cloth before shipping it, and since most imports were luxuries, naturally blossomed as the centre for quality shopping, and as the distribution point from which traders in provincial towns derived their stocks – thus domination of overseas commerce led to control of other sectors of the economy. As the cloth trade faltered in the second half of the sixteenth century and Antwerp fell from grace, London's reliance on cloth exports declined a little, but then its growth became more import-led as the supply of luxuries to an expanding and wealthier elite became more lucrative. Sugar, dried fruit, spices, fine linens, silks and velvets all poured in, with wine imports, for instance, doubling between the 1560s and the 1590s. London merchants were much the most numerous and wealthy of all, and from their capital and natural concerns was derived the capital's development of a money market with insurance and banking facilities which amounted to a virtual national monopoly.

As we have seen, London's domination of foreign trade led to domination of domestic trade – this became clear later in the sixteenth century and was inevitably less clear-cut than in the overseas sphere, because transport factors intervened, with rival regional and local economies continuing to operate long after this period. It was chiefly the trade in foodstuffs over which London towered most clearly, since its supply needs were a direct consequence of its huge size. Probably its clearest virtual

monopoly lay in the provision of luxury goods of all sorts, since it was in the sixteenth century that London established itself as the natural centre for shopping,
entertainment and even permanent residence of the wealthy, powerful and fashion-
conscious. Here the settling of an expanding royal Court in the capital or its immediate area was of primary importance, probably more influential than the location of
the central administration (still surprisingly small) and of the meeting of parliament
(an intermittent occasion). Part cause, part effect of the gathering of wealthy consumers in the capital was the growth of entertainment and leisure facilities in London,
which must have provided employment for many thousands – here inns, taverns and
cook-shops, brothels, jousting, bear-baiting, cock-fighting and the only commercial
theatres in the country, and on a more rarefied level, booksellers and sermons provided much the most varied and numerous feasts which the pleasure-seeker could
hope to find.

In stressing the importance of consumption it is easy to overlook the industrial
strength and variety of the capital; in the fifteenth century there were about 180 distinct crafts and trades, already more than any other town, and during our period the
total increased substantially, perhaps to over three hundred.[10] Those involved in
clothing were the commonest, involved both in the wholesale export trade and in
the provision of personal attire. Next came metal-working of all sorts – London was
the national centre for work in gold and silver, and pewterers supplied much domestic tableware. Leather workers supplied a wide variety of needs, and the construction
and embellishment of the expanding housing stock of the capital provided much
employment. The sheer size of the market encouraged the development of large-scale
enterprises in such areas as brewing and shipbuilding. Specialization of all sorts was
stimulated by this concentration of consumers, so that trades such as tapestry-makers,
hatband-makers, silk-twisters, gold-wire drawers, silver-spinners, oystermen and
costermongers were unlikely to be found elsewhere.

A feature of London's economic strength which is often overlooked is that, in
addition to acting increasingly as the national capital, it was also the regional capital
of the South-east. For a radius of eighty or ninety miles no major city could compete,
and those which lay within this zone were challenged – Canterbury is a good example.
Details of the carrier services which plied between towns show London as the distributive centre and dominant source of traceable commodities such as hallmarked
silver within this region, which spread as far as southern Warwickshire and south-
eastern Worcestershire.[11] The area was not just very large, but contained the densest
population and wealthiest rural districts in the country.

We can add to this London's growing role as the intellectual and artistic centre
of the country. Here most forms of book publishing were concentrated, aided by the
censorship established in the mid-sixteenth century. Most quality crafts were produced here – gold and silversmiths' work, fine furniture, portrait-painting and monumental sculpture, embroidery, engraving, jewellery and all the specialized trades
which were involved in the creation of high-fashion garments. Printers attracted
scholars, as did the Court, Gresham's College, the Inns of Court and the navigators
and cartographers concerned with voyages of discovery and colonization. Provincial
schools of art and architecture declined before the inrush of those new and imported
Renaissance fashions which entered the country through London. The influence of
the capital has been held to be one of the main sources of innovations which were

then distributed through the rest of the nation, and London can be seen as beginning, even before 1600, its role as an engine for growth in the economy as a whole, modernizing and expanding agriculture through the powerful demands of its food supply for instance, or by means of its insatiable appetite for coal, creating a new industrial world (rather resembling the nineteenth century before its time) in the mining and coal-shipping districts around Newcastle upon Tyne.

Ports

Ports were towns with a specialized and distinctive economy. Of the largest English Tudor towns, most were ports – London, Bristol, Newcastle, Exeter, Colchester, Chester – while Norwich and York were connected to the sea by short stretches of navigable river and so could enjoy most of the basic advantages of port status. Of these large towns, only Coventry lay far from the sea, and it is probably significant that it lost much of its industry in the years running up to about 1520, and could not sustain its late-medieval role as a regional distributive centre.[12] In Scotland a similar situation prevailed, with the 'four great towns' all ports (Aberdeen, Perth, Dundee and Edinburgh/Leith), their trade being with northern Europe rather than England: there was no integrated 'British' economic system before the seventeenth century. In Wales there were no large towns of this class but most of its modest urban stock lay beside the sea and traded through large English ports such as Chester and Bristol. In Ireland, most of the towns with any trade were ports, located, like Wexford, Waterford and Cork, along the eastern and southern coast, exporting agricultural produce to England and continental Europe. Economic activity thrived in ports because goods could be moved much more cheaply by water than by road, so trade routes naturally used sea, coastal waters and rivers if possible: ports became the nodes through with most commerce flowed.

Most major ports lay at the centre of complexes of routes which involved navigable rivers as well as the sea: so Bristol co-ordinated goods being brought over a hundred miles down the Severn from as far away as the Welsh borders and the Severn estuary broadened out to include the coastlines of South Wales, Somerset, Devon and Cornwall; London had the Thames, Lynn had the network of East Anglian rivers which opened up a hinterland stretching to the east midlands, and Hull could trade up the Trent to Nottingham and along the Ouse to York. This placed these major ports at the head of a local system of subordinate smaller towns and ports to create local trading systems of considerable importance. To some extent trade flowed within the system, so that grain flowed down the Thames to feed London and raw materials of all kinds supplied the ports' manufactures – barrel staves from the woodlands upriver were shipped down for Bristol's barrel-makers for instance. But more important were the import and export trades which lay at the heart of the port town's economy. England's overseas trade was essentially a matter of exporting cloth and some raw materials in exchange for the importing of luxuries which she could not herself produce, such as wine and spices, silks and velvet plus the specialized manufactures which concentration on cloth made it easier to import than make – metal domestic goods such as frying pans, needles, linen cloth or thread. Some raw materials were also imported: timber, pitch, tar and other forest products from the Baltic; salt, hemp and linen, dyestuffs and oil for the cloth industry; iron from Spain.

In consequence, traders in ports were in an excellent position to capture much of the wholesale trade of the country, and so the merchant class was concentrated very largely in ports. Merchants were much the richest of urban traders, so it is in ports that we find exceptional concentrations of capital, which in turn could form the basis of such primitive banking and insurance services as existed outside London, and in the metropolis could be found sophisticated financial services derived from mercantile capital. Loans were made to large landowners, bills of exchange were issued and London merchants, with stocks of capital far greater than any provincial trader could dream of, frequently raised loans for a crown which was always short of liquidity. Manufactures could be established in ports by the flow of exports such as cloth, which was often finished in London before shipping, and by imported raw materials, such as Bristol's soap industry, which relied on olive oil shipped from Spain.

It would be misleading to assume that all ports were large, for there were many small towns around the coast with very modest quantities of trade but a significant part to play in local urban networks. Some doubled as fishing ports, at a period when preserved and fresh fish supplied a vital element in diet, especially in the winter when meat was scarce. Several south-western towns, like Plymouth, harboured large fleets devoted to fishing for Newfoundland cod by the 1590s, and all up the east coast, from Great Yarmouth to Aberdeen, catches of cod and herring from the North Sea and Baltic were brought home. One common feature of most ports was a distinctive occupational structure, with the crews of ships and those employed at the quayside supplying a proletarian element lacking in inland towns, while merchants formed a dominant elite which was both richer and more sophisticated than could be found inland.

While the commercial success of London went from strength to strength during the course of the sixteenth century, many of the provincial ports experienced difficulties which could be very easily blamed on an over-dominant capital city. London's historian, John Stow, tried in 1598 to defend his native city from the current charge that it had sucked to itself 'both all trade of traffic by sea, and the retailing of wares and exercise of manual arts also.'[13] It seems likely that the contraction of trade found in ports such as Lynn, Southampton and Bristol was partly due to London's competition, but some ports – such as Exeter – flourished because they were too far from the capital to be affected while others benefited from supplying London with its necessities – for example Newcastle with its coal exports and many smaller towns in the south and east which shipped food to London. Some ports competed by developing routes to markets which London was not well sited to exploit, such as Hull with the Baltic, and Bristol to Ireland. And there were independent reasons for troubled ports, such as the silting which slowly strangled access to the quays at Rye and Chester in common with many other harbours along the south-east and southern coasts. The problem here may have been connected with the rising sea level of this time, which caused rivers to drop their silt earlier in their outflow than they had once done, and the absence of a sophisticated dredging technology.

Industry in Towns

We expect to find today that most large towns will have a major industrial element in their economies. But before the industrial revolution what historians have chosen to call 'industry' was almost completely small scale and with limited use for mechanical power, and should be less misleadingly called 'handicrafts' or 'manufacture' in the original sense of the word, meaning the making of things by hand. A majority of urban businesses involved making or processing something which was then sold in a shop, so that in the case of the ubiquitous shoemaker for instance, the workshop in which the footwear was actually made lay at the rear of a display area which may have only amounted to a pole with a few specimens hung from it; when the shop was open the shutters which closed its unglazed window would be lowered to allow transactions to take place across this space. In many cases, the quantity of the completed commodity which was exposed for show would be limited, and most 'shops' would be more accurately described as work spaces with attached facilities for some retailing; some traders would sell from a market stall and use their domestic premises solely for manufacture.

The sort of trades which we are describing here would include bakers and brewers, who would be supplying the country as well as the town, but not consumers at any great distance. Wood was a raw material which would be worked by coopers (sometimes hoopers) into barrels which were essential for a variety of storage and transport purposes. Skins were processed into leather by several different methods, each one a separate trade, whether tanner (who made thick leather by steeping hides in tannin derived from oak bark) or curriers and whittawers (making thinner and more supple leathers by applying organic materials such as dung and bird droppings to skins). The finished leather was sold on, usually through the marketplace, to a variety of specialized trades, shoemakers, makers of purses, belts or girdles, makers of leather clothing such as smiths' aprons, glovers, point-makers (points were the tagged laces which fastened clothing together before buttons and buttonholes became common); saddlers and harness-makers serviced the huge number of horses in the community. A range of manufactures involved metal-working, most commonly the pewterer, who made, from this alloy of lead and tin which was distinctively British, the domestic utensils from which most meals were eaten and drunk, pottery and glass being little used for these purposes at this date.

The most important urban manufacture in this century was the cloth industry, indeed it might well justify the term 'industry' since the scale and complexity of it and the way in which it used raw materials drawn from a distance and supplied faraway markets brings it nearer to the modern concept of an industry than any other contemporary trade. Cloth had usually been made in towns in the high middle ages, but during the fourteenth and fifteenth centuries it tended to migrate to the countryside, allegedly because of high urban overheads and the restrictive practices of the guilds; towns which were seriously affected by this trend included York and Beverley whose cloth manufacture seems largely to have moved to the West Riding of Yorkshire, and Bristol, Winchester and Coventry, which were all damaged in different ways. To compensate for these troubled towns however it is clear that cloth-making was increasing, in Suffolk and Essex at such towns as Colchester, Bury St Edmunds and Lavenham; in Kent; in Wiltshire (Salisbury, Devizes, Trowbridge); and in Somerset and Devon where many of the towns such as Cullompton and Tiverton around the flourishing port and finishing centre of Exeter were dominated by clothing. Further north, Shrewsbury's drapers flourished on finishing and marketing the cheaper cloths made in the North Wales countryside, while Lancashire and the Cumbrian town of Kendal made cottons and friezes – lighter, cheaper fabrics.

Some migration took place between towns; certainly rural industrial centres like the Stroudwater valley in Gloucestershire were significant, but clothing villages often, and naturally, grew rapidly into textile towns. And towns often came to specialize in the lucrative finishing and marketing of textiles, where they had indisputable advantages in their urban facilities, while the activities which operated in the countryside were low-wage, low-skill activities which were often seasonal in nature, allowing craft work to be combined with agriculture, while the urban cloth crafts were pursued throughout the year and at a more professional level.[14] It is often hard to understand exactly how urban craft guilds and regulations hampered the industry, for they certainly kept up quality standards. Probably they discouraged innovation and flexibility, and the maintenance of seven-year apprenticeships may well have added to costs and restricted the supply of skilled labour, but after the 1563 Statute of Artificers the apprenticeship system was extended to the countryside, in theory at least. Not all urban cloth industries were challenged by rural activity – in the case of Worcester, high-quality broadcloth was produced by a trade which seems to have operated at all levels within one settlement, flourishing in the later middle ages and coping quite well until the seventeenth century. The key here may be high quality; it was the pressures which came from trying to compete in the market for cheaper, lighter cloths which encouraged movement to the countryside.

The process of making cloth involved a sequence of skilled operations which relied on the skills of a variety of craftsmen. Wool had to be supplied, often from some distance, and then prepared and spun; this was often undertaken in the countryside, and usually by poor women working in their own homes. Wool was carded prior to spinning, using tools made by card-makers relying on the iron wire made by wire-drawers. Then the spun yarn was made into cloth by weavers with various specialisms and techniques, and then finished by fullers (also walkers) who oiled and matted the cloth using hands, feet or water-driven machinery in fulling mills. Then shearmen smoothed over the surface removing irregularities, and calenderers produced a shiny finish, with the dyer colouring some cloths, though most were exported still white, and dyed abroad. Drapers acted as cloth merchants, handling the buying, transporting and eventual sale of the finished commodity. Many of these tradesmen operated independently, buying raw materials or unfinished cloth, usually in the marketplace, working on it and then selling it on to the next link in the chain. But in many cases the process was controlled by a clothier, who might well begin by buying the wool and then orchestrate the ensuing stages; alternately, one of those engaged in the later finishing stages, or the draper, might oversee part of the process. Clothmaking, directly or indirectly, dominated the economies of many of the towns which came to specialize in it; Norwich, the largest provincial city, had about a quarter of its employment supplied by textiles by 1600, and in some smaller towns the proportion may have been even higher, including Worcester, where over half of the self-employed businesses seem to have been involved in this activity by the later years of the sixteenth century.

One feature of these clothing towns was their instability, liable as they were to periods of marked prosperity when their trade boomed, and to even more pronounced periods of depression when it failed. Rapidly growing prosperity is most marked in the period between the 1460s and the 1540s, when the customs accounts indicate that the total number of cloths exported rose from about 30,000 to about 130,000, a remarkable phenomenon in an age when change was slow and economies relatively unproductive.[15] All that growth needs to be translated into dynamic economic conditions at this date but not necessarily later, in towns like Exeter, Worcester, Bath and Reading. But because they were so reliant on the export trade, English clothing towns were hit hard by foreign wars and trade embargoes which could destroy export markets – typical episodes came in 1569–73 with the deterioration in Anglo-Spanish relations and more generally in the 1590s when much of Europe was convulsed in warfare. A good deal of cloth must have been absorbed by the domestic market, but the decline in the real incomes of poorer people in the second half of the Tudor period cannot have encouraged home sales to compensate for lost foreign markets.

The business was also liable to long-term depressions caused by changes in fashion and demand with which the native industry found it very difficult to cope, partly perhaps because the guild system based on apprenticeship and carefully regulated standards of production discouraged flexibility and innovation. The problem lay essentially in declining demand for the heavy, high-quality broadcloth which had been the mainstay of the traditional industry, in favour of lighter, cheaper cloths which were in demand in warmer climates and among poorer people. These were the 'new draperies' which slowly established themselves in the later sixteenth century. In Norwich, which probably contained the largest urban cloth industry of any major town, traditional manufactures were in the doldrums in the 1560s, and it was only the arrival of several thousand Protestant refugees from the Low Countries in the years after 1568 which rescued the city by introducing new techniques and lighter products, leading on to a positive boom which carried on through most of the following century. Other towns were not so fortunate: Reading slowly lost its trade during the course of the sixteenth century, and it was not alone; Newbury and Salisbury showed that some towns within a prospering regional industry might still experience problems.

Leisure

One major aspect of seventeenth-century town economies which was only just beginning in the Tudor period was the development of towns as leisure and health resorts for the better-off. The spa is the most characteristic of these places, but by 1603 the movement was only just beginning, with Bath attracting wealthy visitors, though perhaps more for medicinal than social reasons. Much clearer was the beginning of the movement of the gentry and its fringes into towns, either seasonally or on a permanent basis. York is a good example, its lacklustre industrial performance leading to a slack demand for housing which provided cheap rented accommodation; here shopping was a major draw, and escape from the isolation of a northern winter; the process was naturally encouraged by the city council, which presented a trophy for the first recorded horse-race at the edge of the city in 1530.[16] The trend did much to rescue the city from its late-medieval depression. The presence of gentry residents, without necessarily much in the way of organized social activity, can be traced in a number of similar county centres at this date, including Chester and Shrewsbury. In time this factor influenced the occupational structure of such places, with more service and luxury trades, such as domestic servants and purveyors of commodities such as grocery and quality clothing. In many towns in continental Europe, the landowning elite naturally made their permanent residence in towns in a way which was unusual in Britain at any time, and certainly at this early period.

Another specialized sort of town which can be tacked on here is the military or naval base. In the modern sense of the expression these were in their infancy, but the investment of governments like that of Henry VIII in the royal navy entailed the designation of some ports as bases, such as Portsmouth, with dry-dock repair facilities. Towns with a strong military element in their lives were rare in England, outside Berwick which was dominated by a remarkable set of sixteenth-century fortifications directed against the Scots, although its garrison was relatively small. Generally in England and Wales the role of towns as centres of fortified security was in decline and walls and gates were allowed to fall into disrepair, but in Scotland, and especially in Ireland, where the general expectation of peace and security was more recent and less well-founded, this aspect of the role of the town was more pronounced: all major Irish towns were walled at some stage, and in places such as Derry the walls were even being extended in the early seventeenth century.

Regulation

These urban economies were the subject of intense and increasing regulation throughout this period, a regime which occupied much of the time of urban governments. Maxima were set for wages and the price of foodstuffs; the right to set up a business was confined to town freemen, who were admitted by town governments on the basis of serving an apprenticeship, having a freeman father or paying a fee; those not so qualified were hounded out. Markets and fairs were subjected to a variety of laws on matters of quality and price; all dealing had to take place in public, and in markets – but not fairs – outsider could not deal with outsider, only a townsman. Market courts sat regularly to fine transgressors and settle civil disputes. Guilds existed for many trades and regulated them at the most detailed level; the apprenticeship system was central to the regulation of the economy and was controlled at guild, town and, after the 1563 Statute of Artificers, at national level. The Protestant attack on the religious role of the guilds weakened them, but they were re-founded in the years after 1548 as 'companies', often with the amalgamation of several hitherto separate trades into a single body, a process which preserved their power, and some of their social dimension, well into the seventeenth century. Above the level of the individual town, a mass of parliamentary legislation attempted to regulate the economy in all sorts of ways; the result was that a mass of restrictions surrounded urban business; some of them may have been supportive but many could have held back its development. Two conspicuously expanding industrial centres, Birmingham and Manchester, never acquired a chartered town government with all its regulatory implications; one is tempted to connect this rapid growth with the lack of controls.

Certainly one could point to a string of further factors which hampered the full development of economic potential. These included the fact that urban wealth tended to be invested in rural land rather than ploughed back into town businesses, as successful traders usually moved out to country estates as soon as they could. Poor road communications were a constant problem which ensured that markets remained relatively small and the movement of goods and people stayed expensive and limited. Towns were subject to periodic disasters – famines and epidemics, often connected, as in 1556–9, undermined capital formation and investment, while fires, like the burning of much of the centre of Nantwich in 1583,[17] additionally destroyed infrastructure and capital equipment. Urban prosperity was compromised by that weakness of consumer demand which was the inevitable consequence of the steady erosion of the living standards of the poorer majority in this period as food prices inflated and wage levels failed to keep up.

Decline or Growth?

For much of the twentieth century the historical orthodoxy was that towns in the early modern period were subject to serious economic pressures. It was accepted that in the later middle ages the phenomenon known as 'urban decline' was general. National population was decreasing or stagnating, and with it the scale of the economy; towns complained to the royal government that their trade was being lost, poverty was increasing and their houses were falling down. There were conspicuous examples of venerable towns in serious trouble, such as Winchester, York and Beverley. And then in the 1960s and 1970s came fine studies of other towns with apparently collapsing economies, the most influential being Charles Phythian-Adams' book on Coventry, where the contraction of its textile industry led to the making of a rare census in the 1520s which revealed the scale of its population loss.[18] The most influential summary of English urban history to be published in the later twentieth century, Clark and Slack's *English Towns in Transition* of 1976, suggested that urban economic problems were general in the first half of the sixteenth century, while the expansion of the national economy after 1560 imposed new problems of poverty and over-population on urban economies which had not completely shaken off their late-medieval stresses.

But as increasing quantities of research and publication followed the wave of interest in the newly defined 'urban history' of these years, a contrary interpretation of urban development emerged, disputing the universality of late-mediaeval decay and viewing the sixteenth century in a rosier light.[19] The problems of the late middle ages were seen by some as confined to a limited number of towns, though admittedly major ones, while much special pleading in the past and over-trusting interpretation of ambiguous sources by modern historians were suggested as misleading influences. Lack of conclusive documentary evidence makes the answering of such questions as 'Were the towns prospering in the sixteenth century?' very difficult to answer, not least because of the challenge of summarizing the fortunes of hundreds of settlements, mostly without good up-to-date histories. What one can suggest is that the middle years of the sixteenth century were certainly a watershed. The Reformation caused much damage and much more change in the towns: it wrecked monastic buildings, undermined or destroyed most of the cultural and social achievement of the middle ages, such as the accumulated art in the parish churches and the mystery-play cycles. Those towns which were centred on great abbeys – like St Albans – or were a focus of pilgrimage – like Canterbury – were temporarily impoverished; but conversely the

Reformation encouraged a wave of grants of self-government to towns which had previously been ruled by bishops (Lichfield, Boston, Banbury) or abbeys (Tewkesbury, Faversham). Protestantism encouraged the foundation of schools and perhaps modernized economic attitudes. If only one factor can be indicated as the turning-point between medieval and early modern in the Tudor town, then this was it.

Although there are indications of economic problems in some individual towns in the earlier decades of the sixteenth century, it seems likely that generally circumstances were improving, not least because cloth exports were booming until the 1550s, with benign effects on the many towns which made, finished or marketed cloth, and steadily rising population from perhaps about 1510 onwards was beginning to expand demand and solve the labour-supply problem which may well have held back the late medieval economy. After 1560 we enter a period when we are on rather surer ground, and it becomes easier to summarize. London was growing strongly, and stimulating provincial towns in turn. Some of the ports were damaged by London competition, but fewer provincial towns appear to be in conspicuous and newly arrived difficulty, and most of the towns which were undoubtedly in trouble in the earlier periods, such as York, Coventry or Winchester, were now stabilized or beginning to recover a little. Domestic trade seems to have been expanding, encouraged by political stability and rising prosperity amongst farmers and landowners. Most of the market towns seem to have expanded as rising demand for foodstuffs brought their basic role as local marketing centres into greater prominence.

But it remains true that with the exception, of course, of London, the fact that urban and rural populations were both expanding meant that the progress of urbanization proceeded rather modestly. It is not until the period after 1660 that we see the larger provincial towns beginning to expand at a faster rate than either the countryside or the market towns. This Tudor English pattern was shared by Wales, with expanding demand for foodstuffs channelled through the towns along the border, but lack of documentation makes it more difficult to see more than a modest economic upswing in Irish towns, and then only in the ports. The Irish economy was held back by the absence of that internal peace which had done so much for Tudor England. In Scotland there is more sign of population increase and a prosperity which spread beyond overseas trade, though large parts of the country remained distinctly under-urbanized by comparison with most of England and Wales. It would be wrong to exaggerate either the degree of change or the success of urban economies in the British Isles during the sixteenth century. The process of change could be painfully slow, so that much remained essentially medieval. The urban systems of Ireland and Scotland remained relatively underdeveloped and it is only in England, and especially London, that we can see clear signs of the highly urbanized and economically innovative future that lay ahead. But there is enough achievement in the urban sphere to point to a recovery from late-medieval problems and the establishment of solid foundations upon which more striking urban growth might take place in the near future.

NOTES

1. Cowan, *Urban Europe*, p. 8.
2. Dyer, 'Small market towns', pp. 430–1, 434.

3. Ibid., p. 432.
4. Proudfoot, 'Markets, fairs and towns in Ireland'.
5. Devine, 'Scotland', p. 153.
6. Clark and Gillespie, *Two Capitals*, p. 1.
7. Schwarz, 'Hanoverian London', p. 93.
8. Clay, *Economic Expansion and Social Change*, vol. II, p. 112.
9. Dietz, 'Overseas trade and metropolitan growth', pp. 115–29.
10. Beier, 'Engine of manufacture', pp. 141–67.
11. Dyer, 'Midlands', p. 93.
12. Berger, *Most Necessary Luxuries*, pp. 59–90.
13. Wheatley, *Survey of London by John Stow*, p. 495.
14. Thirsk, 'Industries in the Countryside'.
15. Clay, *Economic Expansion and Social Change*, vol II, p. 109.
16. Palliser, *Tudor York*, p. 15.
17. Phillips and Smith, *Lancashire and Cheshire*, p. 46.
18. Phythian-Adams, *Desolation of a City*.
19. Dyer, *Decline and Growth in English Towns*.

BIBLIOGRAPHY

Beier, A. L., 'Engine of manufacture: the trades of London', in A. L. Beier and R. Finlay eds, *London 1500–1700: The Making of the Metropolis* (London, 1986).

Berger, R. M., *The Most Necessary Luxuries: The Mercers' Company of Coventry 1550–1680* (Philadelphia, 1993).

Clark, P. and Gillespie, R., eds, *Two Capitals: London and Dublin 1500–1840* (London, 2001).

Clay, C. G. A., *Economic Expansion and Social Change: England 1500–1700* (2 vols, Cambridge, 1984).

Cowan, A., *Urban Europe 1500–1700* (London, 1998).

Devine, T. M., 'Scotland', in P. Clark, ed., *The Cambridge Urban History of Britain*, vol. II, *1540–1840* (Cambridge, 2000).

Dietz, B., 'Overseas trade and metropolitan growth', in A. L. Beier and R. Finlay, eds, *London 1500–1700: The Making of the Metropolis* (London, 1986).

Dyer, A. D., *Decline and Growth in English Towns 1400–1640* (Cambridge, 1995).

Dyer, Alan, 'Midlands', in P. Clark, ed., *The Cambridge Urban History of Britain*, vol. II, *1540–1840* (Cambridge, 2000).

Dyer, Alan, 'Small market towns 1540–1700', in P. Clark ed., *The Cambridge Urban History of Britain*, vol. II, *1540–1840* (Cambridge, 2000).

Palliser, D. M., *Tudor York* (Oxford, 1979).

Phillips, C. B. and Smith, J. H., *Lancashire and Cheshire from A.D. 1540* (London, 1994).

Phythian-Adams, C., *Desolation of a City: Coventry and the Urban Crisis of the Late Middle Ages* (Cambridge, 1979).

Proudfoot, L., 'Markets, fairs and towns in Ireland, c. 1600–1853', in P. Borsay and L. Proudfoot, eds, *Provincial Towns in Early Modern England and Ireland: Change, Convergence and Divergence* (London, 2002).

Schwarz, L., 'Hanoverian London: the making of a service town', in P. Clark and R. Gillespie, eds, *Two Capitals: London and Dublin 1500–1840* (London, 2001).

Thirsk, J., 'Industries in the countryside', in J. Thirsk, *The Rural Economy of England: Collected Essays* (London, 1984).

Wheatley, H. B., ed., *The Survey of London by John Stow* (London, 1912).

FURTHER READING

P. Clark, ed., *The Cambridge Urban History of Britain*, vol. II, *1540–1840* (2000) is now the standard work – detailed and comprehensive (but excludes Ireland). S. M. Jack, *Towns in Tudor and Stuart Britain* (1996) is the only recent shorter introduction. P. Clark and P. Slack, *English Towns in Transition 1500–1700* (1976) was the first attempt at a general thesis when the modern wave of urban history began. C. R. Friedrichs, *The Early Modern City 1450–1750* (1995) provides a European context. *London 1500–1700: The Making of the Metropolis*, ed. A. L. Beier and R. Finlay (1986) is the best introduction to the history of early modern London. S. Rappaport, *Worlds within Worlds: Structures of Life in Sixteenth Century London* (1989) is impressively researched. K. Wrightson, *Earthly Necessities: Economic Lives in Early Modern Britain* (2000) is an up-to-date short survey of the economy, and goes beyond England. *The Tudor and Stuart Town 1530–1688*, ed. J. Barry (1990) reprints some classic articles with a good introduction. C. Galley, *The Demography of Early Modern Towns: York in the Sixteenth and Seventeenth Centuries* (Liverpool, 1998) covers the demographic aspects. D. Woodward, *Men at Work: Labourers and Building Craftsmen in the Towns of Northern England, 1450–1750* (1995) opens up the lives of poorer townsmen. Scottish towns are introduced in M. Lynch (ed.), *The Early Modern Town in Scotland* (1987). R. Tittler, *Townspeople and Nation: English Urban Experiences 1540–1640* (2001) reveals some individual townsfolk. Basic works on individual towns include J. F. Pound, *Tudor and Stuart Norwich* (1988), A. D. Dyer, *The City of Worcester in the Sixteenth Century* (1973), G. Mayhew, *Tudor Rye* (1987) and D. H. Sacks, *The Widening Gate: Bristol and the Atlantic Economy, 1450–1700* (1991).

CHAPTER TWENTY

Metropolitan London

JOSEPH P. WARD

One of the clearest ways to gauge the changes associated with the Tudor period in British history is to look closely at the City of London and its environs. At the start of Henry VII's reign, the City was a medium-sized urban centre confined mostly within its ancient wall on the north bank of the River Thames. Westminster, the seat of English national government, was a largely self-contained community to the west of the City, while the borough of Southwark lay at the southern approach to London Bridge. At the end of Elizabeth I's reign, the extensive development of the City outside its wall to the west had made it less distinctive from Westminster. Additional extra-mural growth to the north and the east as well as urbanization in areas south of the Thames further confirmed the City's status as the centre of a metropolis. Greater London contained around 50,000 people at the start of the sixteenth century, the great majority of whom lived within the City's wall. A century later, there were about 200,000 Londoners, most of whom lived in extra-mural areas. London was one of only eighteen European cities whose population at least doubled during the sixteenth century and, by the year 1600, it was one of the five most populous urban centres in Europe, trailing behind only Paris and Naples.[1]

Such growth in an early modern city would suggest profound changes not only to its own economy and society, but also to those of its region and nation. During the Tudor period, the generally rising stature of the crown, parliament, and the courts of law in national affairs gave growing numbers of people reasons to spend time in the metropolis and encouraged increasing numbers of young men to seek legal training at the Inns of Court. The relative prosperity and desire for social advancement of such visitors to London led many of them to spend their free time patronizing painters and musicians and haunting taverns, shops and theatres, all of which fostered residential and commercial building in Westminster and the western precincts of the City. London's prominence in national commercial networks also increased during the period. In medieval times, London had already established itself as a market whose demands affected a wide variety of commercial activity, especially agriculture, over a considerable portion of England. As the metropolitan population returned to, and then surpassed, the levels it had reached before the great fourteenth-century plague outbreak, it revitalized the trading relationships required to supply the metropolis with its basic needs. The wood–pasture economy of central Suffolk, which comprised two-thirds of that county, focused on supplying London's markets with cheese and butter. At the same time, a farmer in Warwickshire could make a living buying cattle from Wales at Chester, fattening them up on his own property, and selling them to butchers serving the metropolis. Metropolitan demand similarly encouraged developments in the trades of other basic commodities, such as wood and coal, which in turn spurred the expansion of docks, shipyards and the industries that served them.[2]

Such developments challenged the cohesiveness of metropolitan society. The sustained growth of London's population combined with the cultural and political changes associated with the Reformation to loosen the ties that had bound members of London's society to one another. For that reason, the focus of this chapter will be on the metropolis rather than on the City itself because during the course of the Tudor period the challenges, and opportunities, facing London's residents and their governors increasingly crossed the City's legal boundaries.

London's government was a mosaic of overlapping authorities and jurisdictions. At the beginning of the Tudor period, the City of London was divided into twenty-five wards. Most of these lay within London's ancient wall, but three (Aldersgate, Bishopsgate and Cripplegate) contained territory within and without the wall while two others (Farringdon Without and Portsoken) were entirely extra-mural. The citizens of each ward selected one person to represent them on the court of aldermen, the City's primary executive and legislative body, one of whose members would serve as mayor each year. Once chosen, an alderman would serve until he died, resigned, or was removed from his position. The ward was also the unit of the annual selection for members of the common council, which played a subordinate role to the court of aldermen in the City despite the relatively large number of its members. Outside the City lay the counties of Middlesex to the north and Surrey to the south, in which many areas at the outset of the period were still under manorial government. Westminster had the social and economic functions commonly associated with towns but it remained, until the dissolution of the monasteries, a seigneurial manor under the control of the abbot of St Peter's. Its post-Dissolution secular government did not receive formal recognition until an act of parliament was passed for that purpose in 1585. Further complicating the jurisdictional landscape of the metropolis was the presence of more than two dozen precincts known as 'liberties' which were often associated with religious houses and therefore came under the jurisdiction of ecclesiastical authorities rather than of City officials. Ownership of these precincts passed to the crown at the Reformation and, when they were subsequently sold, their immunity from many aspects of civic oversight passed to their new owners, but London's liberties were hardly lawless, for they were subject to royal oversight as well as national legislation.[3]

The City government expanded the area of its legal jurisdiction throughout the Tudor period. The mayor and aldermen leased Moorfields, a marshy area just to the north of the City's wall, in 1309. During the next two centuries, the City government leased the property out to several tenants, requiring them to keep their brook clear of rubbish as well as charging them rent. Much of this area remained relatively undeveloped and used primarily for recreation and the dumping of household and industrial waste, though the rising population of the central City made Moorfields attractive for a mixture of commercial and recreational purposes during the sixteenth century, which included clothes-washing and dyeing, the pasturing of cattle, and gardening. The City government inserted itself even more directly in the affairs of Moorfields' neighbour to the east, Finsbury. In 1514, the mayor and aldermen acquired a lease of the manor of Finsbury from the dean and chapter of St Paul's Cathedral. The manor court continued to operate as it had before, only now the court of aldermen filled the role of overlords of the manor. Most residents of Tudor Finsbury engaged in industries such as cloth-making and brick-making that were increasingly difficult, if not impossible, to accommodate within the City's wall. The most significant extension of the City's authority into neighbouring areas during the sixteenth century came to its south. The term 'Southwark' was, like London itself, open to a variety of meanings in the Tudor period, though generally it referred to five manors on the Surrey side of the Thames: Paris Garden, the Clink, the Guildable manor, the King's manor, and the Great Liberty manor. In 1550, the City purchased the latter three of these, giving it control over a territory that began at the southern end of London Bridge and extended more than 1,000 metres along the main roads into Surrey. These manors were incorporated into Bridge Ward Without, though their inhabitants were not granted the same rights of representation on the courts of aldermen and common council that residents of the City's twenty-five other wards enjoyed.[4]

Religious authority was similarly complex. The metropolis fell under the jurisdiction of the bishops of London (north of the Thames) and Winchester (south of the Thames). The parish was the central unit of religious life, and one of the basic sources of community, in London as it was elsewhere in Tudor Britain. There were over one hundred parishes in the metropolis, with those in the central part of the City often being no more than a few acres in size while those towards the periphery were much larger. Parishes such as St Botolph Aldgate and St Botolph Bishopsgate, which sat at the northern approaches to the City, each contained territory equal to the combined extent of a handful of parishes inside London's wall. This difference in size would prove crucial, for as the open fields in the sprawling extra-mural parishes developed urban characteristics, especially towards the end of the Tudor period, their parochial officers would have growing difficulty serving the needs of their parishioners, many of whom had only recently arrived in the metropolis. The large difference in the territorial extent and, increasingly over time, population of intra-mural and extra-mural parishes also suggests that parishes in the City's centre were better able than outer parishes to foster a sense of community among their members.[5]

The crown took an active interest in the City's affairs throughout the Tudor period. The City government's authority flowed from its royal charter, so it was responsible to the crown for upholding order within its jurisdiction. Concerns about threats to order in the metropolis, especially in the form of vagrancy, were important factors in the crafting of national social policies, most notably in the second half of the sixteenth century. During Elizabeth's reign in particular, the crown asserted its influence in the management of London's economy and society, perhaps most clearly by undertaking a policy to limit the growth of the metropolitan population. In 1580, a royal proclamation prohibited the building of new houses or tenements in the City and within three miles of the City's gates. Anyone who defied this order would be subject to arrest and would be released only after they had taken a bond against future illegal building. Three years later, the privy council scolded London's mayor for failing to see that the queen's order was enforced within his jurisdiction. Such steps may have given contemporaries the impression that the queen's government was committed to restraining London's physical expansion, but in practice it seemed more than willing to grant licences to developers and to collect financial penalties from those who undertook building without royal sanction.[6]

Economic life in the metropolis was regulated primarily through the trade guilds, known as 'livery companies', the most prominent of which were medieval in origin. In 1319, Edward II granted a charter to the City of London specifying that full citizens (the 'freemen') needed to occupy a trade, and made the clearest indication of such status the membership in a livery company. The livery companies, in turn, were also incorporated by royal charter. In the Tudor period, as many as one hundred such companies may have existed at one time or another, although a dozen of the wealthiest of these (the so-called Great Twelve) dominated civic life while perhaps another dozen or two, including companies associated with the building and textile trades, were significantly influential in London's economy. Unlike the vast majority of freemen, London's governors were often involved with overseas trading companies; in 1564, all but five of the City's aldermen were members of the Merchant Adventurers' Company, which controlled the cloth trade with the Low Countries. Despite the gathering of power into elite hands, all of the livery companies were crucial institutions for the integration of young people, and in practice that meant almost exclusively young men, into the political and social fabric of London. Most freemen joined their companies through serving an apprenticeship with a company member, and it was unusual for someone to gain full freeman status before reaching the age of twenty-five. By the mid-sixteenth century as many as three-quarters of adult men in the City of London were members of companies, but it is quite likely that the percentage of freemen declined thereafter.[7]

The close association between citizenship and livery company membership meant that London companies were intimately connected to the City's government, but their influence was not limited to the territory within the lord mayor's jurisdiction. The crown granted companies supervisory powers over trades throughout the metropolis as well as within the City itself. In a typical way, the Vintners' Company charter of 1567 authorized its officers to regulate the business of anyone who occupied a tavern or sold wine in the City of London, its suburbs and all liberties within three miles of the City, a territory that would have encompassed the entire developed area of the metropolis as well as a considerable amount of undeveloped land in the early years of Elizabeth's reign. The legal authority of some companies reached even further afield. For example, the letters patent issued to the Tilers' and Bricklayers' company in 1568 gave its officers the right to inspect the use of tiles and bricks by anyone within fifteen miles of the City's borders. Given that the rate of growth of London neighbourhoods that lay outside of the lord mayor's jurisdiction was, from the middle of the Tudor period, greater than that of areas within the City, it is not surprising that livery companies would want their influence to extend across the metropolis.[8]

As is the case with any type of law enforcement in the early modern period, it is extremely difficult to determine the extent to which livery company regulations were enforced effectively. Company records tend to be inconsistent in this regard and, although at times there is evidence for the collection of fines from those found violating company ordinances, more informal – though potentially more effective – means of regulation, such as verbal warnings to malefactors, may have gone unrecorded. That said, there is no reason to assume that livery companies asserted their control either more effectively or more consistently in the City than they did in the liberties and suburbs. Indeed, given the tendency for company governors to desire to maintain good relations among their members through the ready extension of leniency towards them as well as their wish to assert their authority over rapidly expanding suburban areas, it may well have been the case that many livery companies regulated their trades in suburban areas more aggressively than they did in the City itself.

Beyond the livery companies' purview, informal sectors of the economy provided opportunities for non-citizens. Many crucial tasks, including the loading and unloading of ships at the riverside and the transportation of goods through London's crowded streets, went largely unregulated until the seventeenth century. Ancillary aspects of the building industry, such as hauling supplies or moving earth, were not under the jurisdiction of any livery company. Anecdotal evidence from the Tudor period suggests that such jobs most certainly existed in abundance. Their informal nature provides historians with too little evidence to discuss unregulated occupations in detail, but it seems likely that these types of employment provided opportunities for some of the many thousands of immigrants who never established formal ties to livery companies.

Such opportunities were especially crucial for single women. The custom of London allowed the widow of a freeman to exercise a craft or trade in the City, although company regulations often limited their activity. A study of the binding of apprentices in seven of Tudor London's leading companies indicates that less than 2 per cent of them were engaged by women, most of whom were widows. Beyond the activities that came under livery company supervision, occupations that were open to single women tended to be associated with types of employment considered appropriate to a woman's traditional roles in the household economy, such as nursing infants, caring for the elderly and infirm, washing clothes, cleaning churches and livery halls, preparing food and hawking it in the street. London's civic and ecclesiastical authorities – especially parishes and livery companies – that were always concerned to reduce the numbers of the idle poor in the metropolis gave some structure to the informal economy by allocating casual employment within their control to single women, with a strong preference for widows or daughters of company members.[9]

Crime was a further alternative for those who were not participants in Tudor London's regulated economy. There is abundant contemporary literature, especially concerning Elizabethan London, pointing to the existence of well-established criminal activities such as banditry and prostitution. If this literature were taken at face value, it would suggest that a very substantial segment of London's population subsisted by preying upon immigrants, robbing them of their virtue as well as their property. Research that has placed this literature in the context of efforts by London's civil and ecclesiastical officials to reform metropolitan society offers a more nuanced view of the role of crime in London's society and economy. Literary and archival sources both suggest that crime was commonly associated with youth, as young people may have gradually fallen out with their masters and drifted slowly from small-scale theft to support their pleasurable pastimes to more serious forms of property crime, such as cut-pursing. Many of those who would eventually come to the attention of the authorities for vagrancy or prostitution doubtless first entered metropolitan society as prospective apprentices or maidservants.

The extent to which crime was organized remains uncertain. It is clear that there were from time to time certain houses that developed a reputation for being hospitable to vagrants and petty criminals, and that these provided an opportunity for those who were seeking illicit means to earn a living to form associations with others who shared their goals, but these networks should be characterized as short-term alliances rather than professional enterprises. Still, there certainly were individuals who pursued what may reasonably be considered a career in crime. It is hard not to conclude that John Dytch, who was indicted for nineteen instances of horse-theft during an eighteen-month period in 1582 and 1583, was motivated by more than a fondness for horses, but the boldness of his actions shines brightly against the backdrop of the pettiness, even desperation, of most of the criminal activity undertaken in Tudor London.[10]

An increasingly aggressive regulatory machine took aim at such criminality. When Edward VI chartered Bridewell Hospital in 1552, he empowered its governors to apprehend and discipline those who were threatening social order throughout London and Middlesex. Periodically, such as in a late-1570s sweep of illicit sex that led to the conviction of both prostitutes and their clients, Bridewell authorities played a leading role in establishing order in the metropolis, but more often the burden of law enforcement fell upon the loosely organized, and doubtless overburdened, constables, beadles, surveyors and ward watches. The usual caveats about the limitations of early modern archives are especially important to bear in mind in the discussion of crime for several reasons. First, one must assume that a considerable amount of activity that would have been considered 'criminal' in a strict sense went unreported and therefore unrecorded. The densely packed neighbourhoods of the City and the overlapping jurisdictions of those attempting to apprehend criminals made law enforcement an exceedingly challenging endeavour. It is not surprising therefore that the records of criminal regulation in Tudor London have a sporadic character, reflecting the attempts of London's authorities to crack down on crime during periods of perceived instability, such as times of plague or dearth or following a large-scale demobilization of soldiers, which heightened concerns about groups of vagrants attempting to subsist through crime. Here, the changing tone of religious discussions of social order played a role as godly preachers from the mid-century onwards increasingly challenged London's magistrates to maintain discipline among their subjects by closing down sites of popular entertainment such as bowling alleys and dancing schools as well as unlicensed alehouses and brothels.

The concern with order largely reflected the challenges posed to metropolitan society by its long-term physical growth, but it also was a response to the outbreaks of disease and other catastrophes that regularly struck London. Early modern sources for demographic trends are notoriously difficult to interpret, but it is clear that important epidemics in the 1550s and 1560s had a dampening effect on London's population. An outbreak of sweating sickness took over 800 lives in the summer of 1551, but the worst effect of illness followed the failed harvests of 1555 and 1556, when a combination of typhus, influenza, and other contagious diseases produced a spike in mortality trends. From the 1560s onwards metropolitan population growth accelerated, especially in the areas outside of London's ancient wall.[11]

Immigration fuelled Tudor London's growth. There were two main types of immigrants: 'foreigners' who were born in provincial England and 'aliens' or 'strangers' who came to London from abroad. London was a highly attractive destination for those migrants who were seeking to better their stations in life as well as those who were trying to escape poverty. In order for London's population to have continued to climb steadily despite periodic economic downturns and outbreaks of disease, something in the order of 6,000 immigrants per year were required. It has been estimated that the metropolis absorbed the natural increase (the excess of births to deaths) of half of England's population in the late sixteenth and early seventeenth centuries. As a result, most Londoners – and, in some neighbourhoods, more than three-quarters of them – had been born elsewhere.[12]

Important subsets of non-English immigrants (the 'aliens' or 'strangers') were those who associated themselves with the French and Dutch churches that were created in 1550 to benefit the Protestants who sought refuge in London, especially in the era of the French wars of religion, and which quickly became focal points for the alien communities in the metropolis. As many as 40–50,000 strangers migrated to the metropolis between the years 1550 and 1585, although it is likely that there were no more than 10,000 aliens in London at one time. Such levels of immigration into a society that was struggling to manage its growth could have been highly destabilizing, but the alien churches as institutions succeeded in assisting their members in finding their places in the metropolis. The elders of the French and Dutch churches worked closely with officials of the national and local governments to defuse animosities when they arose. They were quick to defend their brethren from accusations that their immigration was economically rather than religiously motivated and, perhaps most important of all in a society that seemed at times concerned primarily with fostering orderliness, they developed a reputation for their ability to maintain discipline among their members. Indeed, from time to time City authorities would refer strangers who violated the law to the elders of their churches for correction, which suggests the high regard in which London's governors held the leaders of the stranger churches.

The great effectiveness with which the stranger churches assisted immigrants to establish themselves in the metropolis had the effect of creating and maintaining stranger communities that were, to a high degree, separate from the rest of London. A newly arrived immigrant who associated with one of these churches would gain an entry point not only to a familiar community of faith but also to social networks that would provide him or her with important social and economic contacts within an almost exclusively alien world. Such separateness helped to fuel the occasional outbursts of animosity aimed at the strangers – who, it may have appeared to many of London's English residents, had access to a comprehensive range of social services through their churches that were denied to most other Londoners – but it was not so all-encompassing as to prevent strangers from assimilating fully into London society, especially after the first generation gave way to succeeding ones.[13]

Trends in living costs and workers' wages offer some guidance for the underlying challenges that immigrants faced in London. The financial records of livery companies include data on the prices that companies paid for food and drink for their feasts, the rents that they received for tenements they owned, and the wages that they paid to craftsmen and labourers for maintaining their various properties (including the companies' halls). An analysis of these records suggests that there were four distinct phases of price trends in Tudor London. From the 1490s through the early 1540s, living expenses rose fairly gradually. There was a surge in food prices as a result of poor harvests in 1500–3, but better harvests in the succeeding years moderated inflation until the early 1520s. That decade saw sharp price increases at its beginning and end, but prices decreased somewhat during the mid-1520s. Bountiful harvests throughout the 1530s and early 1540s meant that, on the whole, costs for basic foodstuffs in London increased by an average of only 0.5 per cent per year during the first half of the Tudor period. During the second phase, from 1542 to 1551, prices leapt by an average of 6.6 per cent per year, for an aggregate increase of 77 per cent across the decade. The most likely cause for this jump in the cost of living was a combination of currency debasement and the English wars with France and Scotland, which increased demand for commodities as the government sought to feed and equip armies and build fortifications. Price increases moderated somewhat during the third phase, from the early 1550s through the early 1590s. During the 1550s, living costs stabilized at the high levels established in the previous decade. Prices jumped in the wake of successive poor harvests in 1555 and 1556, but they receded a bit thereafter because the harvests for the rest of the decade were quite good. From 1560 to 1590, prices rose no more than 8 per cent from one decade to the next. The final decade of the Tudor period saw wide fluctuations in living costs. The first four harvests of the 1590s were good enough to depress prices by 12 per cent, but between 1593 and 1597, the combination of poor harvests and the demands of the military led to an even more significant inflationary surge than that of the mid-century. The price of flour, which was perhaps the most important commodity to the typical London household, tripled during that brief period. Successful harvests in the following years relieved the inflationary pressure considerably. Wages did not remain stagnant in the face of price increases for basic foodstuffs, but they were not sufficient to keep pace with inflation.

Real wages – the income of skilled and semi-skilled workers adjusted for inflation – declined 19 per cent from the outset of the Tudor period through the early 1540s. During the decade 1542–51, when prices increased by 77 per cent, wages rose only 50 to 60 per cent. Workers made some progress, albeit in fits and starts, from the late 1550s, but by the 1560s real wages had recovered only to the point where they were prior to the debasement. Wages were rather stagnant, with a total decline of only 5 per cent, during the first three decades of Elizabeth's reign, but they plunged during the crisis years of the mid-1590s and recovered slowly thereafter. In summary, the best estimate we have for the trend in real wages for London workers during the Tudor period was a decline of 29 per cent.[14]

It remains difficult to determine whether or not metropolitan society coped effectively with the tension and social stress stemming from economic fluctuations, especially during the serious crisis of the latter part of Elizabeth's reign. London avoided prolonged periods of social and political breakdown – there was no organized effort to overturn the government, for example – but disturbances did occur periodically, some of which challenged the ability of London's governors to maintain order. There were traditions in London, as elsewhere, of young people making merry, not to mention making trouble, on May Day and Shrove Tuesday. The precise origins of these traditions are difficult to determine, which itself reflects the relatively spontaneous nature of such events when compared to the more ritualized times of youthful mischief in some Continental cities. The most famous incident of this sort in Tudor London was the so-called 'Evil May Day' of 1517, in which a crowd of around one thousand people, many but not all of whom were London apprentices, rioted for four hours in St Martin le Grand, a liberty within the City that was home to a largely alien population. The disturbance produced no fatalities, although thirteen of the three hundred people arrested for participating in the riot were convicted of treason and executed soon thereafter. Strangers in London were targeted by much smaller-scale disturbances throughout the remainder of the Tudor period, especially at times of English conflict with Continental powers and when economic crisis made the strangers relatively easy targets for the expression of economic frustration by native workers.

The mid-1590s, and particularly 1595, was an especially tense period in London. Although some historians have interpreted urban protests as a release-mechanism that ultimately helped to keep society on an even keel, riots over the high prices of fish and butter on 12 and 13 June 1595 apparently served only as a prelude to the marching of a crowd of one thousand apprentices in the direction of Tower Hill two weeks later with the rumoured intention of looting gunshops and then overturning the City government. In the event, order was restored, although at the cost of placing the City under martial law for the remainder of the summer. The fact that 1595 marked the high point of disturbances in Tudor London even though the economic crisis inflicting the City would not run its course for another two years suggests that London's governors understood their responsibility to respond – or at the very least to appear to respond – to the hardships faced by their subjects. In this way, riots such as those in June 1595 can best be understood as a form of communication among London's social groups.[15]

The proliferation of faith communities was a further source of social stress in the metropolis. When Henry VII and Henry VIII ascended their thrones, London was a Catholic city that counted among its greatest treasures its many churches, religious houses, and glorious cathedral. Those Londoners who wished to resist theological change could look for leadership to high-ranking officials with strong London ties, such as Sir Thomas More. More was a principal figure in a thriving Christian humanist circle in London that included John Colet, who became dean of St Paul's in 1505 and four years later founded the grammar school that would become one of the most famous in the realm. More had travelled in London's governing circles – he was an under-sheriff at the time of the Evil May Day riot in 1517 – before entering the crown's service. Men such as More called for the spiritual purification of the church, but as the movement for theological reform took, in their view, a divisive turn, they held steadfast to orthodoxy, with many, such as More, sacrificing their lives for their faith. After More's departure, Edmund Bonner, the bishop of London, emerged as a champion of the old faith. Bonner withheld his enthusiastic support from the reformist programme undertaken by Archbishop Cranmer and would emerge as one of the more celebrated – or castigated, depending on one's view – scourges of the Protestants. The initial response of Cranmer was to work around Bonner by building a model of godliness in Westminster, which was given its own diocese in 1540 and which became a centre of Protestant proselytizing in the metropolis. The Westminster diocese was dissolved in 1550 and, with Bonner in prison and deprived of his office, Cranmer took personal direction of the evangelical process in the Diocese of London.

London proved receptive to Cranmer's mission. As a centre of trade with links to the Continent and a relatively high literacy rate, London, like other urban centres in Europe in the middle of the sixteenth century provided the Protestant movement with an environment in which it could take root. Cranmer's careful cultivation ensured that it flourished. In London, as elsewhere in England, the reign of Mary saw the return of Catholic practices in the parishes and livery companies, but the records of the material restoration of the old faith tell us little about the level of enthusiasm for the movement. The queen and her advisers had good reason to be anxious about the true allegiances of many of London's citizens, including those in positions of responsibility for the maintenance of order. As Mary's regime assumed an increasingly hostile stance towards those who refused to give their hearts to Roman Catholicism, London's Protestants grew more steadfast. During Elizabeth's reign, London was one of the strongest centres of the international Protestant movement. Given that public professions of faith were a common requirement for a wide variety of civic office-holders and for members of the livery companies, the mercurial nature of officially sanctioned theology in the mid-Tudor period could be expected to have had a profoundly unsettling effect on Londoners. This was all the more so because neighbourliness rested on the parish, where the rich and poor alike were drawn together as communicants in a shared faith that bound them to the eternal community. Prior to the Reformation, those bounds were reinforced by the hundreds of religious guilds and chantries associated with parishes, livery companies and the many monastic houses in the metropolis.[16]

London served as a centre for Protestant nonconformity in the final decades of the Tudor era. By the late 1560s, the Elizabethan church hierarchy had successfully established control over the beneficed clergy in the metropolis, but it would be from the ranks of the unbeneficed – from preachers supported by endowed lectureships, for example – that many of the leaders of the movement for further godly reform would come. Such men's livings depended directly on their patrons' support, so it proved nearly impossible for the church hierarchy to discipline them. Here the livery companies, institutions that in other contexts lent stability and coherence to the metropolis, could extend their support to those who would, in time, work to undermine the established church. John Field and Thomas Wilcox, authors of the polemic *An Admonition to the Parliament* (1572), participated in the patronage-worlds of London companies, with Field having received help from the Clothworkers' Company during his time at Oxford and Wilcox serving as curate for All Hallows Honey Lane, whose advowson the Grocers' Company owned. These would have an influence not only in the metropolis but also in the broader nation, as they encouraged a generation of successful merchants who had immigrated to London and who would establish endowments to support godly charities – including schools and lectureships – for their home towns and villages, some of which were located in predominantly Catholic areas of England and Wales.[17]

Despite such divisions, there is scant evidence that religious change was fundamentally disruptive of life in the metropolis. Instead, customs and practices evolved both in response to national political developments and London's sheer growth, which put tremendous strains on the parishes that remained the focal points of most Londoners' religious lives throughout the Tudor period. Religious change transformed the nature of charity, as the latter was decoupled from the Catholic doctrine of good works and no longer required that the recipient pray for the soul of the benefactor. The emphasis of godly preachers on the sharp dichotomy between the deserving and the undeserving poor reduced support for the destitute among London's socially marginalized groups, such as young vagrants and single women. At the same time, older commemorative rituals and charitable practices evolved in the later sixteenth century in ways that encouraged charity and linked the living to their deceased benefactors. Livery companies, whose rituals and communal practices often had their origins in lay fraternities, served throughout the sixteenth century as trustees for a variety of their members' charitable bequests. In response to the religious changes implemented during the sixteenth century, the companies could no longer manage endowments for chantries or obits for their deceased members. That did not stop them, however, from encouraging their members' charitable impulses by establishing new, more secular rituals of remembrance that celebrated benefactors of company-centred charitable endowments. In this way, although the communal rituals at the heart of livery-company attempts to maintain cohesion among their members can be seen to have changed dramatically in the wake of the Reformation, they also maintained much of their former emphasis on company traditions and the responsibility of each generation to build upon the charitable reputation of its predecessors.[18]

Recent research into the general quality and quantity of charity in Tudor London suggests that the religious changes of the mid-sixteenth century did not disrupt fundamentally patterns and practices of charitable giving that had been established previously. To be sure, London's charities struggled mightily to keep pace with the demands placed upon them, especially during times of economic distress, and there is no support for the notion that the metropolitan poor were cared for adequately. Even if they were motivated as much by the fear of disorder caused by widespread immiseration as they were by feelings of affection towards their less fortunate fellows, it is essential to recognize that London's elite proved imaginative in responding to the challenges they faced. The governors of Christ's Hospital were authorized by poor-relief legislation in 1563 and 1572 to receive poor-rate collections from across the metropolis. Given discretion to allocate their revenue to parishes as they saw fit, the hospital governors redistributed some of the rates collected from inner City parishes to extra-mural parishes that were in acute distress. Such measures sufficed – perhaps by the barest of margins at times – to ease the stress that periods of pronounced price increases and under-employment placed upon metropolitan society.[19]

Such social pressures did not necessarily diminish – indeed, they may have enhanced – London's cultural vitality. As other chapters have indicated, London was a thriving cultural centre during the Tudor period, influenced by, and contributing to, broader European trends in the visual and performing arts. Here, the combination

of London's political and commercial roles in England was crucial, as the purchasing power of the Westminster elite, the denizens of the Inns of Court and the
City merchants provided sustenance for metropolitan artists. It is particularly with
the theatre, however, that London, especially during the Elizabethan period, made
its greatest mark. More notable, perhaps, than London's ability to accommodate tens
of thousands of immigrants or its adaptability in response to sweeping religious
changes was its emergence as the heart of both puritanism and the theatrical culture
onto which godly preachers poured invective. The success of theatre, and especially
of the public stages, was possible only because London functioned as a metropolis.
The playhouses of Elizabethan London were located in areas outside the City because
its governors seemed largely persuaded by the providentialist argument that the toleration of theatre would invite divine retribution. The godly preacher Thomas White
delivered a sermon in London in 1577, one year after the first public playhouse was
opened, in which he asserted that 'the cause of plagues is sin, if you look to it well,
and the cause of sin are plays; therefore, the cause of plagues are plays.' In an urban
society visited frequently by plague and other disasters, providence could not be easily
dismissed, but nothing prevented freemen, along with their wives and apprentices,
from attending plays, and there is every reason to believe that many of them did so.[20]

Theatre could provoke royal as well as divine displeasure. London's potentially
destabilizing role in national affairs was never clearer than in the final years of
Elizabeth's reign. The second earl of Essex, who fancied himself the upholder of the
codes of aristocratic honour at Court, was caught up in a contest for power at Court
with the Cecil faction, whom he considered upstarts. Having gained, after careful
striving, a place on the privy council as well as the office of earl marshal, Essex lost
most of his prestige in his queen's eye after his inglorious return from a failed mission
to Ireland in the autumn of 1599. Excluded from the royal presence and facing an
investigation into his role in the publication of John Hayward's *The First Part of the
Life and Reign of King Henry IV* (1599) – which was dedicated to him and which
dealt largely with the overthrow of Richard II – Essex began plotting in earnest
against those in power at Court. Having toyed with a number of strategies, including leading an army from Ireland into Wales and eventually on to the capital, he fixed
his fate upon an appeal to his popularity among the citizens of London. Essex believed
that he had the support of key members of the London elite, such as the Puritan-
leaning merchant Thomas Smythe, who held the office of sheriff, and he made Essex
House the centre of a Puritan patronage network in the City. Showing his willingness to lead a broad coalition, Essex also employed the theatre, that object of Puritan
outrage. He supported the performance of a play about Richard II in the streets of
London and, on the eve of the rebellion, his followers attended Shakespeare's
production of *Richard II* at the Globe. In the event, Essex's estimation of London's
utility for his purposes proved unfounded. The earl's grand entrance into the City
on 8 February 1601 astonished more than it inspired the populace, and sheriff
Smythe repulsed the earl's pleas for support. In the meantime, the mayor and aldermen prepared to defend the City against Essex while heralds began spreading the
news that he had been declared a traitor. The earl retreated to Essex House to make
his last stand, but his support dissolved in the face of cannons brought from the
Tower. The Essex rising lasted half a day because London, with all of its cross-
currents of discontent, proved impossible to unite in rebellion.[21]

This chapter has suggested that a combination of factors accounts for Tudor London's ability to absorb the many forces of social, economic, religious and cultural changes thrust upon it. Not the least of these was luck. Surely, it was fortuitous that additional calamities did not occur that might have pushed the metropolis to the breaking point. A successful invasion by the Spanish in the late 1580s or the continuation of poor harvests for another year or two in the following decade might have been too much for London's populace and its governing institutions to have handled. Largely because such calamities did not strike, London was able to grow, in fits and starts and not without long-lasting environmental consequences, from a modest city to a significant metropolis in the space of just over a century. It was one of the more important, and impressive, achievements of the Tudor age.

NOTES

1. de Vries, *European Urbanization*, p. 140 and Appendix I; Harding, *The Dead and the Living*, pp. 14–15.
2. Thirsk, *Rural Economy of England*, pp. 221–2; Overton, *Agricultural Revolution*, pp. 138–9; and Clay, *Economic Expansion and Social Change*.
3. Rappaport, *Worlds Within Worlds*, pp. 31–5 and Rosser, *Medieval Westminster*, pp. 226–48.
4. Levy, 'Moorfields, Finsbury'; Carlin, *Medieval Southwark*; and Rappaport, *Worlds Within Worlds*, p. 34.
5. Discussions of London's parochial structure and detailed maps may be found in Brigden *London and the Reformation*, and Harding, *The Dead and the Living*.
6. Beier, *Masterless Men*, especially pp. 40–4; Ward, *Metropolitan Communities*, pp. 17–18.
7. Archer, *Pursuit of Stability*, p. 47; Rappaport, *Worlds Within Worlds*, pp. 29–54. Rappaport was cautious about his estimate of the percentage of adult men who were livery company members and, citing the work of Boulton for the late sixteenth and early seventeenth centuries, acknowledges that the 75 per cent figure may have been an especially high estimate. Boulton (*Neighbourhood and Society*, p. 151) suggests, quite plausibly, that in the early seventeenth century approximately 50 per cent of adult men in London were freemen. His findings are supported by Ward, *Metropolitan Communities*, pp. 27–44. Given this research, it is surprising to find Rappaport's cautious and admittedly high estimate put forth so confidently by other historians, such as Brigden's recent assertion that 'In Norwich and York about half of the male population were citizens; in London three-quarters' (*New Worlds*, p. 76).
8. For this paragraph, and the next, see Ward, *Metropolitan Communities*, especially pp. 27–44.
9. Rappaport, *Worlds Within Worlds*, pp. 36–42; Mendelson and Crawford, *Women in Early Modern England*; Willen, 'Women in the public sphere'. The most comprehensive study of the lives of women in Tudor London is found in Gowing, *Domestic Dangers*.
10. The discussion of crime and law enforcement discussed here and in what follows is based on Archer, *Pursuit of Stability*, pp. 204–56; Griffiths, 'Structure of prostitution' and 'Overlapping circles'; and Tittler, *Townspeople and Nation*, pp. 156–76.
11. Harding, 'Population of London', is the authoritative discussion of early modern London's demographic trends, but see also her summary of the issue in *The Dead and the Living*, pp. 14–15, 23.
12. Whyte, *Migration and Society*, pp. 63–76.

13. The discussion of the stranger churches is drawn from Pettegree, *Foreign Protestant Communities*.
14. This paragraph is a summary of Rappaport, *Worlds Within Worlds*, pp. 123–50.
15. Rappaport, *Worlds Within Worlds*, pp. 6–18 and Archer, *Pursuit of Stability*, pp. 1–17 and 259–60. Rappaport and Archer disagree about the sources of social stability in Elizabethan London; the summary offered here relies heavily upon Archer's interpretation of events.
16. Brigden, *London and the Reformation*; Rappaport, *Worlds Within Worlds*, p. 16; MacCulloch, *The Boy King*, p. 96–7.
17. Collinson, *The Elizabethan Puritan Movement*, especially pp. 84–91; Seaver, *The Puritan Lectureships*; Ward, 'Godliness.'
18. Jones, *The English Reformation*, pp. 111–15.
19. Archer, *Pursuit of Stability*, and 'Charity'; Schen, *Charity and Lay Piety*.
20. Gurr, *Playgoing*. The quotation is from Ward, *Metropolitan Communities*, p. 11.
21. James, *Society, Politics and Culture*, pp. 416–65; Guy, *Tudor England*, pp. 437–58.

BIBLIOGRAPHY

Archer, Ian W., 'The charity of early modern Londoners', *Transactions of the Royal Historical Society*, 6th series, 12 (2002), 223–44.

Archer, Ian W., *The Pursuit of Stability: Social Relations in Elizabethan London* (Cambridge, 1991).

Beier, A. L., *Masterless Men: The Vagrancy Problem in England 1560–1640* (London, 1985).

Boulton, Jeremy, *Neighbourhood and Society: A London Suburb in the Seventeenth Century* (Cambridge, 1987).

Brigden, Susan, *London and the Reformation* (Oxford, 1989).

Brigden, Susan, *New Worlds, Lost Worlds: The Rule of the Tudors 1485–1603* (Harmondsworth, 2000).

Carlin, Martha, *Medieval Southwark* (London, 1996).

Clay, J. G. A., *Economic Expansion and Social Change: England 1500–1700* (2 vols, Cambridge, 1984).

Collinson, Patrick, *The Elizabethan Puritan Movement* (Berkeley, 1967).

de Vries, Jan, *European Urbanization 1500–1800* (Cambridge, MA, 1984).

Gowing, Laura, *Domestic Dangers: Women, Words, and Sex in Early Modern London* (Oxford, 1996).

Griffiths, Paul, 'Overlapping circles: imagining criminal communities in London, 1545–1645', in Alexandra Shepard and Phil Withington, eds, *Communities in Early Modern England* (Manchester, 2000), pp. 115–33.

Griffiths, Paul, 'The structure of prostitution in Elizabethan London', *Continuity and Change*, 8, 1 (1993), pp. 39–63.

Gurr, Andrew, *Playgoing in Shakespeare's London* (Cambridge, 1987).

Guy, John, *Tudor England* (Oxford, 1988).

Harding, Vanessa, *The Dead and the Living in Paris and London* (Cambridge, 2002).

Harding, Vanessa, 'The population of London, 1550–1700: a review of the published evidence', *London Journal*, 15 (1990), 111–28.

James, Mervyn, *Society, Politics, and Culture: Studies in Early Modern England* (Cambridge, 1986).

Jones, Norman, *The English Reformation: Religion and Cultural Adaptation* (Oxford, 2002).

Levy, Eleanor, 'Moorfields, Finsbury and the City of London in the sixteenth century', *London Topographical Record*, 26 (1990), 78–96.

MacCulloch, Diarmaid, *The Boy King: Edward VI and the Protestant Reformation* (Basingstone and New York, 2001).

Mendelson, Sarah and Crawford Patricia, *Women in Early Modern England 1550–1720* (Oxford, 1998).

Overton, Mark, *Agricultural Revolution in England: The Transformation of the Agrarian Economy 1500–1850* (Cambridge, 1996).

Pettegree, Andrew, *Foreign Protestant Communities in Sixteenth-Century London* (Oxford, 1986).

Prest, Wilfred R., *The Inns of Court under Elizabeth I and the Early Stuarts 1590–1640* (Totowa, NJ, 1972).

Rappaport, Steve, *Worlds within Worlds: Structures of Life in Sixteenth-Century London* (Cambridge, 1989).

Rosser, Gervase, *Medieval Westminster 1200–1540* (Oxford, 1989).

Schen, Claire S., *Charity and Lay Piety in Reformation London, 1500–1620* (Aldershot, 2002).

Seaver, Paul S., *The Puritan Lectureships: The Politics of Religious Dissent, 1650–1662* (Stanford, 1970).

Slack, Paul, *From Reformation to Improvement: Public Welfare in Early Modern England* (Oxford, 1999).

Thirsk, Joan, *The Rural Economy of England: Collected Essays* (London, 1984).

Tittler, Robert, *Townspeople and Nation: English Urban Experiences, 1540–1640* (Stanford, 2001).

Ward, Joseph P., *Metropolitan Communities: Trade Guilds, Identity, and Change in Early Modern London* (Stanford, 1997).

Ward, Joseph P., 'Godliness, commemoration, and community: the management of provincial schools by London trade guilds', in Muriel C. McClendon, Joseph P. Ward and Michael MacDonald, eds, *Protestant Identities: Religion, Society, and Self-fashioning in Post-Reformation England* (Stanford, 1999), pp. 141–57 and 323–6.

Whyte, Ian D., *Migration and Society in Britain 1550–1830* (New York, 2000).

Willen, Diane, 'Women in the public sphere in early modern England: the case of the urban working poor', *Sixteenth Century Journal*, 29, 4 (1988), 559–75.

FURTHER READING

C. M. Barron, 'The parish fraternities of medieval London', in C. M. Barron and C. Harper-Bill (eds), *The Church in Pre-Reformation Society: Essays in Honour of F. R. H. du Boulay* (1985), pp. 13–37.

A. L. Beier and Roger Finlay (eds), *London 1500–1700: The Making of the Metropolis* (1986).

Clive Burgess (ed.), *The Church Records of St Andrew Hubbard Eastcheap c.1450–c.1570* (1999).

Roger Finlay, *Population and Metropolis: The Demography of London, 1580–1650* (1981).

Ian Anders Gadd and Patrick Wallis (eds), *Guilds, Society and Economy in London 1450–1800* (2002).

Paul Griffiths, *Youth and Authority: Formative Experiences in England 1560–1640* (1996).

Paul Griffiths and Mark S. R. Jenner (eds), *Londinopolis: Essays in the Cultural and Social History of Early Modern London* (2000).

Deborah E. Harkness, 'Strange ideas and "English" knowledge: natural science exchange in Elizabethan London', in Pamela H. Smith and Paula Findlen (eds), *Merchants and Marvels: Commerce, Science, and Art in Early Modern Europe* (2002).

Lawrence Manley, *Literature and Culture in Early Modern London* (1995).

Marjorie Keniston McIntosh, *A Community Transformed: The Manor and Liberty of Havering, 1500–1620* (1991).

Lena Cowen Orlin (ed.), *Material London, c. 1600* (2000).

G. D. Ramsey, 'The recruitment and fortunes of some London freemen in the mid-sixteenth century', *Economic History Review*, 2nd series, 31 (1978), 526–40.

CHAPTER TWENTY-ONE

Society and Social Relations in British Provincial Towns

ROBERT TITTLER

This essay presents the subject of provincial urban society in England, Ireland, Scotland and Wales from the perspective of townspeople themselves: their numbers and geographic distribution, their assimilation to the urban milieu and their sociability within it, and the tenor of social relations which characterized the towns and cities of this era. It will begin by considering townspeople in the aggregate: urban population numbers and the movement of people over time; how such urban places came to attract or discourage population movement; and how both newcomers and native-born townspeople were assimilated, or not, into urban society.

The emphasis on migration and assimilation will entail a consideration of some of the points of contact, between newcomer and resident, adolescent and adult, and one status group and another, which facilitated social relations within the provincial town and city. Some such contact points were institutional in nature. They included the household and family (embracing the activities of apprenticeship and service), the guild and fraternity, and the parish and civic governing body. Others were ceremonial. They included social rites of passage, rituals of social harmony and social distinction, forms of address, and even patterns of social seating. They were intended to recognize and affirm social standing within the community and to mark the individual's progress from one rung to another. Some were even spatial and topographical: spaces and places which facilitated the interface between town and hinterland and between different social and economic groups. Behind the discussion of most of these issues lies the prevailing historiographic tendency to see the towns and cities of this era in an almost constant state of economic and social stress. This begs important questions about the actual tenor of social relations, sociability and civility within the urban community, and offers an appropriate note on which to conclude.

It should be clear at the outset that current research on these issues remains heavily weighted towards the English experience, on which seminal work emanates from the early 1970s. Preoccupied with other aspects of their national histories, historians of Ireland, Scotland and Wales have yet to expend equal effort on urban and social issues. Moreover, when they have done so they have tended to deal more with topographical, political and constitutional issues than with social; and more with periods before or after the sixteenth century. The sources which would allow them to give greater attention to urban society in the sixteenth century are also much thinner. Discussion of these areas must therefore remain more speculative and incomplete.

Urban Populations

Notwithstanding numerous exceptions, the broadest tendencies of urban populations over the sixteenth century were their expansion in size, both in absolute terms and in proportion to non-urban populations; their concentration in a slightly smaller number of towns and cities than before; their overall movement from northern and western areas of the British Isles towards more southern and eastern areas; and their tendency to be derived from continued immigration rather than natural growth. A great many factors accounted for these general trends, some of which are treated elsewhere in this volume. Prominent amongst them were a net population increase for the British Isles as a whole, important changes in both the agricultural and manufacturing sectors of the economy, the spectre of poverty, and the migratory search both for temporary subsistence and long-term betterment.

In addition, one of the most powerful magnets for the direction and volume of population flow, especially in the second half of the sixteenth century, was the London metropolis. Already the largest city in the British Isles at the end of the fifteenth century with a population of around fifty to sixty thousand, London rapidly became one of the four largest cities in Europe, with some 80,000 in 1550 and an astounding increase to over 200,000 by 1600. Despite some modest immigration from abroad, especially motivated by religious persecution in France and the Low Countries from the 1560s, most of this growth came from migrants arriving from elsewhere in the British Isles.

Even when this dynamic 'engine' of growth is taken away, despite demographic crises in a number of the older medieval manufacturing and commercial centres such as Coventry, Boston and Gloucester; despite consistent high rates of mortality in most towns and cities; and despite the collapse of some of the very small, marginally urban centres which flourished at an earlier time, the majority of middling and larger *English* towns seem to have experienced a modest net population gain over the period at hand. Though their net populations made them the largest provincial centres in England, the approximate growth over the century – from around twelve to fifteen thousand in Norwich; ten to twelve thousand in Bristol; eight to twelve thousand in York and eight to nine thousand in Exeter – seems typical of the modest increase sustained by many other middling and larger English towns.[1] These figures may pale before London's dramatic rate of growth, especially in the second half of the century, and they failed to keep pace with the rate of population growth across all of England during the same era. Yet with the London totals factored in, they do support the notion of an expanding urban sector of the nation. Clearly the proportion of England's total population which lived in towns and cities was substantially larger in 1600 than in 1500. The sixteenth century marks the first such sustained growth in the English urban sector since before the Black Death.

The details of Scottish or Irish population histories are nowhere as clear as this, and they appear to have mirrored the English patterns only in some respects. Edinburgh resembled London as its kingdom's chief city in that it was more populous than its rivals, but by a very much smaller margin. Even by 1600 it could not yet be counted as one of Europe's principal cities. Yet it did serve as the nation's capital city; it did dominate the nation's export trade (and by a widening margin as the century progressed); it did serve as a strong magnet for migrant populations (especially of the poor and unsettled); and it does seem to have experienced sharp population growth at the end of the century.

Other points of contrast are more vivid. Around 1500, only about half as many Scots (1.6 per cent) lived in urban areas of more than 10,000 than in England and Wales (3.1 per cent).[2] Whereas England's urban population in general probably began to take off around the 1530s and 1540s and possibly even earlier, this was not to happen for another several decades in Scotland. And where the large and middling towns tended to grow more than the smaller ones in England, with London's growth rate towering over all others and smaller centres often finding themselves unable to compete with larger regional rivals, quite a different pattern emerged in Scotland.

Here commercial activity had much more to do with the export trade to the Continent than with the emergence of a capitalized agriculture organized to supply a metropolis on London's scale. Combined with a lively manufacturing sector, and especially in the last decades of the century, Continental trade allowed some of the larger Scottish burghs – especially in the southern Lowlands, south-east and east coast – to flourish and consolidate their position in the urban hierarchy. Though none of them rivalled London in any way, and while Edinburgh remained the largest Scottish burgh with a population around 18,000 by 1600, they nevertheless served as regional magnets for growth, attracting substantial numbers of migrants from their hinterlands especially late in the century. Aberdeen appears roughly to have doubled its size (three thousand to about six or even seven thousand); Dundee grew from around four to around seven thousand; Glasgow expanded from about four to about eight thousand, and St Andrews went from approximately four to something around fourteen thousand over the course of the century, with most growth coming towards the end.[3] These growth rates clearly outstripped those of most comparable provincial centres south of the border.

In still sharper contrast to the English experience, numerous quite small coastal towns were also able to thrive on the overseas export trade of largely unprocessed materials. In addition, the latter decades of the century saw the establishment of scores of new baronial towns, or burghs, the like of which had not been seen in England or most other Western European countries for several centuries. Most of these failed to become truly urban communities, but some did flourish and maintained their meagre populations. Other small burghs in general, mostly of an earlier foundation, remained economically stronger than their populations might suggest. This strength and preponderance of small Scottish towns resembled the Irish or Scandinavian pattern rather than the English.[4]

Ironically, in view of the English experience, it is the middling-sized burghs which seem to have been most vulnerable to economic change in Scotland, and while population growth remained strong at either end of the urban hierarchy, it seems to have been weakest in the middling ranks. Notwithstanding this frailty in the middle, and even without a London to boost its numbers, Scottish urban population as a whole is reckoned to have expanded by 130 per cent over the last half of the sixteenth century.[5]

The Irish picture also failed to mirror the English in most respects, though a very great deal remains to be done before we can speak with confidence on this. Major determinants of Ireland's urban population not only included such common issues as the strength of local manufacturing and, perhaps especially, strong trading ties with several European countries as well as England. They also included the ever-present impact of English colonial policy. This manifested itself from the mid-century in the growing presence of English administration in the Pale of Settlement and in the burgeoning importance of Dublin as the centre of that administration. By the end of the century it began to be seen in the early effects of the Munster plantation, which brought English traders and other settlers into Youghal and Kinsale especially, and in the flight from areas of warfare and conquest. In general, and save for the inland town of Kilkenny, the strongest urban areas remained those older commercial ports, including (in addition to Dublin) Cork, Waterford, Youghal, Drogheda, Dundalk, Galway, Limerick and Sligo, almost all of them acting as points of access and egress for their interior hinterlands. Each drew migrants regularly from those areas, though the extent either of immigration from the bottom rungs of society or of elite emigration outwards, seems less pronounced in these Irish cities than in England.

This allowed for much greater continuity of residence, and of status, from one generation to the next. Each of these middling centres retained a considerable degree of political autonomy from an English crown often occupied with other issues. That autonomy permitted the development of tightly controlled civic oligarchies run by narrow and clearly demarcated social elites.[6] In consequence, for example, all seventy-one mayors of Cork who served between 1558 and 1625, including some who served less than a full year's term, came from a mere twelve families, while in Galway a mere fifteen families controlled the mayoralty in all but a single year between 1484 and 1654![7]

This grip on power by very small elites seems to have been facilitated as well by the stagnant or declining populations of the major Irish cities over the course of the sixteenth century. Dublin, Ireland's largest city, may have had some eight thousand inhabitants around 1500, but most authorities see this as having slipped to around five thousand by 1600. There are substantial indications that the populations of Cork, Londonderry and some other Irish towns also fell off substantially during the course of the century. By around 1600 Galway is thought to have had about 4,200 inhabitants, Limerick between about 2,400 and 3,600, and Waterford and Cork (both of them also once much larger) around 2,400 at the end of the sixteenth century.[8] Though the explanations for these long-term declines have still to be established in full, Galway, along with Armagh, Kilkenny and Kilmallock suffered seriously from the ravages of warfare in the very last years of the sixteenth century.[9]

Finally, it is most difficult of all to write with confidence about the urban population of Wales. The population of the whole principality has been estimated at around 250,000–280,000 by 1540 and as perhaps 400,000 by the end of the century.[10] Wales seems to have had close to fifty market towns around the mid-century mark, though most remained very small. Carmarthen alone, with about 2,150 inhabitants, exceeded a population of 2,000; only a handful more (Brecon, Wrexham, Haverfordwest and perhaps Cardiff) made it up to or over the 1,500 mark at that time, though late-century growth in commerce, mining or manufacturing created increases in Swansea, Caernarfon and perhaps Denbigh and Tenby by about 1600.[11]

Migration, Poverty and Stress

One of the salient characteristics of urban populations throughout the British Isles at this time was the constant ebb and flow of people. Alan Sharlin and Chris Galley have questioned the longstanding assumption that, in the absence of any significant natural population growth, towns and cities grew solely through immigration.[12] Yet the fact remains that, especially in the face of the high urban mortality which prevailed throughout the period, net immigration played a much more substantial role than natural growth in sustaining and expanding urban populations. In many urban communities throughout the British Isles, and especially in the latter half of our era, locally born residents were probably often outnumbered by those born elsewhere.

Migration has thus loomed as a critical feature in urban society, and at least for England it has elicited sustained and relatively conclusive research. In that English milieu and almost certainly elsewhere, migration came in several forms. Peter Clark's study of migration in Kentish towns created a framework for approaching the issue, in which two basic categories came to the fore.[13] 'Betterment migrants' typically travelled less frequently, for shorter distances, and to predetermined destinations. They were more highly skilled to begin with and, though seeking to improve their economic or social standing by their migration, were driven by choice rather than desperation. They counted heavily on kinship ties and/or apprenticeship for their assimilation and anticipated advancement, and they were likely to be adolescents or young adults moving individually rather than in families or other groups.

Against this pattern stood 'subsistence migrants' who, unlike the other type, were substantially new to the scene in sixteenth-century England. Driven by necessity rather than choice, they were chiefly searching for basic subsistence. They did so for many reasons, but perhaps particularly in response to population surpluses in marginal agricultural areas, and particularly in times of agricultural scarcity. Subsistence migrants typically travelled longer distances and moved more often, sometimes even adopting a more or less permanent pattern of movement from one place to another. They were more likely to travel to destinations which were casually or spontaneously chosen, and in which they were less likely to have kinship ties. Their skill levels were lower, nor did they tend to settle long enough to enhance such skills through apprenticeship or stable employment. The least fortunate amongst them – a proportion which expanded rapidly in such difficult decades as the 1550s and 1590s – came to constitute a vagrant population which proved one of the chief domestic concerns of both English and Scottish governments.

Though Clark's proposed dichotomy of betterment and subsistence migration has continuing value, further research has brought a much more complex picture into view. Numerous more specific groups came to be considered which fit comfortably into neither of these categories, and a good many of them began their journeys outside England itself. Aberdeenshire lassies coming annually to pack the autumn herring catch in Great Yarmouth and other East Anglian herring ports; Welsh drovers moving to and from the London market; religious refugees from France and the Low Countries after the 1560s; and impoverished Irish families fleeing the wars of the 1590s, all typify migrations specific to particular areas, industries, seasons or political conditions.

Both contemporary observers and modern historians have emphasized the negative impact which many migrant groups had – or were thought to have had – on their recipient communities. Contemporaries readily identified many migrants as vagrants, linking them, along with the absolute increase in the net population itself, to an attendant increase in urban crime and poverty. These concerns continued to grow, remaining prominent on the political agenda in all parts of the British Isles for the latter half of the century and more. Though the actual extent of poverty and crime cannot be measured precisely, it is hard to deny their growing presence, and even harder to deny contemporaries' growing awareness of the problem.

Paul Slack has reckoned that in times of hardship, like the 1550s and 1590s, as many as 20 per cent of the English urban population may have needed to rely on assistance, as compared to around 5 per cent for the 'chronic' poor who required relief in good times as well as bad.[14] But a number of decaying towns, both outside England and within, clearly had higher proportions both of 'chronic' and occasional poor for long periods at a time. Swansea, for example, one of the few well-documented Welsh towns of the time, may have had at least half its population at or below the poverty line as a general rule through much of the century,[15] and numerous Welsh and Irish towns may have followed suit. The picture was perhaps gloomier still in Scotland, where it was felt with particular intensity in Edinburgh and other centres. Though by 1579 Scotland had adopted legislation to provide for poor relief, those provisions remained largely ignored right into the seventeenth century. In practical terms, the large proportion of impoverished inhabitants were left to the mercies of voluntary parish relief or the dubious potential of subsistence migration.[16] In England itself, the increased perception of poverty and other such symptoms may be tracked chronologically in the written record of both town by-laws and parliamentary statutes, the latter dating from the 1520s and 1530s and culminating in the Elizabethan Poor Laws of 1597 and 1601.

Along with such associated factors as poverty, crime and the fear of unrest, substantial immigration to urban areas directly challenged both the social and political institutions and the economic capabilities of the prevailing order. It pushed hard against the deep-seated insistence on order, hierarchy and social control. Real or imagined waves of 'masterless men' and, indeed, women and children as well, evoked one of the primal fears of Tudor rule: disorder created by a disconnection from the social framework. How indeed, to paraphrase Shakespeare's *Troilus and Cressida*, 'could communities . . . *but by degree* stand in authentic place?' (I. iii, my italics). The value placed on such structure – of preserving

> Degrees in schools and brotherhoods in cities,
> Peaceful commerce from dividable shores,
> The primogeniture and due of birth,
> Prerogative of age, crowns, sceptres, laurels –

lay very deep in contemporary political culture and popular values (I. iii).

Assimilation and Control

Inexperienced in dealing with such problems on this scale, English towns and cities from mid-century onwards found the assimilation of large numbers of migrants a substantial and often overwhelming challenge. That challenge proved even more acute because of the destruction of longstanding mechanisms of social assimilation and relief traditionally provided by religious guilds, fraternities and chantries. As monastic and related bodies disappeared, the schools, almshouses, hospitals and other vital institutions went with them, removing essential safety nets for social activity and life itself.

Civic authorities had to rely not only on the carrot of some remaining assimilatory strategies for those able to make use of them, but also the stick of more punitive mechanisms for those who could not. By mid-century, local initiatives in poor relief and social control emanating from Norwich, Ipswich and elsewhere, served as models for such definitive legislation as the labour code enshrined in the Statute of Artificers of 1563 and the Elizabethan Poor Laws in their most sophisticated expressions of 1597 and 1601. If the socially disconnected could not be joined to the hierarchy in some effective manner, authorities were determined to find ways to control their activities and render them harmless.

Notwithstanding the punitive aspects of this unfolding policy, the greater hope remained with the prospect of effective assimilation. It would be misleading to overlook the many mechanisms – natural and invented; social, economic and political – employed to encourage this process and thus to preserve the social order. In both theory and actual practice, the pathways to assimilation, and thence to mobility, had been clearly marked out in sequential stages for some considerable time. They extended in several, often parallel, directions through a *cursus honorum* provided by the formal structures of traditional urban society. Occupationally, they extended (especially for men) from apprenticeship to journeyman's status to freeman's status as the master of a craft or trade. Domestically (and also especially for men) they extended from the lodging house or (for apprentices) master's household to the journeyman's rooms or cottage, thence to the master's home and household. And for women, they might also extend from household service to marriage and 'rooms' and eventually to a house and household. Men could join in the political life of their communities through entry into the freemanry, thence perhaps to a sequence of offices within the trade or craft guild and, through guild office, to a similar sequence through the offices of town government. And lest we think of Elizabethan legislation as merely punitive, these assimilatory mechanisms were also positively encouraged by a plethora of legislation from about the 1530s on.

It should already be evident that underlying many of these structures, both formal and informal, lay the household itself and the conjugal family unit which ordinarily formed its core. A collectivity best defined as 'all those living under one roof and under the authority of a single head', the household served as the protean unit of all Western societies. It provided the assimilatory functions of kinship, education and apprenticeship; marriage and family; service and employment; as well, of course, as the material benefits of housing and sustenance. An assessment of household composition proves quite revealing of the social structure, the economic condition, and sometimes even the social topography of particular urban communities.

Most households had as their core a conjugal unit of husband and wife, readily extending to the children of that marriage, and occasionally including other relatives. The formation of the conjugal unit, as celebrated publicly in the ceremony of marriage, could perhaps be delayed by a long apprenticeship or, given the English (indeed, Northern European) scruple that a couple did not marry until they could afford a premises of their own, by the length and terms of a journeyman's employment. Wealthier men and women, acquiring the necessary resources at an earlier age, thus married sooner. Because the period of fertility within that marriage therefore extended for a longer time, they also tended to have larger families. Yet whenever it could be undertaken, marriage constituted a milestone of wide social significance as well as a change in personal status. It marked a critical stage towards the establishment of one's own household, and thus to a successive generation of this household-based society.

In some cases, the family unit not only extended to the two generations of parents and children, but also to grandparents who had become too old or infirm for gainful employment or independent living. Guild regulations in most industries and towns allowed freemen's widows to take over the household and run the business, even sometimes to take on apprentices, as their spouses would have done, thus to continue in useful and remunerative employment thereafter. The guild affiliations which accompanied freeman's status often provided certain additional benefits to the elderly, widowed or not, and allowed many such individuals to remain living on their own, or in dwellings with other aged residents, rather than in the households of their married children. Such residences included 'hospitals' or almshouses, either church-run prior to the Reformation or civic-controlled thereafter. A clear preference of the elderly for *not* living with their children runs at least through English society in this era. Though elderly married couples very rarely lived with their married children, it seems to have been more socially acceptable for elderly couples to live with an unmarried child, or for a widowed parent to live with a married child.[17] In this manner the familial core of the household could sometimes be extended to a third generation.

Households also frequently included such non-family members as apprentices, servants and lodgers: a capability directly proportionate to the relative wealth of the family. These larger households especially provided a degree of social contact and sharing of resources amongst all their members which considerably enhanced the process of socialization and reduced the potential for poverty and dislocation. Even in smaller households, apprenticeship and service could provide a broad and intergenerational cultural experience: a preparation for life itself rather than for employment alone.

In smaller towns and in the earlier decades of our period, girls or young women comprised a substantial minority of apprentices in some trades, but these opportunities declined steadily as population pressure erased the labour shortages of those years. Most apprenticeships began in the early to mid-teen years, and had traditionally been construed as seven-year, contractually formalized obligations on the part of both apprentice and master. Incursions on the apprenticeship system by mid-century moved the English parliament, in the Statute of Artificers of 1563, to restate that duration as the legal requirement.

Most often coming from the rural hinterland rather than from within town boundaries – the distance travelled being directly proportional to the size and 'pull' of the urban centre in question – apprentices comprised a large share of betterment migrants. The experience of apprenticeship varied widely with particular masters and households, some of the latter being more conscientious and kindly than others. The young Thomas White, who had been sent by his father in the 1510s from Reading to apprenticeship in London, so impressed his master, the merchant taylor Hugh Acton, that Acton left him £100 to set up on his own at the end of their formal relationship. Never looking back, White became one of the wealthiest men of his time by the 1540s, lord mayor of London by 1554, and a benefactor of unsurpassed generosity before his death in 1567.

As White's experience affirms, the pathways to all sorts of opportunity in the urban milieu could be smoothed from the very beginning with the right sort of family connections and financial resources. Apprenticeships to the better and more lucrative trades cost more than others, and the range widened substantially as the century wore on. By permitting initial access to the better trades, such resources eventually led to more lucrative employment, acceptance into more prestigious crafts and guilds, and thence to greater personal standing and reputation both in the freemanry and the town in general. It was also much easier to succeed in these sequences in smaller towns, whose structures were less highly stratified, than in larger ones, and ease of mobility was almost certainly greater in the earlier than the later decades of the century.[18] Obviously, not all masters were anywhere near as benevolent as Acton. But if White's story remains atypical in that respect it does illustrate the range of possibilities held out by the institution of apprenticeship at this time.

At the other end of the scale, apprenticeships were often initiated by parish officials and other civic authorities who contracted for the apprenticeship of pauper children with local masters, especially in the more cheaply contracted and meaner trades, who were far below Acton's level of affluence. Masters at all levels and of all kinds could sometimes be incompetent, unkindly and even brutal, leading a substantial proportion of apprentices to flee their apprenticeships for a life, as often as not, of poverty.

This reminds us that such theoretical pathways to economic and social mobility were not by any means necessarily followed to their logical ends, nor did they always lead to the desired assimilation or mobility within the urban community. For one reason or another, large numbers of apprentices, even a clear majority in some towns, failed to stay the course. Many of those who did complete it, especially in the latter decades of the century, never acquired sufficient resources to move beyond providing skilled wage labour as a journeyman. Others took their training, complete or not, and returned to the countryside or hinterland, outside the jurisdiction of urban guilds, to set up on their own.[19] In Scotland, merchant guilds were earlier to form and more powerful than crafts guilds, but the merchant trades were so competitive that successfully completed apprenticeships often led to employment abroad rather than at home.

Servants in urban, as opposed to rural, households were almost always domestically rather than occupationally employed. In Coventry and other towns and cities they comprised up to a quarter of the total population. Although, like apprentices, they were also usually taken on at a young age, servants were more likely to be female than male. Indeed, for young women of modest social or economic backgrounds, domestic service had a lot in common with apprenticeship, albeit without the same contractual formalities or stability of employment. A further distinction lay in the fact that the training and supervision of domestic servants fell much more heavily on the woman of the house, usually the master's wife, than on the master himself. Running the domestic side of the household was as much her realm as running the occupational side was his, and much of the art of being a housewife lay in the management of the household and its staff. The more fortunate servants of both sexes thus learned the domestic arts which enhanced their value in marriage and/or future employment. Household service also sometimes facilitated the sorts of contacts which led to courtship and marriage, thence to departure for a place of one's own. Servants, like apprentices, could also be abused: not all households functioned as they were supposed to do, and not all servants had their hopes of assimilation and advancement fulfilled.

Domestic considerations aside, a great many households were also economic units: workshops and places of employment. In addition to the resident members, they often partly included journeymen or wage labourers who dwelt in cottages or rooms of their own, but who spent their working days and ate at least some of their meals under the master's roof . . . and his eye! Thus they formed part of the little community over which that master exercised direct authority. In addition, masters of most households, especially in their occupational capacity, were required to be a member of a craft fellowship or trade guild, and thus of the body of freemanry: those residents with full economic rights and often full political rights within the town itself. That link effectively connected households and their members to the larger structures of local government and civic hierarchy, and implicitly (but just as firmly) with the widely understood social structure of the community. These linkages were just as important to the household's critical role in the local community as the provision of apprenticeship and employment or room and board to those living under its roof.

All things considered, the household remained the best training ground of all for what contemporaries considered the normal patterns of urban life, and the best place to start the climb up the ladder of occupational, domestic, political or social advancement. Newcomers or adolescents who failed to catch the social entrées it offered risked falling out of the social framework entirely. They could then be left to their own devices, or to the casual support of strangers, and/or to the mercies of parliamentary legislation and local by-laws. These last usually meant various forms of parish relief for the 'honest' poor, and punishment, including expulsion, for the 'idle' poor, though Scottish legislation proved much more harsh than the English in this regard. Yet the fact that towns and cities remained reasonably stable communities even at times of the greatest stress suggests that the households of which they were comprised worked most of the time, and in all these dimensions, much as expected.

Social Spaces and Places

Households aside, other aspects of the provincial town or city also encouraged the assimilation and advancement of newcomers. Such possibilities extended beyond actual social or political institutions; some even consisted of spaces and places. In addition to its more conventional functions, the parish church also provided space for guild, fraternity and chantry activities prior to the Reformation, and a meeting place for myriad social as well as religious functions thereafter. In some towns, including Cirencester and, briefly, Hull, parish churches even provided meeting space for town government.[20]

Especially in smaller and middling-sized centres, the market-place constituted another important and universally accessible social space. Its common location at the central crossroads of the community allowed it to bring together all who came to or lived in the town, casually and by chance on most days, and almost without fail on market days. This truly liminal space, positioned both economically and culturally between the town and the world outside, provided an arena for mingling and haggling, gathering news and exchanging gossip, seeking employment and opportunity, attending public events, and making connections. It permitted the performance of ceremonies, rituals and other mimetic activities which were often not permitted elsewhere. At the same time, the limits of acceptable behaviour were represented and proclaimed to the newcomer by particular symbols of authority normally sited there: religious and moral authority by the market cross, seigneurial authority (where it applied) by the market glove – erected on a pole to signal the opening of trade and the lord's authority over such trade – and judicial authority by the lock-up, pillory and stocks.

Many of the same activities and opportunities, if not symbols of authority, accrued as well to the inn and alehouse. Most densely situated on the outskirts and along the roads leading in and out of the centre, they, too, provided liminal spaces between town and hinterland. In fulfilling this function they catered to the traveller's first and most basic needs: food, casual employment, and, despite close monitoring by local authorities, lodging as well. They also provided for the exchange of news and information, for the conduct of business, the services of the local money-lender or scrivener, the temporary storage of trade goods or personal effects, or the performance space for travelling players.

In addition to these liminal areas for the reception of the newcomer, the physical layout of English town, and many Scottish, Welsh and Irish towns as well, also translated into a distinctive social topography. Unlike towns and cities of the industrial era, where larger populations and artificial means of transport applied, most towns and cities of the sixteenth century reflected the necessity of getting about on foot by remaining relatively compact and, especially by century's end, densely settled. Even in smaller towns the ready assumption that the wealthiest inhabitants lived closest to the centre – nearest the market area, the parish church, the town hall or guildhall and other such amenities – while the poorer sort lived further from it, cannot be taken as the *unexcepted* rule. For one, social topography had a vertical as well as horizontal dimension, in which servants, apprentices and sometimes lodgers – none of them anywhere near representing 'the better sort' – might live in the upper stories or solar of a large house near the city centre. Yet as a general statement which applied to most smaller towns, and in all parts of the British Isles, such a rule still has much to commend it.

Larger towns, not to mention the metropolis itself, obviously demonstrated a more complex social topography than smaller ones. Many had multiple nuclei, economic and social focal points and other desirable amenities scattered over broader areas, more than one or two major streets, and housing patterns which were much more varied and often complex. Still, most of the better sort did live in particular, readily identifiable and well-known areas, on main rather than back streets, and mostly in the up-wind west end rather than the down-wind east end. Suburbs and outskirts, by contrast, remained liminal and typically poorer, further from major amenities, and typified by shoddier housing stock, temporary lodgings, cheap food and drink, and dodgier civil behaviour. Their populations remained less residentially stable, less likely to comprise full family units, and more likely to be made up of newcomers without pre-arranged connections and often travelling on their own.

Some urban topographies, and especially those reinforced by parish or natural boundaries, took on characteristics which we may equate with the concept of the neighbourhood. This may not have been as vividly experienced as in open field vils in the countryside, with their constant need to share equipment, beasts of burden and communal tasks. It certainly resembled nothing as distinct and formal as one could find in specific quarters of London or large Continental cities. Yet such a concept did exist in provincial towns, and did bear with it certain distinctive expectations of communal behaviour. Invocations to constructive and sometimes collaborative activity – to clearing ditches, chaining dogs, keeping houses in good repair, respecting quiet hours, avoiding public gossip, maintaining leather buckets against the threat of fire, and sometimes, as in Abingdon, having 'in redynes a good and sufficient clubbe for the conservacion of the peace'[21] – commonly appear in borough council minutes, town assembly books, and local by laws throughout the entire century. Contemporaries sometimes referred to these activities as 'doing good neighbourhood'. We know it as 'civility' or 'citizenship'.

Neighbourhoods were often further defined by affinities of occupation and affluence amongst a large proportion of residents, and by the focal points provided by certain distinctive topographic features. This was most clearly evident in the sixteenth century in parts of London, where wealthy and poorer areas were reasonably well defined, certain industries and occupations had long been topographically concentrated, and where features like the riverside and dockyards, or the areas surrounding St Paul's Cathedral or Smithfield market had established local identities all their own. But we would find it as well in some of the larger and socially more complex provincial towns, in areas like Worcester's Tithing, Oxford's Fisher Row, or the ecclesiastical precincts of, for example, Exeter, Norwich or Canterbury.[22]

Recognizing the Social Structure

In large part because of this concept of collective responsibility and mutual regard, the newcomer's progress into the structures of the urban community remained a matter of general as well as personal interest. Movements from one position to the next – to apprenticeship, freemanry and office; to baptism, marriage and death – tended to be marked by some public recognition or ceremony as well as by private observation. The use of the oath, publicly administered by a figure of authority appropriate to the occasion, was widespread both before and after the Reformation, marking such passages as apprenticeship, marriage, parenthood, and entrance to guild, freemanry and civic office. Coming-of-age rituals, including successful completion of apprenticeship, along with rituals (often including processions or commensality) across boundaries of status, gender and age, helped mark both social and personal stages of life. When widely observed, they bore the potential to smooth relations amongst disparate groups, and to register social and personal milestones in the collective memory of the community. Prior to the Reformation they had operated as extensions of popular religious belief and practice. Sooner or later thereafter, usually after a period of disruption and/or transition, they came to do so in more secular guises. Symbolic expressions of one's status – in local society or in life itself – were also commonly observed, marriage rings and particular forms of dress being amongst the more familiar of such expressions.

These recognitions could also have their spatial element. A particularly graphic projection of status could be found in the English parish church, the single parish of smaller towns often being geographically and socially coterminus with the entire community. Here the newcomer sat or stood furthest from the pulpit, moving up steadily towards the front as his social and economic status came to warrant over the years. By mid-century, pews in most churches were actually numbered and rented out annually, the costliest nearest the pulpit and the least costly furthest away, with a few choice seats being reserved *ex officio* for local governing officials. Surviving lists of pew rentals often display this information for runs of dozens of years at a time.

Even contemporary language had its socially symbolic uses. As if the position of seating were not itself clear enough an indication of the social structure of the parish community, the terminology of address for individual pew-holders (or townspeople in general) reinforced the picture. By the 1580s, the better seats in St Mary's, Reading, for example, all went to men designated as 'Mr', most of whom were members of the civic elite. Middle-range seats went to men designated by their trades and skills ('Ellis the Smith'; 'Payne the Wheler') while the rearmost seats went to those known only by their last names without any honorific or occupational reference: 'Darnne', 'Jones', etc.[23] The seated congregation in many one-parish towns, and the language by which parishioners were described, thus represented with considerable precision the economic and social pecking-order of those communities, with annual adjustments in seating arrangements roughly charting changes in wealth and status amongst parishioners. Burial places in the church aisles or churchyard also provided a locational representation of relative standing, though not, of course, one which could be recalculated year by year.

One might well note here that of all the possible ways in which the churchwardens of St Mary's might have described Ellis and Payne, their occupational designation came most readily to mind. The example reaffirms that, even more in urban than in rural society – the latter having a longer collective memory for family reputations and a deeper awareness of lineage – social status had as much to do with employment and occupation, and thus with economic status, as with any other single criterion. Merchants, and especially long-distance merchants, usually found themselves at the top of the hierarchy in all towns, and perhaps even more so in the less diversified urban economies in Scottish, Irish and Welsh towns than in English. The value placed on other occupations often depended on the particular specialization of a town. It also often changed with time, as economies themselves moved from one to another series of dominant activities, productions and trades. The value placed on particular occupations at particular times may be measured at least in a crude manner by assessing the occupation of those elected mayor in a particular community over time.

The same may be said for the perception of the leading families, with evidence of their turnover through the years lying in the records of mayoral selection. Though such turnover could be very slow in the more static structure of Scottish, Welsh and (as we have seen) Irish towns, it remained rare in English towns for a single family to maintain its position at the top for more than a generation or two, three at the very most, before moving on in one social direction or another and being replaced.

Below the ranks of the merchant elite lay a range of independent tradesman, artificers, and professionals, all of them household heads, most of them masters of known trades and members of the freemanry. Taken together, their households might comprise anywhere from a third to somewhat over half a town's population. Journeymen might typically make up another third, with the remaining third being comprised of wage labourers, the marginally employed and unemployed, the poor (both 'honest' and 'idle'), and the aged and infirm or disabled who were beyond useful work.

Conclusion: Handling Stress

This leads us to one final consideration: the success with which urban communities, especially in England where the research has concentrated, handled social conflict and stress, and the tenor of social relations in normal times. The very title of Peter Clark and Paul Slack's seminal 1972 volume of essays, *Crisis and Order in English Towns, 1500–1700*, and that of a central unit of the 1977 Open University course (A.322) on pre-industrial towns, 'The traditional community under stress', suggests just how centrally concerned that pioneering generation of urban historians were with such issues as inflation, crime, vagrancy, poverty, social conflict and the civil order. The political and economic tensions of the 1960s and 1970s, the coincident influence of the social sciences at the peak of their influence, and perhaps the heavy methodological reliance on the evidence of litigation, no doubt weighed heavily in that approach.

Even after three decades, these works continue to exercise a powerful influence over the agenda of British urban history in the early modern era. Myriad studies have examined at closer range a great many of the ideas and theses of the Clark and Slack school. Its initial perspectives have been poked and prodded, refined and clarified, and sometimes substantially modified. More recent efforts have broadened out to embrace geographic, cultural and political considerations as well. Such issues as social topography, political culture (extending to oral, literary and visual discourses), the effect of religious change on that culture, and the response of both political and cultural institutions to the challenges of the time, have all been fleshed out.

All things considered, it would be foolish to deny that many urban communities throughout the British Isles did face substantial and potentially destabilizing challenges in this era – some of them social and economic, some of them religious and behavioural, still others political and cultural – and that governing authorities sought solutions both time-tested and novel in the effort to meet them. Yet it must also be said that for all this evidence of change and adaptation, crisis and instability, and for all the well-founded fears of the disorder which should have followed, English urban communities especially seem now to have retained reasonably orderly social relations and due political process, to have avoided sustained outbreaks of internal violence, and to have reinvented and formulated a complex, secular civic culture to facilitate those ends. Even in the most difficult decades of the 1590s – rent by harvest failures, Anglo-Irish war, threats of foreign invasion, and widespread disaffection – and especially when compared with urban societies elsewhere in Europe, the urban centre throughout the British Isles bent, and sometimes bent severely, but did not break.

NOTES

1. Wrigley, 'Urban growth and agricultural change', 686, as cited in Galley, *Demography of Early Modern Towns*, p. 5.
2. Whyte, *Scotland before the Industrial Revolution*, table 10.1, p. 173.
3. Ibid., p. 172; Bairoch, et al., *La Population des Villes Européennes*, pp. 32–5; Wrightson, *Earthly Necessities*, p. 36.
4. Devine, 'Scotland', pp. 151–4; Whyte, *Scotland before the Industrial Revolution*, pp. 173–5.
5. Whyte, *Scotland before the Industrial Revolution*, pp. 172–3.
6. Jack, *Towns in Tudor and Stuart Britain*, p. 23; Sheehan, 'Irish towns', pp. 99–105; Bradley, 'From frontier town to renaissance city', p. 32.
7. Sheehan, 'Irish towns', pp. 100–1.
8. Bairoch, et al., *La Population des Villes Européennes*, p. 39; de Vries, *European Urbanization*, p. 271; Sheehan, 'Irish towns', pp. 95–97; Cullen, 'Economic trends', p. 390.
9. Butlin, *Development of the Irish Town*, p. 93, and 'Land and people', p. 158.
10. The lower figures come from Wrightson, *Earthly Necessities*, p. 34; the higher ones from Howells, 'The lower orders of society', p. 239.
11. Everitt, 'Marketing of agricultural produce', p. 472; Griffiths, ' "Very wealthy by merchandise"?', pp. 205–8 and 231, citing Owen, 'The population of Wales', 99–113; Williams, *Renewal and Reformation*, pp. 407–9; and Jenkins, 'Wales', pp. 133–4.
12. Sharlin, 'Natural decrease in early modern cities', pp. 126–38; Galley, *The Demography of Early Modern Towns*.
13. Clark, 'The migrant in Kentish towns', pp. 117–63.
14. Slack, *Poverty and Policy*, pp. 71–2.
15. Griffiths, ' "Very wealthy by merchandise"?', pp. 211–12.
16. Whyte, *Scotland Before the Industrial Revolution*, pp. 167–9.
17. Houlbrooke, *The English Family*, pp. 189–92.
18. See especially Brooks, 'Apprenticeship, social mobility and the middling sort', particularly pp. 52–62; Ben-Amos, *Adolescence and Youth*, pp. 86–94.
19. Ben-Amos, *Adolescence and Youth*, chapters 4–5; Griffiths, *Youth and Authority*, pp. 330–5.
20. Tittler, *Architecture and Power*, p. 32.
21. Abingdon Corporation Minute Book, Berkshire County Record Office MS, D/EP/7/84, p. 163.
22. Boulton, *Neighbourhood and Society*; Prior, *Fisher Row*; Roy and Porter, 'Social and economic structure of an early modern suburb', 203–17; Griffiths et al., 'Population and disease', pp. 225–32.
23. Tittler, ' "Seats of honor, seats of power" ', 218–21.

BIBLIOGRAPHY

Abingdon Corporation Minute Book, Berkshire County Record Office MS. D/EP/7/84.

Bairoch, Paul, Batou, Jean and Chevre, Pierre, *La Population des Villes Européennes de 800 à 1850* (Geneva, 1988).

Ben-Amos, Ilana Krausman, *Adolescence and Youth in Early Modern England* (New Haven, 1994).

Boulton, Jeremy, *Neighbourhood and Society: A London Suburb in the Seventeenth Century* (Cambridge, 1987).

Bradley, John, 'From frontier town to Renaissance city: Kilkenny, 1500–1700', in Peter Borsay and Lindsay Proudfoot, eds, *Provincial Towns in Early Modern England and Ireland: Change, Convergence and Divergence* (Proceedings of the British Academy, no. 108, Oxford, 2002), pp. 29–52.

Brooks, Christopher, 'Apprenticeship, social mobility and the middling sort, 1550–1800', in Jonathan Barry and Christopher Brooks, eds, *The Middling Sort of People: Culture, Society and Politics in England, 1550–1800* (Basingstoke, 1994), pp. 52–83.

Butlin, R. A., ed., *The Development of the Irish Town* (London, 1977).

Butlin, R. A., 'Land and people, c. 1600', in T. W. Moody, F. X. Martin and F. J. Byrne, eds, *A New History of Ireland*, vol. III (Oxford, 1976), pp. 142–86.

Clark, Peter, 'The migrant in Kentish towns', in Peter Clark and Paul Slack, eds, *Crisis and Order in English Towns, 1500–1700* (London, 1972), pp. 117–63.

Clark, Peter and Slack, Paul, eds, *Crisis and Order in English Towns, 1550–1700* (London, 1972).

Cullen, L. M., 'Economic trends', in Moody et al., *A New History of Ireland*, vol. III (Oxford, 1976), pp. 387–407.

de Vries, Jan, *European Urbanization, 1500–1800* (Cambridge, MA, 1984).

Devine, T. M., 'Scotland', in Peter Clark, ed. *The Cambridge Urban History of Britain*, vol. II, *1540–1840* (Cambridge, 2000), pp. 151–66.

Everitt, Alan, 'The marketing of agricultural produce', in Joan Thirsk, *The Agrarian History of England and Wales*, vol. IV, *1500–1640* (Cambridge, 1967), pp. 466–592.

Galley, Chris, *The Demography of Early Modern Towns, York in the Sixteenth and Seventeenth Centuries* (Liverpool, 1998).

Griffiths, Matthew, '"Very wealthy by merchandise"? Urban fortunes', in J. Gwynfor Jones, ed., *Class, Community and Culture in Tudor Wales* (Cardiff, 1989), pp. 197–236.

Griffiths, Paul, *Youth and Authority, Formative Experiences in England, 1560–1640* (Oxford, 1996).

Griffiths, P., Landers, J., Pelling, M. and Tyson, R., 'Population and disease, estrangement and belonging, 1540–1700', in Peter Clark, ed., *The Cambridge Urban History of Britain*, vol. II, *1540–1840* (Cambridge, 2000), pp. 225–32.

Houlbrooke, Ralph, *The English Family, 1450–1700* (London, 1984).

Howells, Brian E., 'The lower orders of society', in J. Gwynfor Jones, ed., *Class, Community and Culture in Tudor Wales* (Cardiff, 1989), pp. 237–60.

Jack, Sybil M., *Towns in Tudor and Stuart Britain* (Basingstoke, 1996).

Jenkins, Philip, 'Wales', in Peter Clark, ed., *The Cambridge Urban History of Britain*, vol. II, *1540–1840* (Cambridge, 2000), pp. 133–50.

Owen, Leonard, 'The population of Wales in the sixteenth and seventeenth centuries', *Transactions of the Cymmrodorion Society* (1959), 99–113.

Phythian-Adams, Charles, Corfield, Penelope, Slack, Paul, and O'Day, Rosemary, eds, *The Traditional Community under Stress* (Milton Keynes, 1977).

Prior, Mary, *Fisher Row; Fishermen, Bargemen and Canal Boatmen in Oxford, 1500–1900* (Oxford, 1982).

Roy, Ian, and Porter, Stephen, 'The social and economic structure of an early modern suburb', *Bulletin of the Institute of Historical Research*, 53, 128 (November 1980), 203–17.

Sharlin, Alan, 'Natural decrease in early modern cities: a reconsideration', *Past and Present*, 79 (1978), 126–38.

Sheehan, Anthony, 'Irish towns in a period of change', in Ciaran Brady and Raymond Gillespie, eds, *Natives and Newcomers: Essays in the Making of Irish Colonial Society, 1534–1641* (Dublin, 1986), pp. 93–119.

Slack, Paul, *Poverty and Policy in Tudor and Stuart England* (London, 1988).

Tittler, Robert, *Architecture and Power: The Town Hall and the English Urban Community, c. 1500–1640* (Oxford, 1991).

Tittler, Robert, ' "Seats of honor, seats of power": the symbolism of public seating in the English urban community, c. 1560–1620', *Albion*, 24, 2 (Summer 1992), 205–23.

Whyte, Ian D., *Scotland before the Industrial Revolution: An Economic and Social History, c. 1050–1750* (London, 1995).

Williams, Glanmor, *Renewal and Reformation: Wales, c. 1415–1642* (Oxford, 1993).

Wrightson, Keith, *Earthly Necessities: Economic Lives in Early Modern Britain* (London and New Haven, 2000).

Wrigley, E. A., 'Urban growth and agricultural change: England and the Continent in the early modern period', *Journal of Interdisciplinary History*, 15, 4 (1985), 683–728.

FURTHER READING

Ian H. Adams, *The Making of Urban Scotland* (1978).

Jonathan Barry and Christopher Brooks (eds), *The Middling Sort of People: Culture, Society and Politics in England, 1550–1800* (1994).

A. L. Beier, *Masterless Men: The Vagrancy Problem in England, 1560–1640* (1985).

Ilana Krausman, Ben-Amos, 'Failure to become freemen: urban apprentices in early modern England', *Social History*, 16, 2 (May 1991), 155–72.

Peter Borsay and Lindsay Proudfoot (eds), *Provincial Towns in Early Modern England and Ireland: Change, Convergence and Divergence* (2002).

Harold Carter, *The Towns of Wales: A Study in Urban Geography* (1965).

Peter Clark and Paul Slack, *English Towns in Transition, 1500–1700* (1976).

Peter Clark and David Souden (eds), *Migration and Society in Early Modern England* (1987).

Nigel Goose, 'Household size and structure in early Stuart Cambridge', *Social History*, 5 (1980), 347–85.

David Harkness and Mary O'Down (eds), *The Town in Ireland* (1981).

J. Gwynfor Jones (ed.), *Class, Community and Culture in Tudor Wales* (1989).

Anne Laurence, *Women in England, 1500–1760: A Social History* (1994).

Michael Lynch (ed.), *The Early Modern Town in Scotland* (1987).

S. G. E. Lythe and J. Butt, *An Economic History of Scotland, 1100–1939* (1975).

T. W. Moody, F. X. Martin and F. J. Byrne (eds), *A New History of Ireland*, vol. III (1976).

John Patten, *English Towns, 1500–1700* (1978).

Margaret Pelling, 'Old age and poverty in early modern towns', *Bulletin of the Society for the Social History of Medicine*, 34, (1984), 42–7.

Charles Phythian-Adams, *Desolation of a City: Coventry and the Urban Crisis of the Late Middle Ages* (1979).

Alexandra Shepard and Phil Withington (eds), *Communities in Early Modern England: Networks, Place, Rhetoric* (2000).

Paul Slack, *From Reformation to Improvement: Public Welfare in Early Modern England* (1999).

T. C. Smout, *A History of the Scottish People, 1560–1830* (2nd edition, 1970).

Robert Tittler, *The Reformation and the Towns in England: Politics and Political Culture, c. 1540–1640* (1998); and *Townspeople and Nation: English Urban Experiences, 1540–1640* (2001).

Ian D. Whyte, *Scotland's Society and Economy in Transition, c. 1500–c. 1760* (1997).

E. A. Wrigley and R. S. Schofield, *The Population History of England, 1541–1871* (1981).

CHAPTER TWENTY-TWO

Women in the British Isles in the Sixteenth Century

ANNE LAURENCE

Writing about Queen Elizabeth I (1533–1603) and Mary Queen of Scots (1542–87) far exceeds in quantity writing about any other sixteenth-century women, either individually or collectively. John Knox's phrase 'the monstrous regiment of women' (regiment meaning rule or regimen) was coined in 1558, when Elizabeth had just succeeded her half-sister Mary Tudor as queen of England, and when the throne of Scotland was occupied by Mary Stewart (though the government was still in the hands of the regent, her mother Mary of Guise). But this was not a time of women's power; these queens ruled over countries in which women's lives were circumscribed by legal systems which advantaged men and where women were substantially excluded from economic power and political decision-making. Nevertheless, women were adaptable and ingenious enough to use such opportunities as were afforded them, though legal and economic differences within the British Isles meant that there was some variation in those opportunities.

Women such as Grace (Gráinne) O'Malley (*c*.1530–1603), Eleanor Countess of Desmond (*c*.1545–*c*.1640), Elizabeth Countess of Shrewsbury (Bess of Hardwick) (1518–1608), Anne Askew (1521–46), and Margaret Clitherow (died 1586) are beginning to be brought out of obscurity through biographical studies, but the very survival of sufficient material to construct a biography makes them exceptional. It is ironic that the home country of one of the most famous women in western European history (Mary Queen of Scots), has produced little else about sixteenth-century Scottish women.

Great strides in the study of women and gender relations have been made by historians, using a wide variety of records and writings to say something about the mass of unnamed women, and about the kind of woman whose name might appear once in a parish register or court deposition. Renaissance literary scholars have enlarged the canon to include letters, memoirs and diaries, as well as poetry and translation by women. Gradually, though more slowly than for later periods, a picture of the lives of women in the sixteenth century is beginning to emerge.

Records and Historiography

English records have been extensively used by historians in the anglophone world, but the (admittedly less numerous) records of Scotland, Ireland and Wales much less so, with the result that the historiography of early modern women's history, feminist history and gender history is overwhelmingly English, and predominantly relates to the period after 1600. Although the low level of women's literacy in the sixteenth century means that there is little writing by women themselves, women are found in many official documents: they paid taxes, rents and market dues, appeared in lay and ecclesiastical courts, and came into contact with the authorities in parish, town and manor. Witness statements and depositions, manor court rolls and wills feature women, as well as parish and kirk registers.

Historians of women have relied particularly heavily on the registers of baptisms, marriages and burials that English and Welsh parishes were required from 1538 to keep, though the negligence of parish clerks and the religious upheavals of the mid-century means that they are rarely complete. Comparable records start to appear in Scotland after the establishment of reformed kirk sessions from the 1560s, but substantial areas of the country had no effective parish organization, and the same is true for much of Ireland. In addition, there was everywhere in the British Isles a secular alternative to church marriage and no official record was kept of such marriages. The lack of records for Gaelic society has led historians to take an interest both in Irish annals and in folkloric sources, and in Scots Gaelic poetry. Traditional Gaelic law has also attracted notice because of the debate about whether traditional Gaelic society offered women more or less freedom than the societies governed by the metropolitan law of Dublin or Edinburgh.

Historians of England have set the agenda for the study of women and gender relations in the sixteenth century, but recent developments promise well for the future, and separate histories of Scotland, Ireland and Wales. Led by Margaret Mac Curtain and Mary O'Dowd's volume of essays on Ireland, which is outstanding for its treatment of women in Gaelic Ireland, Scotland and Wales have followed suit with similar collections.[1] The comprehensive Field Day collection of texts by and on Irish women has been controversial for its organization and selection, but is still a wonderful resource, though with predictably little about the period before 1600.[2] Both the collection of essays and the Field Day texts attempt to address the long-held view that women in Gaelic Ireland had higher status and more political power than women who were subject to English common law, attempting to provide a more nuanced picture of women, and influencing studies of women in Scottish Gaelic society.

The seminal works that have informed the study of women in the sixteenth century have often been primarily concerned with later periods. Alice Clark's classic study of work, for example, has provided an agenda for research on women's working lives in the household. Lawrence Stone's studies of affective relationships have influenced much work on the family, and his examination of noble families' marriage settlements has shaped later historians' views on the relative importance of economics and love in marriage choices. The work of Wrigley and Schofield on the nuclear family has had an impact on historians' views of family networks. Although some of these historians' ideas may have been superseded by later research their influence on the research agenda has been undeniable.

Historians of the sixteenth century have been just as taxed as historians of other periods by the issues with which gender history has been concerned – public and private, 'separate spheres', the 'golden age', and the measurement of historical change in women's lives. A good deal of space has also been devoted to discussing the issue of whether there was a crisis in gender relations in the period, though these debates have not been equally absorbed by historians of the different nations of the British Isles. Anthony Fletcher's consideration of masculinity and femininity and the uncertainties of the boundaries between them in sixteenth-century England has been taken up for Wales, but not yet for Scotland or Ireland.[3]

Discussions about the extent of change in women's lives in the sixteenth century have been particularly concerned with the economic changes of the sixteenth century and with the Reformation. Judith Bennett has, over a number of years, put the case that transformation has assumed too prominent a place as an explanatory device for historians of women in medieval and early modern society, when continuity may prove to be more important. She points out that, even when historians of women have inverted accepted chronologies or subverted ideas of progress or regression, transformations in women's status have been synchronized with major historical turning-points.[4] While Bennett has looked at women's position in society and the economy, Margaret Sommerville has looked at attitudes to women and has concluded that there was little change in the period 1500–1700.[5]

Differences of opinion over the state of the economy in the sixteenth century have necessarily affected the ways in which women's wage-earning has been regarded. Economic opportunities arising from the labour shortages following the Black Death in the 1340s had created favourable circumstances for women's employment in the fifteenth century, but by the early sixteenth century women were in a much less advantageous position and during that century restrictions on their working lives increased as urban guilds sought to protect the employment of men. Opportunities for women's employment fluctuated with the state of the economy, but the study of patterns of female employment suggests considerable continuities with the later middle ages.

The Reformation, as one of the most significant turning-points in western European history, necessarily invites the question: Did it transform the lives of women? To some extent the concerns of historians of women converge with those of revisionist historians of the Reformation such as Christopher Haigh, who argue for continuity between pre- and post-Reformation England. The writings of the reformers emphasized the role of the father as head of the household and the necessity for his wife and children to be obedient, by reference to numerous biblical precedents accessible to the laity in the newly available vernacular translations of the scriptures and in conduct books. In this they were not expressing views radically different from Catholic commentators; English Puritans and Italian Catholics could agree that women were inferior. However, clerical marriage, an increasing emphasis on experiential religion, and growing female literacy did have an impact on women's lives, though gradually and over a long period, suggesting that the institutional and political changes of the Reformation affected women's lives more than changes in religious ideas.

While much of the work on women in the sixteenth century has concentrated on domestic and religious life and women's employment, there has recently been interest in women's access to power. Studies of high-status women have shown how important women were in patronage networks, while studies of lower-status women have shown how they participated in demonstrations about food prices, trade and religion.[6]

Women in the Population

Because women have been so extensively studied in the context of the family, the impact of the work of J. Hajnal and of Wrigley and Schofield on family structure in the British Isles in the early modern period has been seminal.[7] Hajnal's observation that in western Europe from the sixteenth century late marriage for both men and women (that is to say in the mid- to late twenties), with a relatively high proportion of the population not marrying at all, was the usual pattern, in contrast to the youthful marriages of other parts of Europe, has been universally adopted. The studies of Wrigley and Schofield and, more generally, the Cambridge Population Group, have confirmed this for the period from the mid-sixteenth century. Lack of material for the earlier period has inclined historians to behave as if there was a break in the English demographic regime around the beginning of the sixteenth century, but work on poll-tax records for the late fourteenth century suggests that late, companionate marriage preceded by a period of employment was an established pattern in England well before the sixteenth century.

Despite Hajnal's own provisos, there has been an assumption that the British Isles in general was characterized by this pattern of a high age of marriage and a relatively high proportion of non-marriers. However, there was significant regional variation and there were differences between town and country, though demographic studies of Scotland and Ireland are often speculative because of the absence of parish records.

Hajnal's model probably prevailed in most of rural England and Wales, in the Lowlands and the central region of Scotland, in the Pale and amongst the English populations of Irish towns. But Scotland may have had higher birth rates, higher infant mortality and a higher overall death rate than England. The age of marriage in the Highlands and Islands seems to have been lower than that elsewhere in Scotland and patterns of family formation there resembled those of Gaelic Ireland. Anecdotal evidence from travellers to Ireland (mainly English men) emphasized the universality and very young ages at which rural Irish women married and the large families they had.

Social status undoubtedly influenced patterns of family formation. While child marriages made for dynastic reasons declined, noble marriages continued to take place at a younger age than those of non-noble couples, in the early rather than mid-twenties. Younger marriages were also common amongst the elites of the Scottish clans and Irish septs where they were used to cement alliances between leading clan chiefs and clan elites. Likewise, urban marriages tended to take place at a younger age than rural ones and widows and widowers in towns were more likely to remarry than those in the countryside. Wrigley has usefully suggested that the demography of the British Isles consisted of 'a repertoire of adaptable systems' rather than several clearly demarcated ones.[8]

The Cambridge Group's work established that the nuclear family was already in existence by the early sixteenth century and that this was the normal family form, but other historians have demonstrated the importance of kin networks and that, even if it was unusual for more than two generations of a family to live in the same house, other family relationships were often maintained over considerable distances. While neither the nuclear family nor the extent of family relationships is peculiar to women, the tendency to study women primarily in terms of the family means that such historical judgements have a greater impact upon the conclusions that historians draw.[9]

Early modern England and Wales were characterized by their low illegitimacy rate, though births to unmarried women are thought to have peaked at the end of the sixteenth century. However, uncertainty about what constituted valid marriage affected whether a birth was considered legitimate or illegitimate. In Gaelic society, on both sides of the Irish Sea, the nature of marriage meant that, in the eyes of the authorities in Dublin and Edinburgh, many children were considered to be illegitimate. English writers about Gaelic society would refer to the sexual licence of Irish and Highland men and women. Edmund Campion commented of Ireland that

> the honourable state of marriage they much abased, either in contracts unlawful meeting the levitical and canonical degrees of prohibition, or in divorcements at pleasure, or in omitting sacramental solemnities, or in retaining either concubines or harlots for wives. Yea, even at this day, where the clergy is faint, they can be content to marry for a year and a day of probation, and at the year's end to return her home upon light quarrels, if the gentlewoman's friend be unable to avenge the injury. Never heard I of so many dispensations for marriage as these men show.

Campion went on to write of Irish 'strumpets' who were used by noblemen to increase the numbers of descendants carrying their name 'He that can bring most of his name into the field, base or other, triumpheth exceedingly; for increase of which name they allow themselves not only whores, but also choice and store of whores. One I hear named which hath (as he called them) more then ten wives in twenty places'.[10] Even allowing for exaggeration, there is evidence for many of these practices taking place in Ireland, though Campion and other English commentators did not appreciate their cultural significance. The existence of trial marriage in the Orkney and Shetland Islands suggests that the customs Campion described were to be found more widely in the societies of the Highlands, western and northern isles.

Life Cycle

These demographic debates tell us much about the population in general, but little about human and, in particular, female, experience and expectations. While late marriage was the norm for a considerable proportion of the population of Britain and Ireland, women's expectations were affected by differences in the laws and customs regulating marriage, inheritance and succession. Most children were brought up by their parents or a parent and a step-parent, with clearly defined roles for mother and father in the care and discipline of a child, in whom were instilled expectations considered to be appropriate to their gender and class. Children of the nobility and gentry were often nursed by wet-nurses, despite the discouragement of the medical profession.

For most women, such education as they had came not from schools and lessons but from a period of time spent in someone else's household, providing a bridge between childhood and adulthood. Higher-status girls were sent to noble households to learn gentle manners and make connections with families who might provide suitable marriage partners or places at Court. In Ireland this was institutionalized to the point that it was referred to as fosterage and, it was claimed, foster-parents bestowed 'more affection on these children than they do upon their own', while foster-children 'return this love faithfully and warmly'.[11] A spell as a maid-of-honour at Court was another way of making connections with suitable marriage partners. Young noble- and gentlewomen were taught to be modest and obedient to their husbands, but also how to run a household, to command respect from their social inferiors and to be what Linda Pollock has described as selectively deferential and subordinate.[12]

Girls were substantially excluded from the expansion in schools in England; it is unlikely that they attended the grammar schools that educated so many boys, but were probably instead taught in unregulated dame schools, where they learnt basic subjects. London must have been relatively well provided with schools as there were at least forty-seven schoolmistresses who taught in twenty-eight parishes in the period 1560–1603.[13] Ironically, the sixteenth century was a time of important female benefactions for education from grammar schools, such as that founded by Dame Thomasine Percyvale in her home parish of Week St Mary, Cornwall, in 1508, to the Cambridge college (Sidney Sussex) founded from the £5,000 left in 1589 by Frances Sidney, countess of Sussex.

Young plebeian women spent the time after they left their parents' home as farm or domestic servants, living in their employer's household for a contracted period of time, earning a wage and learning some skills; rarely did they take formal apprenticeships. Domestic service became more important as the century progressed and as the large numbers of male servants of the later medieval house were replaced by women. Arable and pastoral farming areas provided different kinds of employment for women, but there was little waged work for them in the cattle-rearing regions of Ireland, Scotland and the English Borders, where there was some transhumance, people moving with their cattle to temporary dwellings while the cattle fed on summer pastures. It is difficult to know what impact this kind of life had on families and on women's lives, but it is likely that in these regions women rarely worked independently of their families and were therefore more likely to marry young.

In England, much of Wales, the Lowlands of Scotland and the counties in the vicinity of Dublin late companionate marriage seems to have been the norm. The exception to this norm seems to have been aristocratic families where strategic alliances required that the arrangement be settled when the parties were young. The age difference between the partners in second marriages was frequently greater than in first marriages, noblemen often marrying women much younger than themselves and widows of urban craftsmen (who were able to pass on their late husband's guild privileges to a second husband) marrying men younger than themselves. Late marriage depended upon the availability of opportunities for work for young women and the harsh economic times of the 1590s may have led to more women getting married younger because of the reduction in opportunities for employment. With the exception of strategic noble and clan alliances, women seem to have had a reasonable amount of freedom in their choice of marriage partner, though friends, family and the local community all contributed to the decision.

Much that is known of marriage in this period is drawn from conduct books, manuals setting out the ideal, usually a specifically Christian ideal of marriage. At the other extreme, cases of matrimonial breakdown reached the courts. In England and Wales problems with the validity of marriage were often dealt with by the church courts, both before and after the Reformation. In Scotland, the jurisdiction of the church courts over marriages and wills passed after 1560 to civil commissary courts, while the new kirk-sessions dealt with offences that had not previously featured much in the courts: adultery, fornication (formerly dealt with by penance), and profaning the sabbath.

Noblemen and women had a reasonable expectation of being married for about twenty years, men and women of lower social status for slightly less time. However, higher-status women's childbearing years were longer because they married younger, and they also had pregnancies at shorter intervals. Bearing children was considered to be the primary purpose of marriage and childbearing was one of the few sources of women's authority in the family. Childlessness was a matter for concern and distress; help was sought to increase the chances of conception not to prevent it.

We have no complete account of the experience of the birth room, we know that women were largely attended by other women, and that men could exercise considerable control over the process. In different parts of the British Isles different customs accompanied the actual birth and observers commented adversely on customs with which they were unfamiliar. English travellers to Scotland and Ireland often noted the speed with which women rose from their beds and were to be found out and about, working in the fields within hours of giving birth, echoing comments made about lower-class English women. It was common for women to have around eight pregnancies, with perhaps four children surviving to adulthood.

Most marriages ended in the death of one of the partners. Technically, marriages made under the Roman Catholic church were indissoluble. However, in the Gaelic custom of secular marriage, which operated on both sides of the Irish Sea, divorce was permitted, the most noteworthy cases being those of noblemen and their wives; John Macgillechallum of Raasay carried off the wife of his chief, Ruari Macleod of Lewis, in 1569 and married her after her divorce.[14] We know little about who initiated divorces, but they permitted remarriage for both parties, creating considerable problems for heirs, especially where the Gaelic custom of inheritance (which could accommodate the complexities of children from different marriages) came into conflict with the law of the state. The reformed churches declared marriage to be no longer a sacrament, thus opening the way for divorce. The Anglican church, however, was the only reformed church in Europe not to recognize divorce. The reformed church of Scotland permitted divorce, though it was administered by a secular court and was more usually used as a way of separating a couple than of allowing remarriage. There seemed little chance of divorce to end the violent and abusive marriage of Lady Margaret Cuninghame, who on one occasion was sent by her husband, with her gentlewoman companion, 'forth of his house naked, and would not suffer us to put on our clothes, but said he would strike both our backs in two with a sword'; the two women had to be taken in by the minister.[15]

Many widows were young women and, especially in towns where they could pass on guild membership rights from a deceased husband, remarriage was common and often took place at quite a short interval after the death of a spouse. Although there is a large ballad and chapbook literature caricaturing the lasciviousness and boldness of widows, for many women widowhood, especially if they were left with young children, meant a descent into poverty from which it was difficult to recover.

Daily Life

Some of the liveliest debates in women's and gender history take place around the subject of work, both waged and unwaged. Driven by the question of whether the industrial revolution changed women's lives for the better or for the worse, historians have tended to concentrate on the later period, but Alice Clark's question, 'Were women more economically valued and independent in pre-industrial Europe than they were later?' has informed much of the research on women's work from the later middle ages.

The principal locus for women's work was the household, not necessarily their own or their family's household, often someone else's. Within it, relationships between individuals replicated those of the patriarchal family even if they were those of employer and employee, and women's working relationships were essentially dependent ones, especially in the different forms of service that employed so many women.

Historians debate the relative proportions of farm servants to day-labourers working in agriculture; it is suggested that around a third of the rural population were labourers. The evidence for Cheshire in the early years of the sixteenth century suggests that farm service was not a particularly attractive form of employment for women: they were more likely to end their contracts early than were men and they were extensively employed as day-labourers, especially at harvest time when at least half of the workforce was female. The pattern for Nathaniel Bacon's estate at Stiffkey in North Norfolk is similar, with two or three women servants working in the dairy, but many more working as day-labourers in seasonal and occasional tasks: weeding, haymaking, planting saffron, shearing and tying up wheat, picking hops and harvesting saffron, sorting wool and picking over seed corn. In addition, there was work in Stiffkey Hall in the house and garden.[16] These figures suggest that the farm servants were probably young women working before they married, and that the casual work was done by women of all ages, at about half the daily pay of men (4 d, as opposed to 8 d). Women worked at different tasks according to the regional specialization, and alongside men, though at different jobs from them.

However, the majority of agricultural work took place on small farms relying on the labour of members of the family of both sexes. It is difficult to see women's hand in the agricultural work of a small land-holding; it is more evident in by-employments, such as spinning and weaving wool, flax and hemp, and localized crafts such as glove-making, lace-making and stocking-knitting. Spinning was almost always done by women; women made woad and worked with clay to make bricks and pots, and often worked in brewing and tanning.

It is much harder to find comparable detail about women's work in Wales, Ireland and Scotland. Lowland Scotland and the east and south of Ireland had not dissimilar kinds of agriculture to England but it is only possible to speculate about the similarity of women's work. However, in the west and north of Ireland and in the west and north of Scotland, there was a very different kind of rural economy, based on cattle-herding. Here, there was virtually no commercial agriculture. Such crops as were grown (chiefly oats) were purely for domestic consumption, as were the cheese and butter that were made.

The advantage of urban life for the working woman was that it offered much more variety and greater opportunity for specialization than agricultural work or the rural industries. The attractions of urban life are evident in the migration of young women to towns, with many towns' populations showing an excess of women over men. Joan Thirsk's observation, that women were often at the forefront of new trades and industries, is borne out by the example of the printing trade. Elizabeth Pickering printed fourteen books in the year 1540–1. Jane Yetsweirt, heir in the 1590s to a patent to print English common-law books, successfully resisted the challenge to her right by the Company of Stationers. Women were also particularly numerous in the victualling trades and in retailing.[17]

Scottish towns had much less varied economies than English towns in the sixteenth century, with fewer trades and a greater dependence on imported manufactured goods. Royal burghs (burghs entitled to trade abroad) relied heavily on exporting such raw materials as hides, wool and fish which cannot have provided many employment opportunities for women except as domestics. Urban life was also economically precarious because of the fluctuations in Scottish urban economies over the century. Edinburgh offered women more opportunity as landladies, money-lenders and pawnbrokers.

Town governments could modify the common-law restrictions on married women's economic activity and did so to make adjustments according to the health of the economy. It was not unusual for towns to have provisions under which married women could trade without their husbands becoming liable for their trading debts. But women were also treated as the flexible sector to be squeezed or encouraged according to the demand for labour, as, for example, when Edinburgh city council in 1532 restricted the setting-up of businesses or renting premises to married women without the council's permission. Women could evade restrictions imposed by town councils and implemented by guilds by private marketing, trade not regulated by the customary provisions, which offered women opportunities to engage in retailing, often selling goods made by someone else.

Work in agriculture changed during the sixteenth century with greater agricultural specialization. Whether farm service became less widespread or whether it became more flexible over the period, it is clear that the distinction between the farm service and other forms of agricultural employment was breaking down. The effect of agricultural specialization was usually to increase the number of jobs in, for example, dairying, rather than to create a wider range of jobs for women. Another significant change during the century was the diminution of rights to common land, which had supplemented the provisions of many rural families and could make the difference between destitution and survival for people in precarious occupations. Poor commoners were the fiercest opponents of Tudor enclosures. At the same time, a number of commons were actually occupied by poor cottagers themselves, often as squatters.

The sixteenth century seems to have seen a diminution in women's ability to support themselves in reasonably paid work in both town and countryside, but the forces that affected women's work also affected men's and undoubtedly the later years of the century saw more families living in poverty.

Women's Material Worlds

One of the great truisms that has undergone radical revision in the last ten years is that because married women were unable to own property in their own right and anything they acquired during their marriage became their husband's to dispose of as he wished, they were entirely at their husband's mercy. In fact, it is possible throughout the period to see that women were able often to circumvent the most oppressive aspects of these provisions by, for example, using one of the jurisdictions that did not recognize the legal doctrine that a married woman was *feme covert*, as was the case under canon law (the church courts), customary law (manorial courts) and in equity (Chancery). While it might be difficult for a woman on her own to exploit differences between jurisdictions, families seem to have used them strategically to ensure their corporate advantage. This is probably most significant in Ireland where the largest number of legal systems and customs co-existed. According to the Spanish ambassador to King James IV, writing in 1498, women in Scotland were 'absolute mistresses of their houses, and even of their husbands, in all things concerning the administration of their property, income as well as expenditure'.[18] In Scotland a wife's moveable property was under her husband's control and he could sell or give away anything except personal clothing and jewels; property that was acquired during the marriage was under the husband's control too. A wife would bequeath her separate possessions, but needed her husband's permission to make a will. Wives could not sell heritable or immovable property without the husband's consent, but husbands could not sell it either without the wife's consent and while husbands could not treat the dowry (or tocher) as their own property, they did control the usufruct. Officially English wives had less control than Scots wives over moveable property or their dowries, but in other respects the provisions were similar.

Under English common law and Scots law women could inherit property, but under Gaelic law, in use in much of the west of Scotland and in Ireland outside the Pale, women were not entitled to inherit clan lands. William Macleod of Harris had to obtain a special dispensation in 1553 to allow his daughter to inherit his estates in Harris, Dunvegan and Glenelg, while other parts of his estate had to pass to his brother as the heir male. At the death of her husband, or the dissolution of the marriage, the only property to which a wife had any right under Gaelic law was what she had brought with her to the marriage and even this could be difficult to secure. Gráinne O'Malley took out sureties for the repayment of her dowry in case her husband died indebted. The Irish court of Chancery was increasingly used by women for mediating between English common law and Gaelic customary law.

Throughout the British Isles women were expected to bring some property at the time of their marriage, either from their own earnings or from the family's property. In England and Wales a women's dowry became her husband's property at marriage, while in Scotland she retained certain rights over it. In Gaelic areas cattle and rights to occupy land (rather than to own it) were the measures of wealth and power, and these were often provided as dowries, though Gráinne O'Malley had a fleet of ships to command and Agnes Campbell a troop of mercenary soldiers.[19]

In England and Wales there was no relationship between dowry (the property a women brought to a marriage) and dower (her entitlement as a widow) and the custom of dower was asymmetrical: the widower was entitled under common law to the whole of his late wife's property, provided she had borne a living child, while the widow was entitled to only a third of her late husband's property regardless of whether she had had any children. Dowry and dower were not just material provision for married or widowed women, they also represented the formation of a new set of alliances forged by the marriage, the nature of which depended much on the social status, the wealth and the location of the families.

Women made up a disproportionately large number of the poor, usually, in England, because of poverty associated with life events and with the recession of the 1590s. Subsistence crises which led to an increase in grain prices were declining in number and severity in England and Wales. Until the Reformation (which involved the dissolution of hospitals, leper houses and religious guilds with charitable aims), much of the charitable provision was in the hands of the religious orders.

The transfer of responsibility to local government was far from satisfactory and lay people's benefactions were an important source of relief, many of them coming from wealthy laywomen, especially childless widows. The poverty of townswomen was recognized in charitable bequests both of almshouses and of money, such as the gift made in 1580 by a London merchant to buy 120 pails so that poor women could supplement their income by carrying water.[20]

The hard times of the 1590s brought the crisis in dealing with the poor to a head. The government took action in 1597 by enacting the first Poor Law which attempted to distinguish between the settled and the vagrant poor. Women were numerous among the settled poor, but there were also women vagrants, often single mothers, sometimes in search of an errant husband. In those places, such as London and Norwich, where it has been possible to identify the numbers of unattached women vagrants the proportion of women seems to have risen steadily over the sixteenth century. In London it rose to as much as a third of all vagrants, in provincial towns the proportion was generally lower. Scotland and Ireland had lower agricultural productivity and less public support for the poor.

Attempts in Scotland to introduce a system similar to that of the English Poor Law, to be administered by the kirk-sessions, were not successful, not least because the Scots were much less used to paying taxes of any kind than the English. Where the Scots system did work, it was more flexible, informal and personal than the English system, and less effective. Unlike England, there was no provision for relief for unemployed people and the modifications made to the English Poor Law legislation to make it more effective were never passed in Scotland. In Ireland, after the dissolution of the religious houses, virtually all poor relief was private and was often restricted to Protestants, being administered through charities left by Protestants.

Women were substantial donors of almshouses and, where these donations were made in their lifetimes, took a close interest in the ways in which the buildings were constructed. Dame Dorothy Pelham built almshouses in Wing, Bucks, in 1596 and Bess of Hardwick founded the Devonshire almshouses in Derby in 1599. Women also showed a conspicuous enthusiasm for commemorating their families, both in funerary monuments and in houses. Bess of Hardwick was not only builder of Hard-wick Hall (at a cost of £80,000), whose internal arrangements include state rooms on the top floor, something that no man who expected a visit from the monarch would dare to have ordered, but also built houses at Oldcotes, Worksop and Bolsover, as well as constructing a Cavendish mausoleum. Ann, widow of Baron Hundson, built a monument for her husband in Westminster Abbey in the 1590s. Margaret Countess of Bath in the 1560s commemorated herself and all of her three husbands on a tomb. These building enterprises brought women into contact with sculptors, masons and the management of money, as well as with contemporary canons of taste; it was an unusual opportunity for them to display their aesthetic judgements in public.[21]

Women and Religion

The Reformation is rightly identified as a transformative moment for women, which had a somewhat different impact on them than on men. By 1539 the medieval reli-gious orders, religious guilds and sisterhoods had been disbanded in England and Wales and devotional activity connected with the Virgin Mary, the Rosary, female saints, relics and shrines was abandoned. This had the effect of removing from women activities which associated them with the practice of their faith, leaving them with church cleaning and the care and repair of textiles such as altar cloths and vestments.

The two thousand nuns in England and Wales in 1500 had fallen in number by 1534 to about 1,600, living in 136 communities. There were, in addition to fully professed nuns, various supernumeraries: lay sisters, pensioners, devout lay women who chose to live in or near a convent.[22] Although many communities were small and poor, a few operated as substantial businesses. The nunnery of St Sexburga in Sheppey maintained ten workers: shepherds, cowherds as well as a carpenter, thatcher, maltster, horse-keeper and carter, all of whom had to find alternative employment at the Dissolution.

Under the Acts which dissolved the religious houses, former members of the orders were granted pensions, though usually these were very small and often paid in arrears. Women religious had much more difficulty than men in finding alterna-tive employment; there was no place for them in the reformed church. Joan Dean, a nun from Syon abbey, where the nuns had a reputation for their learning, was unusual in finding a position as governess in the household of Sir George Gifford.

Ireland had sixty-eight religious houses for women in the early sixteenth century. About half were suppressed in the period 1537–40, but thirty-one survived, some being dissolved in the 1560s, a few even surviving until the seventeenth century.[23] As in England, ex-religious were granted pensions. The surviving houses were impor-tant not just for Irish Catholic women, but also for English Catholic women, as the first English house on the continent was not founded until 1596. The traditional account of the Dissolution in Ireland argues that it was timely because of the moral decay of the religious orders, but recent work is beginning to suggest that the orders were not in such bad shape.

In Scotland, although nuns were far less numerous than in England, they were subject to the most savage satirical attacks by David Lindsay. At the time of the

Reformation there were only eleven religious foundations for women, four having closed down earlier. The surviving houses were of uncertain standing since the Cistercian order seems not to have recognized the nine Cistercian houses. There was no formal dissolution, but in the course of the late sixteenth century much monastic land was alienated to temporal lords and by the 1580s many of the buildings were ruinous, though the prioress of the nunnery at Coldstream, Berwickshire seems to have held office until 1588.

The religious upheavals of the period caused much clandestine religious activity to take place in the household rather than in formal places of worship. Joan Butcher was burned for heresy during Edward VI's reign for being too Protestant in her views, while fifty Protestant women were condemned to death for heresy during Mary's reign. During the reigns of Edward VI and Elizabeth, Catholic women in England and Wales protected priests and Mass vessels. Although, for much of the period, there was de facto toleration of Catholicism in Ireland, there was a noteworthy incident when Margaret Ball, Catholic mother of the mayor of Dublin, was dragged through the streets of Dublin and thrown into gaol where three years later she died.[24]

Protestant women protected ministers during Mary's reign, and exiled reformers corresponded with such influential women as Protector Somerset's daughters. Rose Hickman, wife of a London merchant, took into her own house in London at the start of Mary's reign 'divers godly and well disposed Christians that were desirous to shelter themselves from the cruel persecution of those times'. After the declaration that everyone had to receive the Catholic sacraments Rose Hickman left London, finally joining her husband in exile in Antwerp.[25]

Support for Protestant ministers continued into Elizabeth's reign as the Puritan movement attracted opposition from the authorities. Dorcas Martin and her husband, a lord mayor of London, were the subject of several dedications of Protestant works, including an abridgement of Calvin's *Institutes*, and were noted patrons and protectors of such godly ministers as Thomas Cartwright. Martin and Hickman were both connected with Anne Locke, correspondent of John Knox, who joined Knox in Geneva in 1557 with her two young children to escape the Marian persecution of Protestants, leaving her husband at home. She translated some of Calvin's sermons and returned to London in 1559.

Wives of clergymen found themselves in new, and sometimes very difficult circumstances. When married clergy were cast out of their livings in England and Wales at Mary's accession, the effects were borne by the family as well as by the clergyman. One in eight of the clergymen in the Welsh diocese of St David's and one in six of these in the diocese of Bangor lost his living.[26] In Ireland the marriage of reformed clergy such as Bishop Bale of Ossory and Archbishop Loftus of Armagh caused consternation.

These examples are essentially private ones, but women did go out onto the streets in defence of their religious beliefs. Women took part in mass demonstrations such as the Pilgrimage of Grace (1536–7), the Western Rebellion of 1549 and the Northern Rebellion of 1569. An unusual act of resistance occurred when the nuns of St Clement's convent in York were reinstated during the Pilgrimage of Grace. When, in 1566, the wearing of vestments was enforced, women appeared on the streets of London in protest. A delegation of sixty women supported a Puritan lecturer against the bishop of London in the 1560s. In the 1590s, when James VI made moves to reinstate episcopacy, women took part in the riots in Edinburgh.

Women's Cultures

The study of women's cultures is often dominated by concerns about literacy and its rise or fall, and about the dissemination of literature in English. There is debate about the extent of female literacy in England in the sixteenth century, but little is known about literacy levels in Scotland, Ireland and Wales. While women did not partici- pate in print culture in the same way as men, the oral tradition of bardic poetry was largely closed to them, partly by virtue of the fact that bardic poets were employed to compose public poetry.

Apart from literature in English, there were the Gaelic languages of Scotland and Ireland (hardly, in the sixteenth century, separate languages), the languages of Wales and Cornwall, and the older Scottish tongue (*lalans*, a form of English), as well as writing in Latin and other European languages. That these languages were known to women is apparent from the fact that women feature not only as translators of classical texts, but also as authors.[27]

Female culture was not, of course separate and independent from men's culture; women wrote in the same forms as men, they used writing for communication with men. The tradition of learned women is exemplified by Margaret Roper (*c*.1522–72), translator and daughter of Sir Thomas More, and her kinswoman Margaret Clements (1508–70) who took a special interest in algebra. Writers and artists were dependent on the patronage of women such as the duchess of Norfolk (*c*.1498–1558), patron of the poet Skelton, and Elizabeth Carey (fl.1590s), to whom the poets Spenser and Nashe dedicated works.

Women participated in the male culture of political power from which they were ostensibly excluded, but within which they provided an essential network of con- nections through marriage. A few women were, by virtue of a combination of per- sonality and family connection, able to influence political events, but this influence always owed something to a network of male connections and normally took the form of them playing the role of intermediaries, intercessors, and petitioners.

It is likely that ethnic background was less important in determining the extent of women's political influence than the political culture in which women operated, which differed in different parts of the British Isles. In the Scottish Highlands and Islands, as in Gaelic Ireland, there was no strong central political authority and influ- ence depended more on dynastic networks than it did in metropolitan Scotland or England. There is some evidence that Irish men accepted Irish women's political activity more readily than the English governors of Ireland, who found it threaten- ing. In 1581 a Spanish-born Irish woman was making use of her languages to inter- pret in political negotiations; Thomas Lee's wife acted as interpreter between the English and Irish; and Agnes Campbell, Scottish wife of Turlough Luineach O'Neill, was sent to negotiate with Lord Justice Drury on behalf of her husband. The eighth earl of Kildare used his six daughters to establish his political ascendancy in the early years of the century by strategically arranged marriages. Two of them, Margaret Fitzgerald, wife of Piers Butler, earl of Ormond, and Eleanor Fitzgerald, were active in the rebellious politics of Ireland in the 1530s. Women's part in Irish political life was recognized by the execution of Brian MacPhelim, with his wife, after an attack on a party who had come to parley with the English in 1574. The centralization of the Tudor administration of Ireland was intended to diminish the power of the Gaelic and Old English lordships, with the result that women found themselves less powerful as dynastic connections carried less weight. Dublin Castle provided no equivalent to the possibilities for women's power and patronage that were possible through the English Court, both in positions in the queen's household and as wives of courtiers; the response of Irish noblewomen was to petition the English Court directly.

Women's involvement in politics frequently led to accusations of them exercising undue influence, or influence for the wrong reasons; it carried the cost of rendering them subject to public criticism and of being blamed for their husband's misjudgement. The invocation of plotting wives is a common theme in early modern political discourse; they were used as an evil counsellor trope, and they had a practical function in the case of the husband requiring political rehabilitation. Rarely, however, did they fall as far as Janet Douglas, Lady Glamis (d. 1537) who was accused of supporting her three brothers when they fell into disgrace with James V. She was then charged with poisoning her late husband, found guilty and executed. The countess of Arran was accused of plundering jewels belonging to Mary Queen of Scots, and of having undue influence over her husband, the lord chancellor of Scotland. Miss Drummond, one of Anne of Denmark's women who was secretly receiving a pension from the king of Spain, was allegedly influential in inclining the queen towards Roman Catholicism, as was Henrietta Stewart, countess of Huntly.

Plebeian women had little chance of playing such roles, but they did become involved in public affairs, usually alongside men, taking part in protests concerned with communal grievances. In the hard times of the 1590s women demonstrated against high grain prices, demonstrations which seemed to be aimed at securing fair prices rather than confiscating cornmerchants' stock, and they took part in enclosure riots, protesting at the infringement of ancient rights.

There was a widely held and mistaken popular belief that women protestors could not be prosecuted. Although women were held to be insufficiently responsible to manage property, they were held to be responsible enough for their actions to be able to be prosecuted for crimes, as the history of the courts and of witchcraft clearly demonstrates.

NOTES

1. Mac Curtain and O'Dowd, *Women in Early Modern Ireland*; Ewan and Meikle, *Women in Scotland*; Roberts and Clarke, *Women and Gender in Early Modern Wales*; Meek and Lawless, *Pawns or Players?*.
2. Bourke et al., *Field Day Anthology of Irish Writing*.
3. Fletcher, *Gender, Sex and Subordination*; Roberts, 'More prone to be idle' p. 262.
4. Bennett, 'Confronting continuity', 73–80.
5. Sommerville, *Sex and Subjection*, p. 251.
6. Harris, 'Women and politics', and *English Aristocratic Women*; Brady, 'Political women and reform'; Palmer, 'Gender, violence and rebellion'; Thomas, '"Dragonis Baith and Dowis Ay"'; Grant, 'Politicking Jacobean women'.

7. Hajnal, 'European marriage patterns in perspective', pp. 102–3; Wrigley and Schofield, *Population History of England*; Wrigley et al., *English Population History*.
8. Wrigley, 'Marriage, fertility and population growth', p. 182.
9. Cressy, 'Kinship and Kin interaction'; Chaytor, 'Households and Kinship in Ryton'.
10. Campion, *Two Bokes of the Histories of Ireland*, pp. 21–2, 25.
11. Stanihurst, 'On Ireland's past', p. 157.
12. Pollock, ' "Teach her to live under obedience" ', 245–7.
13. Barron, 'The education and training of girls', p. 149.
14. Gregory, *History of the Western Highlands*, p. 266.
15. Cuninghame, *A Pairt of the Life*, p. 5.
16. Hassall Smith, 'Labourers in late sixteenth century England' 17–29.
17. Thirsk, 'The history women', pp. 1–2; Allen, 'Jane Yetsweirt', pp. 5–12.
18. de Ayala, quoted in Hume Brown, *Early Travellers in Scotland*, p. 47.
19. Simms, 'Women in Gaelic society during the age of transition', pp. 35, 38.
20. Roberts, 'Women and work', p. 93.
21. The details of almshouses come from the various county volumes of the Pevsner Buildings of England series.
22. Knowles and Hadcock, *Medieval Religious Houses*; Cullum, 'Vowesses and female lay piety'.
23. Bradshaw, *Dissolution of the Religious Orders in Ireland*, pp. 47, 61, 144; Gwynn and Hadcock, *Medieval Religious Houses*, p. 309; Casway, 'Irish women overseas', p. 117.
24. Corish, 'Women and religious practice', p. 215.
25. Shakespeare and Dowling, 'Religion and politics'.
26. Gwynfor Jones, *Early Modern Wales*, p. 139.
27. Stevenson and Davidson, *Early Modern Women Poets*.

BIBLIOGRAPHY

Allen, S. M., 'Jane Yetsweirt (1541–?): claiming her place', *Printing History*, 9, 5–12.

Barron, C. M., 'The education and training of girls in fifteenth-century London', in Diane E. S. Dunn, ed., *Courts, Counties and the Capital in the Later Middle Ages* (Stroud, 1996), pp. 139–53.

Bennett, J., 'Confronting continuity', *Journal of Women's History*, 9 (1997), 73–94.

Bourke, A., Kilfeather, S., Luddy, M., et al., eds, *The Field Day Anthology of Irish Writing*: vols V and VI, *Irish Women's Writing and Traditions* (Cork, 2002).

Bradshaw, B., *The Dissolution of the Religious Orders in Ireland under Henry VIII* (Cambridge, 1974).

Brady, C., 'Political women and reform in Tudor Ireland', in Mac Curtain, Margaret and M. O'Dowd eds, *Women in Early Modern Ireland* (Dublin, 1991). pp. 69–90.

Campion, E., *Two Bokes of the Histories of Ireland* (1571), ed. Alphonsus Franciscus Vossen (Assen, Netherlands, 1963).

Casway, J., 'Irish women overseas, 1500–1800', in M. Mac Curtain and M. O'Dowd, eds, *Women in Early Modern Ireland* (Dublin, 1991).

Chaytor, M. 'Households and Kinship in Ryton in the late sixteenth and early seventeeth centuries', *History Workshop Journal*, 10 (1980), 25–60.

Clark, Alice, *Working Life of Women in the Seventeenth Century* (London, 1992 [1919]).

Corish, Patrick, 'Women and religious practice', in M. Mac Curtain and M. O'Dowd, eds, *Women in Early Modern Ireland* (Dublin, 1991).

Cressy, D., 'Kinship and Kin interaction in early modern England', *Past and Present*, 113, 38–69.

Cullum, P. H., 'Vowesses and female lay piety in the province of York, 1300–1530', *Northern History*, 32 (1996), 21–41.

Cuninghame, M., *A Pairt of the Life of Lady Margaret Cuninghame* (Edinburgh, 1828).

Ewan, E. and Meikle, M. M., 'Introduction: a monstrous regiment of women', in E. Ewan and M. M. Meikle, eds, *Women in Scotland c.1100–c.1750* (East Linton, 1999), pp. xix–xxx.

Ewan, E. and M. M. Meikle (eds), *Women in Scotland c.1100–c.1750* (East Linton, 1999).

Fletcher, A., *Gender, Sex and Subordination in England 1500–1800* (New Haven and London, 1995).

Grant, R., 'Politicking Jacobean women: Lady Ferniehirst, the countess of Arran and the countess of Huntly, c.1580–1603', in E. Ewan and M. Meikle, eds, *Women in Scotland c.1100–c.1750* (East Linton, 1999) pp. 95–104.

Gregory, D., *History of the Western Highlands and Isles of Scotland from AD 1493 to AD 1625* (Edinburgh, 1836).

Gwynfor Jones, J., *Early Modern Wales c.1525–1640* (Basingstoke, 1994).

Gwynn, A. and Hadcock, R. N., *Mediaeval Religious Houses: Ireland* (London, 1970).

Haigh, C., 'The recent historiography of the English Reformation', in Margo Todd, ed., *Reformation to Revolution: Politics and Religion in Early Modern England* (London, 1995), pp. 13–32.

Hajnal, J., 'European marriage patterns in perspective', in D. V. Glass and D. E. C. Eversley, eds, *Population in History* (London, 1965) pp. 101–46.

Harris, B. J., *English Aristocratic Women 1450–1550* (New York, 2002).

Harris, B. J., 'Women and politics in early Tudor England', *Historical Journal*, 33 (1980), pp. 259–82.

Hassall Smith, A., 'Labourers in late sixteenth-century England: a case study from North Norfolk, part 1', *Continuity and Change*, 4 (1989), pp. 11–52.

Hume Brown, P., *Early Travellers in Scotland* (1891, reprinted Edinburgh, 1978).

Knowles, D. and Hadcock, R. M., *Medieval Religious Houses: England and Wales* (London, 1971).

Mac Curtain, M. and O'Dowd, M., eds, *Women in Early Modern Ireland* (Dublin, 1991).

Meek, C. and Lawless, C., eds, *Pawns or Players?: Studies on Medieval and Early Modern Women* (Dublin, 2003).

Palmer, W., 'Gender, violence and rebellion in Tudor and early Stuart Ireland', *Sixteenth Century Journal*, 23 (1992), 699–712.

Pollock, L., '"Teach her to live under obedience": the making of women in the upper ranks of early modern England', *Continuity and Change*, 4 (1989), 231–58.

Roberts, M., '"More prone to be idle and riotous than the English?" attitudes to male behaviour in early modern Wales', in M. Roberts and S. Clarke eds, *Women and Gender in Early Modern Wales* (Cardiff, 2000).

Roberts, M., 'Women and work in sixteenth-century English towns', in P. Corfield and D. Keene, eds, *Work in Towns 850–1850* (Leicester, 1990), pp. 86–102.

Roberts, M. and S. Clarke (eds), *Women and Gender in Early Modern Wales* (Cardiff, 2000).

Shakespeare, J. and Dowling, M., 'Religion and politics in mid-Tudor England through the eyes of an English Protestant woman: the recollections of Rose Hickman', *Bulletin of the Institute of Historical Research*, 55 (1982), 94–102.

Simms, K., 'Women in Gaelic society during the age of transition', in M. Mac Curtain and M. O'Dowd, eds, *Women in Early Modern Ireland* (Dublin, 1991), pp. 32–42.

Sommerville, M., *Sex and Subjection: Attitudes to Women in Early-Modern Society* (London, 1995).

Stanihurst, R., 'On Ireland's Past. *De Rebus in Hibernia Gestis* (1584)', in C. Lennon, ed., *Richard Stanihurst the Dubliner 1547–1618* (Dublin, 1981).

Stevenson, J. and Davidson, P., eds, *Early Modern Women Poets: An Anthology* (Oxford, 2001).

Stone, L., *The Family, Sex and Marriage in England, 1500–1800* (Harmondsworth, 1979).

Stone, L., *An Open Elite? England 1540–1880* (Oxford, 1986).

Thirsk, Joan, 'The history women', in M. O'Dowd and S. Wichert, eds, *Chattel, Servant or Citizen: Women's Status in Church, State, and Society* (Belfast, 1995).

Thomas, A., '"Dragonis Baith and Dowis ay in double form": women at the Court of James V, 1515–1542', in E. Ewan and M. M. Meikle, eds, *Women in Scotland c.1100–c.1750* (East Linton, 1999), pp. 83–94.

Wrigley, E. A., 'Marriage, fertility and population growth in eighteenth-century England', in R. B. Outhwaite, ed., *Marriage and Society: Studies in the Social History of Marriage* (London, 1981), pp. 137–85.

Wrigley, E. A., Davies, R. S., Oeppen, J. E. and Schofield, R. S., eds, *English Population History from Family Reconstitution 1580–1837* (Cambridge, 1997).

Wrigley, E. A. and Schofield, R. S., eds, *The Population History of England 1541–1871: A Reconstruction* (1981, repr. Cambridge, 1989).

FURTHER READING

Judith Bennett and Amy Froide (eds), *Singlewomen in the European Past, 1250–1800* (1999).

K. M. Brown, *Noble Society in Scotland: Wealth, Family and Culture from Reformation to Revolution* (2000).

P. Crawford, *Women and Religion in England 1500–1720* (1993; paperback edition, 1996).

D. E. Easson, *Medieval Religious Houses: Scotland* (1957).

A. Everitt, 'Farm labourers', in Joan Thirsk (ed.), *The Agrarian History of England and Wales*, vol. IV, *1500–1640* (1967), pp. 396–465.

E. Ewan, 'Women's history in Scotland: towards an agenda', *Innes Review*, 46 (1995), 155–64.

P. J. P. Goldberg, *Woman is a Worthy Wight*, republished as *Women in Medieval English Society* (1997).

J. Goodare, *State and Society in Early Modern Scotland* (1999).

R. A. Houston and I. D. Whyte (eds), *Scottish Society 1500–1800* (1989).

Olwen Hufton, *The Prospect before Her: A History of Women in Western Europe, 1500–1800* (1995).

P. Kilroy, 'Women and the Reformation in seventeenth-century Ireland', in M. Mac Curtain and M. O'Dowd (eds), *Women in Early Modern Ireland* (1991) pp. 179–96.

Anne Laurence, *Women in England, 1500–1760: A Social History* (1994).

Rosalind K. Marshall, *Virgins and Viragos: A History of Women in Scotland, 1080–1980* (1983).

M. Mates, *Women in Medieval English Society* (1999).

C. E. Meek and M. K. Simms (eds), *'The Fragility of her Sex': Medieval Irish Women in their European Context* (1996).

Sara Mendelson and Patricia Crawford, *Women in Early Modern England, 1550–1720* (1998).

R. Mitchison, *The Old Poor Law in Scotland: The Experience of Poverty 1574–1845* (2000).

M. O'Dowd, 'The political writings and public voices of women, c.1500–1850', in A. Bourke, S. Kilfeather, M. Luddy, et al. (eds), *The Field Day Anthology of Irish Writing*, vols V and VI, *Irish Women's Writing and Traditions* (2002), pp. 6–12.

Diana O'Hara, *Courtship and Constraint: Rethinking the Making of Marriage in Tudor England* (2000).

A. Pacheco (ed.), *A Companion to Early Modern Women's Writing* (2000).

Mary Prior (ed.), *Women in English Society, 1500–1800* (1984).

J. Stevenson and P. Davidson (eds), *Early Modern Women Poets: An Anthology*, Oxford University Press (2001).

M. E. Wiesner, 'Beyond women and the family: towards a gender analysis of the Reformation', *Sixteenth Century Journal*, 28 (1987), 311–21.

D. Willen, 'Women and religion in early modern England', in S. Marshall (ed.), *Women in Reformation and Counter-Reformation Europe: Public and Private Worlds* (1989), pp. 140–65.

D. Woodward, 'Early modern servants in husbandry revisited', *Agricultural History Review*, 48 (2000), 141–50.

PART IV

Culture

Introduction

It seems neither possible nor desirable in a work of this scope to present a comprehensive discussion of all cultural forms. Some subjects integrate with the rest of the volume, and some come to the forefront of current historiographic interest, more than others. We have therefore had to be selective in choosing the most appropriate and current issues, while keeping in mind that there are other companion-surveys to take up those which we leave out.

Once again we have striven to cover the British Isles as best we could though, as we have noted before, the published research concerning cultural activity in England alone far surpasses that pertaining to the rest of the British Isles. We have a sense of writing in the middle of a broad historiographic shift which is still under way, and which will not yield a comprehensive coverage of the Scottish, Irish or Welsh picture until it has run its course. That flow began with the broad scholarly assumptions that most cultural activity of this era took place in London and/or at Court or in aristocratic households; that it mostly consisted of what we would now call 'high' cultural achievements, and that it emanated from patronage by the social and political elites. Over the past generation, scholarly attention has moved ever outwards and downwards, geographically and socially speaking, from those once canonical points of reference.

This great movement has perhaps been most starkly evident in writings on the history of drama, in which the canon of the great playwrights, and of public performances in the London theatres such as the Red Lion, the Theatre, the Curtain and the Rose, largely comprised the contours of the subject. Over the last four decades or so that long tradition came under sweeping challenge, especially by the breathtakingly comprehensive research of the Records of Early English Drama (REED) project, founded in 1975. Now roughly half-way through its mission to retrieve and publish the records of all English and Welsh mimetic activity in every county and major town in the realm up to 1640, REED has fundamentally redirected the research approach to that field, and just as fundamentally redrawn the subject itself. By exhaustively trawling county and borough archives, family records, and previously unexplored files in the Public Record Office, REED brought the methods and sources of historical research to its own subject. These efforts show that London performance was but the tip of the iceberg; that dramatic performance regularly occurred, with notable regional variations, in virtually every nook and cranny of the land; and that – despite its frequently polemical content – mimetic activity was by no means the exclusive purview of aristocratic interest or metropolitan fashion.

The adoption by its sister disciplines of current historical methods and sources has had similar effects on historical investigation of the other arts. The focus of research on other subjects has certainly moved in similar directions: outwards from London, downwards from the fashions of the metropolis and the court, and towards an often polemical (but not necessarily elitist) form and content. Historians of architecture, music, portraiture and historical writing itself, if not yet to the same extent of science, have come to use a wider range of sources than the traditional mainstays of the Public Record Office and British Library. They have similarly expanded the scope of their subjects away from the more or less exclusive concern with high or polite cultural expressions and towards broader perspectives of contextual and polemical significance.

If these current investigatory trends continue in their present direction, we will see them extend not only outwards from London to the rest of England, but from there to the rest of the British Isles. This work may never produce as complete a picture for Scottish or Irish dramatic activity, for example, or for portraiture, or for some of the other cultural forms, as it has for England. Neither the sum of these activities themselves nor the state of the evidence which would describe them weigh heavily enough to sustain such an expectation. Extensive research opportunities nevertheless remain in these areas and fields. The fruits of that future work will bring this historiographic journey to its appropriate conclusion; it will greatly expand what can currently be said.

Daniel Woolf's essay on 'Senses of the Past' moves far beyond the canon of familiar historical writings to describe his subject. In order to emphasize the myriad ways in which sixteenth-century men and women constructed their own pasts he employs the less familiar along with the more familiar written sources, explores the interplay between written and oral traditions, and examines both memories and physical 'sites of memory'. The diverse political and ethnic divisions of Tudor Britain may each have drawn upon some elements of a common, 'ancient British', heritage, but Woolf finds that each nevertheless retained their own historical traditions; distinct in content, polemical in intent, and, to a degree, language of expression; sometimes conflicting with one another. It is something of an understatement to note that he leads us to appreciate more keenly the cultural diversity within the British Isles at this time.

By utilizing unfamiliar sources, exploring the mnemonic element in cultural expression, and emphasizing the extreme cultural diversity of the age, Woolf's essay sounds chords which ring through most of the other essays in this group. Alexandra Johnston's essay, drawn from her unique perspective as founding director of REED, shows how dramatic activity constantly drew upon traditional forms while accommodating to the new, post-Reformation order. She affirms how geographically and socially widespread such dramatic activity proves to have been. She acknowledges the regional diversity of mimetic tradition in England especially, handicapped still by a dearth of comparable research on the Scottish, Irish and Welsh scene.

Similar themes appear as well in Robert Tittler's account of portraiture, by far the principal form of painting at this time, and of its role as a form of political, social and often mnemonic discourse. Like drama, portraiture also proves to have had a vivid non-courtly side to it, and to have reflected local, community-centred inspiration as well as metropolitan, courtly and royal models. It, too, seems far more advanced in England than elsewhere in the British Isles. Its development in England contrasts with the Scottish experience in ways which usefully reflect upon the different social and political realities of those two British kingdoms. Malcolm Airs' essay moves along a similar path in emphasizing the social and political context of his genre, giving due notice to the buildings of the middling sorts of people, and of civic institutions, as well as to the more familiar fruits of royal and aristocratic patronage. John Milsom follows suit, eschewing the tradition-bound canon of the Tudor composers and musical forms and removing the emphasis on the traditional concentration on the impact of the Reformation. He offers instead an extended reflection on music as a varied, popular and universal social activity, indeed, as a pervasive form of oral culture.

And though current research in scientific activity must necessarily depart from some of these patterns, simply because it is not a cultural activity in the same sense as the others, it, too, has usefully departed from the strict canon of great thinkers and discoveries to broader considerations. In addition, as Leslie Cormack's contribution shows, this subject remains more firmly planted on the English side of things than most others, as research on Scottish, Irish and Welsh efforts have much further to go than with most of the other issues under consideration here.

CHAPTER TWENTY-THREE

Senses of the Past in Tudor Britain

DANIEL WOOLF

Over twenty years ago, Sir Keith Thomas drew attention to the distinctive 'perceptions of the past' that could be observed in early modern England. In formulating
his summary, Thomas departed from the usual descriptive methods of historiogra-
phers and their focus on literary historical writing in order to examine the various
informal ways in which the past was conceptualized and discussed. Since that time,
there has been much further work on various matters opened up by Thomas's discussion, including, for instance, work on oral culture and memory by Andy Wood,
Adam Fox and others for England.[1] Moreover, in the intervening time there has been
another historiographical development, namely a much greater awareness that
England was only part – if admittedly an important and politically dominant part –
of a British archipelago which had other components, specifically Scotland, Ireland
and (to the extent that it remained linguistically separate even if politically incorporated) Wales.

Looking back from the perspective of the eighteenth century and a more
united Britain (the 'more' is important) one can see that a significant element in
the 'forging' of a new nation consisted of a number of shared traditions. A British
national identity rested not simply on a united monarchy and, after 1707, a
single parliament, but in large measure on a shared set of perceptions of and
attitudes toward the past in general and, more specifically toward certain key
episodes such as the Norman Conquest, the Reformation and the civil wars.
That unity, and the coherence of those perceptions can be overstated, even for
the eighteenth century, and strong national traditions certainly remained intact.
Moreover, if one examines the formal historiography of the period, it is notable
that some of the Enlightenment's leading historians were Scots – David Hume
and William Robertson among them. It is equally remarkable that they chose to
work in an Anglo-Scottish intellectual environment and, in Hume's case, to write
a history of England, not of Britain. It would take another century, and the
settling of a foreign empire, for a clearer sense of British national identity really
to take hold, itself deriving from a shared pool of the past into which flowed many
tributaries.

We should bear this in mind as we look to the much earlier period covered by this *Companion*. The present chapter will examine, briefly, a variety of aspects of the senses of the past (I shall return to the plural shortly) in 'Tudor' Britain, which of course really means Tudor England and Ireland, Stewart Scotland, and a semi-independent Gaelic Ireland beyond the English Pale. But even these national categories break down on closer inspection. There is, for instance, in England and Wales a distinctive perspective on the ancient 'British' past associated with Wales; the clansmen of the Scottish Highlands or *Gàidhealtachd* had a very different sense of their own past than that shared by the more anglicized and literate Lowlander in Edinburgh; and the Old English settlers whose occupancy of Irish land went back to the twelfth century similarly had (till shared Catholicism brought them closer together) an understanding of their heritage that set them apart from their Gaelic-speaking native-Irish neighbours, as well as from the New English and eventually Ulster Scots settlers who followed in the sixteenth and early seventeenth centuries. While there are many common features in the experience of the past in Britain and Ireland (for instance, the maintenance of both oral and written modes for its preservation and communication), and while there are many good examples of interpenetration of myths and sharing of historical episodes between the separate kingdoms, one will look in vain for a single 'sense'. What was already a set of plural and often *competing* senses within England alone (differences of religion, gender, economic and social status playing a significant role) broadens considerably when one moves into other realms, whether a semi-subjugated one such as Tudor Ireland or a fiercely independent one like Stewart Scotland. And the picture is complicated exponentially by the presence of multiple languages and ethnic backgrounds, Gaelic, Anglo-Saxon, Cambrian (that is, Welsh), Cornish and Anglo-Norman. This chapter will explore a very small number of aspects of this problem.

Ethnicity and Myths of National Origin

Where the past was concerned, nothing more clearly signified the differences among English, Welsh, Scottish, and Irish than the understanding of ethnicity (both one's own and that of others) and the closely related – and in some ways racially definitive – issue of national origins. Early modern thought, which also preferred to identify specific inventors in the past for commonplace things and for civilized accomplishments like writing, came only slowly to more gradualist or evolutionary concepts of social development. A comparable inclination to locate the foundation of kingdoms at a particular time, and with a particular king or line, persisted throughout the sixteenth century, and heated print battles were fought over the relative chronological priority of this or that town or institution (England's two universities for instance), and of monarchies. The English had their longstanding, Galfridian (that is, derived from the writings of 'Galfridus' or Geoffrey of Monmouth, *c.* 1100–54) tradition of an ancient line of British kings, beginning with Brutus the Trojan and including along the way William Shakespeare's (1564–1616) Leir or Lear, and Thomas Sackville's (1536–1608) and Thomas Norton's (1532–1584) Gorboduc. A biblical tradition of ethnic origins that attributed all races to the children of Noah, Shem, Ham and Japhet – technically true if one accepted literally the scriptural account of the extinction of mankind in the Flood – made Japhet's son Gomer the antecedent of British Celts, especially the Welsh. An entire race of giants in 'Albion', the island's supposed pre-British name, was supposed to have been supplanted by Brutus's Trojans. To the leafy stem of these ancient legends, several other competing beliefs were soon grafted in support of the English Reformation: the visit of Joseph of Arimathaea to Britain after Christ's death; the early establishment of Christianity in Britain by a mythical king Lucius (mentioned by both Nennius [*fl.* late eighth century] and Geoffrey), long before Augustine of Canterbury's conversion of the Saxons; and the birth and half-British parentage – via his mother Helen, daughter of King Coel – of the revered Emperor Constantine, a figure identified both with early imperial support for Christianity and with the superiority of the secular over the spiritual arm. John Bale (1495–1563), a learned early Reformation polemicist, borrowed from continental sources such as the pseudo-Berosus of Annius of Viterbo, a spectacular fifteenth-century literary fraud, to introduce into the mix a line of kings descended from Samothes, alternately a grandson of Noah or at least a Celtic prince, and preceding the giant Albion who had in turn been defeated by Brutus. This conveniently filled in the blanks not covered in Geoffrey of Monmouth's *Historia Britonum*, or in the fifteenth-century chronicles collectively known as *The Brut*, a version of which was printed by William Caxton in 1480.[2]

The Welsh, largely subordinated in political terms since the thirteenth century, a process completed by Henry VIII, were not a factor in the various rebellions of the sixteenth century. No latter-day Owain Glyndwr emerged to trouble his fellow-Welsh monarchs. However, they did preserve their own language (more successfully than the Cornish), and with it their own special identification with the Britons pushed into Wales and Cornwall by invading Saxon hosts in the fifth and sixth centuries. Protestant reformers used this history later in the century to identify pure religion with the ancient Britons who, unlike the benighted Saxons, were converted to Christianity long before Augustine's introduction of a corrupt and papalized faith. When tied to the still authoritative if rickety reputation of medieval writers such as Nennius and especially Geoffrey, this meant that a figure such as Arthur, though known all through Britain, had a particularly strong resonance for the Welsh. English authors had since the thirteenth century been evincing some scepticism toward Arthur, and it may have been simply reaction to the Italian emigré Polydore Vergil (1470?–1555) that forced some Tudor English authors to come down off the fence and land firmly on the side of Arthur, Brutus, and the line of fanciful kings in between. Among those British authors who attacked Vergil for doubting the historicity of Brutus and Arthur, Englishmen such as Bale and John Leland (*c.* 1506–52) were joined by a number of Welsh authors. These included Arthur Kelton, Sir John Price or ap Rhys (d. 1573) in his *Historiae Britannicae defensio* (published posthumously in 1573 but written by 1545), Humphrey Lhuyd or Llwyd (1527–68), in *The Breviary of Britayne*, as translated by Thomas Twyne (1543–1612) in 1573, and David Powell (*c.* 1552–98), who edited Lhuyd's English translation of the medieval *Brut y Tiwysogion* ('chronicle of Caradoc of Llancarfan' or 'Chronicle of Princes').[3] Powell's *History of Cambria*, as his edition (Lhuyd's book together with a *Description of Cambria* by Price) was known, amounted in places almost to a new work, such were his corrections and additions. Interest in the remote and hazy pre-Roman past was encouraged not only because of the ruling dynasty's Welsh origins, but because of the interest of some leading English magnates – Lord Burghley would commission Powell to draw up a genealogy of Welsh Cecils – and because of its usefulness in promulgating English 'imperial' expansion in Ireland and overseas, as for instance with John Dee.[4]

As things turned out, Arthur would survive into the seventeenth century, albeit reduced somewhat in proportions. Brutus took a dreadful and ultimately fatal beating, and by the end of the sixteenth century his very existence was being doubted, at least implicitly, by leading antiquaries such as William Camden (1551–1623). By the last years of Elizabeth's reign in England, the whole Trojan legend had been gutted and largely dispensed with in antiquarian circles, in part because of more widespread knowledge and sharpened philological acuity, but also because not very much depended on its veracity: historical interests were focused more urgently elsewhere, for instance on the apostolic and medieval church, or on the dynastic conflicts of the fifteenth century. Even the poets were now rather cautious with respect to the earlier portions of the British myths. Edmund Spenser (*c.* 1552–99), keen on Arthurian mythology in the *Faerie Queene*, was notably more guarded with respect to Brutus. Somewhat later, Michael Drayton (1563–1631) would have the antiquary John Selden (1584–1654) write skeptical annotations to Drayton's own *Poly-olbion* (1612), while the poet-turned-historian Samuel Daniel (1562–1619) flatly refused to look further back than the Norman Conquest in beginning his *First part of the historie of England* (1612).[5]

Scotland, unlike Wales, was independent throughout the sixteenth century, a distinct British monarchy in the seventeenth, and only legislatively integrated from 1707. 'Modern' Scotland was the result of the integration of ancient Picts with invading Scots from Ireland; John of Fordun's fourteenth-century chronicle the *Chronica Gentis Scottorum* (sometimes known as the *Scotichronicon* because it was transplanted at large into a work of that name by the early-fifteenth-century abbot, Walter Bower) had invested the early medieval Dalriadic (that is, west highland) Scots with an ancient monarchy while at the same time contrasting the barbarity of Highlanders with the civility of Lowlanders, and thereby giving rise to a long historiographic tradition distinguishing the two. The Scots had a long national mythology going back via real kings such as the ninth-century Kenneth Macalpin, subjugator of the Picts, to the mythical Fergus MacFerquard. They even had an answer to Trojan Brutus in the Greek prince Gathelos and his Egyptian wife Scota (daughter of Moses' Pharaoh!), the Greeks of course having defeated the Trojans. Gathelos and Scota had settled first in Spain, then in Dalriada. Fordun had initiated an anti-Brutus or at least revisionist approach (eventually adopted by Hector Boece) as early as the fourteenth century, criticizing Geoffrey of Monmouth and rejecting the notion of Scotland as a junior and tributary kingdom once ruled by Brutus' second son – an annoying pseudo-fact cited, among others, by Henry VIII in 1542 as justification for war against his nephew James V.[6]

In Scotland as in England, present values were both projected back on to the past and reinforced by its study and creative reinterpretation: the council in 1552 could refer to the Auld Alliance as dating back to one Achaus, king of Scotland, and Charlemagne. Although mentioned sketchily in medieval sources, the figure of Fergus MacFerquard was most fully developed in the hands of Hector Boece (*c.* 1465–1536) and then George Buchanan (1506–82) – though the latter rejected the earlier,

Gathelos story, largely on philological grounds. An émigré Irish chief, contemporary with Alexander the Great, Fergus had in 330 BC founded a line of forty-five fully independent kings (given much fuller lives by Boece) and, following a brief period of Romano-Pictish disruption, his descendant Fergus II, son of Erc, had re-initiated a kingdom that survived all subsequent incursions, English or Norman. Buchanan also had a quite separate interest in the first Fergus that went beyond national pride: as ruler Fergus was elected by clan chiefs, who were themselves elected by their followers, thereby providing a useful if not absolutely essential historical foundation for Buchanan's radical political theory. (He was obliged, incidentally, to attack the Welshman Lhuyd who, though a fellow Protestant, had scorned Boece's ancient kings in the process of defending the British history against Vergil.) The royalist-inclined Adam Blackwood (1539–1613) would challenge Buchanan's interpretation, making the clan chiefs unfettered rulers of their own territories whose powers had then been transferred to and consolidated the monarchy of Fergus, which in turn was unrestrained in power through its Dalriadic phase until the ninth century. Buchanan's own most illustrious pupil, James VI and I, would later twist Fergus into a model for unrestricted royal authority, and a ruler by conquest rather than election, which was scarcely what his old teacher had intended.[7]

The experience of Ireland was somewhat similar, its various competing groups each having different perspectives on Irish antiquity, though they tended often to borrow from one another. The Gaelic or old Irish, who referred to themselves as Milesians, had a prehistory dating well before the Anglo-Norman conquest of the twelfth century, but acknowledged a prior race of aboriginal giants, which in turn had been superseded by the followers of one Partholón, and then successively by Nemedians, Fir-Bolg and Tuatha-Dé-Danaan. The Gaelic communities, building on a medieval chronicle called *Leabhar gabhála* or the 'Book of Invasions' saw the Irish monarchy as having been founded by King Slangy, one of the Fir-Bolg (in the seventeenth century, this affiliation with Fir-Bolg and Tuatha-Dé-Danaan would be adopted by the Old English also). By that time, all these groups had been absorbed into a collective Gaelic history covering the entire history of the island, and Geoffrey Keating (Gaelic, Séathrún Céitinn, *c.* 1573–1644) would argue – much as contemporary English authors often claimed with respect to the Norman Conquest of 1066 – that the twelfth-century Anglo-Norman conquest was little more than a change of dynasties, preserving Irish independence intact.[8]

The view looked very different from across the Irish Sea or even within the Pale: New English writers like Spenser and Edmund Campion (1540–81) were inclined to attribute Gaelic barbarity to its remote roots in that most useful and much-travelled of ancient ethnic forebears, the Scythians (in Campion's account, the ancestors of Pictish invaders of Ireland). While sceptical of ancient myths at home, they were prone to rest the case for English overlordship not only on the more recent medieval Conquest but on a more ancient imperialism attributed to Arthur and, even earlier, the same Greek/Spanish émigré Gathelos featured, with some differences of detail, in Scottish discussions.[9] Much discussion was devoted to the related question of the nature of the ancient Irish church of St Patrick, and whether it reflected primitive apostolic piety or medieval papal distortion; Keating, again, would maintain that the Irish church had not been subjected to Canterbury since the time of Augustine. The later Irish Franciscan, Peter Walsh or Valesius would defend Irish autonomy against a threat from another quarter, the Scottish assertion (found in Buchanan) that King Gregory of Scotland had conquered Ireland in the ninth century. Other Irish historians asserted the suzerainty of Ireland over the 'Scots' (themselves ethnically Irish) of Dalriada.

The Ancestral Past

In all parts of Britain, family history played a crucial role in constituting a sense of the past, especially for the upper echelons of society both literate and illiterate. Scottish Gaelic culture continued to look to its Irish counterpart culturally, and Highland chiefs tended to project their pedigrees back to Milesian (that is ancient Irish) origins, thereby nurturing a myth of a united Gaelic past. Feudalized Lowlanders played a comparable game, producing in the first third of the seventeenth century (when the creation of new peerages lent genealogy a further impetus) longer works such as David Hume of Godscroft's (*c.* 1560–*c.* 1630) *History of the House of Douglas,* and Sir Robert Gordon's (1580–1656) *Genealogical History of the Earldom of Sutherland* as well as the poet William Drummond of Hawthornden's inflated sense of his family's royal ancestry.

In England, the sixteenth century in particular saw a much greater awareness of family history and genealogy, and the evolution of regulatory controls over its legitimacy. The College of Arms conducted regular visitations of the counties in order to verify claims to gentility, still defined predominantly by birth and ancestry. The advent of such controls, and the increasing upward pressure of new families seeking to join the elite and jostling for place with those whose economic fortunes threatened to drag them down, required local gentry to produce material documentation for their alleged descents. This in turn stimulated greater attention to family muniments, and to details of genealogy, than previously. It is in this period that family bibles began their long history as household records of birth and death, supplementing the parish registers kept by royal injunction from 1538. More than family pride was at stake since often quite immediate, substantive and financial issues turned on establishing legitimate descents, priority of lines, and so on. Such matters as possession of church pews, or the right of privileged admission to schools and universities on the basis of descent from a founder took many a dispute to the College of Arms, the earl marshal's court or other judicial bodies for resolution.

What has been called with some overstatement a 'pedigree craze' in the later sixteenth century made use of antiquarian enthusiasm to project many descents back to the murky reaches of the past, to founders such as Brutus, Noah or even Adam, complete with long lines of fictitious forebears to fill in the gaps in between. Not every interested cultivator of genealogy succumbed to this temptation; against the ancestral fancies of Lord Burghley (quickly disavowed by his son Robert Cecil in the next generation), one must consider the practical views of Robert Furse, a Devon yeoman who encouraged his own children to continue the genealogical record he had begun in 1593. To Furse, thoughts of tracing his ancestry back to illustrious ancestors were entirely subordinated by more basic economic and legal necessities. His book would allow his descendants always to 'be abell to make a perfytt petygree and to understonde the ryght name of your londs and your wrytynges and what you ofte to have and what you ofte to do'. Furse's near-contemporary, the Welsh antiquary George Owen Harry (*fl.* 1590–1604) remarked that even a gentleman of the 'meaner' sort was expected to maintain the written pedigree of his family and ought also to be able to recite the names of his four great-grandfathers and their wives.[10]

As this last example suggests, awareness of the ancestral past was not dependent on writing, for all the greater interest in written pedigrees and other forms of documentation. Much genealogical knowledge continued to circulate right through the early modern period in oral and mnemonic form, transferred from generation to generation (though not as literally and verbatim as even some contemporaries thought). Women consequently, though they had much higher illiteracy rates than males even among the wealthy, were often more valuable sources of information on descent than their husbands. They had a considerably smaller role in more formal oral-genealogical institutions such as the various classes of bards or poets in the Celtic regions. Wales had a bardic tradition, then in decline and virtually extinct by the early seventeenth century; the bards' function merged to some degree with that of the heralds, as genealogies were maintained in both oral and written form. The descent of a patron was compiled into an elegy (*marwnad*) recited by the poet before kin and neighbours, and then a written version was lodged with the kin of the deceased. Sporadic public performances or *eisteddfodau* were held in 1523 and 1567; the Council in the Marches withheld permission for a third in 1594. In a socially motivated attempt to distinguish 'legitimate' bards from mere vulgar minstrels, practitioners were licensed after 1523, and, the 'ordinances' for the *eisteddfod* were given a convenient pseudo-medieval authority, pre-dated through a fictitious statute of Gruffudd ap Cynan, the early-twelfth-century king of North Wales.[11]

The Scottish and Irish experiences were similar in some respects to that of their Celtic cousins the Welsh, but complicated by the greater importance of kinship (in the Highlands identified with the clans and subordinate septs) and by the belief in a common descent, based on blood more than land, not just for the noble but for their most lowly followers. Ancestors were adopted and jettisoned to suit the needs of present circumstances; the clan Macgregor in 1512 swapped their descent from Cormac Mac Oirbertaigh, maintained since the fifteenth century, for one from Kenneth Macalpin, before finally settling on Pope Gregory the Great.[12] Preserving the links in the chain, real and suppositious, was the task of a hereditary caste of bards or *fileadha* in Ireland, and of the 'learned orders' or *aos dána* ('folk of gifts') in the Scottish Highlands.[13] In both instances family history was complicated by a much more expansive sense of blood relation than applied in England or Wales. In Ireland, as Marc Caball has demonstrated, a tradition of verse genealogy increasingly lamented a lost past, but a past increasingly conceded to be both Gaelic and Anglo-Norman. One poem, often ascribed to Tadhg Dall Ó hUiginn, urges one Richard Óg Burke not to surrender an ancient style, 'Richard, son of MacWilliam' for a modern title and confirmation of his inheritances by English authorities. It thereby envelops the ancestry of an Old English family within an older Gaelic social structure, an acculturating tendency that would grow more pronounced in Elizabeth's reign and especially in the mid-seventeenth century, as Gaelic and Old English Catholics made common cause against New English and Scots Protestants.[14]

Popular Beliefs and Traditions

As the treatment of ancestral knowledge reminds us, the various components of Tudor Britain were neither fully oral nor fully literate, and the interplay between spoken and written knowledge forms a critical context in understanding the sense of the past. Certainly, there were wide regional variations: there was a higher level of literacy in Lowland Scotland in the later sixteenth century than in the Highlands or indeed in many parts of England such as the North-west; and urban environments typically developed higher rates of full (reading and writing) literacy than did rural areas. Language differences also mattered – Welsh remained the spoken vernacular of the principality's common people throughout the period, and reformers had to adapt by translating key religious texts into that tongue.

All of this has a great deal to do with Britain's multiple senses of the past, since much knowledge of both recent and more remote ages was circulated and transmitted in spoken form, as stories, tales, songs and oral traditions. Within Scotland, for example, there is a noticeable gulf, as Jenny Wormald has noted, between history and poetry in the hands of Highland bards and of Lowland writers, a major difference being that the Highlanders made little distinction between the two. 'There was developing, in the increasingly literate and record-conscious lowlands, an awareness of the sense of the past, a distinction between past and present, which was absent from Gaelic writing.'[15] Leland, who travelled throughout Tudor England in the 1530s and 1540s derived a wide variety of traditions from what he called 'the common voice'. Indeed, our knowledge of many local traditions from the period is overwhelmingly dependent on Leland's own writings and on those of his later Tudor successors, the various county 'chorographers' who wrote surveys or descriptions of individual counties, and William Camden, whose *Britannia* (1st edition, 1586) more or less covered the whole island (unevenly) with glances across the Irish Sea. Like the chroniclers (see below) who would include local materials in their annals, the antiquaries were less fixated on telling a unified story, and despite their own humanist training, they were untroubled by the strictures of classical history-writing which required only 'great' matters to be recorded. They therefore tended, especially in the sixteenth century, to maintain a degree of confidence in, or at least an open mind to, the things they heard, and to find textual space for them in their published writings. Since the written evidentiary basis for many stories was thin, they were being careful, not credulous, and there is no basis to support an anachronistic dismissal of their willingness to record oral traditions as a mark of inferior or ill-developed historical method. In the mid-seventeenth century reliance on oral tradition would rapidly decline, both for intellectual reasons (a greater reluctance to put into print assertions not supported by documents or other physical evidence) and for social ones. The association of many traditions with 'vulgar' error and popular culture led to an attitude of suspicion on the part of later-seventeenth-century antiquaries in both Scotland and England that is not characteristic of most of their Tudor and early Stuart predecessors.

In spite of this eventual scepticism toward the undocumented, it would be a severe mistake to see oral and written historical writing as opposed, or even as entirely independent streams. Precisely because England and Lowland Scotland, and the settled portions of Ireland, were partially literate, and increasingly subject to print culture, the spoken and the written tended to cross-pollinate. Many of the 'traditional' rituals of mid-Tudor England, such as Hocktide feasts and Robin Hood plays, have relatively recent, late-medieval or early-sixteenth-century, origins. Local heroes such as Guy of Warwick, who survived for generations in oral culture, often derived from earlier written texts. The traffic between the spoken and written (or printed) word thus ran in two directions. A good illustration of how this worked is the stories of the Reformation, and in particular the persecution of Protestants under Henry VIII and especially Mary. These are captured in the colourful and comprehensive account of John Foxe's (1516–87) *Acts and Monuments* (1st English edition, 1563, followed by many subsequent revised editions), perhaps the single most influential work of historical writing throughout Britain and Ireland. A large and expensive tome, it was not nearly so widely available as is often assumed (the 1571 order in Convocation that is often cited mandated its holding in cathedral churches only, not in all parishes). Yet through its vivid woodcuts, its glosses highlighting particular stories for the marginally literate who might not read in detail, and the retelling orally of its stories, it entered and became part of non-literate culture. Although it was in many ways *sui generis* within England (and unduplicated in other kingdoms) in its combination of martyrology, ecclesiastical history and graphic polemical messaging, Foxe's above-mentioned 'Book of Martyrs' was probably the single most important book in the shaping of Anglo-Protestant identity, given particularly its virulent anti-popery.

The impact of religious change on popular belief was undeniably profound yet also highly complicated and uneven. Many popular beliefs had a religious aspect that defied external events such as the Reformation. The citizens of late Tudor Halifax, for example, claimed that their town was originally named Horton and that its modern name derived from the 'hali-fex' (holy hair) of a murdered virgin. Many believed that Halifax was also the burial place of the head of John the Baptist, a tradition acknowledged and perpetuated by town authorities in the borough's corporate seal. Such stories often had Catholic, or even magical overtones which offended more puritanical sensibilities. George Owen, the late-Elizabethan lord of the manor of Kemes, Pembrokeshire, was struck how 'all the inhabitantes, both younge and old' affirmed that the parish of Whitchurch had been free of adders for generations; a similar belief existed in the parish of St David and was ascribed to that familiar nemesis of serpents, St Patrick.[16] A succession of antiquaries beginning with Leland repeat the story of the salt wells at Droitwich, Worcestershire, which had supposedly dried up in the middle ages and been saved through the miraculous intercession of a thirteenth-century bishop, Richard de la Wiche.

The division of sacred from 'civil' history, so tidily laid out in late Renaissance *artes historicae*, was little more than a taxonomical literary convention among historians, and not even universally accepted there. Outside the boundaries of history books, and especially in the world of religious devotion, it could not prevent the intermingling of episodes from the Bible with those from classical, medieval or recent history. Preachers commonly appealed to a wide variety of episodes from the past for the purpose of example. In his notes for a homily on rebellion, Archbishop Thomas Cranmer, for instance, listed Old Testament subversives such as Dathan and Absalom side by side with the architects of more recent 'tumults in England', Jack Cade and Jack Straw.[17] Outside of biblical history, the popular ballad exemplifies the workings of the relationship between oral and printed culture and how, in the Tudor period, the past familiar to the humbler sort had not yet distinguished itself, as it would in subsequent centuries, from the national history consumed by their literate masters.

A great many popular traditions about the past in the sixteenth century had local origins, even if they could sometimes be shoe-horned into the chronology of national history and their characters identified or connected in some way with better-known figures. Locality, in fact, was a force as potent as religion or family in the creation of new historical traditions and the preservation of some older ones throughout the sixteenth century, even at a time of increasing cultural pressure from the centre. Towns and villages had explanations for particular monuments or features of the landscape, and many developed myths of origins or foundation going well beyond the authority that could be found in town charters and other muniments. During one of the first Tudor progresses, in 1486, Henry VII stopped at York where he was greeted by the legendary figure of the 'begynner' of the city, Ebrauk, accompanied by Solomon and David respectively symbolizing royal wisdom and royal power; further along, near the council chamber, stood the figures of six monarchs representing the six previous king Henries.[18]

Ruins often led to traditions of vanished ancient cities, military triumphs over ancient foes, and laments of lost greatness, in which mythical or legendary figures jostled for status with more recent, documentable kings and benefactors. At many points on his *Itinerary* through England and Wales, Leland suspected that a recent building had replaced a more ancient one on the same or a different site. It was no chronicle but the testimony of its monks which told him that 'the old Abbey of Bardeney [Lincolnshire] was not in the very same place wher the new ys, but at a graunge or dayre a myle of.' Leland found the church of Axminster in Devon to be locally renowned for the burial of a number of Danes slain under King Athelstan, probably at the battle of Brunanburgh in AD 937. Several decades later, the town of Windsor, William Harrison (1534–93) noted, was 'builded in time past by King Arthur, or before him by Arviragus, as it is thought, and repaired by Edward the third, who erected also a notable college there'. In Croydon, the inhabitants pointed out to Camden a place where 'in old time' a royal house had once stood. Sixteenth-century inhabitants of Manchester averred that because their ancestors had fought the Danes valiantly, they had been rewarded with the name Manchester or 'city of men'.[19]

Contemporary and recent political events also produced their own sites of historical interest. A long medieval tradition of 'political canonization', often associated with the graves or shrines of 'royal saints' or with victims of authority such as Thomas à Becket or the early-fifteenth-century Archbishop Scrope, had successors in the sixteenth century. The death of Cardinal Wolsey in 1530 near the scene of Richard III's demise two generations earlier almost immediately created a popular tag for his burial place in Leicester Abbey. London would spawn a number of popular beliefs that, because of the city's status as capital and political centre, crystallized around genuinely historical figures rather earlier than was the case in the provinces. These beliefs were also less likely to survive in purely oral form, undisturbed by the influence of written history, because of the city's higher literacy rates and longstanding practice of keeping and collecting records. In London, more than in any other British community, a wide assortment of tales had sprung up concerning men and sometimes women (Edward IV's unfortunate mistress Jane Shore, for instance) who figured in the mythology both of the city itself and also in its sub-communities, such as the guilds and livery companies. Many of these had monuments either officially or traditionally associated with their names. Sir William Walworth, the fourteenth-century mayor who slew the peasant rebel leader Wat Tyler in 1381, turns up again and again in mayoral processions up to the end of the eighteenth century, especially those involving the Fishmongers.[20]

Memories of giants and other monstrous beings in the remote past endured in tradition and folklore from the early modern to the modern era, though it is difficult to date many of the survivals, and folkloric studies generally provide little chronological help. Among the educated classes belief in the existence of real, historical giants began to fade from about 1580. William Harrison was notably suspicious in his contribution to Raphael Holinshed's *Chronicles*, allowing for the likelihood of men with superior stature but taking the legends of a race of giants in early Britain as 'not altogether credible'. As early as the 1590s, Spenser's characters Ireneus and Eudoxus, discussing old Irish burial mounds and stone monuments, dismiss the idea that these were made by giants and ascribe them to pre-Christian burial customs. Spenser's attitude was probably driven as much by his pronounced distaste for certain aspects of Gaelic culture as by historical insight. In the following century, however, antiquaries and virtuosi would come to share in what amounted to an alternative explanation for fossils, artifacts and burial sites, which the great majority of the population still attributed to giants. Foreign travellers like Thomas Platter were regaled with stories of British giants, though it is difficult to tell from their remarks whether these were entirely popular inventions or simply the 'Samotheans' and other literary pre-British beings, such as Gogmagog. This latter figure had evolved in the middle ages from the conflation of ancient giant legends with the biblical character prince Gog of Magog (Ezek. 38–9) and the two nations Gog and Magog which were to lead the forces of Satan at Armageddon (Rev. 20:8). Historical giants figured prominently in sixteenth-century civic processionals and plays, for example the midsummer pageants at Coventry and Chester. Two medieval figures at the Guildhall in London, known as 'Hercules and Samson' in the early sixteenth century, had been renamed Gogmagog and Corineus by Elizabeth's reign.[21]

Historical Writing

It may seem odd to place formal historical writing near the very end of such a survey, but in fact it is to put the cart back firmly behind the horse, in the sense that the various types of literary output covering historical matters (both history proper and antiquarian works of different sorts) must be read against the background of the belief-sets that the previous sections of this essay have discussed. Actual examples of history-writing, though they multiplied during the period, are still relatively easy to number in comparison with the much vaster output in print and manuscript that followed in the seventeenth and eighteenth centuries. In any case, the various genres of historical writing should be regarded as only one product, albeit an important one, of the age's broader historical culture.

In many ways, there is a high degree of continuity between late medieval and Tudor historical writing. In particular, the dominance of the standard form for the recording of stories about the past, the annalistically arranged chronicle, continued well into the century, initially thriving on the arrival of the printing press (in England in 1475, and in Scotland in 1507–8). The major change, which was one of language and style more than substance, was the advent of continental humanist traditions of writing about the past. These appeared early in both Scotland and England, but took hold much more decisively in the former, where humanist historiography began with Hector Boece, who adopted the Latinized name Hector Boethius. Boece's *Scotorum historiae a prima gentis origine* (Paris, 1527) first took a variety of myths of Scottish origin and turned them into a Latin history, basing a good deal of what he wrote upon the authority of a mysterious history by 'Veremundus' that may or may not have actually existed. Boece built on a much longer tradition of medieval Latin chronicle-writing in a patriotic tradition that descends from earlier authors such as Fordun (and which was quite distinct from the chivalric, vernacular Scots tradition of works like John Barbour's *The Bruce* and its later companion epic, *The Wallace*, both of which derived in varying degrees from oral tradition). In one sense, Boece simply modernized Fordun's account, put flesh on its skeletal accounts of ancient kings, and gave it a humanist shape. The literary mould for this was provided by Livy's history of Rome *ab urbe condita*, the ur-text of continental Renaissance historiography, and a classical model that wielded considerably greater influence on Scottish historical writing than it ever enjoyed in contemporary England. Boece's work was in turn more widely disseminated in a vernacular Scots translation by John Bellenden (*fl.* 1533–87), who also published an edition of the Scots chronicles and, at James V's encouragement, would translate Livy.[22]

The essence of Boece's narrative would be taken up, and given both a Protestant and a natural-law spin, by the century's greatest Scottish man of letters, George Buchanan, who was also among the most widely known of Latin poets from either kingdom to make a name for himself in Europe. Though he was probably a native Gaelic speaker, Buchanan was a thorough Renaissance humanist; he had spent most of his career in France prior to the 1560s, and like most sixteenth-century Scottish historians he preferred to publish his works abroad, for a continental audience. Significantly departing from that pattern, Buchanan's Latin-language *Rerum Scoticarum Historia* first saw print at Edinburgh in 1582 shortly after his death (having been composed by stages many years earlier). Like Boece, Buchanan pushed the distinctiveness of Scottish history and its independence from England. This was certainly the majority opinion in Scottish historical writing of the sixteenth century, though it is worth noting that Boece's contemporary, John Mair or Major (1469–1550) presented an alternative view in his *Britanniae Majoris Historia* (published in Paris in 1521). This cast doubt on old-origin myths (including both Brutus and Gathelos), reduced the number of ancient kings, and minimized the Gaelic connection to the Irish. Mair also played down historical Anglo-Scottish differences – not a popular position in the early years after Flodden.

Mair's one-time pupil Buchanan returned to the Boece position, minus Brutus and Gathelos. An erudite classicist and admirer of the Roman republic, Buchanan also championed the ancient form of elective and limited monarchy in his major work of political theory, the *De jure regni apud scotos* (published 1579, but written earlier to justify Mary Stewart's deposition, one of many reasons that his own protégé, James VI, had for disliking his former tutor). What Buchanan did for antiquity was then applied to the more recent past and given a much more obviously presbyterian and apocalyptic spin in the writing of another of Mair's erstwhile students, the great clerical reformer John Knox (1505–72), in particular the vernacular *History of the Reformation of the Church of Scotland*. Knox's *History*, which was published fragmentarily in 1587, began with Lollard persecution – eschewing the establishment of a detailed and lengthy Protestant past in the manner of Foxe – and established a shorter pedigree for a Calvinist kirk and its rebellion against foreign ecclesiastical authority and local episcopal tyranny. It would be countered in the *History of Scotland* (published in Latin at Rome in 1578) by a Catholic, John Leslie (1527–96), bishop of Ross; although written from a very different perspective, Leslie's work nonetheless shared with Buchanan and Boece the common humanist aspiration to use the past as a mirror on the present.[23]

In England and Wales the impact of humanism on historiography occurred at a very different pace. The monastic chronicle tradition was already largely extinguished by the time the last abbey closed. However, a vigorous tradition of urban chronicling, dating from the fifteenth century, had evolved into the 'Great Chronicle' genre by the 1550s. The direct influence of humanism on history-writing was for a long time quite superficial and even ephemeral. The two earliest examples of humanist historical writing in England, Polydore Vergil's *Anglica Historia* and Thomas More's *History of Richard III* initially had rather limited influence. More's work was little known outside courtly and scholarly circles, and in any case was an unfinished biographical study which did not provide much of a model for larger projects, though it did supply an example of a narrative of a single reign, and a treatment of an individual monarch as a psychologically coherent, if hyperbolically evil, subject. Vergil's much longer history was written in Latin, and not translated into English except in pieces. Moreover it was the work of a papal agent whose reputation suffered as a result of the break with Rome, and also because he had dared to question (admittedly on philologically rather shaky grounds) the foundation of Britain by Brutus the Trojan and the historicity of King Arthur.

The dominant historical form in England until the century's close thus remained the chronicle, which assisted by the medium of print was much more widely read from the 1530s to the 1580s. Edward Hall (d. 1548) departed from earlier annalistic models to group his history of the fifteenth century around kings, having clearly profited from reading Vergil. But subsequent authors such as Richard Grafton (*fl.* 1545–72), Raphael Holinshed (d. probably 1580) and John Stow (1525–1605), among others stuck to the old reliable year-by-year scheme, issuing vernacular chronicles in various formats and lengths. These were not worthless throwbacks to medieval times, swimming against an inexorable tide of sound modern scholarship. Stow, better known for his antiquarian *Survey of London*, brought a Londoner's perspective to national history in his various *Summaries, Chronicles* and *Annales*. Grafton was an influential printer of earlier chronicles as well as the author of others in his own right. And the multi-authored chronicle published under the name of Holinshed, its two editions the work of successive editorial teams, is now known to have included local perspectives and material increasingly deemed inappropriate by the canons of 'proper' historiography, but more interesting from the perspective of modern cultural and social history. The chroniclers also succeeded in another important way, as a source of matter for the Elizabethan history play. Holinshed's *Chronicles* in particular would provide the raw ingredients of much of Shakespeare's output (including the English histories and later works such as his sole venture into Scottish history, *Macbeth*).

However inaccurately Shakespeare and other dramatists may have rendered the past, the impact on national historical sensibilities of public re-enactments of prominent scenes from British history was considerable, and it would not have occurred without the earlier flourishing of the chronicles.

It took another half century, a further influx of European models (and especially a vogue for the later Roman historian Tacitus, with his combination of modish stylistic terseness and quasi-Machiavellian political shrewdness), and the advent of pronounced succession anxieties, especially in the 1590s, to establish a more permanent beach-head for humanist-style historical writing which, like the history play, was routinely drawn from the very chronicles that its authors, including Francis Bacon, now affected to despise as a model. The newer prose histories would be organized, like Polydore Vergil's earlier work, around monarchical reigns and rest on a close link between the life of the ruling subject and the nation. They collectively formed a genre of didactic 'politic history' that continued until the eve of the British civil wars. Much of this output, of course, continued to be written from a Protestant and anti-papal perspective, though the existence of an under-studied counter-current of Catholic historiography needs again to be noted, in particular the contribution of writers such as Nicholas Sanders (*c.* 1530–81), Robert Persons (1546–1610) and Richard Broughton (d. 1635).

Irish historiography must be divided into several different categories. Much of it was in fact Anglo-Irish, dating from the *Topographia hibernica* by the late-twelfth-century chronicler and travel-writer Gerald of Wales (Giraldus Cambrensis, a member of the Old English Fitzgerald family), and leading up to the reflections of English observers such as Edmund Spenser and Sir John Davies (1569–1626), who were largely concerned with identifying the reasons why the Irish had never been thoroughly subdued, much less integrated with the English crown. The London-born Edmund Campion contributed a *History of Ireland* (1571) that similarly focused on the need to bring the unruly Irish to civility – shortly before he himself fled to Douai, recanted Protestantism and became a Jesuit. It was the subsequent publication of Campion's work, and its adaptation by the Anglo-Irish and Oxford-educated author Richard Stanyhurst (1547–1618) for Holinshed's *Chronicles* that, Alan Ford comments, first injected a confessional aspect to historical writing about Ireland. Stanyhurst himself was not especially interested in pushing a Protestant agenda, and indeed soon embraced Catholicism, ordination and exile. But the revised version of his work in the second (1587) edition of Holinshed included additions by John Hooker alias Vowell (*c.* 1526–1601), an Exeter antiquary with more obviously anti-Catholic and even apocalyptic views. Stanyhurst's subsequent *De rebus in Hibernia gestis* (Antwerp 1584) had already evinced the notion of an Irish Catholic identity. A full Protestant version of Irish history would soon come from a Welsh minister and émigré to Ireland, Meredith Hanmer (1543–1604). A somewhat disreputable figure who had left England under a cloud, Hanmer made an effort to study Irish history and language; he produced both an English edition of *The Ancient Ecclesiastical Histories . . . written by Eusebius, Socrates and Evagreus* and a manuscript chronicle of Irish history first published in 1633, along with Campion's and other works, by the Dubliner Sir James Ware (1594–1666).[24]

There was also, however, an indigenous tradition of Irish annalistic and genealogical writing, in Gaelic, of which perhaps the outstanding example is the *Annals of*

Loch Cé which covers the period from 1014 to 1599. Whereas the humanist narrative model began to come into vogue in late Tudor English-language writing about the Irish past, Gaelic historical writing remained firmly in the older annalistic tradition, including the later portions of the annals of Loch Cé and the *Annála Connacht* (the annals of Connacht, AD 1224–1544). The first non-annalistic history of Ireland in Gaelic would not appear till Geoffrey Keating's manuscript *Foras Feasa ar Éirinn* (which translates into 'A basis for knowledge about Ireland), written about 1634. Keating's principal rivals were his friend, the secular priest John Lynch (1599–1673), and the group of historians collectively known as the 'Four Masters', actually the O'Clery family, who were hereditary historians to the O'Donnells, princes of Tyrconnel, county Donegal. Their *Annala Rioghachta Éireann* (Annals of the kingdom of Ireland) begins as annals but becomes fuller in its sixteenth-century sections, turning into a connected narrative history by the time it reaches Elizabeth's reign.[25] It is worth observing, in comparing Gaelic regions, that there are no comparable Scottish Highland annals (the earlier epics like *The Bruce* and *The Wallace* belong to the vernacular Scots, not Gaelic tradition, while the chronicles of Fordun and others, composed in medieval Latin, are also Lowland and royalist). Conversely, Gaelic Ireland failed to develop written 'genealogical histories' of the sort that emerged (principally in English) in the Scottish *Gàidhealtachd* after the mid-seventeenth century, in the wake of the decline of the Gaelic learned orders.[26]

Perhaps the most significant development in writing about the past, at least from a modern perspective, is the quite rapid development of the intellectual activities collectively known as antiquarianism. The importance of antiquaries from Leland and Bale in the first half of the sixteenth century to Camden and his much larger circle at the century's end must be acknowledged, though not for the reasons usually adduced (for instance, that they were the first identifiable practitioners of proto-modern historical methods). Their true significance really rests on their establishment of interpersonal networks for the exchange of information about the past, the short-lived Elizabethan 'Society of Antiquaries' being the best known and most formal but by no means the only such venue. Many of them contributed works of fundamental importance to the study of different aspects of the past, for instance the chorographical studies of Sampson Erdeswicke (d. 1603), John Norden (1548–*c*. 1625), William Lambarde (1536–1601), Stow and Camden, the rather different, more ethnographic essay on Cornwall by Richard Carew (1555–1620), and the linguistic enquiries of the exiled Catholic Richard Verstegan, alias Rowlands (*fl.* 1565–1620). But the real impact of the works lay, again, less in the example of pioneering documentary scholarship that they set or in the accuracy of their conclusions than in the road map they established for subsequent antiquaries and indeed for hundreds of interested local gentry and clergy over the next century. The continuity between late-medieval antiquaries such as William Worcestre and early-seventeenth-century scholars such as Sir Robert Cotton (1571–1631) in terms of attitudes to documents is quite striking. However, the social and intellectual contexts of such activities from one end of the Tudor century to the other were very different, in particular the degree to which knowledge of the past had become a subject of discussion, and artifacts from Romano-British, Anglo-Saxon and more recent times (as well as prehistoric artifacts and naturally occurring fossils that were often misinterpreted owing to the rigidity of a scripture-based chronological scheme) began to circulate and coalesce in closets and libraries, the precursors of later institutions such as the British Museum.

In contrast to England, Scottish and Irish antiquarian activities were much less well developed in the sixteenth century. In the case of Ireland, Edmund Spenser's dismissal of Brehon law as 'a certaine rule of right, unwritten, but delivered by tradition from one to an other . . . in many things repugning quite from gods law and mans' is well known (though recent scholarship has pointed out that he was much less hostile to other aspects of ancient Irish culture than has often been supposed).[27] Much of the erudite tradition in Ireland was the work of Anglo-Irish authors. Hanmer's interest in Irish antiquities has been mentioned; later writers included Sir James Ware, who was born late in Elizabeth's reign but did most of his work in the seventeenth century, and James Ussher (1581–1656), the learned future archbishop of Armagh, who is most famous for his tract on the age of the world and its precise dating of the Creation to a particular date in 4004 BC. Ussher was was also an active participant in the historical debate over the Irish church, with his *A Discourse of the Religion Anciently Professed by the Irish and British* (first published in 1622 under a different title and reprinted in 1631).

There was likewise relatively little activity in sixteenth-century Scotland that could be called 'antiquarian', excepting the legal interests of a few authors. These included Sir John Skene (*c.* 1543–1617) of Curriehill, author of *The Lawes and Actes of Parliament maid be King James the First and his successors kings of Scotland* (1597); and Sir Thomas Craig (1538–1608), whose *Jus feudale* (1603) would prove an important work in identifying feudal law as a common source of both English and Scots law, a thesis that would be re-articulated with a unionist spin in a 1605 manuscript entitled *De unione regnorum Britanniae tractatus.* The late discreditation of Boece's mythical ancient rulers had to await the career of an early-eighteenth-century Scottish Catholic priest, Thomas Innes, long after their Anglo-Welsh, Trojan and Samothean counterparts had been sent packing. On the archaeological and naturalist side of antiquarian study, Innes's older contemporary Sir Robert Sibbald (1641–1722) stands out among Britain's late-seventeenth-century scholarly lights, along with a Welshman, Edward Lhuyd – but unlike Lhuyd, Sibbald had not much of a home-grown foundation on which to build. One notes the absence even in the literate Lowlands of anything like the many English and Welsh examples of Tudor antiquarian chorography – with some important exceptions, including the early work of Donald Monro (*fl.* 1550, the 'high dean of the Isles'), in his *Description of the Western Isles* (1550), and eventually of the cartographers Timothy Pont (*c.* 1562–*c.* 1614) and his slightly later successor, Robert Gordon of Straloch (1580–1661). Certain works of history also contain geographical sections which veer into chorography: Buchanan's, borrowing from Monro, begins in this way, and one also finds a 'Descriptione of the Regions' in Bishop Leslie's 1578 *History of Scotland.*[28] More systematic study of particular objects or problems (such as the various Elizabethan discourses on the origins of things like sterling coinage and the shires) are hard to find, much less an organized group such as Camden's Society of Antiquaries.

The obvious explanation for this difference, that Scotland was less exposed to continental scholarly influences, is plainly wrong on two counts: first because Scotland had in general very well-developed international literary and scholarly ties, especially to France, and secondly because we have already seen that humanist influence on narrative historiography in Scotland was well in advance of that in England. Various other circumstances seem more likely, such as the absence of an organized College of Arms (and heraldic visitations) on the English model. Another may be the somewhat later arrival of the Reformation. James IV and V both supported scholarship, and the statutes of Scotland first appeared in print late in the latter's reign. However, there was little to compare with the systematic and intensive crown-sponsored combing through the records that underlay Henry VIII's divorce case and that emerges most clearly in the Act in Restraint of Appeals (1533), with its famous reference to 'divers and sundry histories and chronicles', though James V certainly shared with his Tudor uncle an enthusiasm for imperial kingship.[29] Even Buchanan, though he used history as a cudgel, relied much more on theoretical arguments from natural law.

The differing archaeological environment may also have had an effect. The comparative dearth of former Roman roads and settlements (the focus of much English antiquarianism since it was most easily explicable with reference to classical texts, unlike earlier prehistoric and later medieval remains) north of Hadrian's wall undoubtedly had a negative impact on the development of peripatetic, archaeological antiquarianism since it limited a whole category of visual stimuli from the past, and at that the one most easily explicable by classically trained scholars. Camden covered Scotland and Ireland as well as England, but the sections of *Britannia* dealing with those areas are noticeably thinner, and did not inspire imitation, Timothy Pont aside.

Outside of the paucity of classical visual stimuli, the best explanation for the weakness of Scottish antiquarianism may be that the intellectual issues in sixteenth-century Scotland were different from those in England. They therefore required a different sort of reference to the past, not built upon detailed and usually inconclusive arguments about relative antiquity of the sort that occur with amusing frequency in England. One such strategy (that adopted by Buchanan and, in mirror image, by James VI) rested on establishing a strong link between contemporary political theory and ancient kingship. An overlapping alternative to this derived from apocalyptic visions of the past and future. Versions of this can be found in Knox, in the chronologer Robert Pont (1524–1606, father of the cartographer Timothy), and in the mathematician and inventor of logarithms, John Napier of Merchiston (1550–1617).[30] And where the English inherited a fifteenth-century anxiety about strict dynastic succession in the first third of the century (forebodingly revived at its end), the Scots did not share such worries, given their much more practical if violent habit of displacing or assassinating unpopular monarchs and their regents. Finally, the kind of ethnographic interest in past customs and practices that emerges from late-Tudor antiquarianism presupposes a degree of sympathetic understanding on the part of even English Protestant observers (to say nothing of the significant number of Catholics engaged in such activities), an attitude to the superstitious past that was in short supply in the Scotland of Knox and Napier. Scottish Presbyterians were much less committed than English Protestants to the exercise of identifying havens of pure religion in the middle ages. Indeed, they were largely inclined to view the whole era prior to 1560, in religious terms, as an unsalvageable prehistory of paganism followed by superstition.[31]

This led to a certain detachment from the medieval past that is quite different from the English experience. It perhaps explains why Knox began his history no earlier than the Lollards, and why, too, there is no complete Scottish martyrology in a Foxean vein – though the preacher John Davidson of Prestonpans (*c.* 1550–1604) at one point intended such a work. Similarly, for both Napier and Robert Pont the most usable bits of the past were quite literally its dates, which chronologically aligned, prophetically analysed, and accurately calculated could point ahead to the millennium. Napier's brief reference to an 'utterlie demolished' Roman monument at Musselburgh evoked no tear at its destruction, nor curiosity as to its origin, only the thought that it pointed to an ignorant, pagan past; the inscriptions on Roman coins were to him but 'titles of the pride and vaine-glorie of Rome'.[32]

This is a rather speculative conclusion, in part because detailed comparative work on the historiographies of the three kingdoms and Wales is relatively rare. It does, however, provide us with a further reminder that senses of the past are multiple, variable by region as well as language, and not inevitably tied to the proto-modern forms of historical writing, such as antiquarian chorography and politic history, to which we all too often limit them.[33] A single nation may indeed have emerged in later centuries, but the strength of that union lay to a considerable degree in the complexity, layering and intersection of its constituent peoples' understanding of their pasts.

NOTES

1. Thomas, *The Perception of the Past in Early Modern England*. The growing literature on memory is considerable, and not all of it is directly relevant to the subject of the present essay; but see especially Wood, 'Custom and the social organisation of writing', 257–69; Fox, *Oral and Literate Culture*, and 'Remembering the past in early modern England', 233–56. Some examples in the present essay have been used in my book *The Social Circulation of the Past*.
2. Kendrick, *British Antiquity* remains the fullest account of the various myths and their after-lives; see also Ferguson *Utter Antiquity*, Kidd, *British Identities before Nationalism*.
3. Kelton, *A Comendacion of Welshmen* and *A Chronycle with a Genealogie*, cited in Roberts, 'Tudor Wales, national identity and the British inheritance', p. 15.
4. Anderson, 'The antiquities of fairyland and Ireland', 199–214; Maley, 'The British problem in three tracts', p. 164.
5. Early Stuart English historians such as John Clapham and Edward Ayscu, writing after the accession of a Scottish king to the 'British' throne, and in the early enthusiasm for possible union, pinned their arguments more on the longer history of relations between the two kingdoms than on the veracity of the old Galfridian legends: see Woolf, *The Idea of History in Early Stuart England*, pp. 55–64.
6. Mason, 'Scotching the Brut', pp. 60–84; Boardman, 'Late medieval Scotland and the Matter of Britain', pp. 47–72.
7. Mason, *Kingship and the Commonweal*.
8. Kidd, *British Identities before Nationalism*, pp. 146–7.
9. Hadfield, 'Briton and Scythian', pp. 390–408.
10. Dawson, 'The Gaidhealtachd and the emergence of the Scottish Highlands', pp. 268; Allan, '"What's in a name?"' pp. 147–67; Carpenter, 'Furse of Moreshead', 168–84; Woolf, *Social Circulation of the Past*, chapters 3 and 4.

11. O Riordan, *The Gaelic Mind*; Suggett and White, 'Language, literacy and aspects of identity', pp. 52–83; Suggett, 'Vagabonds and minstrels', pp. 153–9.

12. Smout, *A History of the Scottish People*, p. 41.

13. MacGregor, 'The genealogical histories of Gaelic Scotland', 197.

14. Caball, 'Faith, culture and sovereignty', pp. 119, 127.

15. Wormald, *Court, Kirk and Community*, p. 62.

16. Camden, *Britain*, p. 692; Smith, *Place-Names of the West Riding of Yorkshire*, p. 104; Owen, *The Description of Penbrokeshire*, I, p. 250 and note.

17. Adams, ed., *Dramatic Records of Sir Henry Herbert*, p. 47; Richard Carew recorded the 'Guary miracle', a Cornish interlude, in his *Survey of Cornwall*, fos. 71r–72r; Lancashire, *Dramatic Texts and Records of Britain*, pp. 8, 76, 280; Cox, ed., *Miscellaneous Writings and Letters of Thomas Cranmer*, ii, 188–9.

18. *Records of Early English Drama: York*, I, 139–42, 146–50.

19. Harrison, *Description of England*, p. 226; *Leland's Itinerary*, I, 119, 121, 225, 243, V, 36; Camden, *Britain*, pp. 746–7.

20. J. W. McKenna, 'Popular canonization as political propaganda, and 'Piety and propaganda', pp. 72–88; *Calendar of Letters, Despatches, and State Papers*, p. 833 (for Wolsey).

21. Harrison, 'The Description of Britaine', pp. 8–12; Spenser, *View of the State of Ireland*, pp. 117–18; Platter, *Travels in England*, p. 183. 'Gogmagog' was virtually a byword for giants: the Gogmagog hills near Cambridge were the scenes of recreations and games which university authorities repeatedly tried to suppress. Sixteenth-century Newcastle had an effigy of a giant named Hogmagog, used in its pageants, to the upkeep of which money was regularly contributed by the town officials: *Records of Early English Drama: Cambridge*, pp. 270–2, 276–7; *Records of Early English Drama: Newcastle upon Tyne*, pp. 26–7, 33, 36 and *passim*; Stow, *A Survey of London*, p. 243.

22. For Livy's influence in Scotland see Ferguson, *Identity of the Scottish Nation*, pp. 57–9; Mason, 'Civil society and the Celts', p. 99. At the end of the century, Tacitus became a more popular Roman historian on both sides of the border; the difference was that Polydore Vergil aside, there was not much of a Latin Livian tradition to displace in England, where the vernacular chronicle in annalistic form predominated through most of the sixteenth century.

23. The authoritative treatment of sixteenth-century Scottish historical thought is now Mason, *Kingship and Commonweal*; see especially chapter 2 for a rehabilitation of Mair's reputation; ibid, pp. 166–86 for Knox. Mair is a not especially attractive figure, prone to late-medieval anti-Semitic outbursts, and subscribing to the view that American Indians were natural slaves: McGinnis and Williamson, 'Britain, race, and the Iberian global empire', pp. 70–93.

24. Ware's edition has been republished as *Ancient Irish Histories; Dictionary of National Biography*: sub Hanmer, Meredith; Ford, 'James Ussher and the creation of an Irish Protestant identity'. There was considerable division on issues such as the early Irish church of St Patrick, with Hanmer regarding it as legitimately scriptural and proto-Protestant; others, such as Spenser, saw St Patrick as the Gaelic equivalent of Augustine of Canterbury, that is, as a source *ab origine* of error and of Irish superstition.

25. *Annals of Loch Cé; Annàla Connacht*; Keating, *History of Ireland; Annals of Ireland*. This edition of the annals of the Four Masters covers the period from 1171 to 1616, but the original goes back into the earliest period of Irish history (beginning with the arrival there of a granddaughter of Noah). The principal author, Brother Michael (né Tadght) O'Clery (1575–1643), was also the author of a revised edition of the 'Leabhar Gabhala', or 'Book of Invasions', an account of the several settlements of Ireland. Because he wrote at Donegal Monastery, the *Annals* are sometimes known as the *Annals of Donegal*; its other authors were Cucogry or Peregrine O'Clery, Conary O'Clery and Peregrine O'Duigenan, assisted by two other hereditary historians to the kings of Connacht.

26. MacGregor, 'The genealogical histories of Gaelic Scotland', 197.
27. Highley, *Shakespeare, Spenser, and the Crisis in Ireland*, pp. 20–3.
28. Withers, 'Pont in context', pp. 139–54, and *Geography, Science and National Identity*, pp. 38–56. Withers points out that the geographical introduction to Buchanan's history has features in common with chorography. I owe this reference to Lesley Cormack.
29. Mason, *Kingship and the Commonweal*, p. 128.
30. Firth, *The Apocalyptic Tradition in Reformation Britain*, 111–49; Williamson, *Scottish National Consciousness in the Reign of James VI*, passim.
31. The pro-Unionist Andrew Melville, heir as much to Buchanan's humanism as Knox's Calvinism, penned a poem in praise of 'true history' and began an epic version of the Gathelos myth intended to promote not Scottish independence but pan-British solidarity. However, Melville's historical interests also lay not in locating a legitimate indigenous descent for Scottish reform but rather in finding ancient roots for the climactic union of Scotland and England into a Britain capable of serving as a Protestant counterweight to Spanish global ambitions in the last days of the world. Melville, 'Historiae vera laus' and 'Gathelus, Sive de Gentis origine fragmentum', in *George Buchanan: The Political Poetry*, introduction, pp. 31–36 and appendix C, pp. 282–97.
32. Napier, *A Plaine Discovery of the Whole Revelation*, p. 210. I owe this reference, and helpful comments on the chapter more generally, to Arthur Williamson.
33. I am indebted to Roger A. Mason, Colin Kidd and Elizabeth Ewan for confirming my impressions in this regard.

BIBLIOGRAPHY

Adams, J. Q., ed., *Dramatic Records of Sir Henry Herbert, Master of Revels 1623–1673* (2nd edition, New York, 1964).

Allan, David, *Virtue, Learning and the Scottish Enlightenment: Ideas of Scholarship in Early Modern History* (Edinburgh, 1993).

Allan, David, '"What's in a name?": pedigree and propaganda in seventeenth-century Scotland', in E. J. Cowan and R. J. Finlay, eds, *Scottish History: The Power of the Past* (Edinburgh, 2002), pp. 147–67.

Anderson, Judith H., 'The antiquities of fairyland and Ireland', *Journal of English and Germanic Philology*, 86, 2 (1987), 199–214.

Annála Connacht: The Annals of Connacht (AD 1224–1544), ed. A. M. Freeman (Dublin, 1944).

The Annals of Ireland, translated from the original Irish of the Four Masters, trans. O. Connellan (Dublin, 1846).

The Annals of Loch Cé: A Chronicle of Irish Affairs from AD 1014 to AD 1590, ed. and trans. W. Hennessy (2 vols, London, 1871).

Boardman, Steve, 'Late medieval Scotland and the Matter of Britain', in E. J. Cowan and R. J. Finlay, eds, *Scottish History: The Power of the Past* (Edinburgh, 2002), pp. 47–72.

Bradshaw, Brendan and Roberts, Peter, eds, *British Consciousness and Identity: The Making of Britain, 1533–1707* (Cambridge, 1998).

Caball, Marc, 'Faith, culture and sovereignty: Irish nationality and its development, 1558–1625', in B. Bradshaw and P. Roberts, *British Consciousness and Identity: The Making of Britain, 1533-1707* (Cambridge, 1998), pp. 112–39.

Calendar of Letters, Despatches, and State Papers, Relating to the Negotiations between England and Spain, IV, pt. I (1529–30).

Camden, William, *Britain*, trans. P. Holland (London, 1610), p. 692.

Carew, Richard, *Survey of Cornwall* (London, 1602).

Carpenter, H. J. 'Furse of Moreshead: a family record of the sixteenth century', *Reports and Transactions of the Devonshire Association for the Advancement of Science, Literature and Art*, 26 (1894), 168–84.

Cox, J. E., ed., *Miscellaneous Writings and Letters of Thomas Cranmer*, vol. II of *Works of Thomas Cranmer* (2 vols, Cambridge, 1844–6).

Dawson, Jane, 'The Gaidhealtachd and the emergence of the Scottish Highlands', in B. Bradshaw and P. Roberts, eds, *British Consciousness and Identity: The Making of Britain, 1533–1707* (Cambridge, 1998), pp. 259–300.

Ferguson, Arthur B., *Clio Unbound: Perception of the Social and Cultural Past in Renaissance England* (Durham, NC, 1979).

Ferguson, Arthur B., *Utter Antiquity: Perceptions of Prehistory in Renaissance England* (Durham, NC, 1993).

Ferguson, William, *The Identity of the Scottish Nation: An Historic Quest* (Edinburgh, 1998).

Firth, K. R., *The Apocalyptic Tradition in Reformation Britain* (Oxford, 1979).

Ford, Alan, 'James Ussher and the creation of an Irish Protestant identity', in B. Bradshaw and P. Roberts, *British Consciousness and National Identity: The Making of Britain, 1533–1707* (Cambridge, 1998), pp. 185–212.

Fox, Adam, *Oral and Literate Culture in England 1500–1700* (Oxford, 2000).

Fox, Adam, 'Remembering the past in early modern England', *Transactions of the Royal Historical Society*, 6th series, 9 (1999), 233–56.

Hadfield, Andrew. 'Briton and Scythian: Tudor representations of Irish origins', *Irish Historical Studies*, 28 (1993), 390–408.

Harrison, William, 'The Description of Britaine', in Raphael Holinshed, *The First and Second Volumes of Chronicles* (London, 1587).

Harrison, William, *The Description of England*, ed. G. Edelen (Ithaca, NY, 1968).

Highley, Christopher, *Shakespeare, Spenser, and the Crisis in Ireland* (Cambridge, 1997).

Keating, Geoffrey, *The History of Ireland*, ed. and trans. D. Comyn [and P. Dineen] (4 vols, Dublin, 1902–1914).

Kelton, Arthur, *A Chronycle with a Genealogie declarying that the Brittons and Welshemen are lineallye dyscended from Brute. Newly and very wittely compyled in Meter* (London, 1547).

Kelton, Arthur, *A Comendacion of Welshmen* (London, 1546).

Kendrick, Thomas D., *British Antiquity* (London, 1950).

Kidd, Colin, *British Identities before Nationalism: Ethnicity and Nationhood in the Atlantic World, 1600–1800* (Cambridge and New York, 1999).

Kidd, Colin. *Subverting Scotland's Past: Scottish Whig Historians and the Creation of an Anglo-British Identity, 1689–c. 1830* (Cambridge and New York, 1993).

Lancashire, Ian, *Dramatic Texts and Records of Britain: A Chronological Topography to 1558* (Cambridge, 1984).

Levine, Joseph M., *Humanism and History* (Ithaca, NY, 1987).

Levy, F. J. *Tudor Historical Thought* (San Marino, CA, 1967).

McGinnis, Paul and Williamson, Arthur, 'Britain, race, and the Iberian global empire,' in A. I. Macinnes and J. Ohlmeyer (eds), *The Stuart Kingdoms in the Seventeenth Century* (Dublin, 2002).

MacGregor, Martin, 'The genealogical histories of Gaelic Scotland', in Adam Fox and Daniel Woolf, eds, *The Spoken Word: Oral Culture in Britain 1500–1850* (Manchester, 2002).

McKenna, J. W. 'Piety and propaganda: the cult of King Henry VI', in B. Rowland (ed.), *Chaucer and Middle English Studies in Honour of Rossell Hope Robbins* (Kent, OH, 1974), 72–88.

McKenna, J. W., 'Popular canonization as political propaganda: the cult of Archbishop Scrope', *Speculum*, 45 (1970), 605–23.

McKisack, May, *Medieval History in the Tudor Age* (Oxford, 1971).

Maley, Willy, 'The British problem in three tracts on Ireland by Spenser, Bacon and Milton', in B. Bradshaw and P. Roberts, eds, *British Consciousness and Identity: The Making of Britain 1533–1707* (Cambridge, 1998), pp. 159–84.

Mason, Roger A., 'Civil society and the Celts: Hector Boece, George Buchanan and the ancient British Past', in E. J. Cowan and R. J. Finlay, eds, *Scottish History: The Power of the Past* (Edinburgh, 2002), 95–119.

Mason, Roger A., *Kingship and Commonweal: Political Thought in Renaissance and Reformation Scotland* (East Linton, 1998).

Mason, Roger A., 'Scotching the Brut: politics, history and national myth in sixteenth-century Britain', in R. A. Mason, ed., *Scotland and England 1286–1815* (Edinburgh, 1987), pp. 60–84.

Melville, Andrew, 'Historiae vera laus' and 'Gathelus, Sive de Gentis origine fragmentum', in *George Buchanan: the Political Poetry*, ed. and trans. Paul J. McGinnis and Arthur H. Williamson (Edinburgh, 1995).

Napier, John, *A Plaine Discovery of the Whole Revelation of Saint John* (Edinburgh, 1593).

O Riordan, Michelle, *The Gaelic Mind and the Collapse of the Gaelic World* (Cork, 1990).

Owen of Kemes, George, *The Description of Penbrokeshire*, ed. H. Owen, 4 vols, Cymmrodorion Record Series (1892–1936).

Platter, Thomas, *Thomas Platter's Travels in England, 1599*, ed. and trans. C. Williams (London, 1937).

Pocock, J. G. A. *The Ancient Constitution and the Feudal Law* (Cambridge, 1957; revised edition, 1987).

Records of Early English Drama: Cambridge, ed. A. H. Nelson (2 vols, Toronto, 1989).

Records of Early English Drama: Newcastle upon Tyne, ed. J. J. Anderson (Toronto, 1982).

Records of Early English Drama: York, ed. A. F. Johnston and M. Rogerson, (2 vols, Toronto, 1979).

Roberts, Peter, 'Tudor Wales, national identity and the British inheritance', in B. Bradshaw and P. Roberts, *British Consciousness and Identity: The Making of Britain, 1533–1707* (Cambridge, 1998), pp. 8–42.

Smith, A. H., ed. *The Place-Names of the West Riding of Yorkshire* (Cambridge, 1961).

Smout, T. C., *A History of the Scottish People, 1560–1830* (London, 1969).

Spenser, Edmund, 'View of the State of Ireland' (1595), in H. Morley, ed., *Ireland under Elizabeth and James the First* (London and New York, 1890).

Stow, John, *A Survey of London*, ed. H. Wheatley (London, 1912).

Suggett, Richard, 'Vagabonds and minstrels in sixteenth-century Wales', in Adam Fox and Daniel Woolf, eds, *The Spoken Word: Oral Culture in Britain 1500–1850* (Manchester, 2002), pp. 138–72.

Suggett, Richard and White, Eryn, 'Language, literacy and aspects of identity in early modern Wales', in Adam Fox and Daniel Woolf, eds, *The Spoken Word: Oral Culture in Britain 1500–1850* (Manchester, 2002).

Thomas, Keith, *The Perception of the Past in Early Modern England* (London, 1983).

Ware, James, ed., *Ancient Irish Histories: The Works of Spencer, Campion, Hanmer, and Marleburrough* (2 vols, Port Washington, NY, 1970).

Williamson, Arthur, *Scottish National Consciousness in the Reign of James VI: The Apocalypse, the Union, and the Shaping of Scotland's Public Culture* (Edinburgh, 1979).

Withers, Charles, *Geography, Science and National Identity: Scotland since 1520* (Cambridge, 2001).

Withers, Charles, 'Pont in context: chorography, mapmaking and national identity in the late sixteenth century', in Ian C. Cunningham, ed., *The Nation Survey'd: Essays on Late Sixteenth-Century Scotland as Depicted by Timothy Pont*, (East Linton, 2001).

Wood, Andy, 'Custom and the social organisation of writing in early modern England', *Transactions of the Royal Historical Society*, 6th series, 9 (1999), 257–69.

Woolf, D. *The Idea of History in Early Stuart England* (Toronto, 1990).

Woolf, D. *The Social Circulation of the Past: English Historical Culture 1500–1730* (Oxford, 2003).

Wormald, Jenny, *Court, Kirk and Community: Scotland 1470–1625* (London, 1981).

FURTHER READING

Barrett L. Beer, *Tudor England Observed: The World of John Stow* (1988). Good recent study of London's major antiquary and chronicler.

E. J. Cowan and R. J. Finlay (eds), *Scottish History: The Power of the Past* (2002). Several useful essays on aspects of the Scottish sense of the past.

Arthur B. Ferguson, *Utter Antiquity: Perceptions of Prehistory in Renaissance England* (1993). Useful survey of main antiquity myths, principally English.

F. Smith Fussner, *The Historical Revolution: English Historical Writing and Thought, 1580–1640* (1962). Somewhat anachronistic in assumptions and focus, but contains useful material.

Denys Hay, *Polydore Vergil: Renaissance Historian and Man of Letters* (1952). In need of revision, but still a reliable account; only partially devoted to Vergil's historical writing.

David Loades, (ed.), *John Foxe and the English Reformation* (Aldershot, Ashgate, 1997); and *John Foxe: An Historical Perspective* (1999). Two sets of recent essays on the martyrologist and historian, in whom interest has considerably revived since the mid-1990s.

Hugh A. Macdougall, *Racial Myth in English History: Trojans, Teutons and Anglo-Saxons* (1982). Brief and principally about a later period, but has useful material.

McFarlane, I. D., *Buchanan* (1981). Good study of Scotland's most important humanist.

Annabel Patterson, *Reading Holinshed's Chronicles* (1994). Largely persuasive re-examination of the largest of the late Tudor chronicles on its own merits, rather than as source for Shakespearian drama.

Stuart Piggott, *Ruins in a Landscape: Essays in Antiquarianism* (1976). Only partially about the sixteenth century, but contains excellent essays by the twentieth century's greatest authority on antiquarian archaeological activities.

Retha Warnicke, *William Lambarde, Elizabethan Antiquary, 1536–1601* (1973). Good biography of important Tudor antiquary.

Chapter Twenty-Four

Tudor Drama, Theatre and Society

Alexandra F. Johnston

A year after his victory at Bosworth Field in 1485, Henry VII went in progress through his new kingdom. The entry prepared for him by the city of York resonated with political overtones. Richard III, dead on the field in Bosworth, had lived for many years in York. He and his wife were members of the Corpus Christi Guild, his son had been created prince of Wales in the minster and the city had celebrated his visit as king in 1483 with a special performance of the Creed Play. In 1485, a contingent of soldiers had been on its way from York to Bosworth to fight for Richard when news came of his defeat and death. They had returned home and recorded in the official minutes of the city '. . . that King Richard, late lawfully reigning over us, was, thrugh grete treason . . . pitiously slane and murderd, to the grete hevyness of this Citie'.[1] In 1486, realizing they had need to impress the new king with their support, they hired Henry Hudson, a clerical poet, to write the verses for an elaborate series of pageants to be performed as Henry passed through the streets of York.[2] They presented the most spectacular dramatic compliment to the king they could devise, pouring the expertise of over a century of civic drama into the production.

To seek to impress the new king through drama and spectacle was not unusual in the late fifteenth century. Dramatic presentations were not mere entertainments but were integral parts of religious and political discourse. Christian theology, biblical history and moral rectitude were taught through drama; rulers were advised through drama and important issues of state such as Henry VIII's desire to sell ecclesiastical land, James V of Scotland's attitude to the Reformation and Elizabeth's marriage plans were discussed obliquely through drama in the anonymous *Godly Queen Hester* (1529), David Lindsay's *Ane Satire of the Thre Estates* (1540) and Thomas Sackville and Thomas Norton's *Gorboduc* (1560).

Life in early Tudor Britain was one of ceremony and display. Processions and rituals, both religious and secular marked the year. For centuries, bishops and archbishops in both England and Scotland had served as senior offices of state, knitting church and state together in a common society. Many monastic houses were feudal overlords of market towns as in Reading in Berkshire. The public display of this integrated community was marked by ancient customs with symbolic orders of precedence that were accompanied by music, banners and the processing of pageants and ritual objects. All these activities had mimetic components. The mass itself was often supplemented by what has come to be studied as liturgical drama. Parishes held processions of prophets as part of the late Lenten ceremonies that came to involve costumes and false beards. Lords of Misrule, mock officials to preside over festive seasons, were elected in court and parish and had their ecclesiastical counterparts in the election of choirboys as 'boy bishops' to rule the community for a day. Masking, mumming and disguising took place at all levels of society. Such events were part of the life of the Court, the cathedral, the university, the great secular and ecclesiastical households, the towns and even the villages. The events of the sixteenth century changed all that. In August, 1553, in Ireland, John Bale, English Protestant, playwright and polemicist, the newly appointed bishop of Ossory, refused to be vested in cope, crozier and mitre to walk in a procession in Kilkenny to celebrate the accession of Mary. He chose instead to wear his black Geneva gown while his scandalized clergy carried his mitre and crozier.[3] This symbolic act demonstrated how the ancient cohesion of church and state that had dominated late medieval British society had been irrevocably shattered. Until reformation theology challenged the ancient hierarchy of the church, the social coherence of British society could continue to be reflected in the traditional customs and ceremonies that had evolved over the centuries. This challenge first came in the 1530s when Thomas Cromwell engaged the young John Bale to write polemical plays attacking the bishop of Rome as part of the Henrician reformation. As the religious climate of England changed and evolved over the sixteenth century, the nature of the customs, ceremonies and plays also changed. For this reason, the story of Tudor drama and theatre is inextricably bound in to the political and doctrinal ideologies of the Reformation. The closing of the London theatres by the puritan London city council in 1642 was the 'end-game' of a long and complex struggle.

The importance of play-making, display and ceremony to all levels of Tudor society has emerged only in the last few decades. Play texts before the 1590s are very scarce and, until the mid-twentieth century, were considered grossly inferior to the plays written for the new entertainment industry in London by such playwrights as Christopher Marlowe, Thomas Kyd and William Shakespeare. Three separate though interconnected scholarly approaches to early drama have now converged to allow us to understand more fully the rich and diverse context out of which the work of the later Elizabethan playwrights grew. These are first, the modern stage revival of many of the early plays both religious and secular, secondly, the gathering and editing of all the surviving written evidence for drama, music and ceremony by Records of Early English Drama (REED) and, thirdly, the re-editing of all the surviving play texts.

When the biblical drama was suppressed in 1570s, the prohibitions were most explicitly against the portrayal of any person of the Trinity on the public stage. Although there was never a formal law against such portrayal, until 1951 no professional performance of a play in which Father, Son or Holy Spirit appeared as a character was allowed in England. In 1951, a version of the *York Cycle* was played in the ruins of St Mary's Abbey, York, as part of the Festival of Britain. The effect on the theatrical and scholarly world was electric. More and more productions of biblical plays, morality plays, interludes and early classical adaptations such as *Gammer Gurton's Needle* (c. 1551) were mounted not only (but largely) within academic circles but also in the professional theatre. By the end of the twentieth century all the canon had been performed, many plays had been given more than one interpretation and the vigour and stage-worthiness of early drama was firmly established. This drama on stage had proved to be not an awkward embarrassment to be eclipsed by the professional theatre but a vibrant tradition whose conventions are everywhere in what has come to be called the 'classical' English drama of the period from 1590 to 1642.

Archival research into the surviving records concerning early drama had begun before the Second World War, particularly in the records of the Court and the major cities such as York, Chester and Coventry where the texts of the biblical civic drama survive, at least in part. Scholars had been given their lead by the extraordinary volumes left by Sir Edmund Chambers, who may not have fully understood the significance of the documents he printed and calendared but who made scholars aware that the archival material existed. Some of the documents began to appear haphazardly in the 'Collections' volumes of the Malone Society but the focus of that society on the 'professional theatre' discouraged the collection of the evidence for community drama. After the publication of F. M. Salter's *Medieval Drama in Chester* more and more scholars were led to the provincial archives, now well catalogued and cared for by professional archivists in city and county record offices. By the mid-1970s, major collections were being compiled from the records of York, Chester, Coventry and Norwich but no agreement had been reached about how the material should be transcribed, what material should be transcribed and how it was to be edited and published. All these questions were resolved with the establishment of the REED project in Toronto in 1975. Over a quarter of a century later, with twenty-two volumes in print and more to come, the ubiquity of mimetic activity at every level of British society in the Tudor period has become clear.

Equally clear is the sad fact that only a small fraction of the texts of the plays that once must have existed has survived. This is particularly true of Wales where recent archival research has revealed a widespread tradition of play-making in Welsh similar to the English tradition but with only two surviving texts – a Nativity Play and a Passion Play. Drama was an ephemeral form often written for a special occasion and, all too frequently, once the occasion was passed the texts were discarded. Many religious texts did not survive the Reformation and the plays performed at Court or by the travelling players in guildhalls, churches and great households all over the kingdoms were vulnerable once they began to go out of fashion. One estimate of the number of scripts that must have existed to provide the plays needed for the new purpose-built repertory theatres in London suggests that in the 1570s there would have been approximately 1,200 performances in the eight theatres requiring about 100 or so different scripts per year. Yet between 1576 and 1586 only five or six texts have survived.[4] Commercial playwrights and entrepreneurs were content to reap their profits from the stage rather than the page. Even Shakespeare seems to have had little interest in preserving his plays for posterity. If his fellow shareholders in the King's Men, John Heminge and Henry Condell, had not gathered his plays together and published them in 1623 (seven years after his death), we would not have half of the acknowledged canon.

As the archival scholars of the last few decades have made clear how many texts we have lost, the work of other scholars has been establishing the nature of the texts that *have* survived. New critical editions have appeared of virtually all early drama. The manuscripts that contain the surviving religious drama have been carefully studied and it is now clear that the nature of each manuscript and the circumstances of its creation are unique. For example, the city government of York commissioned a 'register' of the civic Corpus Christi Play to be made from the individual pageant texts held by the craft guilds in the 1470s so that the city council could better control the performance. The several manuscripts of the Chester Whitsun Play were prepared by proud local antiquarians decades after the suppression of the play to preserve what they believed was an important part of the history of their city. Who commissioned the other two large collections of biblical plays is still obscure and the histories of those two manuscripts – the N-Town Plays from East Anglia and the Towneley Plays from West Yorkshire/Lancashire – are uncertain. It appears clear, however, that these manuscripts are compilations and that their component plays and sequences of plays represent a different dramatic tradition from the enormous and expensive extravaganzas of the northern cities. Texts of other plays survive in private 'commonplace' books preserved through the individual interests of antiquarians. Similar new editions have been made of the early printed drama and much work has been done on the printing houses. The work of the textual editors combined with the archival evidence and the renewed sense of the stage-worthiness of this drama has allowed a new appreciation of the place of drama and theatre in Tudor Britain.

Mimetic activities were woven into all aspects of British life. Over the centuries, parish-based customs in the countryside had evolved that were part of the essential money-making activities of the parishes. The churchwardens were responsible for the maintenance of the fabric of the churches west of the chancel or rood screen including the roof, the tower, the porch and the churchyard. Activities typically took place in the 'festive season' between Easter and midsummer when the crops were planted but the harvest had not yet begun. The generic name of the central event is 'church ale' – a festival that sometimes lasted for an entire week. In many parishes, a lord, a lady or both a lord and lady of the summer festival were chosen to preside over the events. Like the 'boy bishops', these 'rulers' were often humbler members of the parish. For example, from Wing in Buckinghamshire we have clear evidence from 1565 that the lord of the manor (Sir William Dormer) chose the lord and lady from among his servants. Puritan pamphleteers attempted to portray these events as near-baccanalian routs but the records evidence suggests much more controlled celebrations focused on raising money. Minstrels, maypoles and morris dancing were all part of the festivities as was Robin Hood and his company in the south and the west of England and in Scotland. At times these legendary figures engaged in simple tom-foolery, at times they took part in archery or other sports competitions or performed short, rowdy plays such as the few that survive. In other parts of the country, the Robin Hood figures seem to be 'gatherers' or licensed beggars for the parish as were the rush-bearers in the north-west and the 'young men' and 'young maids' of the towns and villages farther south who 'hocked' or 'gathered' money from the opposite sex during Hocktide (the week after Easter). Each of the gathering customs had a mimetic component.

Plays sponsored by parishes were also widespread. These were most frequently dramatizations of biblical episodes – shorter versions of the long episodic biblical plays or 'cycles' sponsored by the larger towns. For example, Reading St Lawrence mounted a small sequence of plays based on episodes from Genesis that they played in subsequent years. A parish text from East Anglia of the Christmas sequence was written to follow a similar annual pattern. Some parishes mounted saint's plays or morality plays. Widespread evidence survives for plays associated with the Easter rituals from small embellishments of the Resurrection sequences to large-scale plays on the Passion. The most detailed evidence for a parish passion play comes from New Romney in Kent that bears remarkable similarity to the passion play that survives in the N-Town manuscript. East Anglian plays tend to be large and demand more resources than a single parish could muster. Boxford in Suffolk solved that problem by tapping the resources of as many as twenty-four neighbouring parishes for their play in 1535.

Civic pageantry and drama was also a custom of long standing. Very few cities had full-scale civic processional plays or cycles – at most York, Chester, Coventry, Beverley, Newcastle and Norwich. Many other towns such as Lincoln, Aberdeen and Shrewsbury sponsored large stationary productions. Three major plays survive in Cornish from Cornwall with little documentary evidence concerning where they were performed. Cities such as Hereford, Dublin and Haddington in Scotland had elaborate processions of pageants depicting biblical scenes but the tableaux were dumb shows, that is pageants with action or gesture without words. London had no large civic play but chose to display its civic pride in elaborate annual lord mayor's Shows. Just as the wealth and power of a monarch or a great noble was judged by the nature of the displays and ceremonies he or she sponsored, so the economic and political standing of a city was judged by the nature of its pageantry.

From the surviving evidence it is clear that the performers were both amateur and professional. The guild accounts from York, Chester and Coventry include payment to players in their yearly expenses. From the way the plays from these cities are written, it is possible to deduce that the demanding parts for Christ or his judges would be taken by professionals while the smaller parts would be performed by amateurs. This practice has its analogy in the aristocratic mummings where some of the parts were taken by professionals and some by members of the household. The evidence documenting the widespread custom of travelling entertainers can help us understand where the professional performers in the seasonal civic and parish drama were drawn from. Evidence survives from at least the late fourteenth century of troupes of entertainers criss-crossing the islands, following established routes and stopping at familiar parishes, towns or households where the players knew their skills were valued. These players were sometimes under royal or noble patronage or sometimes came from a particular town or village. For example, there is a company of players 'from Coventry' that is frequently mentioned in the accounts of Maxstoke Priory, Warwickshire.[5] In the later sixteenth century the York chamberlains pay the 'Citties players'. It is possible that these references point to the existence of a core of the local professionals who performed in the seasonal civic drama but made their living touring the neighbouring countryside during the rest of the year.

Theatre and drama also influenced Tudor society through the schools and universities. From the founding of such schools as Eton and Westminster and their sister colleges at the universities, drama had a unique place. The fifteenth-century statutes of Eton and King's, for example, include rules for the boy-bishop ceremonies where a choirboy would be 'elected' on St Nicholas' day (8 December) to be bishop for the day and perform all the duties of the bishop except the administration of the sacraments. Post-Reformation statutes emphasize the importance of play-making for the scholars. Performing plays was not considered idleness but an essential part of the student's training as an orator. The emphasis in the schools and universities was largely on classical texts performed in Latin, since the ability to speak Latin was still seen as an advantage in the legal and diplomatic world. This produced an inevitable bias towards classical forms among university graduates and also, through the human-ist interest in classical dramatic theory, tended to create a bias among graduates against the vibrantly eclectic native tradition of entertainment. Philip Sidney speaks disparagingly of all English drama except *Gorboduc* in his *Apologie for Poetrie* (*c.* 1580) and yet he wrote one of the funniest and most stage-worthy of all the entertainments for Elizabeth, *The Lady of May*, written for the queen's visit to Leicester's house in Wanstead in Essex in 1578. There are no contemporary theorists who analysed the native tradition as an art form and, as a result, centuries of scholarship since the Renaissance have accepted the derogatory assessment of English 'drama' of Tudor university graduates. In all probability, these graduates participated in and learned from the infinitely varied mimetic tradition outside the academy but thought of it as 'entertainment' not 'drama' in the classical sense.

The mimetic traditions of the Courts both in England and Scotland were as eclec-tic and varied as the traditions in the countryside. Henry VIII, in particular, enjoyed Court entertainment and there are two separate accounts of his personal participa-tion in elaborate Robin Hood disguisings. He participated in tournaments, mum-mings, maskings and, as an accomplished musician himself, loved to dance and play with his Court musicians. The records of the Scottish Court provide rich evi-dence for aristocratic morris dancing and elaborate disguising.[6] In the recently pub-lished accounts of the English office of the Revels (1485–1559) W. R. Streitberger gives a detailed picture of the extent and importance of entertainment and display to the first four Tudor monarchs, making clear that Court revels were meant to convey the impression of the monarch's 'estate', and goes on to show how Henry VIII moved 'from image making to overt political commentary and finally to propaganda.'[7]

It was that move to propaganda under the direction of Thomas Cromwell that precipitated a major change in the use of drama in Tudor society. Using drama as a vehicle for political or moral discourse within a household itself had long been part of household revelry. The debates about 'maintenance' in the courtly morality play *Wisdom* (1460–70) or about whether noble birth or honourable behaviour was preferable in a husband in the first truly secular play that survives, John Medwall's *Fulgens and Lucrece* (1496–7), demonstrate the way plays were seen as part of learned and aristocratic discourse. Several plays and interludes survive from the Henrician Court in the 1520s and 1530s that attack or defend Wolsey and his circle. But Cromwell and Bale took the dramatic discourse out of the Court and into the public domain, deliberately using the popular forms of civic and parish drama to attack the hierarchy of the Roman church. These plays set the precedent and with the acces-sion of the boy king Edward VI and his Protestant uncles the established pattern of drama and ceremony began to crumble as the traditions of religious drama and ritual were attacked for their Catholicism and the reformers adopted the stage as one of their instruments of persuasion. As John Foxe, the author of *The Book of Martyrs*, later wrote, wrote 'Players, Printers and Preachers be set up of God as a triple bulwark against the triple crown of the Pope, to bring him down'.[8]

Evidence for much parish dramatic activity begins to disappear soon after 1535. The parish of St Lawrence, Reading, Berkshire, records the last occurrence of their two-part Easter play in 1538, and the last recorded Easter play in the Thames Valley counties was in Thame, Oxfordshire, in 1539. These events pre-date the first official injunction against plays and play-making to survive issued by Edmund Bonner, bishop of London, in 1542, who forbade 'common plays, games or interludes to be played' in the sanctuary of parish churches. All over the country customary practices began to disappear. The last evidence for a procession and pageants in Ipswich in Suffolk is in 1542. The Corpus Christi procession in Boston, Lincolnshire, is last recorded in 1545. In the same year the Corpus Christi procession in Bridgnorth, Shropshire, ended. In 1546–7 the Bristol Corpus Christi procession was suspended and the last event featuring a mimetic representation of St George in the parish of Morebath, Devon, is recorded. In 1547–8, the great St George procession in Norwich with its splendid dragon was reduced to divine service followed by a guild dinner and, in the same year, the town of Louth in Lincolnshire records its last Corpus Christi procession. The effect of these suspensions of ancient community custom can be inferred from the bare accounts of the city of Lincoln. On 13 June 1547 the St Anne's play was ready to go as usual. On 5 November of the same year all the gear for that play was sold off.

With the accession of Edward VI and his Protestant advisers, the situation did not improve. The immediate effect on the biblical cycle in York was the suspension of the plays devoted to the Virgin. The Shrewsbury Corpus Christi procession was cancelled. All records concerning the Christmas play and the Robin Hood activity of Ashburton, Devon, end in 1547–8. The play at Wymondham in Norfolk had its last performance in 1549. The effect on parish secular customs was equally sweeping. The Edwardian injunctions (with the Bonner's prohibitions still in place) turned their attention to activities in church porches and churchyards during service time. Bishop John Hooper's articles for the diocese of Gloucester and Worcester repeated this injunction and added the further stricture that the minister should not be disturbed during divine service with 'plays, games, sports, dancing and such like.' On 1 November 1547 the archdeacons associated with the diocese of Bath and Wells were urged to instruct the parishes in their care to give up holding church ales but at the same time to remind the churchwardens of the financial obligation of the parish for the fabric of the church.

But with the accession of Mary, in July 1553, many of the annual community celebrations were revived with enthusiasm. In York, the plays on the Virgin were reinstated along with the Corpus Christi procession and the St George riding. Lincoln, Louth and Bristol revived their communal customs. An order of the town council of Worcester revived their Corpus Christi procession in 1555–6. There is, also, an excited sense of renewed customary activity at the parish level. Ashburton in Devon revived its old customs and went so far as to mount a new play in this period, as we can deduce from the evidence of gloves bought for 'hym that played god almyghty a Corpus Christi daye'. In Thame, Oxfordshire, the churchwardens responded to the new regime with exuberance, paying their summer lord 6s 6d. for his expenses at Whitsun 1554, and hiring a taborer or drummer from London for the event. Many more Thames Valley parishes revived the customs discreetly suppressed during Edward's reign. Hock gatherings resumed at Lambeth, all three Reading parishes, and Wing, while new evidence for the custom begins at St Botolph, Middlesex, however briefly (1554–5). Parishes also energetically renewed their summer games. An undated Henley account from the mid-1550s has a list of expenses for the refurbishing of the morris costumes and bells. Guildford's summer lord reigned once more in the North Downs, while the rural parishes of Stanford-in-the-Vale, Berkshire, and Pyrton, Oxfordshire, raised summer poles for their ales.

However, although much of accustomed activity in the countryside had been restored under Mary, much was irretrievably lost and continued to be lost under her sister. Suppression of communal activities at the parish level in the early years of Elizabeth's reign was extensive but depended on the zealousness of the diocesan officials, especially the bishop and his archdeacons. Reforming bishops preferred pew rentals, parish levies and other taxes to more convivial ways of raising money. However, these methods did not find favour with many of the parishes of the Thames Valley and the West. Although the churches in Protestant Bristol quickly conformed as did the parishes in the town of Reading that fell under the watchful eye of the local magnate, Sir Francis Knollys, the most puritan of Elizabeth's councillors, many parishes continued their old ways of raising money well into the reign of Elizabeth. For example, Wantage in north Berkshire had morris dancing accompanied by minstrels hired from a sufficient distance to pay them board during revel time. But not every community was united in its revival of old practices. Evidence from archdeacons' courts documents increasingly bitter divisions at the parish level between those who enthusiastically embraced the new religion and the supporters of the old customs as neighbours cited neighbours for such offenses as dancing in service time.

In the 1560s, especially in East Anglia and Kent, several towns mounted elaborate plays that seem not to have been well received by the authorities. At New Romney in Kent, the Passion Play was performed in 1560 and apparently again in 1563–4 but by 1567–8 the play parts were called in. In 1562, the town authorities of Maldon in Essex hired a professional 'property player' (a designation that seems to embrace the functions of both the modern terms 'producer' and 'director') to produce their play but sold the play gear by the end of the year. Bungay in Suffolk mounted a large play between 1566 and 1568 but then all evidence stops. The most famous of these East Anglian extravaganzas was the huge production at Chelmsford in 1562–3 which ended in financial disaster. Elsewhere in the kingdom parish and town drama is also recorded during the decade although sometimes, as with the plays at Ashburton, Devon, for only one last time in 1559–60. Attempts do seem to have been made to make the texts of the traditional plays more palatable to the ecclesiastical authorities either by excising blatantly Catholic sections (such as the plays on the Virgin at York) or by more intrusive tinkering with the texts. Some towns, however, such as Boston, Lincolnshire, and Shrewsbury, Shropshire, mounted new plays written by local schoolmasters, and Lincoln mounted a play based on the story of Tobias from 1563 to 1567. The plays of Thomas Ashton, the headmaster of Shrewsbury School, who is later described as 'a good and godly Preacher' undoubtedly had Protestant themes and it is probable that the others did as well.

In the larger centres where there had been town and guild plays and processions the evidence is mixed. In Norwich in 1558–9 'for pastyme' the famous dragon of the old St George play was allowed 'to come In and shew hym selff as in other yeares'. On 15 April 1565 the Norwich council agreed that 'souche pagentes as were wonte to go in tyme of whitson holydayes shall be Set forthe by occupacions as tymes past haue bene vsyd'. Nothing more is heard of the procession. The last mention of the actual mounting of the procession of pageants in Newcastle is in 1561 although the pageants continue to be mentioned in guild ordinances.

Evidence for parish activity becomes more and more sporadic between 1568 and 1580 as the archdeacons, in some parts of the country at least, became more zealous in their visitations. Nevertheless, ales with their attendant activities continued to be held, though not always every year. The Robin Hood activities in Woodbury, Devon, for example, survived until 1577 and in Yeovil, Somerset, until 1578. More remote parishes, such as tiny Aston Abbots in Buckinghamshire recorded an ale sporadically until 1579 while Wantage and Childrey in Berkshire also continued their ales regularly until after 1589. Town drama in East Anglia gradually disappeared in the 1570s. Braintree in Essex recorded income from play money in 1570, but that same year they began to rent out their costumes. The next year they sold their playbook and in 1579 finally sold the costume stock. In Maldon, in 1573 one Richard Wells and others were fined for performing a play and an archdeacon who preached against the play was given dinner by the town. The next year, however, in the last play evidence to survive from the town, three men were licensed to perform a play. Chelmsford began to sell off its large stock of costumes in 1576 and Bungay in Suffolk, whose play was last performed in 1568, sold off its costumes in 1577.

It was this decade that saw the end of the civic drama. The York Creed Play was suppressed in 1568 by the zealous dean of Yorkminster, Mathew Hutton, and the Corpus Christi Play was mounted for the last time in 1569. The last actual performance of the drama of the old religion in York was the production of the Pater Noster Play in 1572 when two Protestant council members, William Beckwith and Christopher Herbert, were disenfranchised for refusing to see the play with the rest of the council as was the custom. The dispute was taken to the new lord president of the North (the stoutly Protestant third earl of Huntingdon) and the Council of the North, and the playbooks were called in. In 1579, the York city council passed a motion to produce the Corpus Christi Play but took the precaution of sending the text to the dean and archbishop for approval. Nothing is heard of the play that year but the next year, in the last mention of the civic religious drama in York, the common council urged the mayor to see if the authorities would allow the play. But by this time the mayor and aldermen were solidly in the Protestant camp, no action was taken and the play dropped out of sight until the mid-nineteenth century.

Hutton and Grindal also turned to other towns and cities in the archdiocese where play-making had been part of the Catholic past. Hutton signed the letter from the Council of the North's Ecclesiastical Commission to stop a play at Wakefield in 1576 that included a portrayal of the godhead. The plays at Chester were suppressed in 1575 after a struggle between the Catholic and Protestant factions of the city council. The Corpus Christi Play at Coventry in the archdiocese of Canterbury was suspended for one year in 1575 and stopped abruptly in 1580. All evidence supports the argument that the medieval Catholic plays were deliberately suppressed by the new Protestant hierarchy.

To match the deliberate official suppression of community Catholic drama, there is an explosion of evidence in the 1560s documenting the activities of troupes of players travelling under the patronage of prominent members of the new Protestant aristocracy. Acting companies whose repertories were clearly promoting the Protestant cause had first appeared, as we have seen, under the patronage of Thomas Cromwell in the 1530s as part of the strategy of the Henrician reform. The same policy was followed even more vigorously in the 1560s. In his despatches home, the Spanish ambassador, the count of Feria, reported that Cecil was directing the efforts of certain playwrights as Cromwell had done. It seems likely that the government, aware of the power of drama as a tool of propaganda, was using every means at hand to establish, in the countryside, positive responses to the Elizabethan settlement. It was in the countryside, where the roots of traditional religion were deep, rather than in Protestant London that the campaign to persuade the people to embrace the Protestant cause had to be launched. This was the context for John Foxe's comment about plays, preachers and pamphlets bringing down the triple crown of Rome.[9]

During the five years of Mary's reign, evidence for only seventeen performances by travelling companies survives. Yet for the years from 1558 to 1569, 315 performances are recorded by troupes of thirty-one patrons. Of these, over 250 (80 per cent of the total) were by troupes patronized by the Protestant courtiers such as Robert Dudley, earl of Leicester, his brother the earl of Warwick, the duchess of Suffolk, the earls of Oxford and Northampton, Lord Hunsdon and Sir John Fortescue. Other troupes were patronized by staunch Protestants in the provinces such as William Alley, bishop of Exeter, and James Blount, Lord Mountjoy. One of the most active troupes was the one Elizabeth had inherited from her sister. It seems probable that these patrons, zealous as most of them were in the cause of the godly, were prepared to use their actors to carry the Protestant message throughout the kingdom promoting, at the same time, the government policy concerning religion.

Although only a fraction of the plays that must have existed were printed, many plays advancing Protestant arguments were recorded in the *Stationer's Register*, the official record of all publications or proposed publications. Thirty-nine of the eighty-six plays (or 45 per cent) listed by Harbage and Schoenbaum as registered are characterized as moral or religious.[10] Although, it has proved difficult to associate particular plays with particular acting troupes, there are many hints of associations within the tightly knit circle of Protestant writers, patrons, players and printers. Indirect evidence associates Leicester with the plays of William Wager. John de Vere, sixteenth earl of Oxford, whose troupe was active in these years, was the brother-in-law of Arthur Golding, translator of Theodore Beza'a *Abraham's Sacrifice*. William Alley, bishop of Exeter, was himself the author of a play, *Aegio*, registered in 1560. Among other plays 'offered for acting' in this decade were Ulpian Fulwell's *Like Will to Like* and Thomas Garter's *The Most Virtuous and Godly Susanna*. Reaching satisfactory clarity about what was really happening here is hampered by the lack of survival of the texts. Like the evidence for the repertory of the early London theatre, that for the repertory of the players of the powerful nobles in the land in the first decade of Elizabeth's reign can only be conjectured.

Elizabeth's hold on the crown became greatly strengthened when a rebellion sponsored by the northern and largely Catholic earls was suppressed in 1569. After that year, the pattern of performance by the travelling players began to change. The number of named acting companies on the road rose by 50 per cent, but 18 per cent of these companies are recorded fewer than five times and 31 per cent fewer than ten times; 69 per cent of all visits were made by the companies of the queen, four magnates (the earls of Leicester, Sussex and Worcester and Lord Berkeley) and the Stanleys of Derby (both the earl and his son Ferdinando, Lord Strange). The repertory of the companies seems to have changed radically from the previous decade. The pendulum of religious opinion was beginning to make a wider sweep. As Paul White has shown, by the 1570's 'the Word dramatized, as opposed to the Word preached'[11] had come under serious attack from the more extreme wing of the Protestants. Only 15 per cent of the plays for these years listed in Harbage and Schoenbaum have any clear religious content. With the suppression of the rising of 1569, it was no longer as necessary to use drama as part of the propaganda war and the fashion in plays became less political. Leicester's company performed such romances as *Predor and Lucia* and *Panicia* and such comedies as *The Collier*. The company of the earl of Sussex, at this time second only to Leicester's in its provincial visits, added such variants as histories, tragedies and classical themes to their staple of romances.

The companies continued to tour regularly. New evidence is showing that far from abandoning touring when they acquired permanent space in London, the companies continued to exploit their contacts and their customers in the English provinces as well as travelling in to Wales and Scotland and crossing the Irish Sea to perform in Dublin. At the same time they were establishing permanent houses in London. The Red Lion was built in 1567, the theatre at Newington Butts around 1575, the Theatre in 1576 and the Curtain in 1577. Inns that had been used in London for many years (as they had been and were used in the provinces) were the Bull in Bishopsgate Street, the Bell and the Cross Keys in Gracious Street and the Bel Savage on Ludgate Hill. In addition, the boys' companies played in the rectangular halls of Blackfriars and St Paul's. During the 1570s, London was becoming a dramatic centre as it had not been in the earlier period and it is at this point that the history of drama and theatre in Tudor society takes a radical new direction, away from community and towards a market-driven entertainment industry.

But it was an industry that continued to have the deep interest of both the city of London and the royal Court. The city government was hostile to the theatres seeing them as immoral and disruptive, centres of idleness and potential gathering places for the young and restless who might raise rebellion. The court looked on the theatres as a source for their own entertainment. Sir Edmund Chambers characterized these conflicting attitudes as a 'struggle' between the city's increasing puritanism and the queen's delight in drama. But as Scott McMillin has recently put it, 'beyond the queen's love of drama . . . there was a burgeoning city to be governed, and a nation divided over the basic question of religion'.[12] Indeed, although religion was no longer the *subject* of theatrical presentation, public performance of all kinds continued to be tangled in religious issues.

Scott McMillin and Sally-Beth MacLean have argued in their recent book on the Queen's Men that the creation of that troupe was not without political overtones. The troupe called 'the Queen's Men', created as an instrument of policy in 1583, was not the same company as the one known as the 'Queen's Men' from the time of Elizabeth's succession. The new Queen's Men was a specially created company, made up of players from Leicester's Men, Sussex's Men and other major companies by no less a political officer than Sir Francis Walsingham. McMillin and MacLean suggest that both the London city council and the queen's privy council feared the potential power of the public theatre. While the reaction of the city was to prohibit playing, the reaction of the Court was to control it. They further argue that the creation of the Queen's Men on Walsingham's orders had Leicester's full support and co-operation even though it meant the temporary eclipse of his own company. These staunch but moderate Protestants were anxious to glean intelligence from all over the country. The threat from Catholicism continued to be real and equally important was the increasing stridency of the radical Puritans who had by now turned against drama and expressed their distaste for plays in increasingly inflammatory rhetoric. The Queen's Men, a respected group of players under royal patronage travelling widely, were a tool of government policy. Whether or not the players were spies, it served Walsingham's purposes to have them touring around the provinces carrying the honour of the queen's patronage and the support of the strongest political figures in the land.

As the decade of the 1580s unfolded, two important events in the history of Tudor theatre occurred. The first was what William Ingram has called 'the sudden and gratifying appearance in 1586 and 1587, of plays by the group collectively known as the University Wits.'[13] These young men nurtured in play-making at both Oxford and Cambridge had a greater regard for the printed text than did the men who made their living solely through the stage. At last the history of the stage is complemented by at least some of the texts that were being presented by such playwrights as George Peele and John Lyly. The second incident once again emphasized how the business of the public stage was entwined in the religious controversies of the period. Over the two years 1588–90 there appeared a sustained anonymous Puritan attack on the hierarchy of the Church of England that has come to be known as the Martin Marprelate controversy. Whoever Martin was (and it is speculated that he was several people) he chose to ridicule the bishops by using actors and stage routines as the model for his attacks. His satiric, almost slapstick, mode bore a strong resemblance to the style of Richard Tarleton, a clown and one of the leading players of the Queen's Men. As one of the opponents of Martin wrote

> These tinkers termes, and barbers jestes;
> first Tarleton on the stage,
> Then Martin in his bookes of lies
> hath put in every page.[14]

The Admiral's Men, Lord Strange's Men and the Queen's Men all became involved in the battle on the side of the establishment against Martin by lampooning him on the stage. But these efforts tipped over into gross bad taste and they were ordered to desist by the privy council. The boy companies – the Chapel Children and Paul's Boys – both associated with John Lyly, the playwright most active against Martin, were disowned by the authorities and disappeared for almost a decade.

In the provinces in the period after the establishment of the Queen's Men in 1583, the most common reference in town records to dramatic activity is the payment to travelling players carrying the authority of some noble patron. As McMillin and MacLean have so graphically illustrated, the most ubiquitous company was the

Queen's Men, appearing in every corner of the realm. The second most common reference is to city waits or musicians who were employed by many English towns as well as Dublin, Haverfordwest, and Ruthin in Wales. They played for civic functions and, when they were not needed by their primary masters, played for guild feasts, local magnates, neighbouring towns or, in the case of the waits of Oxford, for college functions and plays. Mimetic activity in the parishes continued to decline especially (as in Kent, Sussex, Somerset and Lancashire) where the bishops and their archdeacons were particularly vigilant in their visitations. In other parts of the countryside little changed. Robin Hood, morris dancing and summer lords continued to thrive in Cornwall and in the more remote villages of the Thames valley and the west country while blood sports were enjoyed in Kent, Devon, Somerset and Lancashire. Some of the major towns, deprived of the plays that had given expression to their sense of community, substituted other activities. In the North, Newcastle had a Hogmagog celebration in November while York and Chester mounted midsummer shows. The one in Chester maintained elements from the Whitsun play but York's was simply a martial display. Coventry also substituted a martial display for their play. Until the records of the guild end in 1591–2 there is evidence that St George and the dragon continued to process in Norwich. In the West, Plymouth had a martial display on May Day with morris dancing, Exeter had a midsummer watch, Bristol held special civic events on the queen's accession day and the Shearmen of Shrewsbury raised their 'tree' or maypole even after the extraordinary controversy that surrounded it in 1590–1. Similar local struggles between the more religiously conservative and the more puritanical parishioners flared up at about the same time around the question of raising a maypole at the summer festival in Dover in 1586–7, Englishcombe, Somerset, in 1588, Sandwich in 1588–9, Banbury in Oxfordshire in 1589, Coventry in 1591 and Oxford around 1600. Sir Edward Hoby, writing to Theophilus Higgons about that event, chided him for 'putting your hand to the sawing downe of a poore harmelesse Maypole, because you thought it came out of a Romish forrest . . . .'

Equally divisive for local government was the appearance of travelling players within the jurisdiction of a town, seeking permission to play. A generation before, the struggle to maintain the Catholic civic drama had been fought out by the local aldermen and bailiffs on religious lines. Now, in the final decades of Elizabeth's reign a similar split occurred over tolerating players between those who had become comfortable within the 'via media' of the settlement and the more radical Protestants. As early as 1585, the Kendal town council passed a motion requiring the consent of the majority of the burgesses before any play was performed within their jurisdiction. In Norwich in 1588–9, the council prohibited plays because they 'bee but provocacions and allurements to vices and synnes'. In 1595–6, the council of Great Yarmouth in Norfolk forbade the bailiff to license players because they caused 'great annoyauns & offens of many'. The next year the compiler of the record of payment in Dunwich, Suffolk, recorded his dissent in the account book as he wrote 'Item paid to the Queene her Minstrels, players and yet much discontented by Mr Allen scrivener.' Two years later in Hadleigh, also in Suffolk, an ordinance was passed requiring the written consent of six chief inhabitants before a play could be performed and in the same year the York council began to pass formal motions authorizing players. For centuries payments to players had been made by the chamberlains without question but by 1599 the York council took care to have players formally endorsed. The conflict within the town council of Bridgnorth in Shropshire is silently apparent from the minutes of 1601–2 where all stage plays are banned from the 'Counsell howse or Towne Hall' and then the entry is cancelled with nothing written to replace it. Frequently prohibitions passed one year would be revoked or ignored in subsequent years, reflecting the ongoing factional struggle.

In London, the players had long since lost their battle with the city council. The theatres, except for the halls in St Paul's and Blackfriars that could claim the status of 'liberties' and so outside the jurisdiction of the city, had been banished to the suburbs. The major theatres after 1576, the Theatre and the Curtain, were in Shoreditch north of London. Then, in 1587, Philip Henslowe built the Rose in Southwark across the river and in 1599 the Chamberlain's Men dismantled the Theatre and took it beam by beam across the river to build the Globe. The next year the Admiral's Men closed the Rose and opened a new venue, the Fortune, in the northwest suburbs. Theatre-goers in the capital had what provincial theatre-goers did not have – different civil jurisdictions within walking distance. Despite the steady and growing opposition of the London city council, the suburban playhouses continued to play to ever larger audiences made up, at least in part, of strangers from the provinces seeking work in a city whose economic dominance was increasing. The public had an apparently unquenchable thirst for plays.

It took a while for the companies to recover from the rebuke over the Marprelate controversies. The period 1588–94 was one of uncertainty and flux as they dissolved and re-formed with many of the same players appearing in different configurations in different companies. This is also the period when Marlowe was revolutionizing the nature of English theatre. Although he and his two followers, Thomas Kyd and Shakespeare, relied heavily on the dramaturgical techniques of the drama that had come before them, Marlowe gave the stage a vehicle for language in the blank verse he perfected, allowing his plays to transcend all earlier dramatic writing in imaginative grandeur. He also used exotic plots and created towering characters that captivated audiences. His untimely death in 1593 and Kyd's in 1594 left the field clear for Shakespeare who dominated the decade of the 1590s, encountering no serious new rival until Ben Jonson joined the Admiral's Men in 1597. By that time, by decree of the privy council, there were only two theatre companies active in the London area – the Admiral's Men (Henslowe's company) still resident in the Rose in Southwark and the Chamberlain's Men (Shakespeare's company) at the Theatre in Shoreditch. This company had been formed in 1594 under the patronage of the queen's cousin and close friend and adviser Henry Carey, first Lord Hunsdon who became lord chamberlain in 1585. More than half of Shakespeare's plays were written and performed before the end of the Tudor period in 1603. All the English histories, *Romeo and Juliet*, most of the comedies, *Hamlet* and *Troilus and Cressida* were played by the Chamberlain's Men at the Theatre, then at the Globe and at Court. Although the boys' companies (what Hamlet will call the 'little eyases') were revived at St Paul's and Blackfriars in 1598–9 and two other adult companies, Worcester's and the Duke of York's also appeared at the end of the decade, the Admiral's Men and the Chamberlain's Men continued to dominate. At the accession of James I, the Chamberlain's Men became the King's Men and its members became gentlemen of the chamber.

But the elevation of the players to the status of royal servants came after they came close to being condemned as traitors. The supporters of the earl of Essex had paid the company forty shillings 'more than their ordinary' to revive *Richard II* (a play depicting the deposition of a reigning and legitimate monarch) and perform it on the eve of the rebellion raised by Essex against the queen on 8 February 1601. Charges were not pressed but the very fact that the conspirators thought that the public performance of a play about a political usurpation would aid their cause emphasizes the way that drama continued to be considered part of political discourse even at the end of the Tudor period.[15]

Jacobean society inherited a dramatic tradition that had evolved through the political and religious struggles of the Tudor period from an integral part of communal religious social discourse to a major art form. Yet the character of King Lear bound upon his metaphoric wheel of fire had much in common with the character of Christ hanging on his cross. The visceral power of dramatic performance undertaken with a seriousness of purpose was part of the living legacy that allowed the plays written from 1590 to 1625 to become the 'classical' drama of the English-speaking world. But this magnificent flowering was not only cut off from its communal roots but also under continuing attack from the radical Puritans. During the unhappy reign of Charles I the public stage sank to the portrayal of cynical violence and the court turned to elegant but shallow masques divorced from reality. The closing of the public theatres in 1642 was the final blow to an art form already in decline.

NOTES

1. Raine, *York Civic Records I*, p. 119.
2. Much of this study is based on the primary material contained in the twenty-one collections of records published by Records of Early English Drama (REED); Malone Society Collections, volumes VIII and XI; Mill, *Medieval Plays in Scotland*; Coldewey, 'Early Essex drama'; and my own unpublished research in the records of Berkshire, Buckinghamshire and Oxfordshire and that of two colleagues, Sally-Beth MacLean (Surrey) and Diana Wyatt (Beverley and Oxford). This material is deposited in the offices of REED at the University of Toronto and may be consulted with the permission of the editors. Work is in progress on the Scottish records that is not yet available for analysis. It seems clear, however, that although Wales and Ireland had a richer bardic heritage than England and Scotland, the pattern of the performance of pageants and plays in Wales and the Irish Pale was similar to those in England and Scotland.
3. Fletcher, *Drama and Performance*, p. 167.
4. Ingram, *The Business of Playing*, p. 241.
5. Oxford, Trinity College MS C.84.
6. Mill, *Medieval Plays in Scotland*, pp. 46–59; Forrest, *The History of Morris Dancing*, p. 82.
7. Streitberger, *Court Revels*, p. 6.
8. Cited in White, *Theatre and Reformation*, p. 44.
9. Ibid.
10. Harbage and Schoenbaum, *Annals of English Drama*, pp. 34–40.
11. White, *Theatre and Reformation*, p. 168.
12. McMillin and MacLean, *The Queen's Men*, p. 9.

TUDOR DRAMA, THEATRE AND SOCIETY

13. Ingram, *The Business of Playing*, p. 242.
14. Cited by McMillin and MacLean, *The Queen's Men*, p. 54.
15. Andrew Gurr, *The Shakespearian Playing Companies*, pp. 288–9.

BIBLIOGRAPHY

Anderson, John, ed., *REED: Newcastle upon Tyne* (Toronto, 1982).
Chambers, E. K., *The Elizabethan Stage* (4 vols, Oxford, 1923).
Chambers, E. K., *The Medieval Stage* (2 vols, Oxford, 1903).
Clopper, L. M., ed., *REED: Chester* (Toronto, 1979).
Coldewey, John, 'Early Essex drama: a history of its rise and fall, and a theory concerning the Digby Plays', PhD dissertation, University of Colorado, 1972.
Douglas, Audrey and Greenfield, Peter, eds, *REED: Cumberland/Westmorland/Gloucestershire* (Toronto, 1986).
Fletcher, Alan J., *Drama and Performance and Polity in Pre-Cromwellian Ireland* (Toronto, 2000).
Forrest, John, *The History of Morris Dancing 1458–1750* (Toronto, 1999)
Galloway, David, ed., *REED: Norwich 1540–1642* (Toronto, 1984).
Galloway, David and Wasson, John, eds, *Records of Plays and Players in Norfolk and Suffolk, 1330–1642*, Malone Society Collections XI (Oxford, 1981).
George, David, ed., *REED: Lancashire* (Toronto, 1992).
Gibson, James, ed., *REED: Kent; Diocese of Canterbury* (3 vols, Toronto, 2002).
Gurr, Andrew, *The Shakespearian Playing Companies* (Oxford, 1996).
Gurr, Andrew, *The Shakespearean Stage 1574–1642* (3rd edition, Cambridge, 1992).
Harbage, Alfred and Schoenbaum, Samuel, *Annals of English Drama 975–1700* (Philadelphia, 1964).
Hays, Rosalind Conklin, McGee, C. E., Joyce, Sally L. and Newlyn, Evelyn S., eds, *REED: Dorset/Cornwall* (Toronto, 1999).
Ingram, R. W., ed., *REED: Coventry* (Toronto, 1981).
Ingram, William, *The Business of Playing* (Ithaca, NY, 1992).
Johnston, Alexandra F. and Rogerson, Margaret, eds, *REED: York* (2 vols, Toronto, 1979).
Kahrl, S. J. and Proudfoot, Richard, eds, *Records of Plays and Players in Lincolnshire 1300–1585* (Malone Society Collections VIII, Oxford, 1972).
Louis, Cameron, ed., *REED: Sussex* (Toronto, 2000).
McMillin, Scott and MacLean, Sally-Beth, *The Queen's Men and Their Plays 1583–1603* (Cambridge, 1998).
Mill, Anna J., *Medieval Plays in Scotland* (St Andrews, 1924).
Nelson, Alan H., ed., *REED: Cambridge* (2 vols, Toronto, 1989).
Pilkinton, Mark, ed., *REED: Bristol* (Toronto, 1997).
Raine, Angelo, ed. *York Civic Records I* (Yorkshire Archaeological Society Records Series XCVIII, York, 1939).
Salter, F. M., *Medieval Drama in Chester* (Toronto, 1955).
Somerset, J. A. B., ed., *REED: Shropshire* (2 vols, Toronto, 1994).
Stokes, James, ed. (with Robert Alexander), *REED: Somerset* (2 vols, Toronto, 1996).
Streitberger, W. R., *Court Revels, 1485–1559* (Toronto, 1994).
Wasson, John, ed., *REED: Devon* (Toronto, 1986).
White, Paul Whitfield, *Theatre and Reformation: Protestantism, Patronage and Playing in Tudor England* (Cambridge, 1993).

FURTHER READING

Texts
There are four anthologies that print many of the plays discussed here: David Bevington (ed.), *Medieval Drama* (1975); John Coldewey (ed.), *Early English Drama* (1993); Greg Walker (ed.), *Medieval Drama: An Anthology* (2000); R. A. Fraser and Norman Rabkin (eds), *Drama of the English Renaissance: The Tudor Period* (1976). Critical editions of all the 'medieval' English canon are published by the Early English Text Society except the *The York Plays*, ed. Richard Beadle (1982) and *Everyman*, ed. Arthur Cawley (1961). Critical editions of many sixteenth-century Tudor plays are available through the Revels Plays (Manchester) and the Tudor Interlude series (Cambridge). The Cornish drama is available in three editions: Paula Neuss (ed. and trans.), *The Creation of the World: A Critical Edition and Translation* (1983); E. Norris (ed. and trans.), *The Ancient Cornish Drama* (2 vols, 1859); and Whitley Stokes (ed. and trans.), *The Life of St Meriasek, Bishop and Confessor: A Cornish Drama* (1872). *The Oxford Shakespeare: The Complete Works*, ed. Stanley Wells and Gary Taylor, was published in 1998.

'Medieval'
The best collection of essays that deliberately seeks to use the insights of the new scholarship on the earlier drama is *The Cambridge Companion to Medieval Drama* (1994) ed. Richard Beadle. The most recent general study is Lawrence M. Clopper, *Drama, Play and Game* (2001). East Anglian drama has been studied by John Coldewey in 'The Digby Plays and the Chelmsford records,' *Research Opportunities in Renaissance Drama*, 18 (1975), 103–21 and 'That enterprising property player: semi-professional drama in sixteenth-century England', *Theatre Notes*, 31 (1977), 5–12; Gail Gibson, *The Theater of Devotion* (1989); and Victor I. Scherb, *Staging Faith* (2001). The most recent study of the *Chester Cycle* is David Mills, *Re-Cycling the Cycle: The City of Chester and its Whitsun Plays* (Toronto, 1998). The *York Plays* have been most recently treated in *Early Theatre*, 3 (2000) and by Alexandra F. Johnston, 'The *York Cycle* and the libraries of York', in *The Church and Learning in Late Medieval Society* (2002), pp. 355–70, and 'The city as patron', in *Shakespeare and Theatrical Patronage in Early Modern England*, ed. Suzanne Westfall and Paul White (2002) pp. 150–175. The problems surrounding the Towneley MS has been most recently probed in Barbara D. Palmer, 'Recycling "The Wakefield Cycle": the records', *Research Opportunities in Renaissance Drama*, XLI (2002) 88–130.

Tudor
Two pioneering works on Tudor drama and pageantry were Sydney Anglo, *Spectacle, Pageantry and Early Tudor Policy* (1969) and David Bevington *Tudor Drama and Politics* (1966). More recent work has been done on patronage by Suzanne Westfall in *Patrons and Performance: Early Tudor Household Revels* (1990). W. R. Streitberger's *Court Revels, 1485–1559* (1994) provides essential primary material for Court revels. Greg Walker's two books *Plays of Persuasion: Drama and Politics in the Court of Henry VIII* (1991) and *The Politics of Performance in Early Renaissance Drama* (1998) analyse the politics surrounding early Tudor drama. Paul Whitfield White's *Theatre and Reformation: Protestantism, Patronage and Playing in Tudor England* (1993) is a groundbreaking work connecting drama to the Protestant cause. This is followed up by Alexandra F. Johnston, 'English community drama in crisis: 1535–80', in *European Communities of Medieval Drama: A Collection of Essays*, ed. Alan Hindley (1999) pp. 248–69.

Parish Drama
English Parish Drama edited by Alexandra F. Johnston and Wim Husken (1996) provides a series of essays on the parish material. This should be supplemented by *Festive Drama*, edited

by Meg Twycross (1996), which contains an important article by Sally-Beth MacLean on the hocking customs. MacLean and Johnston also contributed a chapter 'Reformation and resistance in Thames/Severn parishes: the dramatic witness', to *The Parish in English Life*, ed. Katherine L. French, Gary G. Gibbs and Beat Kumin (1997). Two other book chapters by Johnston are useful for this period: 'The inherited tradition: the legacy of provincial civic drama,' and 'Actors and acting in the Elizabethan Theatre', in *The Elizabethan Theatre XIII, Proceedings of the 13th Waterloo International Conference* (1989) eds A. L. Magnusson and C. E. McGee (1994); 'The Robin Hood of the records' in *Playing Robin Hood: The Legend as Performance in Five Centuries*, ed. Lois Potter (Newark, 1998) pp. 27–44.

Professional Theatre

The standard work on the children's companies is still Michael Shapiro, *Children of the Revels: The Boy Companies of Shakespeare's Time* (1974). Scott McMillin and Sally-Beth MacLean's *The Queen's Men and Their Plays 1583–1603* (1998) has opened up a whole new way of studying provincial playing. William Ingram's *The Business of Playing* (1992) adds important depth of detail to the three books by Andrew Gurr that are now the standard introductory works to Shakespeare's theatre: *Playgoing in Shakespeare's London* (1987); *The Shakespearean Stage* (3rd edition, 1992); and *The Shakespearian Playing Companies* (1996).

CHAPTER TWENTY-FIVE

Portraiture, Politics and Society

ROBERT TITTLER

The last few decades have seen art historical scholarship come quite far from its traditionally narrow concentration on questions of style, authorship, patronage and aesthetic context,[1] and towards a deeper concern for the social and political contexts of such works.[2] Over the years, traditional approaches produced a canon of the more aesthetically accomplished works, emanating from the formal and 'polite' fashion of each historical era. Because the better sort of portraits were those commissioned by the better and wealthier sort of people, conventional scholarship on the subject at hand here had been chiefly concerned with what we might term 'courtly portraiture', embracing portraits of royalty, the Court circle, the landed classes, and members of other elites. Whether intentionally or not, less aesthetically accomplished works, often highly vernacular or even naive in style and emanating from much wider social circles, thus tended to be overlooked.

Those traditional, canonical and narrow approaches will not serve us well here. Pursuing an historian's approach to the subject, this essay considers the portrait not so much as an aesthetic creation but rather as an artefact of its time; less as a contribution to the decorative arts and more as a form of social and political discourse. By largely waiving aesthetic considerations, this approach embraces a much wider range of stylistic possibilities and an equally wide range of portrait patrons and subjects. Both vernacular paintings (those which followed no particular formal principles of style) and naive paintings (those vernacular works which exhibit little professional training on their creator's part) come into focus along with the formal and polite. Subjects situated far below the landed classes and Court circle must also command attention. Portraits commissioned not by individuals but by civic institutions, of their founders, officials and benefactors, round out this broader perspective.

This is by no means to deny the central importance of formal and 'polite' painting or of courtly portraiture. They still form the lion's share of the discussion to follow. Royal and Court circles provided the earliest portrait patronage in the British Isles, with the fashion percolating downwards, and taking on different agendas, thereafter. This most elite form of patronage thus provides the obvious place to begin. As the visual arts form one of those subject areas to which there is still no truly pan-

Britannic character in the sixteenth century (and as there is very little to say about the meagre portrait production in Wales or Ireland at this time) this essay first surveys the emergence of English and Scottish portraiture as factors in the shaping of royal imagery in both nations. It then examines the function of portraiture in the social and political discourse of the landed classes and other national elites. Finally, it suggests how portraiture also served urban people of the 'middling sort' and the civic institutions in which they were active. In addition, though the woodcut, manuscript illumination, funerary monument and other portrait forms played their part and will be noted from time to time, the focus rests mostly with the easel portrait, first on panel and eventually also on canvas, as the most visible and representative portrait type at this time.

Whether Scots or English, the people of the British Isles were indeed, as David Piper has said, 'slow to show their faces'.[3] Both courtly and civic portraiture – portraits of the rulers or leaders of such civic institutions as towns, cities and city-states, universities and university colleges, guilds and other civic institutions – had been well established in many parts of Europe for decades and even centuries before Tudor and Stewart kings turned, around the year 1500, to the panel portrait as a form of political, or indeed, personal, expression, and before civic bodies began to do so several decades later.

In their common concern to strengthen royal authority in their respective kingdoms, both James IV of Scotland (1488–1513) and Edward IV of England (1461–83) certainly encouraged a variety of visual art forms, including manuscript illumination and heraldic paintings. Some of the earliest English and Scottish royal portraits came in these forms. A continuing tradition of royal portraits as easel paintings on panel also came at roughly the same time in both kingdoms, with Henry VII's patronage from the mid-1490s being paralleled in James IV's patronage from the first years of the new century. There seems also to have been some early interchange between the two traditions. In 1502 James paid £14 to 'the Inglis payntour' referred to as 'Mynours' for bringing paintings of Henry VII, his wife Elizabeth, and the young Prince Arthur from England, probably as gifts to mark the 'perpetual peace' between the two nations concluded in that year. 'Mynours' may then have stayed on to paint James's new queen, Margaret Tudor, in the following year.[4]

Given anything like an equivalent level of material wealth and a similar concentration of political authority around the monarchy, there is every reason to expect that Scottish courtly portraiture would have continued on a course parallel to England's for a long time to come. But this, of course, was not to happen. Instead, the instability of the Scottish monarchy from the death of James V in 1542 to James VI's coming of age in the 1580s, marked by royal absences and minorities, frequent regencies, and the triumph of the aristocratic periphery rather than the royal centre, precluded such an output. This leads us to turn first to the fuller and much better documented English scene before returning to the Scottish experience later on.

Henry VII (1485–1509) cannot quite be considered the first truly 'Renaissance monarch' in the British Isles, an accolade which properly belongs to his son and namesake. Yet he did begin to take on board Sir John Fortescue's emphasis, in *The Government of England* of about 1479, on the restoration of strong monarchy as the key to stability, and he did see at least something of the role which visual imagery might play in that strategy. Along with patronage devoted to architecture (especially in Richmond Palace and the chapel of King's College, Cambridge) and to manuscript illumination (especially in the royal library established at Richmond), portraiture served Henry as a ready means of accomplishing this end and legitimizing his own rule.

Though easel painting must take pride of place in our discussion of the subject, Henry VII by no means restricted his support of royal portraits to that genre which would become the main and most visible portrait form. In completing his new palace at Richmond around the turn of the century he commissioned frescos of some of the Angevin and Plantagenet kings for the wall spaces between the windows of the Great Hall. Though no trace survives of these Richmond frescos, they clearly served to associate Henry with the long line of his putative forebears, thus emphasizing his rightful place in that line of kings. They provide a link between Henry III's similar commission for the painted chamber of Westminster Palace (*c.* 1267) on the one hand and Holbein's work on Henry VIII's Whitehall on the other.

Other *non*-easel portraiture of this reign proved similarly didactic, contributing additional approaches to the theme of Henry's authority. Naturally, portraits in several forms show Henry wearing a crown. But in many cases that crown is not the open diadem of the French or most other kings. It is instead a revived English use of the closed crown of gold, denoting claims to imperial rather than merely regal authority. This appears again in the king's image on new coinage issued in 1489 and 1504, in a stained-glass image of the royally endowed Magnificat window at Great Malvern, in illuminated manuscripts, including court records, and in woodcut illustrations in printed books.[5]

Though these other forms of portraiture would soon pale before the fuller development of easel-paintings in decades to come, non-easel works still weighed more heavily under Henry VII. Easel portraits of Henry, his wife Elizabeth, and his presumed heir Prince Arthur, certainly state their case for the legitimacy of the line and the extent of its authority. Yet they do so in a relatively low-key manner, and in a style and range of iconographic devices which barely hint at the power-laden imagery of Renaissance kings which followed but a few years later.

Taken together, however, all these portrait forms taken together do stake out many of the discursive themes which would run through Tudor royal portraiture for the duration of the dynasty. These include an emphasis on the legitimacy of the Tudor accession, the continuity of their line, the availability of particular Tudor hands in marriage, and deep-rooted historical claims to both power and authority, even – as we see in the closed crowns – to *imperium.*

For the triumph in England both of easel portraiture itself and of the full-blown reception of Renaissance notions of how kingship should be displayed, we must wait for Hans Holbein the younger to arrive on the English scene, first in his brief visit of 1526–8, and then especially in his permanent settlement of 1532 to his death in 1543. Holbein did more than any other foreign painter to bring England up to speed with continental portraiture. In this he established a path of royal service to be followed by such powerful visual publicists as Rubens under James I and Van Dyck under Charles I. In addition, and right from his first visit, he opened up the fashion for portraiture to social groups beyond the royal family: to members of the landed elite, to churchmen like Archbishop William Wareham, and to 'new men' of a more secular bent, men like Sir Brian Tuke, Sir Thomas Cromwell and Sir Thomas More, who would form the backbone of Tudor government right to the end of the dynasty. He at least held out the availability of portraiture to the middling sorts of people in both agrarian and urban society, painting a number of German merchants of the London steelyard, though – so far as we know – finding no takers amongst their native English counterparts.

Holbein was not the only foreign painter who enjoyed royal patronage under Henry VIII. A number of others, Italians as well as other Northerners, came for short periods of time. A few, including the miniaturists and illuminators Simon Benninck and both Gerard Hornebolte and his son Lucas came with their families in the 1520s to settle for good. Lucas Hornebolte, who came to England by 1524 and stayed on until his death in 1544, actually held the title of King's Painter by royal patent, with a stipend greater than Holbein's. And although, as Sir Thomas Elyot bewailed in *The Boke of the Governour* of 1533, the 'better sort' of people still eschewed training in the fine arts for their children, there were even a few native English portraitists like John Bettes (*fl. c.* 1531–70) who also worked in and around the Court circle. But none of these men, and (with Benninck's daughter Levina Teerlinc) women worked in anywhere near so many different approaches to the craft, were anything like so prolific, or had such a prominent role in conveying the didactic programme of the regime and its principle supporters as the great Holbein.

It may also to be said that Holbein's timing was as impeccable as his taste. At a time when Henry VIII asserted his control over the church and strove to outshine his contemporary rivals Francis I of France and the emperor Charles I, the employment of visual imagery in the service of crown and state called for someone of his abilities as never before. Contemporary aesthetic models for such visual promulgation were also near to hand. Some still invoked the lingering influence of the English Gothic. More of them drew on contemporary Renaissance models, as interpreted both by a few invited painters from the southern, Italian school as well by the larger number of northern Flemish, German and Dutch craftsmen. Besides Holbein, these included such immediate (if lesser) successors as Guillim Scrots (*fl. c.* 1545–52), Gerlach Flicke (*fl. c.* 1547–58) and Hans Eworth (*fl. c.* 1550–74). The turn towards Renaissance style and iconographic programmes also came about through Henry's keen rivalry with Francis I and the cultural milieu of his energetic, lavish and culturally precocious Court. Henry could hardly have ignored or failed to compete with the splendour of the Field of the Cloth of Gold at which the two kings met in 1520, or the work of the French royal portraitist Francois Clouet (*c.* 1485–1540).

Three of Holbein's works, chosen from an impressively large output, illustrate the centrality of his oeuvre to Henry's political programme. They address themes which were central to the dynasty and proclaim images of kings and queens which were dramatically new in their tone, form and style. The first of these is the 1537 Whitehall mural of his father and himself with their wives, Elizabeth of York and Jane Seymour, mother of Henry's son and heir: a painting which we know only from a 1667 copy (Plate 25.1). Holbein has grouped his four figures around a large inscribed plinth whose text proclaims the wisdom and majesty of the Tudor line, a line of which '. . . none greater was ever displayed'. Both plinth and figures stand within an architectural setting associating the group with the grandeur of Renaissance interiors. The figures themselves display personal imagery emphasizing the wisdom and legitimacy of the older generation and the power and determination of the younger. The

Plate 25.1. Remigius van Leemput after Hans Holbein the Younger, 'Henry VII, Elizabeth of York, Henry VIII, and Jane Seymour' ('The Whitehall Mural') 1667. The Royal Collection © 2003 Her Majesty the Queen, Elizabeth II.

portrayal of Henry VIII in this group, modelled directly on a Holbein of Henry alone done the year before, stands as our most familiar and essential image of that king and his reign. Square-jawed and barrel-chested, hands on hips, feet wide apart and pugnacious glare to the forefront, Holbein's Henry VIII stares down any challenge to his rule over state or church. His laconic assertion of power yields not an inch to Clouet's 'Francois I', Titian's Venetian doges, or anything else in the Renaissance portrait catalogue.

The second example, albeit not a portrait in the strictest sense, is the complex title-page woodcut for the Great Bible of 1539, in which Holbein has Henry enthroned at top centre, just below a squeezed-in God. He is handing down to Thomas Cranmer, representing the church, on his right and to Thomas Cromwell, representing secular society, on his left, copies of the new Bible: the word of God to be distributed in turn further down those two chains of command. With all English parish churches obliged to obtain this edition of the Bible, Henry's image as head of both state *and* church came to be distributed to every parish in the land. The era of mass distribution of political imagery had begun.

And the third is Holbein's portrait of the future king Edward VI, presented to Henry in 1538, and intended to proclaim the anticipated succession of Henry's long-awaited male heir. Though only fourteen months of age, Holbein's Edward sports his father's royal trappings and image: a regal, gold-threaded and scarlet over-garment with gold embroidered sleeves protruding, holding an object which seems to be both child's rattle and king's sceptre. His right hand extends, palm outwards, in a sign of benevolent authority, and his feathered cap closely mimics his father's. This, too, has an inscription, with verses by the Henrician publicist Richard Morison. Translated into English they read in part 'Little one, emulate your father and be the heir to his virtue; the world holds nothing greater . . .'.

No painter before Rubens would fill Holbein's shoes as the dominant Court painter of his day, and arguably not even Rubens did as much to form the essential imagery of a reign. It is therefore no slight on their tenure to say that neither Edward nor Mary found an equivalent in their brief reigns. Partly because of their brief time on stage, partly through their necessary preoccupations with the rapid succession of crises which marked those years, and perhaps partly, too, because they lacked their father's understanding of the power of visual imagery, royal portraiture did not play as great a role or receive as much attention in these years.

A number of portraits of Edward, mostly anonymous, assert an imagery of command, but they necessarily speak of promise rather than achievement. With the reign of Mary we come to a new problem in the projection of royal authority, as the awkward reality of the royal youth gave way to the awkward reality of the royal gender. Images of Mary stand in stark contrast to those of Henry in several respects, but the impossibility of duplicating the Henrician image of the warrior king created an obvious iconographic void which would not be successfully worked out until well into the reign of her sister Elizabeth.

That is not to say that royal portraiture took a holiday in this interval, or that some of it did not address Mary's gender very directly. The Catholic sympathizer Hans Eworth in particular painted Mary several times, using a variety of images to denote her royal status, borrowing to create that effect from some of Holbein's devices in portraits of Christina of Denmark and Anne of Cleves.[6] But the reality of an unmarried female monarch bore with it a new set of problems, and there were limits to how much of the muscular, virile and warrior-king imagery attached to her father, or even a delicately masculine imagery attached to her brother, could be applied to her. Ironically, the closest any portraitist came to addressing these problems directly seems to have been the imperial painter Antonis Mor. But his intriguing seated view of the queen may have had much more to do with representing her obedience to Philip of Spain than with reigning over her own realm.[7]

Though one could hardly ignore the implications of queenship for the realities of mid-Tudor policy, those implications did not become an especially dominant preoccupation in royal portraits until Elizabeth's reign. It was not long into her reign before alternative images, taken from both biblical and classical sources, explored the possibilities of feminine virtue instead. Sometimes they did so at Mary's expense. Lucas de Heere's highly allegorical 'Family of Henry VIII' of 1572 has Elizabeth ushered into her father's presence by goddesses of peace and plenty, while Mars, the god of war, ushers Mary and Philip into the opposite side of the scene. The painting of 'Elizabeth and the Three Goddesses' of 1569, possibly by Hans Eworth, places Elizabeth in the company of Juno, Pallas and Venus. And George Gower's 'Sieve Portrait' of around 1579, still finely modelled in the polite fashion of the northern Renaissance, identifies Elizabeth with Petrarch's vestal virgin Tuccia, who proved her virginity by carrying a sieve full of water without it leaking through. Other images included the biblical Deborah, Spenser's chaste huntress Belphoebe, and Ovid's (and others') Astraea the Virgin.

For the first twenty years of so these portraits remained fairly conventional in their composition and aesthetic qualities, relying heavily on foreign painters trained in the northern Renaissance tradition and on a growing number of English craftsmen who often learned from the former. But with works like Marcus Gheeraerts the Elder's full-length portrait of around 1580–5,[8] portraits of the queen begin to leave the mainstream of contemporary European conventions of polite portraiture to reach out in several quite new, complexly allegorical, anatomically distorted, and often wildly unconventional directions. Along this short-lived but fascinating sidetrack in the history of English portraiture we find, for example, the anatomically distorted extremes of William Segar's (?) 'Ermine' portrait of around 1585, the anonymous 'Armada' portrait series of about 1588, and the largest and most surrealistic of all, the younger Gheeraerts's huge and striking 'Ditchley Portrait' of around 1592 (Plate 25.2).

These extremely stylized, two-dimensional, crudely modelled and highly allegorical works, definitely vernacular without precisely becoming 'naive', were no mere accidents, nor did they represent a sudden collapse of available artistic skill. By a royal proclamation of 1563 and other devices, Elizabeth closely controlled her portrait imagery. She forbade unauthorized portraits to be done, and in 1596 prompted the destruction of unauthorized portraits. Rather, these 'distorted' views followed deliberately from the quite remarkable outpouring of imagery, mostly in a highly allegorical literature of devotion, which we think of as 'the cult of Elizabeth'. They followed, too, from the self-imposed cultural isolation of Protestant England from the traditions of Renaissance neo-classicism best exemplified by the Catholic powers of the day. These strident and even shrill images reflect better than most even of the most brilliant literary efforts of that golden age the tension-ridden and wholly insecure apotheosis of Elizabeth's reign. They are driven by the realities of the Spanish Armada and continuing struggles with Spain, or the Irish War, of Essex's revolt, and of an ageing, isolated and childless queen.

Even at its own climax during these same years Scottish royal and courtly portraiture pales in every respect by comparison. Though not lacking for its own tensions at almost any time in the same century, and for reasons noted above, Scotland had simply failed to develop portraiture as a significant form of political discourse. After promising beginnings early in the century it developed, as we have seen, only by fits and starts thereafter. The paucity of Scottish portrait production, and the poorer survival rate of portraits which were produced, makes it impossible to discuss at anything like the same level of detail or with the same degree of confidence as the English.

James V (1513–42), like his near contemporary Henry VIII in England, was the first of his line to encourage a systematic reception of Renaissance style in the

Plate 25.2. Marcus Gheeraerts the Younger, 'Elizabeth I' ('The Ditchley Portrait'). By courtesy of the National Portrait Gallery, London.

humanities and fine arts. But unlike Henry, James concentrated more on architecture than painting, and drew his inspiration, his stylistic models and many of his craftsmen from the very French whom Henry saw as intense rivals. And if royal patronage of the arts in general, and portraiture in particular, slowed down after the death of both monarchs, political instability and economic hardship allowed much less continuity on the Scottish side of the border than on the English. Mary Stewart's thirteen-year childhood absence in France (1548–61), and the consequent rule of her kingdom by a succession of regents, left no commanding centre around which any traditions of courtly portraiture could coalesce.

While Mary's return to her kingdom in 1561 promised a wholesale importation of the French Renaissance Court culture in which she had been raised, her abdication just six years later, followed by the long and troubled regency for her son James VI, nipped such potential in the bud. This is a little ironic, for Mary herself seems to have been the darling of a vibrant French Court culture in its first real blush of Renaissance style. She herself was drawn and painted a number of times in the emerging and very fashionable Fontainebleau style which had come to prominence at the French Court in these years. In addition, there were probably more images drawn and painted of Mary in her English captivity, including two miniatures by Nicholas Hilliard, than in her years in Scotland.

Notwithstanding these long discontinuities, Scotland did develop at least a modest courtly portraiture in the sixteenth century. Following the early years of James VI's reign, as noted above, there was at least one effort at a portrait series of Scottish kings, in which five such worthies were painted on small panels, probably for the triumphant royal entry of the fifteen-year-old James VI in 1579.[9] Though they do aim to connect James with his forbears in the way that Henry VII did at Richmond and Henry VIII at Whitehall, they remain strikingly lifeless in appearance, laconic in imagery, and wholly medieval in style and form (Plate 25.3).

Some conventional portraits of prominent people continued to be done during the 1560s and 1570s, including anonymous depictions of the earl of Bothwell (1566) and George, fifth earl Seton (c. 1570s).[10] Yet it is not until the last twenty years of the century that the work of Arnold Bronkhorst (fl. c. 1578–83) and his successor as royal painter, the Dutchman Adrian Vanson (fl. c. 1581–1601) brought new energy to the genre. As Duncan Thompson has noted, these years mark the point at which Scottish portraiture can be approached fully from the visual rather than primarily from the documentary record.[11]

Bronkhorst first came to Scotland around 1578 not, ironically, to paint, but rather to prospect for gold at the behest of the brilliant English miniaturist Nicholas Hilliard. He is known to have painted several members of the Scottish aristocracy both before and after taking a post as Court painter to James VI in 1580, and completed at least two portraits of the young king before he returned to London in 1583. Bronkhorst cannot be called especially imaginative; he created no particularly polemical or distinctive image of his royal patron. But he did serve to revive the office of the King's Painter, and his portraits show young James as a serious, somewhat stylishly dressed teenaged prince, a wise ruler in the making.

Vanson replaced Bronkhorst as Court painter by 1584 and served to 1602. This span covered James from the ages of eighteen to thirty-six, from young adulthood to what passed for early middle age in that era, from the coming into his own as king of Scotland to the eve of his accession as king of England. While one might have wished for a more vivid imagery of these years, or a larger output to mark them, Vanson's few known portraits of James further enhance the view of James as sagacious, deliberate and dignified. His most significant painting of the king, at age twenty-nine, in 1595, conveys these qualities especially well (Plate 25.4).[12] It may have been done to signal what the English might expect from James as claimant to the English throne, and has been considered the most influential image of James painted prior to that event. Somewhat understated by contemporary English standards, it depicts James alone, with a laconic identifying inscription but no props

Plate 25.3.   Anon., 'James V of Scotland'. Scottish National Portrait Gallery.

or background scenes, in a gold-threaded doublet and ermine cloak. He wears a tall, bejewelled hat instead of a crown, and with the conspicuous letter A, in (somewhat ironic) homage to his consort Anne of Denmark, perched front and centre on the brim. The most striking element is the face, turned slightly downward, eyes staring warily and sceptically out from under slightly closed lids, as if to spy out and reflect on the view before him before taking action. This image of 'the wisest king' had already appeared on coinage of 1590, and would appear again in a Vanson miniature of James also from 1595.[13] Vanson also left his mark as a portraitist to the Scottish nobility at the end of the century, producing what appears to be the largest body of aristocratic portraits painted by a single Scottish painter for the entire century.

Certainly in England and to some extent in Scotland the style, tone and semiotic vocabulary for portraiture of the social elites – the landed gentry, aristocracy, Court figures and some professionals – took their visual cues in one way or another from Court models. Easel portraiture amongst these elites only came into being well after the resumption of political stability in England under Henry VII and, north of the border, James V. In the context of the evolving, Court-centred nature of England's

Plate 25.4. Adrian Vanson, 'James VI of Scotland'. Scottish National Portrait Gallery.

Tudor government especially, the developing relations between the Court and the landed classes, the assertion of a newly risen, often affluent, and increasingly sophisticated element within those classes, and the fashion for portraiture created by Holbein and his contemporaries, all stimulated patronage of polite portraiture even further beyond the Court circle after about the 1530s. In addition, a developing sense of courtly behaviour, emanating from conduct books in general and works like Erasmus's *De Civilitate* and Castiglione's *Book of the Courtier* in particular, helped create conventions of gentility in pose, expression and dress.

Newly risen families bent on announcing their social arrival and older, more established families seeking to defend their accustomed standing began to engage, not in the belligerent activities of the previous century, but rather in an intensely competitive conspicuous consumption. In this fiercely competitive milieu, portraiture, no less than the indulgence in fine clothes, jewellery and the building of country estates, served as common coinage. As the late Lawrence Stone once put it, 'Noblemen and gentlemen wanted above all formal family portraits, which take their place along with genealogical trees and sumptuous tombs as symptoms of the frenzied status-seeking and ancestor worship of the age. What patrons demanded was evidence of the sitter's position and wealth by opulence of dress, ornament, and background.'[14]

'Opulence of dress, ornament and background' was exactly what such patrons got for their money. In addition, as the Tudor state became increasingly Court-centred, and as political opportunity came increasingly to depend on royal favour, service to the crown became an ever more present theme in such paintings. Added to the extremely complex iconographic programmes worked out in contemporary literature and some other discursive forms, and driven by the distinctive Elizabethan mix of neo-chivalric, classical and biblical imagery, English courtly portraiture followed royal models to unparalleled heights of semiotic complexity by the century's end. Most courtly portraits were of individual subjects, done in the formal or polite styles of the age. But a number were multiple portraits, of entire family groups or married couples, parents and children, and other such combinations. Group or double portraits like the anonymous 1567 depiction of 'William Brooke, 10th Lord Cobham and his family' (showing Cobham, his wife and sister-in-law, six children and several pets, surrounded by a strikingly dense and complex imagery of material goods), or Hans Eworth's 1559 'Lady Dacre and her Son', often conveyed complex narrative programmes relating whole chapters in a family's history.[15]

Three examples of such courtly portraiture serve to mark the stages of this visual self-fashioning. One of the earliest and best expressions of the newly risen professional in the service of the Tudor state is magnificently announced in Holbein's 1527 study of Thomas More, now in New York's Frick collection. Anxious to display his skill as a newly arrived continental painter seeking affluent patronage, Holbein spared no effort in presenting More as best (indeed, as monumentally) as he could: sagacious in expression, flamboyant for the time in his brightly highlighted fur-and-velvet dress, and unmistakably associated with the service of the state by his gold livery collar with its Norman portcullis and the Tudor rose. In its northern Renaissance style, drapery-laden setting, and closely observed facial features, indeed in its very choice of a subject outside the circle of the royal family, this was an extremely precocious work for its time.

The well-known if anonymous early Elizabethan (c. 1564) portrait of Robert Dudley, earl of Leicester, lacks some of Holbein's sensitivity, but it shows how rapidly the iconographic complexity of courtly portraiture had evolved over the intervening generation. Here we see another man on the rise, albeit through quite different abilities, and one whose fortunes rested just as much on royal favour as More's. The imagery has become equally more diverse and blatant, alluding by various devices to the earl's personal genealogy and affluence, his ties to crown and state, his cosmopolitan and sophisticated acculturation extending to neo-classical civilization, his ability to command loyalty, his chivalric commitment to defend his mistress, and even his much vaunted horsemanship.[16]

A late Elizabethan (c. 1590) portrait of another would-be servant of the crown, Nicholas Hilliard's miniature of George Clifford, third earl of Cumberland, exemplifies a third stage in Tudor courtly portraiture (Plate 25.5). Here, as in later portraits of the queen herself, the physical features have been distorted for effect and the imagery has become even more complex and less transparent. We see Clifford in

Plate 25.5. Nicholas Hilliard, 'George Clifford, Third Earl of Cumberland (1158–1605)'. © National Maritime Museum.

his role as queen's champion, a product of the neo-chivalric turn taken by Court culture in the 1580s and 1590s. He poses with a lance, his gauntlet thrown down in challenge to all comers, his lady's glove tucked into his hat to proclaim the object of his devotion. Details of costume, pose, setting, colours, landscape all have their complex meanings to the semiotically literate contemporaries who would have seen this work. In its progress from Holbein's More to Hilliard's Clifford, the visual discourse of state service has moved from the laconic and highly focused under-statement to the foothills of caricature itself.

Aside from being fewer in number and slower to appear, late-century portraits of the Scottish landed elite bore roughly the same sorts of intentions, but they remained fewer in number and entirely more conservative in form and semiotic content. They did, however, include one form not seen in England. This was the 'revenge portrait', done of murdered leaders, and preserved as invocations for revenge in the persistent Scottish tradition of the blood feud. The most famous of these is perhaps that of the 'bonny earl of Moray' of 1592, whose near-naked body lies with wounds fully exposed, but several others were also completed before the turn of the century: for example, of the murdered Lord Darnley around 1567, of the regent Moray after his assassination in 1570, and of one of the earl of Mar's murdered servants in 1595, 'with the nomber of the shots and wounds to appeare the maire horrible and rewthfull to the behalders'.[17] Mar later engaged in a variation on the theme by having a picture of his foe, the laird of Johnstone, painted in blood as a means of labelling him a murderer: the portrait as 'wanted poster'!

Especially in England, and perhaps to a limited extent in Scotland, copies of portraits of eminent figures both English and (sometimes) foreign were widely made and sold from at least the half-way mark of the century. While some were painted by regional or itinerant craftsmen in provincial centres or great country houses, others, especially in London, were being produced by large workshops devoted to such work. Fruits of this production were commonly hung in the country houses of the day, in long galleries and other spaces alongside paintings of family and friends. They no doubt served as decoration, but also as declarations of admiration for or devotion to their subjects, and thus often as statements of personal loyalties in matters of politics and religion. By the mid-century it became increasingly common for such copies, in the form of prints as well as paintings, to be purchased and displayed by the middling sorts of people as well, so that even dwellings well below the level of the country house might have their pictures.

Portraits of family members were frequently given as gifts to cement alliances with other families or offered as tokens of friendship. Often they marked milestones in a life, or were simply intended to create a record of what one looked like at a particular occasion or time of life. As early as 1549 the twenty-year-old Somerset yeoman's son and Oxford drop-out Thomas Whythorne could interrupt his search for work as a music tutor in London to visit a portrait shop, purchase a portrait of a woman playing a lute, and then commission one of himself. This would be the first of four portraits Whythorne would have done of himself over his lifetime, collected so that he could have a record of how age changed his appearance through the years.[18]

One portrait type which was developed especially to serve such personal and more intimate motives, and which became more highly developed and enduring in England than anywhere else, is the portrait miniature. This intricate art form came to England at least in part through the influence of Flemish illuminators such as Benninck and Hornebolte in the 1520s, and perhaps as well, though this has yet to be investigated, through native English manuscript illuminators. From that early start its provenance has been traced from Hornebolte and Benninck, through Holbein and Benninck's talented daughter, Levina Teerlinc, and then on to the English masters Nicholas Hilliard and his pupil Isaac Oliver by the end of the century.

Miniatures required a highly specialized technical skill and quite different materials from conventional portraits. Instead of producing an image for semi-public display as with most other portrait types, they conveyed instead an intimate, private image, meant for the eyes of a very small circle of viewers closely associated with the sitter. Instead of being displayed openly, they were conventionally kept in the intimate and closed confinement of a bureau drawer, a locket, or some other such private and dedicated space. Yet even these highly valued and jewel-like objects played their role in contemporary political and social discourse: they were often given as gifts to mark intimate occasions, to show favour or thanks, or to mark personal milestones.

Save perhaps for the allusion to Thomas Whythorne's experiences, all the portrait forms discussed to this point, and many of the actual portraits, will seem broadly familiar. All depicted the elites of the day: royalty, gentry and aristocracy, courtiers, high government officials or similarly prominent figures. Save for the more bizarrely distorted depictions of Elizabeth, most essentially conformed to contemporary aesthetic conventions. They were executed by relatively skilled and experienced, if not necessarily by full-time, 'limners' (painters of portraits). All but the miniature, which played its own political role as a token of affection or loyalty to the recipient but which was often much more candid, served as self-fashioned imagery to a greater or lesser extent. And all seem to have been commissioned by an individual patron, often the sitter him or herself, for motives which were personal as well as implicitly political or social.

Yet these were not the only sort of portraits produced either in England or Scotland during the era at hand. A substantial number were commissioned by groups of people, often by civic institutions, to commemorate figures of civic importance in the past or present life of particular communities or civic bodies. These institutional patrons included the governing bodies of corporate towns and boroughs; of schools, university colleges, and charitable foundations; of livery companies and inns of court. The civic portraiture differed from the personal portrait in its essential purpose, and therefore also in its provenance, places of display, semiotic programmes, and, at least some of the time, in its style. The existence of this type has been recognized in art historical circles slowly if at all, and yet no discussion of portraiture as political discourse can ignore it.

If the people of the British Isles were relatively slow to show their face on board or canvas, civic institutions were even slower. Cities and towns throughout much of western Europe – major centres like Paris, Amsterdam and Venice as well as more modest ones like Toulouse and Urbino – often had well-established traditions of civic portraiture long before the English and Scottish even had portraits of their kings and queens. It would take several decades after the advent of royal portraiture in England and Scotland before most civic institutions would turn to such expression.

In England this tardiness seems to have followed partly from the relatively slow acquisition of civic autonomy in those institutions prior to the Reformation. That tardiness gave way with the assertion of civic authority, especially amongst towns and cities, which followed the seismic upheavals in landholding and local governance marked by that event. In Scotland, where the relative autonomy of at least the major boroughs had been well established well before the Reformation, this tardiness may be due instead to the lack of visual models, or to the simple financial duress in which most towns and cities found themselves.

Whatever the reason, it is nevertheless the case that traditions of civic portraiture as easel paintings do not go back very far before the mid-sixteenth century in either kingdom, nor become well established before the very last decades of that century. They begin to appear in England only in the 1560s, and become relatively common only from about the 1580s.

If the civic portrait arose for different purposes than those commissioned and painted by individual people or their families and friends, we must ask what aims it fulfilled, and how to interpret its discursive role. The most distinguishing mark of the civic portrait is that it exemplifies the virtues of the institution or group rather than the personal virtues of the sitter. While it does not necessarily deny personal achievements, it concentrates on the subject's relationship and contribution to the civic body, his or her exemplifications of civic virtues. The semiotic programme of the civic portrait privileged those attributes, virtues and achievements which contributed to the fame of institution over those which distinguished the person. Towards that end, it often displayed the institution's coat of arms along with or instead of the individual's. The objects or implements held by or displayed near the subject, and the inscriptions on the painting or its frame, speak of the sitter's civic role before addressing his or her personal character. Even familiar props must often be read in a different way in such works: the clutched pair of gloves, for example, which signifying, amongst other things, gentility in the personal portrait but freeman's status, also amongst other things, in the civic. The location of display now typically becomes the courtroom, mayor's or master's parlour, or council chamber rather than the long gallery or stairwell of the country house. As with the Norwich series of mayoral portraits, civic portraits may be framed in a uniform manner, and be of similar size, so to emphasize the institutional continuity of mayors or, less often, college presidents or schoolmasters. Even literal verisimilitude of appearance may have been less important than in personal portraits. In addition, and quite curiously, civic portraits are much more likely to have been done posthumously, sometimes several decades or even a century or more after the death of the subject, making it impossible to achieve a true likeness.[19]

One may well wonder why these portraits were not done during the lifetime of the subject, as would have been the case with the very large majority of portraits of the landed classes, instead of as much as a century after that subject's death. The apparent answer to that question tells us a lot about the wider purposes of civic portraiture *per se*, and to its distinctiveness from other types. Two explanations may be offered. One concerns the disruption of civic memory occasioned by the Reformation; the other concerns the urgent need for civic institutions after the Reformation to reconstruct an alternative civic memory which served their needs. Let us take up these possibilities in turn.

We may think of a 'civic memory' as nothing more than the collective sense of the past which was held in common by members of a particular civic community. Such a sense would have embraced that community or body's identity, its history, its place in the history of the realm, and its own particular heroes and worthies. It would have served as a powerful unifying force, and standard around which to rally local loyalties and identities.

Before the Reformation, part of that memory had to do with being a Christian and with belonging to a particular parish community; it entailed a mnemonic association with particular events and historic figures linked to that faith and community. These might well have included the patron saint for which a parish church or cathedral or religious guild would have been named. Icons and images of various sorts in ecclesiastical buildings, stained-glass windows, plate and other such items, would all have commemorated the religious heritage. Noteworthy individuals would have been remembered by the preservation of funerary brasses, in prayers for their souls offered in obits and anniversaries, and in the periodic reading aloud in the Sunday service of the names on the parish bede-roll. In addition, very important people were commemorated in funerary monuments, by lavish gifts of plate or in statuary on biblical or related themes. These elements of the collective memory obviously played an important part in spiritual terms as a means of encouraging prayers for the souls of the departed. But they also served as important cultural icons of the local identity, and as political markers engendering respect for the community, its traditions and its leaders.

With the wholesale iconoclastic destruction of the material elements of the old faith in both Scottish and English Reformations – of the icons and images, bede-rolls and brasses – many points of reference in the community memory disappeared. Much of the sense of its own particular past went as well. Especially in an English national culture whose traditions of urban identity were relatively weak compared with a number of other northern European traditions, this was a critical loss.[20] It threatened the continuity of a local identity and, with that identity, the continuity of local loyalties, behavioural conventions, and respect for law and order on which civic society depended.

Especially in the era of rapid economic and social change which characterized English life from about the 1540s, when the turnover of urban populations was so quick and so many institutions were refounded or founded anew, civic leaders strove to create or reconstruct whatever elements of local identity they could. They hoped thereby to restore the traditional pride, respect and deference on which their governance depended. When the traditional institutions themselves had been destroyed or dissolved, they strove to create such memories from scratch in the new or refounded analogues. In consequence, the ensuing decades exhibited a highly polemical use of civic architecture and furnishing, and of the writing of civic histories.[21] Civic ruling elites frequently adopted a version of Protestantism which encouraged civic discipline and the perfection of the city or other community as a moral ideal.[22]

The creation of a secular form of civic portraiture, specifically to evoke and commemorate local civic heroes and heroines of both past and present times, worked toward the same end. What had not been necessary in quite the same way prior to the Reformation became more vital in its wake. Traditions of secular and personal portraiture had also by that time become well enough established to serve as discursive models. The infrastructure of portrait production had developed sufficiently to be on hand when required. The need to inculcate local and institutional loyalties against contemporary concerns for disorder and unrest grew rapidly thereafter.

This is the context in which we must interpret the commissioning of civic portraits such as we see, for example, in Norwich. Where individual mayors had been commemorated visually in funerary brasses from at least the early years of the fifteenth century, they came after the Reformation to be commemorated in the more secular form of the portrait. Thus we find, in this particularly heritage-conscious city, the largest collection of civic portraits, beginning around 1560, and including a number whose subjects had been deceased for as much as sixty years. But Norwich's example is unusual only in the number of portraits commissioned. Many of the larger corporate towns followed suit with portraits which often still exist. Portraits of similar intent, some of individuals and some of groups – some of old institutions and some of refounded ones, some of living people and some of those long departed – are often still to be found in their original institutional settings.

We see such paintings of founders, officials and benefactors not only in Norwich's Guildhall and Blackfriars; but in livery company halls such as the Merchant Taylors' and the Mercers'; in ancient schools such as Christ's Hospital (now in Horsham) and its namesake in Abingdon, and in virtually every one of the older college halls of Oxford and Cambridge. When such institutions were founded or refounded after the Reformation, we find them anxious to create a visual history in portraiture as soon as they could. Hence we have group portraits of foundation ceremonies: Holbein's huge 1540 'Great Picture' of the founding of the Barber Surgeons' Company; the much cruder but even larger anonymous group portrait of Edward VI giving the charter to Christ's Hospital; or the small and quite charming 1590s double portrait of John and Joan Cooke, former mayor and mayoress of Gloucester (deceased 1528 and 1543 respectively) marking their founding of St Mary de Crypt School in Gloucester (Plate 25.6).

Plate 25.6. 'John and Joan Cooke'. Courtesy of the Gloucester City Museum and Art Gallery.

In sum, neither English nor Scottish portraiture of the sixteenth century can fruitfully be considered on strictly aesthetic terms, nor were either of them ever considered 'works of art' at that time. Though circumstances permitted one to develop much more fully than the other, both were undeniably intended as forms of social and political discourse, with the vocabularly of that discourse determined by the objectives of the patron and the tenor of the times.

ACKNOWLEDGMENT

I should like to thank Norman Jones, Tarnya Cooper, Michael Wasser, Elizabeth Ewen, Margo Todd and Anne Thackray for their help and suggestions in the preparation of this essay.

NOTES

1. E.g., Auerbach, *Tudor Artists*; Mercer, *English Art*; Waterhouse, *Painting in Britain*.
2. Following in the wake of Sir Roy Strong, notable exemplars include Howard, *Tudor Image*; Howarth, *Images of Rule*; Llewellyn, *Funeral Monuments*; and Cooper, '*Memento mori* portraiture'.
3. Piper, *The English Face*, p. 21.
4. Apted and Hannabuss, *Painters in Scotland*, pp. 68–9.
5. Hoak, 'The iconography of the crown imperial', pp. 65–77.
6. Strong, 'Hans Eworth', pp. 93–134; Hearn, *Dynasties*, pp. 66–7.
7. Woodall, 'An exemplary consort'.
8. Private collection; see Hearn, *Dynasties*, pp. 41 and 86–7.
9. All are oil on panel and roughly 16 in × 13 in; they depict James I (d. 1437), James II (d. 1460) James III (d. 1488) and James V (d. 1542); Smailes, *Concise Catalogue*, nos. PG 682–PG 686.
10. Brown, *Noble Society in Scotland*, pp. 207–8, and Strong, 'Hans Eworth', pp. 103–6. The Bothwell and Seton portraits are, respectively, in the Scottish National Portrait Gallery (PG 869) and the National Gallery of Scotland (no. 309).
11. Thompson, *Painting in Scotland*, p. 7.
12. Scottish National Portrait Gallery PG 156.
13. Ibid., PG 1109.
14. Stone, *Crisis of the Aristocracy*, p. 712.
15. Located respectively in the Marquis of Bath's collection at Longleat and at the National Gallery of Canada, Ottawa.
16. Hearn, *Dynasties*, pp. 96–7 and plate 49.
17. Apted and Hannabuss, *Painters in Scotland*, p. 117.
18. Osborne, *The Autobiography of Thomas Whythorne*. I am grateful to David Dean and Norman Jones for bringing this source to my attention.
19. Tilyard, 'Civic portraits'; Morgan, 'The Norwich Guildhall portraits'.
20. On architecture and furnishing, Manley, *Literature and Culture*, especially p. 15; on civic histories Tittler, *Architecture and Power*.
21. Tittler, *The Reformation and the Towns*, chapter 13.

22. Collinson, *Religion of Protestants*, chapter 4; Collinson, *Birthpangs of Protestant England*, chapter 2; Underdown, *Fire from Heaven*.

BIBLIOGRAPHY

Apted, Michael and Hannabuss, Susan, *Painters in Scotland, 1301–1700: A Biographical Dictionary* (Edinburgh, 1978).

Auerbach, Erna, *Tudor Artists* (London, 1954).

Batschmann, Oskar, *Hans Holbein* (Princeton, NJ, 1997).

Brown, Keith, *Noble Society in Scotland: Wealth, Family and Culture from the Reformation to the Revolution* (Edinburgh, 2000).

Caldwell, David H. and Marshall, Rosalind K., *The Queen's World* (Edinburgh, 1987).

Campbell, Lorne, *Renaissance Portraits: European Portrait Painting in the Fourteenth, Fifteenth and Sixteenth Centuries*, (New Haven and London, 1990).

Collinson, Patrick, *The Birthpangs of Protestant England* (Basingstoke, 1988).

Collinson, Patrick, *The Religion of Protestants* (Oxford, 1982).

Cooper, Tarnya, '*Memento Mori* portraiture: painting, protestant culture and the patronage of middle elites in England and Wales' (PhD thesis, University of Sussex, 2001).

Foister, Susan, 'Paintings and other works of art in sixteenth century English inventories', *Burlington Magazine*, 123 (1981), 273–82.

Frith, Brian, *Twelve Portraits of Gloucester Benefactors* (Gloucester, 1972).

Hearn, Karen, ed., *Dynasties: Painting in Tudor and Stuart England, 1530–1630*, (London, 1995).

Hoak, Dale, 'The iconography of the Crown Imperial', in D. Hoak, ed., *Tudor Political Culture*, (Cambridge, 1995), pp. 54–103.

Howard, Maurice, *The Tudor Image* (1995).

Howarth, David, *Images of Rule: Art and Politics in the English. Renaissance, 1485–1649* (Berkeley, 1997).

Llewellyn, Nigel, *Funeral Monuments in Post-Reformation England* (Cambridge, 2000).

Lloyd, Christopher and Thurley, Simon, *Henry VIII: Images of a Tudor King* (London, 1990).

Macmillan, Duncan, *Scottish Art, 1460–1990* (Edinburgh, 1990).

Manley, Lawrence, *Literature and Culture in Early Modern London* (Cambridge, 1995).

Mercer, Eric, *English Art, 1553–1625* (Oxford, 1962).

Morgan, Victor, 'The Norwich Guildhall portraits: images in context', in Andrew Moore and Charlotte Crawley, eds, *Family and Friends: A Regional Survey of British Portraiture* (London, 1992) pp. 21–30.

Murdoch, John, Murrell, Jim, Noon, Patrick J. and Strong, Roy, *The English Miniature* (London and New Haven, 1981).

Osborne, James, ed., *The Autobiography of Thomas Whythorne* (Oxford, 1961).

Piper, David, *The English Face* (3 vols, London, 1957, 1978, 1992).

Smailes, Helen, ed., *The Concise Catalogue of the Scottish National Portrait Gallery* (Edinburgh, 1990).

Smailes, Helen, ed., *The Queen's Image* (Edinburgh, 1987).

Stone, Lawrence, *The Crisis of the Aristocracy* (Oxford, 1965).

Strong, Roy, *Artists of the Tudor Court: The Portrait Miniature Rediscovered, 1520–1620* (London, 1983).

Strong, Roy, *The Cult of Elizabeth: Elizabethan Portraiture and Pageantry* (London, 1977).

Strong, Roy, *The English Icon: Elizabethan and Jacobean Portraiture* (London and New York, 1969).

Strong, Roy, *Gloriana: The Portraits of Queen Elizabeth I* (London, 1987).

Strong, Roy, 'Hans Eworth: a Tudor artist and his circle', in Roy Strong, ed., *The Tudor and Stuart Monarchy: Pageantry, Painting and Iconography* (Woodbridge, 1995), vol. I, pp. 93–134.

Strong, Roy, *Holbein and Henry VIII* (London, 1967).

Thompson, Duncan, *Painting in Scotland, 1570–1650* (Edinburgh, 1975).

Tilyard, Virginia, 'Civic portraits painted for, or donated to the council chamber of Norwich Guildhall before 1687 . . .', (MA thesis, Courtauld Institute, 1978).

Tittler, Robert, *Architecture and Power: The Town Hall and the English Urban Community, c. 1540–1640* (1991).

Tittler, Robert, 'Civic portraiture and political culture in English provincial towns, ca. 1560–1640', *Journal of British Studies*, 37, 3 (July 1998), 306–29.

Tittler, Robert, 'John and Joan Cooke: civic portraiture and urban identity in Gloucester', in R. Tittler, *Townspeople and Nation, English Urban Experiences, 1540–1640* (Stanford 2001), pp. 81–99.

Tittler, Robert, *The Reformation and the Towns in England, Politcs and Political Culture, 1540–1620* (1998).

Underdown, David, *Fire from Heaven* (London and New Haven, 1992).

Waterhouse, Ellis, *Painting in Britain, 1530 to 1790* (4th edition, Harmondsworth, 1978).

Waterhouse, Ellis, *The Dictionary of 16th and 17th British Painters [sic]* (Woodbridge, 1988).

Woodall, Joanna, 'An exemplary consort: Antonis Mor's portrait of Mary Tudor', *Art History*, 14 (June 1990), 192–224.

Yates, Frances, *Astraea: The Imperial Theme in the Sixteenth Century* (London, 1975).

FURTHER READING

Sydney Anglo, *Images of Tudor Kingship* (1992).

Margaret Aston, 'Gods, saints and reformers: portraiture and Protestant England', in Lucy Gent (ed.), *Albion's Classicism* (1995) pp. 181–220.

Margaret Aston, *The King's Bedpost; Reformation and Iconography in a Tudor Group Portrait* (1993).

Dana Bentley-Cranch and Rosalind K. Marshall, 'Iconography and literature in the service of diplomacy', in Janet Hadley Williams (ed.) *Stewart Style, 1513–1542; Essays on the Court of James V* (1996) pp. 273–95.

Lorne Campbell and Susan Foister, 'Gerard, Lucas and Susanna Hornebout', *Burlington Magazine*, 127 (1986) 719–27.

Mary Edmond, *Hilliard and Oliver: The Lives and Works of Two Great Miniaturists* (1983).

Mary Edmond, 'Limners and picturemakers: new light on the lives of miniaturists and large-scale portrait painters working in London in the sixteenth and seventeenth centuries', *Walpole Society*, 47 (1978–80), 60–242.

Daniel Fischlin, 'Political allegory, absolutist ideology and the 'Rainbow Portrait' of Queen Elizabeth I', *Renaissance Quarterly*, 50, 1 (Spring 1997), 175–206.

Lucy Gent and Nigel Llewellyn (eds), *Renaissance Bodies: The Human Figure in English Culture, c. 1540–1660* (1990).

M. Hackett, *Virgin Mother, Maiden Queen, Elizabeth I and the Cult of the Virgin Mary* (1995).

John N. King, 'The godly woman in Elizabethan iconography', *Renaissance Quarterly*, 38 (1985), 41–84; and 'Queen Elizabeth I, representations of the virgin queen', *Renaissance Quarterly*, 43 (1990), 30–74.

John N. King, *Tudor Royal Iconography* (1989).

Peter Lord, *The Visual Culture of Wales: Imaging the Nation* (2000).

Andrew Moore, with Charlotte Crawley, *Family and Friends: A Regional Survey of British Portraiture* (1992).

John Phillips, *The Reformation of Images: Destruction of Art in England, 1535–1660* (1973).

Elizabeth W. Pomeroy, *Reading the Portraits of Queen Elizabeth I* (1989).

Robert Tittler, 'The Cookes and the Brookes: political uses of portraiture in town and country before the civil war', in G. MacLean, D. Landry and J. Ward (eds), *The Country and the City Revisited* (1999), pp. 58–73.

CHAPTER TWENTY-SIX

Architecture, Politics and Society

MALCOLM AIRS

The central role of buildings in the lives of the British people in the sixteenth century has only begun to be appreciated and explored by mainstream historians over the last generation or so. Previously, with a few notable exceptions, the architecture of the period had been largely studied in isolation from the society that had created it. The buildings of the elite were viewed in aesthetic terms which drew heavily on the classical taste which dominated architectural criticism from the seventeenth century onwards. From this perspective their achievements were scathingly dismissed.

It was only in the second half of the twentieth century that this narrow judgement of the significance of sixteenth-century architecture was challenged. The perception that buildings and the choices made about their form and appearance were primary evidence for understanding past societies was fostered by a new generation of scholars who began to publish in the years after the Second World War. For the first time they brought the techniques of serious historical research to bear in their chosen field and established architectural history as a recognized academic discipline. They went beyond the traditional preoccupation with style and attribution to explore the full potential of the documentary sources that were becoming available in public and private archives. In the process they helped to create a new understanding of the sixteenth century. Not only have they brought an economic and social perspective to the building process but they have also offered fresh insights on the nature of political power and cultural preferences. However, the value of their work is still barely recognized in the general history of the period. It is one of the strengths of this volume that the building history of Tudor Britain is integrated with the more traditional scholarly concerns of the historians of that remarkable age.

The sixteenth century was one of the great ages of building in the history of both kingdoms. Much has been demolished in subsequent centuries but the sheer amount of surviving fabric in both town and country is evidence enough of an extraordinary investment in building at all levels of society. As William Harrison observed in 1577 '. . . if ever curious building did flourish in England, it is in these years . . .'[1]

Once Henry VII had consolidated his hold on the English throne and secured his financial position, he set about a building campaign which created new palaces and ecclesiastical foundations with equal enthusiasm. If he set a standard for ostentatious building, it was comprehensively surpassed by Henry VIII, rightly described by Simon Thurley as 'the most prolific, talented and innovative builder on the English throne'.[2] After the fall of Wolsey in 1529 he devoted a truly remarkable amount of energy and his own personal time to modernizing, extending and new building a portfolio of residences that exceeded sixty properties by the time of his death in 1547. Mainly centred on the home counties around London, they provided the itinerant court with hospitality and hunting in equal measure and placed a great strain on the resources of the office of works.

None of his successors to the English throne was driven by the same impetus to build and under Elizabeth the initiative in architectural magnificence became the clear responsibility of the ambitious nobility. A deep personal rivalry with François I, king of France, had been one of the major motivations for the building programme of Henry VIII and in Scotland a similar ambition to claim a place on the wider European stage drove James IV to employ palatial architecture as an appropriate setting for courtly life. Before his untimely death on Flodden Field in 1513 he carried out major works at Edinburgh, Falkland, Holyrood, Linlithgow and Stirling as he sought to project himself as a Renaissance prince. His son, James V, inherited similar ambitions which were cemented by his marriage first to Madeleine de Valois, eldest daughter of the French king, and, after her death, to the daughter of the duke of Guise. The influence of French culture on the Scottish court was reinforced by the employment of French craftsmen on two of the most remarkable classical buildings in the British Isles, the south range at Falkland Palace and the royal apartments at Stirling Castle. Both were completed in 1541 and the following year James died. Just as in England, the second half of the century saw an hiatus in royal building punctuated only by the Chapel Royal at Stirling.

If royal building was concentrated on the first fifty years of the century, the appetite for new houses amongst the landed classes was spread across the whole period and in terms of sheer numbers probably exceeded that of any other century. The concept of the country house as a centre for the exercise of local power and the carefully fashioned display of learning, gentility and hospitality was essentially a creation of the sixteenth century in which the architecture, the formal gardens and the parkland all played a part. The status of a family was expressed by the house that they occupied and in a hierarchical society it clearly reflected both their public duties and their private culture. In a very real sense, there was an obligation to ensure that their dignity was appropriately maintained by their architectural taste. The form and appearance of the country house changed markedly during the course of the century as the passion for architectural novelty and emulation increased and this in turn acted as a further stimulus to build. The growth in the peerage and the inexorable rise in the numbers of the gentry was another factor which contributed to a country-house building boom. Newly established families of rank sought to announce their arrival by a suitable house and the older dynasties strove to keep up. Relative domestic peace and stability had rendered the castles and fortified houses of the middle ages obsolete and an increasing emphasis on personal comfort demanded new ways of living that could only be satisfied by new houses.

In England and Wales the dissolution of the monasteries in the late 1530s released hundreds of potential building sites onto the market which over the next generation both helped meet an existing demand and stimulated a further desire for new houses. Slightly later in Scotland the Reformation of 1560 had a similar effect as the church lands passed into lay hands. The building of most country houses was financed out of annual revenue and it was the growing economies of both kingdoms which sustained the new architecture. Developments in agriculture and industry and the expansion of overseas trade all contributed to the personal prosperity that was invested in building. And it was not just the great landed families who were rehousing themselves. In the towns and across the countryside, yeomen farmers and prosperous husbandmen, successful merchants and skilled craftsmen were modernizing their existing dwellings or building new ones in forms which announced a radical change in the way that they lived. If we add to all these domestic buildings the new civic buildings of the towns for governance, education and the care of the elderly, and the expansion of the universities, it becomes very clear just how important architecture is in establishing a rounded picture of sixteenth-century life.

Royal Works

Magnificence was the very essence of kingship. As Simon Thurley deftly defines it:

> Being magnificent was the art of being visibly richer and more powerful than the others. It was not enough that a king should rule, he must be seen to be ruling by being surrounded by richness which fitted his elevated state. The concept of magnificence is crucial to the understanding of the buildings and the court culture of the age.[3]

What the Tudor and the Stuart monarchs sought to demonstrate by their domestic buildings was their superiority over their mighty subjects by their ostentatious pursuit of this goal. Magnificence implied not just lavish expenditure but also learning, novelty and skill in the ways that it was expressed. All these qualities are present in the royal palaces. Before he became king, Henry VII spent much of his youth in exile in France where he experienced the courtly culture of the Burgundian legacy at first hand. The opulence and the setting for elaborate etiquette that were an essential part of that culture provided the inspiration for his first major building project at Richmond where he created a new palace out of the fire-damaged ruins of the royal manor of Sheen between 1498 and 1501. Richmond to the west of London was matched by his other great riverside palace at Greenwich to the east and between the two he built a more central house at Baynard's Castle. All of these works together with his additions to the Tower of London and Windsor Castle were in progress at approximately the same time and they mark a determined attempt by Henry to establish the legitimacy of the house of Tudor on the English throne by a building programme that placed him way above his subjects in terms of expenditure and display.

Henry's claim to the throne rested partly on his blood relationship to the Lancastrian King Henry VI and his posthumous popularity was assiduously cultivated by the Tudor monarch. In 1503 he began the construction of a mausoleum at Westminster Abbey to enshrine the bones of Henry VI lying at Windsor and to provide a suitable burial place for himself alongside his 'uncle of blessed memory'. With its elaborate plan of daring fenestration and richly carved walls, its slender towers and flying buttresses it is a remarkable expression of royal munificence. The interior is even more impressive. The massive windows illuminate the delicately fan-vaulted roof and pick out the profusion of statues which line the walls. The confident manipulation of the architectural forms and the iconography of the religious imagery are a superb climax to the English Gothic tradition. In spirit it is a medieval building commissioned by a monarch whose value and culture lay in the past.

However, instead of the traditional canopied tomb to Henry VI which was intended to be the focal point of the chapel and for which the architectural setting was created, the space behind the altar is occupied by a tomb to Henry VII and his queen in a totally different idiom. It is so different that it makes the surrounding sculpture, for all its richness, seem old-fashioned. The body of Henry VI remained at Windsor and in its place Henry VIII commissioned the Florentine sculptor Pietro Torrigiano to create a tomb to his parents which was to bring the Italian Renaissance to England in a complete and fully developed form. The wider European vision of the new monarch could not have been more strikingly expressed than in the contrast between the life-like modelling of the effigies on the tomb and the stiffness of the Gothic images on the building which houses it.

At his accession, Henry VIII was barely eighteen years old. He was slim, handsome, athletic and deeply intellectual. He had a particular talent for music and an enthusiasm for theology, astronomy and geometry. The international reputation of his Court led to an influx of scholars and artists from all over Europe. The commission to Torrigiano was part of this pattern of patronage but the cosmopolitan sophistication that it seemed to promise was never really fulfilled. It was only after the downfall of Wolsey in 1529 that Henry began to take a close personal interest in building. Previously, Wolsey had supervised Henry's building works as well as building on a lavish scale for himself at Hampton Court, York Place and Cardinal College, Oxford. He was in danger of upstaging the king in terms of architectural magnificence and that is surely one of the reasons for his fall. Henry took over Wolsey's projects and made them all bigger and more magnificent. York Place became Whitehall Palace, Cardinal College became Christ Church and Hampton Court over a period of ten years was greatly expanded on a truly palatial scale. One of the most symbolic acts at Hampton Court was the reconstruction of Wolsey's great hall to provide a regal space of epic proportions. Its hammer-beam roof looked to the medieval past but the carved pendants and the decorated spandrels of the trusses reflected the new Italianate taste. This stylistic dichotomy seems to represent a struggle between the new learning and a blatant display of power in which the latter was always going to win. The political and religious affairs of the later years of Henry's reign were to result in isolation from Europe which is reflected in architectural forms as well as the world of diplomacy. Henry was to remain a fanatical builder but, with the tantalizing exception of his hunting lodge at Nonsuch, begun in 1539, his achievements failed to match the sophistication of François I at Blois, Fontainebleau and elsewhere in France. The external carved and stucco decoration of Nonsuch, on which much of its fame rests, was used to demonstrate the virtues of the king and the power of his dynasty but it was to have little influence on the taste of his subjects after his death in 1547.

James IV of Scotland, like his Tudor counterparts, sought to project himself as a Renaissance prince. He expended a vast sum on palace-building to ensure that he was housed in a manner that became his position. At Linlithgow he continued his father's work to complete the courtyard plan and expand the accommodation creating similar public and private apartments to his English rivals. Parallel works were carried out at Holyrood and Falkland. At Edinburgh Castle he built an enormous new hall with a complex hammer-beam roof carried on classical stone consoles. The mingling of medieval form with advanced details pre-dated the same mixture at Hampton Court and is indicative of the deeply felt need of both monarchs to express their lineage as well as their learning. James is known to have had a passionate interest in medieval chivalry and his extensive works at Stirling gave full reign to this enthusiasm. His efforts to create an even grander palace than at Edinburgh can be seen in the damaged remains of the great forework, in his lodging range in the king's Old Building, and, above all, in the great hall with another hammer-beam roof. This was under construction at the time of his marriage to Margaret, the daughter of Henry VII, in 1503 and can be seen as a Scottish response to the great English royal halls such as that at Eltham Palace.

After his death in 1513, he was succeeded by his son, James V, who was to become a far more cosmopolitan architectural patron, directly inspired by his close connections with the French Court. Even before his successive French marriages in 1537 and 1538, he had travelled in France in the company of a French mason, Mogin Martin, and he was clearly deeply impressed by the architectural achievements of François I. The medieval romanticism of his father is still present in his earlier works, such as the gateways at Linlithgow and the towers at Holyrood and Falkland, but from 1537 when he began to remodel the south and east ranges at Falkland his taste had moved towards an altogether more sophisticated European idiom. In the east range he simply refaced the existing building but to the south he added new galleries in front of the chapel. The results were the most advanced classical facades in the whole of the British Isles at that date. The attached columns on high pedestals and flanking portrait medallions are distinctive motifs of the contemporary Loire school and show how profoundly James had come under the spell of his father-in-law. Although medallions had been used as a decorative feature at Hampton Court by Wolsey as early as 1521, at Falkland they are part of a coherent architectural scheme which unified both elevations. They are the product of French workmanship as well as architectural inspiration.

At Stirling from 1538 onwards James built a new quadrangular palace within the castle which reflected the protocol of Court life with a symmetrical pair of royal lodgings at first-floor level. Each of the lodgings had an outer hall, an inner hall, a chamber and then a series of small closets. The diminishing size of the spaces indicated the degree of appropriate public access to the monarch with the closets reserved for the closest intimates and body servants of the king and queen. The external elevations are profusely carved with recessed panels containing statues on twisted columns and waisted baluster shafts. More statues stand on pedestals above the cornice with a crenellated parapet above. The sheer exuberance of the palace contrasts strongly with its fortress surroundings and presents a civilized image of the Scottish Court with knowing references to the architecture of Italy and Germany as well as France. Built under the overall control of Sir James Hamilton of Finnart, the royal master of works, the workmanship was executed by French masons and it represents a fitting climax to a reign of astonishing architectural extravagance.

Plate 26.1. Falkland palace, Fife. French-influenced classical decoration on the south range of the courtyard built for James V, 1537–41. (Photo, Malcolm Airs)

James died in 1542 and, just as in England five years later, the period of excessive royal building was over. The initiative passed to the Court and the only significant royal building in the remainder of the century was the Chapel Royal at Stirling Castle built in 1593–4 by James VI to celebrate the baptism of Prince Henry. A simple and dignified rectangular building, it is lit by pairs of round-arched windows and entered through a centrally placed doorway in the form of a triumphal arch. The crow-stepped gables give it a northern air but its architectural restraint in contrast to the embellished facades of the palace across the courtyard shows how classical confidence had developed in Scotland over the course of a generation.

The Country House

For sixteenth-century builders, classicism was only part of an extensive architectural vocabulary. Undoubtedly, it was perceived as a language of culture and learning but it was absorbed into an equally strong sense of national identity that demanded full recognition of native architectural traditions in fashioning the houses that displayed their proper dignity and status. Only in the mid-century in England was there a moment when it seemed that the example of the Italian Renaissance was to become the accepted expression of courtier taste. But it proved to be a brief interlude before the architecture of the landed classes under both Elizabeth in England and James VI in Scotland entered an exhilarating phase of creativity without parallel in the rest of Europe.

The country house of a powerful man was a visible symbol of his position in society and his political ambition. With the establishment of the strong centralized Tudor state and the growing stability and prosperity of the Stewart kingdom, private houses became the focus for an extraordinary amount of capital investment over the course of the century as the public duties and the private culture of their builders evolved in a variety of complex ways. At the beginning of the century there was no clear break with the architecture of the immediate medieval past. The enclosed courtyard defined by ranges of domestic and service buildings remained the preferred form for the landed elite. The functions were usually separated into a service or base court and an inner court with accommodation for the household and the necessary state rooms. The outer walls were comparatively plain with few windows and little architectural embellishment. The emphasis was on the gatehouse through which the world outside was granted controlled access to the privileged spaces within. Although defence was no longer a consideration, the hierarchical nature of society could not have been expressed more starkly. The gatehouse proclaimed the authority of the owner. Some of the greater houses had two gatehouses: one in the outer court and another, usually more elaborately decorated, in the inner court. It was rank which dictated who was permitted to penetrate these symbolic barriers. Flanked by towers and adorned with the badges of the owner or the monarch as a sign of allegiance, they emphasized the contrast between those who had legitimate business within and those who were kept firmly excluded.

A similar hierarchy was expressed in the architectural form of the buildings within the inner court. The hall was the dominant structure where the whole household and honoured guests could come together in that public display of hospitality which was a fundamental obligation of every great family in the first part of the century. It was invariably placed at the far end of the courtyard directly opposite the gatehouse so that it immediately came into view on entering the court. Access was through a porch which led into a passage with another door at the opposing end. To one side of this through passage would be service rooms such as a buttery, pantry and kitchens. It was separated from the hall itself on the other side by a richly decorated screen which marked the division between the utilitarian area of the house and the areas of privileged access. Within the hall the head of the household was seated at the far end on a raised dais illuminated by a large window which was often given added emphasis in the form of a projecting bay. The prominence of this feature, both externally and internally, was an important element in the layout of the hall and, indeed, the whole house. It announced the superior, or high, end beyond which lay the private parlours, chambers and lodgings of the household. Rising through two storeys to a decorated roof structure, the hall acted as a defining space between the practical and the ritual zones that were necessary for any great household.

With minor variations, this was a standard plan that had evolved through the medieval period and continued to meet the needs of the early-sixteenth-century landed family. For the most ambitious and powerful men, the courtyard house remained the only practical option throughout the period. It was the only way to provide accommodation for the vast households which had been the embodiment of their prestige since the middle ages. The triple courtyard plan of the duke of Buckingham's Thornbury Castle in Somerset, built between 1507 and 1521, was designed to accommodate a household of up to 200 people while Cardinal Wolsey's

Hampton Court had to provide for more than twice that number in a generous double courtyard plan. As the sixteenth century progressed such large permanent households were significantly reduced in size but under Elizabeth the need to provide for the Court on progress maintained the obligation to build extensive accommodation ranges by those who sought her favour. Burghley's great house of Theobalds in Hertfordshire with its five courtyards was, he explained, 'begun by me with a mean measure but increased by occasion of her majesty's often coming.'[4] Unlike her father, she built no palaces of her own. Instead, the considerable financial burden of magnificent building was placed firmly on her mighty subjects. 'God send us both long to enjoy her for whom we both meant to exceed our purses in these,'[5] wrote Burghley to Sir Christopher Hatton in 1579 and the result was houses like Holdenby and Kirby Hall in Northamptonshire, both built around spacious courtyards. It was only in the following reign with Lord Salisbury's Hatfield House of 1607–12 that other options for providing the necessary state apartments and lodgings were being explored but even so men like the earl of Suffolk at Audley End and Sir Henry Hobart at Blickling Hall in Norfolk as late as 1620 adhered to the courtyard form.

The courtyard house was essentially inward-looking. With the exception of the gatehouse, the architectural effect was reserved for the internal elevations to be enjoyed only by those who had access. This sense of exclusiveness was slowly abandoned during the course of the century as a public display of architecture became a necessary sign of the builder's learning and wealth. As the native glass industry rapidly expanded after 1567, large areas of glazing on external elevations became an important symbol of lavish expenditure and flooded the interiors with light. It made it possible to enjoy the elaborate decorative schemes of plasterwork and panelling, the opulence of the tapestries, the painted portraits and the richly carved furniture, all of which proliferated in the second half of the century. Elevated locations were chosen for new buildings so that houses like Wollaton and Hardwick must have glittered like lanterns across the countryside when they were lit up at night. These were houses which were meant to be seen by all and the concealing courtyard no longer had a place in the scheme of things. They were replaced by low retaining walls with decorated gates and garden pavilions taking the place of the gatehouse and towers that had previously expressed the power of the owner. A palpable pride in architectural achievement shines through the most innovative houses of the period. Hardwick Hall, 'more glass than wall', of the 1590s stands in stark contrast to Compton Wynyates of the early part of the century. The latter, built in the years before 1520 for the courtier Sir William Compton, is concealed in a hollow in the landscape. Entered through a now vanished service court, the buttressed inner gatehouse is asymmetrically placed so that it leads directly across the inner court to the screens passage at the lower end of the hall. The tall projecting bay window at the high end of the hall is the dominant architectural feature of the courtyard. The hall itself extends through two storeys with a high battlemented residential tower to the south and other lodgings dispersed around the courtyard. The external elevations are totally irregular and sparely fenestrated with a logic that is determined by the significance of the rooms behind.

Hardwick is the creation of a totally different architectural sensibility. It is placed high up above the surrounding countryside. Its walled forecourt provides an open setting for the towering house behind. All the accommodation is provided in a single

Plate 26.2. Compton Wynyates, Warwickshire. Asymmetrical gatehouse range leading to the inner court of the house built in a hollow for the courtier, Sir William Compton, before 1520. (Photo, Malcolm Airs)

block articulated by six flanking towers. The horizontal hierarchy of earlier houses expressed by the dominance of the hall with its high and low ends is wholly absent. In their place is a much more subtle vertical hierarchy where the relative importance of the rooms behind is expressed by the increasing height of the windows as they rise through the storeys. Hardwick still has a hall but its presence is no longer given any visual expression. Its entrance through the loggia is suppressed and its function as a public room is no longer important. It is surrounded at ground-floor level by service rooms. A spacious stone staircase at the far end winds in a serpentine procession through half-landings and right angles past the family quarters on the first floor to deliver the privileged visitor to the highly decorated rooms of state at the very top of the house. Like other houses of the period, Hardwick was built with an eye to a possible visit from the queen on progress. The state rooms were conceived on a regal scale and decorated with suitable symbols of their purpose. The sequences of high great chamber, withdrawing chamber and best bed chamber deliberately recreate the royal progression from presence chamber through the privy chamber to the royal bedchamber.

In the event, Elizabeth never ventured so far as Hardwick but had she done so she would have instantly recognized the allusions that have been created in her honour. In the high great chamber the royal arms are placed over the fireplace and the gigantic plaster frieze that runs around the room celebrates the story of Diana as an allegory of the qualities possessed by the queen. The elephants are a symbol of her virginity and the trees speak of her virtue. The Cavendish roebuck chasing away the beasts of the forest engage the builder with this allegorical drama and demonstrate her loyalty to the throne. The choice of these images was deliberate in creating a self-fashioning that would have been easily comprehended by her peers.

Plate 26.3. Hardwick Hall, Derbyshire. The towering symmetrical form of Bess of Hardwick's great house with its roof-line emblazoned with her own initials. 1590–98, probably to the designs of the mason Robert Smythson. (Photo, Malcolm Airs)

Above the state rooms was a roof-top terrace from which the geometrical patterns of the gardens below could be enjoyed and views could be obtained of the extent and fecundity of the estate in an after-dinner ritual designed to impress. Here the towers terminated in pavilions crowned with the initials of the builder surmounted by the ducal coronet of her pre-eminent rank as countess of Shrewsbury. To the spectator on the roof the initials would have been back to front. Their message was not for the privileged few but to announce to the world outside that Elizabeth, the daughter of the impoverished minor gentry family of Hardwick, had returned in triumph to the place of her birth and had celebrated her towering achievement with a truly awe-inspiring building of great beauty and enormous wealth.

What is implicit in a house like Hardwick is that by the end of the century the country houses of the landed classes were employed to express a radically different perception of the role of architecture in demonstrating status than their late-medieval predecessors. Sheer size and the trappings of power such as gatehouses and towers were no longer enough. A house also had to display a more civilizing degree of knowledge and learning in ways that might now seem arcane but which were central to the Elizabethan consciousness. The decline in the importance of the hall and of the need to provide lodgings for retainers, the migration of the entertaining rooms to the upper storeys of the house and the proliferation of specialized parlours and chambers marked not only the growing importance of the immediate family and individual privacy at the expense of the extended household, it also liberated house design from the conventions of the past. The opportunities to build in a different way stimulated a passionate interest in architecture which is abundantly clear from contemporary literature and private correspondence. The libraries of builders such as Sir Thomas Smith, Sir Thomas Tresham and Lord Burghley show that they were fully conversant with the architectural treatises of Italy and France. From these books they borrowed the Renaissance concept of symmetry as an essential ingredient of architectural harmony and applied it with increasing rigour to their principal elevations from the middle of the century onwards. At about the same time, under the humanist influence of the duke of Somerset, they began to utilize the classical orders and modular proportion with growing confidence as witnessed by the Strand elevation of Somerset's London house and such buildings as Longleat, Hill Hall in Essex and the early parts of Burghley House. All of these were built for men who had been in the service of Somerset and for a time it seemed as though England would follow the lead of continental Europe and adopt the grammar of classical design. Possibly the execution of Somerset in 1552 stifled the movement before it had time to establish its primacy, but, whatever the reason, fashionable architecture took off in a very different direction under Elizabeth.

The later-sixteenth-century delight in allegory and metaphor, manifest in the literature of Spenser and Shakespeare, the paintings of Hilliard and others, in poetry and dress, in disguises and other entertainments, found full expression in architecture as well. In an age when the symbolism of the emblem was common intellectual currency – defined by Geoffrey Whitney in 1586 as: 'Some wittie devise expressed with cunning woorkemanship, somethinge obscure to be perceived at the first, whereby, when with further consideration it is understood, it maie the greater delighte the behoulder'[6] – building was an irresistible opportunity for such displays of sophisticated wit. The belief that the E-planned house with projecting wings and a central porch were a tribute to Queen Elizabeth may or may not be fanciful but it expressed precisely the sort of effect that could be achieved by the geometry of planning.

It was in this spirit that Sir Thomas Tresham publicly affirmed his Catholicism by building a remarkable triangular lodge on the edge of his estate at Rushton as a play on the Holy Trinity and the abbreviated form of his own name. Whether other triadic buildings, either in the form of triangles such as Longford Castle, Wiltshire, or Y-plans as at Redlynch in the same county or New House in Herefordshire, were similarly motivated is an open question but the delight that was evoked by their geometry was something that could be shared by all. John Thorpe's unbuilt plan for a house based on his own initials is simply an extreme manifestation of a common understanding of the pleasure that could be derived from a conscious manipulation of the form of the house. In both the Thorpe and the Smythson collections of drawings there are plans based on circles, squares, triangles and quatrefoils to amply demonstrate this obsession. Tresham built another lodge on his Lyveden estate in the form of a Greek cross as a symbol of Christ's Passion and the attraction of this symmetrical form is present in a more secular context in other houses such as Hardwick where the plan is based on two Greek crosses separated by the double square of the hall.

Plate 26.4. The Triangular Lodge, Rushton, Northants. Built 1594–7 for the recusant Sir Thomas Tresham as an elaborate Catholic device in celebration of the Holy Trinity. Every element of the design is based on the symbolism of the number three. (Photo, Megan Parry)

Such geometrical conceits are not always readily apparent to the spectator, but a more obvious satisfaction could be achieved from an appreciation of the principal elevation. Whereas at the beginning of the century it was possible to read the disposition of the rooms within from the architectural treatment of the façade, by the end of the century this was no longer so. A rigorous symmetry masked the position of the hall and in some houses, such as Chastleton and Broughton Castle, even the position of the entrance was hidden. Novelty of decoration and a lavish display of glass were the prime considerations, handled with unrestrained self-confidence that speaks of the freedom of a nation that had defeated the Spanish Armada. The light-hearted revival of gothic forms in buildings such as Wollaton Hall and Burghley House are placed side by side with quotations from the classical orders in a romantic demonstration of learning that is quite unique. A house like Montacute, begun in 1599 for Sir Edward Phelips, summarizes this architectural achievement. It is extrovert in its glittering array of showy windows and projecting bays yet disciplined in its symmetry about all four fronts. It has classical references in its pediments and columned chimney-stacks alongside a more mythical pedigree in the statues of the Nine Worthies which separate the continuous grid of windows lighting the long gallery along the whole of the top storey. It is exuberant and even brash in its architectural display but it has an identity that could be found only in England at that particular point in European culture.

A different but equally strong national identity was present in the country houses of Scotland. Despite the strong cultural and trading connections with France, Scandinavia and the Low Countries, the castle-like form of the medieval tower house was creatively adapted during the course of the sixteenth century with a self-confident panache that reflected the growing stability and prosperity of the kingdom. A measure of defensibility remained but the emphasis became increasingly symbolic rather than a practical necessity. Gun loops might have guarded the entrance and the walls might still have been sparsely fenestrated but the wall head became an opportunity for decoration and proud display rather than a platform for defence. Just as in England, but in a different form, the roof was a place for enjoying the view and marking the presence of the house in the landscape. A daring architectural vocabulary evolved of projecting structures on elaborately carved corbels with decorated gargoyles and pedimented dormers which contrasted with the plain harled walls beneath.

In the early part of the century the tower houses were generally rectangular in plan with the accommodation stacked in a vertical fashion. The ground floor was given over to storage and service functions with the hall on the first floor and chambers on the floors above. Internal circulation between the floors was often by a complex arrangement of spiral stairs contrived within the thickness of the walls and providing different routes into the separate rooms. Some towers were augmented by short flanking wings or jambs containing additional chambers or a more spacious stair and with the main entrance in the re-entrant angle. They were usually surrounded by enclosing walls around separate ancillary buildings although true courtyard plans, as in England, were an option for the higher nobility.

It was verticality which gave the Scottish tower house its distinctive form but particularly during the second half of the century there was a fascination with geometry that found full expression in the Z-plan in which two wings were positioned at diagonally opposite corners of the main block as at Claypotts Castle, Angus, of 1569–88. Elevational symmetry was rare, with the outstanding exception of the south front of Fyvie Castle for the first earl of Dunfermline at the very end of the century. The complex of rectangular and circular forms that dominated the roofs was complemented by staircase turrets jutting out from the walls and projecting oriel windows. The only other area of external decoration was above the entrance doorway which became the focus for carved heraldic panels demonstrating the lineage of the builder.

The hall remained the centre of the house long after it had diminished in importance in the English household but the private apartments beyond proliferated in number and in decorative opulence. Plasterwork came late to Scotland but the painted ceilings on wooden boards that flourished from about 1560 onwards provided an opportunity for allegories and texts often taken direct from emblem books like that of Geoffrey Whitney. Like the fanciful skylines and the multiplicity of

Plate 26.5. Claypotts castle, Angus. Z-plan tower house with corbelled and crowstepped caphouses along the roof-line and plain lower walls protected by gun loops. 1569–88 for John Strachan. (Photo, Malcolm Airs)

staircase they invoke a strong national architectural identity based on a self-assured creative energy.

The Farmhouse

The vast majority of the population lived in the countryside and was engaged in agricultural pursuits. Very little survives from Scotland to illustrate how they were housed but the enormous numbers of farmhouses in England and eastern Wales demonstrate a change in domestic arrangements that in many ways was more profound than that which affected their social superiors. At the beginning of the century most of them lived in buildings constructed by local craftsmen in local materials. In lowland areas they were usually of timber and in the uplands of stone. Despite these regional differences in their outward appearance, the dominance of the hall was even more pronounced than in the country houses of the landed classes. It was by far the largest room, open to the underside of the roof and heated by an open fire placed approximately in the centre of the floor. At the low end of the hall was a screens passage with two small service rooms on the other side and at the high end a door would lead into a more private parlour beyond the dais. The only upper storey rooms would be above the service end and the parlour but the great void of the hall prevented any intercommunication between them and access by ladder stairs was difficult. In the more affluent examples the upper-storey chambers were roofed at right angles to the hall and their gables provided an opportunity for decorated framing. Most of them, however, were contained within a single roof often hipped at the ends so that the upper-storey accommodation was minimal.

It was a form that had been common throughout the medieval period and it is clear from inventories as well as the physical evidence that most domestic activity took place on the ground floor centred on the hall. This was the only heated room and it functioned as the principal eating, sleeping and living space. The head of the household might have secured some privacy by sleeping in the parlour but for every-body else it was a communal life around the open hearth with only benches and tables for furniture and wooden shuttered windows that kept the weather out at the expense of the light.

By the end of the period, although many continued to live in this fashion it was becoming increasingly anachronistic. The concept promulgated by W. G. Hoskins of a great rebuilding of rural England concentrated on the period 1575 to 1625 might now seem too simplistic and insensitive to regional variations in timing but its central thesis of a radical change in the organization and furnishing of the house still holds good.[7] Driven by the increase in population and sustained by the Tudor price rise that enabled primary producers to accumulate the capital necessary to build, there was an authentic revolution in rural housing which was made possible by the simple process of enclosing the fireplace and channelling the smoke out of the house by means of a chimney-stack. In his *Description of England* first published in 1577, William Harrison describes the old men of his Essex village of Radwinter marvelling at 'the multitude of chimneys lately erected whereas in their young days there were not above two or three, if so many'.[8] It is a graphic image and all the other changes flowed from it.

By replacing the open hearth with a chimney-stack it was possible to insert a floor at first floor level in the hall to provide an upper-storey chamber which linked the existing upper-storey rooms. It could also provide a support for a proper staircase that made it practical to use the whole of the upper floor for domestic purposes for the first time. The practice of separating sleeping- and living-rooms and going upstairs to bed which is now so deeply entrenched in the modern consciousness was a direct consequence of this change. The existing housing stock could be easily altered to take advantage of these new possibilities for privacy and specialized room functions and through the sixteenth and into the following century most of the surviving medieval examples were modernized in this way.

There was also the opportunity to devise new house types that incorporated these changes from the outset. Throughout much of lowland England and parts of mid-Wales the lobby-entry plan was a common solution. The chimney-stack was placed in the centre of the house forming a small draught-free lobby behind the entrance door with space for a staircase at the rear. The single stack could accommodate sufficient fireplaces to heat the rooms on either side on both floors and provided a decorative central emphasis where it emerged through the roof that signalled to the outside world the modernity of the builder. In its simplest form it had the added advantage of a symmetrical elevation which was only

Plate 26.6. The Old Forge, Dorchester-on-Thames, Oxfordshire. A lobby-entry house of
c.1600 with prominent chimneystacks placed directly in line with the central entrance door.
The lower range to the left is a later addition. (Photo, Malcolm Airs)

compromised if further accommodation was provided in an additional bay at
one end. In southern England it became the most common post-medieval house
type and was exported to the eastern seaboard of America along with the Pilgrim
Fathers.

In upland areas a different choice was made which retained the through
passage and the traditional tripartite division of the medieval house. The service
rooms, which by now included an indoor kitchen, were on one side of the passage
and the principal ground floor room, still known as the hall, was on the other side
with a parlour beyond. Access to the upper floor was usually off the hall which
retained its dominant position in the domestic arrangements. The through-passage
plan suggests a more cautious approach to planning in which symmetry played no
part.

In addition to enclosed fireplaces, the other great advance in comfort was provided by the growing availability of window glass. With no smoke from an open fire
and more light being let into the rooms it was possible to decorate the interior of
the house in a way that never before had been possible. The consequence was an
enthusiasm for wall-paintings, panelling, plaster ceilings and painted cloths that was
almost universal by the end of the century. The opportunity to choose and enjoy personal decorative schemes in their own homes must have been as much a liberation
as sleeping in their own bed-chambers. The amount of furniture and personal possessions greatly increased, as evidenced by probate inventories and duly noted by

Harrison. All of these changes must have meant that life in the farmhouse was a great deal more agreeable and, indeed, civilized in 1600 than it had been a hundred years earlier.

Town Buildings

Due to the economic pressures of later developments the surviving evidence for urban building is more fragmentary than in the countryside but, taking the period as a whole, both north and south of the border towns were flourishing in the sixteenth century. It is impossible to do justice to the vast array of different types of buildings in the available space and in many ways the urban architectural achievement was less innovative than in the country houses of the nobility, the gentry and the farmers. That is not to say that they were unimportant in a process of growing urbanization but that they will inevitably receive a more cursory consideration.

The largest houses that survive in most British towns were generally the residences of the successful merchants and entrepreneurs. They advertise their prosperity by their size and the opulence of their decoration. They would have had rooms set aside for business but they also offered the same domestic comforts of hall and chambers that were demanded by their counterparts in the countryside. The shopkeepers, craftsmen and artisans who made up the mass of the urban population were housed in narrow buildings often only one room wide with a side entry that led both into the house and to the remainder of the burgage plot at the rear. Each unit might have a shop or workshop facing onto the street with living accommodation behind. Various other living-rooms, often sublet or in multiple tenancies, would be on the floors above. The yards at the rear might contain workshops, detached kitchens and further mean tenements. A vivid picture of the crowded nature of the City of London and the chaotic arrangements of tenancies and occupation at the end of the century can be gleaned from the surveys made by Ralph Treswell for Christ's Hospital and the Clothworkers' Company with the majority of houses being no more than two rooms in plan.

Where space was at a premium in the commercial centres of towns, the shops and tenements could only extend in an upward direction, sometimes for as many as four or five storeys. Precious additional floor area could be gained if each successive storey was jettied beyond the floor below. Jettying was only possible for timber-framed buildings and this technical restraint was presumably the reason why so many towns in the sixteenth century were predominantly constructed of this material even where good building stone was available. Although the appearance now might be of architectural disorder, there is a substantial body of evidence that much urban development was the result of controlled speculation with uniform rows of terraced buildings built for rent by bodies capable of assembling the necessary land. The restored row of more than twenty shop units in Church Street, Tewkesbury, developed by the abbey before the Dissolution, is an impressive example of this process. Away from the centre, town buildings were often only two storeys high and spread more generously across wider plots. Contemporary maps of provincial towns, such as that by Ralph Walker of Chelmsford in Essex of 1591, shows how quickly the suburbs were reached from the densely built-up market places. Here there were farm buildings and orchards as well as rows of artisan housing.

Plate 26.7. St Columba's church, Burntisland, Fife. A radical solution to the new liturgical requirements in the form of a square with a central tower. The internal focus was on the pulpit and it was built between 1592 and 1600. (Photo, Malcolm Airs)

At the heart of the community, in the town as well as in the surrounding villages, was the parish church. The opening of the century witnessed the late flowering of the perpendicular gothic tradition and a significant amount of commercial and private wealth was channelled into church building in the years leading up to the Dissolution in England and the Reformation in Scotland. Much of it was spent on chantry chapels with the twofold intention of individual salvation and a public display of generosity. The worldly achievements of the Spring family of clothiers in Lavenham, Suffolk, and of the merchant John Greenway at Tiverton in Devon are proclaimed in their heraldic devices and merchant's marks that decorate the additions that they made to their parish churches. After the religious upheavals, there was little in the way of new church-building with a few exceptions such as the remarkable response to the new form of worship at Burntisland in Fife of 1589, funded by a tax on the import of Baltic pine. Celebration of the lives and virtues of the wealthy focused on their monuments which became conspicuous elements in the internal furnishings of many churches and stimulated the establishment of a number of flourishing sculpture workshops by both émigré and native craftsmen in various parts of the country.

With the decline in church-building, the town and/or market hall in England and the tollbooth in Scotland achieved equal prominence in the urban landscape. In the resonant phrase of Robert Tittler the town hall was 'the seat and symbol of the

Plate 26.8. Market House, Rothwell, Northamptonshire. Built in 1578 at the expense of Sir Thomas Tresham, Sir Christopher Hatton and the burgesses of the town. The pilasters are decorated with the Tresham trefoil and the cornice contains the arms of the county elite. (Photo, Malcolm Airs)

autonomous community' reflecting the growing increase in self-government in towns, particularly in the second half of the century.[9] Large numbers were built or remodelled from the 1540s onwards. They represented significant community expenditure and were the focus for civic pride and local rivalry. The most common form in England was an open ground floor with covered marketing facilities and an upper storey with chambers where the government and administration of the town took place. In Scotland the ground floor was usually enclosed and might contain the town prison or a schoolroom. Their importance to a proper sense of urban dignity is suggested by the fact that where the evidence survives they seem to have invariably been built by the most prominent craftsmen in the locality.

Although they were usually funded from within the community, there are occasional examples of private benefactions which provided an opportunity for the same sort of self-advertisement already noted on the houses and the churches of the period. The inhabitants of Rothwell in Northamptonshire shared the cost of their new market house with Sir Christopher Hatton and Sir Thomas Tresham but it was the latter who negotiated the contract with the mason William Grumbold in 1578 and who claimed full credit for the project in the Latin inscription which runs around the building. Despite the claim that 'nothing but the common weal did he seek . . .' the prominent pilasters that decorate the building are covered with his personal rebus of a trefoil and the entablature is embellished with the arms of his connections among the county gentry.

To the modern sensibility there is something uncomfortable about such blatant proclamations of individual generosity but in the sixteenth century it was an accepted recognition of the public charity that replaced the role of the monasteries in caring for the sick and providing for the educational needs of society. The almshouses that were built in growing numbers as part of that provision invariably carried the names of their donors as did the grammar schools that formed the foundation of an emerging education system geared to meet a demand for literate administrators to service the machinery of the Tudor bureaucracy. In the second half of the century there was an expansion of the universities as an education in the traditional disciplines became an essential attribute for a gentleman of rank. There were new foundations in Oxford and Cambridge and in Scotland new universities were established in Edinburgh and Fraserburgh as well as a second college in Aberdeen. The Inns of Court in London acted as a legal finishing school after university not only for the growing numbers who found employment in the law itself but also for those who were set to inherit the responsibility of managing the family estates. New halls were built at Gray's Inn, Staple Inn and the Middle Temple but all in a medieval tradition complete with hammer-beam roofs. This architectural conservatism, which was present to an even more marked degree in the colleges of the universities, stemmed from the unchanging nature of the facilities that were needed combined with an underlying sense of the traditional dignity of the institution itself. A communal hall, chapel, library and sets of lodgings, arranged around a quadrangle entered through the porter's lodge in the gatehouse, still served the community well as it had done since the middle ages. It was only in the provision of more comfortable lodgings for the head of the college, who after the Reformation was permitted to marry, that any discernable change could be found.

The static forms of the universities are in marked contrast to virtually all the other buildings of the century. From the country houses of the nobility and the peasantry to the town buildings of the mercantile classes, the spirit of architectural adventure stamped an enduring image on the Tudor age. By the end of it both countries had forged a distinct architectural identity that owed little to European precedent and everything to a creative drive in which visual innovation was prized and individual attainment was recognized. Expenditure on building by all classes reached a peak in the latter part of the century and the legacy is an achievement that deserves to be ranked alongside the other creative arts of the era.

NOTES

1. Harrison, *Description of England*, p. 199.
2. Thurley, *Royal Palaces*, p. 39.
3. Ibid., p. 11.
4. Nichols, *Progresses*, p. 205n.
5. Hartshorne, *Memorials of Holdenby*, p. 16.
6. Whitney, *A Choice of Emblemes*, unpaginated introduction.
7. Hoskins, 'Rebuilding of rural England', 44–59.

8. Harrison, *Description of England*, p. 201.
9. Tittler, *Architecture and Power*, p. 89.

BIBLIOGRAPHY

Airs, Malcolm, 'Architecture', in Boris Ford, ed., *The Cambridge Guide to the Arts in Britain: Renaissance and Reformation*, (Cambridge, 1989), pp. 46–97.

Airs, Malcolm, *The Buildings of Britain: Tudor and Jacobean* (1982).

Alcock, N. W., *People at Home: Living in a Warwickshire Village, 1500–1800* (Chichester, 1993).

Barley, M. W., *The English Farmhouse and Cottage* (London, 1961).

Brunskill, R. W., *Illustrated Handbook of Vernacular Architecture* (London, 1970).

Buxton, John, *Elizabethan Taste* (London, 1963).

Dunbar, John G., *The Architecture of Scotland* (London, 1966).

Emery, Anthony, *Greater Medieval Houses of England and Wales*, vol. I, *Northern England* (Cambridge, 1996); vol. II, *East Anglia, Central England and Wales* (Cambridge, 2000).

Harrison, William, *The Description of England*, ed. Georges Edelen (Washington and New York, 1994).

Hartshorne, E. S., *Memorials of Holdenby* (1868).

Hilling, John B., *The Historic Architecture of Wales* (Cardiff, 1976).

Hoskins, W. G., 'The rebuilding of rural England 1570–1640', *Past and Present*, 4 (1953).

Lubbock, Jules, *The Tyranny of Taste: The Politics of Architecture and Design in Britain 1550–1960* (New Haven and London, 1995).

McKean, Charles, *The Scottish Chateau* (Stroud, 2001).

Mercer, Eric, *English Art 1553–1625* (Oxford, 1962).

Mowle, Timothy, *Elizabethan and Jacobean Style* (London, 1993).

Nichols, J., *The Progresses and Public Processions of Queen Elizabeth*, vol. I (London, 1823).

Schofield, John, ed., *The London Surveys of Ralph Treswell* (London, 1987).

Thurley, Simon, *The Royal Palaces of Tudor England* (New Haven and London, 1993).

Tittler, Robert, *Architecture and Power: The Town Hall and the English Urban Community, c. 1500–1640* (Oxford, 1991).

Wells-Cole, Anthony, *Art and Decoration in Elizabethan and Jacobean England: The Influence of Continental Prints, 1558–1625*, (New Haven and London, 1997).

Whitney, Geoffrey, *A Choice of Emblemes* (Leyden, 1586).

FURTHER READING

The focus of most research in recent years has been on the palaces of the monarchy and the country houses of the landowning classes. This is understandable. They are the most striking manifestations of architectural taste and generally they are better documented than other building types. The literature is summarized in a paper by John Newman published in 1988 and updated to 1994 by Maurice Howard: John Newman, 'The Elizabethan and Jacobean Great House: a review of recent research', *Archaeological Journal*, 145 (1988), 365–73; Maurice Howard, 'The Tudor and Jacobean Great House: a summary booklist', in *The Tudor and Jacobean Great House*, ed. Malcolm Airs, 1994, pp. 117–18. The most influential books include Sir John Summerson's pioneering study as part of a broader survey of British architecture (John Summerson, *Architecture in Britain: 1530–1830*, 1953), Sir Howard Colvin's detailed examination of the Royal Works (H. M. Colvin, ed., *The History of the King's Works*,

1485–1660: Part I, 1975, Part II, 1982), complemented by Simon Thurley's *Royal Palaces of Tudor England* (1993), Maurice Howard's account of the country house up to the mid-century (*The Early Tudor Country House: Architecture and Politics 1490–1550*, 1989) and Mark Girouard's continuation of the story in the Elizabethan period (*Robert Smythson and the Elizabethan Country House*, 1983). The social history of the country house in the period is vividly explored in the same author's *Life in the English Country House* (1978). The practical side of design and construction is the principal theme of *The Tudor and Jacobean Country House: A Building History* (1995) by Malcolm Airs. Slightly lower down the social scale, the numerous country seats of the gentry have been comprehensively studied by Nicholas Cooper (*Houses of the Gentry 1480–1680*, 1999). In Scotland a synthesis of the whole architectural spectrum is provided by the two relevant volumes of *The Architectural History of Scotland* – Richard Fawcett, *Scottish Architecture from the Accession of the Stewarts to the Reformation 1371–1560*, (1994), and Deborah Howard, *Scottish Architecture from the Reformation to Restoration 1560–1660* (1995). Both these books cover ecclesiastical buildings and towns as well as the court and the countryside. The houses of the ordinary people, first treated in a cross-disciplinary essay by W. G. Hoskins as long ago as 1953 ('The rebuilding of rural England 1570–1640, *Past and Present*, 4, 1953), have been examined in greater depth for England in two books published in 1975: Eric Mercer, *English Vernacular Houses* and Peter Smith, *Houses of the Welsh Countryside*); and more recently by Anthony Quiney (*The Traditional Buildings of England*, 1990) but the bulk of the later literature is to be found in county and national journals.

CHAPTER TWENTY-SEVEN

Music, Politics and Society

JOHN MILSOM

Introduction

Aristotles resolution touching the civil necessity is, that musick hath relation to these three things, to delectation, to discipline, and to an happy life. To delectation, because musicke with the sweetnesse therof, doth refresh the minde and make it better able to greater labours. To discipline, because it is a cause of breeding in us chastitie, temperance, and other morall virtues. To an happy life, because that cannot consist without judgement and liberall delectations, whereof musicke is the chiefest.[1]

... if you wold have your sonne, softe, womannish, uncleane, smoth mouthed, affected to bawdrie, scurrilitie, filthy rimes, and unsemely talking: brifly, if your wold have him, as it weare transnatured into a woman, or worse, and inclyned to all kind of whordome and abhomination, set hym to dauncing school, and to learne musicke, and then shall you not faile of your purpose.[2]

These arrestingly divergent views – and there are many more on the same subject, each expressing a different nuance of opinion – succinctly show that there was no single or simple attitude towards music in sixteenth-century Britain. Writers on the subject fall broadly into two camps. Many concurred with John Case in believing that the practice and appreciation of music brought true benefit to men, women and children alike, and was to be actively promoted. Others regarded music with mistrust as an idle pursuit that was at best distracting, at worst positively damaging. Disagreement about the value and appropriate place of music led to so much lively debate in Tudor Britain in general, and in Elizabethan England in particular, that it is tempting to quote from it at length in a chapter about music, politics and society. The following passages, for instance, move the debate out of the domestic arena, and express opposed views about the desirability of choirs and organs in the Elizabethan church:

Item because dyvers collegiate, and also some paryshe churches heretofore, there hath ben lyvynges appoynted for the mayntenaunce of menne and chyldren, to use syngynge in the churche, by meanes whereof the lawdable scyence of musicke hath ben had in estimation, and preserved in knowledge: the queenes majestie ... wylleth and com-

maundeth, that fyrst no alteration be made of such assignementes of lyvinge, as heretofore hath bene appoynted to the use of syngynge or musicke in the churche, but that
the same so remayne.[3]

We should be to long to tell your honoures of cathedral churches, the dennes afor-
saide of all loytering lubbers, wher . . . the cheefe chauntor, singing men special favourers of religion, squeaking queresters, organ players . . . etc. live in great idlenesse, and
have their abiding. If you woulde knowe whence all these came we can easely answere
you, that they came from the Pope, as oute of the Trojan horses bellye, to the destruction of Gods kingdome.[4]

Between them, these four statements of opinion raise some of the most important
themes that sound within this chapter. Church music is one of them. In both England
and Scotland, for various reasons, the place of music in worship was radically reorganized during the course of the sixteenth century: the chanting of monks and nuns
was silenced; the medieval liturgy, with its attendant music, was replaced by reformed
vernacular rites; for the first time, congregations were encouraged to sing during
church services; Calvinist attitudes, such as those expressed by Field and Wilcox in
the second extract above, questioned the usefulness of church choirs, seeking to
replace them either with congregational hymnody or with the spoken word alone.[5]
A second important theme explored in this chapter is the significant rise of amateur
music-making that took place during the sixteenth century, principally among the
wealthier and privileged classes. It was fuelled by many factors: the more widespread
availability of secular education; the increase of literacy in general, and the ability to
read music notation in particular; the adoption of humanist models of 'courtesy', in
which the pursuit or appreciation of music was held to be worthy; and a growing
awareness of contemporary social trends on the continent of Europe, especially in
Italy.[6] These two themes – music in the church, and music as social grace – inter-
twine with a third: what might be called a 'history of the music book'. Much mention
is made below of the production, ownership, distribution, importation and use of
notated music, both manuscript and printed, during the period.[7]

Although these three themes are important ones, even when added together they
give rise to only a partial history of music in Tudor Britain. They engage principally
with elite groups – with sites of power, privilege, wealth and education, with the
sophisticated literature of notated compositions, and with the skills, accomplishments
and expenses that went with them: of musical training, connoisseurship, the possession of instruments and music-books, above all the ability to read music notation –
and the debate that surrounded all of this, by men such as John Case, Philip Stubbes,
John Field and Thomas Wilcox, whose views are quoted above. Other social groups
had little or no access to that world; a line must be drawn between what might be
called the 'art music' and the 'popular music' of the age, the former characterized
by authored compositions, the latter by the oral and performative transmission of
unauthored songs, ballads, music for social dance, and those phenomena such as
street-cries and the pealing of bells that occupy the perimeter of the concept of
'music'.

There was a time when the 'popular music' of Tudor Britain was felt to lie largely
beyond study (because so little of it was written down at the time), and in any case
to have existed in a state of relatively stable practice, little affected by external forces

such as regime change, reformation of the church, and the rise of secular education. Recently, however, those views have been challenged in important ways by studies arising from the fields of social history, anthropology and the history of the book, and a new attitude is in the air.[8] Even though the 'popular' music of Tudor Britain is itself largely lost, from the traces of its existence – through, for instance, legal and administrative documents, or the written and printed transmission of words that were once sung to music – a story can be told that shows change to have been as conspicuous a force as continuity. Moreover, the perceived distinction between literate and non-literate music-making in Tudor Britain may have been too rigidly drawn in the past. Meeting-places between those two domains can sometimes be found, if only we know where and how to look.

All this is by way of introduction to the paragraphs that follow. In them, art music inevitably looms large; but an eye and an ear are also kept on the music of the streets, the taverns and the fields, in a bid to gain some sense of overview of Tudor musical experience, and to avoid marginalizing the repertories of popular song. An unconventional narrative strategy has therefore been adopted, one that foregrounds five broad categories of musical activity that were shared by all strata of Tudor society.[9] Pride of place is given to that most widespread of musical pursuits, singing. Less space is devoted to the more specialist skills of playing musical instruments. Then come short surveys of composing and authorship, and the notion of 'ownership' as it may be said to apply to music. Taken separately from those issues is the activity of listening. Running through this structure, as fully as the evidence and constraints of space allow, is one further topic: the relevance of gender to musical activity and repertory. Although many of the observations made here probably apply equally to England and Lowland Scotland, it has to be said that much more information survives about the musical culture of the larger southern nation, and the situation in Scotland is best considered through specialist studies.[10]

Singing

It takes some imaginative effort mentally to reconstruct the soundscapes of Tudor England and Stewart Scotland, filled as they were with orally transmitted song and speech-song, the art-songs of chamber and court, the choral music of the church and, until the dissolution of the monasteries and the suppression of the Latin rite, the chanting of monks, nuns and lay-singers in religious houses. Virtually all of those traditions have faded from modern Britain, so fully replaced by the media of broadcast and recorded sound that the act of singing in a public place might now be regarded by many as unnatural. In Tudor Britain, the opposite was true:

> . . . even the ploughman and cartar, are by the instinct of their harmonicall soules compelled to frame their breath into a whistle, thereby not only pleasing themselves, but also diminishing the tediousnes of their labors. . . . And hence it is, that manual labourers, and mechanicall artificers of all sorts, keepe such a chaunting and singing in their shoppes, the tailor on his bulk, the shomaker at his last, the mason at his wal, the shipboy at his oare, the tinker at his pan, and the tylor on the house top.[11]

So little trace survives of orally transmitted song from Tudor Britain, other than in evocations such as this one, that it is hard to speak with any confidence about (for instance) the ways in which song projected notions of identity and gender, served to bond social groups, and played a part in affirming and challenging ideas. What does seem clear, however, is that the potential of harnessing popular song was recognized by religious reformers in England from at least the 1530s, and that godly or moralizing substitutes for it became, in the words of one modern commentator, 'perhaps the single most effective weapon which the English Reformers possessed'.[12] In the preface to one early attempt to ride new religious thought on the back of popular song, the preacher Miles Coverdale (1488–1568) has this to say:

> O that mens lippes were so opened, that theyr mouthes myght shewe prayse of God. Yee wolde God that . . . oure carters and plow men other thynge to whistle upon, save psalmes, hymnes, and soch godly songes as David is occupied with all. And yf women syttynge at theyr rockes, or spynnynge at the wheles, had none other songes to passe theyr tyme withall, than soch as Moses sister, Elchenas wife, Debbora, and Mary the mother of Christ have song before them, they shulde be better occupied, then with hey nony nony, hey troly loly, and soch lyke fantasies.[13]

Coverdale's own metrical translation of the psalms, fashioned after Lutheran models and provided with notated music, was printed in England but quickly suppressed. Two Edwardine successors, issued by Robert Crowley in 1549 (STC 2725) and Frances Seager in 1553 (STC 2728) – again both with music notation – seem not to have run to more than one edition. Instead it was the metrical psalm translations of Thomas Sternhold, composed initially as courtly verse rather than for popular use, that were taken up by the reformers, and created models for their later Scottish equivalents.[14] In gradually expanding editions, Sternhold's sacred songs (with accretions by John Hopkins and others) became not only a staple of Elizabethan worship, but also by far the most frequently reprinted and widely circulated of all Tudor music-books. The extent to which Coverdale's vision was turned into reality in England, even as early as 1560, can be gauged by a letter sent in March of that year by John Jewel, bishop of Salisbury, to Peter Martyr:

> Religion is somewhat more established now than it was. The people are everywhere exceedingly inclined to the better part. Church music for the people has very much conduced to this. For as soon as they had once commenced singing publicly in only one little church in London, immediately not only the churches in the neighbourhood, but even in distant towns, began to vie with one another in the same practice. You may now sometimes see at Paul's Cross [in London], after the service, six thousand persons, old and young, of both sexes, all singing together and praising God.[15]

What that crowd of 'six thousand persons, old and young' actually sang in 1560 is unknown, nor is it clear how so many people came to know the songs they were able to sing together. What does seem certain, though, is that the mason, the tailor, the shoemaker, their wives and their children all carried those hymns home with them in their heads, to supplement or even oust their 'hey troly loly, and soch lyke fantasies'.

Metrical psalmody apart, the most conspicuous trace of Tudor popular song that survives today is to be found in items of cheap print: single-sheet publications and pamphlets. Songs printed on single sheets, often called 'broadside ballads', cover a wide range of song-types that between them probably addressed an equally wide range of social groups.[16] Pamphlet-sized publications may have a different appearance on account of their folded format, but they overlap significantly with the single-sheet publications in terms of contents, likely desination and durability. Many of these ephemera contain songs made purely for entertainment; others contribute to what one recent writer has called the 'vigorous practice of using songs and ballads as an effective means of communicating political messages among a largely unlettered audience'.[17] Some examples of both categories are sampled below, all of them printed in England. (Scottish examples are very much rarer.) It should be stressed that these may or may not be representative of what once existed. According to recent estimates, as many as 3,000 single-sheet 'ballad' publications may have been issued in Britain during the sixteenth century, each in an edition running to hundreds of copies. Of those 3,000 titles, fewer than 300 survive today, the majority in only a single copy.[18] If that tally is accurate, then lost single-sheet publications massively outnumber the survivals. Almost certainly folded quaterns and slim pamphlets have fared no better.

The classic image of a 'broadside ballad' is of plain-speaking strophic verse on a topical, amorous or moralizing subject that could be sung by a solo singer, male or female, to a popular tune; such a song might move with some circularity between oral performance and written record, and through a printer's initiative could be bought cheaply in single-sheet format. The earliest surviving song-sheets in which all those elements definitely co-exist are in fact rather late; only in the second half of the 1560s do the sheets start to specify tunes, or indeed make any overt reference to singing, and the earliest true ballad-sheet in which music notation is provided dates from 1568.[19] Before the 1560s, almost nothing is known about the music of balladry, nor the extent to which 'ballad' texts were sung. Occasionally there are hints. Some sheets, for instance, have words by known musicians, such as William Forrest and John Heywood. Others clearly parody existing songs, such as the 'songe betwene the Quenes maiestie and Englande' of 1564 (STC 3079), which echoes a much older Tudor song, 'Come over the burn, Bessy'. Ballad-vendors may have supplied through sung example what the sheets themselves failed to specify. And of course there was nothing to stop the owner of a ballad-sheet from marrying its words to any metrically suitable tune. As for the Elizabethan ballad-sheets themselves, some of them specify tunes that were clearly part of Tudor popular culture; 'Greensleeves' and 'Row wel ye Mariners' are examples. In others, a higher register of musical genre is either implied or stipulated, and the choice of music may in some cases have been meaningful. If, for instance, a ballad-text superimposes words upon (or 'ditties') the music of a courtly dance such as 'the Blacke Almaine' or 'new Rogero' – pieces ultimately of Continental origin – it is possible that cross-referential significance or even irony may have been intended. Elsewhere, courtliness is clearly being invoked; examples are the 'famous dittie of the Joyful receaving of the Queens most excellent majestie, by the worthy Citizens of London' of 1584 (STC 12798), in which the tune is 'Wigmores Galliard', and the Armada ballad of 1588 (STC 6557), to be sung 'to the Tune of Mounseurs Almaigne'. Modern ears may not be attuned to the difference of register between those melodies and 'Greensleeves', but an Elizabethan's could well have been.

Falling into a quite different category are what might be called 'part-song ballads': polyphonic pieces that require not one singer but several in order to be performed.

The song printed in 1586 as a 'godly Dittie to be song for the preservation of the Queenes most exclent Majesties raigne' (STC 23926) may look like a 'broadside ballad', furnished as it is with a tune in music notation, but that 'tune' is in fact a polyphonic voice-part, and therefore only one strand of the intended texture. Matching sheets, now lost, must have been printed for the other singers, each of whom would have sung different music (in the same way that each of the four players of a modern string quartet reads different music from a separately printed sheet). Some hint of what that 1586 song was once like can be gleaned from another patriotic 'ballad', the 'godly psalme, of Mary, queene' by Richard Beard, issued in pamphlet form in 1553 (STC 1655); here, four-voice polyphony is printed. Some 'ballads' issued as verse without music turn out to be parodies of polyphonic songs, and they may once have been sung (or intended to be sung) to the music of their models. An example is William Kethe's anti-papal 'Ballet declaringe the fal of the whore of baby-lone intytuled Tye the mare tom boy' (STC 14942), the words of which were printed in about 1548 in pamphlet format; a fragment of its musical model – a polyphonic song by Robert Johnson – survives elsewhere in manuscript.[20]

'Part-song ballads' of this kind move significantly away from the tuneful world of 'Greenesleeves'; instead, they call for a performance situation in which an ensemble of rehearsed singers addressed a listening audience. Who would have sung them, and where? Some must belong to occasions of state, to processions of the monarch through the streets, to royal progresses, and to staged pageants or plays. They might have been sung in the schoolroom, the alehouse, even the home. There is probably some overlap between them and the shadowy genre known as 'three-man songs' (or, sometimes, 'freeman songs'), a forerunner of later repertories such as the catch and the glee (or, in more modern times, barbershop): polyphonic songs owned principally by groups of men, sung for social recreation, not necessarily by singers who could read music notation. Three-man songs evidently penetrated all levels of society. At one extreme they are recorded in taverns; at the other, they were enjoyed at the Tudor court: Henry VIII himself wrote songs that evoke the 'three-man' repertory, and he is said to have joined courtiers in singing 'certeyne songes they called *fremen* songs, as namely "By the bancke as I lay", and "As I walked the wode so wylde"'.[21] Polyphonic pieces such as these might be transmitted orally, but on occasion they also found their way into print; a few simple polyphonic love-songs for three singers have recently come to light, in single-sheet prints issued by John and William Rastall in around 1525–35.[22] Like the later partsong-ballads, these song-sheets appear to have been speculative publications, sold to anyone who cared to buy them. In that respect, they cluster with metrical psalmody and 'broadside ballads' as the music of common experience.

For the rest, we leave behind the singers of the alehouse and the street, and enter instead the singing-world of elite groups. It is, in a sense, a sharp divide, although perhaps today we are much less sensitive to it than would have been the people of Tudor Britain themselves. A strong hint of the divide can be detected in Tudor drama. Shakespeare's plays, for instance, allude often to the repertories of popular song, but they rarely even mention the sophisticated anthems of the church, or the madrigals and songs of Court and chamber, let alone require them to be sung on stage. Shakespeare's ears are fuller of 'Greenesleeves' than the music of Taverner and Tallis, Byrd and Morley, Dowland and Campion. In that respect, he resembles his audiences, who might occasionally have heard those kinds of song, but who would never have sung them themselves. Sophisticated song belonged instead to two special categories of singer: first, professionals; second – but principally at the very end of the Tudor era – educated amateurs.

The professional singer's world was an exclusively male one, and its breeding-house was the church. Before the Reformation, choirs of men and boys were common; ample opportunities existed for employment by parish churches and cathedrals, by colleges with choral foundations (such as those of Cambridge and Oxford, Eton, Fothering-hay and Tattershall), and by the chapels of noble and royal households, the latter crowned by the Chapels Royal of the English and Scottish monarchs. Much has been written about the choral foundations of Tudor Britain;[23] in addition, the world of the professional singing-man is richly evoked by modern recordings, which convey in sound not only an impression of the music's splendour – certainly when compared with the balladry of the streets, or the Elizabethan metrical psalms – but also an idea of the music's stylistic range: simpler music for humbler institutions, or for minor feasts within the liturgical year, magnificent music for the institutions that were most richly endowed. Only a small proportion of the pre-Reformation repertory survives today; most of the books used by church choirs succumbed to the reformers; but those scattered remains, in combination with documentary evidence, project a robust image of choral music-making before the introduction of the Protestant rites.

The size of a choral foundation might be established by statute (as was the case at the colleges of Cambridge and Oxford), but equally it might depend upon the initiative and funding of churchwardens and corporation (in the case of a parish church) or a magnate (in the case of a private household choir). As for the motives that lay behind the maintenance of choirs of singing-men and choristers, they were of various kinds. Statutes, once in place, merely preserved a status quo. In the case of parish churches and cathedrals, civic pride or the wealth of a guild might come into play. Magnates unquestionably vied with one another – and with their peers overseas – in the pursuit of musical excellence. In the early 1520s, for instance, Cardinal Wolsey's household chapel choir was marginally larger even than Henry VIII's, and his plans for Cardinal College, Oxford (later re-founded as Christ Church) were clearly meant to outshine King's College, Cambridge, in terms of chapel size and the provision of a choral foundation.[24]

Before the Reformation, the singing-man's profession offered good opportunities for advancement and mobility. Later in the sixteenth century, matters were quite different; one observer writing in around 1576 reckoned that church music in England was by that date 'so slenderly maintained in the kathedrall chiurches and kolleges & parish chiurches, that when the old stor of the miuzisians be worn owt . . . yee shall hav few or non remaining'.[25] Although a few pockets of local excellence were maintained – at Ludlow parish church, for instance, where the survival of choral services during Elizabeth's reign is particularly well documented[26] – in general the gloomy reports of decline in old choral traditions seem to have been well founded on fact. If Queen Elizabeth's own magnificent Chapel Royal choir seems anomalous, and at odds with Calvinist thinking, that can probably be put down to its role as status symbol, projecting an image that would impress even visiting Catholic dignitaries. Seen in that light, the music written for the Elizabethan Chapel Royal by its gentlemen, such as Thomas Tallis and William Byrd, deliberately sets out to equal the music of foreign princes, and to make full use of the singers and organs maintained out of the royal purse; it does not necessarily tell us much about the queen's own attitude towards music. Elsewhere, however, church authorities seem to have paid more heed to views such as those expressed by reformers John Field and Thomas Wilcox. By 1600, Tudor Britain was no longer richly supplied with 'singing men, squeaking queresters and organ players'. In fact, their total number must have been very small indeed, probably fewer than exists in Britain today.

How, then, is the rich legacy of Elizabethan song to be explained – the madrigals, motets and lute-ayres of the 1570s and beyond? These were, almost exclusively, the property of an amateur elite. From the mid-sixteenth century onwards, there is increasing evidence of musical education being given to the children of the nobility, the gentry and the wealthier merchant class. Payments to music teachers, both for tuition and for the purchase of music-books and instruments, increase significantly in number in household records of the time. For girls and young women, musical skill and connoisseurship were counted among the hallmarks of sophistication and good breeding; and while some Elizabethan parents would have joined Philip Stubbes in his belief that music made a man 'softe, womannish, uncleane, [and] smoth mouthed', others clearly sided with John Case in reckoning it a pathway 'to delectation, to discipline, and to an happy life', by encouraging their sons to learn to sing. For those boys who missed that opportunity, there may have been some shared sense of embarrassment to be felt when they turned to Thomas Morley's self-instruction manual, *A Plaine and Easie Introduction to Practicall Musicke* and found one of the imaginary interlocutors, Philomathes, making this confession:

> . . . supper being ended, and musicke bookes, according to the custome being brought to the table: the mistresse of the house presented mee with a part, earnestly requesting mee to sing. But when, after manie excuses, I protested unfainedly that I could not: everie one began to wonder. Yea, some whispered to others, demaunding how I was brought up: so that upon shame of mine ignorance I go nowe to seeke out mine olde frinde master *Gnorimus*, to make my selfe his scholler.[27]

The art-song repertories of this late Elizabethan age – the madrigals of Thomas Morley, Thomas Weelkes and John Wilbye, the lute-songs of John Dowland and Thomas Campion – tell us much about the sensibilities of their users, and not surprisingly they have been studied in depth. But there is one corner of that late-Elizabethan world that calls for special mention, since it has not always been properly understood or explained in the past. Many of the music-books owned by Elizabethan amateur singers contain significant quantities of sacred music set to Latin words. This is true both of manuscripts (which often include a high proportion of pre-Elizabethan church music, much of it composed for the pre-Reformation rite) and some printed items – specifically the two collections of *cantiones sacrae* or 'sacred songs' published in 1589 and 1591 by William Byrd (STC 4247–8). Several conclusions can be drawn from them. First, in an age of decline in the provision of choral music by the church, some amateurs made a special effort to preserve both the musical works of the past and the musical traditions that had nourished them; a sense of nostalgia tinged with pride is not hard to detect. Second, works that had once been sung by church choirs – and pieces that emulated them, such as the Elizabethan motets by composers like Thomas Tallis, William Byrd and Thomas Morley – were sung in the Elizabethan chamber long after they had largely ceased to sound in the church itself. Third, to Roman Catholics in particular, the genre of the motet became an important medium for the expression of faith and identity, no less than the metrical psalm served to express the Calvinist's point of view.

William Byrd composed many motets for the Catholics, since he was one of them – notwithstanding his professional affiliation to the Chapel Royal, of which he was a gentleman for most of his adult life. Today, Byrd's motets are often performed by church choirs, as if they were church music, and it is easy to overlook the fact that were once used to articulate the thoughts of a suppressed minority, sung behind closed doors by a cluster of women and men who savoured the ideas expressed in their words. The texts of these motets, which derive variously from the Bible, from the Roman Catholic liturgy, and from motets previously set to music by foreign composers, often make historical sense only when they are read as allegories. Help in how to read them that way can be had from non-musical sources – for instance, when those same texts were cited by Jesuits such as Henry Garnet and Robert Southwell, or appear in pamphlets and tracts published by the English Catholics.[28] Themes include the Babylonian captivity, the Egyptian captivity, and Jerusalem laid low. Thus one of Byrd's motets, 'Deus, venerunt gentes' (a setting of Psalm 78:1–4), becomes a musical commentary on the execution of Edmund Campion and other missionary priests in the early 1580s. It is not hard to imagine the power of feeling that might have gone into a performance of that motet by a group of Elizabethan amateur singers in the wake of those executions. Compositions such as this one serve to remind us that music, though sometimes seen as a peripheral ornament in the Tudor world-picture, does sometimes powerfully lock on to the most central issues of the age.

Playing Instruments

In Tudor Britain there were broadly two categories of people who played musical instruments: those who did so for money, and those who played for recreation. Into the first of those categories fell minstrels, city waits, and the various ensembles of largely foreign-born musicians who were employed at the Tudor and Stewart courts. Professional musicians of these kinds were always men, and they formed an artisan class; their skills were sometimes fostered within family groups, and passed on from father to son. The second (amateur) category is inevitably far less well documented. Here, attention tends to focus on the elite groups (such as members of royal families, and those who followed their example) who used music-making as a leisure activity to project a self-image of accomplishment, good breeding and taste. Women no less than men could turn their hands to amateur music-making, a point iconically made by Nicholas Hilliard when he painted his famous miniature of Elizabeth I playing a lute.

Three main functions were performed by the professional minstrels, waits and court instrumentalists of Tudor Britain. First, they signalled ceremony and status; trumpets and other categories of loud instruments were well suited to this role, and they are often mentioned in relation to special events, such as progresses of the monarch, royal weddings, and occasions of national or local rejoicing. Second, minstrels provided recreation for a listening audience, and a convenient blur of background noise against which a private conversation could be held; quieter instruments such as lutes, flutes, viols and keyboards were best suited for indoor use. Third, instrumental music supported dance; for this, the violin band became the preferred ensemble in courtly circles. Records of expenditure for instrumentalists are commonplace; but the music those performers played is today largely lost, for the simple reason that it was never written down. Minstrels and waits played largely or exclusively from memory, learning and transmitting their repertories by ear and through rehearsal. In that respect they contrast with church and amateur musicians, who relied much more upon notation to preserve the pieces they performed.

In provincial Britain, minstrels were largely British-born. At the royal Courts, however, aliens were the dominant presence; instrumentalists recruited from abroad not only had superior skills, but brought fashionable music with them in their heads. Through their presence, a truly international flavour entered some strata of British musical life. The point is well illustrated by 'Greenesleeves', seemingly as English a tune as one could hope to find. Yet this song turns out to be based on a harmonic formula of ultimately Italian origin – the so-called 'romanesca' bass. Almost certainly it found its way to Britain by way of immigrant musicians.

Under the supervision of Court musicians, the children of the English and Scottish royal families learnt to make music. All three of Henry VIII's heirs were taught to play the lute by Philippe van Wilder (d. 1553), a musician of Flemish birth who came to England in the 1520s, and rose in rank to become a gentleman of the privy chamber. Court musicians also taught the royal children to play keyboard instruments; in 1503, prior to their marriage, James IV of Scotland and Margaret Tudor entertained one another by playing the clavichord, and in 1564 Elizabeth I took pains to find out whether her own skills at the virginals surpassed those of Mary Stewart. With models such as these to follow, it is hardly surprising if, by the second half of the sixteenth century, the ability to play a plucked or keyboard instrument had been added to the list of accomplishments to which young people of rank or wealth might aspire.

Composing and Authorship

The craft of composing high-art repertories such as masses and motets, anthems and madrigals, was a specialist one, rich in conventions and rules that add up to the 'grammar' of polyphonic music. This craft was passed on mainly through the traditions of church music; for instance, it was taught to boy choristers as an element in their training, partly through performance and improvization, partly through written exercises. Since the world of professional church music was firmly closed to women and girls, it is no surprise that all known composers of Tudor art music were men, the majority of them church musicians throughout their lives. Amateur composers almost never entered the arena, and when they did so their efforts tend to betray their marginal status. Tudor Britain's most celebrated amateur composer is Henry VIII, who in his youth wrote both church music (lost) and polyphonic songs (still extant); the generally moderate level of his achievement implies only a light brush with formal musical pedagogy.[29] Later in the sixteenth century, amateurs may have had more ready access to the secrets of compositional craft through the church-trained musicians who acted as their teachers; and it was a church musician, Thomas Morley, who published the first English-language manual on the rudiments of music, *A Plaine and Easie Introduction to Practicall Musicke* (1597). Even then, however, we look in vain for any sign of women committing their musical thoughts to paper.

Throughout the Tudor period, it was normal to acknowledge the authorship of high-art music; most of the compositions that survive in manuscript or print bear attributions. Some composers clearly acquired considerable reputations; William Byrd in particular was singled out by his Elizabethan audiences. It may come as a surprise, then, to discover that no Tudor musician was ever employed or salaried specifically as a composer, and that records of remuneration for one-off commissions are very rare. Little is known about the circumstances that might lead a singing man or church organist to create a new piece, nor is it clear to what extent employers and patrons became involved in that process. Almost certainly the employment prospects for a church musician could increase significantly if he happened to have a fertile mind for composition; the upward mobility of some composers (such as Thomas Tallis, William Byrd, and in Scotland Robert Carvor, all of whom held Chapel Royal positions) implies that they were especially valued on this account. But since those men may also have been exceptional performing musicans, and had administrative or other skills to recommend them, the true situation is impossible to assess.

The idea of authorship – and indeed the very notion of 'fixed' compositions – changes materially when we look to other repertories. Song-composers such as Dowland and Campion, who would have accompanied their own singing with a lute, probably refined their works through performance, finally issuing in printed form pieces that they themselves would subsequently have amplified or changed. Composers of keyboard music probably fixed their works principally for the sake of their amateur pupils; sometimes those amateurs themselves were the copyists, writing down what their teacher-composer himself would have reckoned only a version of his work. Music of these kinds moved fluidly between performance and notation, and in manuscript copies of it the extent of anonymity can be relatively high. For professional instrumentalists, such as city waits and court musicians, the situation was more fluid still. 'New' works would often have been built on the substructure of old ones (in the same way that 'Greenesleeves' derives from the 'romanesca' bass), and there must have been much collective improvizing around agreed frameworks, just as jazz musicians do today. In the 'broadside ballad' repertory, the idea of authorship breaks down altogether; ballad-tunes belong to common experience, and the sheets cite them by name, not by composer – much to the glee of modern musicologists, who never tire of trying to track a melody back to its roots.

Owning Music

At that level of common experience, 'ownership' of music relied upon memory alone. A large stock of songs lodged in the minds of the ploughman and carter, tailor and shoemaker, but those songs were never written down; there was no reason why they should be. At the opposite extreme, church musicians depended heavily upon parchment and paper to preserve and transmit their repertories, and educated amateurs who learnt from them followed their example. By the end of the sixteenth century, amateurs had become the principal makers and collectors of music-books; their activities and tastes have been researched in some detail. It should be stressed, however, that the number of people who could read music notation was tiny, certainly when compared with the number who could read verbal texts, and that any history of the music book in Tudor Britain will touch only a small proportion of the British population.

Traditionally, performers of music relied upon manuscript copies to preserve their own selection of pieces, and that practice continued well into the age of print. Church choirs made their own performing manuscripts; church organists played either by ear, or semi-extempore from the same books as the choirs. Although in principle the printing press might usefully and quickly have supplied new, alternative repertories in the wake of reformation and counter-reform, in practice there is little evidence of that happening. John Marbecke's *The Booke of Common Praier Noted* of 1550 (STC 16441), a collection of English-texted plainchant meant for use by church choirs, ran to only a single edition; John Day's *Mornyng and Evenyng Prayer and Communion* (STC 6418–19), a selection of polyphony for church choirs, appeared in 1565 after a long period of gestation, and was evidently no more successful. Nor could the press supply choirs with 'classics' of music, since the notion of a permanent and stable repertory did not exist; new works were constantly being added, old ones dropped. In short, manuscripts met the needs of most musical professionals.

Amateurs were not so easily satisfied. They became the principal importers and collectors of foreign printed music, and it was for them that English composers at the end of the sixteenth century not only composed but also published their collections of motets, madrigals and lute-ayres. Although the number of those publications was small when compared with the production of presses in Italy, France and the Low Countries, they are useful indicators of specifically British trends, since they were printed for local use, not for export, the English language being barely spoken abroad. With their dedications to patrons and effusive prefatory verses, these publications hint at a mini-craze for music ownership in the late years of Elizabeth's reign, specifically for music cast in Italianate forms such as the madrigal, ballett and canzonet. The enterepreneurial Thomas Morley, whose *A Plaine and Easie Introduction to Practicall Musicke* set out to explain the elements of music theory, was also the leading composer of this fashionable new music.

Listening

Beyond generalities, very little is known about the responses of Tudor men and women to the music they heard. Those who mention their listening experiences tend to do so in unspecific terms, by referring (for instance) to the sweetness or splendour of the sound, or the skill of the performers; very rarely does the witness of a performance mention the music's composer by name, or the title of the work, let alone address its content. A disparity therefore existed between the attitude of performing musicians, who clearly cared about the issues of attribution and quality, and the attitude of audiences, whose attention was evidently drawn more to the thrill of the performance. True connoisseurship of musical works was probably the preserve of the very few.

Rather more can be gleaned about the attitudes of listeners from their negative responses to music, such as those quoted at the head of this chapter. For Philip Stubbes, music had an effeminizing influence, and it was clearly unwanted.[30] John Field and Thomas Wilcox, who were concerned that congregations should engage with the Word of God, mistrusted music's insinuation into church services, since it could become an object of adoration in its own right. Although their opinions might be challenged through (for instance) the motets and anthems of William Byrd, which demonstrate how rhetorical a musical setting can be in its projection of a verbal text, the case against listening might always be argued on the grounds that it was a passive activity; a congregation was more fully involved when it sang a psalm from the Sternhold and Hopkins psalter than when listening to a fine anthem by Byrd. Lovers of Byrd's music may instinctively feel that no competition exists here, and that there is justification when, in almost every account of Tudor music, Byrd's music is discussed at length, metrical psalmody barely at all. But in Tudor Britain itself, the balance probably tipped the other way. The issue of participation in music, rather than merely listening to it (as we largely do today), was therefore in some ways an absolutely central one.

Afterword: Dance

The subject of dance falls into the margins of this chapter. Although music accompanies dance, and sometimes evokes it (as is the case with the many stylized dances that were composed for lutes, keyboard instruments and consorts of viols, most of which were not meant for actual dancers to use), in itself music is not the core of this most complex and evanescent of art-forms. Through the combination of music, body-language, gesture, pose, display, choreography and costume, Tudor men and women used dance as a powerfully expressive medium. In courtly dance and the allied genre of the masque, emphasis fell largely on the expression of civility, through codes that evolved at least in part from close reading of the texts and art-works of Antiquity.[31] Even those lofty dance-forms, however, never lost sight of the ground they shared with social dance, namely the expression and projection of gender and sexuality. Within all this, music could play only a supporting role – although in the process it gained some considerable enrichment of its own expressive vocabulary, by being able to allude to meanings that lay beyond its own sounds.

Courtly dance lends itself readily to study today, since so much evidence of it survives in contemporary discussions of the subject, in documentary sources, and through iconography and notated music. By comparison, popular dance is elusive, more known about than known, and musical traces of it are rare. Partly for that reason, partly with the aim of drawing together many strands of discussion that run through this chapter, we might ponder one scrap of evidence that is particularly evocative. It comes from an important but little-known musical work, neglected today largely because only a fragment of it exists – too little to convert into an actual performance (the work is a song originally scored for four singers, but of these, only the soprano part survives).[32] It dates from the mid-sixteenth century, and it describes in narrative form one of the great St Cuthbert's day fairs in the city of Durham. Through words and music that quote from actual songs and dances, it takes us with the crowds through the outskirts of the city, up the narrow streets and into the cathedral precincts. It is hard to imagine richer evidence than this of the ways in which popular song and dance once projected notions of identity and gender, served to bond social groups, and played a part in affirming and challenging ideas; yet this evidence is expressed here, most unusually, in a high-art composition that itself could only have been sung by skilled and literate singers (their identity is unknown), presumably to an audience (also unidentified) of far greater sophistication than the people who are observed by the song itself. The section quoted below, which comes from near the end of this substantial work, begins with a rare evocation of a Robin Hood 'play', in which the participants would have been male. Balancing it is something even rarer: a round-dance or singing-game performed by young women, the words and music of which have evidently been quoted at length. If gaps in the text deny us full access to the song itself, we may at least imagine them being filled authentically with the noises of the crowd and the sound of the dancers' feet:

> ther was dysgysyng / piping and dansyng / and as we cam nere [. . .] which thus began[:] Robyne [. . .] Robyn robyne and many man haith a fayre wyffe that doth him lytill good Robyn robyn robyn and joly roben lend me the bowe[;] / through every strett thus can they go / and every man his horne dyd blowe / tro tro tro tro ro ro ro ro [. . .] / the maydens came [. . .]: /

> > [. . .]
> > when I was in my mothers bower
> > [. . .]
> > I hade all that I wolde
> > > the bayly berith the bell away
> > > [. . .]
> > > the lylle the rose the rose I lay
> > [. . .]
> > the sylver is whit rede is the golde
> > [. . .]
> > the robes they lay in folde
> > > the bayly berith the bell away
> > > [. . .]
> > > the lylle the rose the rose I lay
> > [. . .]
> > and through the glasse wyndow shines the sone
> > [. . .]
> > how shuld I love and I so young
> > > the bayly berith the bell away
> > > [. . .]
> > > the lylle the rose the rose I lay

NOTES

1. John Case, *The Praise of Musicke* (London, 1586; STC 20184).
2. Philip Stubbes, *The Anatomy of Abuses* (London, 1583; STC 23376).
3. Church of England, injunctions (1559; STC 10102.8).
4. John Field and Thomas Wilcox, *An Admonition to the Parliament* (London, 1572; STC 10847).

5. The principal studies of reform in sixteenth-century British church music are (for England) Le Huray, *Music and the Reformation*; Temperley, *The Music of the English Parish Church*; Lehmberg, *The Reformation of Cathedrals*; and (for Scotland) Preece, *'Our awin Scottis use'*. The Tudor Chapel Royal is considered in Kisby, 'The royal household chapel in early-Tudor London', and Page, *Uniform and Catholic*.

6. The richest study of the Elizabethan amateurs is Price, *Patrons and Musicians*.

7. Many of points made in this chapter are amplified in Milsom, 'Music' (for the period up to 1557); and in Krummel, *English Music Printing* (for the later period).

8. See for example Watt, *Cheap Print*, and Fox, *Oral and Literate Culture*.

9. For an alternative overview, see Milsom, 'Music', which considers the high-art music of the elite in greater detail.

10. See in particular Elliott, 'Music of Scotland'; Shire, *Song, Dance and Poetry*; and Preece, *'Our awin Scottis use'*.

11. John Case, *The Praise of Musicke* (London, 1586; STC 20184).

12. MacCulloch, *Tudor Church Militant*, p. 12.

13. Miles Coverdale, *Goostly psalmes and spirituall songes* (London, c.1535; STC 5892).

14. English metrical psalm-singing is considered in Temperley, *The Music of the English Parish Church*, and Leaver, *'Goostly Psalmes'*. The most useful overview of Scottish psalmody remains Patrick, *Four Centuries*.

15. Quoted in Leaver, *'Goostly Psalmes'*, p. 241.

16. The most comprehensive catalogue is Livingstone, *British Broadside Ballads*; the fullest study is Watt, *Cheap Print*.

17. Fox, *Oral and Literate Culture*, p. 385.

18. These estimates are indebted to Watt, *Cheap Print*, chapter 2.

19. 'A newe ballad of a lover/extollinge his ladye', to be sung to the tune of 'Damon and Pithias' (STC 18876); 'Damon and Pithias' refers to the play by Richard Edwards, master of the choristers to the Chapel Royal, and the ballad-sheet's 'tune' seems to be one of his compositions.

20. London, British Library, MS Harley 7578, ff. 111–113v.

21. Stevens, *Music and Poetry*, pp. 44, 286.

22. See Milsom, 'Songs and society'.

23. See in particular Bowers, 'Choral institutions'; Lehmberg, *The Reformation of Cathedrals*; and (for Scotland) Preece, *'Our awin Scottis use'*.

24. See Bowers, 'The cultivation and promotion of music'.

25. Osborn, *The Autobiography of Thomas Whythorne*, p. 245. This eye-witness opinion goes some way towards tempering the view of Lehmberg (*The Reformation of Cathedrals*, p. 182) that 'musical standards remained high'.

26. See Smith, 'Elizabethan church music'.

27. Thomas Morley, *A Plaine and Easie Introduction to Practicall Musicke* (London, 1597; STC 18133).

28. See Monson, 'Byrd, the Catholics, and the motet'.

29. See Fallows, 'Henry VIII as a composer' (which builds upon Stevens, *Music and Poetry*).

30. This point is developed in Austern, ' "Alluring the auditorie to effeminacie" '.

31. The latter point is explored in Franko, *The Dancing Body*.

32. For a discussion and full transcription of this song, see Milsom, 'Cries of Durham'.

BIBLIOGRAPHY

Austern, Linda Phyllis, ' "Alluring the auditorie to effeminacie": music and the idea of the feminine in early modern England', *Music and Letters*, 74 (1993), 343–54.

Bowers, Roger, 'Choral institutions within the English church, 1340–1500' (PhD dissertation, University of East Anglia, 1975).

Bowers, Roger, 'The cultivation and promotion of music in the household and orbit of Thomas Wolsey', in S. J. Gunn and P. G. Lindley, eds, *Cardinal Wolsey: Church, State and Art* (Cambridge, 1991), pp. 178–218.

Elliott, Kenneth, 'Music of Scotland 1500–1700' (PhD dissertation, University of Cambridge, 1958).

Fallows, David, 'Henry VIII as a composer', in Chris Banks, Arthur Searle and Malcolm Turner eds, *Sundry Sorts of Music Books: Essays on The British Library Collections Presented to O. W. Neighbour on his 70th Birthday* (London, 1993), pp. 27–39.

Fox, Adam, *Oral and Literate Culture in England, 1500–1700* (Oxford, 2000).

Franko, Mark, *The Dancing Body in Renaissance Choreography (c. 1416–1589)* (Birmingham, AL, 1986).

Kisby, Fiona, 'The royal household chapel in early-Tudor London' (PhD dissertation, University of London, 1996).

Krummel, D. W., *English Music Printing, 1553–1700* (London, 1975).

Leaver, Robin, *'Goostly Psalmes and Spirituall Songes': English and Dutch Metrical Psalms from Coverdale to Utenhove, 1535–1566* (Oxford, 1991).

Lehmberg, Stanford E., 'Cathedral music and musicians', in *The Reformation of Cathedrals: Cathedrals in English Society, 1485–1603* (Princeton NJ, 1988), chapter 8.

Le Huray, Peter, *Music and the Reformation in England, 1549–1660* (2nd edition, Cambridge, 1978).

Livingstone, Carole Rose, *British Broadside Ballads of the Sixteenth Century: A Catalogue of the Extant Sheets and an Essay* (New York and London, 1991).

MacCulloch, Diarmaid, *Tudor Church Militant: Edward VI and the Protestant Reformation* (Harmondsworth, 1999).

Milsom, John, 'Cries of Durham', *Early Music*, 18 (1989), 147–60.

Milsom, John, 'Music', in Boris Ford ed. *The Cambridge Guide to the Arts in Britain*, vol. III, *Renaissance and Reformation* (Cambridge, 1989, reissued as *16th Century Britain* in 1992), pp. 169–207.

Milsom, John, 'Music', in Lotte Hellinga and J. B. Trapp, eds, *The Cambridge History of the Book in Britain, III: 1400–1557* (Cambridge, 1999), pp. 541–54.

Milsom, John, 'Songs and society in early Tudor London', *Early Music History*, 19 (1997), 235–93.

Monson, Craig, 'Byrd, the Catholics, and the motet: the hearing reopened', in Dolores Pesce, ed. *Hearing the Motet: Essays on the Motet of the Middle Ages and Renaissance* (New York and Oxford, 1997), pp. 348–74.

Osborn, James M., ed., *The Autobiography of Thomas Whythorne* (Oxford, 1961).

Page, Daniel, 'Uniform and catholic: church music in the reign of Mary Tudor (1553–1558)' (PhD dissertation, Brandeis University, 1996).

Patrick, Millar, *Four Centuries of Scottish Psalmody* (London, 1949).

Preece, Isobel Woods, *'Our awin Scottis use': Music in the Scottish Church up to 1603*, ed. Sally Harper, with additional material by Warwick Edwards and Gordon J. Munro (Glasgow and Aberdeen, 2002).

David C. Price, *Patrons and Musicians of the English Renaissance* (Cambridge, 1981).

Shire, Helena Mennie, *Song, Dance and Poetry of the Court of Scotland under King James VI* (Cambridge, 1969).

Smith, Alan, 'Elizabethan church music at Ludlow', *Music and Letters*, 49 (1968), 108–21.

Stevens, John, *Music and Poetry in the Early Tudor Court* (London, 1961).

Temperley, Nicholas, *The Music of the English Parish Church* (Cambridge, 1979).
Watt, Tessa, *Cheap Print and Popular Piety, 1550–1640* (Cambridge, 1991).

FURTHER READING

Some of the pioneering studies of Tudor music, though now showing signs of age, remain important sources of factual information and quotations; they include Walter L. Woodfill, *Musicians in English Society from Elizabeth to Charles I* (1953); Frank L. Harrison, *Music in Medieval Britain* (2nd edition, 1963); and Morrison Comegys Boyd, *Elizabethan Music and Music Criticism* (2nd edition, 1967). Thomas Morley's *A Plaine and Easie Introduction to Practicall Musicke* (1597) is most readily accessible in the modern-spelling version edited by R. Alec Harman (1952).

For up-to-date biographical information about Tudor and Stewart musicians and composers, the most useful resource is the online edition of *The New Grove Dictionary of Music and Musicians* (references in the text used material found were in May 2003, but the website is regularly updated. The print verse is published by OUP in New York and Oxford, 2000). For English Court musicians, see Andrew Ashbee's *Records of English Court Music* (vols I–IV, 1986–91; vols. V–VIII, 1991–5), and Peter Holman, *Four and Twenty Fiddlers: The Violin at the English Court, 1540–1690* (1993).

There is no single comprehensive guide to the surviving sources of the music itself. The most important pre-Reformation English church manuscript sources are all mentioned in Hugh Benham, *Latin Church Music in England, 1460–1575* (1977), although subsequent research has refined much of the information given there. The Elizabethan manuscript sources of Tudor Latin-texted sacred music are broadly surveyed in John Milsom, 'Sacred songs in the chamber', in *English Choral Practice, 1400–1650*, ed. John Morehen (1995), pp. 161–79. For the principal sources of English-texted church music, see Peter Le Huray, *Music and the Reformation*, 1549–1610 (1978); for Scottish church sources, see I. W. Preece, *'Our awin Scottis use': Music in the Scottish Church up to 1603*, ed. Sally Hamper (2002); and for music-books printed in Elizabethan England, see D. W. Krummel, *English Music Printing, 1553–1700* (1975).

Chapter Twenty-Eight

Science and Technology

Lesley B. Cormack

Introduction

The study of nature changed radically during the sixteenth century. Natural philosophy, dedicated to an epistemological and ontological understanding of nature and its underlying concepts, developed new conceptual and theoretical models, especially in astronomy and the physical sciences. The mathematical arts, often seen by contemporaries as a separate branch of philosophy and nature study, began to interact with natural philosophy, as philosophers increasingly saw mathematics as the language of nature. Historians have therefore sometimes characterized this period as the beginning of the mathematization of nature. Methods of investigation also changed during the early modern period as experimentation began to emerge as a legitimate and important method of inquiry and fact determination. Equally, the place of study and the importance of this study to the secular world also changed, from the universities and scholasticism to the courts and more pragmatic princely interests. This was the beginning of what would come to be called the scientific revolution, although this revolution would not be complete until the end of the seventeenth century.

Through most of the sixteenth century English natural philosophers were not major players in this intellectual transformation, and this is even more true of Scottish and Irish scholars, who did not take a lead in natural philosophical pursuits until the late seventeenth and eighteenth centuries. Until the mid-sixteenth century, most English scholars were more concerned with religious and humanistic concerns than with natural philosophical ones. Those interested in natural philosophy received their training or inspiration from the continent and it was really only by the end of the century that an indigenous English natural philosophical and mathematical community began to function robustly. In many ways, the transformation of nature studies in England, which began about 1550, owed more to developing mercantile and artisanal needs than to scholarly imperatives. It was only with the growing interests of mercantile and courtly patrons, a change in educational emphasis, and increasing mathematical understanding on the part of English natural philosophers, that by 1600 Englishmen had joined the European cultural, intellectual and social movement that would become the scientific revolution.

Historians have paid little attention to British participation in the early scientific revolution. Earlier historians of the scientific revolution, such as Alexandre Koyré or Herbert Butterfield, stressed sixteenth-century developments by great Continental thinkers such as Copernicus, Galileo and Kepler.[1] More recent historians, such as Steven Shapin, have changed this emphasis to England, but only by the mid-seventeenth century, when the foundation of the Royal Society and the important work of natural philosophers like Robert Boyle, Robert Hook and Isaac Newton assured England of her prominence in the scientific world.[2] Of course, individual sixteenth-century thinkers, such as John Dee and Thomas Harriot, have been examined, but in studies seeking to understand scientific change in the period, England is conspicuous by its absence. This is even more evident in Scottish historiography, where the Scottish enlightenment has overshadowed earlier developments, which must have existed. Sixteenth-century Scottish natural philosophy thus remains a neglected but potentially fruitful period for future historians, since the path of nature study was undoubtedly quite different from that of England.

The exceptions to the lack of attention to sixteenth-century England came from two mid-twentieth-century historians, Frances Yates and Edgar Zilsel.[3] Yates argued that the importance of neoplatonic or hermetic magic in sixteenth-century intellectual life was an important catalyst for the scientific revolution, and saw the practice of such magic in the studies and laboratories of English magi such as John Dee and Robert Fludd. Zilsel, in contrast, affirmed that a connection between the growth of capitalism in sixteenth-century Europe, especially entrepreneurial England, and the study of nature was responsible for the scientific revolution. Both theories have been rejected or ignored in recent years, again leading to the obscurity of sixteenth-century England. Both Yates and especially Zilsel, however, deserve credit for their examination of the particular world of sixteenth-century English natural philosophy and mathematics, since this era is ripe for re-investigation precisely because there were few luminaries and thus it gives us a much better picture of the practice of natural philosophy before the transformations of the seventeenth century.

The State of the Field Before 1550

Throughout the first half of the sixteenth century, few English scholars were interested in questions of natural philosophy or mathematics, and this is reflected in the current lack of scholarly coverage. Most English thinkers of the period were concerned with a reform of scholarship following the influence of humanism and the Reformation. Even in this, their impact was limited because they were relatively few in number. While Merton College in Oxford had been famous throughout Europe in the thirteenth and fourteenth centuries for its studies of motion, this fame had dwindled by the sixteenth century and scientific study had largely been superceded by more humanistic pursuits. Humanism could and did help recover ancient natural philosophical texts and improve philological techniques, and some humanists, such as Cuthbert Tunstall (1474–1559), promoted mathematical understanding as part of the larger enterprise. Equally, some humanists paid at least lip service to the importance of natural philosophy to the well-rounded education, but most educational theorists and practitioners devoted more time to ancient languages and literatures than to a revival of Aristotle or Ptolemy.

Most humanists, both in England and on the Continent, were more concerned with understanding the books of the Bible and Cicero in their original languages than in predicting the paths of planets, but their enterprise did help infuse new life into natural philosophy. The humanist interest in classical sources led to a wave of rediscovery and translation, but unlike the late-medieval search for Greek philosophy, the humanists treated the sources in a completely new and more sceptical manner. While humanism introduced a new purpose for and mode of scientific discourse, it also fuelled a renewed interest in Aristotelianism. The humanist rediscovery of early Greek versions of Aristotelian texts (formerly known only through Arabic translations) forced scholars to make their arguments and methodology more rigorous. Thus, as Charles Schmitt demonstrated, Aristotle's system did not give way before the humanist onslaught; rather, medieval scholasticism incorporated much of the methodology and rigour of the new humanistic studies, while retaining Aristotle's basic framework. The Aristotelian system had proven extremely fruitful as a research programme; it was all-encompassing, including the study of the physical world – with physics, astronomy, and biology – and the study of the spiritual and social world – with metaphysics, logic, and politics. Until a similarly comprehensive paradigm could be established in the seventeenth century, Aristotelianism remained useful and necessary. Indeed, natural philosophy in England and abroad was essentially an Aristotelian enterprise throughout the sixteenth century. John Case (d. 1599), an important Oxford scholar through the second half of the century, was probably most influential in encouraging a rigorous Aristotelian foundation to English natural philosophy. Case wrote several important Aristotelian textbooks and taught an entire generation of natural philosophers who would go on to influence the study of nature throughout the seventeenth century.[4]

A few humanists actively promoted the *quadrivium* (the mathematical portion of the seven liberal arts) in the first half of the century, most notably Cuthbert Tunstall. Tunstall was a humanist theologian, part of Thomas More's circle, and wrote the first text on arithmetic published in England, *De Arte Supputandi* (1522), before being consecrated bishop of London. Tunstall wrote this book as a final act of secular scholarship, based on his research while on diplomatic missions abroad. Unfortunately, Tunstall's arithmetic was not particularly popular. It was never reprinted or translated into English and, although it was owned by university students and colleges at the end of the century, it had more status as a forerunner than as an actual stimulus to English mathematics.

During the first half of the sixteenth century most educational reformers did not follow Tunstall's lead. Such scholars were interested in introducing humanistic studies to England and only secondarily saw the importance of some natural philosophical and mathematical knowledge. Thomas Elyot (1490?–1546), for example, stressed the need for potential governors of the state to receive a substantial education. In a book designed to win favour with Henry VIII, Elyot suggested that: 'The education or fourme of bringing up of the childe of a gentilman which is to have authoritie in a publike weale' should include an understanding of 'the olde tables of Ptolomee where in all the worlde is paynted' as well as 'the demonstration of cosmographie', not through travel but through reading. 'I can not tell what more pleasure shuld happen to a gentil witte than to beholde in his owne house every thynge that with in all the worlde is contained.'[5] This, however, was Elyot's only foray into the study of nature, in a book of 258 folio pages, and in this case, Elyot argued that the historical and descriptive views of Strabo should take precedence over these maps of Ptolemy's.

Thomas Elyot was a prominent Tudor humanist. His advice on the education of those destined to govern was an interesting blend of neoplatonic idealism and political expediency. While his life was a series of unsuccessful patronage bids, his advice in *The Governor* was that the classics and moral philosophy must be learned and used in the service of the state. Given this overt message that engagement with the world was necessary for the scholar, the study of cosmography and maps, suggested by Elyot, was intended for application. Elyot argued for the introduction of the maps of Ptolemy (after an understanding of the sphere had been achieved) 'to prepare the childe to understandynge of histories.'[6] Such histories, and such maps, were necessary knowledge to someone aspiring to status and power.

Most humanists were afforded little time to study the natural world. Richard Pace (1483–1536), writing in 1517 on *The Benefit of a Liberal Education*, ultimately saw Greek and Roman authors and through them moral philosophy as the guide and guarantor of a moral and upright life. While Pace ranged widely in his recommended areas of study, including medicine and geography for example, he was sceptical of the true value of astronomy (and its sister astrology), arithmetic and alchemy. In a dialogue designed to enliven the pedagogical debate, geometry bemoans her fate as a debased study:

'That's true', said Geometry. 'No one, or almost no one teaches me these days. . . . I'm so kind to the human race that I readily let them transform me from an extraordinary science and field of learning into something used every day and learned by experiences. In that way I cheapened myself even more.'[7]

Pace implied that the original aim of both mathematical and natural philosophical studies was true understanding of the natural world. Unfortunately, this purpose had been lost, but Pace was not particularly interested in the rehabilitation of these debased scientific studies, nor did he see this as a primary responsibility for education. Rather, Pace spent the majority of his text and his argument explaining the importance of the *trivium* (the three literary liberal arts of grammar, rhetoric and logic) and of authors such as Cicero.

By the second half of the century, educational theorists were much more interested in supplying a practical education, including the study of the natural world. For example, Sir Humphrey Gilbert (1539?–1583) proposed a remarkably practical education for Queen Elizabeth's wards, perhaps based on Gilbert's own interests and experiences. Gilbert had been educated at Eton and Oxford and then devoted his life to navigation and a search for the north-west passage before perishing off the coast of Newfoundland. In his proposal, designed to obtain Court patronage, he stressed the need for mathematics and navigational education. Among the instructors to be hired, Gilbert included two mathematicians, one to read cosmography, astronomy and navigation, and the other to teach the art of maps and sea charts.[8] Clearly, imperial aims had overtaken the commonwealth values of earlier educational reformers; Gilbert believed that an ability to understand the world and exploit that knowledge for wealth and country would be more acceptable to Elizabeth and her courtiers than earlier arguments about the good life.

There were several good reasons for educational reformers to change their approach. Goals of education altered dramatically during the century. Where few courtiers, politicians or civil servants were university-trained at the beginning of the century, by 1600 a university education was practically a requirement. This changed the content of education as well as its delivery. The direction of education was also linked to patronage and as patronage patterns changed, natural philosophers and mathematicians were increasingly sought. These patrons, both merchants and courtiers, were responding to an evolving economic imperative, brought about by the rapid expansion of mercantile and trading opportunities. These activities, particularly by the trading companies, were in turn partly made possible by the increasing sophistication of the natural philosophers and mathematical practitioners.

Mathematics and the Muscovy Company

The impetus for increased mathematical education thus came from outside the traditional scholarly community. Merchants and trading companies were interested in applied mathematical practice, especially navigation, surveying and accounting. This need became more pronounced as these merchants changed their focus to the Atlantic trade, putting them in competition with the much better informed Spanish and Portuguese. Algebra was first introduced informally as a practical tool for calculation, but around mid-century merchant companies came to believe that they required a more theoretical grounding in mathematics, especially because they needed to navigate largely uncharted northern waters. This is best illustrated by the patronage of Robert Recorde by the newly founded Muscovy Company in the 1550s.

Robert Recorde (1510–88) was a mathematical practitioner, interested in both practical and theoretical applications of mathematics. He was largely responsible for introducing arithmetic and mathematics to a wider audience in England and for re-establishing a mathematical language and discipline at this time. His career, at once academic and mercantile, shows the importance of the connection between theory and practice in the development of mathematics, navigation and other mathematical studies in the sixteenth century. Recorde, a Welshman, attended Oxford in the late 1520s. He received his BA in 1531, was elected a fellow of All Souls College, and licensed to practise medicine in 1533. He later moved to Cambridge, received his MD, and taught mathematics for a time at both Oxford and Cambridge. It was during his time as an academic that he wrote his first treatise on arithmetic, *The Ground of Artes Teachyng the Worke and Practise of Arithmetike* (1543, enlarged 1552). This was probably the first arithmetic text written in English, and certainly the most popular and influential, going through forty-five editions by 1699. In it, Recorde introduced the symbols for addition, subtraction, and equality, and its popularity guaranteed their gradual acceptance in the larger community. This book established Recorde as a mathematician who could make the connections between the academic world and popular education. Its dialogue form allowed the reader to participate actively and was easy to follow. Recorde claimed that he wrote *Ground of Arts* in order to help the English achieve educational parity with Europe, for

> Sore oftentymes have I lamented with my self the infortunate condition of England, seyng so many great clerkes to aryse in sundry other partes of the worlde, and so few

to apere in this our nation: where as for excellencye of naturall wytte (I thynke) fewe nations dooe matche englyshmen. But I can not impute the cause to anye other thynge, than to the contempt or mysregarde of learnynge.[9]

Recorde later moved to London where he practised as a physician, and in 1549 was appointed comptroller of the Bristol Mint. This move to Bristol was to prove significant, since Bristol merchants had been involved in overseas exploration and trade for several decades, including expeditions in the early 1550s to find a north-east passage, and they formally founded the Muscovy Company there in 1555. They recognized their need for mathematical knowledge and soon commissioned Recorde to write mathematical books for the use of their navigators. In 1551 Recorde published *Pathway to Knowledge*, an explication of geometry through the first four books of Euclid's *Elements*, and in 1556 (reissued 1596) *The Castle of Knowledge, Containing the Explication of the Sphere*, dealing with spherical geometry, astronomy and navigation. The latter was written and printed for the use of the Muscovy Company, and mentioned the Portuguese discoveries in order to illustrate the positions of the earth with respect to the sun. It was based on Ptolemy's astronomy and incorporated more recent astronomical work, including a brief, favourable mention of Copernican theory. Recorde's *Whetstone of Witte* (1557), his explication of algebra, was dedicated to the governors of the Muscovy Company and written, so Recorde claimed, to encourage the great exploration and trading enterprise on which they were embarked: 'I also will show certain means how without great difficulty you may sail to the north-east Indies, and so to Camul, Chinchital, and Balor.'[10] *Whetstone* was never reprinted, perhaps because it dealt with difficult mathematical concepts. It was based on German algebraic texts, including the treatment of the quadratic. Taken as a whole, Recorde's mathematical books contained a full course of mathematical study and many Elizabethan natural philosophers and mathematicians began their education with Recorde's books. In this way, he was hugely influential in developing the English scientific endeavour, an endeavour that therefore owed much to mercantile patronage.

In the end, Recorde's politics were his undoing, since his mercantile support was not matched by any powerful Court patronage. In fact, Recorde made enemies of important courtiers, ensuring his exclusion and downfall. Recorde supported the duke of Somerset in 1549, refusing to send money to armies led by Lord John Russell and Sir William Herbert (later earl of Pembroke). Herbert accused Recorde of treason over this incident and Recorde was confined at court for sixty days in 1550, while the mint ceased production. This was the start of a serious breach with Pembroke. After a series of clashes with the earl, Recorde ended his days in prison, unable to pay the fine Pembroke demanded for libel.

At the same time that merchants began to develop an interest in the mathematical sciences and in the theoretical and practical work of mathematical practitioners such as Recorde, precision instrument-makers began to appear in London. Precision instruments, sometimes called philosophical instruments, required mathematical understanding for their manufacture and therefore could only be made by skilled artisans, often themselves mathematical practitioners. These instruments were necessary for sophisticated navigation, astronomical observation, and natural philosophical experimentation by the seventeenth century. The first philosophical instrument-maker in England was probably Thomas Gemini (*c.* 1510–62), who came from

Louvain to London in the 1540s. In London, Gemini worked as an engraver, printer and publisher as well as manufacturer of mathematical instruments. His business ventures provided a starting-point for an important tradition of London instrument-makers in the second half of the century that included Humphrey Cole (?1530–91) and Emery Molyneaux (*fl.* 1590s), the globe- and map-maker.[11] Cole was probably the most influential instrument-maker of his generation, making instruments for Martin Frobisher's voyages and several other expeditions. Twenty-two instruments made by him are still extant, including a small astrolabe given to Henry, prince of Wales, in the early seventeenth century. In 1568, Cole helped set up the Company of Mineral and Battery Works to manufacture brass, demonstrating the close connections between manufacturing, trade, exploration and mathematical practice. An important mathematical community thus began to develop among instrument-makers, merchants, mathematical practitioners and natural philosophers, a community that requires further investigation than it has yet received from historians.

Navigation and Astronomy

Merchant companies, mathematical practitioners and increasingly courtly patrons were interested in applied mathematical subjects such as navigation, surveying, ballistics and fortification. All were necessary for trans-Atlantic trade, as well as for the increasingly imperial self-fashioning of the monarch, court and government. The most pressing concern was navigation, which required an understanding of the shape and structure of the globe, a coherent mapping system, and an ability to measure distances and calculate routes, all of which was based on spherical geometry and geographical theory, as well as an understanding of astronomy, since the heavens were the logical guide to direction and place. Following Recorde's work, which introduced English scholars and merchants to basic mathematical concepts including astronomy and spherical geometry, several men, most trained at the universities and all involved in mercantile concerns in London and elsewhere, developed introductory treatises on these topics and began to participate in the larger Continental scholarly conversations. These practical concerns, combined with growing theoretical underpinning and interests developed at the universities and in correspondence with Continental natural philosophers, provided an ideal climate for the creation of an English natural philosophical community.

This community began to form through university, Court and London connections. Loose coteries of like-minded scholars grew up, at Oxford, in London and around the households of prominent natural philosophers. Henry Briggs (1561–1630), for example, provided a focal point at Oxford and later at Gresham College in London. He also made connections with Scottish mathematician John Napier of Murchiston (1550–1617), expanding his work on logarithms in the seventeenth century. Likewise, many scholars and practitioners gathered in London and at Mortlake around John Dee, perhaps the most visible natural philosopher in England in the second half of the sixteenth century.

John Dee (1527–1608) was a mathematician, geographer, natural philosopher and Renaissance magus. He attended St Johns College, Cambridge, receiving his BA in 1545, and became a fellow of Trinity College in 1546, achieving his MA soon after. He studied for a time at Louvain, lectured in Paris on Euclid and returned to England to become one of the foremost mathematical practitioners and natural philosophers in the country. Dee numbered among his friends Robert Recorde, Leonard and Thomas Digges, the surveyor Cyprian Lucar, the popular mathematical and equestrian writer Thomas Blundeville, Thomas Harriot and William Camden. Anyone who was anyone in Elizabethan mathematics and natural philosophy knew Dee. Dee was also influential in scholarly, Court and mercantile circles, making connections that would be important to the growth of the natural philosophical community in England. He advised Elizabeth and the privy council on esoteric and practical concerns, as well as briefing every important explorer and merchant-adventurer of his time.

Robert Recorde's important work in mathematical instruction was continued by John Dee. First Dee edited a new version of Recorde's *Ground of Artes* in 1561. Then in 1570, Dee collaborated with Henry Billingsley to produce the first English translation of Euclid's *Elements*. Dee wrote the *Mathematical Preface* to this translated *Elements*, at the request of a number of London practitioners, and in this preface, he provided a blueprint for the use of mathematics to investigate and understand every branch of the natural world.[12] Dee laid out schematically all present and future mathematical subjects and in the process created the objective of the mathematization of the entire study of nature.

In a treatise on navigation, *General and Rare Memorials Pertayning to the Perfect Art of Navigation* (1577), probably intended as a briefing paper for the privy council, Dee continued to argue for the full integration of mathematics and philosophy in imperial and mercantile concerns.[13] He was also interested in the unseen world through Renaissance magic, and devoted much of his life to attempts to uncover esoteric mysteries, especially through crystal-ball communication with angels. Dee thus supplied an important piece of evidence for Frances Yates' assertion of the connection between natural philosophy and magic. Historians such as Nicholas Clulee have since demonstrated that Dee's angelic magic was less integrated with his natural philosophy than Frances Yates once believed. It remains important, however, to stress that natural philosophers were interested in underlying essences, which included spiritual as well as material causes.[14]

Mathematical practitioners connected with Dee continued the work begun by Recorde, just as Dee himself had done. Leonard Digges (–1558?), for example, a close friend of Dee's, was one such mathematical practitioner, skilled in the 'sciences mathematicall', rather than a university-trained scholar. He had some connection to the Court, shown by his dedication of his books to Nicholas Bacon. Leonard Digges wrote books on astrology, surveying and the military sciences, all excellent mixed mathematical topics. His son, Thomas (d. 1595), carried on in his father's footsteps, completing two of Leonard's treatises and becoming a well-known mathematical practitioner in his own right. Significantly, Thomas did receive a university education and achieved significant political and career success, serving as an MP in the 1572 and 1585 parliaments and acting as muster-master-general of English forces in the Netherlands in 1586. Thomas, like his father, was probably a client of Nicholas Bacon, and probably acted as tutor to the young Francis. This father-and-son career trajectory demonstrates the increasing importance of university and specialized knowledge for career advancement, especially by young men from mercantile backgrounds.

The Diggeses produced a series of books explaining the mathematical arts. *A Geometriall Practise Named Pantometria . . . Lately Finished by Thomas Digges* (1571), for example, contained a full introduction to surveying, kinetics and gunnery. To this, Thomas Digges added his own treatise on geometrical solids. *An Arithmeticall Military Treatise Called Stratioticos*, begun by Leonard Digges and finished by Thomas (1579), was dedicated to the earl of Leicester, indicating Thomas' closer connections to the privy council and court. As Thomas stated in his dedication:

> And having spent many of my yeares in reducing the Sciences *Mathematicall*, from *Demonstrative Contemplation*, to *Experimentall Actions*, for the service of my *Prince* and *Countrey*. (beeyng thereto greately ayded by the *Practices, Observations, Monuments,* and *Conferences* of my Father, with the rarest Souldyoures of hys time) have among sundrie other discourses of *Navigation*, of *Fortification*, of *Pyrotechnie*, and great *Artillerie*, long sithence comenced, latelie finished this *Arithmeticall* Treatise, wholy applyed to *Militare* affayres.[15]

Perhaps most significantly, Thomas's 1576 edition of his father Leonard's *Prognostication*, *Alae seu Scalae Mathematicae* (first edition 1553) contained an appendix on the Copernican theory, including the first English translation of part of Copernicus' work. Thomas Digges wrote sympathetically of this theory, making him a very early potential supporter of heliocentrism. Situating this appendix in a work of practical mathematics and astronomy suggests an interesting connection between theoretical innovation and best practice.

There had been much controversy throughout Europe over the structure of the universe and the position of the earth and planets following Nicholas Copernicus's publication of *De Revolutionibus Orbium Coelestium* at his death in 1543. Copernicus claimed that a heliocentric model, with the sun in the centre and the planets orbiting around it, was mathematically equivalent to the earlier geocentric theory and better accounted for the observed phenomena. Copernicus, himself a devout Roman Catholic priest, did not argue that his model represented reality, but this was a clear implication, and one that caused considerable uproar in astronomical and religious circles alike. Many astronomers were happy to use Copernicus' mathematics, but few before Johannes Kepler and Galileo Galilei in the early seventeenth century were willing to commit themselves to heliocentrism as a true representation. In England, Thomas Digges' translation suggests early support for this new planetary model, as did Thomas Harriot's observations and sketches of the phases of the moon (based on Galileo's earlier observations) and Robert Fludd's neoplatonic schema.

Robert Fludd (1574–1637) was a physician, alchemist and astronomer, as well as a famous Rosicrucian and neoplatonist. He was educated at Oxford, receiving both an MA (1598) and an MD (1605), as well as studying alchemy abroad. He was censor of the College of Physicians four times and entered into several controversial exchanges with Kepler, Marin Mersenne and Pierre Gassendi. Fludd was the most vocal supporter of a heliocentric model in early modern England, tying it to a mystical explanation for the formation of the universe involving an angelic hierarchy and the mutually influential macrocosm and microcosm. Fludd's philosophical explanations provide more evidence to support Yates's contention that Rosicrucianism was the key to the origin of modern science, but Fludd represents only a minority opinion for this period. In fact, Fludd's argumentative demeanour may have delayed overall acceptance of Copernicanism in England rather than promoted it.[16]

Changing Patronage Structures

Growing interest in astronomy and mathematics on the part of a increasing segment of the population allowed mathematical practitioners to sell their wares successfully in the second half of the century. Thomas Blundeville (*fl.* 1561–98), for example, a Norfolk gentleman, friend of Dee's, perhaps tutor to Francis Bacon, and popular author of educational treatises for gentry, was one of a growing number of mathematical practitioners able to make his living writing popular books and using these books as advertisements for his private mathematics lessons. In *Exercises Containing Six Treatises...for Young Gentlemen* (1594), Blundeville carefully explained the mathematical arts necessary to anyone interested in the globe, for profit or pleasure. He began with two treatises on arithmetic, written for Elizabeth Bacon, daughter of Sir Nicholas Bacon, and therefore 'I had made this Arithmeticke so plaine and easie as was possible'.[17] He then added a third treatise on the principles of cosmography, first of the heavens and then of the earth. The fourth treatise examined the uses of the globes, both terrestrial and celestial. Fifth, Blundeville explained the use of the astrolabe, and finally, he included a long treatise on navigation, including the finding of longitude and latitude. Blundeville's book was very popular, appearing in several further editions in the seventeenth century, and Blundeville himself appears to have prospered as an author and teacher. Entrepreneurial mathematics-teaching thus went hand in hand with the educational revolution taking place in late sixteenth-century England.

Education was a rapidly changing institution in early modern England. The entrée into governing and public careers was more and more frequently provided by formal education rather than household apprenticeship. Literacy and knowledge of a number of disciplines were viewed as increasingly important attributes for the ambitious man on his way to the top. Therefore, increasing numbers of gentle and mercantile families sent their sons to Oxford and Cambridge, where they would meet the right people and through their studies gain access to the common understanding of the world they would need for governance. As the affairs of state seemed to require more knowledge than could be acquired merely through application, a university education seemed the route to cultural, economic and political success. Natural philosophy, mathematics and geographical knowledge, taught to these aspiring clients, patrons and governors, gave them useful information, a new way of viewing the world, and avenues to career advancement and profit-motivated trading expeditions.

At the same time, the institution of patronage, so important to the governance of the country, expanded to include scholarly patronage more generally and natural-philosophical and mathematical patronage particularly. Both at the royal Court and in aristocratic households, men interested in studies of nature began to dedicate books, donate instruments and devices, and achieve patronage positions. This patronage system as applied to natural philosophy was perhaps most striking on the Continent, where Galileo became the Medici philosopher, and Kepler the astronomer royal to Rudolph II. In England, John Dee worked to achieve a similar position of influence, and men like Walter Raleigh and Henry Percy, ninth earl of

Northumberland, surrounded themselves with natural philosophers and mathematicians. This allowed men of practical knowledge, sometimes skilled artisans and mathematical practitioners, to mingle with university-trained or self-taught natural philosophers. They brought together different ideas and interests and in doing so created new questions and goals for natural knowledge. Most natural philosophers attached to princely Courts gained their reputations by demonstrating both intellectual acuity and practical applications. For example, Johan Kepler and John Dee cast horoscopes for Rudolf II and Elizabeth I respectively. Dee advised Elizabeth on the most propitious day for her coronation, as well as consulting with navigators searching for a north-west passage. Likewise, Galileo's activities as a courtier were both esoteric and applied. These men walked a fine line between theory and practice, since all three were interested in large philosophical systems and desired Court patronage not simply for creating improved telescopes or new armillary spheres. But monarchs wanted results and all investigators of the natural world with Court connections were compelled on occasion to dance for their supper. So claims to utility and the search for topics interesting to those princely patrons changed the orientation of natural philosophy, away from philosophical speculation towards how things worked.

Thomas Harriot (c. 1560–1621) provides an excellent example of the natural-philosophical patronage system at work. Harriot was one of the most able philosophers and mathematical practitioners of his day, although his lack of published results limited his visibility to later natural philosophers and therefore any claims to the priority of his results. Consequently, modern historians were slow to recognize his interest, although this has now changed, and next to John Dee, Harriot is probably the most studied sixteenth-century natural philosopher.[18] During his career, Harriot was connected through patronage with the households of Raleigh, Northumberland, and Henry, prince of Wales. Harriot matriculated from St Mary's Hall, Oxford, in 1577 and received his BA there in 1580. By 1582, Raleigh had recruited Harriot from his old college at Oxford to be his tutor in mathematics. Harriot remained in this position for much of the last two decades of the sixteenth century. He advised Raleigh's captains and navigators, and pursued mathematical research of interest to Raleigh. It was under Raleigh's auspices that Harriot voyaged to Virginia, after having spent time in Ireland surveying and administering Raleigh's concerns. As Richard Hakluyt said of Harriot in 1587, in a dedication to Raleigh:

> By your experience in navigation you saw clearly that our highest glory as an insular kingdom would be built up to its greatest splendor on the firm foundation of the mathematical sciences, and so for a long time you have nourished in your household, with a most liberal salary, a young man well trained in those studies, Thomas Hariot, so that under his guidance you might in spare hours learn those noble sciences.[19]

Raleigh sent Harriot to Virginia in 1585 and Harriot used his time in the New World well. His description of Virginia, in his *Brief report of . . . Virginia* (1588), was an impressive assessment of the native flora and fauna and their potential for exploitation. It was reprinted a number of times in Continental compilations and was Harriot's chief claim to popular fame. Harriot was fascinated by the natives he encountered and was concerned that English colonists treat them as legitimate occupants of the land. He argued for co-operation with the natives and compiled the first word-list of any North American Indian language (probably Algonquin). This compilation shows his desire for communication, while at the same time classifying the world in order to understand and control it. His advice concerning Virginian settlement was to prove prophetic as the Virginia companies of the seventeenth century were established. This was the work of a man very aware of the practical and economic ramifications of the intellectual work of describing the larger world, as well as the imperial imperatives at work.

Harriot ranked an investigation of the mathematical structure of the globe as more important than exploration or navigation. His mathematics reflected his imperial attitude in general and the experience of his Virginian contacts in particular. He was deeply concerned about astronomical and physical questions, including the imperfection of the moon and the refractive indexes of various materials. Harriot was inspired by Galileo's telescopic observations of the moon and produced several fine sketches himself after *The Starry Messenger* appeared. He also investigated one of the most pressing problems of seventeenth-century mathematical geography – the problem of determining longitude at sea. Harriot worked long and hard on the longitude question and on other navigational problems, relating informally to many mathematical geographers his conviction that compass variation contained the key to unravelling the longitude knot. This latter problem was of particular interest to Raleigh, and to Henry Percy, who pensioned Harriot in 1597 and in whose house (Sion House near London) Harriot spent much time working on mathematical and philosophical problems. Harriot worked for both Raleigh and Percy during their respective years in the tower as state prisoners, and was imprisoned himself for a short time in connection with the Gunpowder Plot. Despite the hazards of a poor choice in patrons, however, Harriot by necessity maintained his connection with these men, and the natural philosophy and mathematics that he investigated owed much to their support.

Natural Philosophy Comes of Age

From early mercantile support of mathematical education and innovation at mid-century to the expansion of opportunities for university-educated gentlemen within the courts and patronage circles soon after, natural philosophy in England became a much more frequently practised and multifaceted enterprise by the end of the century. Astronomy and the mathematical sciences continued to flourish, especially in connection with exploration and European competition. Investigations of the motion of the compass needle, important for navigation, led to new interpretations of the unseen forces of magnetism and a new appreciation for the importance of such occult forces. A number of different areas of investigation, including medicine and anatomy, biological studies, geography and antiquarianism, called for a methodology of incremental fact-gathering. This inductive method would be described by Francis Bacon in the seventeenth century, but really developed in the sixteenth as more people became interested in observing the world around them. Finally, collecting sciences, connected with this methodology, produced an interest in display of exotic artifacts and the classification of nature, to be seen through the genesis of scientific displays and collections.

In the mathematical sciences, navigation, geography and cartography continued to occupy many thinkers. Edward Wright (1558?–1615), the most famous English geographer of the period, was very concerned with the problems of modern navigation. Wright was educated at Gonville and Caius College, Cambridge, receiving his BA in 1581 and his MA in 1584. He remained at Cambridge until the end of the century, with a brief journey to the Azores with the earl of Cumberland in 1589. Wright's greatest achievement was *Certaine Errors in Navigation* (1599), in which he enumerated the problems still remaining for modern navigation and argued that a mathematical solution was necessary. In this book, Wright explained Mercator's map projection mathematically for the first time, providing an elegant Euclidean proof of the geometry involved. He also published a table of meridian parts for each degree that enabled cartographers to construct accurate projections of the meridian network, and offered straightforward instructions on map construction.[20] Likewise, he constructed his own map using this method. Wright's work placed English mathematicians, for a time, in the vanguard of European mathematical geography. His books and mapping projects were equally significant for the close communication Wright advocated between theoretical mathematicians and practical navigators.

One of the problems identified by Wright and several others was the changing declination of the compass needle. In fact, the compass needle had a number of odd characteristics, including the 'dip', first identified by Robert Norman (*fl.* 1590), which indicated that the lodestone was attracted to the earth in a peculiar manner. William Gilbert (1540–1603) took up these problems with the lodestone (although there is much controversy as to his supposed debts to both Wright and Norman).[21] Gilbert demonstrated experimentally the existence and properties of terrestrial magnetism, arguing that the earth itself was a lodestone. Gilbert published his findings in *De Magnete* (1600), a book steeped in neoplatonic cosmology and full of experimental descriptions. It includes a positive assessment of Copernicanism and a suggestion that magnetism might provide the mechanism by which the earth was kept in orbit around the sun. This suggestion was taken up by Kepler, although Gilbert was much more hesitant in his support for a realist heliocentric position than Kepler was to be. Unfortunately, we know very little about Gilbert, since all his papers were destroyed, either during the civil war or later during the Great Fire of London. He was a gentleman, educated at Cambridge, and he practised medicine in London, becoming physician to Elizabeth and briefly to James. He was president of the College of Physicians from 1600 until his death. His work on terrestrial magnetism, with his discussion of that other imponderable fluid, electricity, established the parameters for such research well into the eighteenth century.

Gilbert's work is sometimes seen as an early model of experimental method, a path to be taken up repeatedly in the seventeenth century.[22] Likewise, several natural-philosophical pursuits used the methodology of collecting and categorization (taxonomy) and incremental fact-gathering or induction. Anatomical work, although largely a Continental enterprise, for example, might be seen as taxonomic in method. Most of the sixteenth-century English investigation of human anatomy developed from the work of John Caius (1510–73). Caius had attended Gonville Hall, Cambridge, in the 1530s, and then received his medical training in Padua, studying under the great anatomist Andreas Vesalius. He lived with Vesalius for eight months and through Caius's humanist goal of producing a pure edition of Galen, encouraged the famous anatomist to look again at the human body. Unlike Vesalius, however, Caius was convinced that Galen was correct, and spent much of his life arguing for a better understanding of that classical source. Caius was president of the College of Physicians of London from 1555 to 1571 and insisted on higher standards for licensing practitioners. He also encouraged dissections and ensured that both the universities and the College received bodies of executed criminals on a yearly basis to promote anatomical education and research.

Proto-Baconian sciences such as collections of botanical species, antiquities, local history, and even early anthropological descriptions of other peoples gained ground in the latter part of the sixteenth century. William Camden (1551–1623), for example, developed a whole industry of antiquarian collecting. Geographical descriptions of European and far-off lands carefully enumerated differences and similarities of different countries, customs and commodities. It is in this branch of the study of nature that we know most about the Scottish scene, since local historians such as Hector Boece (*fl.* 1520s), John Major (*fl.* 1520s), and George Buchanan (1506–82) were all looking at Scotland's natural history during the sixteenth century. Buchanan was probably the most important Scottish natural philosopher of the sixteenth century. By the early seventeenth century, the Englishman John Tradescant (d. 1637?) was collecting exotic artefacts from Britain and abroad, in order to display them for paying visitors. By 1683, this display would become the Ashmolean Museum. Increasingly, natural philosophers were interested in collecting exotic and rare books, coins, biological specimens, rocks and philosophical instruments, for display and investigation. This had ties with the growing mercantile economy and with the growing culture of display and ostentation at Court. By the mid-seventeenth century, taxonomies would develop in all the areas which began with collecting in the sixteenth.

Conclusion

A relatively small group of men promoted the study of the natural world in sixteenth-century England. They all knew each other and helped form a coherent community that in the seventeenth century would expand to take a significant role in the development of natural philosophy both in England and abroad. This sixteenth-century community was deeply influenced by mercantile and practical concerns, although it would be a mistake to ignore the philosophical and transcendental interests of scholars like John Dee or William Gilbert. Through the work of this small coterie, a social and cultural groundwork was laid for the important developments of the next century.

In the first instance, Francis Bacon, who was tutored by several important mathematical practitioners and gained his political and patronage connections in the sixteenth century, would in the seventeenth help define English scientific culture for the next hundred years. Bacon too played the patronage game, although perhaps instructively he wrote his natural philosophical work while exiled from the royal Courts. Bacon was able to articulate a method, an epistemology, and a scientific culture that reflected much of the work done by natural philosophers in the sixteenth century, and his model became a standard against which English science would be measured. After Bacon, an explosion of interest in natural philosophy occurred throughout the seventeenth century, leading eventually to the foundation of the Royal Society and the work of scores of natural philosophers including Sir Isaac Newton.

There are good reasons that this period in the history of science has been so little studied. European science was not transformed in England or in Scotland in the sixteenth century. There were few major discoveries, few natural philosophers whose fame pronounces them as part of the scientific revolution. But it is just the existence of 'normal science', to borrow a term from Thomas Kuhn, that should make the sixteenth century an ideal focus for understanding the place of science in society.[23] Just as the eighteenth century has proven a fertile ground for historians of science looking for the construction of scientific knowledge in society, historians should now look at sixteenth-century Britain. The nexus of interests – scientific, mercantile, imperial, national – would provide a rich and evocative story of the development of a natural philosophical community and culture. Perhaps through a full understanding of sixteenth-century British natural philosophy, historians will find a key to explaining and describing the scientific revolution.

NOTES

1. Koyré, *From a Closed World to an Infinite Universe*; Butterfield, *Origins of Modern Science, 1300–1800*.
2. Shapin, *The Scientific Revolution*; also Shapin and Schaffer, *Leviathan and the Air Pump*.
3. Yates, *Rosecrucian Enlightenment*; Zilsel, 'Sociological Roots of Science'.
4. Schmitt, *John Case and Aristotelianism*.
5. Elyot, *The Boke named the Governor*, sigs. 15b, 37a,b.
6. Elyot, f. 37a.
7. Pace, *Ed Fructu qui ex Doctrina Percipitur*, p. 77.
8. Gilbert, *Queen Elizabethe's Achademy*, p. 5.
9. Recorde, *Grounde of Artes*, sig. A2a.
10. Recorde, *Whetstone of Witte*, sig. A1a.
11. Johnston, 'Mathematical practitioners and instruments'.
12. Dee, *Mathematical Preface*.
13. Sherman, *John Dee*.
14. Yates, *Rosicrucian Enlightenment*. Clulee, *John Dee's Natural Philosophy: Between Science and Religion*.
15. Thomas Digges, dedication, in Leonard Digges, *An Arithmeticall Military Treatise*, sig. A2a.
16. Yates, *The Rosecrucian Enlightenment*.
17. Blundeville, *Exercises Containing Sixe Treatises*, sig. A5a.
18. See especially Shirley, *Thomas Harriot* and more recently Fox, ed., *Thomas Harriot*.
19. Richard Hakluyt, introduction to Peter Martyr, as quoted in Shirley, 'Science and Navigation', p. 80.
20. Wright, *Certaine Errors in Navigation*, sigs. D3a–E4a.
21. Pumfrey, *Latitude and the Magnetic Earth*.
22. Zilsel, 'The origins of Gilbert's scientific method'; Henry, 'Animism and empiricism: Copernican physics and the origins of William Gilbert's experimental method'.
23. Kuhn, *Structure of Scientific Revolutions*.

BIBLIOGRAPHY

Blundeville, Thomas, *His Exercises Containing Sixe Treatises* (London, 1594).
Butterfield, Herbert, *The Origins of Modern Science, 1300–1800* (London, 1949).

Clulee, Nicholas, *John Dee's Natural Philosophy: Between Science and Religion* (London, 1988).

Dee, John, *The Mathematical Preface to the Elements of Geometrie of Euclid of Megara* (London, 1570).

Digges, Leonard, *An Arithmeticall Military Treatise called Stratioticos* (London, 1579).

Elyot, Thomas, *The Boke named the Governor* (London, 1531).

Fox, Robert, ed., *Thomas Harriot: An Elizabethan Man of Science* (London, 2000).

Gilbert, Humphrey, *Queen Elizabethe's Achademy* (London, 1869).

Henry, John, 'Animism and empiricism: Copernican physics and the origins of William Gilbert's experimental method', *Journal of the History of Ideas*, 62, 1 (2001), 99–119.

Johnston, Stephen, 'Mathematical practitioners and instruments in Elizabethan England', *Annals of Science*, 48 (1991), 319–44.

Koyré, Alexandre, *From the Closed World to the Infinite Universe* (Baltimore, 1957).

Kuhn, Thomas, *The Structure of Scientific Revolutions* (Chicago, 1960).

Pace, Richard, *Ed Fructu qui ex Doctrina Percipitur (The Benefit of a Liberal Education)* (Basel, 1517; ed. and trans. Frank Manley and Richard S. Sylvester, New York, 1967).

Pumfrey, Stephen, *Latitude and the Magnetic Earth* (Cambridge, 2002).

Recorde, Robert, *The Grounde of Artes* (London, 1542).

Recorde, Robert, *Whetstone of Witte* (London, 1557).

Schmitt, Charles B., *John Case and Aristotelianism in Renaissance England* (Kingston, Ontario, and Montreal, 1983).

Shapin, Steven, *The Scientific Revolution* (Chicago, 1996).

Shapin, Steven and Schaffer, Simon, *The Leviathan and the Air Pump: Hobbes, Boyle, and the Experimental Life* (Princeton, NJ, 1985).

Sherman, William H., *John Dee: The Politics of Reading and Writing in the English Renaissance* (Amherst, 1995).

Shirley, John W., 'Science and navigation in Renaissance England', in John W. Shirley and F. David Hoeniger, eds, *Science and the Arts in the Renaissance*, pp. 74–93 (Washington, DC, 1985).

Shirley, John W., *Thomas Harriot: A Biography* (Oxford, 1983).

Wright, Edward, *Certaine Errors in Navigation* (London, 1599).

Yates, Frances A., *The Rosecrucian Enlightenment* (London, 1972).

Zilsel, Edgar, 'The origins of Gilbert's scientific method', *Journal of the History of Ideas*, 2 (1941), 1–32.

Zilsel, Edgar, 'The sociological roots of science', *American Journal of Sociology*, 47 (1942), 552–5.

FURTHER READING

Amir Alexander, *Geometrical Landscapes: The Voyages of Discovery and the Transformation of Mathematical Practice* (2002).

Peter Barber, 'England I: pageantry, defense, and government: maps at Court to 1550', and 'England II: monarchs, ministers, and maps 1550–1625', in *Monarchs, Ministers, and Maps: The Emergence of Cartography as a Tool of Government in Early Modern Europe*, ed. David Buisseret, pp. 26–56, 57–98 (1992).

William Barr, 'The world view of Robert Record: a brief study of Tudor cosmology', *Albion* 1, 1 (1969), 1–9.

James A. Bennett, 'The challenge of practical mathematics', in Steven Pumfrey et al. (eds), *Science, Belief, and Popular Culture in Renaissance Europe* (1991), pp. 176–90; and 'The mechanic's philosophy and the mechanical philosophy', *History of Science*, 24 (1986), 1–28.

Mario Biagioli, 'Galileo's system of patronage', *History of Science*, 28(1990), 1–62.

Desmond Clarke, 'An outline of the history of science in Ireland', *Studies: an Irish Quarterly Review*, 62 (1973), 247–8, 287–302.

Lesley B. Cormack, *Charting an Empire: Geography at the English Universities 1580–1620* (1997); and 'Good fences make good neighbors: geography as self-definition in early modern England', *Isis*, 82 (1991), 639–61.

Allen Debus, 'Renaissance chemistry and the work of Robert Fludd', *Ambix*, 14 (1967), 42–59.

Mordechai Feingold, *The Mathematicians' Apprenticeship: Science, Universities, and Society in England, 1560–1640* (1984).

Robert Frank, 'Science, medicine and the universities of early modern England', *History of Science* 11 (1973), 194–216, 239–69.

Richard W. Hadden, *On the Shoulders of Merchants: Exchange and the Mathematical Conception of Nature in Early Modern Europe* (1994).

Deborah Harkness, *John Dee's Conversations with Angels: Cabala, Alchemy, and the End of Nature* (1999).

P. D. A. Harvey, *Maps in Tudor England* (1993).

A. G. Howson, *A History of Mathematics Education in England* (1982).

Lynette Hunter and Sarah Hutton (eds), *Women, Science and Medicine 1500–1700: Mothers and Sisters of the Royal Society* (1997).

Stephen Johnston, *Making Mathematical Practice: Gentlemen, Practitioners, and Artisans in Elizabethan England* (PhD thesis, University of Cambridge, 1994).

Berhard Klein, *Maps and the Writing of Space in Early Modern England and Ireland* (2002).

David Lindberg and Robert Westman (eds), *Reappraisals of the Scientific Revolution* (1990).

Bruce T. Moran (ed.), *Patronage and Institution: Science, Technology, and Medicine at the European Court* (1991).

Katherine Neal, *From Discrete to Continuous: The Broadening of Number Concepts in Early Modern England* (2002).

Vivian Nutton, 'John Caius and the Eton Galen: medical philology in the Reniassance', *Medizinhistorisches Journal*, 20 (1985), 227–52.

E. G. R. Taylor, *Mathematical Practitioners of Tudor and Stuart England* (1954).

Sarah Tyacke (ed.), *English Map-Making 1500–1650* (1983).

Charles W. J. Withers, *Geography, Science and National Identity: Scotland since 1520* (2001).

Bibliography

Abbott, L. W., *Law Reporting in England 1485–1585* (London, 1973).

The Acts of the Parliaments of Scotland (London, 1816).

Adams, I. H., *The Making of Urban Scotland* (London and Montreal, 1978).

Adams, J. Q., ed., *Dramatic Records of Sir Henry Herbert, Master of Revels 1623–1673* (2nd edition., New York, 1964).

Adams, S., 'Eliza enthroned? The court and politics', in C. Haigh, ed., *The Reign of Elizabeth I* (London, 1984).

Adams, S., 'Favourites and factions at the Elizabethan Court', in R. Asch and A. M. Birke, eds, *Princes, Patronage and the Nobility* (Oxford, 1991).

Adams, S., 'Favourites and factions at the Elizabethan Court', in J. Guy, ed., *The Tudor Monarchy* (London, 1997).

Adams, S., *Leicester and the Court: Essays on Elizabethan Politics* (Manchester, 2002).

Adams, S., 'The Protestant cause: religious alliance with the West European Calvinist communities as a political issue in England, 1585–1630' (D.Phil. thesis, Oxford university, 1973).

Airs, M., 'Architecture', in B. Ford, ed., *The Cambridge Guide to the Arts in Britain: Renaissance and Reformation* (Cambridge, 1989).

Airs, M., *The Buildings of Britain: Tudor and Jacobean* (London, 1982).

Airs, M., *The Tudor and Jacobean Country House: A Building History* (Stroud, 1995).

Alcock, N. W., *People at Home: Living in a Warwickshire Village, 1500–1800* (Chichester, 1993).

Alexander, A., *Geometrical Landscapes: The Voyages of Discovery and the Transformation of Mathematical Practice* (Stanford, 2002).

Alford, S., *The Early Elizabethan Polity: William Cecil and the British Succession Crisis, 1558–1569* (Cambridge, 1998).

Allan, D., *Virtue, Learning and the Scottish Enlightenment: Ideas of Scholarship in Early Modern History* (Edinburgh, 1993).

Allan, D., ' "What's in a name?": Pedigree and propaganda in seventeenth-century Scotland', in E. J. Cowan and R. J. Finlay, eds, *Scottish History: The Power of the Past* (Edinburgh, 2002).

Allen, S. M., 'Jane Yetsweirt (1541–?): claiming her place', *Printing History*, 9.

Anderson, J., ed., *Records of Early English Drama: Newcastle upon Tyne* (Toronto, 1982).

Anderson, J. H., 'The antiquities of fairyland and Ireland', *Journal of English and Germanic Philology*, 86, 2 (1987).

Anglo, S., *Images of Tudor Kingship* (London, 1992).

Anglo, S., *Spectacle, Pageantry and Early Tudor Policy* (Oxford, 1969).

Annála Connacht: the Annals of Connacht (AD 1224–1544), ed. A. M. Freeman (Dublin, 1944).

The Annals of Ireland, Translated from the Original Irish of the Four Masters, trans. O. Connellan (Dublin, 1846).

The Annals of Loch Cé: A Chronicle of Irish Affairs from AD 1014 to AD 1590, ed. and trans. W. Hennessy (2 vols, London, 1871).

Apted, M. and Hannabuss, S., *Painters in Scotland, 1301–1700: A Biographical Dictionary* (Edinburgh, 1978).

Archer, I. W., 'The art and acts of memorialization in early modern London', in J. F. Merritt, *Imagining Early Modern London: Perceptions and Portrayals of the City from Stow to Strype, 1598–1720* (Cambridge, 2001).

Archer, I. W., 'The charity of early modern Londoners', *Transactions of the Royal Historical Society*, 6th series, 12 (2002).

Archer, I. W., *The Pursuit of Stability: Social Relations in Elizabethan London* (Cambridge, 1991).

Archer, J., *Sovereignty and Intelligence: Spying and Court Culture in the English Renaissance* (Stanford, 1993).

Arthurson, I., *The Perkin Warbeck Conspiracy 1491–1497* (Stroud, 1994).

Asch, R. and Burke, A., eds, *Princes, Patronage and Royalty, 1450–1800* (London, 1977).

Ascham, R., *English Works*, ed. W. A. Wright (Cambridge, 1904).

Ashbee, A., *Records of English Court Music* (vols I–IV, Snodland, 1986–91; vols V–VIII, Aldershot, 1991–5).

Aston, M., 'English ruins and English history: the Dissolution and the sense of the past', *Journal of the Warburg and Courtauld Institutes*, 36 (1973).

Aston, M., 'Gods, saints and reformers: portraiture and Protestant England', in L. Gent, ed., *Albion's Classicism* (New Haven and London, 1995).

Aston, M., *The King's Bedpost; Reformation and Iconography in a Tudor Group Portrait* (Cambridge, 1993).

Auerbach, E., *Tudor Artists* (London, 1954).

Austern, L. P., ' "Alluring the auditorie to effeminacie": music and the idea of the feminine in early modern England', *Music and Letters*, 74 (1993).

Aveling, H., 'The Catholic recusants of the West Riding of Yorkshire, 1558–1790', *Transactions of the Leeds Philosophical and Literary Society*, 10 (1963).

Aveling, H., ed., *The Papers of the Meynell Family* (London, 1964).

Ayre, J., ed., *Works of John Jewel* (Cambridge, 1854).

Ayre, J., ed., *Works of John Whitgift* (3 vols, Cambridge, 1851–3).

Baildon, W. P., ed., *Les Reportes del Cases in Camera Stellata, 1593 to 1609, from the Original MS of John Hawarde* (London, 1893).

Bailey, M., 'Demographic decline in late medieval England: some thoughts on recent research', *Economic History Review*, 49 (1996).

Bainbridge, V., *Gilds in the Medieval Countryside: Social and Religious Change in Cambridgeshire c.1350–1558* (Woodbridge, 1996).

Bairoch, P., Batou, J. and Chevre, P., *La Population des Villes Européennes de 800 à 1850* (Geneva, 1988).

Baker, J. H., *An Introduction to English Legal History* (4th edition, London, 2002).

Baker, J. H., *The Legal Profession and the Common Law: Historical Essays* (London, 1986).

Baker, J. H., *The Oxford History of the Laws of England*, vol. VI, *1483–1558* (Oxford, 2003).

Baker, J. H. and Milsom, S. F. C., eds, *Sources of English Legal History: Private Law to 1750* (London, 1986).

Balfour, J., *The Practicks of Sir James Balfour of Pittendreich*, ed. P. G. B. McNeill (Edinburgh, 1962).

Barber, P., 'England I: pageantry, defense, and government: maps at court to 1550', and 'England II: monarchs, ministers, and maps 1550–1625', in D. Buisseret, ed., *Monarchs, Ministers, and Maps: The Emergence of Cartography as a Tool of Government in Early Modern Europe* (Chicago, 1992).

Bardgett, F., *Scotland Reformed: The Reformation in Angus and the Mearns* (Edinburgh, 1989).

Barley, M. W., *The English Farmhouse and Cottage* (London, 1961).

Barnes, T. G., 'Deputies not principals, lieutenants not captains: the institutional failure of the lieutenancy in the 1620s', in M. C. Fissel, ed., *War and Government in Britain, 1598–1650* (Manchester, 1991).

Barr, W., 'The world view of Robert Record: a brief study of Tudor cosmology', *Albion* 1, 1 (1969).

Barrell, A. D. M., *Medieval Scotland* (Cambridge, 2000).

Barron, C. M., 'The education and training of girls in fifteenth-century London', in D. E. S. Dunn, ed., *Courts, Counties and the Capital in the Later Middle Ages* (Stroud, 1996).

Barron, C. M., 'The parish fraternities of medieval London', in C. M. Barron and C. Harper-Bill, eds, *The Church in Pre-Reformation Society: Essays in Honour of F. R. H. du Boulay* (Woodbridge, 1985).

Barry, J., ed., *The Tudor and Stuart Town, 1530–1688* (London, 1990).

Barry, J. and Brooks, C., eds, *The Middling Sort of People: Culture, Society and Politics in England, 1550–1800* (Basingstoke, 1994).

Batschmann, O., *Hans Holbein* (Princeton, NJ, 1997).

Beadle, R., ed., *The Cambridge Companion to Medieval Drama* (Cambridge, 1994).

Beadle, R., ed., *The York Plays* (London, 1982).

Bearman, R., ed., *The History of an English Borough: Stratford-upon-Avon 1196–1996* (Stratford-upon-Avon, 1997).

Beer, B. L., *Tudor England Observed: The World of John Stow* (Stroud, 1988).

Beier, A. L., 'Engine of manufacture: the trades of London', in A. L. Beier and R. Finlay, eds, *London 1500–1700: The Making of the Metropolis* (London, 1986).

Beier, A. L., *Masterless Men: The Vagrancy Problem in England 1560–1640* (London, 1985).

Beier, A. L. and Finlay, R., eds, *London 1500–1700: The Making of the Metropolis* (London, 1986).

Bellamy, J. G., *The Tudor Law of Treason: An Introduction* (London, 1979).

Bellamy, J. G., *Criminal Law and Society in Late Medieval and Tudor England* (Gloucester, 1984).

Ben-Amos, I. K., *Adolescence and Youth in Early Modern England* (New Haven, 1994).

Ben-Amos, I. K., 'Failure to become freemen: urban apprentices in early modern England', *Social History*, 16, 2 (May 1991).

Benham, H., *Latin Church Music in England, 1460–1575* (London, 1977).

Bennett, J., 'Confronting continuity', *Journal of Women's History*, 9 (1997).

Bennett, J. and Froide, A., eds, *Singlewomen in the European Past, 1250–1800* (Philadelphia, 1999).

Bennett, J. A., 'The challenge of practical mathematics', in S. Pumfrey, P. Rossi and M. Slawinski, eds, *Science, Belief, and Popular Culture in Renaissance Europe* (Manchester, 1991).

Bennett, J. A., 'The mechanic's philosophy and the mechanical philosophy', *History of Science*, 24 (1986).

Bennett, M. *Lambert Simnel and the Battle of Stoke* (Stroud, 1987).

Bentley-Cranch, D. and Marshall, R. K., 'Iconography and literature in the service of diplomacy', in J. H. Williams, ed., *Stewart Style, 1513–1542: Essays on the Court of James V* (East Linton, 1996).

Beresford, M., 'The common informer, the penal statutes and economic regulation', *Economic History Review*, 2nd series, X, 2 (1957).

Berger, R. M., *The Most Necessary Luxuries: The Mercers' Company of Coventry* 1550–1680 (Philadelphia, 1993).

Bernard, G. W., ed., *The Tudor Nobility* (Manchester, 1992).

Bernard, G. W., *War, Taxation and Rebellion in Early Tudor England* (Hassocks, 1986).

Bevington, D., ed., *Medieval Drama* (Boston, MA, 1975).

Bevington, D., *Tudor Drama and Politics* (Boston, MA, 1966).

Biagioli, M., 'Galileo's system of patronage', *History of Science*, 28 (1990).

Bindoff, S. T., *Tudor England* (London, 1960).

Blundeville, T., *His Exercises Containing Sixe Treatises* (London, 1594).

Boardman, S., 'Late medieval Scotland and the Matter of Britain', in E. J. Cowan and R. J. Finlay, eds, *Scottish History: The Power of the Past* (Edinburgh, 2002).

Bonner, E., 'The French reactions to the rough wooings of Mary Queen of Scots', *Journal of the Sydney Society for Scottish History*, 6 (1998).

Bonner, E., 'The *politique* of Henri II: de facto French rule in Scotland', *Journal of the Sydney Society for Scottish History*, 7 (1999).

Booty, J., ed., *The Book of Common Prayer 1559: The Elizabethan Prayer Book* (Washington, DC, 1976).

Borsay, P. and Proudfoot, L., eds, *Provincial Towns in Early Modern England and Ireland: Change, Convergence, and Divergence* (Oxford, 2002).

Bossy, J., *The English Catholic Community 1570–1850* (London, 1975).

Boulton, J., *Neighbourhood and Society: A London Suburb in the Seventeenth Century* (Cambridge, 1987).

Bourke, A., Kilfeather, S., Luddy, M. et al., eds, *The Field Day Anthology of Irish Writing*: vols V and VI, *Irish Women's Writing and Traditions* (Cork, 2002).

Bowers, R., 'Choral institutions within the English church, 1340–1500' (PhD dissertation, University of East Anglia, 1975).

Bowers, R., 'The cultivation and promotion of music in the household and orbit of Thomas Wolsey', in S. J. Gunn and P. G. Lindley, eds, *Cardinal Wolsey: Church, State and Art* (Cambridge, 1991).

Bownde, N., *Medicines for the Plague* (London, 1604).

Boyd, M. C., *Elizabethan Music and Music Criticism* (2nd edition, Philadelphia, 1967).

Brachlow, S., *The Communion of the Saints: Radical Puritan and Separatist Ecclesiology, 1570–1625* (Oxford, 1988).

Braddick, M. J., *State Formation in Early Modern England, c.1550–1700* (Cambridge, 2000).

Braddock, R. C. 'The rewards of office-holding in Tudor England', *Journal of British Studies*, 14 (1975).

Bradley, J., 'From frontier town to Renaissance city: Kilkenny, 1500–1700', in P. Borsay and L. Proudfoot, eds, *Provincial Towns in Early Modern England and Ireland: Change, Convergence and Divergence* (Oxford, 2002).

Bradshaw, B., *The Dissolution of the Religious Orders in Ireland under Henry VIII* (Cambridge, 1974).

Bradshaw, B., 'The English Reformation and identity formation in Ireland and Wales', in B. Bradshaw and P. Roberts, eds, *British Consciousness and Identity: The Making of Britain, 1533–1707* (Cambridge, 1998).

Bradshaw, B., *The Irish Constitutional Revolution of the Sixteenth Century* (Cambridge, 1979).

Bradshaw, B., 'The Tudor Reformation in Wales and Ireland: the origins of the British problem', in B. Bradshaw and J. Morrill, eds, *The British Problem, c.1534–1707* (New York, 1996).

Bradshaw, B. and Roberts, P., eds, *British Consciousness and Identity: The Making of Britain, 1533–1707* (Cambridge, 1998).

Brady, C., *The Chief Governors: The Rise and Fall of Reform Government in Tudor Ireland* (Cambridge, 1994).

Brady, C., 'Political women and reform in Tudor Ireland', in M. Mac Curtain and M. O'Dowd, eds, *Women in Early Modern Ireland* (Dublin, 1991).

Brigden, S., *London and the Reformation* (Oxford, 1989).

Brigden, S., *New Worlds, Lost Worlds: The Rule of the Tudors, 1485–1603* (Harmondsworth and New York, 2000).

Brooks, C., 'Apprenticeship, social mobility and the middling sort, 1550–1800', in J. Barry and C. Brooks, eds, *The Middling Sort of People: Culture, Society and Politics in England, 1550–1800* (Basingstoke, 1994).

Brooks, C. W., *Pettyfoggers and Vipers of the Commonwealth: The 'Lower Branch' of the Legal Profession in Early Modern England* (Cambridge, 1986).

Brooks, P. N., *Thomas Cranmer's Doctrine of the Eucharist* (2nd edition, Basingstoke, 1992).

Brown, A. D., *Popular Piety in Late Medieval England: The Diocese of Salisbury, 1250–1550* (Oxford, 1995).

Brown, A. L., *The Governance of Late Medieval England 1272–1461* (Stanford, 1989).

Brown, K. M., 'Aristocratic finances and the origins of the Scottish revolution', *English Historical Review*, 104 (1989).

Brown, K. M., *Bloodfeud in Scotland, 1573–1625: Violence, Justice and Politics in an Early Modern Society* (Edinburgh, 1986).

Brown, K. M., *Noble Society in Scotland: Wealth, Family and Culture from Reformation to Revolution* (Edinburgh, 2000).

Bruce, J., ed., *Correspondence of Matthew Parker* (Cambridge, 1853).

Brunskill, R. W., *Illustrated Handbook of Vernacular Architecture* (London, 1970).

Burgess, C., ed., *The Church Records of St Andrew Hubbard, Eastcheap c.1450–c.1570* (London, 1999).

Burgess, C., 'A fond thing vainly invented: an essay on purgatory and pious motive in later medieval England', in S. J. Wright, ed., *Parish, Church and People: Local Studies in Lay Religion, 1350–1750* (London, 1988).

Burgess, C., 'London parishioners in times of change: St Andrew Hubbard, Eastcheap, c.1450–1570', *Journal of Ecclesiastical History*, 53 (2002).

Burgess, C., 'Shaping the parish: St Mary at Hill, London, in the fifteenth century', in J. Blair and B. Golding, eds, *The Cloister and the World: Essays in Medieval History in Honour of Barbara Harvey* (Oxford, 1996).

Burns, J. H., *The True Law of Kingship: Concepts of Monarchy in Early Modern Scotland* (Oxford, 1996).

Burton, J. H. et al., eds, *Register of the Privy Council of Scotland* (38 vols, Edinburgh, 1877–).

Bush, M. L., *The Government Policy of Protector Somerset* (London and Montreal, 1975).

Bush, M. L., 'The problem of the far north: a study of the crisis of 1537 and its consequences', *Northern History*, VI (1971).

Butlin, R. A., ed., *The Development of the Irish Town* (London, 1977).

Butlin, R. A., 'Land and people, c.1600', in T. W. Moody, F. X. Martin, and F. J. Byrne, eds, *A New History of Ireland*, vol. III (Oxford, 1976).

Butterfield, H., *The Origins of Modern Science, 1300–1800* (London, 1949).

Buxton, J., *Elizabethan Taste* (London, 1963).

Byrne, M. St. Clare, ed., *The Lisle Letters* (London, 1983).

Caball, M., 'Faith, culture and sovereignty: Irish nationality and its development, 1558–1625', in B. Bradshaw and P. Roberts, eds, *British Consciousness and Identity: The Making of Britain, 1533–1707* (Cambridge, 1998).

Calderwood, D., *The History of the Kirk of Scotland by Mr. David Calderwood*, ed. T. Thomson (8 vols, Edinburgh, 1842–9).

Caldwell, D. H. and Marshall, R. K., *The Queen's World* (Edinburgh, 1987).

Calendar of Letters, Despatches, and State Papers, Relating to the Negotiations between England and Spain (20 vols, London, 1862–1954)

Calendar of State Papers Foreign, Reign of Elizabeth, ed. J. Stevenson et al. (23 vols, London, 1863–1950).

Camden, W., *Annals* (London, 1688).

Camden, W., *Britain*, trans. P. Holland (London, 1610).

Cameron, A. I., ed., *The Scottish Correspondence of Mary of Lorraine, 1543–1560* (Edinburgh, 1927).

Cameron, J., ed., *The First Book of Discipline* (Edinburgh, 1972).

Cameron, J., *James V: The Personal Rule, 1528–1542* (East Linton, 1998).

Campbell, B. M. S. and Overton, M., 'A new perspective on medieval and early modern agriculture: six centuries of Norfolk farming, c.1250–c.1850', *Past and Present*, 141 (1993).

Campbell, L., *Renaissance Portraits: European Portrait Painting in the Fourteenth, Fifteenth and Sixteenth Centuries* (New Haven and London, 1990).

Campbell, L., and Foister, S., 'Gerard, Lucas and Susanna Hornebout', *Burlington Magazine*, 127 (1986).

Campion, E., *Two Bokes of the Histories of Ireland* (1571), ed. A. F. Vossen (Netherlands, 1963).

Canny, N., *Making Ireland British, 1580–1650* (Oxford, 2001).

Caraman, P., ed., *The Hunted Priest: The Autobiography of John Gerard* (London, 1959).

Carew, R., *Survey of Cornwall* (London, 1602).

Carlin, M., *Medieval Southwark* (London, 1996).

Carpenter, C., *Locality and Polity: A Study of Warwickshire Landed Society, 1401–1499* (Cambridge, 1992).

Carpenter, C., *The Wars of the Roses: Politics and the Constitution c.1437–1509* (Cambridge, 1997).

Carpenter, H. J., 'Furse of Moreshead: a family record of the sixteenth century', *Reports and Transactions of the Devonshire Association for the Advancement of Science, Literature and Art*, 26 (1894).

Carter, H., *The Towns of Wales: A Study in Urban Geography* (Cardiff, 1965).

Casway, J., 'Irish women overseas, 1500–1800', in M. Mac Curtain and M. O'Dowd, eds, *Women in Early Modern Ireland* (Dublin, 1991).

Cawley, A., ed., *Everyman* (Manchester, 1961).

Chambers, E. K., *The Elizabethan Stage* (4 vols, Oxford, 1923).

Chambers, E. K., *The Medieval Stage* (2 vols, Oxford, 1903).

Chaney, E., *The Evolution of the Grand Tour* (London, 1998).

Chaytor, M., 'Households and Kinship in Ryton in the late sixteenth and early seventeenth centuries', *History Workshop Journal*, 10 (1980).

Chrimes, S. B., *Henry VII* (London, 1972; 2nd edition, New Haven, 1999).

Cicero, M. T., *De Legibus*, trans. C. W. Keyes (London, 1928).

Clark, A., *Working Life of Women in the Seventeenth Century* (London, 1992; [1919]).

Clark, P., ed., *The Cambridge Urban History of Britain*, vol. II, *1540–1840* (Cambridge, 2000).

Clark, P., *English Provincial Society from the Reformation to the Revolution: Religion, Politics and Society in Kent, 1500–1640* (Hassocks, 1977).

Clark, P., 'The migrant in Kentish towns', in P. Clark and P. Slack, eds, *Crisis and Order in English Towns, 1500–1700* (London, 1972).

Clark, P. and Gillespie, R., eds, *Two Capitals: London and Dublin 1500–1840* (London, 2001).

Clark, P. and Murfin, L., *The History of Maidstone: The Making of a Modern County Town* (Stroud, 1995).

Clark, P. and Slack, P., eds, *Crisis and Order in English Towns, 1500–1700* (London, 1972).

Clark, P. and Slack, P., *English Towns in Transition, 1500–1700* (Oxford, 1976).

Clark, P. and Souden, D., eds, *Migration and Society in Early Modern England* (London, 1987).

Clarke, D., 'An outline of the history of science in Ireland', *Studies: An Irish Quarterly Review* 62 (1973).

Clay, C. G. A., *Economic Expansion and Social Change: England 1500–1700* (2 vols, Cambridge, 1984).

Cliffe, J. T., *The Yorkshire Gentry from the Reformation to the Civil War* (London, 1969).

Clopper, L. M., ed., *Records of Early English Drama: Chester* (Toronto, 1979).

Clopper, L. M., *Drama, Play and Game* (Chicago, 2001).

Clulee, N., *John Dee's Natural Philosophy: Between Science and Religion* (London, 1988).

Cockburn, J. S., *A History of English Assizes 1558–1714* (Cambridge, 1972).

Cockburn, J. S., ed., *Calendar of Assize Records: Home Circuit Indictments, Elizabeth I and James I, Introduction* (London, 1985).

Cockburn, J. S. and Green, T. A., eds, *Twelve Good Men and True: The English Criminal Trial Jury, 1200–1800* (Princeton, NJ, 1988).

Cogswell, T., *Home Divisions: Aristocracy, the State and Provincial Conflict* (Manchester, 1998).

Coke, E., *The Third Part of the Institutes of the Laws of England* (London, 1644).

Coke, E., *The Fourth Part of the Institutes of the Laws of England* (London, 1644).

Coldewey, J., 'The Digby Plays and the Chelmsford records', *Research Opportunities in Renaissance Drama*, 18 (1975).

Coldewey, J., ed., *Early English Drama* (New York, 1993).

Coldewey, J., 'Early Essex drama: a history of its rise and fall, and a theory concerning the Digby Plays' (PhD dissertation, University of Colorado, 1972).

Coldewey, J., 'That enterprising property player: semi-professional drama in sixteenth-century England,' *Theatre Notes*, 31 (1977).

Cole, M., *The Portable Queen: Elizabeth I and the Politics of Ceremony* (Amherst, 1999).

Coleman, C. and Starkey, D. R., eds, *Revolution Reassessed* (Oxford, 1986).

Coleman, D. C., 'The "gentry" controversy and the aristocracy in crisis, 1558–1641', *History*, 51 (1966), 165–78.

Collinson, P., *Archbishop Grindal, 1519–1583* (Berkeley, 1979).

Collinson, P., *The Birthpangs of Protestant England* (Basingstoke, 1988).

Collinson, P., '*De Republica Anglorum* or history with the politics put back', reprinted in P. Collinson, *Elizabethan Essays* (2nd edition, London, 2003).

Collinson, P., 'Ecclesiastical vitriol: religious satire in the 1590s and the invention of Puritanism', in J. Guy, ed., *The Reign of Elizabeth I: Court and Culture in the Last Decade* (Cambridge, 1995).

Collinson, P., *Elizabethan Essays* (London, 1994; 2nd edition, 2003).

Collinson, P., *The Elizabethan Puritan Movement* (London and Berkeley, 1976).

Collinson, P., *The Religion of Protestants* (Oxford, 1982).

Collinson, P., ed., *The Short Oxford History of the British Isles: The Sixteenth Century* (Oxford, 2002).

Colvin, H. M., ed., *The History of the King's Works, 1485–1660* (2 vols, London, 1975 and 1982).

Condon, M., 'Ruling elites in the reign of Henry VII', in C. D. Ross, ed., *Patronage, Pedigree and Power in Late Medieval England* (Gloucester, 1979).

Cooper, J. P., 'Henry VII's last years reconsidered', *Historical Journal*, 2 (1959).

Cooper, J. P., 'Ideas of gentility in early modern England', reprinted in J. P. Cooper, *Land, Men and Beliefs: Studies in Early Modern History* (London, 1983).

Cooper, N., *Houses of the Gentry 1480–1680* (New Haven and London, 1999).

Cooper, T., '*Memento Mori* portraiture: painting, Protestant culture and the patronage of middle elites in England and Wales' (PhD thesis, University of Sussex, 2001).

Cooper, T. M., ed., *Regiam Majestatem and Quoniam Attachiamenta* (Edinburgh, 1947).

Corish, Patrick, 'Women and religious practice', in M. Mac Curtain and M. O'Dowd, eds, *Women in Early Modern Ireland* (Dublin, 1991).

Cormack, L. B., *Charting an Empire: Geography at the English Universities 1580–1620* (Chicago, 1997).

Cormack, L. B., 'Good fences make good neighbors: geography as self-definition in early modern England', *Isis*, 82 (1991).

Cowan, A., *Urban Europe 1500–1700* (London, 1998).

Cowan, E. J., and Finlay, R. J., eds, *Scottish History: The Power of the Past* (Edinburgh, 2002).

Cowan, I. B., 'Church and society', in J. M. Brown, ed., *Scottish Society in the Fifteenth Century* (New York, 1977).

Cowan, I. B., *The Scottish Reformation: Church and Society in Sixteenth Century Scotland* (London, 1981; New York, 1982).

Cowan, I. B. and Easson, David E., *Medieval Religious Houses, Scotland* (2nd edition, London, 1976).

Cox, J. E., ed., *Works of Thomas Cranmer*, vol. II, *Miscellaneous Writings and Letters of Thomas Cranmer* (2 vols, Cambridge, 1844–6).

Craig, J., *Reformation, Politics, and Polemics: The Growth of Protestantism in East Anglian Market Towns, 1500–1610* (Aldershot, 2001).

Crawford, P., *Women and Religion in England 1500–1720* (London, 1996).

Cressy, D., 'Kinship and Kin interaction in early Modern England', *Past and Present*, 113.

Croft, P., ed., *Patronage, Culture and Power: The Early Cecils* (New Haven and London, 2002).

Cross, C. and Vickers, N., *Monks, Friars and Nuns in Sixteenth Century Yorkshire* (York, 1995).

Cross, C., Loades, D. M. and Scarisbrick, J. J., eds, *Law and Government under the Tudors* (Cambridge, 1988).

Crouch, D. J. F., *Piety, Fraternity, and Power: Religious Gilds in Late Medieval Yorkshire, 1389–1547* (Woodbridge, 2000).

Crowson, P. S., *Tudor Foreign Policy* (London, 1973).

Cullen, L. M., 'Economic trends', in T. W. Moody, F. X. Martin and F. J. Byrne, eds, *A New History of Ireland*, vol. III (Oxford, 1976).

Cullum, P. H., 'Vowesses and female lay piety in the province of York, 1300–1530', *Northern History*, 32 (1996).

Cunich, P., 'The dissolution of the chantries', in P. Collinson and J. Craig, eds, *The Reformation in English Towns, 1500–1640* (London, 1998).

Cunich, P., 'The ex-religious in post-Dissolution society: symptoms of Post-Traumatic Stress Disorder?', in J. G. Clark, ed., *The Religious Orders in Pre-Reformation England* (Woodbridge, 2002).

Cunich, P., 'Revolution and crisis in English state finance, 1534–47', in M. Ormrod, M. Bonney and R. Bonney, eds, *Crises, Revolutions and Self-Sustained Growth: Essays in European Fiscal History, 1130–1830* (Stamford, CA, 1999).

Cuninghame, M., *A Pairt of the Life of Lady Margaret Cuninghame* (Edinburgh, 1828).

Cunningham, S., 'Henry VII and rebellion in north-eastern England, 1485–1492: bonds of allegiance and the establishment of Tudor authority', *Northern History*, 32 (1996).

Cunningham, S., 'Henry VII, Sir Thomas Butler and the Stanley family: politics and the assertion of royal influence in north-western England, 1471–1521', in T. Thornton, ed., *Social Attitudes and Political Structures in the Fifteenth Century* (Stroud, 2000).

Currin, J. M., 'Henry VII and the treaty of Redon (1489): Plantagenet ambitions and early Tudor foreign policy', *History*, 81 (1996).

Currin, J. M., 'Persuasions of peace: the Luxembourg–Marigny–Gaguin embassy and the state of Anglo-French relations, 1489–90', *English Historical Review*, 113 (1998).

Currin, J. M., 'Pro expensis ambassatorum: diplomacy and financial administration in the reign of Henry VIII', *English Historical Review*, 108 (1993), 589–609.

Curteys, R., *Two Sermons* (London, 1576).

Curtis, E., *A History of Medieval Ireland from 1086 to 1513* (2nd edition, London, 1938).

Cust, R., 'Honour and politics in early Stuart England: the case of Beaumont *v.* Hastings', *Past and Present*, 149 (November 1995).

Davie, N., 'Chalk and cheese? "Fielden" and "Forest" communities in early modern England', *Journal of Historical Sociology*, 4 (1991).

Davies, C. S. L., 'England and the French war', in J. Loach and R. Tittler, eds, *The Mid-Tudor Polity, c.1540–1560* (London, 1980).

Davies, C. S. L., 'Richard III, Brittany and Henry Tudor, 1483–1485', *Nottingham Medieval Studies*, 37 (1993), 110–26.

Davies, C. S. L., '"Roy de France et Roy d'Angleterre": the English claims to France 1453–1558', in *L'Angleterre et les Pays Bourguignons*, Centre européen d'Etudes bourguignonnes, 35 (1995).

Davies, N., *The Isles: A History* (Oxford, 1999).

Davies, R. R., *The First English Empire: Power and Identities in the British Isles 1093–1343* (Oxford, 2000).

Dawson, J., 'The Gaidhealtachd and the emergence of the Scottish Highlands', in B. Bradshaw and P. Roberts, eds, *British Consciousness and Identity: The Making of Britain, 1533–1707* (Cambridge, 1998).

Dawson, J. E. A., 'Calvinism in the *Gaidhealtachd* in Scotland', in A. Pettegree, A. Duke and G. Lewis, eds, *Calvinism in Europe, 1540–1620* (Cambridge, 1994).

Dawson, J. E. A., *The Politics of Religion in the Age of Mary, Queen of Scots: The Earl of Argyll and the Struggle for Britain and Ireland* (Cambridge, 2002).

Dawson, J. E. A., 'William Cecil and the British dimension of early Elizabethan foreign policy', *History*, 74 (1989).

Dawson, J. P., 'The privy council and private law in the Tudor and early Stuart periods: parts I and II', *Michigan Law Review*, XLVIII, 4 (1950).

de Ayala, Dom P., in P. H. Brown, *Early Travellers in Scotland* (1891, reprinted Edinburgh, 1978).

de Parmiter, G., *Elizabethan Catholic Recusancy at the Inns of Court* (London, 1976).

de Vries, J., *European Urbanization, 1500–1800* (Cambridge, MA, 1984).

Dean, D. M., *Law-Making and Society in Late Elizabethan England: The Parliament of England, 1584–1601* (Cambridge, 1996).

Dean, D. M. and Jones, N. L., eds, *The Parliaments of Elizabethan England* (Oxford, 1990).

Debus, A., 'Renaissance chemistry and the work of Robert Fludd', *Ambix*, 14 (1967).

Dee, J., *The Mathematical Preface to the Elements of Geometrie of Euclid of Megara* (London, 1570).

Dee, J., *The Perfect Arte of Navigation* (London, 1577).

Dent, A., *The Plaine Man's Pathe-way to Heaven* (London, 1601).

Devine, T. M., 'Scotland', in P. Clark, ed., *The Cambridge Urban History of Britain*, vol. II (Cambridge, 2000).

Dialogue Concerning Strife in Our Churche (London, 1584).

Dickens, A. G., *The English Reformation* (2nd edition, London, 1989).

Dickinson, W. C., ed., *John Knox's History of the Reformation in Scotland* (2 vols, London, 1949).

Dietz, B., 'Overseas trade and metropolitan growth', in A. L. Beier and R. Finlay, eds, *London 1500–1700: The Making of The Metropolis* (London, 1986).

Digges, L., *An Arithmeticall Military Treatise called Stratioticos* (London, 1579).

Dillon, A, *The Construction of Martyrdom in the English Catholic Community 1535–1603* (Aldershot, 2002).

Dilworth, M., *Scottish Monasteries in the Late Middle Ages* (Edinburgh, 1995).

Donaldson, G., *All the Queen's Men: Power and Politics in Mary Stewart's Scotland* (London, 1983).

Donaldson, G,. 'Foundations of Anglo-Scottish union', in G. Donaldson, *Scottish Church History* (Edinburgh, 1985).

Donaldson, G., *Scotland: James V–VII* (Edinburgh, 1978).

Donaldson, G., *Scottish Church History* (Edinburgh, 1985).

Donaldson, G., ed., *Scottish Historical Documents* (Edinburgh, 1970).

Donaldson, G., *The Scottish Reformation* (Cambridge, 1960).

Doran, S., *Elizabeth I and Foreign Policy* (London, 2000).

Doran, S., *England and Europe 1485–1603* (London, 1986, rev. 1996).

Doran, S., *England and Europe in the Sixteenth Century* (London, 1999).

Doran, S., *Monarchy and Matrimony: The Courtships of Elizabeth I* (London, 1996).

Doran, S., ' "Revenge her foul and most unnatural murder?": the impact of Mary Stewart's execution on Anglo-Scottish relations', *History*, 85 (2000).

Douglas, A. and Greenfield, P., eds, *Records of Early English Drama: Cumberland/Westmorland/Gloucestershire* (Toronto, 1986).

Downhame, J., *Guide to Godlynesse or a Treatise of a Christian Life* (London, 1629).

Duffy, E., 'The parish, piety, and patronage in late medieval East Anglia: the evidence of rood screens', in K. L. French, G. G. Gibbs and B. A. Kümin, eds, *The Parish in English Life, 1400–1600* (Manchester, 1997).

Duffy, E., *The Stripping of the Altars: Traditional Religion in England, c.1400–c.1580* (New Haven and London, 1992).

Duffy, E., *The Voices of Morebath: Reformation and Rebellion in an English Village* (New Haven and London, 2001).

Dunbar, J. G., *The Architecture of Scotland* (London, 1966).

Dunbar, L., *Reforming the Scottish Church: John Winram (c.1492–1582) and the Example of Fife* (Aldershot, 2002).

Dunlop, D., 'The politics of peacekeeping: Anglo-Scottish relations from 1503 to 1511', *Renaissance Studies*, 8 (1994).

Dunlop, I., *Palaces and Progresses of Elizabeth I* (London, 1962).

Dyer, A. D., *Decline and Growth in English Towns 1400–1640* (Cambridge, 1995).

Dyer, A. D., *The City of Worcester in the Sixteenth Century* (Leicester, 1973).

Dyer, A. 'Midlands', in P. Clark, ed., *The Cambridge Urban History of Britain*, vol. II, *1540–1840* (Cambridge, 2000).

Dyer, A. 'Small market towns 1540–1700', in P. Clark ed., *The Cambridge Urban History of Britain*, vol. II, *1540–1840* (Cambridge, 2000).

Eales, J., 'The rise of ideological politics in Kent, 1558–1640', in M. Zell, ed., *Early Modern Kent, 1540–1640* (Woodbridge, 2000).

Easson, D. E., *Medieval Religious Houses: Scotland* (London, 1957).

Edington, C., *Court and Culture in Renaissance Scotland: Sir David Lindsay* (Amherst, 1994).

Edington, C., 'Knox and the Castilians: a crucible or reforming opinion?', in R. Mason, ed., *John Knox and the British Reformations* (Aldershot, 1998).

Edmond, M., *Hilliard and Oliver, the Lives and Works of Two Great Miniaturists* (London, 1983).

Edmond, M., 'Limners and picturemakers: new light on the lives of miniaturists and large-scale portrait painters working in London in the sixteenth and seventeenth centuries', *Walpole Society*, 47 (1978–80).

Edwards, D., 'Collaboration without anglicisation: the MacGiollapadraig lordship and Tudor reform', in P. J. Duffy, D. Edwards and E. Fitzpatrick, eds, *Gaelic Ireland: Land, Lordship and Settlement, c.1250–c.1650* (Dublin, 2001).

Elliott, K., 'Music of Scotland 1500–1700' (PhD dissertation, University of Cambridge, 1958).

Ellis, H., ed., *Original Letters of Eminent Literary Men of the Sixteenth, Seventeenth, and Eighteenth Centuries* (London, 1843).

Ellis, S. G., 'A Border baron and the Tudor state: the rise and fall of Lord Dacre of the North', *Historical Journal*, XXXV, 2 (1992).

Ellis, S. G., 'Civilizing Northumberland: representations of Englishness in the Tudor state', in *Journal of Historical Sociology*, xii (1999).

Ellis, S. G., *Ireland in the Age of the Tudors 1447–1603: English Expansion and the End of Gaelic Rule* (2nd edition, London, 1998).

Ellis, S. G., *Reform and Revival: English Government in Ireland, 1470–1534* (London, 1986).

Ellis, S. G., *Tudor Frontiers and Noble Power: The Making of the British State* (Oxford, 1995).

Ellis, S. G. and Barber, S., eds, *Conquest and Union: Fashioning a British State 1485–1725* (London, 1995).

Elton, G. R., *England under the Tudors* (3rd edition, London, 1991).

Elton G. R., 'Henry VII: rapacity and remorse', *Historical Journal*, 1 (1958).

Elton, G. R., 'Henry VII: a restatement', *Historical Journal*, 4 (1961).

Elton, G. R., *The Parliament of England, 1559–1581* (Cambridge, 1986).

Elton, G. R., *Policy and Police: The Enforcement of the Reformation in the Age of Thomas Cromwell* (Cambridge, 1972).

Elton, G. R., *Reform and Renewal: Thomas Cromwell and the Common Weal* (Cambridge, 1973).

Elton, G. R., *Reform by Statute: Thomas Starkey's Dialogue and Thomas Cromwell's Policy* (London, 1970).

Elton, G. R., *Studies in Tudor and Stuart Politics and Government* (4 vols, Cambridge, 1974–1992).

Elton, G. R., *The Tudor Constitution* (Cambridge, 1960).

Elton, G. R., 'Tudor government: the points of contact', reprinted in G. R. Elton, *Studies in Tudor and Stuart Politics and Government*, vol. III, *Papers and Reviews* (Cambridge, 1983).

Elton, G. R., *The Tudor Revolution in Government* (Cambridge, 1953).

Elyot, T., *The Boke named the Governor* (London, 1531).

Emery, A., *Greater Medieval Houses of England and Wales*, vol. I, *Northern England* (Cambridge, 1996).

Emery, A., *Greater Medieval Houses of England and Wales*, vol. II, *East Anglia, Central England and Wales* (Cambridge, 2000).

Emmison, F. G., *Elizabethan Life: Home, Work and Land* (Chelmsford, 1976).

Evans, J. T., 'The decline of oligarchy in seventeenth-century Norwich', *Journal of British Studies*, 14 (1974).

Evans, J. T., *Seventeenth-Century Norwich: Politics, Religion and Government, 1620–1690* (Oxford, 1979).

Evans, J. X., ed., *The Works of Sir Roger Williams* (Oxford, 1972).

Everitt, A., 'Farm labourers', in J. Thirsk, ed., *The Agrarian History of England and Wales*, vol. IV, *1500–1640* (Cambridge, 1967).

Everitt, A., 'The marketing of agricultural produce', in J. Thirsk, ed., *The Agrarian History of England and Wales*, vol. IV, *1500–1640* (Cambridge, 1967).

Ewan, E., Women's history in Scotland: towards an agenda, *Innes Review*, 46 (1995).

Ewan, E. and Meikle, M. M., 'Introduction: a monstrous regiment of women', in E. Ewan and M. M. Meikle, eds, *Women in Scotland c.1100–c.1750* (East Linton, 1999).

Ewan, E. and Meikle, M. M., eds, *Women in Scotland c.1100–c.1750* (East Linton, 1999).

Ewart, G., *Scottish Archaeological Internet Reports 1: Dundrennan Abbey: archaeological investigation within the south range of a Cistercian house in Kirkcudbrightshire (Dumfries & Galloway), Scotland* (Society of Antiquaries of Scotland, 2001, at http://www.britarch.ac.uk/sair/sair1.html).

Fallows, D., 'Henry VIII as a composer', in C. Banks, A. Searle and M. Turner, eds, *Sundry Sorts of Music Books: Essays on The British Library Collections Presented to O. W. Neighbour on his 70th Birthday* (London, 1993).

Farnhill, K., *Guilds and the Parish Community in Late Medieval East Anglia* (Woodbridge and Rochester, NY, 2001).

Fawcett, R., *Scottish Architecture from the Accession of the Stewarts to the Reformation 1371–1560* (Edinburgh, 1994).

Feingold, M., *The Mathematicians' Apprenticeship: Science, Universities, and Society in England, 1560–1640* (Cambridge, 1984).

Fenner, D., *Counter-Poyson* (London, 1584).

Fenner, D., *Sacra Theologia sive Veritas quae est Secundum Pietatem* (London, 1585).

Ferguson, A. B., *Clio Unbound: Perception of the Social and Cultural Past in Renaissance England* (Durham, NC, 1979).

Ferguson, A. B., *Utter Antiquity: Perceptions of Prehistory in Renaissance England* (Durham, NC, 1993).

Ferguson, W., *The Identity of the Scottish Nation: An Historic Quest* (Edinburgh, 1998).

Ferguson, W., *Scotland's Relations with England: A Survey to 1707* (Edinburgh, 1977).

Fifoot, C. H. S., *History and Sources of the Common Law: Tort and Contract* (London, 1949).

Finch, M. E., *Five Northamptonshire Families* (Northampton, 1956).

Finlay, R., *Population and Metropolis: The Demography of London, 1580–1650* (Cambridge, 1981).

Firth, K. R., *The Apocalyptic Tradition in Reformation Britain* (Oxford, 1979).

Fischlin, D., 'Political allegory, absolutist ideology and the 'Rainbow Portrait' of Queen Elizabeth I', *Renaissance Quarterly*, 50, 1 (Spring, 1997).

Fissel, M. C., *English Warfare 1511–1642* (London and New York, 2001).

Fleming, D. H., ed., *Register of the Minister, Elders and Deacons of the Christian Congregation of St Andrews 1559–1600* (2 vols, Edinburgh, 1889–90).

Fletcher, A., *Gender, Sex and Subordination in England 1500–1800* (New Haven and London, 1995).

Fletcher, A., 'Honour, reputation and local office-holding in Elizabethan and early Stuart England', in A. Fletcher and J. Stevenson, eds, *Order and Disorder in Early Modern England* (Cambridge, 1985).

Fletcher, A., *Reform in the Provinces: The Government of Stuart England* (New Haven, 1986).

Fletcher, A. and MacCulloch, D., *Tudor Rebellions* (4th edition, Harlow, 1997).

Fletcher, A. J., *Drama and Performance and Polity in Pre-Cromwellian Ireland* (Toronto, 2000).

Flynn, T. S., *The Irish Dominicans 1536–1641* (Dublin, 1993).

Foister, S., 'Paintings and other works of art in sixteenth century English inventories', *Burlington Magazine*, 123 (1981).

Forbes, P., *A Full View of the Public Transactions in the Reign of Elizabeth* (2 vols, London, 1740–1).

Ford, A., 'James Ussher and the creation of an Irish Protestant identity', in B. Bradshaw and P. Roberts, eds, *British Consciousness and National Identity* (Cambridge, 1998).

Forrest, J., *The History of Morris Dancing 1458–1750* (Toronto, 1999).

Foster, W. R., *The Church before the Covenants: The Church of Scotland 1596–1638* (Edinburgh, 1975).

Fox, A., *Oral and Literate Culture in England, 1500–1700* (Oxford, 2000).

Fox, A., 'Remembering the past in early modern England', *Transactions of the Royal Historical Society*, 6th series, 9 (1999).

Fox, A. and Guy, J., eds, *Reassessing the Henrician Age: Humanism, Politics and Reform, 1500–1550* (Oxford, 1986).

Fox, R., ed., *Thomas Harriot: An Elizabethan Man of Science* (London, 2000).

Frank, R., 'Science, medicine and the universities of early modern England', *History of Science*, 11 (1973).

Franko, M., *The Dancing Body in Renaissance Choreography (c.1416–1589)* (Birmingham, AL, 1986).

Fraser, R. A. and Rabkin, N., eds, *Drama of the English Renaissance: The Tudor Period* (New York, 1976).

French, K., *People of the Parish: Community Life in a Late Medieval Diocese* (Philadelphia, 2001).

Frere, W. H. and Douglas, C. E., eds, *Puritan Manifestoes* (New York, 1972).

Friedrichs, C. R., *The Early Modern City 1450–1750* (London, 1995).

Frith, B., *Twelve Portraits of Gloucester Benefactors* (Gloucester, 1972).

Fulke, W., *The Text of the New Testament of Jesus Christ Translated out of the Vulgar Latine by the Papists* (London, 1589).

Fuller, T., *The Holy State and the Profane State*, ed. M. G. Walten (New York, 1938).

Fussner, F. S., *The Historical Revolution: English Historical Writing and Thought, 1580–1640* (New York, 1962).

Gadd, I. A. and Wallis, P., eds, *Guilds, Society and Economy in London 1450–1800* (London, 2002).

Galley, C., *The Demography of Early Modern Towns: York in the Sixteenth and Seventeenth Centuries* (Liverpool, 1998).

Galloway, D., ed., *Records of Early English Drama: Norwich 1540–1642* (Toronto, 1984).

Galloway, D. and Wasson, J., eds, *Records of Plays and Players in Norfolk and Suffolk, 1330–1642* (Oxford, 1981).

Gent, L., and Llewellyn, N., eds, *Renaissance Bodies: The Human Figure in English Culture, c.1540–1660* (London, 1990).

George, D., ed., *Records of Early English Drama: Lancashire* (Toronto, 1992).

Gibson, A. and Smout, T. C., 'Food and hierarchy in Scotland, 1550–1650', in L. Leneman, ed., *Perspectives in Scottish Social History: Essays in Honour of Rosalind Mitchison* (Aberdeen,1988).

Gibson, G., *The Theater of Devotion* (Chicago, 1989).

Gibson, J., ed., *Records of Early English Drama: Kent; Diocese of Canterbury* (3 vols, Toronto, 2002).

Gibson, S., ed., *Statuta Antiqua Universitatis Oxoniensis* (Oxford, 1931).

Gifford, G., *A Briefe Discourse of Certaine Points of the Religion which is among the Common Sort of Christians, which may bee termed the Countrie Divinitie, with a Manifest Confutation of Same* (London, 1581).

Gilbert, H., *Queen Elizabethe's Achademy*, ed. F. J. Futrivall, Early English Text Society, extra series 8 (London, 1869).

Gillespie, R., *Devoted People: Belief and Religion in Early Modern Ireland* (Manchester, 1997).

Gillespie, R., 'Explorers, exploiters and entrepreneurs: early modern Ireland and its context, 1500–1700', in B. J. Graham and L. J. Proudfoot, eds, *An Historical Geography of Ireland* (London, 1993).

Girouard, M., *Life in the English Country House* (Harmondsworth and New Haven, 1978).

Girouard, M., *Robert Smythson and the Elizabethan Country House* (New Haven and London, 1983).

Giry-Deloison, C., 'La diplomatie anglaise 1485–1603' in L. Bély and I. Rochefort, eds, *L'invention de la diplomatie: Moyen-Age – Temps Modernes* (Paris, 1998).

Giry-Deloison, C, 'Henry VII et la Bretagne', in J. Kehervé, ed., *Bretagne Terre d'Europe* (Brest/Quimper, 1992).

Giry-Deloison, C, 'Money and early Tudor diplomacy: the English pensioners of the French kings (1475–1547)', *Medieval History*, 3 (1993).

Giry-Deloison, C., 'Le personnel diplomatique au début di XVIe siècle: l'exemple des relations franco-anglaises de l'avènement de Henry VII au camp du drap d'or (1485–1520)', *Journal des Savants* (July–September 1987).

Giry-Deloison, C., ed., *François Ier et Henri VIII: Deux Princes de la Renaissance (1515–1547)* (Lille, n.d.).

Glennie, P. D., 'Industry and towns, 1500–1730', in R. A. Dodgshon and R. A. Butlin, eds, *An Historical Geography of England and Wales* (2nd edition, London, 1990).

Goldberg, P. J. P., *Woman is a Worthy Wight*, repub. as *Women in Medieval English Society* (Stroud, 1997).

Goodacre, J., *The Transformation of a Peasant Economy: Townspeople and Villagers in the Lutterworth Area, 1500–1700* (Aldershot, 1994).

Goodare, J., 'James VI's English subsidy', in J. Goodare and M. Lynch, eds, *The Reign of James VI* (East Linton, 2000).

Goodare, J., ed., *The Scottish Witch-hunt in Context* (Manchester, 2002).

Goodare, J., *State and Society in Early Modern Scotland* (Oxford, 1999).

Goodare, J. and Lynch, M., 'James VI: universal king?', in J. Goodare and M. Lynch, eds, *The Reign of James VI* (East Linton, 2000).

Goose, N., 'Household size and structure in early Stuart Cambridge', *Social History*, 5 (1980).

Goring, J. and Wake, J., eds, *Northamptonshire Lieutenancy Papers, 1580–1614* (Northampton, 1975).

Gowing, L., *Domestic Dangers: Women, Words, and Sex in Early Modern London* (Oxford, 1996).

Graham, M., 'Conflict and sacred space in Reformation Scotland', *Albion*, 33 (2001).

Graham, M., *The Uses of Reform: 'Godly Discipline' and Popular Behavior in Scotland and Beyond, 1560–1610* (Leiden, 1996).

Grant, R., 'Politicking Jacobean women: Lady Ferniehirst, the countess of Arran and the countess of Huntly, c.1580–1603', in E. Ewan and M. M. Meikle, eds, *Women in Scotland c.1100–c.1750*, (East Linton, 1999).

Graves, M. A. R., *Burghley* (Basingstoke, 1999).

Graves, M. A. R., *Early Tudor Parliaments* (London, 1990).

Graves, M. A. R., *Elizabethan Parliaments 1559–1601* (2nd edition, London, 1996).

Graves, M. A. R., *Thomas Norton : The Parliament Man* (Oxford, 1994).

Graves, M. A. R., *The Tudor Parliaments: Crown, Lords and Commons, 1485–1603* (London, 1985).

Gray, C. M., *Copyhold, Equity, and the Common Law* (Cambridge, MA, 1963).

Green, T. A., *Verdict According to Conscience: Perspectives on the English Criminal Trial Jury* (Chicago, 1985).

Gregory, D., *History of the Western Highlands and Isles of Scotland from AD 1493 to AD 1625* (Edinburgh, 1836).

Griffiths, R. A., ed., *The Boroughs of Medieval Wales* (Cardiff, 1978).

Griffiths, M., ' "Very wealthy by merchandise"? Urban fortunes', in J. G. Jones, ed., *Class, Community and Culture in Tudor Wales* (Cardiff, 1989).

Griffiths, P., 'Overlapping circles: imagining criminal communities in London, 1545–1645', in A. Shepard and P. Withington, eds, *Communities in Early Modern England* (Manchester, 2000).

Griffiths, P., 'The structure of prostitution in Elizabethan London', *Continuity and Change*, 8, 1 (1993).

Griffiths, P., *Youth and Authority: Formative Experiences in England 1560–1640* (Oxford, 1996).

Griffiths, P. and Jenner, M. S. R., eds, *Londinopolis: Essays in the Cultural and Social History of Early Modern London* (Manchester, 2000).

Griffiths, P., Fox, A. and Hindle, S., eds, *The Experience of Authority in Early Modern England* (London and New York, 1996).

Griffiths, P., Landers, J., Pelling, M. and Tyson, R., 'Population and disease, estrangement and belonging, 1540–1700', in P. Clark, *The Cambridge Urban History of Britain*, vol. II (Cambridge, 2000).

Griffiths, R. A., *The Boroughs of Medieval Wales* (Cardiff, 1978).

Griffiths, R. A. and. Thomas, R. S., *The Making of the Tudor Dynasty* (Gloucester, 1985).

Grummitt, D., ed., *The English Experience in France c.1450–1558: War, Diplomacy and Cultural Exchange* (Aldershot, 2002).

Grummitt, D., ' "For the Surety of the Towne and Marches": early Tudor policy towards Calais 1485–1509', *Nottingham Medieval Studies*, 44 (2000).

Grummitt, D., 'Henry VII, 'Chamber finance and the "New Monarchy": some new evidence', *Historical Research*, 72 (1999).

Guevara, A., *The Diall of Princes*, trans. T. North (New York, 1968).

Guide to the Contents of the Public Record Office, vol. I, *Legal Records, etc.* (London, 1963).

Gunn, S. J., 'The accession of Henry VIII', *Bulletin of the Institute of Historical Research*, 64 (1991).

Gunn, S. J., 'The courtiers of Henry VII', *English Historical Review*, 108 (1993).

Gunn, S. J., *Early Tudor Government, 1485–1558* (Basingstoke and New York, 1995).

Gunn, S. J., 'The French Wars of Henry VIII', in J. Black, ed., *The Origins of War in Early Modern Europe* (Edinburgh, 1987).

Gunn, S. J., 'Sir Thomas Lovell (c.1449–1524): a new man in a new monarchy?', in J. L. Watts, ed., *The End of the Middle Ages* (Stroud, 1998).

Gunn, S. J., 'Wolsey's foreign policy and the domestic crisis of 1527–8', in S. J. Gunn and P. G. Lindley, eds, *Cardinal Wolsey: Church, State and Art* (Cambridge, 1991).

Gunn, S. J. and Lindley, P. G., eds, *Cardinal Wolsey: Church, State and Art* (Cambridge, 1991).

Gurr, A., *Playgoing in Shakespeare's London* (Cambridge, 1987).

Gurr, A., *The Shakespearian Playing Companies* (Oxford, 1996).

Gurr, A., *The Shakespearean Stage 1574–1642*, (3rd edition, Cambridge, 1992).

Guy, J., *The Cardinal's Court: The Impact of Thomas Wolsey in Star Chamber* (Hassocks, 1977).

Guy, J., 'Introduction: the 1590s: the second reign of Elizabeth I', in J. Guy, ed., *The Reign of Elizabeth I: Court and Culture in the Last Decade* (Cambridge, 1995).

Guy, J., *Politics, Law and Counsel in Tudor and Early Stuart England* (Aldershot, 2000).

Guy, J., 'The privy council: revolution or evolution', in C. Coleman and D. Starkey, eds, *Revolution Reassessed: Revisions in the History of Tudor Government and Administration* (Oxford, 1986).

Guy, J., ed., *The Reign of Elizabeth I: Court and Culture in the Last Decade* (Cambridge, 1995).

Guy, J., 'Thomas Wolsey, Thomas Cromwell and the reform of Henrician government', in D. MacCulloch, ed., *The Reign of Henry VIII: Politics, Policy and Piety* (Basingstoke and New York, 1995).

Guy, J., *Tudor England* (Oxford, 1988).

Gwynfor Jones, J., *Early Modern Wales c.1525–1640* (Basingstoke, 1994).

Gwynn, A. and Hadcock, R. N., *Medieval Religious Houses: Ireland* (London, 1970).

Gwynn, P., *The King's Cardinal: The Rise and Fall of Thomas Wolsey* (London, 1990).

Gwynn, P, 'Wolsey's foreign policy: the conferences at Calais and Bruges reconsidered', *Historical Journal*, 23 (1980).

Hackett, M., *Virgin Mother, Maiden Queen: Elizabeth I and the Cult of the Virgin Mary* (New York, 1995).

Hadden, R. W., *On the Shoulders of Merchants: Exchange and the Mathematical Conception of Nature in Early Modern Europe* (Albany, NY, 1994).

Hadfield, A., 'Briton and Scythian: Tudor representations of Irish origins', *Irish Historical Studies*, 28 (1993).

Haigh, C., 'Catholicism in early modern England: Bossy and beyond', *Historical Journal*, 45 (2002).

Haigh, C., 'The Church of England, the Catholics and the people', in C. Haigh, ed., *The Reign of Elizabeth I* (London,1984).

Haigh, C., 'The continuity of Catholicism in the English Reformation', *Past and Present*, 93 (1981).

Haigh, C., *Elizabeth I* (2nd edition, London, 1998).

Haigh, C., *The English Reformations: Religion, Politics, and Society under the Tudors* (Oxford, 1997).

Haigh, C., 'From monopoly to minority: Catholicism in early modern England', *Transactions of the Royal Historical Society* (1981).

Haigh, C., 'The recent historiography of the English Reformation', in Margo Todd, ed., *Reformation to Revolution: Politics and Religion in Early Modern England* (London, 1995).

Haigh, C., 'The taming of the Reformation: preachers, pastors, and parishioners in Elizabethan and early Stuart England', *History*, 85 (2000).

Hajnal, J., 'European marriage patterns in perspective', in D. V. Glass and D. E. C. Eversley, eds, *Population in History* (London, 1965).

Hammer, P. E. J., *The Polarisation of Elizabethan Politics: The Political Career of Robert Devereux, 2nd Earl of Essex, 1585–1597* (Cambridge, 1999).

Harbage, A. and Schoenbaum, S., *Annals of English Drama 975–1700* (Philadelphia, 1964).

Harding, A., *A Social History of English Law* (Harmondsworth, 1966).

Harding, V., *The Dead and the Living in Paris and London* (Cambridge, 2002).

Harding, V., 'The population of London, 1550–1700: a review of the published evidence', *London Journal*, 15.

Harkness, D., *John Dee's Conversations with Angels: Cabala, Alchemy, and the End of Nature* (Cambridge, 1999).

Harkness, D. and O'Down, M., eds, *The Town In Ireland* (Belfast, 1981).

Harkness, D. E., 'Strange ideas and "English" knowledge: natural science exchange in Elizabethan London', in P. H. Smith and P. Findlen, eds, *Merchants and Marvels: Commerce, Science, and Art in Early Modern Europe* (New York, 2002).

Harris, B. J., *English Aristocratic Women 1450–1550* (New York, 2002).

Harris, B. J., 'Women and politics in early Tudor England', *Historical Journal*, 33 (1980).

Harrison, C. J., 'The petition of Edmund Dudley', *English Historical Review*, 87 (1972).

Harrison, F. L., *Music in Medieval Britain* (2nd edition, London, 1963).

Harrison, W., 'The Description of Britaine', in R. Holinshed, *The First and Second Volumes of Chronicles* (London, 1587).

Harrison, W., *The Description of England: The Classic Contemporary Account of Tudor Social Life*, ed. G. Edelen (Ithaca, NY, 1968).

Harriss, G. L., 'Medieval government and statecraft', *Past and Present*, 24 (1963).

Hartley, T. E., *Elizabeth's Parliaments: Queen, Lords, and Commons, 1559–1601* (Manchester, 1992).

Hartley, T. E., *Proceedings in the Parliaments of Elizabeth I* (Leicester, 1981).

Hartshorne, E. S., *Memorials of Holdenby* (Newcastle, 1868).

Harvey, P. D. A., 'Estate surveyors and the spread of the scale-map in England, 1550–80', *Landscape History*, 15 (1993).

Harvey, P. D. A., *Maps in Tudor England* (Chicago, 1993).

Hassel, R. C., *Renaissance Drama and the English Church Year* (Lincoln, 1979).

Hay, D., *Polydore Vergil: Renaissance Historian and Man of Letters* (Oxford, 1952).

Haynes, S., ed., *Collection of State papers . . . Left by William Cecil, Lord Burghley* (2 vols, London, 1740–59).

Hays, R. C., McGee, C. E., Joyce, S. L. and Newlyn, E. S., eds, *Records of Early English Drama: Dorset/Cornwall* (Toronto, 1999).

Head, D. M., 'Henry VIII's Scottish policy', *Scottish Historical Review*, 61 (1982).

Heal, F., *Reformation in Britain and Ireland* (Oxford, 2003).

Hearn, K., ed., *Dynasties: Painting in Tudor and Stuart England, 1530–1630* (London, 1995).

Helgerson, R., *Forms of Nationhood: The Elizabethan Writing of England* (Chicago, 1992).

Helmholz, R. H., *Roman Canon Law in Reformation England* (Cambridge, 1990).

Helmholz, R. H., *Select Cases on Defamation to 1600* (London, 1985).

Henderson, G. D., ed., *The Scots Confession, 1560 and the Negative Confession, 1581* (Edinburgh, 1937).

Henry, J., 'Aminism and empiricism: Copernican physics and the origins of William Gilbert's experimental method', *Journal of the History of Ideas*, 62, 1 (2001).

Hey, D. G., *An English Rural Community: Myddle under the Tudors and Stuarts* (Leicester, 1974).

Higgs, L., *Godliness and Governance in Tudor Colchester* (Ann Arbor, 1998).

Highley, C., *Shakespeare, Spenser, and the Crisis in Ireland* (Cambridge, 1997).

Hilling, J. B., *The Historic Architecture of Wales* (Cardiff, 1976).

Hindle, S., 'Custom, festival and protest in early modern England: the Little Budworth Wakes, St Peter's Day, 1596', *Rural History*, 6 (1995).

Hindle, S., 'Dearth, fasting and alms: the campaign for general hospitality in late Elizabethan England', *Past and Present*, 172 (August 2001).

Hindle, S., 'Hierarchy and community in the Elizabethan parish: the Swallowfield articles of 1596', *Historical Journal*, XLII, 3 (1999).

Hindle, S., 'The political culture of the middling sort in English rural communities, *c.*1550–1700', in T. Harris, ed., *The Politics of the Excluded, 1500–1850* (Basingstoke, 2001).

Hindle, S., *The State and Social Change in Early Modern England, 1550–1640* (Basingstoke, 2000).

Hirst, D., *Authority and Conflict, 1603–58* (London, 1986).

Historical Manuscripts Commission, *Calendar of Salisbury Manuscripts at Hatfield House* (London, 1883–1923).

Hoak, D., 'The iconography of the Crown Imperial', in D. Hoak, ed., *Tudor Political Culture* (Cambridge, 1995).

Hoak, D., *The King's Council in the Reign of Edward VI* (Cambridge, 1976).

Hoak, D., 'The king's privy chamber, 1547–1553', in D. Guth and J. McKenna, eds, *Tudor Rule and Revolution: Essays for G. R. Elton from his American Friends* (Cambridge,1982).

Hoak, D., ed., *Tudor Political Culture* (Cambridge, 1995).

Holman, P., *Four and Twenty Fiddlers: the Violin at the English Court, 1540–1690* (Oxford, 1993).

Holmes, C., 'Statutory interpretation in the early seventeenth century: the courts, the council and the commissioners of sewers', in J. A. Guy and H. G. Beale, eds, *Law and Social Change in British History: Papers Presented to the British Legal History Conference, 14–17 July 1981* (London, 1984).

Holmes, P., 'The Great Council in the reign of Henry VII', *English Historical Review*, 101 (1986).

Horrox, R., 'Yorkist and early Tudor England', in C. Allmand, ed., *The New Cambridge Medieval History*, Vol. 7, *c.1415–c.1500* (Cambridge, 1998).

Hoskins, W. G., *The Age of Plunder: King Henry's England, 1500–1547* (London, 1976).

Hoskins, W. G., 'The rebuilding of rural England 1570–1640', *Past and Present*, 4 (1953).

Houlbrooke, R. A., *Church Courts and People During the English Reformation, 1520–1570* (Oxford, 1979).

Houlbrooke, R. A., 'Debate: Henry VIII's wills: a comment', *Historical Journal*, 37 (1994).

Houlbrooke, R. A., *The English Family, 1450–1700* (London, 1984).

Houston, R. A., *The Population History of Britain and Ireland, 1500–1750* (Basingstoke, 1992).

Houston, R. A., 'Women in the economy and society of Scotland, 1500–1800', in R. A. Houston and I. D. Whyte, eds, *Scottish Society 1500–1800* (Cambridge, 1989).

Houston, R. A. and Whyte, I. D., eds, *Scottish Society 1500–1800* (Cambridge, 1989).

Howard, D., *Scottish Architecture from the Reformation to Restoration 1560–1660* (Edinburgh, 1995).

Howard, M., *The Early Tudor Country House: Architecture and Politics 1490–1550* (London, 1989).

Howard, M., 'The Tudor and Jacobean Great House: a summary booklist', in M. Airs, ed., *The Tudor and Jacobean Great House* (Oxford, 1994).

Howard, M., *The Tudor Image* (London, 1995).

Howard, S., ' "Ascending the riche mount": performing hierarchy and gender in the Henrician masque', in P. Herman, ed., *Rethinking the Henrician Era: Essays on Early Tudor Texts and Contexts* (Urbana, 1994).

Howarth, D., *Images of Rule: Art and Politics in the English Renaissance, 1485–1649* (Berkeley, 1997).

Howells, B. E., 'The lower orders of society', in J. Gwynfor Jones, ed., *Class, Community and Culture in Tudor Wales* (Cardiff, 1989).

Howson, A. G., *A History of Mathematics Education in England* (Cambridge, 1982).

Hoyle, R. W., 'The origins of the dissolution of the monasteries', *Historical Journal*, 38 (1995).

Hoyle, R. W., 'Agrarian agitation in mid-sixteenth century Norfolk: a petition of 1553', *Historical Journal*, 44 (2001).

Hoyle, R. W., *The Estates of the English Crown, 1558–1640* (Cambridge, 1992).

Hoyle, R. W., *The Pilgrimage of Grace and the Politics of the 1530s* (Oxford, 2001).

Hoyle, R. W., 'Tenurial litigation in England, 1540–1640: the evidence of the Chancery decrees' (in preparation).

Hoyle, R. W. and Winchester, A. J. L., 'A lost source for the rising of 1536 in northwest England', *English Historical Review*, 118 (2003).

Hudson, A., *The Premature Reformation: Wycliffite Texts and Lollard History* (Oxford, 1988).

Hufton, O., *The Prospect Before Her: A History of Women in Western Europe, 1500–1800* (London, 1995).

Hughes, P. L. and Larkin, J. F., *Tudor Royal Proclamations*, vol. III, *The Later Tudors (1588–1603)* (New Haven and London, 1969).

Hume Brown, P., *Early Travellers in Scotland* (1891, repr. Edinburgh, 1978).

Hunter, L. and Hutton, S., eds, *Women, Science and Medicine 1500–1700: Mothers and Sisters of the Royal Society* (London, 1997).

Hurstfield, J., 'County government: Wiltshire, c.1530–1660' (1957), reprinted in J. Hurstfield, *Freedom, Corruption and Government in Elizabethan England* (London, 1973).

Hurstfield, J., ed., *The Historical Association Book of the Tudors* (London, 1973).

Hutton, R., *The Rise and Fall of Merry England* (Oxford, 1994).

Ingram, M., *Church Courts, Sex and Marriage in England, 1570–1640* (Cambridge, 1987).

Ingram, R. W., ed., *Records of Early English Drama: Coventry* (Toronto, 1981).

Ingram, W., *The Business of Playing* (Ithaca, NY, 1992).

Ives, E. W., 'Henry VIII: the political perspective', in D. MacCulloch, ed., *The Reign of Henry VIII: Politics, Policy and Piety* (Basingstoke and New York, 1995).

Ives, E. W., *The Common Lawyers in Pre-Reformation England: Thomas Kebell, a Case Study* (Cambridge, 1983).

Jack, S. M., *Towns in Tudor and Stuart Britain* (New York and Basingstoke, 1996).

James VI, *The Basilikon Doron of King James VI*, ed. J. Craigie (2 vols, Edinburgh, 1944–50).

James, M. E., 'The concept of order and the Northern Rising', reprinted in M. E. James, *Society, Politics and Culture: Studies in Early Modern England* (Cambridge, 1986).

James, M. E., *Family, Lineage and Civil Society: A History of Society, Politics and Culture in the Durham Region 1500–1640* (Oxford, 1976).

James, M. E., *Society, Politics and Culture: Studies in Early Modern England* (Cambridge, 1986).

Jenkins, P., 'Wales', in P. Clark, *The Cambridge Urban History of Britain*, vol. II, *1540–1840* (Cambridge, 2000).

Johnston, A. F., 'The city as patron', in S. Westfall and P. White, eds, *Shakespeare and Theatrical Patronage in Early Modern England* (Cambridge, 2002).

Johnston, A. F., 'English community drama in crisis: 1535–80', in A. Hindley, ed., *European Communities of Medieval Drama: A Collection of Essays* (Turnhout, 1999).

Johnston, A. F., 'The inherited tradition: the legacy of provincial civic drama', in A. L. Magnusson and C. E. McGee, eds, *Actors and Acting in the Elizabethan Theatre: The Elizabethan Theatre XIII, Proceedings of the 13th Waterloo International Conference, 1989* (Toronto, 1994).

Johnston, A. F., 'The Robin Hood of the records', in L. Potter, ed., *Playing Robin Hood: The Legend as Performance in Five Centuries* (Newark, Delaware and London, 1998).

Johnston, A. F., 'The *York Cycle* and the libraries of York', in A. F. Johnston, *The Church and Learning in Late Medieval Society* (Donnington, 2002).

Johnston, A. F. and Husken, W., eds, *English Parish Drama* (Amsterdam and Atlanta, 1996).

Johnston, A. F. and Rogerson, M., eds, *Records of Early English Drama: York* (2 vols, Toronto, 1979).

Johnston, S., *Making Mathematical Practice: Gentlemen, Practitioners, and Artisans in Elizabethan England* (PhD thesis, University of Cambridge, 1994).

Johnston, S., 'Mathematical practitioners and instruments in Elizabethan England', *Annals of Science*, 48 (1991).

Jones, E., *The English Nation: The Great Myth* (Stroud, 1998).

Jones, G., *History of the Law of Charity, 1532–1827* (Cambridge, 1969).

Jones, J. G., ed., *Class, Community and Culture in Tudor Wales* (Cardiff, 1989).

Jones, M. K., *Bosworth 1485: Psychology of a Battle* (Stroud, 2002).

Jones, M. K., 'Henry Tudor and the myth of 1485', in D. Grummitt, ed., *The English Experience in France: War, Diplomacy and Cultural Exchange, c.1450–1558* (Aldershot, 2002).

Jones, M. K., 'The myth of 1485: did France really put Henry Tudor on the throne?', in D. Grummitt, *The English Experience in France: War, Diplomacy and Cultural Exchange, c.1450–1558* (Aldershot, 2002).

Jones, M. K., 'Sir William Stanley of Holt: politics and family allegiance in the late fifteenth century', *Welsh History Review*, 14 (1988).

Jones, M. K. and Underwood, M. G., *The King's Mother: Lady Margaret Beaufort, Countess of Richmond and Derby* (Cambridge, 1992).

Jones, N., *The Birth of the Elizabethan Age: England in the 1560s* (Oxford, 1993; repr. 1995).

Jones, N., 'Elizabeth's first year: the conception and birth of the Elizabethan political world', in C. Haigh, ed., *The Reign of Elizabeth I* (London, 1984).

Jones, N., *The English Reformation: Religion and Cultural Adaptation* (Oxford, 2002).

Jones, N., *Faith by Statute: Parliament and the Settlement of Religion, 1559* (London, 1982).

Jones, W. J., *The Elizabethan Court of Chancery* (Oxford, 1967).

Jones, W. R. D., *The Mid-Tudor Crisis, 1539–1563* (London, 1973).

Kahrl, S. J. and Proudfoot, R., eds, *Records of Plays and Players in Lincolnshire 1300–1585*, (Oxford, 1972).

Keating, G., *The History of Ireland*, ed. and trans. D. Comyn and P. Dineen (4 vols, Dublin, 1902–1914).

Kelly, H. A., *The Matrimonial Trials of Henry VIII* (Stanford, 1976).

Kelton, A., *A Chronycle with a Genealogie declarying that the Brittons and Welshemen are lineallye dyscended from Brute. Newly and very wittely compyled in Meter* (London, 1547).

Kelton, A., *A Comendacion of Welshmen* (London, 1546).

Kendrick, T. D., *British Antiquity* (London, 1950).

Kenny, A., ed., *The Responsa Scholarum of the English College, Rome, 1598–1621* (London, 1962).

Kerridge, E., *Agrarian Problems in the Sixteenth Century and After* (London, 1969).

Kershaw, S., 'Duty and power in the Elizabethan aristocracy: George, earl of Shrewsbury, the Glossopdale dispute and the council', in G. W. Bernard, ed., *The Tudor Nobility* (Manchester, 1992).

Kidd, C., *British Identities before Nationalism: Ethnicity and Nationhood in the Atlantic World, 1600–1800* (Cambridge and New York, 1999).

Kidd, C., *Subverting Scotland's Past: Scottish Whig Historians and the Creation of an Anglo-British Identity, 1689–c.1830* (Cambridge and New York, 1993).

Kilroy, P., 'Women and the Reformation in seventeenth-century Ireland', in M. Mac Curtain and M. O'Dowd, eds, *Women in Early Modern Ireland* (Dublin, 1991).

King, J. N., 'The godly woman in Elizabethan iconography', *Renaissance Quarterly*, 38 (1985).

King, J. N., 'Queen Elizabeth I: representations of the Virgin Queen', *Renaissance Quarterly*, 43 (1990).

King, J. N., *Tudor Royal Iconography* (Princeton, NJ, 1989).

Kipling, G., *Enter the King: Theatre, Liturgy and Ritual in the Medieval Civic Triumph* (Oxford, 1998).

Kipling, G., *The Triumph of Honour: Burgundian Origins of the English Renaissance* (Leiden, 1977).

Kirk, J., *Patterns of Reform: Continuity and Change in the Reformation Kirk* (Edinburgh, 1989).

Kirk, J., ed., *The Second Book of Discipline* (Edinburgh, 1980).

Kisby, F., 'The Royal Household Chapel in early-Tudor London' (PhD dissertation, University of London, 1996).

Kisby, F., '"When the king goeth a procession": chapel ceremonies and services, the ritual year, and religious reforms at the early Tudor court, 1485–1547', *Journal of British Studies*, 40 (2001).

Kissack, K., *Monmouth: The Making of a County Town* (London, 1975).

Kitching, C. J., 'The quest for concealed lands', *Transactions of the Royal Historical Society*, 4th series, XXIV (1974).

Klein, B., *Maps and the Writing of Space in Early Modern England and Ireland* (Basingstoke, 2002).

Knafla, L., *Law and Politics in Jacobean England: The Tracts of Lord Chancellor Ellesmere* (Cambridge, 1977).

Knecht, R. J., *Renaissance Warrior and Patron: The Reign of Francis I* (Cambridge, 1994).

Knowles, D., *The Religious Orders in England*, vol. 3, *The Tudor Age* (Cambridge, 1959).

Knowles, D. and Hadcock, R. N., *Medieval Religious Houses: England and Wales* (London, 1994; 1st edition, 1971).

Kouri, E., *England and the Attempt to Form a Protestant Alliance in the Late 1560s: A Case Study in European Diplomacy* (Helsinki, 1985).

Koyré, A., *From the Closed World to the Infinite Universe* (Baltimore, 1957).

Kreider, A., *English Chantries: The Road to Dissolution* (Cambridge, MA, 1979).

Krummel, D. W., *English Music Printing, 1553–1700* (London, 1975).

Kuhn, T., *The Structure of Scientific Revolutions* (Chicago, 1960).

Kümin, B. A., *The Shaping of a Community: The Rise and Reformation of the English Parish, c.1400–1560* (Aldershot, 1996).

Lake, P., *Anglicans and Puritans? Presbyterianism and English Conformist Thought from Whitgift to Hooker* (London, 1988).

Lake, P., 'Constitutional consensus and Puritan opposition in the 1620s: Thomas Scott and the Spanish match', *Historical Journal*, XXV, 4 (1982).

Lake, P., *Moderate Puritanism and the Elizabethan Church* (Cambridge, 1982).

Lake, P. and Questier, M., *The Antichrist's Lewd Hat: Protestants, Papists, and Players in Post-Reformation England* (New Haven, 2002).

Lamb, J., ed., *Collection of Original Documents from the Manuscript Library of Corpus Christi College, Illustrative of the History of the University of Cambridge, 1500–1572* (London, 1838).

Lambarde, W., *Eirenarcha: Or, Of the Office of the Justice of the Peace* (London, 1583).

'Lamentable Complaint of the Commonaltie', in *A Parte of the Register* (Middleburg, 1593).

Lancashire, I., *Dramatic Texts and Records of Britain: A Chronological Topography to 1558* (Cambridge, 1984).

Lander, J. R., 'Bonds, coercion and fear: Henry VII and the peerage', in J. G. Rowe and W. H. Stockdale, eds, *Florilegium Historiale: Essays Presented to Wallace K. Ferguson* (Toronto, 1971).

Larner, C., *Enemies of God: The Witch-Hunt in Scotland* (London, 1981).

Laurence, A., *Women in England, 1500–1760: A Social History* (London, 1994).

Leaver, R., *'Goostly Psalmes and Spirituall Songes': English and Dutch Metrical Psalms from Coverdale to Utenhove, 1535–1566* (Oxford, 1991).

Lee, M., Jr, *Great Britain's Solomon* (Urbana, 1990).

Lee, M., Jr, *John Maitland of Thirlestane and the Foundation of the Stewart Despotism in Scotland* (Princeton, NJ, 1959).

Lehmberg, S. E., 'Cathedral music and musicians', in *The Reformation of Cathedrals: Cathedrals in English Society, 1485–1603* (Princeton, NJ, 1988).

Lehmberg, S. E., *The Reformation Parliament 1529–1536* (Cambridge, 1970).

Le Huray, P., *Music and the Reformation in England 1549–1660* (2nd edition, Cambridge, 1978).

Lennon, C., 'The chantries in the Irish Reformation: the case of St Anne's Guild, Dublin, 1550–1630', in R. V. Comerford, M. Cullen, J. R. Itril and C. Lennon (eds) Religion, Conflict and Coexistence in Ireland (Dublin 1990).

Lennon, C., 'The rise of recusancy among the Dublin patricians, 1580–1613', in W. J. Sheils and D. Wood, eds, *The Churches, Ireland and the Irish* (Dublin, 1989).

Lennon, C., *Sixteenth-Century Ireland: The Incomplete Conquest* (Dublin, 1994).

Letters and Papers, Foreign and Domestic, of the Reign of Henry VIII, 1509–47, ed. J. S. Brewer, J. Gairdner, R. H. Brodie (21 vols, London, 1862–1932).

Levack, B. P., *The Civil Lawyers in England 1603–1641* (Oxford, 1973).

Levin, C., Heart and Stomach of a King: Elizabeth and the Politics of Sex and Power (Philadelphia, 1994).

Levine, J. M., *Humanism and History* (Ithaca, NY, 1987).

Levy, E., 'Moorfields, Finsbury and the City of London in the sixteenth century', *London Topographical Record*, 26 (1990).

Levy, F. J., *Tudor Historical Thought* (San Marino, CA, 1967).

Linaker, R., *A Comfortable Treatise for the Relief of such as are Afflicted in Conscience* (London, 1595).

Lindberg, D. and Westman, R., eds, *Reappraisals of the Scientific Revolution* (Cambridge, 1990).

Livingstone, C. R., *British Broadside Ballads of the Sixteenth Century: A Catalogue of the Extant Sheets and an Essay* (New York and London, 1991).

Llewellyn, N., *Funeral Monuments in Post-Reformation England* (Cambridge, 2000).

Lloyd, C. and Thurley, S., *Henry VIII: Images of a Tudor King* (London, 1990).

Lloyd, H., *The Rouen Campaign, 1590–92* (Oxford, 1973).

Loades, D. M., *England's Maritime Empire: Seapower, Commerce and Policy* (Harlow, 2000).

Loades, D. M., ed., *John Foxe: An Historical Perspective* (Aldershot, 1999).

Loades, D. M., ed., *John Foxe and the English Reformation* (Aldershot, 1997).

Loades, D. M., *The Mid-Tudor Crisis, 1545–1565* (London, 1992).

Loades, D. M., *Politics and Nation: England 1450–1660* (5th edition, Oxford, 1999).

Loades, D. M., *Power in Tudor England* (New York, 1997).

Loades, D. M., *The Tudor Court* (London, 1986).

Loades, D. M., *Tudor Government: Structures of Authority in the Sixteenth Century* (Oxford, 1997).

Loades, D. M., *The Tudor Navy: An Administrative, Political and Military History* (Aldershot, 1992).

Lockyer, R., *Tudor and Stuart Britain 1471–1714* (2nd edition, New York, 1985).

Lord, P., *The Visual Culture of Wales: Imaging the Nation* (Cardiff, 2000).

Louis, C., ed., *Records of Early English Drama: Sussex* (Toronto, 2000).

Lubbock, J., *The Tyranny of Taste: The Politics of Architecture and Design in Britain 1550–1960* (New Haven and London, 1995).

Luckett, D. A., 'Crown office and licensed retinues in the reign of Henry VII', in R. Archer and S. Walker, eds, *Rulers and Ruled in Late Medieval England* (London and Rio Grande, OH, 1995).

Luckett, D. A., 'Crown patronage and political morality in early Tudor England: the case of Giles, Lord Daubeney', *English Historical Review*, 110 (1995).

Lynch, A., 'Religion in late medieval Ireland', *Archivium Hibernicum*, 36 (1981).

Lynch, M., 'Court ceremony and ritual during the personal reign of James VI', in J. Goodare and M. Lynch, eds, *The Reign of James VI* (East Linton, 2000).

Lynch, M., 'The Crown and the burghs 1500–1625', in M. Lynch, ed., *The Early Modern Town in Scotland* (London, 1987).

Lynch, M., ed., *The Early Modern Town in Scotland* (London, 1987).

Lynch, M., *Edinburgh and the Reformation* (Edinburgh, 1981).

Lynch, M., 'John Knox, minister of Edinburgh and commissioner of the kirk', in R. A. Mason, ed., *John Knox and the British Reformations* (Aldershot, 1998).

Lynch, M., ed., *Mary Stewart: Queen in Three Kingdoms* (Oxford and New York, 1988).

Lynch, M., 'Religious life', in M. Lynch, ed., *The Oxford Companion to Scottish History* (Oxford, 2001).

Lynch, M., *Scotland: A New History* (London, 1991).

Lyons, M. A., Franco-Irish Relations, 1500–1600 (Woodbridge, 2003).

Lythe, S. G. E. and Butt, J., *An Economic History of Scotland, 1100–1939* (Glasgow and London, 1975).

MacCaffrey, W., 'The Anjou match and the making of Elizabethan foreign policy', in P. Clark, A. G. T. Smith, and N. Tyacke, eds, *The English Commonwealth, 1547–1640* (Leicester, 1979).

MacCaffrey, W., *Elizabeth I* (London, 1993).

MacCaffrey, W., *Elizabeth I: War and Politics 1588–1603* (Princeton, NJ, 1992).

MacCaffrey, W., *Exeter* (Cambridge, MA, 1958).

MacCaffrey, W., 'Place and patronage in Elizabethan politics', in S. T. Bindoff, J. Hurstfield and C. H. Williams, eds, *Elizabethan Government and Society: Essays Presented to Sir John Neale* (London, 1961).

MacCaffrey, W., *Queen Elizabeth and the Making of Policy, 1572–1588* (Princeton, NJ, 1981).

MacCaffrey, W., 'The Newhaven Expedition, 1562–63', *Historical Journal* 1 (1997).

MacCaffrey, W., *The Shaping of the Elizabethan Regime: Elizabethan Politics 1558–72* (London, 1969).

MacCaffrey, W., 'Talbot and Stanhope: an episode in Elizabethan politics', *Bulletin of the Institute of Historical Research*, 33 (1960).

MacCarthy-Morrogh, M., *The Munster Plantation: English Migration to Southern Ireland, 1583–1641* (Oxford, 1987).

McClendon, M., *The Quiet Reformation: Magistrates and the Emergence of Protestantism in Tudor Norwich* (Stanford, 1999).

McCoog, T., 'The English Jesuit mission and the French match, 1579–1581', *Catholic Historical Review*, 87 (2001).

MacCulloch, D., *The Boy King: Edward VI and the Protestant Reformation* (New York, 2001).

MacCulloch, D., ed., *The Reign of Henry VIII: Politics, Policy and Piety* (New York and Basingstoke, 1995).

MacCulloch, D., *Suffolk and the Tudors: Politics and Religion in an English County 1500–1600* (Oxford, 1986).

MacCulloch, D., *Thomas Cranmer: A Life* (New Haven, 1999).

MacCulloch, D., *Tudor Church Militant: Edward VI and the Protestant Reformation* (Harmondsworth, 1999).

Mac Curtain, M. and O'Dowd, M., eds, *Women in Early Modern Ireland* (Dublin, 1991).

MacDonald, A. A., Lynch, M. and Cowens, I., eds, *The Renaissance in Scotland: Studies in Literature, Religion, History, and Culture* (Leiden, 1994).

MacDonald, A. R., *The Jacobean Kirk, 1567–1625: Sovereignty, Polity and Liturgy* (Aldershot, 1998).

Macdougall, H. A., *Racial Myth in English History: Trojans, Teutons and Anglo-Saxons* (Montreal, 1982).

Macdougall, N., *An Antidote to the English: The Auld Alliance 1295–1560* (East Linton, 2001).

Macdougall, N., *James IV* (Edinburgh, 1989).

Macdougall, N., ed., *Church, Politics and Society: Scotland 1408–1929* (Edinburgh, 1983).

McEntegart, R., *Henry VIII, the League of Schmalkalden and the English Reformation* (Boydell, 2002).

Macfarlane, Alan, *Witchcraft in Tudor and Stuart England: A Regional and Comparative Study* (London, 1970).

McFarlane, I. D., *Buchanan* (London, 1981).

McFarlane, K. B., The Nobility of Later Medieval England (Oxford, 1973).

McGinnis, P. and Williamson, A., 'Britain, race, and the Iberian global empire', in A. I. Macinnes and J. Ohlmeyer, eds, *The Stuart Kingdoms in the Seventeenth Century* (Dublin, 2002).

McGrath, P., 'Elizabethan Catholicism: a reconsideration', *Journal of Ecclesiastical History*, 35 (1984).

MacGregor, M., 'The genealogical histories of Gaelic Scotland', in A. Fox and D. Woolf, eds, *The Spoken Word: Oral Culture in Britain 1500–1850* (Manchester, 2002).

Macinnes, A. I., *Clanship, Commerce and the House of Stuart, 1603–1788* (East Linton, 1996).

Macinnes, A. I. and Ohlmeyer, J., eds, *The Stuart Kingdoms in the Seventeenth Century: Awkward Neighbours* (Dublin, 2002).

McIntosh, M. K., *A Community Transformed: The Manor and Liberty of Havering, 1500–1620* (Cambridge, 1991).

McIntosh, M. K., *Controlling Misbehaviour: England 1370–1600* (Cambridge, 1998).

McKean, C., *The Scottish Chateau* (Stroud, 2001).

McKechnie, H., ed., *An Introductory Survey of the Sources and Literature of Scots Law* (Edinburgh, 1936).

McKenna, J. W., 'Piety and propaganda: the cult of King Henry VI', in B. Rowland, ed., *Chaucer and Middle English Studies in Honour of Rossell Hope Robbins* (Kent, OH, 1974).

McKenna, J. W., 'Popular canonization as political propaganda: the cult of Archbishop Scrope', *Speculum*, 45 (1970).

McKisack, M., *Medieval History in the Tudor Age* (Oxford, 1971).

McLaren, A. N., *Political Culture in the Reign of Elizabeth I: Queen and Commonwealth 1558–1585* (Cambridge, 1999).

MacLean, S.-B. and Johnston, A. F., 'Reformation and resistance in Thames/Severn parishes: the dramatic witness', in K. L. French, G. G. Gibbs and B. A. Kümin, eds, *The Parish in English Life, 1400–1600* (Manchester, 1997).

Macmillan, D., *Scottish Art, 1460–1990* (Edinburgh, 1990).

McMillin, S. and MacLean, S.-B., *The Queen's Men and Their Plays 1583–1603* (Cambridge, 1998).

MacQueen, H. L., ed., *The College of Justice: Essays by R. K. Hannay* (Edinburgh, 1990).

MacQueen, H. L., ed., *Miscellany Four* (Edinburgh, 2002).

McRae, A., *God Speed the Plough: The Representation of Agrarian England, 1500–1660* (Cambridge, 1996).

McRee, B. R., 'Religious gilds and civic order: the case of Norwich in the late middle ages', *Speculum*, 67 (1992).

McSheffrey, S., *Gender and Heresy: Women and Men in Lollard Communities, 1420–1530* (Philadelphia, 1995).

Maley, W., 'The British problem in three tracts on Ireland by Spenser, Bacon and Milton', in B. Bradshaw and P. Roberts, eds, *British Consciousness and Identity: The Making of Britain 1533–1707* (Cambridge, 1998).

Maltby, J., *Prayer Book and People in Elizabethan and Early Stuart England* (Cambridge, 1998).

Maltby, W. S., *The Black Legend in England: The Development of Anti-Spanish Sentiment, 1558–1660* (Durham, NC, 1971).

Manley, L., *Literature and Culture in Early Modern London* (Cambridge, 1995).

Manning, R. B., 'The making of a Protestant aristocracy: the ecclesiastical commissioners of the diocese of Chester, 1550–98', *Bulletin of the Institute of Historical Research*, XLIX (1976).

Manning, R. B., *Religion and Society in Elizabethan Sussex* (Leicester, 1969).

Manning, R. B., *Village Revolts: Social Protest and Popular Disturbances in England, 1509–1640* (Oxford, 1988).

Marcus, L., Mueller, J. and Rose, M. B., eds, *Elizabeth I: Collected Works* (Chicago, 2000).

Marprelate Tracts, facsimile ed. (Menston, 1970).

Marsh, C., *The Family of Love in English Society, 1550–1630* (Cambridge, 1994).

Marsh, C., 'Piety and persuasion in Elizabethan England: the Church of England meets the Family of Love', in N. Tyacke, ed., *England's Long Reformation, 1500–1800* (London, 1998).

Marsh, C., *Popular Religion in Sixteenth-Century England: Holding Their Peace* (New York, 1998).

Marshall, P., *The Catholic Priesthood and the English Reformation* (Oxford, 1994).

Marshall, R. K., *Virgins and Viragos: A History of Women in Scotland, 1080–1980* (London, 1983).

Martin, C. and Parker, G., *The Spanish Armada* (London, 1988).

Mason, R. A., 'Civil society and the Celts: Hector Boece, George Buchanan and the ancient British past', in E. J. Cowan and R. J. Finlay, eds, *Scottish History: The Power of the Past* (Edinburgh, 2002).

Mason, R. A., ed., *John Knox and the British Reformations* (Aldershot, 1998).

Mason, R. A., *Kingship and Commonweal: Political Thought in Renaissance and Reformation Scotland* (East Linton, 1998).

Mason, R. A., 'Scotching the Brut: politics, history and national myth in sixteenth-century Britain', in R. A. Mason, ed., *Scotland and England 1286–1815* (Edinburgh, 1987).

Mason, R. A., ed., *Scotland and England 1286–1815* (Edinburgh, 1987).

Mates, M., *Women in Medieval English Society* (Cambridge, 1999).

Mathew, D., *Catholicism in England: The Portrait of a Minority, its Culture and Tradition* (London, 1936).

Mayer, T., *Thomas Starkey and the Commonweal: Humanist Politics and Religion in the Reign of Henry VIII* (Cambridge, 1989).

Mayhew, G., *Tudor Rye* (Falmer, 1987).

Meek, C. E. and Lawless, C., eds, *Pawns or Players? Studies on Medieval and Early Modern Women* (Dublin, 2003).

Meek, C. E. and Simms, M. K., eds, *'The Fragility of her Sex': Medieval Irish Women in their European Context* (Dublin, 1996).

Meigs, S. A., *The Reformations in Ireland: Tradition and Confessionalism, 1400–1690* (Basingstoke and New York, 1997).

Melville, A., 'Historiae vera laus' and 'Gathelus, sive de gentis origine fragmentum', in P. J. McGinnis and A. H. Williamson, eds and trans., *George Buchanan: The Political Poetry* (Edinburgh, 1995).

Mendelsohn, S. and Crawford, P., *Women in Early Modern England 1550–1720* (Oxford, 1998).

Mercer, E., *English Art 1553–1625* (Oxford, 1962).

Mercer, E., *English Vernacular Houses* (London, 1975).

Merriman, M., *The Rough Wooings: Mary Queen of Scots, 1542–1551* (East Linton, 2000).

Mill, A. J., *Medieval Plays in Scotland* (St Andrews, 1924).

Mills, D., *Re-Cycling the Cycle: The City of Chester and its Whitsun Plays* (Toronto, 1998).

Milsom, J., 'Cries of Durham', *Early Music*, 18 (1989).

Milsom, J., 'Music', in B. Ford, ed., *The Cambridge Guide to the Arts in Britain*, vol. III, *Renaissance and Reformation* (Cambridge, 1989; reissued as *16th Century Britain*, 1992).

Milsom, J., 'Music', in L. Hellinga and J. B. Trapp, eds, *The Cambridge History of the Book in Britain*, vol. III, *1400–1557* (Cambridge, 1999).

Milsom, J., 'Sacred songs in the chamber', in J. Morehen, ed., *English Choral Practice, 1400–1650* (Cambridge, 1995).

Milsom, J., 'Songs and society in early Tudor London', *Early Music History*, 19 (1997).

Mitchison, R., *The Old Poor Law in Scotland: The Experience of Poverty 1574–1845* (Edinburgh, 2000).

Monson, C., 'Byrd, the Catholics, and the motet: the hearing reopened', in D. Pesce, ed., *Hearing the Motet: Essays on the Motet of the Middle Ages and Renaissance* (New York and Oxford, 1997).

Moody, T. W., Martin, F. X. and Byrne, F. J., eds, *A New History of Ireland*, vol. III (Oxford, 1976).

Moore, A., with Crawley, C., *Family and Friends: A Regional Survey of British Portraiture* (London, 1992).

Moore, P., 'The heraldic charge against the Earl of Surrey, 1546–47', *English Historical Review*, 116 (2001).

Moran, B. T., ed, *Patronage and Institutions: Science, Technology, and Medicine at the European Courts* (Woodbridge, 1991).

Moreton, C., *The Townshends and their World: Gentry, Law and Land in Norfolk, c.1450–1551* (Oxford, 1992).

Morgan, D. A. L., 'The king's affinity in the polity of Yorkist England', *Transactions of the Royal Historical Society*, 5th Series, 23 (1973).

Morgan, V., 'The Norwich Guildhall portraits: images in context', in A. Moore and C. Crawley, eds, *Family and Friends: A Regional Survey of British Portraiture* (London, 1992).

Morley, T., *A Plaine and Easie Introduction to Practicall Musicke*, ed. R. A. Harman (London, 1952 [1597]).

Moryson, F., 'Introduction', in *An Itinerary Containing his Ten Years' Travel* (Glasgow, 1907–8).

Mowle, T., *Elizabethan and Jacobean Style* (London, 1993).

Mullan, D., *Episcopacy in Scotland: The History of an Idea, 1560–1638* (Edinburgh, 1986).

Mullan, D., *Scottish Puritanism, 1590–1638* (Oxford, 2000).

Mullett, M., *Catholics in Britain and Ireland, 1558–1829* (Basingstoke, 1998).

Murdoch, J., Murrell, J., Noon, P. J. and Strong, R., *The English Miniature* (London and New Haven, 1981).

Napier, J., *A Plaine Discovery of the Whole Revelation of Saint John* (Edinburgh, 1593).

Naunton, R., *Fragmenta Regalia, or Observations on Queen Elizabeth, Her Times and Favorites*, ed. J. S. Cerovski (Washington, 1985).

Neal, K., *From Discrete to Continuous: The Broadening of Number Concepts in Early Modern England* (Dordrecht and Boston, MA, 2002).

Neale, J. E., *Elizabeth I and her Parliaments* (2 vols, London, 1953 and 1955).

Neale, J. E., *The Elizabethan House of Commons* (London, 1949).

Nelson, A. H., ed., *Cambridge: Records of Early English Drama* (2 vols, Toronto, 1989).

Neuss, P., ed. and trans., *The Creation of the World: A Critical Edition and Translation* (New York, 1983).

Neville, C. J., *Violence, Custom and Law: The Anglo-Scottish Border Lands in the Later Middle Ages* (Edinburgh, 1998).

The New Grove Dictionary of Music and Musicians (London and New York, 2000; also online).

Newman, J., 'The Elizabethan and Jacobean Great House: a review of recent research', *Archaeological Journal*, 145 (1988).

Newton, R., 'The decay of the borders: Tudor Northumberland in transition', in C. W. Chalklin and M. A. Havinden, eds, *Rural Change and Urban Growth 1500–1800: Essays in English Medieval History in Honour of W. G. Hoskins* (London, 1974).

Nichols, J., *A Collection of Ordinances and Regulations for the Government of the Royal Household, Made in Divers Reigns.* (London, 1790).

Nichols, J., *The Progresses and Public Processions of Queen Elizabeth* (3 vols, London, 1823).

Nicholls, M., *A History of the Modern British Isles, 1529–1603* (Oxford, 1999).

Nicholson, R., *Scotland: the Later Middle Ages* (Edinburgh, 1974).

Nicholson, W., ed., *Remains of Edmund Grindal* (Cambridge, 1843).

Nolan, J., 'The militarisation of the Elizabethan state', *Journal of Miitary History*, 58 (1994).

Norris, E., ed. and trans., *The Ancient Cornish Drama* (2 vols, Oxford, 1859).

Nutton, V., 'John Caius and the Eton Galen: medical philology in the Renaissance', *Medizinhistorisches Journal*, 20 (1985).

O'Day, R., *The Professions in Early Modern England, 1450–1800: Servants of the Commonweal* (Harlow, 2000).

O'Dowd, M., 'Gaelic economy and society', in C. Brady and R. Gillespie, eds, *Natives and Newcomers: Essays on the Making of Irish Colonial Society, 1534–1641* (Dublin, 1986).

O'Dowd, M., 'The political writings and public voices of women, c.1500–1850', in A. Bourke, S. Kilfeather, M. Luddy et al., eds, *The Field Day Anthology of Irish Writing*, vols V and VI, *Irish Women's Writing and Traditions* (Cork, 2002).

O'Hara, D., *Courtship and Constraint: Rethinking the Making of Marriage in Tudor England* (Manchester, 2000).

O Riordan, M., *The Gaelic Mind and the Collapse of the Gaelic World* (Cork, 1990).

Orlin, L. C., ed., *Material London, c.1600* (Philadelphia, 2000).

Osborn, J. M., ed., *The Autobiography of Thomas Whythorne* (Oxford, 1961).

Outhwaite, R. B., 'Progress and backwardness in English agriculture, 1500–1650', *Economic History Review*, 39 (1986).

Overton, M., *Agricultural Revolutions in England: The Transformation of the Agrarian Economy, 1500–1850* (Cambridge, 1996).

Overton, M. and Campbell, B. M. S., 'Norfolk livestock farming, 1250–1740: a comparative study of manorial accounts and probate inventories', *Journal of Historical Geography*, 18 (1992).

Owen, L., 'The population of Wales in the sixteenth and seventeenth centuries', *Transactions of the Cymmrodorion Society* (1959).

Owen of Kemes, G., *The Description of Pembrokeshire*, ed. H. Owen (4 vols, 1892–1936).

Pace, R., *De Fructu qui ex Doctrina Percipitur* (Basel, 1517; ed. and trans. as *The Benefit of a Liberal Education*, F. Manley and R. S. Sylvester, New York, 1967).

Pacheco, A., ed., *A Companion to Early Modern Women's Writing* (Oxford, 2000).

Page, D., 'Uniform and catholic: church music in the reign of Mary Tudor (1553–1558)' (PhD dissertation, Brandeis University, 1996).

Palliser, D. M., 'Tawney's century: brave new world or Malthusian trap?', *Economic History Review*, 35 (1982).

Palliser, D. M., *Tudor York* (Oxford, 1979).

Palliser, D. M., ed., *The Cambridge Urban History of Britain*, vol. 1, *600–1540* (Cambridge, 2000).

Palmer, B. D., 'Recycling "The Wakefield Cycle": the records', *Research Opportunities in Renaissance Drama*, XLI (2002).

Palmer, W., 'Gender, violence and rebellion in Tudor and early Stuart Ireland', *Sixteenth Century Journal*, 23 (1992).

Parker, K. L. and Carlson, E. J., *Practical Divinity: The Works and Life of Reverend Richard Greenham* (Aldershot, 1998).

Paton, G. C. H., ed., *An Introduction to Scottish Legal History* (Edinburgh, 1958).

Patrick, M., *Four Centuries of Scottish Psalmody* (London, 1949).

Patten, J., *English Towns, 1500–1700* (London, 1978).

Patterson, A., *Reading Holinshed's Chronicles* (Chicago, 1994).

Patterson, C., *Urban Patronage in Early Modern England: Corporate Boroughs, the Landed Elite, and the Crown 1580–1640* (Stanford, 1999).

Peck, F., ed., *Desiderata Curiosa* (2 vols, London, 1732).

Peck, L. Levy, 'Peers, patronage and the politics of history', in J. Guy, ed., *The Reign of Elizabeth I: Court and Culture in the Last Decade* (Cambridge, 1995).

Peel, A., ed., *The Seconde Parte of a Register* (Cambridge, 1915).

Peel, A. and Carlson, I. H., eds, *The Writings of Robert Harrison and Robert Browne* (London, 1953)

Pelling, M., 'Old age and poverty in early modern towns', *Bulletin of the Society for the Social History of Medicine*, 34 (1984).

Peltonen, M., *Classical Humanism and Republicanism in English Political Thought, 1570–1640* (Cambridge, 1995).

Percy, H., earl of Northumberland, *Advice to his Son by Henry Percy, Ninth Earl of Northumberland*, ed. G. B. Harrison (London, 1930 [1609]).

Perkins, W., 'The foundation of the Christian religion', in *Workes of that Famous and Worthy Minister of Christ in the University of Cambridge, Mr. William Perkins*, vol. 1 (London, 1616).

Perkins, W., 'A treatise of Man's imaginations', in *Workes of that Famous and Worthy Minister of Christ in the University of Cambridge, Mr. William Perkins*, vol. 2 (London, 1617).

Perkins, W., 'A treatise tending unto a declaration whether a man be in the estate of damnation or in the estate of grace', in *Workes of that Famous and Worthy Minister of Christ in the University of Cambridge. Mr. William Perkins*, vol. 1 (London, 1616).

Pettegree, A., *Foreign Protestant Communities in Sixteenth-Century London* (Oxford, 1986).

Phillips, C. B. and Smith, J. H., *Lancashire and Cheshire from A. D. 1540* (London, 1994).

Phillips, G., *The Anglo-Scots Wars 1513–50* (Woodbridge, 1999).

Phillips, J., *The Reformation of Images: Destruction of Art in England, 1535–1660* (Berkeley, 1973).

Phythian-Adams, C., *Desolation of a City: Coventry and the Urban Crisis of the Late Middle Ages* (Cambridge, 1979).

Phythian-Adams, C., Corfield, P., Slack, P. and O'Day, R., eds, *The Traditional Community under Stress* (Milton Keynes, 1977).

Piggott, S., *Ruins in a Landscape: Essays in Antiquarianism* (Edinburgh, 1976).

Pilkinton, M., ed., *Records of Early English Drama: Bristol* (Toronto, 1997).

Piper, D., *The English Face* (3 vols, London, 1957, 1978 and 1992).

Platter, T., *Thomas Platter's Travels in England, 1599*, ed. and trans. C. Williams (London, 1937).

Pocock, J. G. A., *The Ancient Constitution and the Feudal Law* (Cambridge, 1957; revised edition Cambridge, 1987).

Pollard, A. J., *Late Medieval England, 1399–1509* (London, 1999).

Pollen, J. H., ed., 'The Bedingfield Papers' in *Miscellanea* 6 (Catholic Record Society 7, London, 1909).

Pollock, L., ' "Teach her to live under obedience": the making of women in the upper ranks of early modern England', *Continuity and Change*, 4 (1989).

Pomeroy, E. W., *Reading the Portraits of Queen Elizabeth I* (Hamden, CT, 1989).

Potter, D., 'Anglo-French relations 1500: the aftermath of the Hundred Years War', *Franco-British Studies*, 28 (1999).

Potter, D., 'The duc de Guise and the fall of Calais', *English Historical Review*, 98 (1983).

Potter, D., 'Foreign policy', in D. MacCulloch, ed., *The Reign of Henry VIII: Politics, Policy and Piety* (Basingstoke and New York, 1995).

Potter, D., 'French intrigue in Ireland during the reign of Henri II, 1547–59', *International Historical Review*, 5 (1983).

Potter, D., 'Mid-Tudor foreign policy and diplomacy, 1547–1563', in S. Doran and G. Richardson, eds, *Tudor England and its Neighbours* (Basingstoke, 2004).

Potter, D., 'The treaty of Boulogne and European diplomacy', *Bulletin of the Institute of Historical Research*, LV, 131 (May, 1982).

Pound, J. F., *Tudor and Stuart Norwich* (Chichester, 1988).

Power, D. and Standen, N., eds, *Frontiers in Question: Eurasian Borderlands, 700–1700* (Basingstoke, 1999).

Preece, I. W., *'Our Awin Scottis Use': Music in the Scottish Church up to 1603*, ed. S. Harper, with additional material by W. Edwards and G. J. Munro (Glasgow and Aberdeen, 2002).

Prest, W. R., *The Inns of Court under Elizabeth I and the Early Stuarts 1590–1640* (Totawa, NJ, and London, 1972).

Price, D. C., *Patrons and Musicians of the English Renaissance* (Cambridge, 1981).

Prior, M., *Fisher Row: Fishermen, Bargemen and Canal Boatmen in Oxford, 1500–1900* (Oxford, 1982).

Prior, M., ed., *Women in English Society, 1500–1800* (London, 1984).

Proudfoot, L., 'Markets, fairs and towns in Ireland, c.1600–1853', in P. Borsay and L. Proudfoot, eds, *Provincial Towns in Early Modern England and Ireland: Change, Convergence and Divergence* (Oxford, 2002).

Pugh, T. B., 'Henry VII and the English nobility', in G. Bernard, ed., *The Tudor Nobility* (Manchester, 1992).

Pulman, M. B., *The Elizabethan Privy Council in the Fifteen-Seventies* (Berkeley, 1971).

Pumfrey, S., *Latitude and the Magnetic Earth* (Cambridge, 2002).

Questier, M., *Conversion, Politics and Religion in England 1580–1625* (Cambridge, 1996).

Quiney, A., *The Traditional Buildings of England* (London, 1990).

Quinn, D., *England and the Discovery of America, 1481–1620* (London, 1974).

Quintrell, B. W., ed., *Proceedings of the Lancashire Justices of the Peace at the Sheriff's Table During the Assizes Week, 1578–1694* (Lancashire and Cheshire, 1981).

Raab, F., *The English Face of Machiavelli : A Changing Interpretation, 1500–1700* (London and Toronto, 1964).

Raine, A., ed., *York Civic Records I* (York, 1939).

Raleigh, Sir Walter, *Selected Prose and Poetry*, ed. A. M. Latham (London, 1965).

Ramsey, G. D., 'The recruitment and fortunes of some London freemen in the mid-sixteenth century', *Economic History Review*, 2nd series, 31 (1978).

Rappaport, S., *Worlds within Worlds: Structures of Life in Sixteenth-Century London* (Cambridge, 1989).

Rastell, J., *The Exposicions of Termys of Law of England and the Nature of the Writts* (London, 1523).

Read, C., *Lord Burghley and Queen Elizabeth* (London, 1960).

Read, C., *Mr. Secretary Cecil and Queen Elizabeth* (London, 1955).

Read, C., *Mr. Secretary Walsingham and the Policy of Queen Elizabeth* (3 vols, Oxford, 1925).

Recorde, R., *The Grounde of Artes* (London, 1542).

Recorde, R., *Whetstone of Witte* (London, 1557).

Records of Early English Drama (21 vols, Toronto, 1976–).

Reid, R. R., *The King's Council in the North* (London, 1912).

Reid, R. R., 'The rebellion of the earls, 1569', *Transactions of the Royal Historical Society*, 2nd series (1906).

Rex, R., 'Thomas Vavasour MD', *Recusant History*, 20 (1991).

Richards, J. M., 'Love and a female monarch: the case of Elizabeth Tudor', *Journal of British Studies*, 38 (April 1999).

Richardson, G., *Renaissance Monarchy: The Reigns of Henry VIII, Francis I and Charles V* (London, 2002).

Richardson, W. C., *History of the Court of Augmentations, 1536–1554* (Baton Rouge, 1961).

Rigby, S. H., 'Urban "oligarchy" in late medieval England', in J. A. F. Thomson, ed., *Towns and Townspeople in the Fifteenth Century* (Stroud, 1988).

Rigby, S. H. and Ewan, E., 'Government, power and authority 1300–1540', in D. M. Palliser, ed., *The Cambridge Urban History of Britain*, vol. 1, *600–1540* (Cambridge, 2000).

Ritchie, P., *Mary of Guise in Scotland* (East Linton, 2002).

Roberts, J., 'Parliamentary representation of Devon and Dorset, 1559–1601' (MA thesis, University of London, 1958).

Roberts, M., ' "More prone to be idle and riotous than the English?" Attitudes to male behaviour in early modern Wales', in M. Roberts and S. Clarke, eds, *Women and Gender in Early Modern Wales* (Cardiff, 2000).

Roberts, M., 'Women and work in sixteenth-century English towns', in P. Corfield and D. Keene, eds, *Work in Towns 850–1850* (Leicester, 1980).

Roberts, M. and Clarke, S., eds, *Women and Gender in Early Modern Wales* (Cardiff, 2000).

Roberts, P., 'Tudor Wales, national identity and the British inheritance', in B. Bradshaw and P. Roberts, eds, *British Consciousness and Identity: The Making of Britain, 1533–1707* (Cambridge, 1998).

Robinson, H., ed., *Zurich Letters*, vol. 1 (London, 1842).

Robinson, O. F., Fergus, T. D. and Gordon, W. M., *European Legal History: Sources and Institutions* (London, 1994).

Rodríguez-Salgado, M. J. and Adams, S., ed. and trans., 'The Count of Feria's dispatch to Philip II of 14 November 1558', *Camden Miscellany*, XXVIII (1984).

Rodriguez-Salgado, M. J. and Adams, S., eds, *England, Spain and the Gran Armada, 1585–1604* (Edinburgh, 1991).

Rosser, A. G., 'The town and guild of Lichfield in the late middle ages', *Transactions of the South Staffordshire Archaeological and Historical Society*, 27 (1987).

Rosser, G., 'Communities of parish and guild in the late middle ages', in S. J. Wright, ed., *Parish, Church and People: Local Studies in Lay Religion, 1350–1750* (London, 1988).

Rosser, G., *Medieval Westminster 1200–1540* (Oxford, 1989).

Rowlands, M. B., ed., *Catholics of Parish and Town 1558–1778* (London, 1999).

Roy, I. and Porter, S., 'The social and economic structure of an early modern suburb', *Bulletin of the Institute of Historical Research*, 53, 128 (November, 1980).

Rubin, M., *Corpus Christi* (Cambridge, 1991).

Rushton, N., 'Monastic charitable provision in Tudor England: quantifying and qualifying poor relief in the early sixteenth century', *Continuity and Change*, 16 (2001).

Russell, C., *Parliament and English Politics, 1621–29* (Oxford, 1979).

Russell, J., *Diplomats at Work: Three Renaissance Studies* (Stroud, 1992).

Russell, J., *The Field of Cloth of Gold: Men and Manners in 1520* (New York and London, 1969).

Russell, J., *Peacemaking in the Renaissance* (London, 1986).

Sacks, D. H., *The Widening Gate: Bristol and the Atlantic Economy, 1450–1700* (Berkeley and Los Angeles, 1991).

St German, C., *St German's Doctor and Student*, ed. T. F. T. Plucknett and J. L. Barton (London, 1974).

Salter, F. M., *Medieval Drama in Chester* (Toronto, 1955).

Sanderson, M. H. B., *Ayrshire and the Reformation: People and Change, 1490–1600* (East Linton, 1997).

Sanderson, M. H. B., 'Catholic recusancy in Scotland in the sixteenth century', *Innes Review*, 21 (1970).

Sanderson, M. H. B., *Scottish Rural Society in the Sixteenth Century* (Edinburgh, 1982).

Scarisbrick, J. J., 'Cardinal Wolsey and the Common Weal', in E. W. Ives, R. J. Knecht and J. J. Scarisbrick, eds, *Wealth and Power in Tudor England: Essays Presented to S. T. Bindoff* (London, 1978).

Scarisbrick, J. J., *Henry VIII* (London, 1968).

Scarisbrick, J. J., *The Reformation and the English People* (Oxford, 1984).

Schen, C. S., *Charity and Lay Piety in Reformation London, 1500–1620* (Aldershot, 2002).

Scherb, V. I., *Staging Faith* (Madison, NJ, 2001).

Schmitt, C. B., *John Case and Aristotelianism in Renaissance England* (Kingston and Montreal, 1983).

Schofield, J., ed., *The London Surveys of Ralph Treswell* (London, 1987).

Schofield, R., 'Taxation and the political limits of the Tudor state', in C. Cross, D. M. Loades and J. J. Scarisbrick, eds, *Law and Government under the Tudors* (Cambridge, 1988).

Schwarz, L., 'Hanoverian London: the making of a service town', in P. Clark and R. Gillespie, eds, *Two Capitals: London and Dublin 1500–1840* (London, 2001).

Scott, H. S., ed., 'The journal of Sir Roger Wilbraham', in *Camden Miscellary*, 10, Camden 3rd ser., 4 (1902).

Seaver, P. S., *The Puritan Lectureships: The Politics of Religious Dissent, 1650–1662* (Stanford, 1970).

Shagan, E. H., 'Protector Somerset and the 1549 rebellions: new sources and perspectives', *English Historical Review*, 114 (1999).

Shakespeare, J. and Dowling, M., 'Religion and politics in mid-Tudor England through the eyes of an English Protestant woman: the recollections of Rose Hickman', *Bulletin of the Institute of Historical Research*, 55 (1982).

Shakespeare, W., *The Oxford Shakespeare: the Complete Works*, ed. S. Wells and G. Taylor (Oxford, 1998).

Shapin, S., *The Scientific Revolution* (Chicago, 1996).

Shapin, S. and Schaffer, S., *The Leviathan and the Air Pump: Hobbes, Boyle, and the Experimental Life* (Princeton, NJ, 1985).

Shapiro, M., *Children of the Revels: The Boy Companies of Shakespeare's Time* (New York, 1974).

Sharlin, A., 'Natural decrease in early modern cities: a reconsideration', *Past and Present*, 79 1978).

Sharpe, B., *In Contempt of all Authority: Rural Artisans and Riot in the West of England, 1586–1660* (London, 1980).

Sharpe, J. A., *Instruments of Darkness: Witchcraft in England, 1550–1750* (London, 1996).

Sharpe, J. A., 'Social strain and social dislocation, 1585–1603', in J. Guy, ed., *The Reign of Elizabeth I: Court and Culture in the Last Decade* (Cambridge, 1995).

Sharpe, K., 'Culture, politics and the English civil war', reprinted in Sharpe, *Politics and Ideas in Early Stuart England* (London, 1989).

Sharpe, K., *The Personal Rule of Charles I* (New Haven, 1992).

Shaw, A. N., 'The involvement of the religious orders in the Northern Risings of 1536/7: compulsion or desire?', *Downside Review*, 117 (1999).

Sheehan, A., 'Irish towns in a period of change', in C. Brady and R. Gillespie, eds, *Natives and Newcomers: Essays on the Making of Irish Colonial Society, 1534–1641* (Dublin, 1986).

Sheils, W. J., 'Catholics and their neighbours in a rural community: Egton chapelry 1590–1780', *Northern History*, 41 (1999).

Shell, A., *Catholicism, Controversy, and the English Literary Imagination, 1558–1660* (Cambridge, 1999).

Shepard, A. and Withington, P., eds, *Communities in Early Modern England: Networks, Place, Rhetoric* (Manchester and New York, 2000).

Sherman, W. H., *John Dee: The Politics of Reading and Writing in the English Renaissance* (Amherst, 1995).

Shire, H. M., *Song, Dance and Poetry of the Court of Scotland under King James VI* (Cambridge, 1969).

Shirley, J. W., 'Science and navigation in Renaissance England', in J. W. Shirley and F. D. Hoeniger, eds, *Science and the Arts in the Renaissance* (Washington, DC, 1985).

Shirley, J. W., *Thomas Harriot: A Biography* (Oxford, 1983).

Sil, N. P., *Tudor Placemen and Statesmen: Select Case Histories* (Madison, NJ, 2001).

Simms, K., 'Women in Gaelic society during the age of transition', in M. Mac Curtain and M. O'Dowd, eds, *Women in Early Modern Ireland* (Dublin, 1991).

Slack, P., 'Dearth and social policy in early modern England', *Social History of Medicine*, 5, 1 (1992).

Slack, P., *From Reformation to Improvement: Public Welfare in Early Modern England* (Oxford, 1999).

Slack, P., *Poverty and Policy in Tudor and Stuart England* (London, l988).

Slack, P., 'Poverty and social regulation in Elizabethan England', in C. Haigh, ed., *The Reign of Elizabeth I* (London, 1984).

Slavin, A. J., *The Precarious Balance: English Government and Society* (New York, 1973).

Smailes, H., ed., *The Concise Catalogue of the Scottish National Portrait Gallery* (Edinburgh, 1990).

Smailes, H., ed., *The Queen's Image* (Edinburgh, 1987).

Smith, A., 'Elizabethan church music at Ludlow', *Music and Letters*, 49 (1968).

Smith, A. G. R., *The Government of Elizabethan England* (London, 1967).

Smith, A. H., *County and Court: Government and Politics in Norfolk, 1558–1603* (Oxford, 1974).

Smith, A. H., 'Labourers in late sixteenth-century England: a case study from North Norfolk, part 1', *Continuity and Change*, 4 (1989).

Smith, A. H., *The Place-Names of the West Riding of Yorkshire* (Cambridge, 1961).

Smith, H., *Works of Henry Smith*, vol. 2 (Edinburgh, 1867).

Smith, P., *Houses of the Welsh Countryside* (Aberystwyth, 1975).

Smith, R. M., 'Geographical aspects of population change in England, 1500–1730', in R. A. Dodgshon and R. A. Butlin, eds, *An Historical Geography of England and Wales* (2nd edition, London, 1990).

Smith, T., *De Republica Anglorum: A Discourse of the Common Weal of this Realm of England* (ed. E. Lamond, Cambridge 1929; ed. M. Dewar; Cambridge, 1982).

Smout, T. C., *A History of the Scottish People, 1560–1830* (London, 1969; 2nd edition, 1970).

Smuts, R. M., *Culture and Power in England, 1585–1685* (New York, 1999).

Smythe, J., *Certain Discourses Military*, ed. J. R. Hale (Ithaca, NY, 1964).

Somerset, J. A. B., ed., *Shropshire: Records of Early English Drama* (2 vols, Toronto, 1994).

Sommerville, M., *Sex and Subjection: Attitudes to Women in Early-Modern Society* (London, 1995).

Spedding, J., ed, *The Letters and Life of Francis Bacon* (7 vols, London, 1861–74).

Spedding, J., Ellis, R. L. and Heath, D. D., eds, *The Works of Francis Bacon* (17 vols, London, 1857–74).

Spenser, E., *View of the State of Ireland* (1595), in H. Morley, ed., *Ireland under Elizabeth and James the First* (London and New York, 1890).

Spufford, M., *Contrasting Communities: English Villagers in the Sixteenth and Seventeenth Centuries* (Cambridge, 1974).

Spufford, M., ed., *The World of Rural Dissenters, 1520–1725* (Cambridge, 1995).

Stanihurst, R., *On Ireland's Past: De Rebus in Hibernia Gestis* (1584), in C. Lennon, ed., *Richard Stanihurst the Dubliner 1547–1618* (Dublin, 1981).

Stanyhurst, R., 'The description of Irelande', in L. Miller and E. Power, eds, *Holinshed's Irish Chronicle* (Dublin, 1979).

Starkey, D., 'Intimacy and innovation: the rise of the privy chamber, 1485–1547', in D. Starkey, J. Murphy, P. Wright, N. Cuddy and K. Sharpe, eds, *The English Court from the Wars of the Roses to the Civil War* (London and New York, 1987).

Starkey, D., *The Reign of Henry VIII: Personalities and Politics* (London, 1985).

Starkey, T., *A Dialogue between Pole and Lupset*, ed. T. F. Mayer (London, 1989).

Stater, V., *Noble Government: The Stuart Lord Lieutenancy and the Transformation of English Politics* (Athens, GA, 1994).

Stevens, J., *Music and Poetry in the Early Tudor Court* (London, 1961).

Stevenson, J. and Davidson, P., eds, *Early Modern Women Poets: An Anthology* (Oxford, 2001).

Stokes, J., ed., (with Robert Alexander), *Records of Early English Drama: Somerset* (2 vols, Toronto, 1996).

Stokes, W., ed. and trans., *The Life of St Meriasek, Bishop and Confessor: A Cornish Drama* (London, 1872).

Stone, L., *The Crisis of the Aristocracy* (Oxford, 1965; abridged edition, 1967).

Stone, L., *The Family, Sex and Marriage in England 1500–1800* (Harmondsworth, 1979).

Stone, L., *An Open Elite? England 1540–1880* (Oxford, 1986).

Storey, R. L., *The Reign of Henry VII* (New York, 1968).

Streitberger, W. R., *Court Revels, 1485–1559* (Toronto, 1994).

Strong, R., *Artists of the Tudor Court, the Portrait Miniature Rediscovered 1520–1620* (London, 1983).

Strong, R., *The Cult of Elizabeth: Elizabethan Portraiture and Pageantry* (London and Berkeley, 1977).

Strong, R., *The English Icon: Elizabethan and Jacobean Portraiture* (London and New York, 1969).

Strong, R., *Gloriana: The Portraits of Queen Elizabeth I* (London, 1987).

Strong, R., 'Hans Eworth: a Tudor artist and his circle', in R. Strong, ed., *The Tudor and Stuart Monarchy: Pageantry, Painting and Iconography* (3 vols, Woodbridge, 1995).

Strong, R., *Holbein and Henry VIII* (London, 1967).

Suggett, R., 'Vagabonds and minstrels in sixteenth-century Wales', in A. Fox and D. Woolf, eds, *The Spoken Word: Oral Culture in Britain 1500–1850* (Manchester, 2002).

Suggett, R. and White, E., 'Language, literacy and aspects of identity in early modern Wales', in A. Fox and D. Woolf, eds, *The Spoken Word: Oral Culture in Britain 1500–1850* (Manchester, 2002).

Summerson, J., *Architecture in Britain: 1530–1830* (Harmondsworth, 1953).

Sutherland, N. M., *The Massacre of Saint Bartholomew and the European Conflict, 1559–72* (London, 1973).

Sutherland, N. M., 'The origins of Queen Elizabeth's relations with the Huguenots, 1559–62', *Proceedings of the Huguenot Society of London*, 20 (1958–64).

Sutherland, N. M., *Princes, Politics and Religion* (London, 1984).

Swanson, R. N., *Church and Society in Late Medieval England* (Oxford, 1989).

Swanson, R. N., 'Problems of the priesthood in pre-Reformation England', *English Historical Review*, 105 (1990).

Taylor, E. G. R., *Mathematical Practitioners of Tudor and Stuart England* (Cambridge, 1954).

Temperley, N., *The Music of the English Parish Church* (Cambridge, 1979).

Thirsk, J., 'Enclosing and engrossing', in J. Thirsk, ed., *The Agrarian History of England and Wales*, vol. IV, *1500–1640* (Cambridge, 1967).

Thirsk, J., 'The history women', in M. O'Dowd and S. Wichert, eds, *Chattel, Servant or Citizen: Women's Status in Church, State, and Society* (Belfast, 1995).

Thirsk, J., 'Industries in the countryside', in J. Thirsk, *The Rural Economy of England: Collected Essays* (London, 1984).

Thirsk, J., *The Rural Economy of England: Collected Essays* (London, 1984).

Thirsk, J., ed., *The Agrarian History of England and Wales*, vol. IV, *1500–1640* (Cambridge, 1967).

Thomas, A., '"Dragonis baith and dowis ay in double form": women at the court of James V, 1515–1542', in E. Ewan and M. Meikle, eds, *Women in Scotland c.1100–c.1750*, (East Linton, 1999).

Thomas, K., *The Perception of the Past in Early Modern England* (London, 1983).

Thomas, K., *Religion and the Decline of Magic: Studies in Popular Beliefs in Sixteenth- and Seventeenth-Century England* (London, 1971).

Thomas, W. S. K., *The History of Swansea: From Rover Settlement to the Restoration* (Llandysul, 1990).

Thompson, D., *Painting in Scotland, 1570–1650* (Edinburgh, 1975).

Thompson, E., *Customs in Common* (London, 1991).

Thomson, D., *An Introduction to Gaelic Poetry* (2nd edition, Edinburgh, 1989).

Thomson, G. S., *The Lords Lieutenants in the Sixteenth Century* (London, 1923).

Thomson, J. A. F., ed., *Towns and Townspeople in the Fifteenth Century* (Stroud, 1988).

Thomson, T., ed., *Acts and Proceedings of the General Assemblies of the Kirk of Scotland*, (3 vols, Edinburgh, 1839–45).

Thurley, S., *The Royal Palaces of Tudor England* (New Haven and London, 1993).

Tilyard, V., 'Civic portraits painted for, or donated to the council chamber of Norwich Guildhall before 1687 . . .' (MA thesis, Courtauld Institute, 1978).

Tittler, R., *Architecture and Power: The Town Hall and the English Urban Community c.1500–1640* (Oxford, 1991).

Tittler, R., 'Civic portraiture and political culture in English provincial towns, ca. 1560–1640', *Journal of British Studies*, 37, 3 (July 1998).

Tittler, R., 'The Cookes and the Brookes: political uses of portraiture in town and country before the Civil War', in G. MacLean, D. Landry and J. Ward, eds, *The Country and the City Revisited* (Cambridge, 1999).

Tittler, R., 'John and Joan Cooke: civic portraiture and urban identity in Gloucester', in R. Tittler, *Townspeople and Nation: English Urban Experiences, 1540–1640* (Stanford, 2001).

Tittler, R., *The Reformation and the Towns in England: Politics and Political Culture, c.1540–1640* (Oxford, 1998).

Tittler, R., ' "Seats of honor, seats of power": the symbolism of public seating in the English urban community, c.1560–1620', *Albion*, 24, 2 (Summer, 1992).

Tittler, R., *Townspeople and Nation: English Urban Experiences, 1540–1640* (Stanford, 2001).

Todd, M., *The Culture of Protestantism in Early Modern Scotland* (New Haven and London, 2002).

Travers, W., *An Answere to a Supplicatorie Epistle of G. T. for the Pretended Catholiques* (London, 1583).

Trim, D., ' "Fin de siècle": the English soldier's experience at the end of the sixteenth century', *Military and Naval History Journal*, 10 (1999).

Trim, D., 'The foundation-stone of the British army? The Normandy campaign of 1562', *Journal of the Society for Army Historical Research*, 77 (1999).

Trim, D., 'The "Secret War" of Elizabeth I: England and the Huguenots during the early Wars of Religion, 1562–77', *Proceedings of the Huguenot Society of London*, 27, ii (1999).

Twemlow, J. A., ed., *Liverpool Town Books. Proceedings of Assemblies, Common Councils, Portmoot Courts, etc., 1550–1862*, vol. I, *1550–1571* (London, 1918).

Twycross, M., ed., *Festive Drama* (Cambridge, 1996).

Tyacke, Nicholas, ed., *England's Long Reformation, 1500–1800* (London, 1998).

Tyacke, S., ed., *English Map-Making 1500–1650* (London, 1983).

Underdown, D., *Fire from Heaven* (London and New Haven, 1992).

Wabuda, S. and Litzenberger, C., eds, *Belief and Practice in Reformation England* (Aldershot, 1998).

Walker, D. M., *A Legal History of Scotland*, vol. III, *The Sixteenth Century* (Edinburgh, 1995).

Walker, G., ed., *Medieval Drama, an Anthology* (Oxford, 2000).

Walker, G., *Plays of Persuasion: Drama and Politics in the Court of Henry VIII* (Cambridge, 1991).

Walker, G., *The Politics of Performance in Early Renaissance Drama* (Cambridge, 1998).

Wall, A., 'Faction in local politics, 1580–1620: struggles for supremacy in Wiltshire', *Wiltshire Archaeological Magazine*, LXXII–LXXIII (1980).

Wall, A., 'Patterns of politics in England, 1558–1625', *Historical Journal*, 31 (1988).

Wall, A., *Power and Protest in England 1525–1640* (London, 2000).

Walsham, A., *Church Papists: Catholics, Conformity and Confessional Polemic in Early Modern England*, (Woodbridge and Rochester, NY, 1993).

Walter, J., 'A "rising of the people"? The Oxfordshire Rising of 1596', *Past and Present*, 107 (1985).

Walter, J., 'The social economy of dearth in early modern England', in J. Walter and R. S. Schofield, eds, *Famine, Disease and the Social Order in Early Modern Society* (Cambridge, 1989).

Ward, J. P., 'Godliness, commemoration, and community: the management of provincial schools by London trade guilds', in M. C. McClendon, J. P. Ward and M. MacDonald, eds, *Protestant Identities: Religion, Society, and Self-Fashioning in Post-Reformation England* (Stanford, 1999).

Ward, J. P., *Metropolitan Communities: Trade Guilds, Identity, and Change in Early Modern London* (Stanford, 1997).

Ware, J., ed., *Ancient Irish Histories: The Works of Spencer, Campion, Hanmer, and Marleburrough* (2 vols, Port Washington, NY, 1970).

Warnicke, R., *William Lambarde, Elizabethan Antiquary, 1536–1601* (Chichester, 1973).

Wasson, J., ed., *Devon: Records of Early English Drama* (Toronto, 1986).

Waterhouse, E., *The Dictionary of 16th and 17th British Painters* [sic] (Woodbridge, 1988).

Waterhouse, E., *Painting in Britain, 1530 to 1790* (4th edition, Harmondsworth, 1978).

Watson, A., *Legal Transplants: an Approach to Comparative Law* (2nd edition, Athens, GA, 1993).

Watt, T., *Cheap Print and Popular Piety, 1550–1640* (Cambridge, 1991).

Watts, J., 'A New Fundacion of is Crowne': monarchy in the reign of Henry VII', in B. Thompson, ed., *The Reign of Henry VII* (Stamford, 1995).

Watts, S. J., *From Border to Middle Shire: Northumberland 1586–1625* (Leicester, 1975).

Waylye, J., *An Introduction to the Knowlege and Understundyng aswel to make as also to perceyve the Tenour and Forme of Indentures: Obligations, Quyttances, Bylles of Payment, Letters of Lycence, Letters of Sale, Letters of Exchange, Protections, Supplycatyons, Complayntes, a Certificat, and the Copy of Save Condyte* (London, 1550).

Webb, S. and Webb, B., *English Local Government*, vol. 2, *The Manor and the Borough* (Hamden, CT, 1963).

Wells-Cole, A., *Art and Decoration in Elizabethan and Jacobean England: The Influence of Continental Prints, 1558–1625* (New Haven and London, 1997).

Wernham, R. B., *After the Armada* (Oxford, 1984).

Wernham, R. B., *Before the Armada: the Emergence of the English Nation, 1485–1588* (London, 1972).

Wernham, R. B., 'English policy and the revolt of the Netherlands', in J. S. Bromley and E. H. Kossmann, eds, *Britain and the Netherlands* (London, 1960).

Wernham, R. B., *The Making of Elizabethan Foreign Policy, 1558–1603* (Berkeley, 1980).

Wernham, R. B., *The Return of the Armadas* (Oxford, 1994).

Westfall, S., *Patrons and Performance: Early Tudor Household Revels* (Oxford, 1990).

Wheatley, H. B., ed., *The Survey of London by John Stow* (London, 1912).

White, A., 'The regent Morton's visitation: the Reformation of Aberdeen, 1574', in A. A. MacDonald, M. Lynch and I. Cowan, eds, *The Renaissance in Scotland: Studies in Literature, Religion, History, and Culture* (Leiden, 1994).

White, A. B., *Self-Government at the King's Command: A Study in the Beginnings of English Democracy* (Minneapolis, 1933).

White, B., ed., *The Eclogues of Alexander Barclay from the Original Edition by John Cawood* (London, 1928).

White, P. W., *Theatre and Reformation: Protestantism, Patronage and Playing in Tudor England* (Cambridge, 1993).

Whiting, R., *The Blind Devotion of the People: Popular Religion and the English Reformation* (Cambridge, 1989).

Whitney, G., *A Choice of Emblemes* (Leyden, 1586).

Whittle, J., *The Development of Agrarian Capitalism: Land and Labour in Norfolk, 1440–1580* (Oxford, 2000).

Whyte, I. D., *Migration and Society in Britain 1550–1830* (New York, 2000).

Whyte, I. D., *Scotland before the Industrial Revolution: An Economic and Social History c.1050–c.1750* (London, 1995).

Whyte, I. D., *Scotland's Society and Economy in Transition, c1500–c.1760* (Basingstoke, 1997).

Wiesner, M. E., 'Beyond women and the family: towards a gender analysis of the Reformation', *Sixteenth Century Journal*, 28 (1987).

Willen, D., 'Women and religion in early modern England', in S. Marshall, ed., *Women in Reformation and Counter-Reformation Europe: Public and Private Worlds* (Bloomington, 1989).

Willen, D., 'Women in the public sphere in early modern England: the case of the urban working poor', *Sixteenth Century Journal* 29, 4 (1988).

Williams, G., *Recovery, Reorientation and Reformation: Wales c.1415–1642* (Oxford, 1987).

Williams, G., *Renewal and Reformation: Wales c.1415–1642* (Oxford, 1993).

Williams, G., *Wales and the Act of Union* (Bangor, 1992).

Williams, J. H., ed., *Stewart Style, 1513–1542: Essays on the Court of James V* (East Linton, 1996).

Williams, P., *The Tudor Regime* (Oxford, 1979).

Williamson, A., *Scottish National Consciousness in the Age of James VI: The Apocalypse, the Union, and the Shaping of Scotland's Public Culture* (Edinburgh, 1979).

Wilson, C., *Queen Elizabeth and the Revolt of the Netherlands* (London, 1970).

Withers, C. W. J., *Geography, Science and National Identity: Scotland since 1520* (Cambridge, 2001).

Withers, Charles, 'Pont in context: chorography, mapmaking and national identity in the late sixteenth century', in I. C. Cunningham, ed., *The Nation Survey'd: Essays on Late Sixteenth-Century Scotland as Depicted by Timothy Pont* (East Linton, 2001).

Wolffe, B. P., *The Royal Demesne in English History: The Crown Estate in the Governance of the Realm* (London, 1971).

Wood, A., 'Custom and the social organisation of writing in early modern England', *Transactions of the Royal Historical Society*, 6th series, 9 (1999).

Woodall, J., 'An exemplary consort: Antonis Mor's portrait of Mary Tudor', *Art History*, 14 (June, 1990).

Woodfill, W. L., *Musicians in English Society from Elizabeth to Charles I* (Princeton, NJ, 1953).

Woodward, D., 'Early modern servants in husbandry revisited', *Agricultural History Review*, 48 (2000).

Woodward, D., *Men at Work: Labourers and Building Craftsmen in the Towns of Northern England, 1450–1750* (Cambridge, 1995).

Woodward, G. W. O., *The Dissolution of the Monasteries* (London, 1966).

Woolf, D. R., *The Idea of History in Early Stuart England* (Toronto, 1990).

Woolf, D. R., 'Little Crosby and the horizons of early modern historical culture', in D. R. Kelley and D. H. Sacks, eds, *The Historical Imagination in Early Modern Britain: History, Rhetoric and Fiction 1500–1800* (Cambridge, 1997).

Woolf, D. R., *Reading History in Early Modern England* (Cambridge, 2000).

Woolf, D. R., *The Social Circulation of the Past: English Historical Culture 1500–1730* (Oxford, 2003).

Wormald, J., *Court, Kirk and Community: Scotland 1470–1625* (Toronto and London, 1981).

Wormald, J., *Lords and Men in Scotland: Bonds of Manrent, 1442–1603* (Edinburgh, 1985).

Wormald, J., *Mary Queen of Scots: Politics, Passion and a Kingdom Lost* (London, 2001).

Wright, E., *Certaine Errors in Navigation* (London, 1599).

Wright, L. B. and Fowler, E. E., eds, *English Colonization of North America* (London, 1968).

Wright, P., 'A change in direction: the ramifications of a female household, 1558–1603', in D. Starkey, J. Murphy, P. Wright, N. Cuddy, and K. Sharpe, eds, *The English Court from the Wars of the Roses to the Civil War* (London and New York, 1987).

Wrightson, K., *Earthly Necessities: Economic Lives in Early Modern Britain* (London and New Haven, 2000).

Wrightson, K., 'The politics of the parish in early modern England', in P. Griffiths, A. Fox and S. Hindle, eds, *The Experience of Authority in Early Modern England* (New York and London, 1996).

Wrightson, K., 'Two concepts of order: justices, constables and jurymen in seventeenth-century England', in J. Brewer and J. Styles, eds, *An Ungovernable People: The English and their Law in the Seventeenth and Eighteenth Centuries* (London, 1980).

Wrightson, K. and Levine, D., *Poverty and Piety in an English Village: Terling, 1525–1700* (London, 1979; paperback edition, Oxford, 1995).

Wrigley, E. A., 'Marriage, fertility and population growth in eighteenth-century England', in R. B. Outhwaite, ed., *Marriage and Society: Studies in the Social History of Marriage* (London, 1981 and New York, 1982).

Wrigley, E. A., 'Urban growth and agricultural change: England and the Continent in the early modern period', *Journal of Interdisciplinary History*, 15, 4 (1985).

Wrigley, E. A. and Schofield, R. S., *The Population History of England, 1541–1871: A Reconstruction* (London and Cambridge, MA, 1981).

Wrigley, E. A., Davies, R. S., Oeppen, J. E. and Schofield, R. S., eds, *English Population History from Family Reconstitution 1580–1837* (Cambridge, 1997).

Yates, F. A., *Astraea: The Imperial Theme in the Sixteenth Century* (London, 1975).

Yates, F. A., *The Rosecrucian Enlightenment* (London, 1972).

Youings, J., *The Dissolution of the Monasteries* (London, 1971).

Youngs, F. A., *The Proclamations of the Tudor Queens* (Cambridge, 1976).

Youngs, F. A., 'Towards petty sessions: Tudor JPs and divisions of counties', in D. J. Guth and J. W. McKenna, eds, *Tudor Rule and Revolution: Essays for G. R. Elton from His American Friends* (Cambridge, 1982).

Zilsel, E., 'The origins of Gilbert's scientific method', *Journal of the History of Ideas*, 2 (1941).

Zilsel, E., 'The sociological roots of science', *American Journal of Sociology*, 47 (1942).

Index

Printed in Great Britain
by Amazon